RJ 134 .E93 1967 v.2

Exceptional infant

3-27-97

D1230397

From the

Highland Hospital
Collection

Asheville, North Carolina

donated by
National Medical Enterprises, Inc.
1994

EXCEPTIONAL INFANT
Studies in Abnormalities

Volume 2

Jerome Hellmuth, Editor

EXCEPTIONAL INFANT

STUDIES IN ABNORMALITIES

BRUNNER/MAZEL New York
BUTTERWORTHS London

Copyright © 1971 by Brunner/Mazel, Inc.
80 East 11th Street
New York, N. Y. 10003

Library of Congress Catalog Card Number: 68-517
SBN 87630-034-4

MANUFACTURED IN THE UNITED STATES OF AMERICA

CONTENTS

PART III: BEHAVIOR DISORDERS AND
PSYCHOPATHOLOGY

INTRODUCTION

Gerald D. LaVeck, M.D.

Director, National Institute of Child Health and
Human Development
Bethesda, Maryland

During the last ten years the tremendous importance of the first few years of life has become increasingly clear. The psychiatric significance of the first two or three years has been stressed for a long time. More recently, the crucial nature of events of this period for physical, social, and cognitive development has become recognized. What happens to the neonate can have a lasting, possibly lifelong, influence on his development.

A hopeful note is an increased capability today to deal diagnostically and correctively with an increasing number of conditions present at birth or detectable soon after. This statement is not meant to be overly optimistic. Many malformations present at birth do not have greatly improved prognoses. However, in many fields such as mental retardation and cognitive development generally there are significant advances in management and therapy. Improved diagnostic methods, some of them behavioral, for recognizing damage or deviancy are becoming available. In short the ability to assess the newborn and to take remedial action in many instances has greatly increased. This volume will reward the reader with a clear statement of many of these advances although complete coverage is not claimed.

An interesting point is the fact that the recent research emphasis upon infancy and the early childhood years has produced a convergence of those interested in normal development and those concerned with the detection and correction of deviancy. These studies have produced related efforts by behavioral experimentalists, clinically oriented workers, whether medical or not, those concerned with scientific advances in learning, and those having the concerns of the educator. These contributors have not always worked together in the same laboratory or clinic, but the pattern of research fits nicely together and is mutually supplemental. This volume brings together an assortment of distinguished writers of great professional and scientific heterogeneity. The chapters, though, hang together and give the reader a fresh and comprehensive view of some of the promising leads in diagnosis, prevention, and treatment. Not very many years ago this book would have been very heavily medical and biological. Actually, the largest input is from the behavioral, educational, and speech areas, but a perusal of the chapter titles shows that these contributions are data laden and experimentally oriented. The advances of medicine are also well represented. It is gratifying that research work as diverse as that reported here can be brought to bear on the exceptional infant and that no real communication gap between the various areas appears to exist.

It should be noted, however, that this book is both a book of beginnings and a book of refinements. The coverage of the neurological examination of the newborn and the report of neonatal behavior represent refinements and valuable comprehensive statements. The chapters using behavioral indices of damage, behavioral corrective approaches, or new formulations of complex human speech developments are at the edge of new understandings of child development. They do, however, go beyond theoretical and academic concern to diagnostic and therapeutic device.

In an introduction one cannot summarize the entire content of the publication. There is, however, a host of issues in child development which are in need of research, and one could talk about specific issues at great length. The need in nearly all cases is for cross discipline integration. Many of these problems are discussed in this book. An important example of the convergence of biological, medical, and behavioral concerns lies in the field of malnutrition and its relationship to intellectual development. Animal studies clearly indicate a relation between severe malnutrition and reduced body growth and brain size and altered behavioral patterns and learning ability. In humans, severe protein-calorie malnutrition during the first two years of life adversely affects head and body growth. Learning ability and behavioral patterns are compromised in children who recover from severe protein-calorie malnutrition. The degree of deprivation shown to cause these changes is not frequently seen in the United States. Whether the types or severity of malnutrition currently being described by the National Nutrition Survey affect intellectual competence is unknown.

Malnutrition exists in company with many other environmental factors, each of which may adversely influence intellectual development. Research is needed to separate the effects of malnutrition from the effects of physical, biological, and sociocultural environment in the United States population. This is a superb illustration of a type of research endeavor that is needed and requires participation by scientists from many disciplines.

Early childhood development is critical to man's performance in the adult years. Undesirable events, both behavioral and biological, can occur during infancy which may later be reversible only with difficulty or not at all. We are all aware of the need to intervene and to prevent these undesirable occurrences. Intervention, however, is fraught with dangers of greater harm than good. It is essential, therefore, that intervention be based on scientific knowledge of early development, and that application of this knowledge in social, health, and educational programs for both the privileged and underprivileged be under continuing review, development, and evaluation to insure that the goals of intervention are achieved.

The National Institute of Child Health and Human Development has had a continuing concern in these problem areas. In 1969 it published a document entitled, *Perspectives on Human Deprivation: Biological, Psychological, and Sociological* (1). For help in the assessment of the impact of deprivation, the Institute turned to the scientific community, and over 50 scientists contributed papers on various aspects of the phenomena of psychosocial deprivation. The scientists who prepared the reviews unanimously concluded that research on biological and psychological insult during the early years of childhood should receive high priority. Specific areas in need of exploration included nutrition; multidisciplinary studies of children during the first three years of life in such significant areas as neurological and endocrine changes with age and the development of cognition, language, personality, and social role. Also considered were early child care arrangements based on the differentiated developmental needs of newborns, infants, toddlers, and preschool children; the biological and genetic basis of learning and behavior; institutions and social structural factors which determine and maintain dependence and deprivation; and personality development and motivation with special concern with the role of parent surrogates. The Institute's publication supplies some data and brings together available knowledge, but more important it makes clear the need for further progress. The present volume meets some of these needs and is therefore an important contribution.

Exceptional Infant, Volume 1, concerns itself with the normal infant. Volume 2 stresses the deviations from normal development and focuses on the identification of "high risk" infants, diagnosis, prevention, and management of infants with many types of handicapping disabilities. This publication will have appeal to many disciplines including practitioners and investigators.

Luther Burbank said many years ago, "If we had paid no more attention to plants than we have to our children, we would now be living in a jungle of weeds." This volume relates to the emerging scientific and professional efforts of our society on behalf of the special child with disability.

---

1. U. S. Government Printing Office, Washington, D.C., 1969.

EXCEPTIONAL INFANT
Studies in Abnormalities

Part I

Examination
and
Observation

1

NEUROLOGICAL EXAMINATION
OF THE NEWBORN

A. H. Parmelee, M.D.

Professor of Pediatrics
Head, Division of Child Development
Department of Pediatrics
School of Medicine, University of California at Los Angeles

and

R. Michaelis, M.D.

Department of Pediatrics
University of Göttingen, Germany

In the past, neurologists and pediatricians were discouraged from any predictive assessment of the newborn by the concept that the newborn functioned only at a brain stem level of nervous organization (Peiper, 1928, 1963). This concept was reinforced by studies of anencephalic and hydrancephalic infants who had only a brain stem (Gamper 1926, Andre-Thomas and Saint-Anne Dargassies 1952). It was recognized that these infants had the familiar reflex responses such as Moro, rooting and sucking. However, the reflex responses in these infants are qualitatively different than in the normal infant. Their responses are either partially expressed or exaggerated and stereotyped (Robinson and Tizard, 1966). The function of the cortex and other higher brain centers in the normal newborn is to modify various response components through partial inhibition or facilitation. Thus the qualitative evaluation of reflex responses in the newborn may be more important than determining their presence or absence. Most current neurological examinations provide scoring systems for rating these qualitative differences.

Pediatricians have also been discouraged by their clinical experiences about the possibility of assessing the nervous system of the newborn. Each has seen a newborn infant in serious neurological difficulty in the first

This research was supported in part by U.S.P.H.S. Grants No. B-3131, HD-00351 and Deutsche Forschungsgemeinschaft Grant No. M: 115/1.

3

days of life, perhaps semi-comatose with no sucking or Moro response, who was quite normal several years later, and also a newborn judged as neurologically normal who in childhood had obvious cerebral palsy or was mentally retarded.

There are some possible explanations for this paradox. For example, acute perinatal stress may cause brain trauma without permanent damage, but the immediate adaptation of the infant to his environment is poor. He may have a low Apgar score, unstable respirations, poor feeding and be unresponsive for a few hours or a few days but recover fully. The immediate threat to survival is great but if the baby survives the long term outcome can be good. The best prognostic indicator of the long term outcome in such a case seems to be the speed of recovery during the first days or weeks of life (Amiel-Tison 1969, Drillien 1968). On the other hand, prenatal complications of a chronic nature that involve the fetus or placenta or both tend to cause more permanent damage to the central nervous system when it is affected. The fetus, if it survives, has time to make a functional adaptation in the uterus, so that the heart rate, respirations and color can be quite normal at birth. The baby eats reasonably well, sleeps and cries and has no obvious motor defects, so he is judged normal. However, later he may develop obvious evidence of cerebral palsy or mental retardation (Amiel-Tison 1969, Drillien 1968). We assume that these infants display qualitative differences in their responses in the newborn period that are persistent over time and that this persistent difference will have diagnostic significance, making it possible to identify this child by means of a newborn neurological evaluation concerned with the quality of behavioral response.

APPROACHES TO NEWBORN NEUROLOGICAL EVALUATION

For many years, neurologists and pediatricians interested in the neurological and behavioral responses of the newborn described various isolated reflexes, some of which bear their names. These have recently been reviewed by Taft (1967). Albrecht Peiper (1928, 1963) was one of the first to attempt to view all aspects of the behavior of the newborn and young infant and to conceptualize an organizing schema. To him, the postural and righting reflexes were the underlying organizers of all newborn behavior. This is not surprising since his work was contemporary with, and strongly influenced by, the classic studies of Magnus on the postural reflexes of animals (Magnus 1924). Peiper concluded from his observations of the newborn and Magnus's animal studies that the newborn infants' highest level of central nervous system control was the pallidum. He did not organize and define a systematic neurological examination of the newborn but laid the ground work for this.

Andre-Thomas also made detailed neurological observations of the newborn with special reference to the significance of muscle tone. During a life time of work as an adult neurologist, he was particularly interested in muscle tone. He divided muscle tone assessment into three categories: 1) active tone that is evident during all voluntary or spontaneous movement; 2) passive tone as tested by extending a limb to the limit at each joint; 3) passive tone as tested by swinging the extremity at each joint (essentially a test of the stretch reflex). Normally one would expect all three types of muscle tone to vary in the same direction. However, in certain neurological conditions he observed discordance in the response to these three tests and attached great clinical significance to this discordance (Andre-Thomas and Ajuriaguerra 1949, Andre-Thomas and Saint-Anne Dargassies 1952).

Saint-Anne Dargassies organized Andre-Thomas's observations and techniques into a systematic examination of the newborn (Saint-Anne Dargassies 1954, 1955, 1966, Andre-Thomas et al. 1960). She also adapted her examination to the premature infant, for whom it is particularly appropriate. Changes in muscle tone with maturation are very dramatic in the premature and, since neurological problems readily interfere with the evolution of these changes in muscle tone, they can be identified by this technique.

Graham developed the first systematically organized newborn neurological examination in this country. She took great pains to establish reliable scoring techniques for each item and selected the items carefully to test various types of behavior in the shortest time possible with the least disturbance to the baby. Included were tests of motor activity and strength, auditory, visual, tactual and pain stimulus responses and measures of irritability and tension. The pain threshold test was subsequently eliminated from the examination by most workers because it required a special instrument for electrical stimulation. Using a history of perinatal trauma as the criterion, she was able to establish the validity of this examination in the newborn period (Graham 1956, Graham et al. 1956).

A newborn neurological examination having widespread influence on recent studies in this field was constructed by Prechtl (Prechtl and Dijkstra 1960, Prechtl and Beintema 1964). They stressed the importance of the infant's state of arousal at the time of testing behavioral responses, as did Graham. The more subtle the gradations of the behavioral responses and the more complex the behavior response patterns, the more likely that shifts in state of arousal will alter the response (Prechtl et al. 1967). Prechtl was also interested in comparing the responses on the two sides of the body for any evidence of laterality, as were Andre-Thomas and Saint-Anne Dargassies.

A major contribution of Prechtl's approach was the clustering of response patterns into diagnostic syndromes, which he called: apathy

TABLE I

DEFINITION OF SYNDROMES ACCORDING TO PRECHTL

HYPEREXCITABILITY	APATHY	HEMISYNDROME	COMA
Low-frequency, high amplitude tremor, high or medium intensity of tendon reflexes and Moro with low threshold. There may also be hyperkinesis, increased resistance to passive movement, and prolonged crying.	Low intensity of and high threshold for responses, many responses absent, hypokinesis and decreased resistance to passive movements. The baby shows prolonged quiet wakefulness. (State 3)	At least three asymmetric findings in motility, posturing and response to stimulation or manipulation.	Slow or abnormal respiration, absent or weak arousal to various stimuli, including vestibular stimulation.

Prechtl, H., and Beintema, D.: The Neurological Examination of the Full-Term Newborn Infant. Little Club Clinics in Developmental Medicine No. 12. London: William Heineman Medical Books Ltd., 1964.

TABLE II

DEFINITION OF SYNDROMES ACCORDING TO SCHULTE

HYPEREXCITABILITY	APATHY	HYPERTONIA	HYPOTONIA	HEMISYNDROME	SEIZURES	COMA
Easily obtained long lasting myoclonus of the extremities, nystagmus easily elicited, and brisk tendon and skin reflexes.	Spontaneous movements slow and rare; tendon and skin reflexes sluggish and easily fatiguable, infrequent crying.	Strong resistance to passive movements, tonic-myotatic reflexes strong. Tendon reflexes variable.	Weak resistance to passive movements. Tonic-myotatic reflexes feeble, tendon reflexes feeble or absent.	Unilateral hypo- or hypertonia and cranial nerve weakness or paralysis and unilateral seizures.	Tonic or clonic seizures, often with apnea and nystagmus.	Reflexes extinguished, eye movements uncoordinated. Reflex responses absent and deviant eye positioning.

Schulte, F. J., Michaelis, R., und Filipp, E.: Neurologie des Neugeborenen. I. Mitteilung. Ursache und klinische Symptomatologie von Funktionsstörungen des Nervensystems bei Neugeborenen. Zeit. f. Kinderheilk., 93:242, 1965.

syndrome, hyper-excitability syndrome, hemi-syndrome, and coma. The criteria are given in Table I. Schulte et al. (1965a, b) and Joppich and Schulte (1968) adapted Prechtl's examination for use with the very sick newborn as well as the suspect infant, extending the diagnostic syndromes as indicated in Table II.

SUGGESTIONS FOR THE NEUROLOGICAL EVALUATION OF THE NEWBORN

The neurological examination of the newborn must serve three major purposes, each requiring a slightly different technique and mode of analysis:

1) The immediate diagnosis of an evident neurological problem, such as extreme hypotonia, convulsions, coma or localized paralysis, to determine what therapy to institute.

2) The evaluation of the day to day changes of a known neurological problem to determine the evolution of a pathological process, such as an hypoxic episode, or to follow the evolution of the neurological signs of a systemic disease such as respiratory distress.

3) The long term prognosis of a newborn who is recovering from some neonatal neurological problem or is considered at risk due to abnormalities of the pregnancy, labor, or delivery.

One would like an examination that serves all three purposes. Since most of the current newborn neurological examinations do not meet the requirements for all these functions, they have not been completely satisfactory.

Before one can discuss any detailed techniques for the neurological evaluation of the newborn one must consider several general factors that influence the assessment of the findings.

First of all, to judge the significance of any neurological finding in the newborn period, one needs to know the gestational age of the infant. A 1500 gram baby at term (small-for-dates) does not have the same degree of hypotonicity and lethargy as a true premature of this weight. Similarly a 2600 gram baby of 35 weeks gestation (large-for-dates) will not be as responsive or have as much flexor tone as a term baby of this weight. In most instances we may rely on the mother's history of her last menstrual period to determine the duration of the pregnancy. Recently, with greater understanding of the characteristics of small- and large-for-dates infants, we have discovered that the mother's histories are more reliable than we had thought in the past. Intrauterine growth charts are particularly helpful in evaluating the relation of gestational age to weight, height, and head circumference (Fig. 1) (Lubchenco et al. 1963, 1966, Hoseman 1948, Parmelee et al. 1964). One can also use well defined physical or neurological criteria for estimating the gestational age (Farr et al. 1966, Robinson, 1966, Graziani

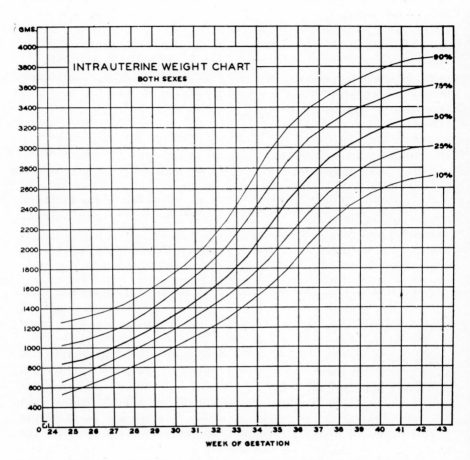

FIG. 1. The weights of live born Caucasian infants at gestational ages from 24 to 42
weeks graphed as percentiles.
    Lubchenco, L. O., Hansman, C., Dressler, M., and Boyd, E.: Intrauter-
    ine growth as estimated from liveborn birthweight data at 24 to 42
    weeks of gestation. *Pediatrics.* 32:793, 1963.

et al. 1968, Saint-Anne Dargassies 1955, 1966) within the limitations found by Michaelis (1970). In addition, there are EEG criteria of gestational age (Dreyfus-Brisac et al. 1958, Dreyfus-Brisac 1968, Parmelee et al. 1968, and Graziani et al. 1968). Unfortunately, in our experience, all of these measures are distorted if the baby is ill in any way and particularly so if he has a neurological problem. The criterion of gestational age that is most independent of the infant's health is the nerve conduction velocity (Fig. 2). In the future this will undoubtably become a primary criterion of gestational age (Schulte et al. 1968a, Dubowitz et al. 1968, Blom and Finnström 1968).

A second important general consideration in the neurological examination of the newborn is the baby's state of arousal. The responses of an irritable baby will be quite different from those of a baby asleep and to a lesser degree so will those of an alert quiet baby compared with a drowsy baby.

Environmental factors, such as temperature, lighting, and sound level, are important primarily because they influence the baby's state of arousal. A cold environment can be sufficiently stimulating to a baby to make him cry or be very irritable and tense. On the other hand, a very sick baby who is chilled may become less active. The examination should be done in a warm, well-illuminated, quiet environment.

A third area of concern is the examiner's skill and experience, especially when the examination technique and response scoring are not well defined. Every doctor can do a newborn neurological examination based on his general knowledge of neurology and medicine but only those highly experienced with the newborn are likely to be successful. The accumulated knowledge of the characteristics of newborn responses provides a standard for comparative assessment. Ideally the technique of examination and response scoring should be so well defined that even the beginner can be successful. In other words, one would like to reduce to a minimum the variability of the results that may be due to the examiner's experience and skill.

Finally, an unavoidable problem is the fact that one cannot use a long and complicated neurological examination on a very sick baby. Thus, it is important to try to build an examination of items that are the most informative and discriminating and, at the same time, are minimally disturbing to a sick baby.

These general considerations are applicable in all three types of situations in which a neurological evaluation is desired: immediate diagnosis, short- and long-term follow-up.

(1) *Obvious neurological problems*

Some neonatal neurological problems are obvious because of the presence of symptoms and signs never found in the normal infant. The

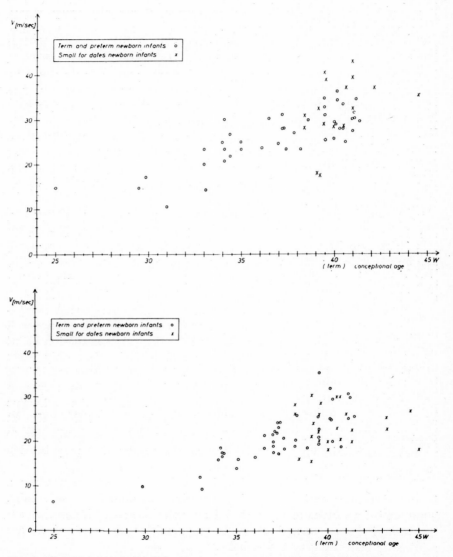

Fig. 2. Ulnar (top) and tibial (bottom) motor nerve conduction velocity increases with conceptional age.

Schulte, F. J., Michaelis, R., Linke, I., and Nolte, R.: Motor nerve conduction velocity in term, preterm, and small-for-dates newborn infants. *Pediatrics,* 42:17, 1968.

problem is to determine the etiology if possible so that appropriate therapy may be instituted promptly. Some symptoms and signs of neurological problems never present in the normal infant are: coma, severe lethargy, constant crying, convulsions, recurrent apnea, a bulging fontanel, rapidly increasing head size, unequal pupils, absent corneal reflexes, and paralysis of any extremity, facial muscle or eye muscle.

It is not always easy to decide by observation alone whether the baby is sleeping profoundly or is very lethargic or comatose, but this can be determined on examination. The comatose child does not arouse with foot withdrawal to painful pinching or pinprick, whereas the sleeping infant is easily brought to wakefulness by these procedures. The head drop stimulation for the Moro reflex is one of the most massive stimulations one can give a baby and normally brings him from a quiet to a crying state. In coma, the Moro reflex is absent, and in lethargy the response is limited or may require repeated stimulation to be elicited.

Other signs that are always pathological but take some experience to evaluate are: (1) an obligatory asymmetric tonic neck reflex. Normal newborns may have an asymmetric tonic neck reflex but it is never obligatory (Clark 1964, Critchley 1968); (2) an exaggerated Babinski response with an extended reflexogenic area. A Babinski response is normally present in the newborn but has a limited reflexogenic area.

Having established the clinical nature and severity of the neurological disorder from the signs and symptoms, there remains the problem of determining the etiology of the disorder. This is more difficult, and frequently a definite diagnosis of the cause of the neurological problem cannot be made and therapy is symptomatic. The remaining concern is whether the brain has been only temporarily injured or has sustained some degree of permanent damage. A judgment on this matter can best be obtained by following the evolution of the process over time. In general, rapid recovery in the first 2 to 4 weeks of life is a good prognostic sign.

(2) *Following the neurological progress*

The items most important for the day-to-day assessment of the infant's neurological condition can be grouped in the following categories:

1) States of sleep and vigilance
2) Sensory responses
3) Muscle tone
4) Integrated motor activities

Commonly observed items related to states of sleep and vigilance are amount of crying, general motor activity and amount of wakefulness or sleep. More detailed evaluations can be made by using polygraphic recordings of eye movements, body movements, respirations, heart rate, electromyographic activity of selected muscles and EEG (Stern et al. 1969, Prechtl et al. 1968, Parmelee et al. 1967).

Normal responsiveness to sensory stimulation includes: (1) withdrawal of the foot to light touch or magnate response of the foot to hand touch; (2) rooting reflex response to face stimulation; (3) glabellar reflex; (4) blinking response to light and loud sounds; (5) visual following of a light or an object. More specific evaluations can be made by obtaining EEG evoked responses to light, sound, touch, and movement (Akyama et al. 1969, Ellingson 1967, Hrbek et al. 1968a, 1968b).

Muscle tone can be evaluated by the observation of spontaneous posture, passive manipulation of the extremities, and by precipitating movement to assess the vigor of the response. The normal full term infant spontaneously holds his arms and legs in flexion. A child who is hypotonic usually lies with arms and legs extended. A resumption of flexion posturing signals a return of normal tone. A hypertonic child generally is in an excessively flexed posture and makes few extensor movements. A relaxing of such excessive flexion and the appearance of many spontaneous extensor movements signal improvement. Passive manipulation of the arms and legs serves to confirm the impressions given by the spontaneous posturing. The Moro reflex also gives some information regarding the balance of flexor and extensor tone. The hypotonic child (e.g., Mongols and small premature infants) may have only extension of the arms as a response. Hypertonic infants have primarily a flexor Moro response with the arms immediately brought against the chest or across the chest. The normal Moro has a nice balance with limited extension of the arms and hands first, and gradual flexion next, neither overshooting the mark. This can be measured with greater refinement by recording EMG activity during the Moro response (Schulte and Schwenzel 1965, Schulte et al. 1968b).

Performance of integrated motor activities is probably the best indicator of the infant's degree of recovery. The most commonly used and most useful integrated motor activities to observe are those related to feeding, the components of which are the rooting reflex, the searching for and capturing of the nipple, the strength, duration and rhythm of sucking, and successful coordination of swallowing with respirations without aspiration of the liquid. Other integrated motor activities are the walking response, straightening of the back and neck when the infant is placed upright on his feet, hand grasping and arm traction, head control in the seated position, raising of the head from the prone position, creeping movements in prone position, and the Moro reflex.

By careful daily observation of the infant's behavior on the items in these four categories one can readily assess his degree of improvement. Rapid improvement in all four categories indicates satisfactory recovery

TABLE III

COMPARISON OF NORMAL AND TRAUMATIZED GROUPS ON FIVE NEONATAL TESTS

TEST	N	Variables Controlled	Mean Scores	Comparison Statistic	p
Pain Threshold					
Normal	55	Age	165	t test	.01
Traumatized	55		270		
Maturation Scale					
Normal	28	Age, race	13.0	F test	.05
Traumatized	28		10.6		
Vision Scale					
Normal	37	Age, race	6.8	t test	.01
Traumatized	37		4.2		
Irritability					
Normal	91	—	.12	Chi square	.01
Traumatized	29		.61		
Tension					
Normal	103	—	.08	Chi square	.01
Traumatized	29		.48		

Graham, F. K., Matarazzo, R. G., and Caldwell, B. M.: Behavioral differences between normal and traumatized newborns. II. Standardization, reliability, and validity. Psychol. Monogr. 70:17, 1956.

and reason for prognostic optimism. Delay in improvement in all or even one category is cause for concern.

(3) *Predictive neurological evaluation*

The development of a predictive neurological examination for newborn infants who appear essentially well but are considered at risk because of prenatal, perinatal, or neonatal problems has been a most difficult and challenging task. The principal studies in this area are those of Graham (1956), Saint-Anne Dargassies (1954, 1955, 1966), Andre-Thomas et al. (1960), Prechtl (1965), Prechtl and Beintema (1964), Schulte et al. (1965a, b) and Joppich and Schulte (1968).

Graham et al. (1956) were able to distinguish babies with histories of pre- or perinatal problems from those with none by their newborn neurological examination (Table III). In a three year follow-up study, the incidence of neurological, intellectual and behavioral problems was found to be related to the pre- and perinatal history but not to scores on the newborn neurological examination. At the seven year follow-up none of the correlations were significant (Graham et al. 1962, Corah et al. 1965). Rosenblith (1966), on the other hand, found a significant correlation between her modification of the Graham test and the results of the Bayley infant development test done at 8 months of age.

Saint-Anne Dargassies (1955, 1966) has devised the only neurological examination for premature infants. Follow-up neurological examinations at two to six years showed a significant correlation with the neonatal examination (Table IV) (Parmelee et al. 1970).

TABLE IV

INFANTS WITH BIRTH WEIGHTS ≦ 2500 GMS

Newborn Neurological		Childhood Neurological		
		Normal	Suspect	Pathological
Normal	(n=52)	22	27	3
Suspect	(n=75)	36	33	6
Pathological	(n=32)	9	13	10
		—	—	—
		67	73	19

$$X^2_4 : p < 0.01$$

Parmelee, A. H., Jr., Minkowski, A., Saint-Anne Dargassies, S., Dreyfus-Brisac, C., Lezine, I., Berges, J., Chervin, G., and Stern, E.: Neurological evaluation of the premature infant. Biol. Neonat., 15:65, 1970.

Prechtl devised a subtle, detailed examination that has been particularly successful in predicting the outcome in risk babies. The results of a follow-up study of 252 babies who had all had pre- or perinatal complications and had been examined in the newborn period are presented in Table V (Prechtl 1965).

TABLE V

NEUROLOGICAL EXAMINATIONS

NEWBORN		AT 2-4 YEARS		
Normal	102	Normal	88	(86%)
		Abnormal	14	(14%)
Abnormal	150	Normal	40	(27%)
		Abnormal	110	(73%)

$$p = 0.001$$

Prechtl, H. F. R.: Prognostic value of neurological signs in the newborn infant. Proc. Roy. Soc. Med., 58:3, 1965.

Donovan et al. (1962) in a one year follow-up also found that babies with normal neonatal neurological examinations remained normal. However, 80% of the neonates with abnormal neurological examinations were also normal at one year of age. They suggested that subtle neurological signs probably could not be detected at one year of age but might be found in later childhood.

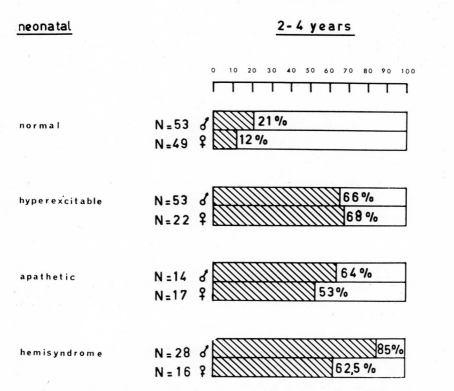

Fig. 3. Incidence of neurological signs for each neonatal syndrome after 2-4 years. Prechtl, H. F. R.: Prognostic value of neurological signs in the newborn infant. *Proc. Roy. Soc. Med.,* 58:3, 1965.

As previously stated, one of the most useful concepts to come from these studies is that of neonatal neurological syndromes as proposed by Prechtl and Beintema (1964) and elaborated by Schulte et al. (1965a) and Joppich and Schulte (1968).

Apathy is the most commonly found syndrome associated with severe pre- or perinatal complications. It has the worst prognosis of all the syndromes particularly when combined with hypotonia, as it usually is. The abnormal neurological sequelae in childhood are very diverse.

Prechtl found the hyperexcitability syndrome most commonly associated with lesser degrees of perinatal complications. The infants who have this syndrome have a good prognosis. It is usually combined with

TABLE VI

FOLLOW-UP NEUROLOGICAL FINDINGS

NEWBORN SYNDROMES	N	GROUP A Normal	Mildly Abnormal	Severely Abnormal	Died	N	GROUP B Normal	Mildly Abnormal	Severely Abnormal	Died
Normal	39	30	9							
Hyperexcitable	8	1	7			10	1	8		1
Apathy	20	9	10			46	11	14	7	14
Hypertonia	3	2	1			17	1	4	6	5
Hemi-syndrome	2					32	1	7	13	11
Seizures & Coma	6	3		3		29	3	1	8	15
Hypotonia	2		1		1	27	1	5	5	16

GROUP A—Infants only had a single neonatal syndrome.
GROUP B—Infants had multiple neonatal syndromes but are classified by dominant syndrome.
Schulte, F. J., Filipp, E., und Michaelis, R.: Neurologie des Neugeborenen. II. Mitteilung. Die Prognose von Funktionsstörungen des zentralen Nervensystems beim Neugeborenen. Zeit. f. Kinderheilk., 93:264, 1965.

hypertonia. He also demonstrated a significant correlation between this syndrome and choreiform uncontrolled twitching of the arms and fingers and hyperkinetic behavior problems at 2 to 4 years of age.

Schulte et al. (1965b) found the hemisyndrome more often in infants with abnormal deliveries and neonatal meningeal or encephalitic infections and asphyxia. Prechtl found a significant incidence of this syndrome with perinatal hypoxia. There is a very high correlation between this syndrome in the neonate and the same syndrome in the child. This is the only syndrome that significantly predicts the type of neurological problem in childhood.

The hypertonia syndrome alone has a good prognosis. The hypotonia syndrome alone has a somewhat worse prognosis. As previously stated, these are usually associated with other syndromes. The risk of neurological abnormality in childhood increases with the number of neonatal syndromes found in combination.

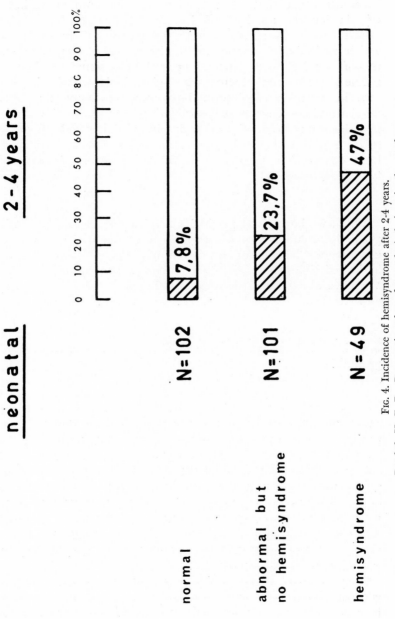

Fig. 4. Incidence of hemisyndrome after 2-4 years.
Prechtl, H. F. R.: Prognostic value of neurological signs in the newborn infant. *Proc. Roy. Soc. Med.*, 58:3, 1965.

Figures 3 and 4 illustrate the relation of these syndromes to follow-up findings in Prechtl's study and Table VI those for Schulte et al. It should be remembered that these two investigators use somewhat different criteria for the apathy and hyperexcitability syndromes. There are numerous factors, in addition to those discussed in the next section, which undoubtably contribute to the difficulty of prediction. One of these is our lack of understanding of the functional development of the nervous system and of the neurological basis of behavioral evolution seen in the maturing infant. Thus attempts to make a direct correspondence between narrowly defined responses in the newborn and homologous responses in the older infant have had disappointing results. The fact that Saint-Anne Dargassies, Prechtl and Schulte have been successful in predicting neurological outcome in early childhood is very encouraging.

DISCUSSION

While we have given particular emphasis to studies of the long term predictive value of newborn neurological examinations, all of the methods discussed have usefulness in the other situations in which assessment is desired, immediate diagnosis and assessment of immediate progress. We have also stressed those approaches felt to be the most systematic and detailed, of which there are only a few. The differences in the approaches that have been used to devise newborn examinations stem partially from the varying requirements of the situations for which they were intended and partially from differences in the investigators' backgrounds.

Saint-Anne Dargassies was primarily interested in organizing a thorough clinical neurological examination that would be useful in establishing an immediate diagnosis and in following the progress of the illness in the neonatal period. The assessment of muscle tone is a significant aspect of her examination technique, derived from the work of Andre-Thomas. While it is a unique contribution, great skill and experience are required, making it difficult for others to use successfully. The primary drawback is that good standards for the normal range of muscle tone in the newborn are as yet lacking. Saint-Anne Dargassies has been able to successfully extend her examination for use with premature infants. However, here again great skill and experience are required because we have so little information about the normal response variation at different gestational ages.

Graham was the first to use an organized research technique in the development of a newborn neurological examination, carefully establishing a reliable scoring system, the day to day stability of scores and their validity within the newborn period. She was one of the first to stress the importance of the state of arousal at the time of examination.

Her focus was more on the development of a research tool and on the predictive aspect of the examination and less on clinical diagnosis.

Prechtl proceeded much as Graham did in standardizing techniques and testing neonatal validity. He also took account of the baby's state and devised a system for scoring levels of arousal. He included more of the traditional neurological examination technique than Graham, such as testing monosynaptic tendon reflexes and polysynaptic skin reflexes, but he recognized the importance of the more complicated motor responses of the Moro and rooting reflexes, etc. Since the latter require greater integration of the nervous system, they are more easily disturbed by abnormal conditions, which also makes them more discriminating than the simpler reflexes. Beintema (1968), working with Prechtl, has provided information on the range of normal responses from day to day.

Recognizing that it is generally futile to attempt to make a diagnosis or prediction from a single pathological finding or a few isolated findings that are unrelated to each other, Prechtl introduced the concept of clustering signs and symptoms into syndromes. Prechtl's examination is useful both for clinical purposes and research but may be too detailed for some clinicians.

The examination described by Schulte was derived from Prechtl's and to some extent from Saint-Anne Dargassies's. It was designed to be an effective short examination, easily applicable in all clinical situations. The scoring system is less elaborate and contains more items directed at immediate lesional diagnosis.

Except for Graham, a psychologist, the other investigators all had training in classical neurology, yet the examination techniques they devised tend to rely heavily on behavioral observations. One reason for this may be that it is difficult to transfer the tools and ideas of classical neurology to the examination of the newborn. Using a more classical neurological approach has not been as successful as in adults in localizing the neurological lesion to a particular part of the central nervous system. Because of these failures, many experienced neurologists and investigators feel that there may never be a satisfactory neurological examination for the newborn.

It is true that the more behaviorally oriented neurological assessments of the newborn result in general, rather than specific, diagnoses, such as the apathy or hyperexcitability syndromes. Yet there is evidence that such diagnoses are clinically useful in the neonatal period and in making tentative prognoses for later years. This usefulness may very well derive from the special characteristics of the developing brain.

Insults or injuries to the infant's brain are often caused by intra-uterine, labor, or delivery difficulties that compromise the physiological stability of the entire organism. These are more likely to result in the dysfunction of more complex integrated behavior, state of arousal or total body muscle tone than in the elimination of specific tendon or skin reflexes. At the same time, these general physiological disturbances to the fetus and newborn may also result in discrete lesions that remain undetected. Because the newborn's brain is unorganized from the stand-point of localized control of specific functions, a discrete lesion need not interfere with later normal functioning. Thus, assuming one could develop a newborn neurological examination, analogous to the classical adult examination, that identified localized brain lesions, there might still be some question of its prognostic usefulness. The developing brain seems to possess tremendous plasticity and adaptive capacity to re-program function in uninjured portions of the brain, depending of course on the size and location of the brain lesion.

Many recent follow-up studies have found a large percentage of in-fants with perinatal complications, who function normally, if not within the first weeks of life, within the first years of life (Graham et al. 1962, Thurston et al. 1960, Corah et al 1965, Prechtl 1965, Niswander et al. 1966a, b, c, d, 1968, Drage 1970). More of the children in Graham's sample displayed sequelae at three years than at seven years. We do not know whether these infants fully recovered from temporary neo-natal brain insults or whether they compensated for permanent brain lesions.

Much more needs to be known about how the brain compensates for brain injury by reprogramming the nervous system. Such information would perhaps enable us to adjust the infant's environment to maximally assist this process, since we know that infants with perinatal problems are more vulnerable to the effects of an adverse environment than normal children (Drage 1970).

The pessimism of some concerning the possibility of constructing a successful newborn neurological examination has been well expressed by Clark (1964). "It is not difficult to compose long lists of reflexes which may be elicited from infants, or devise detailed schemata of exam-inations by scratching, thumping, spinning, or otherwise invading their privacy. It is a good deal harder to find signs which reliably predict lasting CNS damage."

Although at present no completely satisfactory methods for newborn neurological assessment exist, we believe considerable progress has been made in new conceptions of approach and refinement of established techniques.

For the present, therefore, it seems that the predominantly behavioral approach may provide the most useful information about the degree of CNS dysfunction during the neonatal period and serve to indicate potential developmental problems.

REFERENCES

1. AKIYAMA, Y.. SCHULTE, F. J., SCHULTZ, M. A., and PARMELEE, A. H., JR.,: Acoustically evoked responses in premature and full term newborn infants. *Electroenceph. Clin. Neurophysiol.,* 26:371, 1969.

2. AMIEL-TISON, C.: Cerebral damage in full-term new-born. Aetiological factors, neonatal status and long-term follow-up. *Biol. Neonat.,* 14:234, 1969.

3. ANDRE-THOMAS ET DE AJURIAGUERRA, J.: Étude Sémiologique du Tonus Musculaire. Paris: Éditions Médicales Flammarion, 1949.

4. ANDRE-THOMAS ET SAINT-ANNE DARGASSIES, S.: Études Neurologiques sur le Nouveau-Né et le Jeune Nourrisson. Paris: Masson et Cie., 1952.

5. ANDRE-THOMAS, CHESNI, Y., and SAINT-ANNE DARGASSIES, S.: The Neurological Examination of the Infant. Little Club Clinics in Developmental Medicine No. 1. London: National Spastics Society, 1960.

6. BEINTEMA, D. J.: A Neurological Study of Newborn Infants. Clinics in Developmental Medicine No. 28. London: William Heinemann Medical Books, Ltd., 1968.

7. BLOM, S., and FINNISTROM, O.: Motor conduction velocities in newborn infants of various gestational ages. *Acta Paediat. Scand.,* 57:377, 1968.

8. CLARK, DAVID B.: Abnormal neurological signs in the neonate. In Physical Diagnosis of the Newly Born. Report of the Forty-sixth Ross conference on Pediatric Research. Columbus: Ross Laboratories, 1964. Pp. 65-71.

9. CORAH, N. L., ANTHONY, E. J., PAINTER, P., STERN, J. A., THURSTON, D. L.: Effects of perinatal anoxia after seven years. *Psychol. Monogr.,* 79: Whole No. 596, 1965.

10. CRITCHLEY, E. M. R.: The neurological examination of neonates., *J. Neurol. Sci.,* 7:427, 1968.

11. DONOVAN, D. E., COUES, P., and PAINE, R. S.: The prognostic implications of neurologic abnormalities in the neonatal period. *Neurology,* 12: 910, 1962.

12. DRAGE, J. S., BERENDES, H. W., and FISHER, P. D.: The 5-minute Apgar scores and 4-year psychological examination performance. A report from the collaborative study of cerebral palsy, mental retardation and other neurological and sensory disorders of infancy and childhood. *N.I.N.D.S., N.I.H.* Presented at the Eighth Meeting of the Pan American Health Organization Advisory Committee on Medical Research. Washington, D.C., June, 1969. (Published in the proceedings of the P.A.H.O., W.H.O. Scientific Publication No. 185, Oct. 1969.)

13. DREYFUS-BRISAC, C., SAMSON, D., BLANC, C., and MONOD, N.: L'EEG de l'infant normal avant 3 ans. Aspect bioélectrique fonctionnel de la maturation nerveuse. *Études Neonat.,* 4:143, 1958.

14. DREYFUS-BRISAC, C.: The bioelectric development of the central nervous system during early life. In Human Development, Ed. F. Falkner. Philadelphia and London: W. B. Saunders Co., 1966, pp. 286-305.

15. DRILLIEN, C. M.: Studies in mental handicap. II. Some obstetric factors of possible etiological significance. *Arch. Dis. Childh.,* 43:283, 1968.

16. DUBOWITZ, V., WHITTAKER, G. F., BROWN, B. H., and ROBINSON, A.: Nerve conduction velocity—an index of neurological maturity of the newborn infant. *Develop. Med. Child Neurol.,* 10:741, 1968.

17. ELLINGSON, R. J.: Methods of recording cortical evoked responses in the human infant. In Regional Development of the Brain in Early Life, Ed. A. Minkowski. Oxford and Edinburgh: Blackwell Scientific Publications, 1967.

18. FARR, V., MITCHELL, R. G., NELIGAN, G. A., and PARKIN, J. M.: The definition of some external characteristics used in the assessment of gestational age in the newborn infant. *Develop. Med. Child. Neurol.,* 8:507, 1966.

19. GAMPER, E.: Bau und Leistungen eines menschlichen Mittelhirnwesen. (Arrinencéphalie und Encéphalocèle) Part II. *Z. ges Neurol. Psychiat.,* 104:49, 1926.

20. GRAHAM, F. K.: Behavioral differences between normal and traumatized newborns: I. The test procedures. *Psychol. Monogr.,* 70:1, 1956.

21. GRAHAM, F. K., MATARAZZO, R. G., and CALDWELL, B. M.: Behavioral differences between normal and traumatized newborns: II. Standardization, reliability, and validity. *Psychol. Monogr.*, 70:17, 1956.

22. GRAHAM, F. K., ERNHART, C. B., THURSTON, D., and CRAFT, M.: Development three years after perinatal anoxia and other potentially damaging newborn experiences. *Psychol. Monogr.*, Vol. 76, 1962.

23. GRAZIANI, L. J., WEITZMAN, E. D., and VELASCO, M. S. A.: Neurologic maturation and auditory evoked responses in low birth weight infants. *Pediatrics*, 41:483, 1968.

24. HOSEMANN, H. A.: Schwangerschaftsdauer und Neugeborenengewicht. *Archiv. f. Gynakologia*, 176:109, 1948.

25. HRBEK, A., PRECHTL, H. F. R., HOBKOVA, M., LENARD, H. G., and GRANT, D. K.: Proprioceptive evoked potentials in newborn infants and adults. *Develop. Med. Child Neurol.*, 10:164, 1968a.

26. HRBEK, A., HOBKOVA. M., and LENARD, H. G.: Somato-sensory evoked responses in newborn infants. *Electroenceph. clin. Neurophysiol.*, 25:433, 1968b.

27. JOPPICH, G., and SCHULTE, F. J.: Neurolgie des Neugeborenen. Berlin, Neidelberg, New York: Springer-Verlag, 1968.

28. LUCHENCO, L. O., HANSMAN, C., DRESSLER, M., and BOYD, E.: Intrauterine growth as estimated from liveborn birth weight data at 24 to 42 weeks of gestation. *Pediatrics*, 32:793, 1963.

29. LUBCHENO, L. O., HANSMAN, C., and BOYDE, E.: Intrauterine growth in length and head circumference as estimated from live births at gestational ages from 26 to 42 weeks. *Pediatrics*, 37:403, 1966.

30. MAGNUS, R.: Körperstellung. Berlin: Julius Springer, 1924.

31. MICHAELIS, R., SCHULTE, F. J., and NOLTE, R.: Motor behavior of small for gestational age newborn infants. *J. Pediat.*, 76:208, 1970.

32. NISWANDER, K. R., FRIEDMAN, E. A., HOOVER, D. B., PIETROUSAI, H., and WESTPHAL, M. C.: Fetal morbidity following potentially anoxigenic obstetric conditions. I. Abruptio placentae. *Amer. J. Obstet. Gynec.*, 95:838, 1966a.

33. NISWANDER, K. R., FRIEDMAN, E. A., HOOVER, D. B., PIETROWSKI, H., and WESTPHAL, M. C.: Fetal morbidity following potentially anoxigenic obstetric conditions. II. Placenta previa. *Amer. J. Obstet. Gynec.*, 95:846, 1966b.

34. NISWANDER, K. R., FRIEDMAN, E. A., HOOVER, D. B., PIETROWSKI, H., and WESTPHAL, M. C.: Fetal morbidity following potentially anoxigenic obstetric conditions. III. Prolapse of the umbilical cord. *Amer. J. Obstet. Gynec.*, 95:853, 1966c.

35. NISWANDER, K. R., FRIEDMAN, E. A., HOOVER, D. B., PIETROWSKI, H., and WESTPHAL, M. C.: Fetal morbidity following potentially anoxigenic obstetric conditions. IV. Occult prolapse of the umbilical cord. *Amer. J. Obstet. Gynec.*, 95:1099, 1966d.

36. NISWANDER, K. R., BERENDES, H. W., DEUTSCHBERGER, J., WEISS, W., LIPKO, N., and KANTOR, A. G.: Fetal morbidity following potentially anoxigenic obstetric conditions. VI. Rupture of the marginal sinus. *Amer. J. Obstet. Gynec.*, 100:862, 1968.

37. PARMELEE, A. H., JR., STERN, E., CHERVIN, G., and MINKOWSKI, A.: Gestational age and the size of premature infants. *Biol. Neonat.*, 6:309, 1964.

38. PARMELEE, A. H., JR., WENNER, W. H., AKIYAMA, Y., STERN, E., and FLESCHER, J.: Electroencephalography and brain maturation. In Regional Development of the Brain in Early Life. Ed. A. Minkowski. Oxford and Edinburgh: Blackwell Scientific Publications, 1967, pp. 459-476.

39. PARMELEE, A. H., JR., SCHULTE, F. J., AKIYAMA, Y., WENNER, W. H., SCHULTZ, M. A., and STERN, E.: Maturation of EEG activity during sleep in premature infants. *Electroenceph. Clin. Neurophysiol.*, 24:319, 1968.

40. PARMELEE, A. H., JR., MINKOWSKI, A., SAINT-ANNE DARGASSIES, S., DREYFUS-BRISAC, C., LEZINE, I., BERGES, J., CHERVIN, G., and STERN, E.: Neurological evaluation of the premature infant. *Biol. Neonat.*, 15:65, 1970.

41. PEIPER, A.: Die Hirntätigkeit des Säuglings. Berlin: Julius Springer, 1928.

42. PEIPER, A.: Cerebral Function in Infancy and Childhood. (Translation of the

3rd revised German edition by B. Nagler and H. Nagler) New York: Consultants Bureau, 1963.

43. PRECHTL, H. F. R., and DIJKSTRA, J.: Neurological diagnosis of cerebral injury in the newborn. In Prenatal Care, Ed. B. S. ten Berge. Groningen: Noordhoff, 1960.

44. PRECHTL, H., and BEINTEMA, D.: The Neurological Examination of the Full-term Newborn Infant. Little Club Clinics in Developmental Medicine No. 12 London: William Heinemann Medical Books Ltd., 1964.

45. PRECHTL, H. F. R.: Prognostic value of neurological signs in the newborn infant. *Proc. Roy. Soc. Med.*, 58:3, 1965.

46. PRECHTL, H. F. R., VLACH, V., LENARD, H. G., and GRANT, D. K.: Exteroceptive and tendon reflexes in various behavioral states in the newborn infant. *Biol. Neonat.*, 11:159, 1967.

47. PRECHTL, H. F. R., AKIYAMA, Y., ZINKIN, P., and GRANT, D. K.: Polygraphic studies of the full-term newborn: I. Technical aspects and qualitative analysis. In Studies in Infancy. Clinics in Developmental Medicine No. 27. London: William Heinemann Medical Books Ltd., 1968, pp. 1-21.

48. ROBINSON, R. J.: Assessment of gestational age by neurological examination. *Arch. Dis. Child.* 41:437, 1966.

49. ROBINSON, R. J., and TIZARD, J. P. M.: The central nervous system in the newborn. *Brit. Med. Bull.*, 22:49, 1966.

50. ROSENBLITH, J. F.: Prognostic value of neonatal assessment. *Child Develop.*, 37: 623, 1966.

51. SAINT-ANNE DARGASSIES, S.: Méthode d'examen neurologique du nouveau-né. *Études Neonat.*, 3:101, 1954.

52. SAINT-ANNE DARGASSIES, S.: La maturation neurologique des prématures. *Études Neonat.*, 4:71, 1955.

53. SAINT-ANNE DARGASSIES, S.: Neurological maturation of the premature infant of 28 to 41 weeks' gestational age. In Human Development, Ed. F. Falkner. Philadelphia and London: W. B. Saunders Co., 1966, pp. 306-325.

54. SCHULTE, F. J., MICHAELIS, R., und FILIPP, E.: Neurologie des Neugeborenen. I. Mitteilung Uraschen und klinische Symptomatologie von Funktionsstörungen des Nervensystems bei Neugeborenen. *Zeit. f. Kinderheilk.*, 93:242, 1965a.

55. SCHULTE, F. J., FILIPP, E., und MICHAELIS, R.: Neurologie des Neugeborenen. II. Mitteilung. Die Prognose von Funktionsstörungen des zentralen Nervensystems beim Neugeborenen. *Zeit. f. Kinderheilk.*, 93:264, 1965b.

56. SCHULTE, F. J., and SCHWENZEL, W.: Motor control and muscle tone in the newborn period: electromyographic studies. *Biol. Neonat.*, 8:198, 1965.

57. SCHULTE, F. J., MICHAELIS, R., LINKE, I., and NOLTE, R.: Motor nerve conduction velocity in term, preterm, and small-for-dates newborn infants. *Pediatrics*, 42:17, 1968a.

58. SCHULTE, F. J., LINKE, I., MICHAELIS, R., and NOLTE, R.: Electromyographic evaluation of the Moro reflex in preterm, term, and small-for-dates newborn infants. *Developm. Psychobiol.*, 1:41, 1968b.

59. STERN, E., PARMELEE, A. H., AKIYAMA, Y., SCHULTZ, M. A., and WENNER, W. H.: Sleep cycle characteristics in infants. *Pediatrics*, 43:65, 1969.

60. TAFT, L. T., and COHEN, H. J.: Neonatal and infant reflexology. In Exceptional Infant. Vol. I. The Normal Infant, Ed. J. Hellmuth. New York: Brunner/ Mazel, Inc. 1967, pp. 79-120.

61. THURSTON, D., GRAHAM, F. K., ERNHART, C. B., EICHMAN, P. L., and CRAFT, M.: Neurologic status of 3-year-old children originally studied at birth. *Neurology*, 10:680, 1960.

2

NEUROBEHAVIORAL ORGANIZA-
TION OF THE HUMAN NEWBORN

Gerald Turkewitz, Ph.D.
and
Herbert G. Birch, M.D., Ph.D.
Department of Pediatrics
Albert Einstein College of Medicine,
Yeshiva University (New York)

Almost all students of development are dissatisfied with the degree to which our techniques for the assessment of deviance permit us to identify abnormal functioning very early in life. Such identification is not at all difficult in severely damaged newborns but lesser degrees of impairment go unnoticed when standard methods of clinical assessment are used. Over 20 years ago Monnier and Willi (1947 a & b) were able to demonstrate that, with the exception of the visual following response, reflex organization appeared to be grossly normal even in anencephalic infants. Therefore, if we are to develop more sensitive techniques for the early identification of handicap we must go beyond standard examinations and direct our attention to properties of more complex neurobehavioral organization. Our aim in this chapter is to suggest an approach to this problem together with some of the findings that have derived from it.

A number of alternative strategies have been used in the effort to increase diagnostic sensitivity. André-Thomas and his associates (André-Thomas, Chesni & Dargassies, 1960) as well as others such as Beintema (1968), Prechtl and Beintema (1964), and Taft and Cohen (1967) have all sought to modify the pediatric neurological schedule so as to include such factors as tonus, and lateral equality as well as more standard reflexes in their examination of infant status. Other workers such as Dreyfus-Brisac (1957, 1962), Ellingson (1957, 1967), Engel (1965), Harris and Tizard (1960), Hrbek and Meres (1964), and Parmelee et al (1970)

The research reported was supported in part by the National Institutes of Health, Institute of Child Health and Human Development (#HD-00719), the Association for the Aid of Crippled Children, and the National Association for Retarded Children.

have approached the problem through the incorporation of electrophys-
iologic measures ranging from EEG through sleep patterns to evoked
cortical responses.

Finally although there has as yet been no attempt to identify atypical
infants on the basis of their learning ability the recent development and
application of more successful techniques for producing learning in infants (Kaye, 1965; Lipsitt, 1966; Siquiland & Lipsitt, 1966) will undoubtedly result in the exploration of this approach in the not too
distant future.

Although each of these approaches has its own merits and should therefore be pressed there are certain limitations which attach to each of
them. Since the demands for higher level integrative behavior placed
upon the infant in the investigation of his reflexes and his muscle tonus
are normally quite minimal such indicators are frequently insensitive to
even marked neurologic deficiencies. Although the examination of neu-
roelectrical activity is promising with respect to identifying individuals
with immature or defective neurointegrative organization it is limited
by our imperfect understanding of the relationship between such neuro-
electrical activity and behavior. Although the findings that the alpha
rhythm of the EEG of puppies do not appear until the puppies are three
weeks old (Charles & Fuller, 1956), when examined in relation to Fuller
et al's (1950) failure to obtain evidence of learning in puppies at ages
younger than three weeks, were taken as indicating a relationship between maturity of EEG activity and learning capacity, more recent findings, that under appropriate conditions learning could be accomplished by
puppies during the first week of life (Stanley et al, 1970) while the EEG
pattern is still quite immature, raises serious questions about the nature
of the relationship between EEG findings and neurointegrative organization. Similarly Shapiro et al's (1970) findings that infant rats exhibiting
precocial evoked potential patterns show a depression in certain types
of learning at latter ages indicates that any assessment of neurointegrative intactness based upon the appearance of electrocortical events
is at the present time on somewhat shaky ground. When Shapiro administered thyroxine to infant rats these animals showed mature patterns
of evoked cortical potentials earlier than did non-treated controls. However thyroxine treated animals also showed poorer learning ability when
tested at older ages. Finally, although the study of learning during early
infancy may well enable us to detect individuals whose neurointegrative
competence is atypical both at the time of testing and at latter ages,
the time required to train infants might prove to be prohibitive with
respect to its general use for evaluative purposes.

In view of these possible limitations our strategy has attempted to
identify behaviors that: 1) require a relatively high degree of integration,

2) the infant is capable of exhibiting without any special training and 3) are potentially important for the future development of the infant.

Since many patterns of normal behavior ranging from speech and reading through fine motor coordination seem to require stable patterns of lateral differentiation, it appeared likely that lateralization of functioning during the neonatal period might represent a sensitive indicator of neurobehavioral organization and one which is of more than minor importance for the subsequent organization of behavior. We therefore focused our attention on the identification of lateralized aspects of behavioral organization in the newborn infant.

In selecting a particular aspect of lateral differentiation for study we were guided by certain principles of development. It has long been recognized that there is a gradient of development which occurs along a cephalocaudal axis such that development at the head end is more advanced than that of the trunk or extremities. It therefore seemed likely that those responses which occurred at or near the infant's head end would be more advanced than other responses and that head end responses being of a higher level of organization would represent maximally sensitive indicators of neurointegrative organization. We therefore concentrated our attentions on head end responses of the infant e.g. head turning and eye movements. Furthermore, very early in our search for organized behaviors in newborns we came to recognize that directional responses to spatially distributed stimuli are among the earliest organized patterns of behavior to emerge in ontogeny. The early emergence of such patterns is evidenced by their appearance in the embryo, foetus and neonate of such diverse vertebrate forms as salamanders (Coghill, 1929), rats (Angulo y Gonzalez, 1932; Crozier & Pincus, 1937), guinea-pigs (Windle, 1944), cats (Coronios, 1933), and man (Minkowski, 1921). In view of their prevalence and early appearance directionalized behaviors appeared to represent a potential source of sensitive indicators of neurointegrative organization.

Our principle strategy has therefore been to seek for sensitive indicators of neurointegrative organization among laterally differentiated directional responses of the infant's head end. This strategy has led us to investigate lateral differences in the infant's head turning response to laterally applied somesthetic stimulation of the perioral region and to compare infants whose developmental history has been unexceptional with infants whose histories suggest that they are at an elevated risk of neurointegrative disturbance.

The results of an investigation of normal infants between 24 and 72 hours of age indicates that the head turning response to laterally applied somesthetic stimulation of the perioral region is not equivalently manifested when a stimulus is applied to the infant's left side and when it is applied to his right side (Turkewitz et al, 1965b). Although the response typically elicited by stimulation of either side is a turn in the direction of stimulation (Prechtl, 1958) we found such ipsilateral responses to be more readily elicited by stimulation of the infant's right than by stimulation of his left side. Furthermore, although contralateral responses are infrequently made to stimuli applied at either locus they are significantly more common when the stimulus is applied at the infant's left side.

Having identified an early appearing pattern of lateral differentiation in normal infants we compared infants at different degrees of exposure to antecedent conditions associated with later manifestations of CNS damage with respect to this pattern of lateral differentiation.

Although infants whose condition at birth is suboptimal frequently appear to be normal by the second day of life, there is evidence that such infants exhibit a relatively high frequency of abnormalities in motor, language and intellectual functions during later infancy and childhood (Edwards, 1967; Graham et al, 1962; Klatskin et al, 1966). It therefore appeared possible that the effects of poor condition at birth were not evanescent and that there was continuing disorganization which was masked by the insensitivity of routine clinical evaluation. To explore this possibility we compared the neurointegrative competence of infants who had been in poor condition at birth but who according to routine clinical assessment had completely recovered with that of infants whose condition at birth and thereafter was good (Turkewitz et al, 1968). Birth condition was assessed by means of Apgar scores (Apgar & James, 1962) and neurointegrative competence by means of tests of lateral differences in the head turning response to somesthetic stimulation of the perioral region. The tests consisted of the presentation of 30 lateralized stimuli (15 to each side) in a predetermined random order. On the basis of their Apgar scores (taken within one minute after birth) 130 infants (all of whom were judged by pediatric examination to be in good condition at the time of testing) were divided into three groups: a High Apgar Group (score of 9-10); an Intermediate Apgar Group (score of 7-8); and a Low Apgar Group (score of 1-6).

The data indicated that infants in poor condition at birth made head turns as frequently as did normals. However, they exhibited differences in the lateral organization of these responses. Infants in both the Intermediate and High Apgar Groups made significantly more responses to stimulation at the right than at the left whereas infants in the Low Apgar Group exhibited no such lateral difference in responsiveness and in fact were slightly more responsive to stimulation of the left than of the right. As may be seen in Figure 1 the percentage of infants who were preponderantly responsive to stimulation of the right was highest in the High Apgar Group and lowest in the Low Apgar Group. In addition, as may also be seen in the figure, the percentage of subjects who

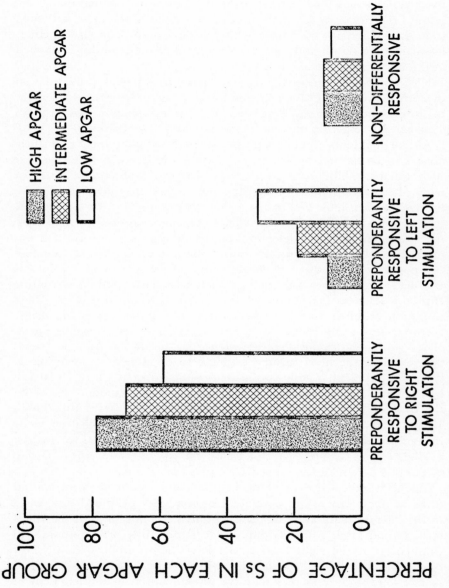

FIGURE 1

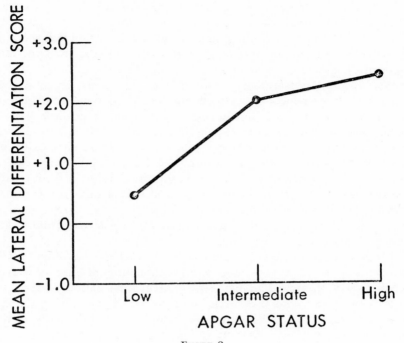

FIGURE 2

were more responsive to stimulation of the left than of the right was significantly higher in the Low than in the High Apgar Group.

To achieve a more refined analysis of lateral differences in the frequency of responses a differentiation score was calculated for each baby. This was done by subtracting the number of responses to stimulation of the left perioral region from the number of such responses to stimulation of the right perioral region. A positive score reflected an excess of right responses and a negative score an excess of left responses. As may be seen in Figure 2 the mean lateral differentiation score increased as Apgar level rose. The magnitude of lateral differentiation was significantly higher in both the Intermediate and High Apgar Groups than in the Low Apgar Group.

Not all infants whose condition was poor at birth showed atypical lateral differentiation but even those babies who showed typical overall patterns showed them less clearly than did babies whose condition at birth was normal with the amount of disturbance associated with Apgar level. Thus, even those infants in the Low Apgar Group who exhibited the same direction of lateral difference as did normal infants, showed a lesser degree of differentiation than did normal subjects.

These findings suggest that either the recovery of the infants whose condition at birth had been suboptimal was more apparent than real or that the early malfunctioning had contributed during the perinatal period to a sequence of development which did not lead to the establishment of typical patterns of lateral differences.

It is tempting to speculate about the possible developmental consequences of disturbances in early lateral differentiation. The early appearing lateral differentiation of behavior provides a possible basis for the subsequent development of more far-reaching and functionally significant lateral differences. The early lateralization of responsiveness may result in the establishment of a leading side in dealing with the environment and either directly or via a learning process result in the increasing permanence of lateral preference. It is possible that this suggested developmental sequence may be modified by the failure of early lateral differentiation to occur, and that infants who are in poor condition at birth are at this type of developmental risk.

It is obvious to us that the examination of early lateral differentiation represents a useful approach to the identification of infants who are exceptional with regard to neurointegrative organization. Although it appears likely that lateral differentiation or its absence during the early postnatal period affects subsequent development it is equally obvious that examination of the relationship between early lateral differentiation and subsequent functioning is required before we can assume that the disturbance of lateral differentiation which we have observed in the young infant is related to the association which has been found between a variety of functional disabilities and disturbances in laterality in older children and adults.

Normal lateralization in the young infant may be dependent upon a whole set of underlying factors. A series of investigations in our laboratory has served to identify the head position of the infant as one important contributor to the early development of lateral differences in responsiveness.

One of the most easily observed and prevalent types of lateral differentiation which the young infant exhibits is a marked propensity to lie with his head turned to the right (Gesell & Ames, 1947; Turkewitz et al, 1965a). In one series of observations during which we made systematic sample observations of the head positions of 100 infants ranging in age from several minutes to slightly over 100 hours, it was found that on more than 3000 observations during which the infants were observed while in the supine position their heads were turned to the right of the body midline during 88.0 per cent of them. The heads of the infants were in a midline position during 2.8 per cent of the observations and to the left of the body midline during only 9.2 per cent of these observations. Not only was it true that when in the supine position infants in general spend roughly 10 times as much time with their heads turned to the right as to the left but it was found that most individual infants spend well over 90 per cent of the time in which their head is not in a midline position with their heads maintained to the right of the body midline. None of the infants was found to have his head turned to the left of the midline more frequently than to the right. These observations in which two types of infants were identified, i.e. those with a marked preference for a head right posture and those in whom there was a less clearly defined position preference, are in agreement with findings from an earlier study (Turkewitz et al, 1965a) in which we also found that babies either exhibited clear-cut preferences for a head right posture or no clearly defined lateral head position preference. In the earlier study we found that approximately 85 per cent of a group of infants who were continuously observed for a defined time period maintained their head exclusively to the right of the body midline; the remaining infants showed no clear-cut lateral preference.

Although all of the reported observations were made while the infants were in the supine position and consequently in the position in which they could most readily determine their own head posture it was possible that the disproportionately high incidence of a head right posture resulted from a systematic bias in the way in which the infants were placed in their bassinettes by the nursing staff and had little or nothing to do with the infants' own preferential behavior. To examine this question, the spontaneous position preferences of a group of two- and three-day-old infants were examined by placing the infant's head in a midline position, releasing it, and continuously noting its position during the next 15 minutes. These tests in which the infants spent approximately 75 per cent of the test period with their heads turned to the right clearly indicate that by the time the infant is two days old asymmetrical placement is not required to produce a systematic preference for a head right posture.

The systematic assumption of a head right posture is closely associated with the reception of sensory input during the neonatal period. We as well as others have found that the human newborn is more responsive to auditory (Turkewitz et al, 1966a), tactile (Siqueland & Lipsitt, 1966; Turkewitz et al, 1965b), and visual (Wickelgren, 1967) stimuli presented at his right than at his left side. In the case of tactile and auditory stimulation the infants prior maintenance of a head right posture at least in part determines this lateral difference in responsiveness and while an assessment of the effect of the infant's head right posture on lateral differences in response to visual stimulation has yet to be undertaken, it is quite possible that the infant's prior head position affects his responsiveness to laterally presented visual stimuli as well.

Investigation of the infant's lateral conjugate eye turning in response to laterally presented auditory stimulation (Turkewitz et al, 1966a) indicates that he is more responsive to stimuli applied at his right than at his left ear. Although a 66 db white noise stimulus is sufficient, when applied at the right ear, to produce a significant increase in the number of infants turning toward the stimulus, no such effect is obtained when the same stimulus is applied at the infant's left ear. A more intense stimulus (87 db) when applied at the infant's left ear produces the same effect as does the weaker stimulus applied at the infant's right ear, i.e. significantly more ipsilateral than contralateral responding.

The principal determinant of the lateral differences in the infant's responsiveness to auditory stimuli appears to be his prior asymmetrical head position. We postulated that when the infant lies with his head in its characteristic position the right ear is occluded and the ambient level of stimulation at this ear is consequently lower than at the left ear. The difference in the degree to which each ear has become adapted to ambient levels of sound then eventuates in lateral differences in responsiveness when objectively equal lateralized sound stimuli are subsequently applied. We carried out an experiment to test this hypothesis (Turkewitz et al, 1966b). One group of infants was subjected to an adaptation procedure designed to equalize the level of ambient stimulation to which the two ears were exposed. This was accomplished by holding the infant's head in a midline position with both ears equally exposed to ambient sound. A control group was allowed to maintain spontaneous head positions and was not given the equal exposure treatment. Following this procedure both groups received identical tests of responsiveness to auditory stimulation. Although infants in the Control Group showed clear evidence of a lateral difference in responsiveness to the test stimuli those in the Experimental Group i.e. those whose two ears had been equally exposed to the ambient auditory stimuli showed no such evidence of lateral differentiation.

Since the infant's asymmetrical head position may result in asymmetries of somesthetic input as well as of auditory input a study was conducted in order to determine whether the effect of prior head position on lateral differences in responsiveness was restricted to a teloreceptor system (audition) or whether its effects were more general and applied to a proximoreceptor system (somesthesis) as well. We therefore sought to determine whether maintenance of the infant's head in the midline would also reduce or eliminate the characteristic lateral difference in his responsiveness to somesthetic stimulation of the perioral region. In this experiment (Turkewitz et al, 1967) infants in one group had their heads held in a midline position and infants in another group were allowed to maintain their head in any position spontaneously chosen. Immediately following this period both groups were examined in an identical manner for lateral differences in head turning responses to laterally presented somesthetic stimulation of the perioral region. The results of this investigation were very clear in showing that the infants who maintained spontaneous asymmetrical head positions exhibited the characteristic lateral differences in both ipsilateral (Table 1) and contralateral (Table 2) responses whereas those who had been

TABLE 1

THE INFLUENCES OF PRIOR HEAD POSITION ON THE DIFFERENTIAL EFFECTIVENESS OF RIGHT AND LEFT STIMULATION IN PRODUCING IPSILATERAL HEAD TURNS

| Group | More Responsive to | | Number of Infants | |
	Right stimulation	Left stimulation	X^{2*}	Equally responsive to right and left stimulation
Spontaneous	19	5	7.04***	2
Restricted	8	10	.06	7
X^{2*}		3.99**		

* corrected for continuity
** p < .05
*** p < .01

TABLE 2

THE INFLUENCE OF PRIOR HEAD POSITION ON THE DIFFERENTIAL EFFECTIVENESS OF RIGHT AND LEFT STIMULATION IN PRODUCING CONTRALATERAL HEAD TURNS

| Group | More Responsive to | | Number of Infants | | |
	Right stimulation	Left stimulation	X^{2*}	Equally responsive to right and to left stimulation	Making no contralateral responses
Spontaneous	5	15	4.04**	2	4
Restricted	6	9	.26	4	6

* corrected for continuity
** p < .05

prevented from assuming an asymmetrical head position exhibited neither type of lateral difference (Tables 1 and 2). Since it was possible that the failure to obtain lateral differences in the restricted group stemmed from the effects of head restriction *per se* rather than from the prevention of an asymmetrical posture and its associated asymmetries of input, another group of infants who had their heads held to the right of the body midline was included in the study. The results from this group were no different from those obtained in the group allowed spontaneous head right postures, indicating that the failure to obtain evidence of lateral differences in the infants not allowed an asymmetrical head posture stemmed from the absence of such asymmetry rather than from any effect of head restriction as such.

It was possible that the infants' asymmetrical head position resulted in lateral differences in responsiveness to subsequently applied lateral stimulation of the perioral region by producing differential adaptation to different levels of ambient somesthetic input. It was also possible that the infants' characteristic posture resulted in lateral differences in muscle tonus which then produced an increased motor readiness to turn to the right even in the absence of applied stimulation. Alternatively, differential tonus could by virtue of its afferent consequences, contribute summatively to subsequent input and result in a lateral difference in responsiveness. Since keeping the head in the midline not only reduces asymmetry of stimulation but also reduces asymmetry of muscle tone, it was not possible to determine whether the experimentally induced changes in responsiveness were based upon the modification of prior asymmetries of ambient stimulation, upon changes in the asymmetry of muscle tone, or upon the interaction of both factors. A further study (Turkewitz et al, 1969) was therefore designed to permit a separate consideration of the effects of asymmetries of tonus and of prestimulation in order to determine whether the infant's asymmetrical head position results in lateral differences in responsiveness because it produces lateral differences in somesthetic input or because it results in lateral differences in muscle tone. To this end infants were randomly assigned to four groups.

Infants in two of the groups were given differential somesthetic stimulation but were prevented from maintaining lateral differences in tonus by having their heads held in a midline position. Infants in a third group had a lateral difference in tonus induced by holding their heads to the right but differential somesthetic stimulation was avoided by not allowing either cheek to contact the substrate and by preventing self-stimulation. Infants in a control group were treated in a manner designed to eliminate asymmetries of both somesthetic input and muscle tone and so had their heads held in a midline position with no contact made with the infant's face. Following these treatments all infants were given identical tests of responsiveness to laterally applied somesthetic stimulation of the perioral region.

The results revealed that both differential muscle tonus and differential somesthetic stimulation of the face can contribute to the lateral differences in responsiveness to somesthetic stimulation which are typically associated with a head right posture. Subjects in the Control Group made essentially the same number of ipsilateral responses to stimulation of the two sides whereas subjects in the Tonus and Somesthetic Right Groups made significantly more responses to stimulation of the right than of the left. Infants in the Somesthetic Left Group were not more responsive to stimulation of the left than of the right and in fact made slightly more responses to stimulation of the right than of the left. In view of the non-equivalent effects of prior stimulation of the right and of the left it appears likely that there is an additional factor other than prestimulation or tonus which affects lateral differences in response to somesthetic stimulation. Whatever the basis for this additional factor it is clear that the assumption of a head right posture by an infant has marked consequences for his subsequent responsiveness to stimulation and that the effect of his asymmetrical head position can be mediated by both asymmetrical tonus and differential stimulation.

It is possible that such lateral differences may contribute to the subsequent development of lateral dominance, lateral preference, and hemispheric differentiation and that the failure of normal lateral differences to appear early in life may have marked consequences for subsequent development. Although we have not yet attempted to determine which factors or mechanisms are lacking or disturbed in those infants who fail to develop typical patterns of lateral differences, the identification of factors leading to normal lateral differentiation makes this line of investigation very promising both for identifying and understanding certain types of exceptional infants.

The study of lateral differences in responsiveness does not exhaust the potentially profitable areas for the investigation of neurointegrative functioning in the newborn. Normal functioning in both children and adults appears to involve specific relationships between excitation and inhibition as well as a typical hierarchical relationship between stimulus modalities (Birch, 1962). Since the relationship between excitation and inhibition seems to be disturbed in certain instances of malfunctioning (Birch, Belmont & Karp, 1967) and since atypical hierarchical relationships among stimulus inputs seems basic to a variety of dysfunctions in children (Hermelin & O'Connor, 1964), investigation of both of these areas would appear to repay study in the poorly functioning newborn. However, since there is virtually nothing known about either excitation-inhibition relationships or hierarchical relationships among stimuli in the newborn, it is necessary to establish normative baselines before attempting to evaluate infants who are potentially deviant with regard to either of these sets of relationships. Therefore, concurrently with our investigations of lateral differences we have been pursuing a line of investigation which has as its focal point an examination of the relationships both among stimuli in different modalities and among different responses to the same stimulus.

In order to determine the nature of the relationships between various responses to the same stimulus we carried out a study (Turkewitz et al, in press) in which we examined the effect of a series of laterally presented, white noise stimuli, of graded intensities, on one autonomic response (heart rate acceleration) and two musculoskeletal responses (lateral conjugate eye movements and finger movements). The results of this investigation indicate that stimulation increases the occurrence of each of these responses so that across the range of stimulus intensities used (70 to 98 db) there is a positive linear relationship between the occurrence of each of the responses and the intensity of the stimuli. However, the thresholds indicated by each of the measures is not the same and of even greater significance is the finding that the occurrence of one response is not related to the occurrence of any of the other responses. If the occurrence or non-occurrence of each of the responses was determined by the operation of a mechanism common to all of the responses, those stimuli which elicited one response should also have tended to elicit other responses more (facilitation) or less (inhibition) frequently than was the case when the response in question was not elicited. Such was not the case, and responses did not co-occur more or less frequently than would be expected if the responses were determined by independent mechanisms. That is, the frequency with which responses co-occurred was no greater than the frequency of co-occurrence to be expected from the independent frequency of occurrence. These findings raise serious questions about the appropriateness of concepts such as generalized arousal and a unitary orienting response for explaining the facts of infant behavior since each of these concepts postulates the existence of a mechanism which simultaneously affects the occurrence of a variety of behaviors (Duffy, 1957; Magoun, 1964; Anohkin, 1958; Sokolov, 1958, 1960; Voronin & Sokolov, 1960). The apparent independence of responses from each other suggests exciting possibilities with respect to the differential diagnosis of infants with neurointegrative disturbances. The independence of responses might make it possible to distinguish between infants having hearing difficulties and those having integrative difficulties of one or another type. Thus, if an infant were deaf or had a hearing loss one would anticipate an absence or reduction of all types of response to auditory stimuli. If, on the other hand, hearing were intact but autonomic functioning were disturbed we might anticipate normal eye turning and finger movements together with atypical or no heart rate responses. Conversely there could be intact autonomic functioning but impairment of orientation which would be exhibited by normal cardiac responses and atypical eye turning. Although the potential value of this type of application is obvious it has yet to be attempted.

Although we know something about the attributes of the environment to which the young infant is responsive we as yet have little information on the hierarchical relationships which exist among stimuli in different modalities. A complete understanding of the relationships between stimuli would entail a detailed examination of the thresholds for effective stimulation in all sense modalities, the relation of such thresholds to ambient levels of stimulation, and the interactions and hierarchical relationships among modalities under conditions of multimodal input. Although we can lay no claim to any such exhaustive analysis of sensory relationships we have begun just such a program of research by investigating the relative durability of effectiveness of stimulation in two different sensory modalities. This investigation (Moreau et al, 1970) involved the repeated presentation of initially equivalent stimuli in two different modalities. Infants in one group received successive presentations of a lateralized white noise stimulus and infants in the other group the same number of lateralized somesthetic stimulation. Initially, that is on the first presentation, the auditory stimulus and the somesthetic stimulus were equally effective in eliciting cardiac responses. Despite their initially equivalent effect, the results clearly indicate that the auditory and somesthetic stimuli used were not equally effective for the subsequent elicitation of the cardiac response. Auditory stimulation had a more persistent effect on heart responsiveness than did somesthetic stimulation. Somesthetic stimulation resulted in the immediate habituation of the cardiac response i.e. by the second trial there was a significant reduction in responses whereas it was not until the fourteenth trial that a similar reduction in responsiveness was noted in those infants who were subjected to repeated auditory stimulation. The greater persistence of response to auditory than to somesthetic stimulation in the normal infant can have marked consequences for determining those aspects of the environment to which the infant will continue to respond and so play a major determinative role in his subsequent development. Any failure for a typical pattern of responsiveness to develop could then have marked consequences for the infant's course of development and result in a variety of atypical modes of functioning.

If habituation were a ubiquitous phenomenon with habituation of one response occurring simultaneously with habituation of other responses the task of determining whether an infant exhibited typical habituation would be greatly simplified. If, on the other hand, habituation was specific to given stimulus response configurations, characterizing an infant with respect to his rate of habituation would be much more involved but as a compensation for complexity there would be advantages for differential diagnosis.

In order to determine whether habituation is ubiquitous or whether there are different rates of habituation for different responses, the lateral conjugate eye movements of those infants who were presented with the successive auditory stimuli were recorded simultaneously with the measurement of their cardiac changes. Although to the initial presentation of the stimulus there was no difference in the percentage of infants making ipsilateral eye turns and the percentage making cardiac acceleration responses, subsequent presentations of the stimulus resulted in a more rapid habituation of the eye turning response than of the cardiac acceleration response. As has previously been stated, habituation of the cardiac response did not occur until the fourteenth trial whereas a significant reduction in the eye turning response was noted by the fifth stimulus presentation. These results indicate that, even when different responses are elicited by the same stimulus, habituation of the various responses does not proceed at the same rate. This state of affairs might make it possible to elaborate a quite extensive typology of infants having different habituation characteristics.

Although we have just begun to explore some of the relationships among stimuli and between them and responses in very young infants, it is already apparent that the complexities of interrelationships found offer a wide spectrum of possible individual differences even during the newborn period. These provide possibilities for identifying a variety of patterns of individual functioning which may in turn provide the opportunity for a fuller understanding of neonatal competence than that which derives from more conventional modes of behavior analysis in infants and so provide the basis for early identification of children at risk for abnormal development.

REFERENCES

1. ANDRE-THOMAS, CHESNI, Y., and SAINT-ANNE DARGASSIES, S. The neurological examination of the infant. Little Club Clinics in Developmental Medicine No. 1. National Spastics Society, London, 1960.
2. ANGULO Y GONZALEZ, A. W. The prenatal development of behavior in the albino rat. *J. Comp. Neurol.*, 55:395, 1932.
3. ANOHKIN, P. K. The role of the orienting-exploratory reaction in the formation of the conditioned reflex. In L. G. Voronin, A. N. Leontiev, A. R. Luria, E. N. Sokolov and O. S. Vinogradava (Eds.) *Orienting reflex and exploratory behavior.* Moscow: *Acad. Ped. Sci.*, RSFSR, 1958, pp. 3-16.
4. APGAR, V., and JAMES, L. S. Further observations on the newborn scoring system. *Amer. J. Dis. Child.*, 104:419, 1962.
5. BEINTEMA, D. J. A neurological study of newborn infants. Little Club Clinics in Developmental Medicine No. 28. National Spastics Society, London, 1968.
6. BIRCH, H. G. Dyslexia and the maturation of visual function. In J. Money (Ed.) *Reading disability.* Johns Hopkins Press, Baltimore, Maryland, 1962, pp. 161-169.
7. BIRCH, H. G., BELMONT, I., and KARP, E. Delayed information processing and extinction following cerebral damage. *Brain,* 90:113, 1967.
8. CHARLES, M. S., and FULLER, J. L. Developmental study of the electroencephalogram of the dog. *EEG Clin. Neurophysiol.*, 8:645, 1956.
9. COGHILL, G. E. The early development of behavior in Amblystoma and in man. *Arch. Neurol. Psychiat.*, 21:989, 1929.
10. CORONIOS, J. D. Development of behavior in the fetal cat. *Genet. Psychol. Monogr.*, 14:283, 1933.
11. CROZIER, W. J., and PINCUS, G. Photic stimulation of young rats. *J. Genet. Psychol.*, 17:105, 1937.

12. DREYFUS-BRISAC, C. Actvité électrique cérébrale du foetus et du très jeune prématuré. *Proc.* 4th Int. Congr. Electroencephalog. *Clin. Neurophysiol.*, 163, 1957.
13. DREYFUS-BRISAC, C. The electroencephalogram of the premature infant. *World Neurol.*, 3:5, 1962.
14. DUFFY, E. The psychological significance of the concept of "arousal" or "activation." *Psychol. Rev.*, 64:265, 1957.
15. EDWARDS, N. The relationship between physiological factors immediately after birth and mental and motor performance at four years. Paper read at 38th Annual Meeting of the Eastern Psychological Association, Boston, April 1, 1967.
16. ELLINGSON, R. J. "Arousal" and evoked responses in the EEGs of newborns. *Proc. 1st Int. Congr. Neurol. Sci.*, 3:57, 1957.
17. ELLINGSON, R. J. The study of brain electrical activity in infants. In L. P. Lipsitt and C. C. Spiker (Eds.) *Advances in child development and behavior*, 3:1967, pp. 53-97.
18. ENGEL, R. Maturational changes and abnormalities in the newborn electroencephalogram. *Develpm. Med. Child Neurol.*, 7:498, 1965.
19. FULLER, J. L., EASLER, C. A., and BANKS, E. M. Formation of conditioned avoidance responses in young puppies. *Amer. J. Physiol.*, 160:462, 1950.
20. GESELL, A., and AMES, L. B. The development of handedness. *J. Genet. Psychol.*, 70:155, 1947.
21. GRAHAM, F. K., ERNHART, C. B., THURSTON, D., and CRAFT, M. Development three years after perinatal anoxia and other potentially damaging newborn experiences. *Psychol. Monogr.*, 76: Whole No. 522, 1962.
22. HARRIS, R., and TIZARD, J. P. M. The electroencephalogram in neonatal convulsions. *J. Pediat.*, 57:501, 1960.
23. HERMELIN, B., and O'CONNOR, N. Effects of sensory input and sensory dominance on severely disturbed, autistic children and on subnormal controls. *Brit. J. Psychol.*, 55:201, 1964.
24. HRBEK, A., and MARES, P. Cortical evoked responses to visual stimulation in full-term and premature newborns. *EEG Clin. Neurophysiol.*, 16:575, 1964.
25. KAYE, H. The conditioned Babkin reflex in human newborns. *Psychon. Sci.*, 2:287, 1965.
26. KLATSKIN, E. H., McGARRY, M. E., and STEWARD, M. S. Variability in developmental test patterns as a sequel of neonatal stress. *Child Develop.*, 37:819, 1966.
27. LIPSITT, L. P. Learning processes of human newborns. Merrill-Palmer *Quart. Beh. Develp.*, 12:45, 1966.
28. MAGOUN, H. W. *The waking brain*. (2nd Ed.) Charles C. Thomas, Springfield, Ill., 1964.
29. MINKOWSKI, M. Sur les mouvements, les réflexes, et les réactions musculaires du foetus humain de 2 à 5 mois et leurs relations avec le système nerveux foetal. *Rev. neurol.*, 37:1105, 1921.
30. MONNIER, M., and WILLI, H. Die integrative tätigkeit des nervensystems beim normalen säugling und beim bulbospinalen anencephalen (Rautenhirnwesen). *Annales Paediatrici*, 119:289, 1947a.
31. MONNIER, M., and WILLI, H. Die integrative tätigkeit des nervensystems beim mesorhombospinalen anencephalus (mittel-hirnwesen). I. *Physiologischer Teil. Mschr. Psychiat. Neurol.*, 126:239, 1947b.
32. MOREAU, T., BIRCH, H. G., and TURKEWITZ, G. Ease of habituation to repeated auditory and somesthetic stimulation in the human newborn. *J. Exp. Child Psychol.* 9:193. 1970.
33. PARMELEE, A. H., JR., WENNER, W. H., AKIYAMA, Y., SCHULTZ, M., and STERN, E. Sleep states in premature infants. *Developm. Med. Child Neurol.*, 9:70, 1970.
34. PRECHTL, H. F. R. The directed head turning response and allied movements of the human baby. *Behaviour.*, 13:212, 1958.
35. PRECHTL, H., and BEINTEMA, D. The neurological examination of the full term newborn infant. Little Club Clinics in Developmental Medicine No. 12. National Spastics Society, London, 1964.
36. SHAPIRO, S., SALAS, M., and VUKOVICH, K. Hormonal effects on ontogeny of swim-

ming ability in the rat: Assessment of central nervous system development. *Science*, 168:147, 1970.

37. SIQUELAND, E. R., and LIPSITT, L. P. Conditioned head-turning in human newborns. *J. Exp. Child Psychol.*, 3:356, 1966.

38. SOKOLOV, E. N. The orienting reflex its structure and mechanisms. In L. G. Voronin, A. N. Leontiev, A. R. Luria, E. N. Sokolov and O. S. Vinogrodava (Eds.) *Orienting reflex and exploratory behavior.* Moscow: Acad. Ped. Sci., RSFSR, 1958, pp. 141-152.

39. STANLEY, W. C., BACON, W. E., and FEHR, C. Discriminated instrumental learning in neonatal dogs. *J. Comp. Physiol. Psychol.*, 70:335, 1970.

40. TAFT, L. T., and COHEN, H. J. *Neonatal and infant reflexology.* In J. Hellmuth (Ed). Exceptional Infant, Vol. 1. Brunner/Mazel, New York, 1967, pp. 79-120.

41. TURKEWITZ, G., BIRCH, H. G., MOREAU, T., LEVY, L., and CORNWELL, A. C. Effect of intensity of auditory stimulation on directional eye movements in the human neonate. *Anim. Behav.*, 14:93, 1966a.

42. TURKEWITZ, G., GORDON, E. W., and BIRCH, H. G. Head turning in the human neonate: spontaneous patterns. *J. Genet. Psychol.* 107:143, 1965a.

43. TURKEWITZ, G., GORDON, E. W., and BIRCH, H. G. Head turning in the human neonate: effect of prandial condition and lateral preference. *J. Comp. Physiol. Psychol.*, 59:189, 1965b.

44. TURKEWITZ, G., MOREAU, T., and BIRCH, H. G. Head position and receptor organization in the human neonate. *J. Exp. Child Psychol.*, 4:169, 1966b.

45. TURKEWITZ, G., MOREAU, T., and BIRCH, H. G. Relation between birth condition and neuro-behavioral organization in the neonate. *Ped. Res.*, 2:243, 1968.

46. TURKEWITZ, G., MOREAU, T., BIRCH, H. G., and CRYSTAL, D. Relationship between prior head position and lateral differences in responsiveness in the human neonate. *J. Exp. Child Psychol.*, 5:548, 1967.

47. TURKEWITZ, G., MOREAU, T., BIRCH, H. G., and DAVIS, L. Relationships among responses in the human newborn: the non-association and non-equivalence among different indicators of responsiveness. *Psychophysiology,* (in press).

48. TURKEWITZ, G., MOREAU, T., DAVIS, L., and BIRCH, H. G. Factors affecting lateral differentiation in the human newborn. *J. Exp. Child Psychol.*, 8:483, 1969.

49. VORONIN, L. G., and SOKOLOV, E. N. Cortical mechanisms of the orienting reflex and its relation to the conditioned reflex. In H. H. Jasper and G. D. Smirnov (Eds). *Moscow Colloquium on electroencephalography of higher nervous activity. EEG. Clin. Neurophysiol.* Suppl., 13, Serial E, 1960, pp. 335-346.

50. WICKELGREN, L. W. Convergence in the human newborn. *J. Exp. Child Psychol.*, 5:74, 1967.

51. WINDLE, W. F. Genesis of somatic motor function in mammalian embryos: a synthesizing article. *Physiol. Zool.*, 17:247, 1944.

3

NEUROPSYCHOLOGY EXAMINA-
TIONS IN YOUNG CHILDREN

Henry J. Mark, Sc.D.

and

Shirley Alpern Mark, M.S.

Department of Pediatrics
Johns Hopkins University

Many parents and their pediatricians are secretly concerned about the development of an infant or young child but are reluctant to consider the administration of formal mental measurements. A frequently-asked series of questions is "At what age is it possible to obtain valid and reliable developmental examinations?", "How often should they be repeated?", and "Who is qualified to administer such an examination?"

These questions cannot be answered without knowing the purpose of the developmental examination. If the purpose is to make long range I.Q. predictions in a "non-suspect" normal infant, then we would favor delay of mental measurements until school age. If on the other hand the purpose is to establish normalcy vs. non-normalcy and/or to detect handicaps and areas of relative intellectual strength and weakness, then we favor early examinations. Certainly, all infants and children who are considered to be at higher-than-average risk of having some Central Nervous System (CNS) dysfunctions should be given one and possibly two comprehensive neuropsychology examinations before the age of two.

The early neuropsychology examinations may be constructed around popular developmental test batteries such as the Gesell (1954), Cattell (1940), Bayley (1969), Binet (Terman & Merrill, 1960), etc., because these contain a wealth of normative data (standardized test scales and items) which a clinician can use as comparison baselines for judging an infant's progress in many areas. However, the standard developmental batteries must be modified both in test administration as well as in analysis and interpretation of test performances. To be of practical clinical value they must be sensitive and specific to the known "grosser"

41

disorders in intellectual development which are detectable in infants and young children and which affect the major channels or avenues of learning.

Disorders in Learning Channels

In children with CNS dysfunctions it must be recognized that the grosser types of disorders in intellectual development may affect the important avenues or channels of learning either singly, or in specific combinations, including the combination of affecting all channels "evenly all across the board." The frequently affected avenues of learning in young children may be divided into a) *sensorimotor modalities* and b) *languages*. Among the major *sensorimotor modalities* frequently affected are the visual, hearing, tactile and kinesthetic "input" modalities, and the gross-motor, fine-motor and vocalizing-motor "output" modalities. Among the most frequently affected *languages* in infants and young children are the "first" or primitive languages involving gesture and sound recognition, as well as the more complex or formal "spoken language" which in normal man is the primary avenue of learning and channel of communication.

The clearly established fact that CNS dysfunction may *differentially* affect some skill areas while leaving others intact (Mark, 1969, 1970) means that all skill areas may have to be examined separately. For example, some children with CNS dysfunction have perfectly adequate vision and good motor skills, but develop no, or very poor, gesture language (i.e., two-way communication via gesture or pantomime). Such a major disorder in a "first" or primitive gesture language is easily detectable in the first year of life when we administer test combinations which distinguish between visual-motor and gesture language.

Other infants with CNS dysfunction may develop normal visual or gesture language skills, but may *not develop* (or develop poorly) the ability to understand and use *spoken* language, in spite of good hearing acuity and sound imitation abilities (word and sentence parroting). Such disorders are easily detected in the second and third years of life with proper selection of test combinations.

Current national attention remains focused on those school age children in whom CNS dysfunctions mainly affect the development of academic languages (dyslexias, etc.) while leaving other major avenues of learning (such as spoken language or mechanical abilities) intact, or even at superior levels. Here again, proper test combinations can detect this academic "language-specific" disorder.

It is clear, then, that the primary purpose of an early neuropsychology examination in *suspect* infants and young children, is to identify disorders in learning channels for the purpose of finding management guidelines. The goal, of course, is to "cure" or minimize the disorder itself, to isolate its effect upon "better" avenues of learning wherever possible, and to exploit optimally all capabilities in all channels of learning and communication. Even in those cases where early detection does not gain valuable treatment time, it often prevents the rise of unnecessary secondary emotional and social problems in the child and his family.

THE NEUROPSYCHOLOGY EXAMINATION

Limit Testing Helps Identify Psychosocial Factors

One difficulty with identifying CNS effects is that they frequently mimic and/or compound the effects of psychosocial factors such as cultural deprivation and emotional disturbance. Thus, CNS dysfunction just as cultural deprivation may result in evenly retarded development such as a 10 point lowering of I.Q. equivalent (I.Q.E.) scores all across the board—i.e., on all of the subscales of developmental or I.Q.-type batteries. Similarly, CNS dysfunction just as emotional disturbance may give rise to "hyperactivity" or extreme fidgetiness which may result in evenly lowered performance scores on only those tasks requiring continuous attention.

For example, a mentally subnormal, hyperactive, young child may achieve successes on a block-design test under standard testing conditions which earn him an I.Q.E. of 50. This score will reflect the hyperactivity resulting in inattentiveness to the task. To find the relative importance of organic and psychosocial factors, we may then limit-test the child by refocusing his attention on the problem a number of times or by attempting different methods of motivation. Under such limit-testing conditions a small but important percentage of children will improve their scores by ten or more I.Q.E. points. A very small percentage of children (less than 1 in 100) might improve their performance by 30 or 40 I.Q.E. points. Thus, testing the limits (optimizing) and observing the changing score patterns give us some basis for making initial judgments about the child's attention. When the scores do *not* change under a variety of optimizing conditions, then there is some basis for a tentative clinical assumption that the child has a) biological (organic) limitations in paying continuous attention and solving problems and/or b) biological limitations in analyzing problems in sufficient detail required for solutions. In contrast, when the scores do change significantly, then it is more reasonable to assume that environmental factors tend to detract from the child's ability to pay continuous attention to the problem; such factors, then, may contribute toward other "secondary" failures and it may well be that the child could really do better and analyze problems in greater depth in many other areas if he could be trained in the mechanics of paying attention. We frequently send such children with mental ages of 3 or 4 to well-structured nursery schools for a few months and then re-evaluate the child to obtain a more stable and accurate estimate of his potential over the next few years.

Testing the limits, thus, is a miniature teaching-learning paradigm or behavior-shaping effort in which quite a large number of common-sensible approaches to teaching and management can be pre-tested.

How much psychosocial factors alone can suppress cognitive or intellectual development is not known, and we personally favor all programs aimed at early stimulation and exposure to optimal learning opportunities. As clinicians, however, we must also bear in mind that many children from severely deprived homes develop very well intellectually. Our experience with children who live at home suggests that unless the environment is grossly bizarre (e.g., locking a child in dark rooms for long periods), psychosocial factors alone will not depress Developmental Quotient (D.Q.) or I.Q. levels by more than 15 points below the mean of the parental I.Q.s. Thus, children who perform significantly below this value should always be considered at high risk of having an organic CNS type involvement, even when there is clear evidence of emotional or psychosocial components. Such children should always be limit-tested until stable success-failure boundaries are established in all areas.

Failure to test the limits altogether in neurogenic children has some hidden consequences. It often leads to exaggerated claims on the part of a therapist or treatment agent. There is no easier way to delude oneself and others than to report capabilities based on standard-tested scores at the beginning of a treatment and capabilities based on limit-tested scores at the end of a treatment. The "before-and-after difference" may look like the child made giant strides or acquired a new capability as a result of treatment efforts, when in fact the capability may have been demonstrable all along had the "limits been tested."*

Skill Profiles Help Identify Patterns of Strength and Weakness

Once the limits are tested and the more easily modifiable failures have been identified, the neuropsychology examination must attempt to classify the remaining more stable success-failure patterns. Testing strategies (data collection) and test data analyses aimed at identifying specific areas of strength and deficit in an infant or child must cover *all* important sensorimotor and/or language areas (avenues of learning) systematically, comprehensively, and if need be singly. Similar to the systems-

---

* A more technical justification for using standardized tests to generate a distribution of limit-tested scores in clinical examinations of neurogenic patients is presented in the (Mark, 1969) U. S. Department of Health, Education and Welfare paper.

methods used by a television technician searching for the malfunctioning tube, the diagnostician must be prepared to use systems-methods for analyzing the success and failure patterns of the child to determine which sensorimotor modalities and/or languages contain the handicaps and which operate relatively well. Thus, the diagnostician's report must yield a "profile" on the child. In substance, the profile must reflect the diagnostician's willingness to make a number of separate estimates regarding rate of development in different learning channels and along a number of different dimensions.

This, of course, is common practice in pediatrics. A pediatrician handling a child with spastic cerebral palsy will automatically attempt to distinguish between motor handicaps vs. intellectual handicaps. In his assessment of the child and in his prognostications of intellectual development, he will be careful not to contaminate assessment of intellect by judging the child on tests dependent upon motor performance.

Perhaps somewhat less well known is the fact that the diagnostician must be equally sensitive to the reverse possibility. For example, in a microcephalic child a diagnostician might have to make one set of estimates indicating that he expects early sensorimotor development to progress relatively well, (perhaps even at or near normal rate), while making a second set of estimates indicating that the intellectual development of the child will progress at grossly abnormal rates in most or all areas.

Thus, as with older children, the evaluation of the infant or young child with suspected neurogenic dysfunction should yield a *profile* of areas of strength and weakness. Only in those children whose sensorimotor and/or higher language functions are not affected at all by CNS dysfunctions, or whose functions are *evenly* "depressed," can cognitive skill levels be reported as a single I.Q.-type value. Even in those children who show comparable developmental rates all across the board but who have some other medical symptom to place them at higher-than-average risk of "minimal cerebral dysfunction," diagnostic vigilance should be maintained until the child does "as well as expected" in all academic learning areas. The need for such vigilance is most dramatically illustrated in dyslexia. It is by now well known that a key milestone such as a "reading skill" may fail to emerge as expected even when there are no other irregularities in the emergence rate of previous milestones.

In brief, when a child is suspect of CNS dysfunction, two rules should be borne in mind. First, the clinician must think of skill *profiles*. Single developmental rate values such as I.Q.s or D.Q.s may be misleading. Second, until a child "does as well as expected" in all academic skills, the possible emergence of an organic-type learning disability such as a mild dyslexia or acalculia cannot be ruled out. In the case of infants and young children in whom understanding and use of spoken sentences is suspect, an examination between the ages of 2 and 2½ is particularly important. Such an examination must be aimed at assessing (psycho) linguistic functions. Specifically, the examination must be designed to differentiate between parroting-without-understanding vs. true sentence-using skills (sentence understanding and sentence construction skills). When psycholinguistic tests are successfully passed at that age level, diagnostic vigilance with respect to intelligence or higher cognitive functions can be somewhat relaxed until age of about 5½ to 6, when the pre-reading and reading skill milestones are expected.

Best Cognitive Skills Set Standard and Anchor Profile

A child's very *best* intellectual or cognitive ability should be of prime interest to a diagnostician and educator because it sets a standard of performance for the child. In normal children we expect all cognitive skills to fall within a relatively narrow range of this standard or top skill value. However, in children with CNS dysfunction, many important skills may be significantly below this top skill value or "intra-patient" standard (I.P.S.). Thus, the neuropsychology examination must first be aimed at eliciting the child's best intellectual capabilities and obtaining a reliable top skill or I.P.S. value. This value in turn sets the standard and anchors the child's profile of areas of *relative* strength (compatible with the I.P.S.) and *relative* weakness (incompatible with the I.P.S.).

In infants and young children, special care must be taken to assure that the I.P.S. which anchors the diagnostic profile is based on the child's best *cognitive* skills, as contrasted to his best sensorimotor skills. The distinction is equally important in older children, but the confusion-likelihood between cognitive vs. sensorimotor skills is much greater in the young. For practical clinical purposes, the criterion which distinguishes best between sensorimotor vs. cognitive skills in the young child is the test specification that a child must engage in "two-way communication" before he can be credited with cognitive-skill success. This "two-way communication" need be nothing more elaborate than a willingness to engage in a most primitive gesture language; for example, looking for an instruction *from* an examiner, following the instruction *for* the examiner *and* waiting for approval *from* the examiner meet that specification. A test item such as "cooperates in games" found at the 7-months level on most developmental scales is one of the earliest formal test items for such communication, problem-sharing, or cognitive skills.

In brief, to calculate an I.P.S. for a child above 7 months of age, pure sensorimotor skills such as parroting, manual dexterity, etc., must be excluded. The resultant I.P.S. value can be expressed as a mental age and/or in I.Q.E. rate units. All cognitive skills which are some significant percent (e.g. 20%) below the I.P.S. value may then be considered specific learning disabilities (S.L.D.s). Such a use of cognitive skill indices is compatible with the definition of learning disabilities suggested by the National Advisory Committee on Handicapped Children of the Office of Education in the U. S. Dept. of Health, Education and Welfare.

A carefully obtained I.P.S. on a child suspect of CNS dysfunction is useful as an estimate of general rate of CNS development. For example, an athetoid or motor handicapped 3-year-old may have normal psycholinguistic skills which will yield an I.P.S. of 100 or more in I.Q.E. units. Because of the motor handicaps, such a child often appears to be much more "immature" than he really is. The I.P.S. then gives us a guideline, suggesting that we must provide the child with all the learning opportunities we provide to other 3-year-olds; our demands and expectations in all areas except those requiring gross and/or fine motor control must be similar to those we would make of a 3-year-old. Conversely, the 3-year-old with relatively normal motor development but an I.P.S. of 50 cannot be expected to behave better than a 1½-year-old in social, emotional and cognitive functions—except in those specific areas where he has been "trained to the task," i.e., received special training as is frequently the case in toilet habits.

In many ways the I.P.S. yielded by our neuropsychologic examination is comparable to the altitude scores obtained by Jastak's (1952) techniques, and we find that both indices are related to what psychologists often call a G factor of general intelligence. In many children, our I.P.S. is almost exactly 10 points higher than a G factor-type I.Q. obtained on formal developmental or I.Q. tests. This frequently-found 10-point difference represents the fact that we are deliberately reporting the top end of a distribution of cognitive skills as a "goal" toward which we direct our training efforts and toward which we hope to improve some of the S.L.D.s the child may manifest.

It should now be recalled that the concept of I.Q. and D.Q. represents a rate factor comparing mental age to chronological age. Reporting skills in I.Q.E. terms, therefore, may be viewed as reporting the rate at which the child passes important developmental and cognitive skill milestones in various sensorimotor and/or language avenues of learning. Thus, the profile of I.Q.E. values may be viewed as consisting of descriptors and quantifiers which show which modalities and language combinations in the child are relatively good and which are relatively poor "avenues of learning"; that is to say, the profiles show various channels for receiving instruction and the rate at which the child can be expected to learn in each channel.

Proper Use of Profiles Based on Learning Rates

Many professionals react negatively as soon as such terms as I.Q., D.Q., or I.Q.E.s are mentioned. They question the validity and relia- bility of such indices and generalize their opposition to the use of such statistics to include all formal mental measurements. These professionals justify the avoidance of all measurements on the basis that I.Q.-type scores are often used to "label" or categorize children, and, therefore, tend to generate self-fulfilling prophesies affecting the child's devel- opment.

As already stated, there is nothing inherent in neuropsychologic exam- inations which requires permanent classification or labeling of a child. Properly used, a neuropsychologic examination should help the special educator to focus on the child's "success-failure" boundary and thereby suggest where to start a teaching effort. An efficiency minded special educator who seeks to tailor his teaching strategies to the child's needs will use such a starting point to initiate what statisticians call an "Up- and-down Method" (Dixon & Massey, 1951) of teaching-testing. Such a method is essential to keep the child optimally motivated toward achieving specified educational goals. If the educator starts significantly below the boundary, or fails to move up at the proper rate, the child will not only fail to reach important educational milestones, but even more important, the child may get bored and be "turned off." In contrast, if the educator starts significantly above the boundary, the child will lack prerequisite skills and will have excessive failure experiences which will also "turn him off." Ideally, then, the neuropsychologist and spe- cial educator must work hand-in-hand and develop a rather formal schedule for exchanging information on the stability of the diagnostic profiles, as well as on the rate of the child's progress.

An educator using an up-and-down testing-teaching method will deter- mine very rapidly whether the initial diagnostic profile is stable and valid. Suppose, for example, a diagnostician examines a 10-month-old child who hears well but for whom sound has no meaning. He suspects an auditory agnosia. A careful history also shows the child *does not recognize,* but *does alert to* environmental sounds—sometimes even to sounds occurring at low intensity levels. A diagnostician should then use a common "paired associative conditioning" paradigm to determine whether the child can be conditioned to sound (i.e., form auditory associations). Such conditioning is demonstrable in normal 6-month-old children using non-instrumented office procedures. If the 10-month-old child fails to condition, the diagnostician must then pursue a differential diagnosis between a more severe "peripheral" hearing loss vs. a more central association disorder.

Again, a simple office procedure often suffices to yield the critical data so that the diagnostician frequently need not wait for the results of the audiologist-specialist for that aspect of the differential diagnosis. The key question is "Does the child imitate sounds well enough to show that his hearing monitors his vocalizations?" If the answer is "yes," then a conditioning paradigm using grossly different sounds (such as a noise-maker and a human voice) which fails to elicit conditioned responses is pathognomonic for a central language disorder such as an agnosia. If the child is otherwise normal, as reflected in an I.P.S. of 100 based on gesture language responses, the diagnostician must then mention auditory agnosia as a tentative diagnosis to the "educator" (parents, teachers, etc.).

The proper use of that label by the educator, then, involves a brief (perhaps five or ten minute) daily "treatment and testing" procedure to determine whether paired-associative auditory conditioning is still not possible. Also, periodically (perhaps once a month) a more formal extensive experimental "treatment-testing" session should be used in an attempt to "upset" that diagnosis. It may well be that the child is found a month later to identify different environmental sounds and the diagnosis of "agnosia" should no longer be carried.

It is unfortunately more likely that the agnosia will not remit a month later. In such a case, the diagnosis serves an extremely useful purpose for the educator. It counter-indicates all those training procedures which would deprive the child of sensory input information in other channels (e.g., visual) based on the popular theory that he "must be motivated to listen." Quite on the contrary, the dignosis suggests that we circumvent the auditory agnosia handicap by providing the child *visually* with compensatory and equivalent learning opportunities wherever possible. Just as with deaf children, our aim should be to minimize the penalties for a poorly functioning auditory communication and learning channel. At the same time, we must monitor as described the status of the agnosia handicap.

TRANSLATING DIAGNOSTIC PROFILES INTO TREATMENT PRESCRIPTIONS

To illustrate methods of translating diagnostic profiles into training and teaching procedures in young children, let us consider a severely defective "autistic-type" 2½-year-old. Our diagnostic profile shows him to do well in visual manipulative and visual discrimination tasks. He fits pegs into a pegboard and blocks into the recesses of a formboard with as much dexterity as a normal 2½-year-old. However, when we apply more formal criteria for determining whether the child's response is a two-way communication attempt with another person (i.e., the examiner), we find that it is not. Thus, the child never displays his solutions specifically to an examiner; he never looks for a reward, approval or feedback information after completing the task. He does not form adequate eye contact with an examiner to receive gestured instructions. When he does not pick the test object up spontaneously it is not possible to focus his attention on the task. His success appears to be based primarily on object manipulation. Corroborating this impression are failures on more formal tests found at lower age levels which are specifically designed to reveal two-way communication processes (such as "cooperates in games" at the 7-months level or "responds to gestures" at the 9-months level). The test data show that the child's responses are not consistent enough to earn credit at the 9-months level (approximately 30 I.Q.E. for a 2½-year-old).

Similarly, formal testing in the spoken language area frequently shows such a child's abilities to be even poorer. Often the child will not even make differential responses to voice vs. non-voice sounds, even though he can occasionally be overheard to parrot vocalizations spontaneously. Such a finding will place the child's spoken language abilities significantly *below* the 9-months or 30 I.Q.E. level.

For reasons already presented, we therefore base our I.P.S. for such a child on the best *language* skill levels, which in this case are in the gesture language area with I.Q.E. values of somewhat less than 30. As noted, we deliberately exclude from calculations of the I.P.S. the relatively well developed sensorimotor skills, some of which (visual-motor and rote parroting) are at or near normal levels.

We can translate the profile just described into teaching strategies by considering more specifically the mental age values associated with various skill levels. Testing suggested that two-way communication with this child can be expected only in the visual modality; in this modality communication is still limited to the relatively small amount of gesture language one expects in a 9-month-old. Actually, a child with such a handicap usually does not perform as consistently or as well as a 9-month-old, and one of the major treatment aims with such a child is to elicit more consistent responses. A multi-sensory approach of synchronizing input information from the visual channel with auditory or sound information may be useful; it may help the child alert to (space-orient towards) the sound source. This orientation, in turn, may help to improve the child's visual-motor "focus-and-lock" functions necessary for visual tracking and gesture communication. However, until the child recognizes the special character of the human voice, spoken language will not facilitate gesture language communication. The spoken language channel itself is certainly not a useful learning channel for the child at that stage.

We frequently place such children into a "pat-a-cake class" where the first milestone for the child is to imitate gestures on command. Hopefully, this will improve his ability to make responses and learn to establish a two-way communication channel during a "response-expected" interval. A second milestone is passed when the child directs specific "pat-a-cake gestures" to an examiner as evidenced by the fact that he waits for a reinforcing response from the examiner. This would be the beginning of two-way communication. If we are successful, we will try to enlarge the response repertoire. For example, we might focus attention on the examiner's face, lips and mouth movements to determine whether we can accelerate the emergence of spoken language functions in the child.

It is no doubt apparent that one of the diagnostician's most important jobs is to discuss the areas of relative strength and weakness with those who will work with the child. Such children are often reported by parents and others in the environment as having good "mechanical abilities." Parents must be told that well developed sensorimotor capabilities are often mistaken for mechanical capabilities and are frequently found in children who are mentally severely handicapped. Parents must be told that unfortunately we must make our predictions regarding future intellectual development of the child on the slow emergence rate of all *languages* (gesture and spoken languages) rather than on the relatively normal emergence rate of sensorimotor skills.

We must hasten to explain to the family that failure to learn the gesture language—the most concrete and primitive of the languages— in a child with adequate visual abilities is itself chief evidence for severe mental subnormality. It is not likely to be the result of emotional or psychosocial factors. We would point out that similar failure to learn a spoken language (aphasia) which is now recognized as an organic condition had in the past also been frequently mistaken for a disorder of volition with psychosocial components or etiology. We can hardly overemphasize that many self-doubting parents of children who have been classified as "autistic" breathe a sigh of relief when they learn that they do not bear primary responsibility for the condition of the child.

The examples cited so far illustrate only grossly simplified clinical reasoning processes. Each of the examples discusses only a small number of data points. In practice, clinical neuropsychology examinations in children with chronological ages below 10 years often yield between 30 and 100 or more measurements. Without such measurements we cannot identify modality-specific disorders such as memory disorders which affect only the auditory modality or memory disorders which affect only the visual modality or memory disorders which affect only sound-producing skills (verbal apraxia), etc.; nor could we identify "cross-modality" effects such as memory disorders for *recent* as contrasted to *distant* events which often affect combinations of modalities —auditory, visual, motor, etc.—in homologous fashion.

"Relative" success-failure combinations of a large number of data points yield a much more finely differentiated profile, which in turn can be translated into much more specific management and teaching recommendations. Even the more finely differentiated profiles, however, can only serve as guidelines for where and how to initiate management and teaching strategies and what first set of goals to establish. A resourceful therapist or teacher will invariably modify suggested teaching methods; he will use his own observations of the rate at which the child learns under a variety of conditions or teaching options as the basis for continued efforts. Nevertheless, use of diagnostic techniques to scratch out the problem in order to generate starting point guidelines is an important step in (re)habilitation and education. The fact that strategies may have to be changed radically in a day or month or year can be no excuse for failure to make formal measurements.

SAMPLING VERSUS SYSTEMATIC AND COMPREHENSIVE SURVEYS

It is clear that with normal non-suspect children careful developmental and psychometric testing can rely heavily on good sampling techniques. In contrast, the discussion on the nature of CNS dysfunction presented here should make it clear that to be clinically useful an examiner must sample all important avenues of learning and assess the emergence rate of key developmental milestones in each channel. To omit certain channels or milestones or factors from a list to be considered (i.e., reducing the sample) in neuropsychology examinations with children at high risk of CNS dysfunction would be no more acceptable than to reduce the data sample in a neurologic examination of these children. Thus, we cannot ask a neurologist who examines a child with suspected traumatic head injury to choose between examining the child's eye ground vs. examining his reflexes. His answer invariably will be that he needs to look at both channels. In neuropsychology, as in medicine, an increase in treatment options may well justify an increase in diagnostic sampling.

Failure to be systematic and comprehensive may well lead to failure to detect an important skill in an omitted channel, thereby changing the intra-patient standard and with it the entire cognitive profile of the child. Failure to search all channels for handicaps, and failure to search systematically and comprehensively for pseudo-skills and pseudo-failures may well obscure the neuropsychologic basis for wrong expectation levels for the child. Such a failure may obscure the etiology and possible "cure" of avoidable social, emotional and behavioral problems which are so frequently secondary to poorly diagnosed organic-type learning disabilities.

In nearly all clinical settings there is, of course, real pressure to reduce to a minimum the time and effort spent on a neuropsychological survey. The effort is motivated by the need to reduce the cost of the examination in manpower, time and money. At the present we believe that a systematic and comprehensive neuropsychologic examination in infants and young children takes only one hour or one-and-a-half hours longer than a thorough standard developmental or psychometric examination. We describe in other publications (Mark, 1969, 1970) that the search for true and pseudo-capabilities and handicaps can be conducted entirely by technicians directed by an on-line digital paper-and-pencil computer. The computer also analyzes and reports the data, and extensive quality control checks permit a professional examiner to monitor whether the clinical diagnostic data collection analysis and reporting procedure in each case "meets his own professional standards." We, therefore, believe that techniques for reducing the cost of thorough neuropsychologic examinations are available which make these examinations competitive with standard developmental or psychometric examinations. However, it is our strong conviction that even when such technology is not employed and a clinician must himself expand a *standard* psychometric examination into a longer *neuropsychologic* examination, the increase in cost and effort is well worth it. It should be remembered that many of the high-risk children will turn out to require careful clinical decision-making over many years, and a thorough systematic and comprehensive examination can get such a process off to a well-focused start.

REFERENCES

BAYLEY, N. *Bayley scales of infant development.* New York: The Psychological Corp., 1969.

CATTELL, P. *The measurement of intelligence of infants and young children.* New York: The Psychological Corp., 1940.

DIXON, W. J., & MASSEY, F. J. JR. *Introduction to statistical analysis.* New York: McGraw-Hill, 1951, p. 279.

GESELL, A., & AMATRUDA, C. S. *Developmental diagnosis, Ed. 2.* New York: Paul B. Hoeber, 1954.

JASTAK, J. Psychological tests, intelligence, and feeblemindedness. *Journal of Clinical Psychology,* 1952, 8, 107-112.

MARK, H. J. Psychodiagnostics in patients with suspected minimal cerebral dysfunction (s) (MBD), in *Minimal brain dysfunction in children.* N&SDCP Monograph, U. S. Dept. of Health, Education and Welfare, PHS Publication No. 2015. 1969.

MARK, H. J. Some requirements for translating psychological diagnoses into teaching programs, in Dr. P. Black (Ed.), *Brain damage in children: etiology, diagnosis, management.* Baltimore, Md.: Williams and Wilkins Co., in press. 1970.

TERMAN, L. M., & MERRILL, M. A. *Stanford-Binet intelligence scale.* Cambridge, Mass.: The Riverside Press, 1960.

4

LEARNING OF MOTOR SKILLS ON THE BASIS OF SELF-INDUCED MOVEMENTS

Emmi Pikler, M.D.

*Director, National Methodological Institute
for Infant Care and Education,
Budapest, Hungary*

This paper is an account of the gross motor development of 722* normal children, brought up at the National Methodological Institute for Infant Care and Education, Budapest, Hungary, under defined conditions. The children—contrary to the customary way— attained each new stage of motor performances on their own initiative, without direct help of adults, as a result of self-induced movements in the course of independent play-activity.

Development of readiness to assume more and more advanced static postures and to be active in these new postures, the course of acquiring mastery over different forms of locomotion, has been the subject of numerous investigations. The developmental range of self-induced active movements occurring in everyday life during playtime and the concomitant occurrences of the different forms of such motor actions have not been the subject of systematic investigations so far.

Despite the increasing importance that is attributed to self-induced motor actions in the development of certain psychic functions (e.g. 5, 20, 21, 22, 23, 43, 47), most researchers dealing with the gross motor development of infants disregard the spontaneous occurrence of these abilities in the child's everyday life. Whether the child practices newly acquired motor abilities on his own initiative independently or whether he is only more or less a passive object while the adult makes him move is also not differentiated by researchers. Data collected on the pattern of infant motor development recorded motor skills achieved independently along with those not achieved independently, and in-

---

* The first processing of this material included 736 children. However, 14 of them proved to be abnormal, so data relating to them have been discarded.

cluded them as stages of normal development in the developmental scales. We find this in special papers dealing with the development of certain motor skills (e.g. 34, 35), as well as in most of the pediatrical (e.g. 8, 12, 14, 17, 36) and developmental-psychological (e.g. 15, 30, 31, 44) works, in the majority of the well known developmental scales (e.g. 4, 10, 11, 19) and popular books written for mothers (e.g. 6, 13, 24, 45).

Adult help is often considered so important that the lack of direct interference is referred to as one of the primary reasons for the delay in the gross motor development in children brought up in certain institutions (e.g. 16, 42).

A synthesis of the customary descriptions of the typical course of motor development indicates that the usual course of achieving the various stages (lying prone, sitting, standing, walking) is the following:

First stage: When the mother considers it timely (according to schedules) she introduces a new posture to the child. The infant, who is only capable of lying with good balance, mobile on his back, is placed in the prone position. Later, whenever the mother or her adviser considers the child to be ready for a more advanced stage, the child is put in sitting or standing posture, and when his legs are able to support him he is led by hand as an exercise during walking. (In different countries different supporting equipment is also used.)

Second stage: The infant is exercised by an adult or with the aid of an apparatus, such as special chair, swing, baby-walker etc., to attain the ability of remaining in the new posture or to move according to the new way. In the beginning of these exercises the child is more or less rigid, spasmodic, his coordination is unsure. As time advances, he moves and stays increasingly in the newly-acquired postures appropriately.

In this period the adult keeps the child in sitting or standing postures or makes him walk, leading him by the hand over increasingly longer periods of time and with increasingly less support. At the end of this period the child is able to remain in the new posture without support, and when raised to standing position by the adult he is able to manage a few steps independently. (Some authors when describing the development of sitting, also illustrate the needed various supporting methods. [2, 18, 27, 33].)

Third stage: The child learns to take on, abandon and practice new forms of motions and postures, on his own, independently.

Thus, *after* the child has learned to be *prone,* he learns *to turn prone* and back again. *After* having learned *to sit,* he learns *to sit up* and get down; *after* having learned *to stand,* he learns *to stand up* and get down; and *after* having *learned to take some steps independently,* he learns *to stand up without support and to start* and stop walking and to get down.

Only after he has learned these, is the child able to use the advanced motor skills in everyday life on his own initiative. Only after this third period does he really become independent in the more advanced postures and motions.

EDUCATIONAL CONDITION OF THE CHILDREN

The motor development of the 722 children to be described below happened quite differently from the above described customary way. These children attained all stages of the motor development independently on their own (self-induced) initiative without any direct interference by adult or aid of supporting equipment. These children were reared in our research institute founded in 1946 with capacity for 70 children in residential care from 0 to 2½ years of age.

Conditions of gross motor development

The Institute ensures the following conditions for the children:

a) *Non-restrictive clothing:* Starting with the newborn child, clothing is used which does not restrict free activity of the upper limbs with regard to bending, stretching or turning. It is also suitable for the peculiar initial position of the lower limb (abduction and flexion of the hip and flexion in the knees) and as far as possible does not restrict movement, such as stretching, turning, bending, nor the activity of the feet. Even after the postnate period, during sleeping and resting hours in the daytime or at night, indoors or outdoors, a wide sleeping-bag is used which is longer and wider than the usual one, at least 30 cm (11.7 inches) longer than the length of the child and at least 60 cm (23.4 inches) wide, so that he can kick inside the bag or practise other activities peculiar to his age. The child is never tucked in or wrapped in blankets. No clothing is used that limits the free movement of the head. (For the same reason the child lies from the very first days of his life on a smooth —not sagging—base in his cot without a pillow.)

When the child begins to turn to the side, he is dressed in pants to facilitate free activity in tumbling and rolling. As soon as he tries to stand up, he is provided with pants reaching only to the ankles. If the feet have to be protected against cold, soft light footwear is provided, made of linen or knitted material and following the shape of the feet. As long as the child cannot walk well, he never wears rigid, hard-soled shoes. He wears them later only when weather conditions demand it outdoors.

The child spends his waking time with the least clothing necessary depending on the weather conditions. In summer he usually stays outdoors without any clothing at all. (The temperature of his room during daytime in the winter is about 18 degrees C (64.4 degrees F) at the level of the child's playing space, close to the floor.)

b) *Suitable space to facilitate movements*: The area of the cot used in the first two years of life is: 60 x 90 cm (23.62 inches x 35.43 inches) except during the newborn period when a cot of 45 x 90 cm (17.71 inches x 35.43 inches) is used. As soon as the child can turn from back to side, but not later than the age of three months, he spends his waking time indoors as well as outdoors in a play-pen. But when a child gets tired or sleepy or is disinclined to play for any other reason, he is taken back to his cot. The play-pen has a hard base which is either on the floor or slightly elevated and is surrounded with vertical bars of a height of about 50-60 cm (19.50-23.62 inches) depending on the child's age. The pen has an area of at least 120 x 120 cm (47.24 x 47.24 inches). As soon as the child is capable of changing his location in the pen by tumbling about or rolling, a space of 2 x 2 m (78.74 x 78.74 inches) is at his disposal. When—and this is usually the case—several infants are placed in a common big play-pen, an area of at least 1 m² (1550 square inches) is allotted to each child. When they are more advanced in movement or in case they are playing with bulky toys, more than this amount of space is allotted for each child.

From the end of the first year, after having learned to change location easily by crawling, creeping or rolling, children are placed in a fenced-in floor area or, during the summer, in a fenced-in grassy area in the garden.

c) *Appropriate toys*: It has been the aim of the Institute to provide the children from about the age of 8-10 weeks with toys which they can seize and handle at their respective levels of development, on their own initiative without the help of an adult. Naturally those toys are chosen that cannot harm the children in the course of their spontaneous playing activity.

d) *No "teaching" (direct help) by adults*: The Institute withholds "teaching" in any form. Under "teaching" we understand systematic practice of certain motor-skills by holding or keeping the child in a certain position, whether by adult or by various equipment, or in any way helping him to make movements that he is not yet able to execute by himself in his daily life.

For example, the infant is always put down lying on his back. He spends his waking time as well as his sleeping time in this position until he is able to achieve another position on his own initiative and without any help. At this age adults carry the infant lying on their arms. While being fed, he lies on the lap of the nurse, obliquely, leaning his trunk and head against her shoulder.

A child who is not yet able to turn from supine to prone is put in prone position only for some minutes daily after bathing for drying his back or if medical examination is needed. As long as the child spends his time lying supine or prone, all toys are placed more or less near to the child on the bottom (base). At no stage of his development are toys placed in the child's hand to introduce them to him. Neither are toys hung above his head in the crib, nor fixed on the railing of his crib or play-pen.

A child who cannot yet attain a sitting position is never put in this position either during medical examination or during caretaking (feeding, bathing, dressing) or while playing. It is also forbidden to give him help in order to cause him to complete a tentative form of activity. Nurses do not take the child by the hand in order to aid him in sitting up. Further, there is nothing in the Institute resembling a chair in which the child can be incarcerated, such as a chair with two holes for the infant's legs. Nor is the child ever placed in a corner of his cot, propped up with pillows.

Nobody puts the child who cannot attain a standing position in this position, not even for medical examination or caretaking. Neither do nurses use any aid to keep the child in standing position. If the child is able to manage only a few steps, he is not held by his hand even if he wants help for a longer walk. The child is led by the hand only after he has learned walking quite well, when he wants a hand as a means of establishing contact with the adult. (The fact that adults do not help the child to move and that they avoid encouraging him to move in some particular way does not mean that they do not enjoy the child's attempts and progress, nor do they avoid showing their feelings.)

About the educational conditions in general

Naturally, our work concerning the gross motor development is only a small part of the educational work conducted in the Institute. The determining basic condition to which we attribute the absence of signs of hospitalism is the specialized kind of infant care that is done in the Institute. Building up an adequate relation between the child and the nurse is indispensable for the normal development of the child. This is a most important aspect of our educational work.

The optimum rapport between the child and his caretaker is formed primarily—and especially during infancy—while caring for the child (37). Therefore, besides trying to meet everyday problems (what kind of food and clothing does the child need, when and how much time should he spend out of doors,* etc.) equal importance is given to the

---

* From the very beginning the schedule was designed to allow children to be in open air as much as possible. During the summer they spend nearly the entire day outdoors. In the winter, even the youngest nap in the open air.

quality of caretaking (the way children are handled while their needs are provided for). Thus our interest is not only concentrated on *what* particular food the child is given, but *how* it is to be offered to him, *how the child accepts it, how both the nurse and the child behave* during feeding (38) and *what kind of interaction (collaboration, cooperation) comes into being.* The same attention is paid to the cooperation between nurse and child during bathing (39), changing diapers, dressing or any other activity. The Institute endeavors to form the best possible interaction between child and adult from the newborn period on. Thus *the child should never be only the subject of caretaking* procedures but—as much as possible—an active partner of the adult from the very beginning.

Furthermore, the Institute attempts to keep the membership and the supervising nurse of a given group constant. (One group of nine children is attended by a stable team of three caretakers alternately.)

The Institute endeavors further to ensure suitable calmness while the children sleep. The schedule made for the caretakers enables them to spend the needed time for caring in the expected way.

ABOUT THE DEVELOPMENT IN GENERAL OF CHILDREN REARED IN THE INSTITUTE

Judging from 24 years' experience, the results are satisfying. The children reared in the Institute from their newborn period on developed by and large normally both somatically and psychically. They proved not to be more often ill in general than in average families (32). Special research work, e.g. investigations on the development of manipulation of children reared in the Institute, proved that it follows the generally accepted norms (3, 46). Reexaminations (so far few were made) did not show any well-known typical later damages (7, 25). At this time a more extensive reexamination is under way with the support of a World Health Organization Medical Grant.

Children admitted shortly after birth to and brought up in the Institute are, in general, active and interested in their environment. Their development and their behavior are, by and large, like those of children reared in good families. Typical institutional negative symptoms cannot be observed. The Institute considers these facts (i.e. that the children are active in general and interested) as preliminary conditions for the normal motor development under the above-defined conditions. On the other hand, the manner of motor development reported below is considered by us as one of the important preliminary conditions of attaining active and interested behavior in children reared in institutions.

The observed children

The 722 children stayed in the Institute between 1947-1964. They were admitted, in general, before three (premature ones four) months of age. They spent at least three months in the Institute. Of the 722 children, 393 arrived younger than two weeks of age. 199 stayed there at least till walking age. There were 591 children whose birthweights were above 2500 g (5.5 lb.), 131 under 2500 g (5.5 lb.) and 12 children's birthweights were unknown.

Method of recording

The main motor developmental stages which could be seen and verified by everybody were recorded. The records were made as part of the everyday procedure. The recorded motor developmental stages were part of the phenomena of self-induced independent motor activities in the course of spontaneous play activities. Finer details—e.g. the different way of sitting, standing or walking—were not recorded. Neither was the development of reflexes recorded, partly because this was not the object of our observations and partly because in that time-period we did not want (even for the sake of experiment) to make the child stand, sit or turn repeatedly, weekly or monthly.

The nurse who was responsible for and cared for the child made the recording. A pediatrician or pedagogue who knew the children well verified the accuracy of the data. In this way, records which did not reflect the facts were avoided. It could happen, however, that the recording of some motor developmental stages happened somewhat later than they actually emerged; thus it is possible that our data show some lateness in respect to reality.

The results

The children without exception attained the age-appropriate motor skills similarly to those children who were reared under similar conditions in families supervised by the author as their pediatrician for a period of 10 years.

The recorded stages of motor development in children reared under the specified conditions are defined as follows: a) turns from back on the side and returns to back; b) turns from supine to prone; c) turns from prone to supine, tumbles about; d) crawls (without lifting the trunk); e) creeps on hands and knees or hand and feet on level as well as on rising terrain; f) sits up by self; g) kneels up by self and lets himself down; h) stands up by self and lets himself down; i) starts

TABLE 1

THE MAIN DATA OF GROSS MOTOR DEVELOPMENT BY GROUPS OF BIRTHWEIGHT

Forms of gross motor activity	Mean age of attaining the principal stages of motor development — Completed wee's			Median[4]			Standard Deviation Weeks			Coefficient of variation %		
	B¹	C²	D³	B¹	C²	D³	B¹	C²	D³	B¹	C²	D³
Turns on side (from back)	16.97	19.91	22.85	16.5	20.5	21.5	4.58	5.17	7.12	27.0	26.0	31.2
Turns from supine to prone	23.88	28.55	31.88	23.5	28.5	30.5	5.01	5.51	6.79	21.0	19.3	21.3
Turns from prone to supine	28.72	34.67	37.13	28.5	35.5	35.5	6.00	6.72	5.98	20.9	19.4	16.1
Crawls	38.52	43.92	49.66	37.5	42.5	48.5	7.47	8.02	10.83	19.1	18.3	21.8
Creeps	44.19	48.51	58.14	43.5	49.5	55.5	7.99	9.13	10.83	18.1	18.8	18.6
Sits up	44.39	49.91	58.33	43.5	49.5	58.5	6.46	8.07	10.07	14.6	16.2	17.3
Kneels up	45.35	50.04	57.89	44.5	50.5	57.5	7.42	8.20	10.44	16.4	16.4	18.0
Stands up	48.60	53.56	62.39	47.5	52.5	61.5	7.89	8.98	11.15	16.2	16.8	17.9
Starts walking	66.21	72.32	83.02	65.5	70.5	79.5	11.37	11.63	14.18	17.2	16.1	17.1
Walks well	72.08	78.15	87.13	69.5	77.5	85.5	11.90	11.72	14.62	16.5	15.0	16.8

B¹—birthweight above 2500 g (5.5 lb.) 591 children
C²—birthweight from 2001 to 2500 g (4.4-5.5 lb.) 75 children
D³—birthweight 2000 g, under 2000 g (4.4 lb.) 44 children
⁴—the middle of the one-week interval in which the median falls

walking without clinging to objects; j) walks well, uses walking in everyday life for locomotion.

In regard to the sequence of the stages: the turning on side and to prone (tumbling about) always precedes all further stages. The sequence of the stages—crawling, creeping, sitting up, kneeling up, standing up —is not stable, but kneeling up always precedes standing up; creeping and sitting up occur approximately at the same time. Sitting up precedes standing up in 90% of the cases. In the remaining 10%, standing up precedes sitting up or both occur at the same time.

Table 1 contains occurrence-data of the different stages concerning all children (except the 12 whose birthweight was unknown) grouped according to their birthweight.*

Among the 591 children with birthweight above 2500 g (5.5 lb.), turning to the side occurred on the average at the age of 17 weeks; turning prone at 24 weeks; turning from prone back again at 29 weeks; crawling at 39 weeks; creeping at 44; sitting up at 44 weeks; kneeling up at 45 weeks; standing up at 49 weeks; first free steps at 66 weeks; safe walking at 72 weeks (17 months). All numbers are average; there are remarkable and frequent deviations in both directions. Parallel with growing ages, the dispersion becomes more and more scattered in time. While at turning prone the standard deviation is $\pm$ 4½ weeks, the difference is 9 weeks; at the time of walking well the deviation is $\pm$ 12 weeks, the difference being nearly ½ year.

Figure 1 shows the average ages when these principal stages have been reached. The distribution in question approaches the normal distribution. About 70 per cent of all cases fall within one standard deviation of the mean: consequently, this interval on either side of the mean indicates the characteristic time for the acquisition of each stage of motor ability.

Table 2 shows the percentile distribution of the appearance of different stages of motor development.

The motor development of the group of children with birthweight under 2500 g (5.5 lb.) follows the same sequence as that of the group with higher birthweight but shows delay in time. The delay of children with birthweight between 2000-2500 g (4.4-5.5 lb.) can be regarded as by and large even and it amounts in general to 4-6 weeks. In the group with birthweight under 2000 g (4.4 lb.) the delay is greater and grows with increasing age. While turning on side shows on the average 6

---

* Motor developmental data of children admitted in various calendar years did not differ. For this reason the data are processed together. Data were examined for two groups: Group A, all the children, and Group B, the children who remained in the Institute until they started walking. Since, while in the Institute, Group B did not differ in gross motor development from the remainder of Group A, data for the entire 722 children are here processed.

Figure 1

Mean age of attaining the principal stages of motor development

(591 children with normal birthweight)

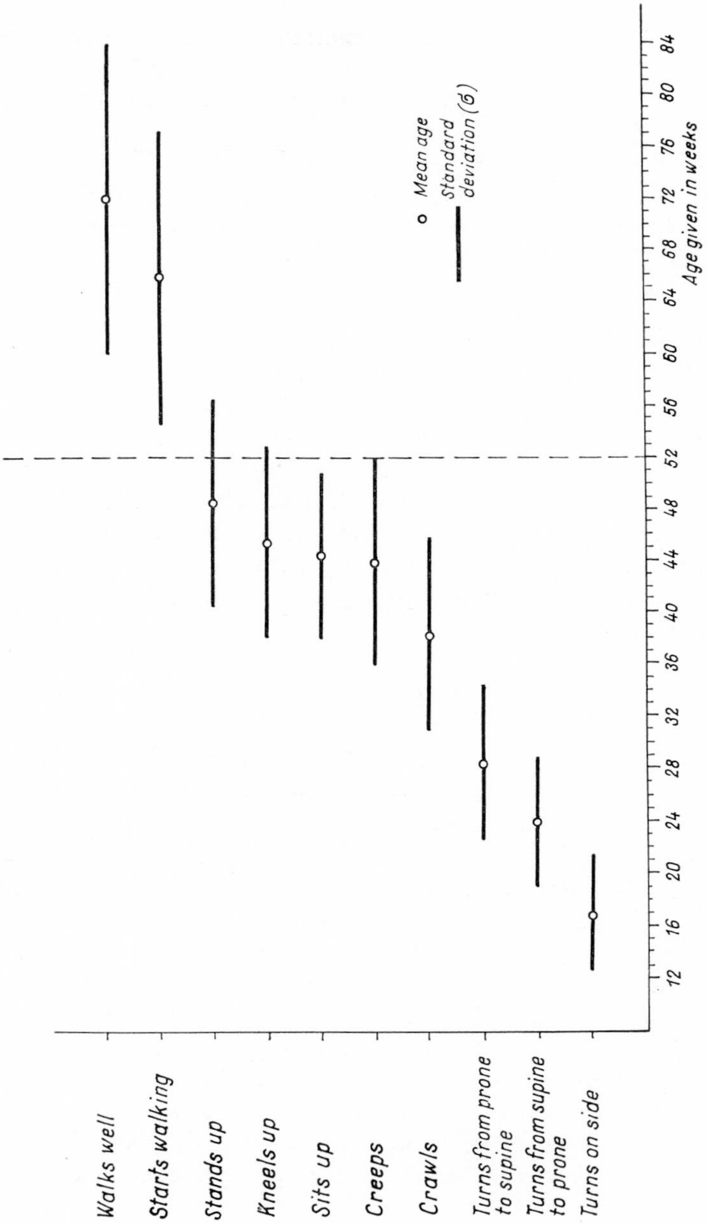

TABLE 2

The Percentile Division for the Time of Appearance
for Each Movement
(The data are given in weeks completed)

Movements	Number of children	10%	25%	50%	75%	90%
Turns to side	487	11.0	14.2	16.7	19.7	22.9
Turns to prone	471	18.0	20.4	23.6	26.9	30.0
Turns back from prone	327	20.9	24.9	28.0	32.5	36.9
Crawls	252	29.2	33.3	37.9	43.2	46.9
Creeps	240	35.2	38.7	43.1	48.6	55.0
Sits up	233	35.7	38.7	43.4	49.1	54.4
Kneels up	227	36.6	40.3	44.8	49.7	54.5
Stands up	229	40.0	42.7	47.8	52.8	59.8
Starts walking	144	54.1	59.6	65.4	71.1	79.9
Walks	128	59.2	64.3	69.9	78.4	84.2

weeks delay compared to the children with normal birthweight (approximately 1½ months), the time of the first independent steps lags 17 weeks behind (about four months). That is: the time of learning motor skills in the latter group is gradually more and more prolonged. See Figure 2.

COMPARISON OF THE MOTOR DEVELOPMENTAL DATA OF THE OBSERVED CHILDREN WITH DATA FOUND IN FOUR STANDARD DEVELOPMENTAL SCALES

We have compared the average data of the motor development of 591 children with normal birthweight with the corresponding data* of four (10, 11, 19, 29) of the well-known developmental scales (see Table 3). Though their subject matter cannot be regarded as homogeneous (as the data are gathered from children reared under various conditions), they agree in one single fact: supposedly, all the children have been helped to sit, to stand, to walk, and have been put prone in the first months of their life.

The data of appearance of independent motor activity by the observed children proved to move about in the same range as the corresponding data of one or another of the scales. Those of turning prone agree with Gesell-Amatruda and precede the data given by Illingworth and Brunet-Lézine. Data of crawling precede by one week; those of

---

* The correspondence refers merely to the appearance of the skills as the circumstances are different. Our children performed these motor skills not only independently, but they also came into the starting postures independently on their own initiative; thus each new stage could occur only after the former stage had been completed.

FIGURE 2

Cumulative Distribution of Age Appearance of the Different
Motor Skills by Groups of Birthweight

SIGNS USED

———————Birthweight over 2500 g (5.5 lb.)
———————Birthweight between 2000-2500 g (4.4-5.5 lb.)
— · — · —Birthweight under 2000 g (4.4 lb.)

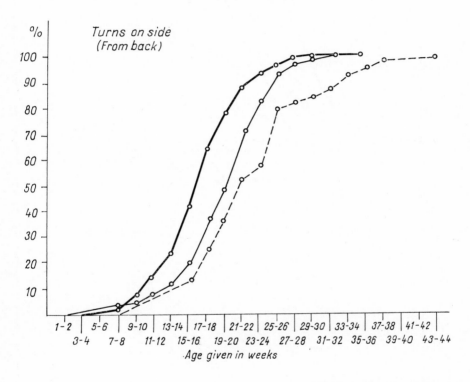

(*Fig. 2 continued next page*)

FIGURE 2 *continued*

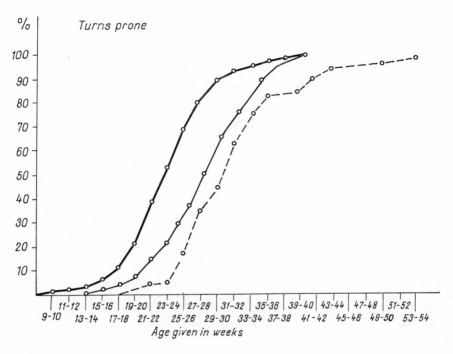

% — Turns prone

Age given in weeks

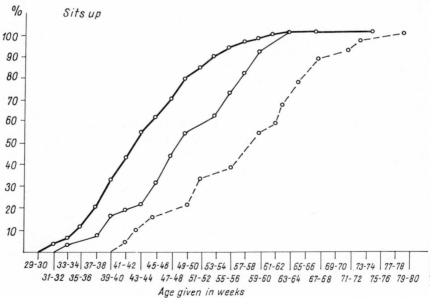

% — Sits up

Age given in weeks

(Fig. 2 continued on next page)

FIGURE 2 *continued*

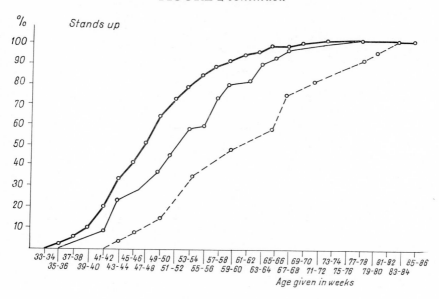

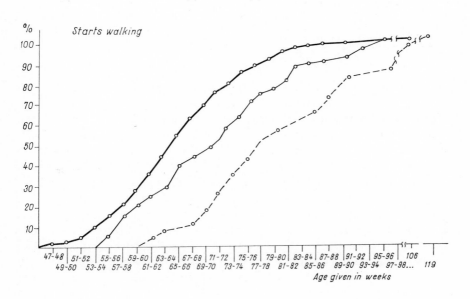

TABLE 3

The Comparison of the Main Data of Motor Development

	Pikler[1]	Brunet-Lézine	Bühler-Hetzer	Gesell	Illingworth
			Completed weeks[2]		
Turns from back to side	17	—	28	20	—
Turns from supine to prone	24	32	—	24	28
Turns from prone to supine	29	—	—	24	24
Crawls	39	—	—	—	40
Creeps on level ground	44	62	39	40	44
Sits up	44[3]	—	47	44[3]	40
Kneels up by self	45	—	—	—	—
Stands up by self	49	41	47	40	36
Starts walking	66	62	69	65	56
Walks well (uses walking for locomotion)	72	—	—	78	—

[1] Data of 591 children with normal birthweight
[2] Age data given in different units were translated into completed weeks. In cases where being in a certain week or in a certain month was quoted, the mean ages were computed.
[3] Sits up from prone

creeping agree with the data of Illingworth and precede those of Brunet-Lézine (which are remarkably late). Data of sitting up agree with those of Gesell-Amatruda and precede data of Bühler-Hetzer. Data of the first independent steps occur three weeks earlier than indicated by Bühler-Hetzer and one week later than by Gesell-Amatruda; data of walking well precede by six weeks those indicated by Gesell-Amatruda.

There are only two stages of motor development that appear later in our children than in all of the cited scales. These are: "turning from prone, back again" and "standing up." The former may be due to the fact that according to our conditions "turning from prone back" can occur only after the child has learned to master turning prone. The relative lateness of standing up may be related to the availability of adequate space and freedom for our children to move in it. According to our experience, children who spent practically no waking time in cots and have enough space for creeping show the tendency to get in vertical position at a later time.

Some developmental stages that are found in a number of scales obviously do not occur in our population, owing to the conditions of the Institute. Stages like "sits with help," "persists in sitting position," "stands with help," "remains standing when helped up," "walks with help," "makes some steps alone, when placed in standing position," etc., do not occur.

Some other stages did not occur in spite of the fact that the children had the opportunity to execute them. Thus either sliding on the bottom or sliding on bent legs in sitting position did not occur, although they are described by some authors as physiological stages of motor development (9, 26, 28). Lying in supine position and raising the head from the base, which is described in the majority of publications, occurs only sporadically with us. It has also been rare for our infants to raise themselves into a sitting position from lying on back by holding onto the railing. It was only observed exceptionally when the child for some reason, such as long illness, was kept in bed for long periods of time. Children at the Institute usually sit up by first turning to prone position, then half side, and from this position rise into sitting position.

On the other hand, there are motor skills which occur regularly with our children but are not even mentioned in the scales. For example: they are regularly kneeling up and playing in kneeling position; this precedes standing up. Some of them walk on knees, but this is an exception.

Data on creeping show differences, too. Our children creep regularly before walking, not only on level terrain but also climbing on stairs, on ladders, and up and down slopes, Brunet-Lézine, for example, do not even mention creeping on level ground, while other authors (Gesell-Amatruda, Illingworth) differentiate between creeping on level ground and creeping up and down ladders, putting the former immediately after sitting up and the latter at the time walking begins or later.

SOME TYPICAL FEATURES OF GROSS MOTOR DEVELOPMENT ON THE BASIS OF SELF-INDUCED MOVEMENTS

1) The child first learns to assume a new posture, and only after this to stay in it or, starting from it, to experiment with movements (this is opposite to the customary way described in the preface).

2) The child practices preparatory motor actions for several weeks. He practically prepares himself for the new movement before trying to attain a new posture or perform a new motion (he plays on his side for some weeks before assuming the prone position). Later, he makes crawling-creeping exercises for some weeks and plays in the prone position or sitting half way before sitting up completely. Then he spends some weeks in the kneeling posture before he first attempts to stand up. In this way, the infant is generally able to move and coordinate

The drawing-series illustrates the most often experienced motor developmental sequences of our children. In demonstrating these it has to be pointed out that the motor performances of these children show great diversity; each child having an individual way of moving. The sequences shown are much simplified. (I am indebted to Mrs. Klara Pap, graphic artist, steady collaborator of the Institute, who made the drawings.)

Starting positions which represent basic skills needed for the performance of the following sequence of movements indicated in the same row.

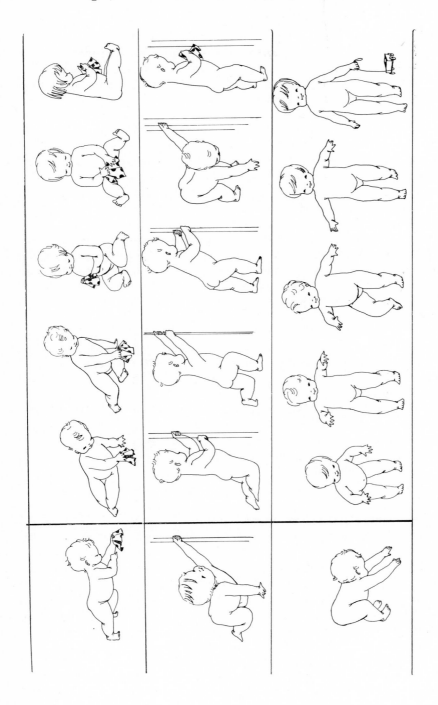

all his muscles with dynamic balance while learning new motor skills. Harmonious movement is typical for him; he does not move rigidly or spasmodically. This is contrary to the customary course of motor development in which the children first learn to keep a new posture which they are unable to adopt yet and keep it but with an inappropriate coordination. When they learn to move in a new way, they do it spasmodically, rigidly, with the aid of the adult or instrument. Only later are they able to correct, more or less, the inappropriate performances.

3) *New postures and motions occur only gradually more and more often and for longer and longer periods of time* because in the beginning the child is not usually comfortable in them and returns to the foregoing, less advanced but more comfortable positions and motions for play. If the posture is a transitory one (playing prone or creeping), the amount of time the child stays in them gradually decreases.

In this relation we gathered data on eight children reared in our Institute, observed longitudinally (40, 41). In every case records were made of each child three times a week with fifteen seconds precision within a period of 30 minutes. Gross motor performances of children from the stage of turning on their side till walking well were recorded during the usual playtime and in the regular surroundings.

Graphs 3 and 4 demonstrate the time that two of the children spent at different ages in different postures while recorded. Graphs 5 and 6 illustrate the development of the same children's frequency of locomotion activity. B. J. is a slow developer, H. Z. is an average according to our range.

4) Another characteristic feature of the children is *independence*. They do not expect help from adults either in order to change place or to change postures. As for their play activities, they usually apply the already well-known former performances and not the newest performances they are just learning.

(This does not mean that these children do not need the help of adults in general. The inexperienced infant exercising new ways of activity or while playing often gets into unexpected situations in which he cannot help himself. For instance, his clothing may slide down or he may meet other unexpected accidents, in which case the child becomes uncomfortable, unhappy and seeks help. The adult ought to give this help as soon as possible, otherwise the child becomes timid and loses the pleasure in being active. But the difference between giving this needed help and having the adults put the child in different positions is that here the need for help is always accidental and the help rendered is limited to putting the child back in the familiar starting position, or helping him get rid of the unexpected trouble.)

5) The ability to change place begins at a very early age. Children are very *mobile* during the whole time of infancy while absorbed in

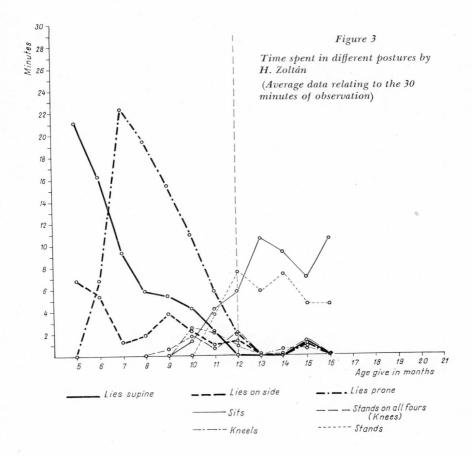

Figure 3

Time spent in different postures by
H. Zoltán

(Average data relating to the 30
minutes of observation)

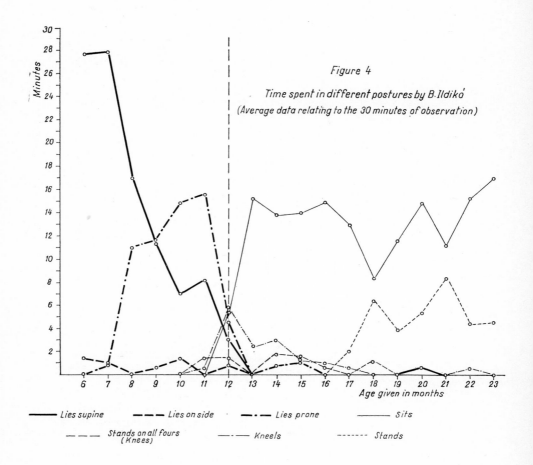

Figure 4

Time spent in different postures by B.Ildikó

(Average data relating to the 30 minutes of observation)

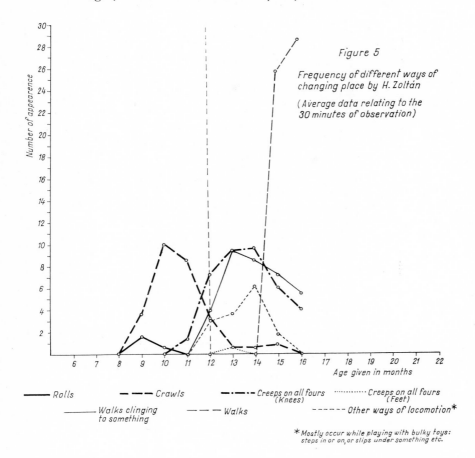

Figure 5

Frequency of different ways of
changing place by H. Zoltán

(Average data relating to the
30 minutes of observation)

——— Rolls   — — — Crawls   —·—·— Creeps on all fours   ············ Creeps on all fours
                                              (Knees)   (Feet)

———— Walks clinging   — — — Walks   — — — — Other ways of locomotion*
          to something

*Mostly occur while playing with bulky toys:
steps in or on, or slips under something etc.

their play activity. They accompany play activity with manifold postures
and motions, always trying to attain the most comfortable and economical
one.

The longitudinal study mentioned above shows that the changing
of posture (turning prone, turning back, rising on all fours, kneeling
up, sitting up, standing up and getting down from all these postures)
occurs on the average 53.3 times per 30 minutes. That means the children change their postures on average at least once per minute. This
change of postures occurred most often in the motor developmental
period between sitting up, kneeling up and standing up respectively
(see Table 4).

Graph 7 shows the variety of postures assumed and the frequency
with which these postures were taken up within 30 minutes of observation. From turning to side on up to walking, no period occurred in
which the child assumed only one single position. In the time space

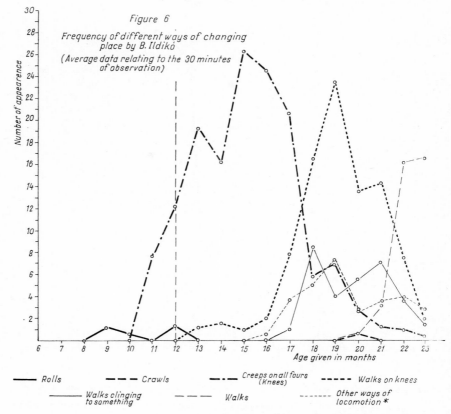

Figure 6

Frequency of different ways of changing place by B. Ildikó

(Average data relating to the 30 minutes of observation)

───── Rolls   ─ ─ ─ Crawls   ─··─ Creeps on all fours (Knees)   ····· Walks on knees

───── Walks clinging to something   ─ ─ ─ Walks   ----- Other ways of locomotion *

* Mostly occur while playing with bulky toys: steps in or on, or slips under something etc.

between sitting up, rising on all fours and standing up there were periods in which, within one recording time, five or seven postures were taken up respectively (on back, on side, prone, on all fours, kneeling, sitting half way, sitting). On the average the children spent two minutes without interruption in one posture. They spent less than one-and-a-half minutes in the period after rising on all fours or sitting half way. (Postures in which they stayed less than half a minute are regarded as transitory and were not counted.)

6) Another feature of the children is being *cautious*. Experimenting independently, they not only have learned to start and change postures and to move in a great variety of ways, but also how to fall. Falling is unavoidable during their agile activity. Though the children are very mobile and courageous and fall fairly often, only one fracture has occurred in the Institute since its establishment in 1946. This happened to a child who did not go through his gross motor development at the Institute as he could walk when admitted.

TABLE 4

TIME SPENT IN ONE POSTURE WITHOUT INTERRUPTION AND THE NUMBER
OF TAKING NEW POSTURES BY PHASES OF DEVELOPMENT

Phases of development	Time spent in one posture without interruption			Number of taking new postures		
	In minutes		Coefficient of variation %	Average	Standard deviation	Coefficient of variation %
	Average	Standard deviation				
I.	7.77	1.951	25.1	22.5	4.17	18.5
II.	2.26	0.332	14.7	56.7	2.70	4.8
III.	1.34	0.072	5.4	44.7	3.14	7.0
IV.	1.35	0.053	3.9	64.6	2.62	4.0
V.	1.40	0.061	4.3	57.8	1.88	3.2
VI.	1.43	0.106	7.4	39.9	2.33	5.9
Total	1.99	0.162	8.1	53.3	1.16	3.2

COMMENTARY

Developmental phases	from	to	Dominant way of changing place
I.	turning to the side	turning prone	happens by chance
II.	turning prone	rising on all fours or sitting up half way	rolling
III.	rising on all fours or sitting half way up	kneeling up or sitting up	crawling
IV.	sitting up or kneeling up	standing up	creeping
V.	standing up	starting to walk	still creeping
VI.	starting to walk	safe walking	walking

(Naturally the children are not permitted to explore situations that would mean danger: for instance, there are bars on the window when their height from the ground outdoors is greater than indoors. Furniture, wardrobes, shelves, which are not stable and which may tumble down when the child clings on, are fastened securely. On the other hand, the corners of the furniture are not rounded, leaving the edges exposed.)

SUMMARY AND CONCLUSIONS

It has been established that in the course of motor development based on self-induced motor activity, under suitable conditions, children—both with normal and with low birthweight—attain all motor skills needed from lying on their back till walking well. Those with normal

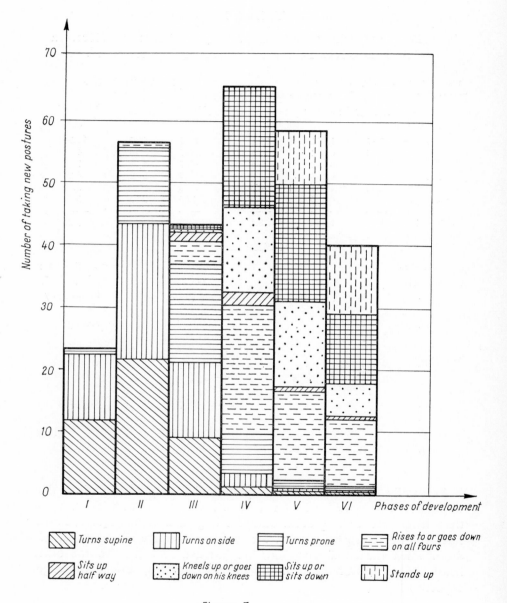

Figure 7

Number of taking new postures by phases of development
(Average data concerning the 30 minutes of observation)

birthweight attain turning on the side and walking well—the first and the last station of primary motor development—without delay compared to well-known data considered as standards. The stages in between differ in time and in sequence from the customary, described ones.

This course of motor development creates adequate possibilities for learning motor skills with appropriate coordination and for maintaining a stable high activity level during the whole period of learning new motor skills.

We deem the described motor developmental way to be especially favorable for children with constitutional difficulties in motor development, e.g. prematures. In general, it is favorable for all children whose motor development in infancy is delayed for various reasons. In the described way of motor development, these children—similarly to children with normal developmental range—are able to spend their infancy in an active fashion with plenty of successful experiences. They, too, learn all basic skills like those with normal developmental rate with good coordination—only a little later in time—and are not compelled, as they are when the adult determines what and when motor skills shall be performed. They are not compelled to spend more or less time in postures more advanced than their developmental level, in uncomfortable positions which they can attain only with help and with improper coordination. They do not have to become frustrated by repeatedly experiencing failure to move adequately.

The fact is that the level of mobility is high, even at the time of learning basic motor functions and while getting acquainted with surroundings. Also, on the basis on self-induced independent motions, further suitable conditions are created for favorable emotional and intellectual development. In general, these factors facilitate favorable psychosomatic development both in familial and institutional environments.

PICTURES

The following picture-series was taken of four children while they were playing independently on their own initiative. Two of them, R. Anna and K. Attila, are slow developers; N. Tibor is advanced, and E. István shows an average motor developmental time according to our developmental range. All pictures were taken in the children's usual environment during their usual activities.

With the picture-series I would like to demonstrate both the psychosomatic state of the children reared in the Institute and the smoothness and carefulness of their motion, as well as the frequency of changing postures while manipulating or solving motor tasks.

I am indebted to Mrs. Marian V. Reisman, master photographer, steady collaborator of the Institute, who has taken the pictures.

R. Anna born May 14, 1966. Birthweight 2400 g (5.3 lb.). She had been reared in the Institute in residential care since 24 days old.

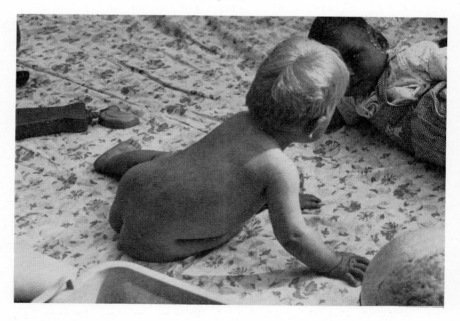

This picture-series was taken May 11, 1967, when Anna was 52 weeks old. At this time her most advanced motor skills were: *playing in a half-way-sitting position and creeping.*

K. Attila born Dec. 19, 1967. Birth-weight 3400 g (7.5 lb.). He had been reared in the Institute in residential care since 17 days old. This picture-series was taken April 1, 1969, when Attila was 67 weeks old. At this time his most advanced motor skills were: *playing in a sitting position between bent knees or above the heels, kneeling, creeping.* (*Continued on facing page.*)

Tibor (1)

Tibor (2)

Tibor (3)

N. *Tibor* born Feb. 5, 1968. Birth-weight 3800 g (8.4 lb.). He had been reared in the Institute in residential care since 14 days old. This picture-series was taken Oct. 2, 1968, when Tibor was 39 weeks old. At this time his most advanced motor skills were: *playing in a sitting position, creeping, walking while clinging to objects.*

Tibor (4)

Tibor (5)

Iststatus (2)

E. István born June 20, 1964. Birthweight 3760 g (8.3 lb.). He had been reared in the Institute in residential care since 19 days old. This picture-series was taken Sept. 15, 1965, when István was 65 weeks old. At this time his most advanced motor skills were: *playing in a sitting position, creeping, walking while clinging to objects.*

István (1)

Istyán (5)

Istyán (4)

Istyán (3)

REFERENCES

1. This paper is an abridgement of the book: "Adatok a csecsemo mozgásának fejlodéséhez" (Data on the gross-motor development of the infant.) Published by the Publishing House of the Hungarian Academy of Science, Budapest, Hungary 1969. Short summaries of earlier versions were published in *The Journal of Genetic Psychology,* 1968. 113. 27-39.; and presented at the XVIII. International Congress of Psycsology, Moscow, 1966; The XVI. International Congress of Applied Psychology, Amsterdam, 1968; The Sixth International Study Group on Child Neurology and Cerebral Palsy, Oxford, 1968.
2. ANDRE-THOMAS & AUTGARDEN, S.: Psycho-Affectivité des premiers mois de nourisson. Masson et Cie Éditeurs. Libraires de l'Académie de Médicine, Paris. 1959. Pp. 117.
3. BARKOCZI, I.: Adatok a csecsemok manipulációs fejlodéséhez. Pszichológiai Tanulmányok, 1964. 6. 65-80.
4. BAYLEY, N.: Manual of Direction for an Infant and Preschool Scale of Motor Development. Child Study Center. Institute of Human Development. University of Calif., Berkeley, 1961.
5. BERGERON, M.: Psychologie du premier âge de la naissance à trois ans. Presses Universitaires de France, Paris. 1961. Pp. 85.
6. BOUFFARD, P.: L'enfant jusqu'à trois ans. Édition du Seuil. 1965. Pp. 19-24.
7. BOWLBY, J.: Child Care and the Growth of Love. Penguin Books, London, 1957. Pp. 34.
8. Brennemann's Practice of Pediatrics. Hagerstown, W. F. Prior Company, Maryland. 1957. I., Chapter VIII. Pp. 11., Chapter IX. Pp. 4., 9., 16.
9. BROCK, J.: Biologische Daten für den Kinderarzt. Springer Verlag. Berlin-Göttingen-Heidelberg. 1954. II. Pp. 734.
10. BRUNET, O. & LEZINE, I.: Le développement psychologique de la première enfance. Presses Universitaires de France. 1951.
11. BUHLER, CH. & HETZER, H.: Kleinkindertests vom 1. bis 6. Lebensjahr. Johann Ambrosius Barth. München. 1953.
12. COURT, S. D. M.: The Medical Care of Children. London, Oxford University Press, New York, Toronto. 1963. Pp. 212.
13. DAVID, M.: L'enfant de O à 2 ans. Éduard Privat, Éditeur. 1960. Pp. 25.
14. DEBRE, R., LESNE, E. & ROHMER, P.: Pathologie Infantile. Doin et Cie. Paris, 1954, I. Pp. 26., II. Pp. 773-774.
15. DENNIS, W. & DENNIS, M. G.: Behavioral Development in the First Year as Shown by Forty Biographies. *The Psychological Record,* 1937. Vol. 1. No. 21. Pp. 349-361.
16. DENNIS, W. & NAJARIAN, P.: Readings in Child Psychology. Prentice-Hall, Inc., Englewood Cliffs, N. J. 1963. Pp. 329.
17. DIECKHOFF, J.: Pädiatrie und Ihre Grenzgebiete. Edition Leipzig, 1965. I. Pp. 15., II. Pp. 938.
18. FRONTALI, G.: Manuela di Pediatria. Edizioni Minerva Medica S.A. Torino, 1954. Vol. 1. Pp. 160.
19. GESELL, A.-AMATRUDA, C.: Developmental Diagnosis. Harper and Row, Inc., New York, 1964.
20. HELD, R.-FREEDMANN, S. J.: Plasticity in Human Sensorimotor Control. *Science,* 1963. Vol. 142. No. 3591, 455-462.
21. HELD, R.-HEIN, A.: Movement-Produced Stimulation in the Development of Visually Guided Behavior. *J. Comp. Physiol. Psychol.* 1963. Vol. 56. No. 5. 872-876.
22. HELD, R.-REKOSH, J.: Motor-Sensory Feedback and the Geometry of Visual Space. *Science,* 1963. Vol. 141. No. 3582. 722-723.
23. HELD, R.-BAUER, J. A. JR.: Visually Guided Reaching in Infant Monkeys after Restricted Rearing. *Science,* 1967. Vol. 155. No. 3763, 718-720.
24. HERZKA, H. S.: Das Gesicht des Säuglings. Schwabe und Co. Verlag, Basel-Stuttgart, 1965. Pp. 14-17.

25. HIRSCH, M.: A szüloktol elszakadt, gyermekotthonban, majd családi környezetben nevelkedo gyermekek személyiségvizsgálata. Pszichológiai Tanulmányok, 1964. 6. 595-614.
26. HOLT, L. E.-McINTOSH, R.: Holt Pediatrics. Appleton Century Crofts Inc., New York, 1953. Pp. 24.
27. HURLOCK, E. B.: Modern Ways with Babies. J. B. Lippincott Company, Philadelphia, 1937. P. 68.
28. HURLOCK, E. B.: Child Development. McGraw-Hill Book Company, New York, 1964. P. 117.
29. ILLINGWORTH, R. S.: The Development of the Infant and Young Child, Normal and Abnormal. E. and S. Livingstone Ltd., Edinburgh, 1960.
30. ILLINGWORTH, R. S.: An Introduction to Developmental Assessment in the First Year. Little Club Clinics in Developmental Medicine 3. National Spastics Society, London 1962. P. 26.
31. KOUPERNIK, C.: Développement psycho-moteur du premier âge. Presses Universitaires de France, Paris. 1954. P. 59.
32. KOZPONTI STATISZTIKAI HIVATAL: Az egészségügyi helyzet 1963-ban. Statisztikai idoszaki közlemények 1964. P. 27.
33. LANDRETH, C.: The Psychology of Early Childhood. Alfred A. Knopf, Inc., New York. 1959. P. 82.
34. McGRAW, M. B.: Neuromuscular Development of the Human Infant as Exemplified in the Achievement of Erect Locomotion. *J. Pediat.* 1940. 17. 747-770.
35. McGRAW, M. B.: Neuro-motor Maturation of Anti-gravity Functions as Reflected in the Development of a Sitting Posture. *J. Genet. Psychol.* 1941. 59. 155-175.
36. NELSON, W. E.: Textbook of Pediatrics. Saunders Company, Philadelphia, 1964. P. 45.
37. PIKLER, E.: A prevenció általános kérdéseirol a bölcsodekben es csecsemootthonokban. Népegészségügy 1955, 36. évf. 2. 31-38.
38. PIKLER, E.: Az etetéstechnika néhány részletkérdése. Gyermekgyógyászat 1958. 4-6. 121-123.
39. PIKLER, E.: A hospitalizáció elleni küzdelem egyik részletkérdésérol. Orvosi Hetilap 1966, 4. 166-168.
40. PIKLER, E.-TARDOS, A.: Megfigyelések a csecsemo nagymozgásos aktivitasanak alakulásáról az oldalrafordulastol a biztos járásig. Magyar Pszichológiai Szemle 1968. XXV. 1-2. 69-86.
41. PIKLER, E.-TARDOS, A.: Some Contributions to the Study of Infant's Gross Motor Activities. XVI. International Congress of Applied Psychology, Amsterdam. Swets and Zeitlinger, 1969.
42. PROVENCE, S.-LIPTON, R. C.: Infants in Institutions. International Universities Press, Inc., New York, 1962. P. 48.
43. RUBINSTEIN, SZ. L.: Az általános pszichológia alapjai. Akadémiai Kiadó. 1964. I. P. 324.
44. SHIRLEY, M. M.: The First Two Years. Minnesota University Press, Minneapolis, 1933. Vol. 1.
45. SPOCK, B.-REINHARDT, J.: A Baby's First Year. Pocket Books, Inc., New York, 1962. P. 43.
46. TARDOS, A.: A 3-12 hónapos csecsemo optikus és taktilmotoros viselkedése. Magyar Pszichológiai Szemle, 1967. XXIV. 1. 57-70.
47. WHITE, B. L.-HELD, R.: Plasticity of Sensorimotor Development in the Human Infant. Readings in Child Development and Educational Psychology. Ed. by Judy F. Rosenblith and Wesley Allinsmith, Boston, Allyn and Bacon, Inc. 2nd ed. 1966.

5

FACTORS IN VULNERABILITY FROM INFANCY TO LATER AGE LEVELS

Grace M. Heider, Ph.D.

Professor, Department of Psychology
University of Kansas (Lawrence)

The purpose of this chapter is to argue against some of the absolutes that enter into our thinking about child development, especially about deficits and liabilities in a behavior pattern. It is based on a study that attempted to tease out factors, both positive and negative, that are related to functioning in infancy, and to find out how far infant vulnerability is to be taken as an indicator of later weakness. The term *vulnerability* as it is used here is what may be called a dispositional concept, not necessarily describing an existing deviation from optimal functioning or forecasting later malfunction in a given case, but indicating a potentiality that may or may not be realized, depending on the occurrence or non-occurrence of conditions, often unpredictable conditions, in the child's life. In ordinary usage at this time it is often taken to refer to possibility of deterioration of function under conditions of stress, and it is interesting to note that *stress,* in turn, is relatively new as a topic of direct study by psychologists. We still lack an entirely satisfactory definition of what we mean by the term. It first appeared in the index of the Psychological Abstracts in 1944 shortly before Grinker and Spiegel published *Men Under Stress* as a by-product of work that was carried on during World War II (1945), though certainly many studies had dealt with phenomena related to it during the preceding years. Since that time there has been an increasing number of investigations of stress effects and of susceptibility to stress, but most of them have dealt with single aspects of the problem, e.g. with conditions under which stress effects appear, or with manifestations of stress, or with the relationship of physical and psychological characteristics to stress susceptibility. A recent book by Lazarus, *Psychological Stress and the Coping Process* (1966), gives a survey of this work.

The present study is specialized in the sense that it deals primarily

with data from studies of infants and young children,* but this difference may be less important than the fact that it is an attempt to treat
several different aspects of the problem within a single frame. It also
differs from many studies in that its data include not only results of
formal tests and measurements but also descriptions of behavior, and
that the behavior that is described occurred in relatively free situations
rather than in situations contrived for the purpose of laboratory study.
Herbert Wright has treated the place of this kind of study for child
psychology (1960, 1967) and Tinbergen gives a graphic example of its
significance in the field of animal behavior (1965, p. 130). The studies
treated in this paper were carried out in the conviction that data from
such work, difficult as they are to deal with in a quantitative way, play
an important part in structuring a new field of investigation and in the
discovery of relevant variables, many of which can then be studied under
the more exactly controlled conditions of the laboratory. It is believed
further that just such approaches probably provide the most direct way
of resolving the apparent contradictions that have arisen from earlier
investigations in the same field.

The present analysis will begin with a description of two investigations
in which the writer participated, one of infants and one of young children. Both were sponsored jointly by the Menninger Foundation in
Topeka, Kansas, and by the National Institute of Mental Health, and
have been described in a number of publications (Escalona and Leitch,
1952; Escalona and Heider, 1959; Murphy, 1962; Heider 1966). The
data of the Infancy Study are used here in an attempt to define the
factors that seemed important for the balance between stress susceptibility and stress resistance that determines level of vulnerability at that
age level. The data from the second study are records describing some
of the original subjects during their preschool years. The data of these
two studies make it possible to compare level of vulnerability and loci
of vulnerability effects in one sample of children at different age levels;
and beyond this, they suggest that the same factor may have both positive and negative potential, depending on its place in the total picture
at a particular point in the development of an individual. Glimpses of
later work with the same children give further hints of this relativity of
value as regards some of the factors that are seen as related to vulnerability.

The Infancy Study was initiated in 1947 by Sibylle Escalona and Mary
Leitch, then members of the staff of the Menninger Foundation. It had
as its subjects 128 "normal, healthy, well-developing" infants, eight boys
and eight girls of each four-week age level from four weeks through

---

* Most of the earlier work had been with adults, but an important exception is
a series of studies by Elizabeth Duffy with preschool children during the thirties
(1930, 1932a, 1932b).

thirty-two weeks of age. The study of preschool children, headed by Lois B. Murphy, was begun when the children of the Infancy Study were three, four, and five years of age, and included 31 of the original sample, casually selected on the basis of their availability during the summer months when contacts were being made. The second group was limited in size because a more intensive study was planned of each child. At the earlier age level each child was seen once with his mother for a single four-hour period at the project nursery. At this time, information was obtained from the mother about the child's history and the family setting, and detailed observations of the child were made by a team consisting of interviewer and two observers, usually a psychiatrist with pediatric training and two psychologists. This prolonged observation and interview were followed within a week by a home visit made by one member of the team to obtain supplementary information and to observe behavior of the infant in his usual setting. A pediatric examination and psychological tests were made during these contacts, partly to give assurance that the infant's development fell within the normal range, partly because they added variety to the situations to which each infant was exposed during the observation.

During the preschool study each of the 31 children who had been studied as infants was seen a number of times and in a wide range of situations with different examiners. A second member of the project staff was present at each session to make notes on the behavior of the child and the interaction between child and examiner. The series usually began with two or more sessions in which a permissive woman examiner gave psychological tests, administering them in such a way as to obtain both normative information about the child's cognitive functioning and to afford opportunity to observe how the child dealt with experiences of success and failure and with the challenge of new demands in a relatively structured situation. Several projective tests, including the Rorschach and the Child's Thematic Apperception Test, were given by a male examiner in a more impersonal fashion and under greater time pressure. Lois Murphy's Miniature Life Toy procedure (Murphy, 1956) offered a relatively unstructured situation in which the child had the responsibility for organizing material and using play materials on his own initiative, while a psychiatric play session involved interaction with a male examiner who elicited a fairly wide range of affect, although always leaving the child feeling comfortable about the situation. Pediatric examinations were conducted by a woman physician in an examining room of the state health center at a local hospital, and again offered a range of experiences that involved some degree of stress for most of the children, as did a study made by an associate of Sheldon's for the purpose of studying body build (Sheldon, 1940). Beyond these sessions, there were a few situations in which groups of children were seen together and there were informal home visits in which children were seen with members of their families and neighborhood play groups.

While precautions were taken in every phase of the study to avoid undue strain for both mothers and children, stress effects were inevitable, different for different children. The mere fact of going with or without the mother to a strange place with strange people seemed to involve some degree of strain for most of the children of the group. With some, the first session seemed the most stressful, whether or not the mother had chosen to accompany the child. In other cases a first occasion with the mother at hand seemed easy and the break came the first time the mother decided that the child was ready to go without her. For some, the structured tests seemed to offer a haven of security; for others, their demands were a serious threat. Some children found the freedom and wealth of materials of the play sessions a special delight; for others, they seemed almost overwhelming at first. Some children were relatively comfortable as long as project contacts were limited to adults, but showed utter misery at being with a group of unfamiliar children. For a few, the matter of undressing for the physical examination was a matter of high stress, while some who were shy in other situations took this as a matter of course. Differences as regards susceptibility to stress, the locus in which stress characteristically showed itself, and in the ways in which it was handled formed an important part of the records that were made of each contact. Altogether, this material from the preschool years is broad enough to serve as a sound basis for assessments of each child and to throw light on the significance of some of the factors that had been considered in the earlier assessments. It should be noted that by the time the children were seen in the second study the records from the Infancy Study were filed away and all but one member of the new team made their assessments without any knowledge of what a child had been as an infant or of his home setting.

The procedure used to deal with the descriptive records of behavior that formed much of these data was to decide on relevant variables after a detailed reading of all the records for a child and to bring together all the examples of acts and verbalizations by the child and comments of observers that seemed relevant to each variable. Under "sensory reactivity," for example, there would be notes from the infancy material about each occasion on which a baby startled, or failed to startle, at a sudden sound, with an indication of the intensity and source of the sound and the baby's condition, whether he was sleepy, wide-awake, content or fretful at the moment. There were also the mother's comments on how the baby responded to household noises and what disturbed his sleep, and an observer's summarizing comment such as, "Steve was a baby to whom every sort of stimulation seemed a kind of affront." All the information included under a heading was then studied and a rating was given on a five-point scale.

A weakness of the study is the fact that the final ratings on a considerable portion of the infancy material and on a few variables of the preschool material were made by a single investigator, the writer. This happened because it was not possible, within the limits of the project resources, for a second person to give the time that would have been needed to make comparable ratings. However, the fact that the data on which ratings are based comes from the records of several trained observers who made independent records and overall assessments, that there were also available the results of tests and measurements, and that analyses and ratings of some parts of the data, more of preschool than of infancy data, were made by other members of the staff or by teams of staff members add to the reliability of the procedure, though certainly the work remains within the category of exploratory studies which have their greatest usefulness in suggesting hypotheses for further and more controlled work.

The immediate starting point of the first study of vulnerability based on material from these projects (Heider, 1966) was the observation made during the preschool sessions of differences among children in degree of susceptibility to whatever aspects of a situation proved stressful. It was also notable that many children, whether or not they showed a high degree of stress susceptibility, tended to show effects consistently in one functional area rather than another. For example, there were children who showed stress effects initially and predominantly in the ways in which they handled their bodies and others in whom stress effects could be noticed primarily in their manner of talking. When the change was a matter of deterioration in motor control it was sometimes most noticeable in larger skeletal movements, in other cases in fine coordination. In speech the change might show itself in a stutter or a stammer, in what seemed to be a highly uncomfortable inhibition of speech, or in gross changes of voice quality. There were also children who showed a striking loss of perceptual clarity or a loss of spatial orientation but it seemed likely that this aspect of behavior was often cloaked by ongoing activity and that we did not have sufficient evidence of its presence or absence to study it with the material that was available.

The observations of behavioral deterioration in the preschool children led to two specific questions regarding continuity of behavioral style from infancy through the preschool years. First, would the earlier records show that those children who seemed highly susceptible to stress at the age of three or four or five had also been specially vulnerable in this respect as infants and vice versa? Second, would earlier records indicate that preschool children who showed stress effects predominantly either in speech or in motor behavior had shown the same tendency as infants?

In order to reduce the series of ratings that were made for each child to overall appraisals that could be compared for the two ages the variables were classified under three comprehensive headings. Two of these were aspects of the child's own functional pattern which were designated respectively as *Equipment* and as *Management Processes.* The first included factors like energy level, sensory reactivity, and autonomic stability, the second what at the later age would be called coping and defensive behavior, and referred to the readiness of the child to reach out and utilize the offerings of the world and to the ways in which he dealt with stressful situations. A third heading, designated as *Environmental Factors,* referred for infants primarily to the social factors that affected the child, largely the mother's overall stability and her sensitivity to the needs and temperament of the particular child.

Several points should be noted about this avowedly exploratory selection of variables. Some were suggested by previous studies or based on theoretical assumptions, especially assumptions derived from psychoanalytic theory. This is true, for example, of several variables related to sensory threshold. Other variables that proved interesting, for example the infant's activity level, as it was judged under different conditions, emerged from the study of the infancy data and would probably never have been included in an a priori list of items (Heider, 1966, p. 32-34).

Further, some factors could be seen both as causes of susceptibility to stress and also as indicators that a condition of stress existed, producing a circularity in categorization within this study that had already proved difficult to deal with in surveys that attempted to bring preceding work together. In other cases, for example under the heading *Environment* at the infancy age level, "Attitude of the mother toward breast feeding" was only a special case of "Mother's attitude toward natural functions in general," yet seemed worth examining separately because of its specific relevance to the mother-child relationship.

Ratings of the variables also reflected the preliminary character of the investigation. They were made on a five-point scale, the variables derived from previous studies and from theoretical considerations being appraised according to the ideology of the source from which they were taken while ratings of other factors were based on preliminary analyses of our own data. Where value judgments were seen as linear, as in the case of "The mother's respect for the infant's autonomy" a rating of 1 was considered highly favorable, of 5 highly unfavorable. In other cases, for example, "Level of sensory reactivity," both the child who showed maximum reactivity with a rating of 1 and the child who was described as relatively insensitive to the sights and sounds of his environment with a rating of 5 were seen as functioning less favorably than the child with mid-ratings.

The work was further complicated by the extent to which close study

of the 31 cases showed that the final appraisal at either age was determined by the interwoven fabric of variables rather than by a summation
of values assigned to single items. For example, a high degree of bodily
contact with the mother might be a favorable aspect of the mother-child
interaction for a child of moderate skin sensitivity or for a child who
welcomed a good deal of restraint, but less so for the infant with highly
sensitive skin or the infant who seemed to demand full autonomy of
bodily movement. Bell, for example, has pointed to the way in which
infants of different characteristics need and often elicit different kinds
of treatment from the same mother (1968). All this meant that in a
preliminary survey with a relatively small number of cases it would not
have been meaningful to try to determine an exact numerical index
of vulnerability for each child. Instead, an overall appraisal was made
for the pattern of variables listed in each of the three categories, *Equipment, Management Processes,* and *Environment,* taking into account
interactions between factors within categories and across categories, as
in the example above, of the relationship between the kind of child and
the kind of treatment offered by the mother. At each age the 31 children
were then assigned to five levels of overall vulnerability, with those who
had negative assessments in all three categories assigned to Level 1, those
who had positive or neutral assessments in all three to Level V, with
others falling between.

A full list of the variables included in each category is presented in
the original report (Heider, 1966, pp. 171-213). Following is a list of
the variables that proved most significant in the infancy assessments,
some identified briefly, others described in more detail where they were
understood in ways that went beyond the ordinary usage of the name
by which the variable was designated. These descriptions often include
mention of the relationships among variables that were taken into
account in the appraisals.

Equipment Variables

1. Physique, based on judgments of body build, energy of movement, and fatiguability.
2. Vegetative functioning, based on the results of the pediatric
   examination and the child's physical history as given by the
   mother. This factor was considered important in itself and as
   an indication of stresses that had been part of the child's experience. Erikson's discussion of the relationship between a child's
   physical history and the development of attitudes like "basic
   trust" suggests that this factor may have significance beyond
   its mere physical results (1950, 1959).
3. Sensory reactivity. This factor seems important in itself as regards
   the child's commerce with his environment. Freud's treatment
   of the sensory apparatus as a "protective barrier" (1924) pointed

to this factor as a focal variable as did Frank's monograph on tactile sensitivity (1957) and other work in this area.

In appraising sensory reactivity an effort was made to distinguish between genuinely high sensory thresholds and what may sometimes have been low thresholds cloaked by defensive operations. Studies by Bell (1968) and by Escalona and Heider (1959) had pointed to some of the special problems in judging sensory reactivity. Our data suggested that high fatiguability out of proportion to apparent physical robustness might be an indication that factors like sensory reactivity were being controlled, at a cost to the child, by defensive controls. As has been noted, ratings for this factor were probably non-linear, with the optimal point near the middle of the scale.

4. Drive level. A factor called "drive level," probably equivalent to "external cathexis" in psychoanalytic terms, indicated the extent to which the child was reaching out perceptually or physically toward the external world, the extent of his interest in bodily activity, for example in the mastery of new motor skills, and the extent of his interest in his own body as a perceptual object.

Ratings for this factor, like ratings for sensory threshold, were probably non-linear, with the optimal point somewhere between the two extremes. The charts included ratings for each child and indications of areas of especially high and especially low cathexis.

It seems likely that drive level, also, was reduced in some children by defensive controls. The evidence for this in individual cases was, again, partly a matter of fatiguability that seemed out of proportion when the child's general health and vigor were taken into account.

5. Activity level. Estimates of activity level were made by each member of the team of observers during the original session with an infant and his mother and were supplemented by material of the full record. These estimates were based on the child's activity within his own age group. A four-week old who was judged to be highly active would usually move about less than an only moderately active thirty-two week old. One unexpected factor emerged from the analysis of the data of activity level. It was noted that some infants were given approximately the same ranking within their own age groups when they were awake and asleep. Others showed a marked discrepancy in age group ranking awake and asleep. A comparison of this difference with differences in "Ease of vegetative functioning" showed a statistically significant relationship between the two. Infants whose physical development had proceeded without special incident from birth tended to show the same relative level of activity when awake and asleep, while infants whose physical history had been marked by disturbance tended to show differences in relative activity within their own age groups when they were awake and when they were asleep. One example of a child who showed such a discrepancy was Terry, an active, almost "driven" baby who had great difficulty in slowing down enough to fall asleep but who,

once asleep, slept with a minimum of movement. Another was Vernon, a complicated, almost inhibited baby whose waking activity level was judged low for his age but who showed a high degree of activity during sleep, almost as though he was then free to behave in a more "natural" fashion. Neither of these infants had highly favorable ratings on the variable "Vegetative functioning," the one being rated 5 and the other 3.

The sample was, of course, too small for this finding to be accepted as having general validity, but it was taken as grounds for treating a consistent sleep-waking activity level as a positive indication and an inconsistent one as negative for the purposes of this study. Beyond this, it seemed possible that this relationship, like the combination of apparently high sensory threshold and low drive with unduly high fatiguability, pointed to the operation of something like the defense mechanisms of psychoanalytic theory during this period of life (Anna Freud, 1946).

It should also be noted that the three factors, sensory reactivity, drive level, and activity level had to be viewed in relation to each other in the assessment of equipment factors. High sensory reactivity coupled with high drive, for example, often meant that a child was pushing himself into activity beyond the point of efficient and comfortable functioning. Appraisals of activity level also involved relationships among these factors and ease of functioning in the area under consideration (Heider, 1966, pp. 76-77).

6. Balance in developmental level. Previous studies had suggested that developmental scatter may be a source of vulnerability (Leitch and Escalona 1949, Hellersberg 1957), and infants were rated on degree of consistency of developmental level within the four areas of the Gesell Developmental Scale, motor, adaptive, language, and personal-social behavior, with the assumption that a high degree of consistency was favorable, inconsistency less favorable.

7. Functional stability. This term was used to mean freedom from the massive shifts in autonomic, motor, and perceptual functioning to which some infants were subject and which they were able to handle with greater or less great success. This factor was seen as a linear variable with a rating of 1 indicating a high degree of stability, 5 low stability. In connection with this, the areas in which loss of stability characteristically showed itself were charted. One child might show heightened sensitivity to external stimulation, another marked cardio-vascular change, and another loss of motor control.

8. In addition to these factors that could be rated for each child were several that seemed significant when they were noted but for which the data often failed to provide basis for an evaluation. These include *Tendency to delay* in response which is treated in psychoanalytic theory in relation to intellectual development (Hartmann, 1958). In some cases it could not be distinguished from *Activity level* for purposes of rating, in some it was a clear-cut factor in its own right and was rated accordingly. Another such factor was called *Areas of maximal and*

minimal differentiation and referred to the fact that some children, for example Ray at 16 weeks, responded differently to different people, yet in a highly stereotyped way to objects, while another child might seem to notice particular aspects of objects and be relatively unconcerned with people.

A third factor, very noticeable in a few children, was a tendency to respond with discomfort to aspects of stimulation other than high intensity. Brennie, for example, at 28 weeks, startled at some sounds of rather low intensity and seemed quite unaware of much louder sounds at which most of his peers showed startle effects.

Management processes

What were called management variables were classified under three headings, 1) those in which the child met discomfort and frustration in a relatively passive fashion, 2) those in which he used active ways of handling a situation, and 3) a possibly overlapping heading of cases in which a child made use of special sources of support. The principal items under these headings were:

Passive approach

1. Escape. Several infants seemed to find a way to "leave the field" under conditions that appeared stressful to most in the sample. In some cases it was a matter of closing the eyes in a way that observers described as more or less deliberate rather than a merely reflex blinking. In other cases the child actually fell asleep in the midst of the administration of the psychological test or the pediatric examination which more often resulted in heightened irritability.
2. Avoidance, a similar, perhaps more differentiated kind of behavior, that occurred when an infant seemed to disregard one kind of stimulation or stimulus object while responding happily to others. This occurred with Darlene at eight weeks when she first showed mild distress at the sight of the shiny cup, then paid little attention to it when it was presented a second time, but attended immediately when the red cube was offered. The examiner commented on this rather striking behavior, "In view of her ability to focus on things I don't see how she could have avoided it."
3. Accepting substitutes. Some infants, once engaged with an object, found a certain degree of difficulty in giving it up, but there was a striking difference between two 32-week-olds, Tommy, who could readily exchange one object for another, and Terry, who held the first in a grip that could hardly be broken.

Active approach

1. Protest. Even by the age of four weeks there was a clear-cut distinction between the child whose crying was an outgoing and

wholehearted protest and the child whose behavior was characterized more by whining or whimpering that seemed an almost self-directed expression of discontent.

2. Rejection. It was usually possible to distinguish between children who characteristically used active rejection when they were confronted with an object that they did not want and those who used what we have described as avoidance. In the case of unwanted food, one child might merely turn his head, another might spit the food out or at a later stage push a spoon or bottle away.

3. Action to attain. Sally, at 28 weeks, initiated rocking activity when she was on her mother's lap or managed to slide off and make walking movements to which her mother responded by helping her walk about the room. A more doubtful case, but interesting because it may have been of the same kind, was Vivian, who at four weeks, seemed to move about in her bed until she had made a comfortable nest for herself.

Utilization of sources of support

1. Some children found it easy to accept comfort from the mother while others could not do this until they had reached a stage of extreme discomfort. Ratings of this factor were confused, of course, by differences in the mother's awareness of the child's need and the sensitivity of her response.

2. Utilization of support from own functioning. The child who could attain comfort and support from food intake, from sucking a thumb, from touching a nearby object, rhythmic movements of his own body, or vocalization had a resource that others lacked. Sheila, for example, at four weeks seemed able to divert herself by effortful perceptual activity, and eight-week-old Greg found diversion in the sight of lights and colors. At higher age levels, this capacity showed in the way in which a hungry or uncomfortable child could broaden his base through involvement in the outside world, perhaps with people.

Environmental Variables

At this age factors of the environment were largely a matter of the quality of mothering that a child was receiving, not in absolute terms but in terms of the way in which the mother offered what a particular child appeared to need. This factor, of course, involved information about the mother herself and her personal situation. To give as rounded a picture as possible of this group of factors three headings were used, 1) *The mother-child relationship,* 2) *the mother as a person,* and 3) *the relationship between the parents.* The items listed under each heading are not all equally important, and often overlapped to some extent. Some, like degree of satisfaction with the infant's sex, are included because they seemed to recur through the series of records and could be rated in a way that showed a close relationship to some of the less ratable impressions of observers about the mother's feeling toward her shild.

Mother-child relationship

1. Awareness of the infant's needs. One mother would shift the infant's position whenever she herself became restless, regardless of his state, or restrain the movements of a child for whom freedom of movement seemed important, while others almost automatically tuned their actions to the baby's temperament and momentary state.

   b. Mother-child viability. This term has been used by Lois Murphy to describe a basic physiological and psychological compatibility between mother and child. Schaefer has pointed to something similar suggesting that maternal behavior appropriate to a child of one age may be less so to one of another age (1960). In our data this factor seemed to outweigh others like tenderness and gentleness that are ordinarily taken as characteristic of the "good" or the "natural born" mother. Lennie, for example, who was seen at four weeks, had a mother who showed a certain "toughness" in the way she treated him. Lennie was a sturdy, well-knit baby who fully gratified his mother's longing for a boy and the relationship between the two seemed sounder than mere "sensitivity" in the usual sense. In contrast was Tommie, a high-threshold, active baby with a mother who suggested the stereotype of what a mother is expected to be, gentle, sensitive, and tender. In this case observers felt that the driven, insatiable quality of Tommy's behavior might have been reduced by the stimulation of "tougher" handling.

2. Degree of acceptance of the infant. A rating of 1 was used for the almost exultant feelings of the mother who had herself been a foundling and who glowed as she said, "This is the first person of my own flesh and blood I have ever had," a rating of 2 when the mother seemed altogether warm and positive, but in a more matter-of-fact way, of 3 for simple comfortable acceptance that was not described as notably positive or negative, of 4 when the mother's behavior and words suggested a feeling of doubt or distance and of 5 when she expressed definite uncertainty, perhaps about the kind of person he was. The sample of volunteers was, of course, selected in such a way that a deeply rejecting mother would probably not have taken part.

3. Degree of satisfaction with the infant's sex. Here our mothers ranged from the exultant mother of Lennie who told of greeting her husband after the delivery with the exclamation, "My God, we've got a *boy*" to Gordon's petite, feminine mother who had openly wanted a little girl and who continued to treat her baby like a doll.

4. Respect for the baby's autonomy. Many mothers assumed that they knew the posture in which the baby should fall asleep, how much he should eat and the like, and acted with little regard to clues that the baby seemed to offer. Others in a matter-of-course way let the baby take the lead in these matters and adjusted their approaches to him.

5. Acceptance of the infant's developmental pace; absence of a tendency to accelerate the baby's development. A rating of 1 in this factor did not imply failure to offer suitable stimulation,

but rather that a mother offered only what a baby was ready to enjoy and showed no tendency to impose goals. A mother who received a lower rating made the typical remark, "He ought to be sitting up by now. My sister's baby does, and he is a week younger."

6. Role of the infant in the mother's life. Ratings were made of this factor with a rating of 1 used for the mother who saw the baby as a person in his own right and as an object of special pleasure and admiration; 2 indicated a comfortable natural relationship in which the child was more or less taken for granted; a rating of 3 that a baby was seen as a piece of property for whom certain things had to be done; 4, a responsibility to be given conscientious care, or an object for the gratification of her own needs—for example the mother who constantly fed the baby or fondled him to cover her own restlessness; 5, an object of somewhat negative value; an extension of herself from which she obtained narcissistic pleasure with little regard for its individuality.

7. Mother's goals for the infant as an infant, with a rating of 1 used for the mother who wanted the baby to develop comfortably in his own way and 5 for the mother who tried to fit the baby into the pattern of what she herself was or wanted to be.

The mother as a person

This heading included several items such as the mother's acceptance of natural functions, her attitude toward breast feeding, and the changing of a soiled diaper, and her report on her pregnancy and the delivery of the baby.

Relationship between the parents

No questions were asked during the interview that referred directly to the relationship between the parents. However, incidental remarks in the course of the contacts often gave indications that were confirmed if the parents were seen together, as they were in some of the home visits, or later, if they wished to come to project headquarters to see the pictures that were made during the principal project session. Questions that were pertinent included the degree of agreement between the parents in their wishes, before the child's birth, about his sex, and their feelings afterwards about matters of handling him, schedule, and the like.

The factors used to assess level of vulnerability in the preschool children followed the same general pattern, with *Equipment, Management Processes,* and *Environment* again treated as principal categories. A list follows of the more significant variables in each category, but with less description of single variables since more of the terms were used much as they were for the infancy appraisal or carried more common connotations.

Equipment

1. Physique
2. Vegetative functioning
3. Energy reserves
4. Sensory reactivity and perception. Under this item were included ratings of general sensory reactivity, degree of variability in sensory responsiveness, tendency to be overwhelmed by sensory stimulation, vs. a preference for strong, definite sensory qualities.
5. Motor behavior. Ratings on this factor included activity level, motor coordination, special pleasure in smooth, easy motor functioning, resistance to stress effects in this area, use of motor channels for discharge of tension, and motor function as an area of special cathexis.
6. Developmental level. Actual test results were more reliable at these ages and were given greater weight than they were during infancy. Balance among test results in different areas and areas of special acceleration or retardation were again noted.
7. Speech. Developmental level was judged from test data and from the records of behavior. Talkativeness, resistance to deterioration under conditions of stress, absence of persistent problems in the speech area, and use of speech as a channel of tension discharge were evaluated.
8. Sex role. This factor included surface acceptance of sex role, also apparent freedom from underlying ambiguity or conflict regarding sex role.
9. Social behavior. Social ease, social skill, interest in social interaction, and degree of positive satisfaction obtained from social interaction.
10. Cognitive functioning. Cathexis for cognitive activity, speed of orientation, length of attention span, spatial orientation, creativity, and need for cognitive clarity were judged.
11. Fantasy elaboration. Assessments based on observations of the child during the Miniature Life Play and the Psychiatric Play sessions as well as general contacts with the children formed the basis of ratings on "Degree of fantasy elaboration" and "Fantasy in everyday life."
12. Affect. These ratings included range of affect, pervasiveness, frequency of affect storms, and dominant affective tone.
13. Drive. Ratings on this factor included strength of interest in objects and other people; drive for mastery.
14. Special sources of stress. Strange situations and the presence of basic imbalances in the child's make-up were frequently mentioned here. For example, one four-year-old was described as having cognitive drive and interest out of proportion to his intellectual potential as measured by tests, and one three-year-old showed a great desire for attention from others coupled with little capacity to make herself an object of interest to them.

Management Processes

The term "management processes" had been used in the evaluation of the infants and was used again but with the understanding that it now included both Lois Murphy's "coping capacity" and much that is explicitly thought of in psychoanalytic terms as defensive behavior. It was judged on the basis of ratings of two aspects of coping made by Dr. Lois Murphy and Dr. Alice Moriarty, one referring to the child's ability to deal with the external environment and its demands, the other to internal integration. Beyond this, several special factors were rated, including ability to protest, to make a direct attack on a situation, to fend off unwanted stimulation, capacity to mobilize energy under pressure, to make good use of own capacities, to use external support, to make use of evasion and escape, or to find positive ways of tension discharge.

Environmental Variables

Relevant environmental factors included the child's physical setting, his relationship with his parents, largely with the mother, the relationship between the parents, the child's relationship with siblings, the role of the extended family unit in the child's life. "Family atmosphere" included freedom from financial needs, whether the family was sufficiently child-oriented to give the child security, and whether it allowed sufficiently for adult needs. Finally notes were made of special conditions and events like separations from the mother, health of the parents, physical trauma suffered by the child, family problems involving siblings, and trauma associated with death.

The ratings on these variables were used, like those from the infancy records, to make appraisals of vulnerability for the 31 children of the original sample when they had reached preschool ages. The next step was to compare the judgments from the two ages to answer the questions about continuity of degree of vulnerability and locus of vulnerability effects for this segment of the life span. There were, as would be anticipated, cases in which there had been considerable change by the time the child was seen for the second time. Fifteen children showed increases of vulnerability, two an increase from Level V (highly resistant to stress effects) to Level I (highly vulnerable) ; eight showed an increase of a single level, and five an increase of two levels.

Eleven children, or slightly more than one-third of the sample remained at the same level, and five were judged as less vulnerable. There was a Spearman rank difference correlation of .531 (p<.01) between the two series of judgments.

Changes in the direction of increased vulnerability seemed principally to come from two causes: In some cases developmental deficits that were probably present but not affecting the child's behavior to any great extent had become focal, for example a moderate visual defect in a child who was seen at four weeks and again at three years. In some, illnesses had occurred between the two contacts and left the child at a markedly lower energy level than could have been anticipated, and in other cases there had been changes in environmental pressures that may have come at a critical period. An example of this last was the breakdown and hospitalization of a mother who had earlier been judged as only slightly unstable. Another case was that of a little girl in a family into which two lively and time-consuming brothers had been born in the interval. This child was no longer the determined, resilient person she had seemed at 28 weeks and even her cognitive level seemed lower than infant tests predicted.

Obviously, the effects of occurrences like these depended in each case on the interaction between the nature of the event itself and the overall pattern of strengths and weaknesses of the particular child. It is likely that in some of these cases we were dealing with interactions between variables whose significance we had not sufficiently noted, or that we had failed to give adequate weight to a recognized liability that later affected the behavior pattern of the particular child. Evidences of instability in the mother or in the relationship between the parents, for example, may not have been given sufficient weight. A re-reading of the first records with the later picture in mind pointed to factors of these sorts in several cases where they had been given rather little weight in the infancy evaluation.

Further, and this was certainly unpredictable, the exact age at which unfavorable events occurred probably played an important part in the intensity of their effects. Erikson's idea of periods of special susceptibility as related to turning points, or crises, in the developmental pattern is doubtless important here in suggesting an explanation for the fact that some children seemed to weather pressures that others who had seemed equally resistant found traumatic (Erikson, 1959, 1963).

The five cases of children who were judged more stress-resistant at the later age may be the most significant, in spite of the small number in the whole sample. Four of these were children who had been judged highly vulnerable as infants. In spite of functioning sufficiently within the normal range to be acceptable for the study, they had seemed to be seriously threatened by the constellation of inner and outer factors to which the assessment had pointed; the fifth child had been placed at a mid-level, III, in the infancy assessment but had suffered a disabling illness from which she was making a slow and difficult recovery when she was seen as a preschool child. What seems significant in these cases is that the gain in each case seemed the result of the child's own struggle to survive in the face of threat. Each of these children certainly had had support, some more than others, from his environment, but the result seemed in large part a matter of the child's own response to what seemed, psychologically, a life or death battle.

An analysis of the records at the two ages also gave a tentative answer to our question regarding the locus of stress effects, specifically whether preschool children who showed stress effects in the motor area had also shown effects in that area as infants, and whether children who showed stress primarily in their speech and vocalizations had shown such effects in pre-speech behavior as infants. In studying this question we made the assumption that an area that became the locus of stress effects might be expected to show some degree of developmental retardation and took relative retardation in the one area or the other, as measured on the Gesell schedule during infancy, as one indicator of locus of stress effects. Beyond this we principally took into account behavior descriptions of quality of performance and changes in quality in situations that appeared generally stressful to the child. For the preschool ages the records of the observers gave copious descriptions of the usual quality of each child's speech and motor behavior and changes that occurred under stress.

A comparison of infancy and preschool data for motor performance showed no significant relationship between the two age levels, though certainly there were a few striking cases in which developmental level and degree of deterioration under stress remained constant. Lacey's work with autonomic stability has shown that continuity may be characteristic of some individuals without being significant as a general factor for a sample (1953).

In the speech area, however, there was considerable evidence that relative retardation in vocal behavior as compared to other aspects of functioning in infancy was related to stress susceptibility in this area at a later age, and it may be significant that Rousey and Moriarty (1965) in a postdictive study of 24 children of the same sample found evidence of continuity from preschool to prepuberty ages.

We have considered questions related to continuity and overall level of vulnerability and locus of the area in which stress effects characteristically show themselves from infancy through the preschool years, and have found evidence of such continuity in the data of two studies. In doing this we have seen the importance of using patterns of factors rather than indices obtained by adding a number of discrete positive and negative values.

The next questions concern still later development, for example, how far the evidences that we found of continuity, are to be taken as indications, however tentative, that we can expect a vulnerable infant to develop into a vulnerable adult and vice versa. The answer, clearly, in the light of the shifts of vulnerability level that had already occurred by the time the children had moved from infancy through the preschool years is that even though some physiologically-based factors, e.g. sensory threshold, may remain relatively constant for an individual, changes in environmental pressures and in ways of dealing with deficits and liabilities, and in ways of utilizing assets in self and environment will still further change the picture for many individuals. As with our small sample over a short span of time, some individuals will become somewhat more vulnerable, some will suffer serious disintegration, while others will become less vulnerable. The promising aspect of the picture was suggested in our sample by the five children who, under severe threat, developed resources and utilized support to handle the stress and in doing that seemed to reach a more effective integration of their overall functioning.

Another facet of this picture, and only more extended studies of individuals and groups will give evidence on this, is the long-term role of the factor that appears to be the focus of threat at any period. Some evidence from our material, supported by later studies of children in the sample, suggests that just the factor that is sufficiently salient to have become focal in a negative way may also have positive potential, that its significance in the one sense may augur for either good or ill in later stages. This may be especially true in the cases that were conspicuous in our group, those in which high sensory reactivity, high drive, and low autonomic stability seemed to work together to produce disintegrative threat. Helen, one of the children who showed maximum vulnerability in infancy, was described in this way. In addition, she received unfavorable ratings on *physique* and had had a history of digestive problems with a proneness to infection. She displayed a constant hunger for contact and social interaction which a somewhat distant mother, already pregnant for a fourth time, did little to satisfy. At five years she was classified as Level II, still stress-susceptible but as having gained somewhat in terms of the appraisal. At that time the pediatrician described her as one of the least healthy children in the sample. She still tended to push herself beyond the limits of easy and effective functioning. For example, high sensory reactivity continued and with it she showed a preference for the kind of strong and crude sensory stimulation that a less reactive child often seems to need. She still showed what was described as a craving for social attention and close physical contact, and while she was capable of genuine enjoyment, her strong affect expression often carried an angry or unhappy feeling tone. The staff psychiatrist spoke of disintegrative tendencies as high, constrictive tendencies as low, with coping capacity more effective in dealing with the external world than with inner stability. Sex role identification had become a source of conflict, Helen often seeming torn between an interest in feminine toys and ruffly dresses that were far from suiting her build, and a tomboyishness that seemed to reflect her need to compete with her brothers for the attention of her father.

Going beyond the two investigations described in this chapter into material from early puberty we find that the direction of change from infancy to five years had continued. Improved physical health was certainly a factor in the change, but cannot fully describe what had happened. The vulnerable baby had developed into a frank, warm young person, able to communicate insights and feelings, serious beyond her years, perhaps to protect herself still from the rebuffs from outside, but to an unusual extent able to understand and offer support to others. Her history showed how the process of developing the inner integration that she had needed for self-preservation had taken her through phases of aggression and competitive relationships with others, and a period of considerable concern with right and wrong, into near-adulthood. Lois Murphy gives a detailed analysis of Helen's history in a forthcoming book entitled *Development, Vulnerability, and Resilience.* For the purpose of the present study what seems important is the relationship between the positive features of the later picture and the sources of threat in the early one. In many ways the same factors related to sensory reactivity, drive, autonomic stability, and social responsiveness that seemed out of hand in the infant and young child served as the foundation of the enriched awareness and capacity of reaching other people in the older child. The caution and mild anxiety that were also evident seemed residues of the early picture, an unavoidable price, perhaps, of the controls that made possible the positive balance of the later period.

BIBLIOGRAPHY

BELL, R. Q. A reinterpretation of the direction of effects in studies of socialization. *Psych. Rev.,* 1968, 75, 81-95.

DUFFY, E. Tensions and emotional factors in reaction. *Genet. Psychol. Monog.,* 1930, 7, 1-79.

————— Muscular tension as related to physique and behavior. *Child Development,* 1932, 3, 200-206.

————— Relation between muscular tension and quality of performance. *Amer. J. Psychol.,* 1932, 44, 535-546.

————— *Activation and behavior.* New York: Wiley, 1962.

ERIKSON, E. H. *Childhood and Society.* New York: Norton, 1950 (Second Edition, 1963).

————— Identity and the Life Cycle. *Psychol. Issues,* 1959, 1.

ESCALONA, S. & HEIDER, G. M. *Prediction and Outcome.* New York: Basic Books, 1959.

ESCALONA, S. & LEITCH, M. et al. Early phases of personality development: A non-normative study of infant behavior. *Mong. Soc. Res. Child Development,* 1952, 17 (No. 1).

FRANK, L. K. Tactile communication. *Genet. Psychol. Monog.,* 1957, 56, 209-255.

FREUD, A. *The ego and the mechanisms of defence.* New York: Int. Universities Press, 1946.

FREUD, S. *Beyond the pleasure principle.* New York: Boni & Liveright, 1924.

GRINKER, R. R. & SPIEGEL, J. P. *Men Under Stress.* Philadelphia: Blakiston, 1945.

HARTMANN, H. *Ego psychology and the problem of adaptation* (trans. by D. Rapaport). New York: International Universities Press, 1958.

HEIDER, G. M. Vulnerability in infants and young children: A pilot study. *Genet. Psychol. Mono.*, 1966, 73, 1-216.

HELLERSBERG, E. F. Unevenness of growth in its relation to vulnerability, anxiety, ego weakness, and schizophrenic patterns. *Amer. J. Orthopsychiat.*, 1957, 27, 577-586.

LACEY, J. I., BATEMAN, D. E., & VAN LEHN, R. Autonomic response specificity. *Psychosomat. Med.*, 1953, 15, 8-21.

LAZARUS, R. S. *Psychological Stress and the Coping Process.* New York: McGraw-Hill, 1966.

LEITCH, M. & ESCALONA, S. The reaction of infants to stress. *Psychoanalytic study of the child* (Vol. 3-4) New York: Internat. Universities Press, 1949, 121-140.

MORIARTY, A. E. *Constancy and I. Q. change.* Springfield, Ill.: Thomas, 1966.

MURPHY, L. B. *Personality in young children* (2 vols.) New York: Basic Books, 1956.

———— et al. *The widening world of childhood: Paths toward mastery.* New York: Basic Books, 1962.

———— *Development, vulnerability and resilience.* San Francisco: Jossey-Bass (In Press).

ROUSEY, C. L. & MORIARTY, A. E. *Diagnostic implications of speech sounds.* Springfield, Illinois: Thomas, 1965.

SCHAEFER, E. S. Converging conceptual models for maternal behavior and for child study. Paper read at Conference on Research on Parental Attitudes and Child Behavior. Second Annual Conference of the Social Science Institute, Washington University, St. Louis, Missouri, 1960.

SHELDON, W. H., STEVENS, S. S., & TUCKER, W. B. *The varieties of human physique.* New York: Harper, 1940.

TINBERGEN, N. *Social Behavior in Animals.* New York: Wiley, 1965.

WRIGHT, H. F. Observational child study. *In* P. H. Mussen (Ed.), *Handbook of Research Methods in child development.* New York: Wiley, 1960.

———— *Recording and analyzing child behavior.* New York: Harper & Row, 1967.

6

SMILING AND STRANGER REACTION IN BLIND INFANTS

Selma Fraiberg

Professor of Child Psychoanalysis, Department of Psychiatry
Director, Child Development Project
Children's Psychiatric Hospital, University of Michigan

I

We have strong evidence in the study of human infancy that the healthy, sighted baby establishes his human bonds during the first eighteen months of life. From the maternal deprivation studies we know that the absence of human partners or a rupture in the early love ties during this period may produce permanent impairment in the capacity to form enduring bonds in later life.

When we consider the central role of vision in the process of human attachment—in the differential responses to the human face, the development of recognition memory and the acquisition of a stable mental representation of the mother—we can see that the study of human object relations in the blind infant can afford an extraordinary opportunity to examine the non-visual components and the extent to which these can lead to adaptive substitutions in human attachment.

Since 1963 we have been engaged in a series of longitudinal studies of blind infants at Children's Psychiatric Hospital, University of Michigan Medical Center. Our study covers these areas of development: human object relations, behavior toward inanimate objects, language, gross motor development, prehension, object concept, affectivity, body and self image, self-stimulating behaviors, sleep patterns, eating patterns.

This research has been supported since 1966 by Grant #HD01-444 from the National Institute of Child Health and Development and, since 1969, by Grant #OEG-0-9-322108-2469 (032) from the Office of Education.

I wish to express my gratitude to colleagues in The Child Development Project who have participated in the primary research. I am specially indebted to Edna Adelson, Lyle Warner, Evelyn Bruckner and Marguerite Smith of our staff, for examining problems of criteria with me and for reading and criticizing the first drafts of this paper.

In this essay, we have selected items from our study of human object relations which are generally accepted as indicators on a scale of human attachment: (a) differential smiling and (b) stranger reactions.

II

The sample: The data which are summarized in this report are derived from a study of ten babies, seven boys and three girls. So far as possible we have brought babies into the study soon after birth, but the actual age at the point of first observation has ranged from twenty-three days to seven months for eight children and two children were first seen at nine months and eleven months respectively. Within the range of medical certainty we have selected babies who are totally blind from birth or who have light perception only and no other defects.

Our sample, then, is highly selective and our findings cannot be generalized for the total blind infant population. (A typical blind population includes children with a range of useful vision who are still legally classified as "blind," and children who have other sensory and motor handicaps and neurological damage.) Our babies, then, are advantaged in a blind child population by the intactness of other systems and are disadvantaged as a group by having no pattern vision. (These restrictive criteria have given us a small population even though we called upon the referral network of a major medical center.)

It is important to note that we have provided a concurrent educational and guidance service for all babies in the research program. We know that the early development of blind babies is perilous. In the general blind child population we see a very high incidence of deviant and non-differentiated personalities and arrested ego development (even when we exclude cases of brain damage and multiple handicaps which are also common to this population). As our own research progressed we were able to link certain developmental road-blocks with a clinical picture seen in the older blind child (Fraiberg and Freedman, 1964), (Fraiberg, 1968). As these findings became available to us they were readily translatable into a program of prevention and education. We felt that no benefits to the research could justify withholding this knowledge and began to provide a home-based educational program which has been highly effective in promoting the development of our blind babies (Fraiberg, Smith and Adelson, 1969).

We can say then that the observations in this report are derived from a group of healthy, otherwise intact infants; their families represent a good range of socioeconomic conditions; their mothers are at least adequate and, in four cases, would be rated as superior. The development of these babies has probably been favored by our intervention.

Observational Procedures

Observers: Each baby is assigned to a team of two observers. The primary responsibility for observation is placed in the senior staff member who is present at each visit.

Methods: The baby is visited in his home at twice monthly intervals for an hour and a half session. (We travel within a radius of one hundred miles to cover our home visits.) We try to time our visits to coincide with a morning or afternoon waking period and to fit our observations into the normal routine of that period. Nearly all of the data required for our study can be obtained through observing a feeding, a bath, a playtime with mother, a diapering or clothes changing and a period of self-occupation with or without toys. A small amount of time in each session may be employed for testing procedures by the examiner in the areas of prehension and object concept.

The observers record a continuous narrative with descriptive detail. Once a month we record a fifteen minute 16 mm. film sample covering mother-child interaction, prehension, and gross motor development which will be employed for close analysis by the staff using a variable speed projector.

Since the areas we are studying have not been previously researched, our data collection procedures had to insure coverage of hundreds of items for comparative study, yet needed to be open, flexible and rich in detail for qualitative study.

Our study of human attachment was, of course, one of the central areas of this study. Since nothing was known regarding the characteristics of human attachments in the blind infant we had to design a study which permitted the blind baby to teach us what kinds of sense information he used when he made selective responses to his mother, his father and other familiar persons, how he differentiated mother and stranger, how he reacted to separation from his mother, how he demonstrated affection, joy, need, grief, anger and the range of human emotion that will normally tell us about the quality of human bonds during the first eighteen months.

Our observations, then, covered differential responses (smiling, vocalizing, motor responses) to the human voice, to touch, to holding, to lap games, with familiar and unfamiliar persons, with mother present and, when appropriate for testing, with mother absent. The data covering the first eighteen months of life were classified, yielding twenty-five categories which could be employed for analysis of differential responses.

From these data we have selected two areas which afford interesting comparisons between the blind child and the sighted child in the sequence that leads to the establishment of human bonds: smiling and stranger reactions. In the following sections we will present brief summaries of the literature pertaining to normal development in each of these areas and brief summaries of our findings in the study of the blind infant.

The Sighted Child

Wolff (1963) reports a response smile to the human voice in the third week of life, and a selective response to the mother's voice in the fourth week. Emde and Koenig (1969) describe *irregular* smiling at three weeks to two months as a "response to unpatterned kinesthetic, tactile, auditory and visual stimulation" leading to a *regular* smiling response at two to two and a half months. There appears to be general agreement among investigators that by the second month the response smile to the configuration of the human face appears and that it is the most successful stimulus for regularly evoking the smile (Spitz and Wolf, 1946), (Gewirtz, 1965).

Between four and six months Benjamin (1963) reports that the experimenter's smile will elicit a smile from the baby, and that discrimination of faces will appear during the same period. Emde and Koenig speak of the further differentiation of the smile during the period two and a half to six months with more frequent and intense smiling to mother than to unfamiliar persons. During the period six to eleven months there is a marked decline in the smiling response to strangers reported by Spitz and Wolf, 1946; Ambrose, 1961; Polak, Emde and Spitz, 1964. Emde and Koenig speak of this period as an "all or none" smiling, that is, smiling occurs only to mother and familiar persons. There is some disagreement among investigators regarding this last point (Gewirtz, 1965 and Morgan and Ricciuti, 1969). Since the experimental conditions in these two sets of studies were not identical, the "not smiling to the stranger" or the "smiling to the stranger" may be related to variations in the introductory stage of the stranger-reaction testing.

The differentiation of the smile, then, gives information regarding the baby's increasing selectivity and valuation of human partners during the first year and may be taken, as Spitz and Wolf (1946) long ago proposed, as a key indicator of stages in the growth of human attachment during the period of ego formation. The negative demonstration is seen in the institutional baby, where the absence, or infrequency, or non-differentiation of the smile can be regarded as a sign of impoverishment in human relations. The indiscriminate smile for all-comers, seen by Provence and Lipton (1962) in year-old babies in an institution was regarded by these investigators as a sign of failure or absence of human connections, speaking for no valuation of one person over another.

Exceptional Infant: Studies in Abnormalities

The Blind Infant

D. G. Freedman (1964) reported on the characteristics of smiling in response to touch and voice in four congenitally blind infants tested under six months of age. He described the smiles of these infants as "fleeting," that is they quickly formed and disappeared, as in normal infants during the first month. In two cases observed by Freedman through six months of age, the fleeting smiles gradually changed to normal prolonged smiling. In this study Freedman did not test differential smiling and his observations did not extend beyond the six month level. S. Fraiberg and David A. Freedman* (1964) reported a longitudinal study of one blind infant followed from 5 months to 36 months of age, in which selective smiling to the voice and touch of mother and familiar persons was described in some detail. Studies by Thompson (1941), which included smiling in twenty-six children, employed a mixed population of children with congenital and acquired blindness and his findings are not applicable to the problem we are investigating in the present study.

Four of our ten babies were seen by us under three months of age. These babies were able to demonstrate a clear response smile to the sound of the mother's voice in the early weeks of life. Our findings show close correspondence with those of Peter Wolff (1963) as cited above, in which he demonstrates that the sighted baby shows a selective smile to the sound of his mother's voice as early as four weeks of age.

> Example: Ronny, at 0:0:28 days, just wakening from his nap, drowsy, briefly alert with eyes open, then slipping back into sleep. Mother calls his name. A smile appears, eyes open briefly. Father calls his name. A smile appears. Mother and Father take turns calling his name. After calling his name several times, either of the parents can elicit a smile. The observer now calls his name several times. There is no smile. Mother calls. The smile returns. Observer tries repeatedly to elicit his smile without success. Parents in several repetitions can nearly always elicit the smile.

At this age, as Emde and Koenig (1969) point out, the familiar voice as well as a number of other stimuli can irregularly elicit a smile in the sighted child. And, while it is impressive to see how the blind Ronny can respond selectively to the sound of one or another of his parent's voices, we should note that this is not an automatic or a regular response. Even with the familiar voices, several repetitions are required to elicit the smile. At this point, however, where voice is the stimulus for the smile, there is good equivalence between the blind baby's smiling response and that of the sighted baby.

---

* Not to be confused with D. G. Freedman whose work is cited above.

But at two to two and a half months, where the visual stimulus of the human face evokes an automatic smile with a high degree of regularity, there is no equivalence in the blind baby's experience. The blind baby's smiling becomes more frequent from the second month on, and the pattern of selective smiling for the familiar voice or sound becomes increasingly demonstrated in favor of the mother, but even the mother's voice *will not regularly* elicit the smile. There is no stimulus in the third month or later that has true equivalence for the human face gestalt in the experience of the sighted child.

At a meeting in May 1969 with René Spitz, Robert Emde and David Metcalf, we presented some of our data and were satisfied that this constituted the essential difference between the smile of the blind baby at two to three months and that of the sighted baby. Robert Emde proposed that what we saw in the blind child's smile was an adaptive modification of the characteristics of smiling observed in sighted children between the ages of three weeks and two months in which the human voice was one of a pool of stimuli which elicited *irregular* smiling. Out of this pool, only the visual stimuli will be differentiated for automatic response in the third month to the stimulus of the human face gestalt. In the case of the blind baby, the human voice afforded the means for selective smiling but lacked the sign value of the visual stimuli which release the automatic smile.

Between three and six months (now reporting on seven babies), the smile remains selective for the parents' voices and we have only isolated instances in our record in which the smile was elicited by the observer's voice. Yet, in this period, too, it is never an automatic smile to the sound of the parent's voice.

Now, in our records of this period, we begin to see that the most reliable stimulus for evoking a smile or laughter in the baby is gross tactile or kinesthetic stimulation. As observers, we were puzzled and concerned by the amount of bouncing, jiggling, tickling and nuzzling that all of our parents, without exception, engaged in with the baby. In several cases, we had to judge the amount of such stimulation as excessive by any standards. We had rarely seen, among parents of sighted babies in such a range of homes, so much dependence upon gross body stimulation. Then we began to understand; these games provided the almost certain stimulus for the smile, while the parents' voices, alone, provided at best, an irregular stimulus. The parents' own *need* for the response smile, which is normally guaranteed with the sighted baby of this age, led them to these alternative routes in which the smile would be evoked with a high degree of reliability.

During the same period, lap games, particularly "patty-cake," provided patterned motor stimulation which almost always elicited a smile from the baby. Such games had the advantage, of course, of giving the baby some means of regulating stimuli through anticipating pattern and rhythm and became favorite games for all of our children in the second half of the first year.

Smiling and pleasure in the game were clearly linked to the mother. When we tested differential responses through our observers by repeating a favorite game, we were unable to elicit a smile or responsive vocalizations, except in rare instances.

> Ronny, at 0:4:6, is playing pat-a-cake with mother. (In our region this game is played with five sequences, usually involving five motor patterns. Patta cake, patta cake, Baker's man. Bake me a cake as fast as you can./ Roll it/ and pat it/ and mark it with a T;/ put it in the oven for baby and me.) As soon as mother begins the first sequence with hand clapping, Ronny smiles. As the shift in rhythm is about to appear in the second sequence, there is anticipatory excitement on his face. As the new pattern appears, a big smile. At the conclusion of the game, laughter and vocalizations, then distress, which mother reads as "more." Mother resumes the game. At one point in repetition of the game with mother, mother interrupts the game to address a comment to the observers. There is a loud outcry from Ronny and mother must resume.
>
> Later, the observer plays patty-cake with Ronny, using the same chant and motor patterns. There is no smile and no active participation. When the observer experimentally interrupts the game at a point where a shift in rhythm and motor pattern would occur (a high point in the game with mother) there is no discernible reaction. Ronny maintains his hands limply in the posture of the point of interruption.

During the period six to twelve months (now reporting on ten babies) our records of smiling show no patterns of further differentiation, and parallels with the smiling of sighted infants break down at several points. For each child known to us in the first and second quarters, our records show an increase in the number of observations of smiling during this period. The pattern of preferential smiling for parents and familiar persons remains unchanged. The stimuli themselves, voice, tactile, kinesthetic, nearly always united with the familiar person, remain unchanged, except that the range of smile eliciting experience now enlarges to include a variety of games, which had not been in the child's repertoire in the earlier period. (A notable favorite among games, a sure stimulus for joyful smiling and laughter is a version of "peek-a-boo" in which a cloth is pulled over the blind baby's face with the ritual, "Where is . . . Johnny?")

When we consider the course of the differentiated smile in the case of the sighted infant, an attempt to find further parallels with our blind infants would be spurious. Smiling in the sighted infant is differentiated through vision. The automatic smile to the sign gestalt of the human face becomes a differentiated smile as recognition memory discriminates facial characteristics; it becomes a preferential smile for the face of intimate persons, and some observers (Benjamin (1963), Spitz and Wolf (1946), Emde and Koenig (1969)) report that in the second half of the first year the smile is reserved for mother, and familiar persons and not elicited by unfamiliar persons.

Now, of course, since the blind infant's smile to voice is selective from earliest infancy on, the differentiating criteria which we employ for sighted infants later in the first year have no meaning in the study of the blind infant. Since, in our observations, unfamiliar persons rarely elicited the smile, "not smiling" to the stranger in the second half of the first year had no value as a criterion for stranger reaction. (Other criteria were employed for stranger reactions, as we shall see in the next section.)

Actually, as we studied the characteristics of the blind baby's positive attachment to mother in the second half of the first year, we found that responsive vocalizations offered more differentiating criteria for valuation of the mother than the smile itself. The recorded "dialogues" between mother and child with "question and answer" cadence, play on sound, imitation of sound, could not be elicited by an observer experimentally reproducing cues with the baby. We have isolated examples in our record in which, for example, a blind baby says "Hi!" in response to the observer's "Hi!", but no examples of the extended "dialogue" with an observer in cases where we had clear demonstrations in relation to the mother or father.

When we exclude vision as a factor in the socialization of the smile, other differences in smiling emerge. Since the sign value of the smile in greeting can only be a visual sign (the exchange of smiles) the blind baby does not automatically smile in greeting; the blind baby does not *initiate* or invite contact with a smile.. Our babies do not smile as frequently as sighted babies do (the consensus of our own staff and a very large number of independent observers who have reviewed film with us over the years). And even when we have all the criteria for a mutually satisfying mother-child relationship, the smile of the blind infant strikes us as a muted smile. The joyful, even ecstatic, smile that we see in a healthy sighted baby is a comparatively rare occurrence among blind babies. This suggests that the smile on the face of "the other" is a potent re-inforcer—even in infancy—of one's own smile. The contagion of smiling is clearly dependent upon visual experience.

And what about the contagion of laughter? Since laughter is vocal, we should expect not only imitation, but the possibility of contagion. All of our babies laughed, of course. Typically, laughter was associated with peaks of excitement in games.

Under what circumstances did laughter of "the other" evoke laughter in the baby? We have only isolated examples in our records of laughter in response to laughter! We have a report from Ronny's mother that Ronny "laughs when his father laughs," at the age of ten months. But we never observed this. Was he imitating the sound of laughter (mechanically) or was this, properly speaking, laughter evoked by the laughter of "the other"? We have an observation of Teddy at eight months in which he laughed in response to laughter. We have an example of contagious laughter in Paul at the age of two years. We have this example in Robbie's records.

> Robbie: age 2:6:0. His mother reported during our visit that Robbie had been taught to say his prayers. "God bless Mama, God bless Daddy." Recently, Robbie invented his own litany: "God bless Mama, God bless Daddy, God bless television!" This, of course, broke up the research team and we all roared with laughter. Robbie, hearing our laughter, began to laugh. To get more mileage out of his joke, he repeated the litany, and we laughed again. One of us said, still laughing, "Robbie, you are a clown." "I'm a clown," he said, squealing with laughter. We kept up this nonsense for a few moments, in which one wave of laughter from us initiated another wave of laughter from Robbie. . . .
> After we left the session and drove back home, we realized that this was the first time we had ever encountered "contagious laughter" in Robbie.

These exceptional examples lead to some reflections. Is the contagion of laughter related to the contagion of the smile? In the absence of the visual signs that lead to the contagious smile, is the evolution of contagious laughter altered or impeded?

STRANGER REACTIONS

The Sighted Child

On the scale of increasing differentiation and valuation of the mother and other human partners, a complementary series of reactions toward the unfamiliar person begins to emerge before the middle of the first year. Benjamin (1963) describes "fear of the strange" during the period four-to-five months, which he discriminates from "stranger anxiety proper" at approximately seven months of age. At this age, fear of the stranger is closely connected with, or identical with, "fear of the strange" and has little to do with the human attributes of the stranger. It may be related to the sudden movement of the unfamiliar person, or a loud voice, reactions which can also be elicited by unfamiliar toys at the same age. There will also be reactions to physical handling by the unfamiliar person where shifts in the postural mode of holding, or differences in feeding techniques will elicit fear reactions.

The phenomenon of "stranger anxiety" or "negative reaction to the stranger" which appears between six and ten months of age has been variously described in the literature. Some of the differences among writers regarding "onset" and "peaks" may be related to differences in criteria and experimental procedures. Spitz, who has written extensively on the subject, uses the term "stranger anxiety" to cover a broad spectrum of behaviors which he referred to most recently under the more general term "negative reaction to the stranger" (1969). As described to us by Spitz, his procedures for eliciting stranger anxiety involve a direct approach by the experimenter to the child, preferably without mother in the room, in which the experimenter brings his face close to the child and speaks. The reactions of the child may range from "sobering," "averting the head" to "distressed crying." Any of these reactions are scored as negative reactions to the stranger. Morgan and Ricciuti (1969) employed distance and a gradual approach in the introduction of the stranger and scored "sobering" as neutral rather than negative. In their sample, the intensity peak for negative reactions to the stranger appeared at twelve months while Tennes and Lampl's (1964) sample (using procedures and criteria that involved a direct approach to the child) demonstrated a peak at nine months.

On a scale of human attachment, the negative reaction to the stranger is regarded as a significant criterion for the assessment of the positive bonds to the mother and other human partners (Spitz (1957), Benjamin (1963), Provence and Lipton (1962)). It speaks for another level in valuation of the mother in which the positive affect is bound to a partner, in which persons are no longer "interchangeable."

It is significant, again, that in the institutional studies of Provence and Lipton the non-attached babies showed no negative behavior toward the stranger in the last quarter of the first year and, as previously noted, smiled and vocalized indiscriminately for all-comers. Ainsworth (1967), in her Uganda study, rated her sample on an attachment scale and found a significant correlation between the rating of attachment and the manifestation of stranger anxiety in the last quarter of the first year, while the babies rated as "non-attached" did not, as a group, manifest negative reactions toward the stranger.

The Blind Baby

During each twice monthly visit, we recorded in descriptive detail differential responses to mother and the observers. Reactions to the observer's voice and to being held in the observer's arms were recorded at each visit. In several cases, too, where a game and vocal dialogue were important elements of mother-child interaction, we experimentally reproduced the conditions of the game, substituting an observer, and recorded the baby's participation and response. Our longitudinal findings were then classified on the basis of (1) discrimination of mother and unfamiliar persons, (2) negative reactions to the stranger in which we attempted to discriminate between (a) fear of the strange and (b) fear of the unfamiliar person.

Discrimination of Mother and Strangers

During the first year, the blind baby in our sample shows increasingly selective and well-differentiated responses to his mother, his father, to other intimate persons and to strangers. In addition to voice cues, the blind baby begins to inform himself through his fingers around five months of age and explores the face of familiar persons with his hands. Not only does he smile more frequently for mother and father, but his responsive vocalizations are far richer and more fluent with his parents or siblings than with the stranger, even after a warm-up period. Similarly, when we as observers attempted to play games with the baby, attempting to approximate in every way discernible to us the motor pattern employed in the game with parents, or the song or chant that accompanied the game, there were discernible differences, as described earlier, in the baby's response, his participation, and the registration of interest or pleasure on his face, compared to the game with one of the parents.

Negative Reactions to the Stranger

In the analysis of our data we have tried to differentiate (following Benjamin) between "fear of the strange" and "fear of the stranger." Thus, we have a large number of observations during the first year which show that the blind baby will react to "something different" in the situation, or in a voice characteristic, or in being held, or in touching an object that has novel tactile properties. The parallels with sighted babies are close here. During this period, as Benjamin has said, "a stranger is best defined as someone who does things differently." We have reserved the term "stranger anxiety" for manifest fear reactions to unfamiliar persons, following criteria which exclude the element "fear of the strange" and which offer fair evidence that the unfamiliar *person* is the object of distress.

There are obvious difficulties in setting up criteria. "Fear of the strange" flows into "fear of the stranger" in the case of the blind child as well as the sighted child. For example: Nine of our ten babies reacted to being held in the observer's arms in ways that contrasted with the easy molding to the mother's body. These babies quieted, stiffened, strained away and showed discomfort or distress in the stranger's arms. When the baby was then returned to the arms of his mother, he settled and relaxed. (This behavior is, of course, very close to that described by Benjamin (1963) and Ainsworth (1967) in sighted babies of the same age. The baby reacts to subtle postural differences in the stranger's arms.) We have classified these reactions as "fear of the strange," that is, something new has been introduced into a familiar situation.

Between 7 and 18 months, we find that something new begins to emerge in the behavior—manifest fear, struggling, crying—which, for the majority of the babies in our sample, occurs when the observer holds the baby. As we will see later, these fear reactions appear even though the observer, a twice-monthly visitor, is not, strictly speaking, a stranger. At the same time that these reactions are manifest in relation to the observer, we have parallel reports from the mothers, showing that fear of strangers has emerged with other visitors to the house as well.

In examining differential reactions to unfamiliar persons, we recorded, beginning with the first observational session, (a) reactions to the voice of the observer in the first encounter of the session, (b) reactions to being held in the observer's arms.

Reactions to voice alone: Among those children who were observed under six months of age, we have already mentioned that smiling was rarely evoked by the stranger's voice and appeared as a selective response to the voice of the mother and other intimate persons from the earliest weeks on. During the first six months, the baby was attentive to the sound of the stranger's voice. We have no reports of negative reactions to the stranger's voice.

Between six and thirteen months, we obtained reactions in all ten babies which we have called "quieting" in response to the stranger's voice, i.e. a cessation of action or vocalizing (without signs of distress) which may last for several minutes, or longer. Mothers have told us that this is a typical reaction to strange voices. Indeed, we were to learn, the quality of vocalizations was affected by the presence of unfamiliar persons, something mothers had told us, but we were unable to verify until recently.

> When Teddy was seven months old, the observer became concerned by the sharp drop in vocalizations in a child who had been one of our most vocal and "conversational" babies. His dialogue had been almost exclusively with mother but now, during the past two visits, the observer was impressed to see how little vocal exchange was present even in relation to the mother. The observer found a way to make tactful inquiry regarding Teddy's language and the mother, perhaps amused, assured the observer that Teddy was as talkative as ever—he just shut up when strangers were around. To prove her point, Teddy's mother tape recorded some samples of Teddy's "conversations" during the day. There was no question in listening to the tapes that mother was right. Teddy was reacting to

strangers by a constriction of vocalizations and exchange with his mother.

The meaning of "quieting" for all of our babies during this period is open to several possible interpretations. We should state at the outset that we have not scored "quieting" as a negative reaction or as stranger anxiety. However, it regularly precedes the period in which a manifest stranger anxiety occurs. "Quieting" is also one of the characteristics of the reactions to strangers among sighted children in the period before the onset of fear of the stranger. For the sighted child, too, there is a reduction in vocalizations and vocal exchanges when strangers are present, as Ronald Tikofsky tells us (1970). Is "quieting" in the blind child an equivalent of "staring" in the sighted child, which Ainsworth and others describe in the period that precedes fear of the stranger? Is it a form of focused listening, as the blind child sorts out the information coming to him from familiar and unfamiliar voices, as Edna Adelson of our staff suggested? (Dorothy Burlingham (1964) also describes the intent listening of older blind children as a characteristic orienting device.) Is the immobilization at the sound of unfamiliar voices a defensive posture on the part of the blind child who has a limited repertoire of mechanisms for regulating or "turning off" novel, unexpected or excessive stimuli? (Another possibility proposed by Mrs. Adelson.) At the present, we cannot provide answers to these questions, but as we move into other areas of data evaluation, the characteristics of "quieting" as defense will be studied in an extended range and we may obtain further clues.

Reactions to being held: In addition, to "voice alone," we tested the reaction of the baby to being held in the observer's arms at each of the twice-monthly visits. Typically, the observer spoke to the baby while holding him. (This was not by design, but intuitively we felt that to hold the blind baby without speaking to him would introduce another factor of strangeness and produce a shock reaction that could not be discriminated from stranger reaction—without vision, the baby cannot anticipate the stranger's approach signs, the open arms, for example, that signify "I would like to pick you up." Without the voice the blind child cannot have information regarding the person who is holding him.) So, while "holding without speaking" would have been a procedure that would differentiate between the reactions to voice and the reactions to being held, it would not have provided fair analogies to the situation with the sighted child and would probably have been an unwarranted disturbance for the baby.

The cumulative record for each child on "reactions to being held" was analyzed for each of our ten babies. Our problem, then, was to discriminate between those reactions that could be classified as "fear of the strange" and those that were, properly speaking, "fear of the stranger." Thus, if "stiffening" and "straining away" are characteristic reactions in our sample from the early months on (fear of the strange), we will need other criteria to define "stranger anxiety" as such at a later stage.

A number of criteria employed for stranger reactions in sighted child studies are not applicable to the blind child at all. "Sobering," for example, is inapplicable because there is actually not enough contrast in the facial expressions of blind children to produce a valid judgment of "sobering." The blind child typically wears a "sober" (solemn, serious) look. And since his smiles, too, are rare for the stranger, *not* smiling to the stranger, or regarding him solemnly, have no value in assessment. "Frowning" is not an expressive sign for all of our blind babies, and we have some evidence that when it appears at all, it occurs among those babies who have light perception. But, as an infrequent or atypical sign in our sample we cannot use "frowning" as a criterion of negative response.

We are left, then, with a limited number of signs in our blind children that can fairly be called "fear responses" or "negative reactions" to the stranger. Vocal displeasure—whimpering, crying, screaming—remains the same for the blind baby as the sighted baby. Motor resistance and avoidance to the approach of the unfamiliar person, followed by active seeking of the mother, will also provide fair equivalence to the behavior of the sighted child.

As we analyzed the protocols of each child for differential responses to strangers, eight of the ten children showed fear and avoidance reactions to the observer between the ages of seven and sixteen months, even under the circumstances in which the observer had been a twice-monthly visitor in the home. Since holding the baby or approaching the baby for games and testing had been part of the regular observational procedure, the appearance of the first fear reactions could be placed against a background in which no fear reactions had been observed in previous visits. There was close correspondence, too, between our first observations and the parents' reports of fear of strangers.

The following examples represent, in each case, the first appearance of fear of the stranger in eight cases which provided unambiguous evidence.

> Toni: age 0:7:2 Soon after the observer (a woman) picks her up, she freezes, then bursts into tears. She frantically fingers the face of the observer; registers increasing distress on her face, strains away from the observer's body, turns her head and trunk as if seeking to locate her mother by voice. She claws at the examiner's arms. She begins to scream loudly. When she is returned to her mother, she buries her head in the mother's neck and is gradually comforted.

Teddy: age 0:8:18   During an observation session at the project office, S. F. was used to test stranger reactions. Teddy had not previously met her. Teddy was lying supine on a rug, playing a game in which he brought his clasped hands to his mouth. He was vocalizing "gaga" and "ah" and seemed very comfortable with three observers and his parents nearby. When S. F. spoke to him he seemed attentive to her voice; there was no smile or responsive vocalizations as we observed with the parents. S. F., while talking with Teddy, now picked him up, speaking throughout. Teddy now became very still and quiet. Then he began to finger her mouth. He stiffened more and more and then began a quiet whimper which got louder and louder. He mouthed her scarf. S. F. continued to talk to him and his whimper became louder. He began to cry. S.F. handed him to his mother. He snuggled in her arms and was soon comforted.

Jamie: age 0:9:12   E.L. is visiting with the team today. Jamie has never met him before. E. L. picks up the baby and begins to talk to him. As soon as he is picked up, Jamie begins to cry. He is handed to his mother who diverts him with a game and succeeds in comforting him.

Paul: age 1:1:5   Later in the morning, when he was standing on the floor, I offered him my hand while talking to him. Once again, he listened but made no move on his own to approach closer. Both with S. F. (second observer) and myself, he turned away from us as soon as he heard his father's voice, and reached toward his father.

Cathy: age 1:1:16   The observer speaks to Cathy. She is attentive. Now the observer picks her up. Cathy stiffens, feels the observer's face with her right hand, clutches her shirt with the other hand, whimpers, is transferred to her mother's arms.

Joan: age 1:3:17   As the observer began to engage Joan in play, he noticed fear and withdrawal for the first time in his regular visits. When he spoke to Joan and touched her, she drew his hand away. Later, too, when he attempted to place her on his lap, Joan withdrew from contact and tried to get away from him. When he offered her objects in a testing situation during this session, she was unwilling to touch and explore any of the items.

Ronny: age 1:3:29   . . . While mother went to get coffee, Ronny was still in his teeterbabe. He was fretful and upset. I (observer) asked him if he wanted to get out and he instantly raised his arms (as he does when mother askes him this question). However, as soon as I had him in my arms, he stiffened and arched away and didn't want to have any contact with me at all and began to cry noticeably. . . . I was talking to him. "Mama's coming right back." He still very definitely and angrily kept pushing away from me and mother then takes him from me. . . .

Jackie: age 1:6:21   Jackie is sitting on his mother's lap, not at the moment engaged with mother or the observers. The observer picks him up and brings him to stand, holding his hands. There is not an immediate negative reaction. On film we see an initial smile on his face. But this is followed by constraint and motor signs of discomfort (observer's own notes). Now, on film he turns in the direction of mother, on the couch, correctly orienting himself, and holds out his arms to mother. Mother offers her hand and as soon as Jackie makes contact with the hand he begins to crawl upon his mother's lap. Once on mother's lap he makes chance contact with the observer's hand, fingers it, then turns back toward mother, very actively climbing on mother, and settles in a supine position on her lap. He then engages mother in a favorite game.

This leaves two cases out of ten children who have not given evidence of stranger anxiety during the first eighteen months. It may be worth reporting briefly on each of them to give a picture of the sample:

> Karen provided no clear examples of fear of the stranger at any point in the second year. Since she had always resisted being held, and did not enjoy being held in her own mother's arms, the examples of protest in the stranger's arms had no meaning in assessing differential responses. On the other hand, her positive attachment to the mother could be seen in following the mother when she became mobile and in frequent excursions to mother to "touch base."

> Robbie provided one example of "quieting" to the observers' voices at 1:0:0 and no other examples of negative reactions to strangers at any time in the second year. During the second year he allowed our own observers and other unfamiliar persons to hold him and to play with him. We have examples in our hospital waiting room and other unfamiliar places in which his indiscriminate friendliness to strangers is recorded. He is also the one child in our group whose attachment to his mother was regarded by us as unstable, without signs of active seeking of the mother for pleasure or comfort.

If we can accept, then, those differences in testing stranger reactions which were required when we needed to translate procedures for testing sighted infants into procedures for blind infants, there is fair equivalence in the characteristics of stranger anxiety in our blind baby sample and those reported for sighted children.

However, if our criteria are fair, there is a marked difference in age of onset of fear of the stranger in our blind group. For five of the eight children the first observations of fear of the stranger appeared between the ages of 13 and 15 months. The one child (Toni) who showed the most extreme fear of strangers, at 7 months, 2 days, sustained a fear of strangers that I would now regard as pathological in its intensity. As late as four years of age, when Toni was last seen, this otherwise healthy and bright child, reacted to strangers through the most complete withdrawal. We have always felt that the early and intense stranger anxiety must have been related to other events, very possibly a brief separation from the mother.

The full significance of these differences between the age of onset of stranger anxiety in our blind sample and age of onset in sighted children awaits further study. The links with separation anxiety will be described in a separate report. The relevance of locomotor achievements, prehension and object concept (in Piaget's terms) will be examined as our data analysis moves ahead.

BIBLIOGRAPHY

1. AINSWORTH, M. D. Infancy in Uganda: Infant Care and the Growth of Love. Baltimore: Johns Hopkins U. Press, 1967.
2. ———— The Development of Infant-Mother Interaction Among the Ganda. *Determinants of Infant Behavior*, Vol. II, pp. 67-104. Ed. B. M. Foss. London: Methuen, 1963.
3. AMBROSE, J. A. The Development of the Smiling Response in Early Infancy. *Determinants of Infant Behavior*. Vol. I, pp. 179-196. Ed. B. M. Foss. London: Methuen, 1961.
4. BENJAMIN, J. D. Further Comments on Some Developmental Aspects of Anxiety. *Counterpoint*, pp. 121-153. New York: International Universities Press, 1963.
5. BOWLBY, J. The Nature of the Child's Tie to His Mother. *Int. J. Psychoanalysis*, 39:350-373, 1958.
6. ———— Separation Anxiety. *Int. J. Psychoanalysis*, 41:89-113, 1960.
7. ————Attachment. *Attachment and Loss*, Vol. I. New York: Basic Books, Inc., 1969.
8. BURLINGHAM, DOROTHY. Hearing and Its Role in the Development of the Blind. *Psychoanalytic Study of the Child*, Vol. XIX, pp. 95-112. New York: International Universities Press, 1964.
9. EMDE, R. N. & KOENIG, K. L. Neonatal Smiling, Frowning, and Rapid Eye Movements States: II Sleep-Cycle Study. *Journal of the American Academy of Child Psychiatry*, Vol. IV, 1969.
10. ESCALONA, S. Emotional Development in the First Year of Life. *Problems of Infancy and Childhood*, pp. 11-92. Ed. M. Senn. New York: Josiah Macy Foundation, 1953.
11. FRAIBERG, S. Libidinal Object Constancy and Mental Representation. *Psychoanalytic Study of the Child*, Vol. XXIV. New York: International Universities Press, 1969.
12. ———— Parallel and Divergent Patterns in Blind and Sighted Infants. *Psychoanalytic Study of the Child*, Vol. XXIII, pp. 264-300. New York: International Universities Press, 1968.
12a. FRAIBERG, S. & FREEDMAN, D. A. Studies in the Ego Development of the Congenital Blind Child. *Psychoanalytic Study of the Child*, Vol. XIX, pp. 133-169. New York: International Universities Press, 1964.
13. FRAIBERG, S., SIEGEL. B. & GIBSON, R. The Role of Sound in the Search Behavior of Blind Infants. *Psychoanalytic Study of the Child*, Vol. XXI, pp. 327-357. New York: International Universities Press, 1966.
14. FRAIBERG, S., SMITH, M. & ADELSON, E. An Educational Program for Blind Infants. *Journal of Special Education*, Vol. III, No. 2, pp. 121-139, 1969.
15. FREEDMAN, D. G. Hereditary Control of Early Social Behavior. *Determinants of Infant Behavior*, Vol. III, pp. 149-161. Ed. B. M. Foss. London: Methuen, 1965.
16. ———— Smiling in Blind Infants and the Issue of Innate vs. Acquired. *J. Child Psychol. and Psychiat.*, Vol. V, pp. 171-184, 1964.

17. GEWIRTZ, J. L. The Course of Infant Smiling in Four Child-Rearing Environments in Israel. *Determinants of Infant Behavior,* Vol. III, pp. 205-248. Ed. B. M. Foss. London: Methuen, 1965.
18. GOUIN-DECARIE, T. Intelligence and Affectivity in Early Childhood. New York: International Universities Press, 1953.
19. MORGAN, GEORGE A. & RICCIUTI, HENRY N. Infant's Responses to Strangers During the First Year. *Determinants of Infant Behavior,* Vol. IV. Ed. B. M. Foss. London: Methuen, 1969.
20. POLAK, P. R., EMDE, R. N. & SPITZ, R. A. The Smiling Response to the Human Face: I Methodology, Quantification and Natural History. *J. Nerv. Ment. Dis.,* 139:103-109, 1964.
21. PROVENCE, S. & LIPTON, R. Infants in Institutions. New York: International Universities Press, 1962.
22. SCHAFFER, H. R. & EMERSON, P. E. The Development of Social Attachments in Infancy. *Monogr. Soc. Res. Child Develop.,* 28, No. 1: Serial No. 94, 1964.
23. ——— Some Issues for Research in the Study of Attachment Behavior. *Determinants of Infant Behavior,* Vol. II, pp. 179-199. Ed. B. M. Foss. London: Methuen, 1963.
24. SPITZ, R. A Genetic Field Theory of Ego Formation: Its Implications for Pathology. New York: International Universities Press, 1950.
25. SPITZ, R. A. & WOLF, K. A. The Smiling Response: A Contribution to the Ontogenesis of Social Relations. *Genet. Psychol. Monogr.* 34:57-125, 1946.
26. ——— Anxiety in Infancy: A Study of Its Manifestations in the First Year of Life. *Int. J. Psychoanal.* 31:138-143, 1950.
27. ——— No and Yes: On the Beginnings of Human Communication. New York: International Universities Press, 1957.
28. ——— The First Year of Life. New York: International Universities Press, 1965.
29. ——— *Personal Communication,* 1969.
30. TENNES, K. H. & LAMPL, E. E. Stranger and Separation Anxiety. *J. Nerv. Ment. Dis.* 139:247-254, 1964.
31. THOMPSON, J. Development of Facial Expression of Emotion in Blind and Seeing Children. *Arch. Psychol.* No. 264, 1941.
32. TIKOFSKY, RONALD. *Personal Communication,* 1970.
33. WOLFF, P. H. The Early Development of Smiling. *Determinants of Infant Behavior,* Vol. II. Ed. B. M. Foss. London: Methuen, 1963.

7

THE MATERNAL PERSONALITY INVENTORY

An Objective Instrument for Assessing Personality Attributes in Relation to Maternal Behavior and Infant Development

Nahman H. Greenberg, M.D.
Associate Professor of Psychiatry

and

Jesse Hurley, M.A.
Research Assistant
Child Development Clinical and Research Unit
Department of Psychiatry, College of Medicine
of the University of Illinois at the Medical Center

I. INTRODUCTION

This is a report of the Maternal Personality Inventory (MPI), an objective questionnaire designed to test mothers for attributes of personality associated with maternal behavior thought to adversely influence the development of infants. Individual questionnaire items, scales and

From: The Child Development Clinical and Research Unit, Department of Psychiatry, College of Medicine of the University of Illinois at the Medical Center, P.O. Box 6998, Chicago, Illinois 60680; and in collaboration with the Maternal, Infant and Preschool Child Health Center (MIPC Health Center) of the Chicago Board of Health.

Supported in part by Project 1723, "Psychosomatic Differentiation During Infancy," Psychiatric Training and Research Authority, Department of Mental Health, State of Illinois, and in part by Project 502, "Growth and Development of High-Risk Infants," Maternal and Child Care Projects, City of Chicago Board of Health and the Childrens Bureau, Department of Health, Education, and Welfare.

Supported in part by a Research Scientist Development Award MH-13,984. from the National Institute of Mental Health, Department of Health, Education and Welfare.

Acknowledgements: Contributions to this study were made by various persons including Robert Lipgar, Ph.D., Sandra Incorvia, B.A., Adrienne Lieberman, B.S., Mr. Joel normative statistics, including reliabilities, are presented. Correlations with the Eysenck (Maudsley) Personality Inventory and with an overall score of atypical infant behavior are presented as examples of the usefulness of the MPI in suggesting attributes of maternal personality which may anticipate maternal behavior found in association with the development of atypical behavior during infancy.

II. PERSONALITY, MATERNAL BEHAVIOR, AND ATYPICAL INFANT BEHAVIOR: SOME COMMENTS AND A REVIEW OF LITERATURE

A. *Introduction*

The personality of parents and the interaction with their infants and children are assumed to have an inordinate influence on early development and on adult personality. Parental personality has been studied and attempts made to correlate them with earlier and later aspects of development. In general there has been limited documentation in understanding how parental factors, especially maternal personality and behavior, influence the growth and development of infants and young children.

Major traumata occurring during infancy have been implicated in the origins of character disorders, psychosomatic illnesses, psychotic and prepsychotic diseases. Pathogenic experiences originating in faulty infant-mother relationships have been considered necessary preconditions for the later development of major disorders including childhood schizophrenia. Mothers, for example of schizophrenic children, have been variously described as overstimulating, intrusive and disruptive rather than protective and regulating.

Atypical behavior during infancy is assumed to appear when the care and stimulation of babies are inadequate, insufficient, inappropriate, faulty or abusive. Such undesirable conditions are thought to come about by mothers' behavior and especially in their choices or failures to select stimulations and techniques of infant care which will regulate behavior state, satisfy needs, and comfort. The actual care and stimulation patterns constitute the maternal behaviors which can be directly observed as infant-mother interactions and which, in large measure, are thought to be derivatives of maternal personality and of cultural and subcultural factors.

These assumptions are difficult to support or refute since the infor-

Heineman and Mr. Charles L. Ririe. The assistance of Mrs. Sharon Reznicek and Mrs. Johnnie Williams was particularly helpful. We are especially grateful to the Public Health nurses, clinic staff nurses, and the clerical staff of the MIPC Health Center for their consistent and conscientious dedication to the task of systematic and complete data collection.

mation needed to test them is not yet available. The data which are required include direct observations of maternal behavior and of the specific care techniques and stimulations of these infants by their parents, particularly their mothers, as well as studies on subculture and personality factors.

It is important to separate out negligence and abuse ascribed to cultural conditions from those due directly to the person responsible for infant care. If neglect is thought of in terms of deficiencies, restrictions or the absence of specific environmental stimulations and care needed for an infant to thrive, then various circumstances qualify for such conditions. Ignorance, famine and poverty may result in infant neglect. Faulty information combined with insufficient resources for educating an uninformed mother engaged in undesirable infant care practices may also contribute to infant neglect. A withdrawn mother suffering from a serious mental disorder may create conditions of infant negligence. In the sense of actual experiences, the babies in each of the three conditions may go through very similar, perhaps almost identical experiences in their care and sensations. Maternal attitudes and emotions influence the characteristics of infant care and stimulation; the background and personality of a mother might be the roots of negligence or of her failure to respond with warmth and nurturance. Culture and subcultural factors must also be independently assessed especially if an understanding of the relative importance of their contribution is to be utilized in prevention and treatment. The use of a comparative design should aid the discovery of significant differences between mothers and subcultures whose infants thrive and mothers and subcultures whose infants do not thrive.

B. *Prenatal and Postnatal Maternal Emotions*

Emotional stress and anxiety during pregnancy are thought to be associated with less favorable infant adjustment. Gravid infrahuman subjects have been experimentally subjected to extreme stimulations resulting in morphologically damaged offsprings. It is difficult to extrapolate such findings for application to humans although it is reasonable to seriously entertain the general idea that rather alien emotional and environmental conditions impinging on gravid women, especially during the critical first trimester of pregnancy, may sufficiently alter inner physiological and biochemical conditions and the processes of embryogenesis as to cause untoward events for a developing fetus. The nature of such alterations and the emotional conditions necessary and sufficient to bring them about are not known in the human.

It is assumed that a favorable mother-child relationship involves mutual satisfaction and pleasure and that the mother's capacity to recognize and evaluate the needs of her own child, and her ability to achieve gratification within her own unique personality pattern influence the development of adequate maternal behavior. The effect of childhood events and experiences, such as one's own mother-child relationship and the woman's identification with her own mother on subsequent mothering, is important to emphasize (Benedek, 1956). The reciprocal element of the mother-child relationship and the importance of the mother's experience are indicated by Benedek's statement that:

> "the capacity of the mother to receive from the child, her ability to be consciously gratified by the exchange and to use this gratification unconsciously in her emotional maturation is the specific quality and function of motherliness."

For both infant and mother, developmental processes are intensively interactive and begin at conception. Therefore a psychological assessment of the mother during pregnancy may help anticipate future maternal behavior. The mother who gains gratification from interaction with her infant is thought to acquire confidence in her mother abilities and this may greatly influence not only future mother-child interaction, but also aid in the fulfillment of her role as a woman.

C. *Some Maternal and Cultural Factors Associated with Patterns of*
    Infant Atypical Behavior—Body-rocking, Failure-to-thrive, and Pica

The origins of severe body-rocking have been ascribed to understimulating and/or overstimulating environments. The high incidence of body-rocking among deprived and neglected infants supports the idea that insufficient somatic stimulation may be an important precondition for severe body-rocking although body-rocking can develop in infants exposed to excesses of kinesthetic stimulation while relatively lacking stimulation in other sensory modalities. These are also conditions in which faulty or insufficient affectional ties with a maternal person are assumed to emerge. In one study (Spitz, 1945), about one-fourth of the mothers of the "Nursery" infants with body rocking were evaluated with psychological tests and were described as generally "infantile, extroverted with alloplastic tendencies, lacking the faculty to control their aggression . . . presenting outbursts of negative emotion, of violent hostility." Spitz observed that the babies were alternately exposed to intense outbursts of love and equally intense outbursts of hostility and rage. The mothers of the "Nursery" infants were characteristically inconsistent, impulsive and subject to swift changes in mood.

Failure-to-thrive or a severe retardation in the rate of weight gain (Greenberg, 1970) may involve a complex interaction of physical, nutritional, and psychological factors such as in failure-to-thrive associated with pica and nutritional anemia. Most reports do not clearly delineate failure-to-thrive from maternal deprivation. In infants reared at home by their own mothers, failure-to-thrive has been related to neglect and rejection, and to poor infant-mother relations. Disturbances in the mother-child relationship are considered the primary problem, and the failure-to-thrive is thought to reflect resulting "emotional" disturbances on body functioning. Although the circumstances of the families varied, most were of low socioeconomic status. This may well be a sampling bias since most cases are drawn from clinic populations. The marital status of mothers varied; the absence of the father was observed in a number of cases and there are reports of family violence. The mothers are often described as depressed, lacking emotional warmth toward the infant and unable to provide protective care for the infant. Some of the mothers are also described as anxious, indifferent, rejecting, inadequate, or unable to experience gratification in their maternal role.

The interaction between poverty and parental behavior, between sub-cultural and cultural forces, is dramatically observed in infants with pica. Pica or perverted appetite in the absence of organic causes is assumed to have psychological or mental origins. Poor economic conditions and faulty housing are associated with the greater availability of paint and plaster chips and the mothers of children with pica are thought to be unable to watch their children. The following social factors have been found to be significant: more unmarried mothers, geographic instability and families with major emotional problems. Most cases of paint poisoning in children occur in areas characterized by overcrowded living quarters, by low economic status of the resident, by poor maintenance of housing and by non-parental supervision of young children.

D. *Psychological Assessments of Parents of Atypical Children*

Clinical interviews, projective tests and structured inquiries (questionnaires) have been used individually and in combinations to study the personality of parents and, indirectly, to study parent-child relations and interaction. It has been extremely difficult to develop objective techniques which simultaneously assess parental personality and indicate or predict specific facets of parent-child interactional behavior. Although projective and objective tests of parental personality have revealed personality correlates of parent-child behavior, the interactions and parent-child relations demonstrated tend to be broad in dimensions and too general to contribute to an understanding of relations between parent personality and behavior and how they influence children's development.

The personality of parents of typical infants has been studied using clinical interviews (Greenberg, 1970) and semi-structured questionnaires (Greenberg, 1971). The personality of parents of older atypical children has also been studied using non-projective instruments such as the Minnesota Multiphasic Personality Inventory (MMPI). Some MMPI studies have found promising leads, while others have not proved useful in discriminating between parent groups where, on the basis of theory, personality differences might have been expected. There is some question whether the failure of these MMPI studies to come up with more definitive results lies mainly in the test itself, the theory and hypotheses being tested, in the research design, e.g., errors in the selection or sampling of parent Ss or in methods of analysis. An MMPI study of two groups of parents (Adrian, 1957) revealed the MMPI profiles of parents of disturbed children to be more abnormal than those of non-disturbed children. From these differences criteria were developed for selecting prospective adoptive parents, and social workers, independent of the MMPI criterion, accepted or rejected these prospects as suitable adoptive parents. Mothers rejected were identified by this criterion as similar to the mothers of disturbed children. An MMPI study of matched groups of parents of disturbed and non-disturbed children (Liverant, 1959) found that the mothers of disturbed children scored significantly higher than mothers of non-disturbed children on the D (depression), Hy (hysteria), Pd (psychopathic deviated), Pa (paranoia), Pt (Psychasthenia) and Taylor Anxiety Scales. A description of the "average" mother of a disturbed child was of an anxious, depressed, angry woman, likely to act out her destructive feelings in relation to others. No significant differences were found in MMPI profiles between parents of cerebral palsied and non-cerebral palsied children, (Williams, 1954) and between parents of stuttering and non-stuttering children (Goodstein and Dahlstrom, 1956).

Our experience with the MMPI is limited to a study of sixteen mothers of infants with atypical behavior who were given the MMPI. The mean score for each of nine clinical scales, based on the 16 Ss scores, is above the normal population mean and all but the Mf (masculinity-femininity) and Ma (hypomania) scales are more than one T-score above the population mean.

III. PREVIOUS WORK

A. *Introduction*

A number of clinical studies of maternal personality and observational studies of infant-mother interaction were carried out prior to work on the Maternal Personality Inventory (MPI). These investigations were designed around a set of ideas which attempted to link maternal personality and characteristics of infant care and stimulation with the differentiation of normal infant behavior and the emergence or onset of atypical infant behavior. The examination of these ideas required a variety of data and necessitated a multimethod approach. Clinical interviews, projective psychological tests including The Rorschach, The Thematic Apperception and Draw-A-Person tests, a personal history questionnaire, and direct and film-recorded observations of infant-mother interaction were used to provide the data for evaluating our concepts and to suggest related hypotheses.

Clinical studies have unique contributions to make and clinical methods including projective tests provide data that enrich conceptualization and stimulate new ideas and hypotheses. The findings obtained from our clinical investigations were valuable contributions as guides to more specific areas of inquiry, to better delineated dimensions of maternal personality which seem related to those characteristics of infant-mother interaction influencing the development of atypical infant behavior. Clinical techniques have limitations. They are very elusive in yielding unambiguous, quantitative information, in testing hypotheses, and in making systematic case to case comparisons. They are, moreover, complex in interpretation and time consuming to employ.

B.   *Clinical Interviews*

From an assessment of clinical interview data, mothers of infants with atypical behavior were found to have impaired and limited psychological defenses, reality-testing and capacity for self-observation. They suffered from an intolerance of frustration and anxiety. The capacity for emotional involvements with others was restricted and they maintained a low concept of self (Greenberg, 1970). Their adjustment to pregnancy and maternal attitudes seemed disturbed (Greenberg, 1971).

C.   *Rorschach Assessments of Mothers of Infants with Atypical Behavior: A Summation of Findings*

Projective instruments such as the Rorschach do not lend themselves readily to objective quantitative methods of content analysis although they are a rich source of date on personality. We elected to use the Rorschach with an initial sample of mothers and planned to develop techniques to order the Rorschach data for statistical treatment.

Three studies based on Rorschach data were carried out on mothers of infants with atypical behavior. The first was an assessment of the mothers' Rorschach responses using standard scoring systems and interpretive approaches. The second study was an examination of Rorschach data for maternal violence, and the third study was a comparison of the Rorschach data from mothers of infants with atypical behavior and mothers of battered babies.

The *first study* was a statistical analysis of the Rorschach structural scores of twenty-nine mothers of infants with atypical behavior and a group of thirty controls drawn from a larger population of normal women forming the subjects of an earlier study (Beck, 1949), and matched to the experimental group for age, education, and socioeconomic class. Protocols were independently scored by two psychologists experienced with the Rorschach and re-scored to rule out clerical errors and to reconcile differences in the application of scoring rules. The Beck scores of the two mother groups were found to differ significantly, by t-test, on four of the Rorschach determinants; R, F+%, A%, and P. The mothers of infants with atypical behavior revealed reduced expressiveness and less intellectual investment in the environment (lower R), somewhat less effective intellectualized approach in maintaining reality contact (higher F+%), a lower scope of flexibility of imagination (higher A%), and less conformity with conventional percepts (lower P).

Clinical interviews and direct observations of maternal behavior made us increasingly aware that many mothers of the atypical infants demonstrated overt hostile behavior towards their infants. Impatience, unwarranted rejections, icy aloofness, angry recriminations, insensitivity to the baby's responses of distress, which sometimes were activated by excessive handling and prodding of the infants by mothers, were often observed. Repeated viewing of filmed interactions between infants and mothers revealed cases of excessive handling which verged on abusivness; vigorous rubbing seemed more like an effort to mold the infant's body as if it were modeling clay and its message of destruction was made clear when one of our first infant subjects was killed by her mother.

To examine the specific hypothesis that maternal destructiveness or hostility was more pronounced among mothers of infants with atypical behavior, a *second* study was carried out using a scale devised to measure destructive or violent percepts and applied to Rorschach data from mothers of battered babies, mothers of infants with atypical behavior, and from normal controls. The four-point (0-3) "violence-destructiveness" (*v-d*) scale, based in part on the work of other investigators (Elizur, 1949; Murstein, 1956), was used to score each response in the Beck scoring system (Beck, 1949), according to the content of each response. The scores for each subject are totaled and divided by the number of responses. The hypothesis states that if this scale differentiates among the groups described, then the mothers of battered babies should have the highest *v-d* scores, the controls the lowest, and the mothers of infants with atypical behavior should have intermediate scores.

The *v-d* scores divided by the number of responses were computed for each subject. An analysis of variance was performed to test for group differences and the pooled intergroup variances were used to compute a standard error. Each of the group means is significantly different at the 0.01 level of significance. Since any pair of group means is significantly different, a significant regression occurs when the group means are ordered, results which support the hypothesis. To estimate control, the ratio of the frequency of the response scored 3 occurring to the total number of responses for each group was computed and by Chi-square was found significant beyond the 0.05 level of statistical significance.

In a *third* study, the Rorschach protocols were used to estimate probable infant abuse. The question was posed as to how well clinicians experienced in the Rorschach technique could differentiate among the three mother groups without knowledge of the *v-d* scores and, if successful, what criteria would they use. Twenty-four Rorschach protocols were selected; eight protocols from the mothers of battered babies; eight from the mothers of infants with atypical behavior and eight from among the controls. Using a 6-point scale, three Rorschach diagnosticians were asked to rate the probability that each maternal subject would physically injure or severely abuse her infant. The raters, working independently, were told only that there was at least one protocol from a mother of a battered baby; no other information was provided.

Analysis of variance indicated that, on the average, the raters considered the possibility of physical infant abuse by the mothers of battered babies and the mothers of infants with atypical behavior to be nearly the same, and significantly greater than that of the controls (statistically significant at a 99% level). No significant differences were found for the general level of scoring between raters. One rater stressed the importance of structure (Beck's scores) in rating the subjects, but also indicated that hostile and childish content, impulsiveness and the adequacy of controls were taken into account. The second rater emphasized the importance of content as well as structure. He also attempted to assess the subject's impulsiveness and the adequacy of her controls. He also looked at role comfort as a variable—i.e. how comfortable a woman was with the feminine role and at what level she was comfortable (as a child, wife, mother, etc.).

The third rater thought the criterion of psychotic pathology would be helpful and considered the presence of pathologically depressed states, delusional ideation, poor reality testing, and severely regressive-preoccupation to increase the likelihood of physically abusive acting-out against infants. He also searched for evidence of "primitive personality organization" with poor control of aggressive impulses as heightening expectation of abuse against children.

D. *Infant-Mother Interactional Behavior*

Descriptions of maternal behavior and infant-mother interaction were obtained during interviews with the mothers, from observers' narratives of infant-mother interaction during these interviews, and from narrative and quantitative assessments of behavioral interaction recorded by motion film (Greenberg, 1971). There were rather distinct differences in the patterns of maternal behavior and in the characteristics of infant stimulation between mothers of infants with atypical behavior and mothers of normal infants. The nature of these differences was consistent with some of our prior conceptualizations which linked maternal personality, infant care and stimulation patterns, and the occurrence of atypical infant behavior.

E. *Summary*

The data from clinical interviews, projective tests and questionnaires appeared rather consistent and indicated that the mothers of infants with atypical behavior suffered from serious emotional disturbances, had limited range of defenses, an overall inflexibility associated with insufficient psychological differentiations, severely impaired judgment and poor reality testing. While many appeared depressed, most seemed distant, apathetic, withdrawn, and impoverished. Empathy and closeness were not in evidence and gratifying relations with other adults seemed almost non-existent. Their fantasy life was usually sparse and most often consisted of rather primitive notions and fears with hostility and violence the principal themes. The world seemed portrayed as cruel, where people get stung, neglected, gobbled up, hurt and taken advantage of even as they consciously appear to seek nurturance and closeness. These mothers impressed us as being severely hostile, yet seemed amazingly unaware of and unable to acknowledge hostile impulses. This was an unmistakable feature even in the mothers whose infants were the victims of violence and suffered severe physical injury. The findings in general indicated interactions between atypical behavior of infants, serious abnormalities in the personality of their mothers, and concurrent faulty and inadequate maternal care including neglect and understimulation or distinct, perhaps, abusive, kinesthetic overstimulation.

One of the next directions which seemed reasonable and natural to take was the construction of an objective questionnaire relevant to these behavioral dimensions and focused on areas of maternal personality and behavior tentatively associated with the development of atypical infant behavior. Thus, the decision to construct an objective instrument to assess maternal personality was based on a number of needs and considerations and was preceeded by a number of clinical studies on maternal behavior and infant development. Such a test has several characteristics which are advantageous in research dealing with parents, particularly when subject groups are drawn from a public clinic. (1) They are pencil and paper tests which do not presume a high degree of literacy on the subject's part; therefore they can be used with a wide range of subjects. (2) They are self-administered; they do not require the presence of an examiner but can be answered by the subject at his leisure. (3) The test can provide objective scores which facilitate easy comparisons among diverse groups and can prove useful in detecting personality differences between various subject groups. (4) The test can provide data which can be interpreted projectively to generate hypotheses about parental personality and behavior. These hypotheses can then be explored more fully using other techniques. (5) The test can be used to screen for psychologically "high-risk" mothers and to consider preventive interventions.

IV.   CONSTRUCTION OF THE MATERNAL PERSONALITY INVENTORY (MPI)

A. *Introduction*

Our goal was an instrument to assess personality and capable of general utility by mothers. In designing the MPI, special attention was given to examining variables of maternal behavior tentatively associated with the development of atypical behavior during infancy. Many of the statements of the MPI had origins in interview data, psychological test responses, and in narratives of observed infant-mother interactional behavior. There were many revisions of the test items with additional efforts made to insure that the items were phrased to make them readily understandable to the broadest socio-economic spectrum. This is of particular importance since the MPI was to be used extensively at the Maternal, Infant, and Preschool Child Health Center (MIPC Health Center) which served Appalachian and Southern Whites, Afro-Americans, American Indians, Spanish Americans, and Oriental-Americans. The test items needed to be simple and clear, and made up of familiar words. It was also necessary for the MPI to be self-administered.

B. *Test Items and Scales*

The MPI consists of 152 true-false statements many of which incorporate obvious or veiled references to aggressive, abusive, hostile, neglectful and rejecting maternal behavior. Some of the MPI test items are listed in Table I to illustrate these characteristics.

Scales were designed to evaluate some broad dimensions of personality, including femininity, and to assess maternal behavior, especially maternal aggression. The scales were established by grouping of the test items. There are eighteen scales in current use and their names, which are listed in Table II, are descriptive of the psychological importance. One group of scales (15-18) was designed to assess specific characteristics of aggression.

TABLE I. <u>SELECTED ITEMS FROM THE MATERNAL PERSONALITY INVENTORY</u>

ITEM NUMBER	STATEMENTS
2.	I think pregnant women should be seen in public as little as possible.
3.	It bothers me to use a knife or anything sharp.
11.	Relatives sometimes treat babies like they were of iron.
12.	My feelings are not easily hurt.
23.	I have spells when I feel like breaking things to pieces.
26.	Sometimes I'm afraid I will hurt my baby.
29.	I sometimes feel like spanking a crying baby.
38.	I got along very well with my mother.
44.	It isn't easy for me to talk when I meet people.
50.	I would have done better in life if other people had not been against me.
55.	My mother was affectionate toward me.
71.	When my periods first started I was afraid I would bleed to death.
80.	It takes a lot to make me mad.
101.	The best thing for a child that says dirty words is to wash his mouth with soap.
122.	When someone helps me out, I often wonder what their real reasons is for doing it.
128.	Sometimes I get a strong urge to do something mean.
137.	I suffer from backaches.
143.	If a child bit me, I would teach it that biting hurts by biting it back.

C. *Characteristics of the Sample of Ss Used to Standardize the MPI*

The MPI was administered to 1171 pregnant women receiving prenatal maternal services at the MIPC Health Center. They also completed a family information questionnaire and 1021 of the 1171 maternal Ss completed the Eysenck Personality Inventory. Some of the characteristics of this sample of women are included in Table III.

D. *Analytical Treatment of the Raw Data*

Raw scores were computed and distributions for the eighteen scales were obtained. The scales were found to have fairly good distributions

TABLE II.. **SCALES OF THE MATERNAL PERSONALITY INVENTORY**
Statistics, tests of reliability and correlational studies.

SCALES OF THE MATERNAL PERSONALITY INVENTORY	NO. OF TEST ITEMS IN EACH SCALE	MEAN ($\bar{X}$) SCORES AND STANDARD DEVIATIONS (S.D.) FOR EACH OF THE MPI SCALES		TESTS OF RELIABILITY		CORRELATIONS BETWEEN SCALES OF THE MATERNAL PERSONALITY INVENTORY AND: THE EYSENCK PERSONALITY INVENTORY		THE INFANT BEHAVIOR INVENTORY
		$\bar{X}$	S.D.	SPLIT-HALF (N=1519)	TEST-RETEST (N=67)	1. E SCALE	2. N SCALE	TOTAL SCORES
(1. Lie)	9	4.7	±2.0	0.461	0.476	0.036	-0.056	
2. Somatic Complaints	11	5.7	2.4	0.520	0.596	-0.011	0.322 *	0.265 +
3. Menstruation	6	2.4	1.4	0.488	0.811	-0.051	0.268 *	0.181 +
4. Adjustment-Conformity	7	3.5	1.8	0.566	0.625	0.027	-0.085 *	-
5. Inferiority-Inadequacy	35	15.2	5.2	0.724	0.776	-0.158 *	0.381 *	0.213 +
6. Shame and Guilt	13	5.3	2.4	0.595	0.748	-0.142 *	0.244 *	0.202 +
7. Phobic Anxiety	17	7.2	2.8	0.592	0.765	-0.098 *	0.329 *	-
8. Depression	8	3.4	1.7	0.532	0.684	0.035	0.323 *	-
9. Suspicious-Secretive	7	3.0	1.6	0.557	0.717	-0.085 *	0.293 *	0.206 +
10. Marital Adjustment	15	4.5	2.8	0.730	0.721	-0.065 *	0.248 *	0.208 +
11. Relations with Mother	11	3.7	2.4	0.717	0.827	-0.026	0.182 *	0.192 +
12. Conflicts re: Femininity	16	6.3	2.5	0.540	0.701	-0.036	0.308 *	0.228 +
13. Rejection of Pregnancy	12	5.9	2.1	0.516	0.660	0.036	0.232 *	-
14. Infants and Children	25	0.67	0.72	0.667	0.726	0.015	0.108 *	-
15. General Hostility	25	8.6	3.8	0.659	0.504	-0.015	0.402 *	0.277 +
16. Overt Hostility	27	9.8	3.7	0.634	0.521	-0.056	0.271 *	0.197 +
17. Resentment-Hatred	19	6.6	3.1	0.699	0.658	0.037	0.367 *	0.331 +
18. Phobic re: Sadism	13	5.6	2.6	0.598	0.586	0.033	0.289 *	0.257 +

all correlations with either (*) or (+) markings are statistically significant at the 0.05 level or better.

TABLE III. SOME CHARACTERISTICS OF THE SAMPLE OF WOMEN Ss USED TO STANDARDIZE THE MATERNAL PERSONALITY INVENTORY

N OF WOMEN Ss	AGE OF Ss	FAMILY INCOME (Yearly)	ETHNIC BACKGROUND		FORMAL SCHOOLING		MARITAL STATUS	
			ETHNIC GROUP	PERCENT OF SAMPLE	LEVEL REACHED	PERCENT OF SAMPLE	CATEGORY	PERCENT OF SAMPLE
1171	$\bar{X}$ = 22.0 years SD = ±5.9 years	$\bar{X}$ = $3,000.00	APPALACHIAN AND SOUTHERN WHITES	62.5	NONE	0.4	MARRIED NOT SEPARATED	60.8
			AFRO-AMERICANS	27.2	1 - 4 years	1.7	MARRIED, SEPARATED	12.5
			AMERICAN INDIANS	6.9	5 - 8 years	7.2	SINGLE	23.1
			ORIENTAL-AMERICANS	0.5	ELEMENTARY SCHOOL GRADUATION	14.6	DIVORCED	2.9
			UNKNOWN	2.9	9 - 12 years	49.8	WIDOWED	0.7
					HIGH SCHOOL GRADUATION	19.5		
					COLLEGE	6.4		
					COLLEGE GRADUATION	0.7		

FIGURE 1.   MATERNAL PERSONALITY INVENTORY

DISTRIBUTION OF SCORES

SCALE 14:   PERTAINING TO INFANTS AND CHILDREN

RAW SCORE	NUMBER OF Ss	CUMULATIVE FREQUENCY	T-SCORE	FREQUENCY DISTRIBUTION (*) = 5 = SCALE
0	35	0.035	33	********
1	7	0.042	34	**
2	7	0.049	34	**
3	9	0.057	35	**
4	20	0.077	36	*****
5	24	0.101	38	******
6	49	0.149	40	***********
7	85	0.235	43	*********************
8	95	0.330	46	***********************
9	108	0.438	48	*************************
10	114	0.553	51	***************************
11	116	0.669	54	****************************
12	98	0.767	57	***********************
13	71	0.838	60	******************
14	68	0.906	63	*****************
15	35	0.941	66	********
16	20	0.961	68	*****
17	10	0.971	69	**
18	14	0.985	72	***
19	6	0.991	74	*
20	4	0.995	76	*
21	3	0.998	79	*
22	0	0.998	79	
23	1	0.999	81	
24	0	0.999	81	
25	1	1.000	**	

FIGURE 2. MATERNAL PERSONALITY INVENTORY

DISTRIBUTION OF SCORES

SCALE 15: GENERAL HOSTILITY

RAW SCORE	NUMBER OF Ss	CUMULATIVE FREQUENCY	T-SCORE	FREQUENCY DISTRIBUTION (*) = 5 = SCALE
0	38	0.038	33	********
1	8	0.045	34	**
2	14	0.059	35	***
3	25	0.084	37	*******
4	61	0.144	40	*************
5	65	0.209	42	*************
6	78	0.287	44	****************
7	86	0.373	47	*****************
8	108	0.482	50	**********************
9	116	0.598	52	***********************
10	103	0.701	55	*********************
11	86	0.787	58	*****************
12	50	0.838	60	**********
13	61	0.898	63	*************
14	36	0.934	65	********
15	37	0.971	69	********
16	17	0.988	73	****
17	9	0.997	78	**
18	2	0.998	79	
19	2	1.000	**	

FIGURE 3.   MATERNAL PERSONALITY INVENTORY

DISTRIBUTION OF SCORES

SCALE 17:   RESENTMENT – HATRED

RAW SCORE	NUMBER OF Ss	CUMULATIVE FREQUENCY	T-SCORE	FREQUENCY DISTRIBUTION (*) = 5 = SCALE
0	39	0.039	33	*********
1	15	0.054	35	***
2	39	0.093	37	*********
3	73	0.166	40	*******************
4	94	0.260	44	*************************
5	114	0.373	47	******************************
6	110	0.483	50	*****************************
7	114	0.598	52	******************************
8	137	0.734	56	**************************************
9	91	0.826	59	*************************
10	67	0.893	62	******************
11	50	0.943	66	**************
12	24	0.967	68	******
13	25	0.991	74	******
14	5	0.997	78	*
15	2	0.998	79	
16	1	0.999	81	
17	1	1.000	**	

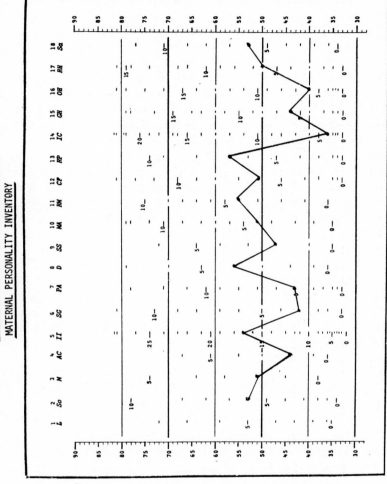

FIGURE 4. A SAMPLE PROFILE (PSYCHOGRAM) OF THE
MATERNAL PERSONALITY INVENTORY

as illustrated in the distributions of three scales (Figures 1, 2, 3). Table II lists the scales by name, the number of items contributing to any single scale, and the mean (X) scores and standard deviations for each of the MPI scales. The raw scores were converted to T-scores which were recorded on the MPI scales. The MPI scales were used to prepare an MPI Profile Sheet. By plotting the T-scores of individual Ss on the appropriate MPI scales, a psychogram is produced (Figure 4).

Mothers of different ethnic backgrounds were compared according to scores on the MPI scales and it was found that no statistically significant differences existed between White and Black prenatal Ss. The MPI scales also failed to discriminate between women pregnant for the first time and those who had delivered previously. There were rather high intercorrelations among the MPI scales as might be expected from overlap and the large sample size.

Tests of reliability were carried out and included both a split-half and a test-retest test for each of the eighteen MPI scales (Table II). Reliabilities were adequate but the test-retest results suggested that there was some attenuation of reliabilities which in part may be due to a more advanced stage of pregnancy since the test-retest measurements were obtained about two months apart.

It was also assumed that elevated MPI profiles aside from locating the at-risk mother should be associated with some degree of psychopathology as measured by independent and standard instruments. To test this idea, the Eysenck Personality Inventory was also administered to 1021 Ss of the 1171 who completed the MPI. These tests were completed at the same time and it was found that the MPI scales in general correlated well with the *E* (extroversion-introversion) scale and the *N* (neuroticism) scale (Table II).

V.   ELEVATED MATERNAL PERSONALITY INVENTORY PROFILES
AND ATYPICAL INFANT BEHAVIOR

The detection and measurement of atypical behavior among infants have been very much facilitated by the development of the Infant Behavior Inventory (IBI). This is a two-part questionnaire to detect and record specific forms of atypical behavior, to trace their chronology, and to determine patterns or combinations of behavior. Part I contains thirty-nine items for use with infants up to six months of age. Part II contains an additional twenty-eight items and with Part I is administered to infants between the ages of ten and twenty-four months. The thirty-nine items of Part I are ordered into six scales such as feeding problems, disturbances in habit formation and mood; the twenty-eight items of Part II together with the thirty-nine items in Part II are ordered into 11 scales. High scores on the IBI would be descriptive of atypical infant development.

A comparison of MPI and IBI scores was accomplished in a study of 350 mothers who already had children at the time of testing. These mothers completed the MPI and the IBI and scores were obtained for eighteen MPI scales and eleven IBI scales. Intercorrelations among these scales were relatively high and by way of illustration the MPI scales correlations with the IBI total score are presented in Table II. Although all of these correlations are statistically significant at the 0.05 level or better, the highest of the significant correlations are in the "hostility-hatred-sadism" scales. The highest correlation with MPI scales is with "resentment-hatred," the second highest is with "general hostility," and the fourth highest correlation is with "phobic re: sadism." It is most interesting that the MPI scale "overt hostility" ranks tenth among twelve correlations while "somatic complaints" ranks third highest and suggesting that the covert and less obvious forms of hostility, fears of inner aggressive urges and hatreds may be more important during early development for the onset of atypical development than direct and un-disguised forms or acts of hostility.

A selection of 38 maternal Ss with the highest IBI scores and another 38 maternal Ss with average IBI scores was made from among the 350 maternal Ss. The MPI scores of these Ss were then plotted and the profiles of the two groups compared (Table IV). It is apparent that the mothers of infants with high IBI scores also have a much higher frequency of MPI T-scores which exceed 70. Of the 38 high IBI Ss, 14 had one or more T-scores in excess of 70, while 4 of the average scores IBI Ss had T-scores over 70. Moreover, of the high IBI Ss with T-scores over 70, there is a clustering of the high MPI scales in an area of the "hostility" scales. Only one of the IBI Ss in the average score group had a single MPI scale exceed a T-score of 70 in the "hostility" group of scales (Figure 5).

VI.   CONCLUSIONS

The findings reported here are preliminary and additional statistical work on the data collected from the 1171 Ss and from the prenatal cases tested in subsequent sampling will probably result in the revision of scales and in the number of items employed for the MPI. These early observations suggest that the MPI may be of value in estimating the risk of atypical infant development for individual mothers. There appears to be a special importance in the association of "hostility-hatred-sadism" attributes of maternal personality with the existence of atypical infant behavior. It must be emphasized that this is an initial impression and does not constitute the result from an analysis of the other dimensions of maternal personality reflected in the MPI scales. That work is in progress and the findings are yet unknown.

TABLE IV. A COMPARISON BETWEEN HIGH SCORES ON THE MATERNAL PERSONALITY INVENTORY AND AVERAGE AND HIGH SCORES ON THE INFANT BEHAVIOR INVENTORY

| THE NUMBER OF MATERNAL PERSONALITY INVENTORY SCALES WITH T-SCORES $\geq$ 70 | INFANT BEHAVIOR INVENTORY (IBI) GENERAL SCORES | | | |
| | INFANT Ss (N=38) WITH AVERAGE IBI GENERAL SCORES | | INFANT Ss (N=38) WITH HIGH IBI GENERAL SCORES | |
	N of Ss	SCALES WITH T-SCORES $\geq$ 70	N of Ss	SCALES WITH T-SCORES $\geq$ 70
ONE	2	10,16	6	5,11,12,15,16,18
TWO	1	12,13	4	3,11,12,13,13,15,16,17
THREE	1	3,5,6,10,12,13	4	5,5,6,7,10,10,10,11,11,12,13,13,14,15,15,15,16,16,17,17,17,18,18
TOTALS	4	10	14	37

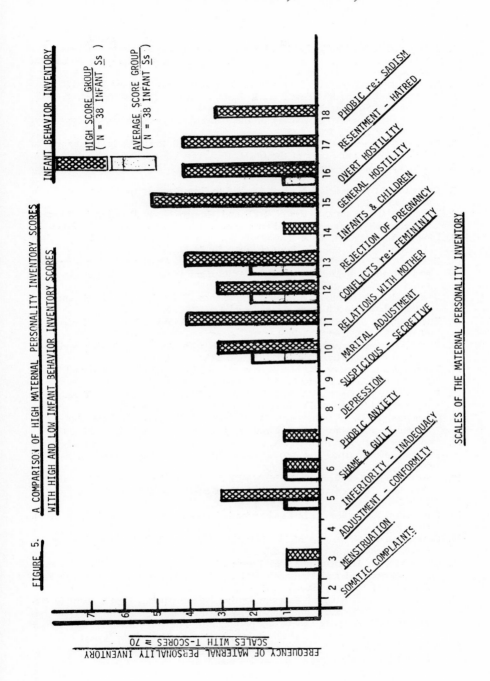

FIGURE 5. A COMPARISON OF HIGH MATERNAL PERSONALITY INVENTORY SCORES WITH HIGH AND LOW INFANT BEHAVIOR INVENTORY SCORES.

REFERENCES

1. ADRIAN, R. J. The Relationship of Parental Personality Structures to Child Adjustment and Adoption Selection. Ph.D. dissertation, University of Minnesota, 1957. (*Dissert. Abstr.*, 1957, 17, 1386)
2. BECK, S. J. The Rorschach Experiment. Grune and Stratton, New York, 1960.
3. BECK, S. J. Rorschach's Test, Vol. I, Basic Processes. (Second edition, revised), Grune and Stratton, New York, 1949.
4. BENEDEK, T. Toward the Biology of the Depressive Constellation. *J. Amer. Psychoanalytic Assoc.*, 1956, 4, 389.
5. BIBRING G. Some Considerations of the Psychological Processes in Pregnancy. In the Psychoanalytic Study of the Child, 1959, 114, 113-121.
6. BOLIN, B. J. Anxiety and the Duration of Delivery. *J. Mental Science,* 1959, 105, 1045.
7. CRONBACH, L. J. Statistical Method Applied to Rorschach Scores: A Review. *Psych. Bull.,* 1949, 46, 393-429.
8. DAVIDS, A. & DeVAULT, S. Use of TAT and Human Figure Drawing in Research of Personality, Pregnancy and Perception. *J. Proj. Tech.,* 1960, 24, 362-366.
9. DAVIDS, A., DeVAULT, S. & TALMADGE, M. Anxiety, Pregnancy and Childbirth Abnormalities. *J. Consult. Psychol.,* 1961, 25, 74-77.
10. DAVIDS, A., HOLDEN, R. H. & GRAY, G. B. Maternal Anxiety During Pregnancy and Adequacy of Mother and Child Adjustment Eight Months Following Birth. *Child Developm.,* 1963, 24, 993.
11. DYK, R. B. & WITKIN, H. A. Family Experiences Related to the Development of Differentiation in Children. *Child Developm.,* 1955, 36, 21-55.
12. EISENBERG, M. D., et al. A Prognostic Study of Neurotic Pregnant Patients. *J. Mental Science,* 1960, 106, 1099.
13. ELIZUR, A. Content Analysis of the Rorschach with Regard to Anxiety and Hostility. *Rorschach Res. Esch.,* 1949, 13, 247-284.
14. FARINA, A., & BUNHAM, R. M. Measurement of Family Relationships and Their Effects. *Arch. Gen. Psychiat.,* 1963, 9, 64-73.
15. FERREIRA, A. J., WINTER, W. D., & POINDEXTER, E. Some Interactional Variables in Normal and Abnormal Families. *Family Process,* 1966, 5, 60-75.
16. GOODSTEIN, L. D. & DAHLSTROM, W. G. MMPI Differences between Parents of Stuttering and Nonstuttering Children. *J. Consult. Psychol.,* 1956, 20, 365-370.
17. GOODSTEIN, L. D. & ROWLEY, V. N. A Further Study of MMPI Differences between Parents of Disturbed and Nondisturbed Children. *J. Consult. Psychol.,* 1961, 26, 460.
18. GOODSTEIN, L. D. & ROWLEY, V. N. MMPI Profiles on the Parents of Behaviorally Disturbed Children and Parents from the General Population. *J. Clin. Psychol.,* 1966, 30, 39.
19. GREENBERG, N. H. Studies in Psychosomatic Differentiation During Infancy. *Arch. Gen. Psychiat.,* 1962, 7, 17.
20. GREENBERG, N. H. Origins of Head-Rolling (Spasmus Nutans) During Early Infancy. *Psychosom. Med.,* 1964, 26, 162.
21. GREENBERG, N. H. Developmental Effects of Stimulation During Early Infancy: Some Conceptual and Methodological Considerations. *Annals of the New York Academy of Sciences,* 1965, 118, 831-859.
22. GREENBERG, N. H. Atypical Behavior During Infancy: Infant Development in Relation to the Behavior and Personality of the Mother. In The Child in His Family. E. J. Anthony and C. Koupernik, Eds. *The International Yearbook for Child Psychiatry and Allied Disciplines,* Volume 1, New York, Wiley, 1970.
23. GREENBERG, N. H. A Comparison of Infant Mother Interactional Behavior in Infants with Atypical Behavior and Normal Infants. In Exceptional Infant, *this volume,* Studies in Abnormalities. J. Hellmuth, Ed., New York, Brunner/Mazel, 1971.
24. GREENBERG, N. H., LOESCH, J. G., & LAKIN, M. Life Situations Associated with the

Onset of Pregnancy: 1. The Role of Separation in a Group of Unmarried Pregnancy Women. *Psychosom. Med.*, 1959, 21, 296-310.

25. HANVIK, L. J. & BYRUM, M. MMPI Profiles of Parents of Child Psychiatric Patients. *J. Clin. Psychol.*, 1959, 15, 427-43.

26. HASMER, J. S. Traits Predictive of the Successful Outcome of Unmarried Mothers' Plans to Keep Their Children. Smith College Studies in Social Work, 1942, 12, 263-301.

27. LIVERANT, S. MMPI Differences between Parents of Disturbed and Nondisturbed Children. *J. Consult. Psychol.*, 1959, 23, 256-260.

28. LOESCH, J. G. & GREENBERG, N. H. Some Specific Areas of Conflicts Observed During Pregnancy: A Comparative Study of Married and Unmarried Pregnant Women. *Amer. J. Orthopsy.*, 1962, 32, 624-636.

29. LOESCH, J. G. & GREENBERG, N. H. Patterns of Maternal Behavior During Early Infancy. Presented at the Annual Meetings, American Psychiatric Association, Los Angeles, Calif., 1964.

30. LOVELAND, N. T. The Relation Rorschach: A Technique for Studying Interaction. *J. Nerv. Ment. Dis.*, 1967, 145, 93-105.

31. LUBIN, B., LEVITT, E. E., & ZUCKERMAN, M. Some Personality Differences between Responders and Non-responders to a Survey Questionnaire. *J. Consult. Psychol.*, 1962, 26, 192.

32. MURSTEIN, B. I. The Projection of Hostility on the Rorschach, and as a Result of Ego-Threat. *J. Proj. Tech.*, 1956, 20, 418-428.

33. MURSTEIN, B. I. Theory and Research in Projective Techniques. John Wiley & Sons, Inc., New York & London.

34. ROME, R. A Method of Predicting the Probable Disposition of Their Children by Unmarried Mothers. Smith College Studies in Social Work, 1940, 10, 167-201.

35. SPITZ, R. Hospitalism: An Inquiry into the Genesis of Psychiatric Conditions in Early Childhood. *Psychoanal. Study of the Child.* 1945, 1, 33-72.

36. WALLIN, R. & RILEY, R. P. Reactions of Mothers to Pregnancy and Adjustment of Offspring in Infancy. *Amer. J. Orthopsy.*, 1950, 20, 616.

37. WILLIAMS, H. L. Comparison of the Rorschach and MMPI by Means of Factor Analysis. *J. Consult. Psychol.*, 1954, 193-197.

38. ZEMLICK, M. & WATSON, R. Maternal Attitudes of Acceptance and Rejection During and After Pregnancy. *Amer. J. Orthopsy.*, 1953, 23, 570-584.

Part II
Learning
and
Language

8

PRENATAL AND PERINATAL FACTORS WHICH INFLUENCE LEARNING

Murray M. Kappelman, M.D.

Associate Pediatrician-in-Chief, Sinai Hospital, Baltimore
Associate Professor, Pediatrics
University of Maryland Medical School and
Assistant Professor, Pediatrics, Johns Hopkins School of Medicine

There is an increasing awareness among pediatricians and educators of the vast number of children whose educational progress is seriously hampered and interfered with by a specific learning disability. The recently established *Journal of Learning Disabilities* called these children "The obsolescent child." The *Journal* stated that "Learning disabilities are found in every socio-economic strata of life. The statistics, even though uncertified, are too massive to be ignored" (1).

The term, specific learning disability, encompasses a spectrum of conditions which prevent the adequate accumulation, retention, and utilization of knowledge by the educationally involved youngster. This group of etiologic conditions leading to a learning disorder ranges over a wide area of diverse problems, each of which must be meticulously delineated before an appropriate approach to the child's problem can be undertaken. Often overlapping of suspected etiologic causes for an individual child's learning difficulty will occur; and each aspect of the overall situation must be handled in the most beneficial manner.

It is important to recognize that underlying the overt school performance difficulty, no matter how it manifests itself externally, may be either an organic or functional basis. Although both are often discernible in the same child, it is usually possible to decide which area contributed first to the problem and which diagnosis is currently most disabling after thorough work-up.

There can be little doubt that certain functional categories can be directly incriminated as the primary causation of learning disorders in

155

specific children. Significant emotional disturbance without organic central nervous system disease can seriously impede learning and cause youngsters to function well below their measurable potential. Testing of these children often uncovers pathologic dependency needs, anger toward parents, and low self-esteem. Cultural deprivation is another functional area which can be viewed as undermining the child's ability to learn. These children are felt to be adversely affected by severe degrees of deprivation of environmental stimulation. "Pseudo-retardation" based on low I.Q. results stemming from a limited fund of information about the world in general and particularly poor verbal skills is characteristic of this phenomenon. Emotional immaturity usually based upon a manipulative resistance to maturation as a response to home environment will prevent a young person from attempting to maintain his chronologic-education balance. Occasionally, the investigator is forced to use the term "educational immaturity" to describe the delayed development of learning skills which may subsequently be expected to mature by an age significantly later than is usually anticipated. The familial dyslexia which tends to affect the generations of males in specific families and is self-limited in time is an important example of this particular category (2).

As long ago as 1917, Henschelwood noted that a brain disorder might precipitate abnormalities in reading ability, arithmetic, orientation of right versus left and in other aspects of learning (3). In 1927, J. Gerstmann reiterated this supposition in the world psychiatric literature (4). Paine suggests that a prevalent concept among workers in this specialized field today is that this organic disorder of learning affects 5% or more of the entire random child population, which would therefore make it the commonest neurological diagnosis among children, exceeding the problem of seizures and uncomplicated mental retardation (5).

A recent study done by this author and others in the inner city of Baltimore among disadvantaged children showed that over half of the children referred to a comprehensive School Health Team for diagnosis and evaluation of their learning disorders had organic pathology diagnosed as the primary, basic cause of the educational difficulty (6). Coleman and Sandhu demonstrated that among their socially heterogeneous group of children with learning problems: 24% had experienced birth difficulties and 8% had had prenatal difficulties (7). This helps place in the proper perspective the decidedly important role that the unstable neurologic state of the child plays in the overall problem of specific learning disabilities. It will be the elucidation of the factors which contribute significantly to the development of these neurologic dysfunctions on which this article will concentrate.

DESCRIPTION OF ORGANIC MANIFESTATIONS

It is presumptuous to suggest that one can sharply delineate the various manifestations that minimal organic brain injury can produce. Such categorization fails to take into consideration the frequent overlapping of symptomatology in the same child and the dynamic changes that time and stress can produce in any specific brain-injured child. However, it is essential to have guidelines upon which one can depend if one is to attempt to designate the child as having a symptom-complex that fits into the organic category. Therefore it would be pertinent to mention the types of problems considered by the diagnostic team involved in this clinic as being the broad areas of expression of organic learning disorders.

The child so often brought to the attention of the parent early in the educational continuum is the hyperkinetic brain-injured child. The parent is often aware that their child is distractible, has a shortened attention span, has problems in memory retention, and is often overtly disruptive because of an inability to exercise impulse control. This youngster may respond quite favorably to specific medications, amphetamine and ritalin being particularly helpful among others.

A small percentage of children with organic central nervous system dysfunction will present as withdrawn, depressed, pathologically shy, and uncommunicative pupils. They may easily be confused with the emotionally autistic child or the intellectually obtunded child. Their neurologic problems must be delineated if they are to be helped appropriately.

The child with organically based perceptual handicaps may not present until the school years have progressed to the level of conceptual reasoning, phonetic reading, and need for complex recall. There are several specific manifestations of impaired perception which can be separated from the confusing encompassing term "perceptual handicap." First one sees the deficient reader who has difficulty because of a visual-motor impairment. This is generally known as organic dyslexia. Another manifestation of visual-motor imbalance is the inability to correctly assess and then convert visual impression into meaningful information (8). The inability to understand and correctly answer complex written problems in arithmetic would be a cogent example of this type of problem. Another perceptual handicap is expressed in an overall inability to conceptualize and utilize already learned information. These youngsters can return to their teachers only that specific information taught them. They have great difficulty in displacing the original facts into a new and challenging situation or problem. Another problem which has an organic basis and can be considered in the area of perceptual disorders is the central communication syndrome. These youngsters have an organic interruption in their ability to express verbally or in a written sense what they know intellectually to be the accurate response. Unusual responses by the child eliciting class scorn, stuttering, and written work of irrelevant or abortive quality are trademarks of this type of child. These can become deeply frustrated children who literally discontinue any attempts at educational response due to their repeated failures and rebuffs despite being conscious of the appropriate answer.

One must include in any list of children with organic causes for their inability to learn that group of children who have diminished intellectual potential. One may not consider a youngster with an intelligence quotient of 80 measured by our current standards of testing as being mentally retarded but the child's performance in a normally progressive learning situation may demonstrate severe limitations and must be recognized so that appropriate special education can be provided. Some of these children demonstrate observable neurologic abnormalities either on physical examination or in overt performance (i.e. severe hyperkinesis and impulsivity) while others may not. A view of factors which lead to the manifestation of organic learning problems must also consider some which give rise to measurable lowered potential that is not remedial by medication or specialized instruction, i.e.: the moderate to severely retarded child.

PRENATAL FACTORS WHICH AFFECT LEARNING

I. *Maternal Infection*

It is a well established fact that certain of the viral infections as well as one of the protozoan infections cross the placenta and adversely affect the infant in utero from a neurological standpoint. The pediatric literature is replete with discussions and case demonstrations of the effects of the cytomegalic virus infection upon the developing fetus in the prenatal state. The occurrence of microcephaly, microopthalmia and mental retardation are noted in these children. Radiologic investigation of the skull in these young people demonstrates intracranial calcifications which bear witness to the cerebral effects of this maternal infection on the intrauterine infant (9). Similar problems arise in the child whose mother has had toxoplasmosis during her pregnancy. Pathologically, focal disseminated areas of necrosis and miliary granulomatous inflammation are found in the periventricular and aqueductal tissue of the brain. These lesions may calcify and result in radiologic evidence of intracranial calcifications similar to those in cytomegalic inclusion disease. Thus in congenital toxoplasmosis, microcephalus, progressive hydrocephalus, psychomotor disorders, and/or mental retardation are noted as the significant sequelae (10). Recently, South et al. pointed out that intrauterine infection with the herpes simplex virus mimics the cytomegalic virus in its effect upon the fetus in many ways. The intracranial calcifications, microcephaly, microopthalmia, and mental retardation may appear indistinguishable between the three aforementioned conditions although the infant suffering from intrauterine herpetic disease will often display areas of cutaneous vesiculation rather characteristic of herpes in general (11). Desmond and her associates reported that among 60 children with the congenital rubella syndrome at birth who were followed to eighteen months of age, 11 (18%) were classified as mentally retarded and 31 others had mild to severe cerebral palsy. This was noted during the 1964 epidemic. The spectrum of central nervous system involvement after congenital rubella at eighteen months included motor deficits, seizures, hyperactivity, restlessness, stereotyped movements, motor delay and lack of progress in adaptive behavior (12). One need only to visualize such a child as he approaches the age of classroom learning to envision the problems he will bring into the classroom and those classroom problems he will create because of his neurological impairment secondary to the intrauterine infection with the rubella, herpes simplex, or cytomegalic virus or the toxoplasma gondii protozoan.

II. *Radiation*

It is now well known that ionizing radiation in sufficient dosage and time span can induce microcephaly with mental retardation in man. In Hiroshima, there were 15 children with microcephaly whose mother's last menstrual period was 7 to 15 weeks before the bomb (13). Ionizing radiation to that degree is not a common problem, for which we can be thankful, but the Hiroshima experience alerts us to the dangers of extensive radiation therapy or inadvertent radiation exposure during the early months of pregnancy and the effects upon the fetus. Wood et al. in a review of the twenty-year follow up of mental retardation after the Hiroshima atomic bomb and Yamazaki in his review of the effects of radiation on the central nervous system point up also the dangers of microcephaly and mental retardation that the intrauterine infant faces when exposed to significant doses of radiation (14, 15).

Yamazaki suggested that the behavioral effects are dependent upon the gestational age at the time of irradiation, the dose, and the age at the time of testing. Morphologic lesions in animals can be correlated with some of the behavioral effects; but, for others, no morbid anatomy can be detected. Maze learning with rats suggested decreasing abilities to master the maze with increasing age after intrauterine irradiation. The meager data with humans suggests that the developing human neural tissue behaves toward ionizing radiation as does the developing neural tissue of animals. Although extrapolation is not fully warranted, the potential hazards to the human fetus central nervous system from even small exposures to irradiation must be borne in mind when evaluating the prenatal history of a youngster presenting with intellectual problems in learning and also when contemplating the exposure of the pregnant female to radiation.

III. *Maternal Nutrition*

Today the world is becoming acutely aware of the states of malnutrition and undernutrition that exist unnoticed and unheeded in the overall population. Kwashiorkor, rickets, scurvy and other visible states of nutritional deficiency announce themselves overtly, alerting the clinician, nutritionist, and politician to note and remedy the situation whether individually or collectively. But there exist subclinical states of poor nutrition throughout the world that go unrecognized and may be perpetuating silent destruction upon the learning skills of the world's population. The significance of that statement is reflected in the work of Harrel et al. who found that the state of nutrition during pregnancy influenced the subsequent intellectual performance of the child. When vitamin supplementation was given to a low socioeconomic group of pregnant and lactating women with previously poor nutritional environment, the offspring at 4 years of age had an average intelligence quotient score 8 points greater than the average score of the children of mothers given a placebo over the same period (16). Experiments on various animals have indicated that nutrition inadequate in calories and protein, coinciding with the period of life in which the brain is growing most rapidly, produces a brain which is not only smaller at maturity than in control animals but also one which matures biochemically and functionally at a slower rate (17). There is a strong suggestion that inadequate protein nutrition or synthesis or both during brain development could result in changes in function and that, if the degree of deprivation were sufficiently severe and prolonged, the changes in function may be permanent (18). Another important feature of maternal undernutrition which has a direct bearing on the subsequent learning skills of the offspring is the rate of prematurity among poorly nourished pregnant females. Drillien suggested that the mother's nutritional history influenced her subsequent pregnancy, with increased prematurity among the poorly nourished, and thus increased central nervous system problems and diminished I.Q. among this group's off-spring (19). The latter possibility will be discussed next.

IV. *Premature Birth*

In 1956, Knobloch and her group studied a group of Baltimore children who were prematurely born to assess the intellectual dangers that such premature birth created. The study revealed findings of multiple visual, neurologic and intellectual deficits among these children who were prematurely born. They further noted the highest incidence of abnormalities to be among those children with the lowest birth weight (20). Margaret Dann and her group studied the intelligence quotient results of 100 low birth weight prematures (660-1280 grams) compared to the I.Q. of 49 full term siblings. There was only a mild difference in intelligence by testing (94.8 among the premies compared to 106.9 among the full term sibs). Two factors are to be remembered in evaluating Dann's work; first, she was dealing with a special population, that of a primarily higher socioeconomic level than Knobloch was in her study; and more importantly, of the 83 children excluded from the ultimate examination, 32 were known to be mentally retarded. These facts and their interpretations tend to corroborate the assumption that very low birth weight increases the chance of neurologic and intellectual handicaps (21). The latest of two fine review articles by C. M. Drillien performed in Scotland and published in this country revealed data relating to 50 children whose weight at birth was 3 lb. (1360 gm.) or less and who were five years or older at the time of the study. On individual testing, 41% had I.Q. scores of 90 or over, 40% had scores of 70 to 89 and 19% had scores of less than 70. Fifty-eight percent attended normal schools but half required special modalities of teaching. Thirty percent were not educable or required special schooling primarily because of mental handicap and 10% required special schooling because of physical handicap. She noted that children reared in the best homes less often showed handicap than children reared in average or poor homes. Drillien succinctly states that though the survival rate had improved between the publication of her two studies (32% to 56% in a ten year span), there had been no improvement in the lowered later intellectual status of low weight infants (22).

V. *Oversized newborn*

Babson, Henderson, and Clark recently published an interesting analysis of all infants born of low-income white mothers in Oregon over a specified time. They were placed in three groups. One was a high birth weight group (over 4250 grams—9 lbs. 6 oz.); another was a group of infants of normal weights; the third was a group of low birth weight infants (under 2501 grams). There were 74 infants in the high birth weight group and only 1 had a known diabetic mother. The mean gestational age of the group was 41.4 weeks. A careful study of this population revealed that high birth weight is associated with an increased incidence of subsequent mental subnormality indicated by an intelligence quotient below 80 on the Stanford-Binet Form L-M administered at four years of age. Twenty-three percent of the high birth weight babies had

I.Q.'s under 80 compared to 16.6% in those of usual expected birth weight. These figures proved statistically significant (23). One may conjecture on the etiologic basis for these findings and raise such problems as birth trauma due to size, prolonged intrauterine existence with end-stage placental incompetence and undiagnosed maternal gestational diabetes with neonatal hypoglycemia as possibilities. Whatever the underlying cause, attention must now be paid to both extremes of infant's birth weight as potential causes of subsequent incompetent learning skills.

VI.   *Maternal Complications During Pregnancy and Labor*

Drillien in her studies states that severe and potentially hypoxia producing complications of later pregnancy were associated with a higher proportion of handicapped children, this being particularly true of the low birth weight infant (22). Such maternal pregnancy complications as toxemia of pregnancy with or without eclamptic seizures, bleeding particularly early in the pregnancy, trauma to the mother during pregnancy and difficult delivery resulting in birth trauma or excessive hypoxia have long been known to result in high risk infants as far as intellect and physical structure were concerned. Pregnancy complications such as mentioned above were noted in 67% of the low birth weight prematures tested by Dann and her group (21). Thus pregnancy complications, prematurity and lowered intellect as a consequence of both are inter-related. Problems of labor resulting in infant anoxia or infant trauma also are known precursors to serious defects in intelligence and subsequent learning problems. Kawi and Pasamanick revealed that 16.6% of children with reading problems had been exposed to four or more maternal complications (24). The perinatal infant problems will be subsequently discussed. Pasamanick and Knobloch found that four specific neurobehavioral entities were significantly associated with complications of pregnancy including prematurity. These were cerebral palsy, epilepsy, mental deficiency and reading disabilities. They also noted that the children with I.Q.'s below 80 had higher rates of abnormalities during pregnancy than did a carefully selected control group (25).

PERINATAL FACTORS WHICH AFFECT LEARNING

VII.   *Birth Trauma and Hypoxia*

Honzik et al. found that twenty-three babies who were rated highly suspect on the basis of perinatal complications scored significantly lower than 39 who were rated only suspect, 68 possibly suspect and 67 rated as normal. They were tested by the Bayley Mental and Motor Scales at

8 months. The highly suspect babies based on perinatal stress were rated significantly more often as hypoactive or hyperactive, distractible, and poorly coordinated and they had special difficulty with items requiring problem-solving and eye-hand coordination (26). Schacter and Apgar demonstrated significant relationships between a multiple clinical criterion of perinatal complications (prolonged labor, difficult delivery, neonatal complications, maternal illness during pregnancy) and an eight-year-old WISC I.Q. as well as with special tests of brain damage (Bender-Gestalt). The percentage of children with intelligence quotients under 100 is higher for the children with severe perinatal complications (86%) compared to the children without perinatal complications (43%). Thus with increasing perinatal stress the psychological examinations showed an increase in the percentage of children with below normal mental and social development (27).

Graham evaluated 355 infants who were divided into three groups: normal full-term, anoxic full-term, and other complications (such as prematurity, erythroblastosis and trauma). The anoxic group was further subdivided into three divisions: prenatal anoxia, perinatal anoxia, or a combination of both. At three years of age, the anoxic major group scored significantly lower on all tests of cognitive functioning including the Stanford-Binet and concept tests. The impairment was greatest in the area of conceptual ability. The findings were most pronounced in the postnatal anoxia group, suggesting that perinatal anoxia carries an onus even greater than that of intrauterine hypoxia (28).

Pasamanick and Knobloch found no difference between the neurologic behavior disorders and the matched controls in the incidence of prolonged and difficult labor and of operative procedures at the time of delivery, such as the use of forceps, Caesarean section or breech extraction. Rather the associations occurred with the prolonged and probably anoxia-producing complications of pregnancy, such as the toxemias and bleeding (25). This study does not negate the previous findings of the severity of perinatal hypoxemia but also stresses that intrauterine anoxia is a prime causation for subsequent neurologic learning and behavioral disorders.

VIII. *Perinatal Malnutrition*

The problem of perinatal and neonatal malnutrition must be considered whether it be secondary to feeding difficulties, congenital intestinal structural or enzymatic abnormalities, or generalized or specific intestinal infection. It has been shown that the intellectual attainments of children who have recovered from a clinically severe episode of protein-calorie malnutrition are consistently lower than those of individuals with adequate nutrition during infancy (29). This has significance not only in the neonate but obvious importance throughout the learning period of the child's life. Thus nutrition and learning assume an inter-relationship both prenatally and neonatally that signals the involvement not only of the medical but also of the social and political professionals as well.

IX. *Infection of the Central Nervous System*

There is a very high mortality among those infants diagnosed as having purulent meningitis in the newborn period. One small study by Dyggve found 47% mortality (30). The complications among those that survive are both formidable and frequent. Dyggve found that hydrocephalus developed in 35% of his cases of purulent meningitis while Yu and Granang found 42% of the survivors in their study had developed hydrocephalus (31). Fifty percent of the survivors in Dyggve's study were left with significant residual findings; of the twelve survivors, three were retarded, one had impaired hearing and two had behavior problems. Follow-up by Yu and that group on their surviving children revealed moderate disability among 31% of the children with behavior problems, partial deafness, and backward development of a moderate to severe degree. Despite the development of antibiotics and skills that enable the rapid diagnosis and treatment of the neonatal central nervous system infection, the overall outlook for recovery without impairment of intellectual or social potential is not good. Thus such infection becomes a serious consideration in the etiology of subsequent learning disorders.

X. *Hyperbilirubinemia*

Kernicterus is a syndrome characterized by extrapyramidal involvement of the central nervous system and subsequent intellectual limitation which has been regarded as a sequel to the yellow staining and necrosis of the brain cells. The overall incidence in later life of the various manifestations of central nervous system involvement in infants recovering from the hyperbilirubinemia of acute hemolytic disease was first assessed in 1946 to be 6.5%. The figure was an accelerating one, higher values of central nervous system abnormalities occurring with the more prolonged exposure of the central nervous system to higher levels of unconjugated bilirubin (32). Evidence has accumulated that the early institution of treatment via exchange transfusion to reduce the brain cell staining by unconjugated bilirubin will reduce the percentage of children demonstrating central nervous system damage. However, Day and Haines found that the mean intelligence quotient of children who recovered from erythroblastosis fetalis since the introduction of exchange transfusions was still somewhat less than the mean scores of a control group consisting of older previously unaffected sibs of the patients in the test group (33).

The question has always arisen as to whether hyperbilirubinemia when it occurs unassociated with hemolytic disease will result in significant central nervous system involvement when treated without intervention. Bjure et al compared 113 full term infants with bilirubin values of 18 mgm% or more during the neonatal period with 51 full term, non-icteric infants at ages of 2-3 years. They found that the hyperbilirubinemia alone did not give rise to any cerebral lesions. The I. Q. distribution was the same. No central deafness was noted as is the case in the kernicterus syndrome (34). This work in 1961 was corroborated by the work of Holmes et al in 1968 which studied virtually the same problem and reached the same conclusions (35). Shiller and Silverman studied the problem with prematures and failed to demonstrate a significant correlation between uncomplicated hyperbilirubinemia in premature infants and neurologic deficits at three years of age (36). Complications such as anoxia, sulfa drugs, vitamin K overdosage, hypoglycemia, and sepsis alter the outlook in non-hemolytic disease hyperbilirubinemia and heighten the possibility of central nervous system involvement.

XI. *Hypoglycemia*

Cornblath et al. state that the available data indicate that the hypoglycemic infants as a group function ten points lower on the Stanford Binet intelligence test than do their controls when tested at three to five years of age (37). Eeg-Olofson et al. studied 24 children who had clinical manifestations and laboratory evidence of hypoglycemia (blood glucose value below 20 mgm/100 ml.) starting between 12-72 hours of age and lasting no longer than one week. They were reexamined at between eight months and six years. None of these infants were from mothers with diagnosed diabetes, actual or gestational. Ten out of 24 had developmental quotients below 85, with three of the children scoring below 50. The ultimate prognosis did not seem to be different among those with or without relapses of hypoglycemia. Neither has any difference been detected between children with different weights at birth (38). Haworth and McRae evaluated 22 infants (at 8-30 months of age) who presented with laboratory evidence of hypoglycemia in the newborn period for adverse neurologic and developmental sequelae. Of the eight neonates who had overt symptoms of hypoglycemia, six (75%) demonstrated actual or probable impairment in the later study. Only two (17%) of the fourteen neonates who were asymptomatic with their low blood sugar during the first days of their lives had possible but not definite impairment demonstrated on subsequent testing. Their work refined the problem even more, suggesting that hypoglycemia associated with neurological symptoms in the newborn period carries a poor prognosis with respect to permanent neurological damage while asymptomatic hypoglycemia may have a decidedly better long term developmental-behavioral prognosis (39). Thus the occurrence of symptomatic hypoglycemia during the neonatal period is an important historical point in the analysis of any youngster suffering from a learning disability.

DISCUSSION

One of the major problems facing the clinician when confronted with the problem of specific learning disabilities is the establishment of the diagnosis when presented with a retrospective history taken usually from a parent unsophisticated in many of the intricate medical subtleties that comprise the important prenatal and perinatal predisposing factors discussed here. Even those physicians fortunate enough to have the previous hospital or office chart of maternal pregnancy and delivery plus infant birth and perinatal history will discover how inadequate many of our peer group are in noting important prenatal and perinatal problems that are either undetected or considered too insignificant or unimportant to warrant recording. Thus the physician who sees the child with a learning disorder for the first time has little information in the area of past history to aid him in making the correct diagnosis. Retrospective studies are fraught with the inherent dangers of omissions, incorrect assumptions, and purposefully withheld information. A complete understanding (by the obstetrician or the pediatrician or their counterparts) of the factors that will later affect the infant is essential if the hospital records and office notes will ever be of real value in retrospectively analyzing the events around the child's birth to see if they are pertinent to his current learning problem.

The family physician or pediatrician has the advantage of attending the infant immediately after birth and, in some areas, watching over the mother during her pregnancy. Thus he has the advantage of the immediacy of the information, and this, combined with the knowledge of the important factors involved in the expression of this problem, enables him to predict and observe and later make a diagnosis more readily and with greater accuracy than anyone else. One need not be a super-specialist in neurological disorders to put the pieces of this particular puzzle together if awareness of the etiological possibilities is combined with an acutely sensitive ability to detect them as they occur during the intrauterine and immediate extrauterine period. Thus the preceding discussion is of paramount importance to the practicing physicians in our communities.

Parents are entitled to know the possible problems they may face with any high risk child if they specifically request such information. Prognosis of the outcome of any disease begins with the knowledge of other studies done prospectively to ascertain the usual percentage of satisfactory and unsatisfactory outcomes and what particular factors have the most influence on the ultimate outcome. Thus with a severe postnatal hypoxic episode lasting for a prolonged period of time, one can honestly predict that there is a significant chance that learning difficulties, especially perceptual problems of concept formation, may develop in the future. Prematurity with very low birth weight (under 2000 grams) carries a reasonable risk for subsequent learning disabilities. Maternal malnutrition has been found to have a profound effect upon future learning in the offspring, as has excessive exposure to radiation. All of these factors when present require the physician's attention to be focused upon the child's educational progress, behavioral manifestations, and social demeanor in the future. The parent can be forewarned of the risks if the physician feels that the cooperation of a mature parent will aid in early diagnosis and remediation.

Prevention assumes the position of being the prime target that must be focused upon if meaningful diminution of this vast problem is to be accomplished. Remediation is a long, arduous and often emotionally and financially taxing procedure. Prevention makes much better sense in the long range view. Rubella prevention is now being undertaken in many of the major urban areas on a large scale. The rubella vaccine is available and is recommended for the child population, hoping to diminish the immediate spread of the viral disease to pregnant adult women as well as hopefully immunizing the next generation of child-bearers. The careful obstetrical prenatal and delivery management of the woman with herpes genitalis might obviate the spread of this disease to the intrauterine and extrauterine infant, preventing the intrauterine passage of the virus to the developing fetus with its cytomegalic virus-like picture and the extrauterine contamination through the birth canal and postnatal herpes encephalitis and sepsis with the dire central nervous system possibilities.

Meticulous care as to the use of radiation and diagnostic radiologic procedures to the pregnant woman warrants the attention of the physician in order to prevent the intrauterine effects of radiation upon the fetus. Maternal nutrition is particularly important since this is not only a medical condition but a social disease as well as a political shame. The vicious cycle of poverty leading to malnutrition which then causes severe learning problems in the offspring which in turn results in the inability of the subsequent generations to improve their state of poverty because of lack of educational improvement is a danger that faces the world today. Improvement in food distribution; better means and mechanisms for measuring malnutrition; better population education as to proper diet; and active physician, social scientist, and politician cooperation and participation in assuring that these improvements materialize are our only hope to end this major cause of intellectual deprivation.

Learning to cope with and conquering malnutrition will aid in preventing some of the instances of prematurity which is another of the factors leading to a significant number of poor learners. The causes of the initiation of labor and thus the underlying causes for premature extrusion of the fetus must be delineated in the future so that fetal wastage as well as eventual intellectual handicaps among the survivors can be minimized.

Efforts on the part of obstetrician, anesthesiologist, and pediatrician must be made to reduce the incidence of prenatal and perinatal hypoxia to an absolute minimum. The careful monitoring of the intrauterine infant for fetal distress and immediate attention to cause and subsequent delivery by the most expeditious method; the immediate recognition of perinatal difficulties and the use of techniques and instruments to deliver oxygen to the lungs and subsequently to the brain during the first few minutes of life; and the subsequent utilization of vigorous methods to prevent neonatal hypoxia via special incubator with monitored blood gases and artificial ventilatory machines with similar monitoring of blood gases would appear to be essential pathways for the physicians attending the intra- and extra-uterine infant to follow in order to prevent subsequent neurological imbalances leading to impaired learning.

The early detection of meningitis in the neonate by recognizing the protean and often seemingly mild initial presentations and the subsequent use of the appropriate antibiotics in adequate dosage for the specified number of days will help eradicate the high incidence of sequelae after recovery. In addition, careful isolation procedures as well as good general nursery techniques will help prevent the introduction and spread of infection within the nursery itself.

The ability to prevent kernicterus with the use of exchange transfusions, particularly in the infants with hemolytic disease of the newborn, makes the intelligent monitoring of the bilirubins in this specific entity essential. The decision to perform exchange transfusions particularly in the cases with erythroblastosis fetalis should take into consideration not only the severe overt signs of kernicterus which can be prevented and which often give warning with early neurological signs but also the discrete central nervous system staining and damage which may not manifest itself until inadequacies in learning surface during the immediate preschool and school years. Thus vigorous handling of hyperbilirubinemia in the erythroblastotic infant is a means of potentially preventing specific learning disorders.

In certain specific cases, hypoglycemia in the newborn can be prevented. The early use of intravenous glucose solutions in the infants of diabetic mothers will help prevent the appearance of the low blood sugar seen so often after birth to twenty-four hours of age in these infants. It is also important to establish the careful monitoring of the serum glucose in the premature, the septic or anoxic full term, and the infant of normal length of gestation but low birth weight suggesting intrauterine malnutrition. The rapid treatment and prolonged observation of the known hypoglycemic infant are also mandatory as the extent and severity of damage depend upon the extent of time exposed to the low blood sugar. It is very important for all physicians handling the newborn to know the protean manner in which hypoglycemia may express itself. Convulsions and jitteriness are symptoms not often overlooked but the pale, sweaty, irritable, listless or vomiting baby may have many other procedures undertaken before an astute physician recognizes the possibility of hypoglycemia. The prevention of permanent central nervous system damage and subsequent learning problems is contingent on the prevention, recognition, and vigorous management of this hypoglycemic phenomenon in the newborn.

Thus an understanding of the entities occurring in the prenatal and perinatal periods that lead to specific learning disorders in the older child is essential in the areas of prevention, diagnosis and early prognosis and remediation of the neurologic reasons for educational failure. One can only hope that such understanding will take an equal place in the armamentarium of the physician next to his culture plates, immunizations, and antibiotics. The ultimate wastage of human intellect and progress will continue to be overwhelming and eventually debilitating to society unless we fully understand the causative factors leading to defects in learning and attempt prevention and modification of these factors.

BIBLIOGRAPHY

1. Editorial: *J. Learn. Disabs.* 1:124-127, 1968.
2. SNYDER, RUSSELL D., & MORTIMER, JOAN: Diagnosis and Treatment: Dyslexia. *Pediatrics,* Vol. 44, No. 4, 1969.
3. HENSCHELWOOD, J.: Congenital Word Blindness. London, H. K. Lewis and Co., 1917.
4. GERSTMANN, J.: Fingeragnosie und isolierte Agraphie ein Neves Syndrome. *Neurol. Psychiat.* 108:152-177, 1927.
5. PAINE, RICHMOND S.: Syndromes of Minimal Cerebral Damage. *Ped. Clinics N. Amer.* Vol. 15, No. 3, 1968.
6. KAPPELMAN, M. N., KAPLAN, E., GANTER, R. L.: A Study of Learning Disorders Among Disadvantaged Children. *J. Learn. Disab.* Vol. 2, No. 5, 1969.
7. COLEMAN, JAMES, C. & SANDHU, MALATHI: A Descriptive Relational Study of 364 Children Referred to a University Clinic for Learning Disorders. *Psychological Reports.* 20:1091-1105, 1967.
8. GOLDBERG, H. K. & DRASK, P. W.: The Disabled Reader. *J. Ped. Opth.,* pp. 11-24, February 1968.

9. MEDEARIS, DONALD N.: Observations Concerning Human Cytomegalic Infection and Disease. Bulletin of the Johns Hopkins Hospital. 114-115:181, 1964.
10. FELDMAN, HARRY A.: Toxoplasmosis (Concluded): *N. Eng. J. Med.* 279:1431, 1968.
11. SOUTH, M. A., TOMPKINS, W. A., MORRIS, C. R., RAWLS, W. E.: Congenital Malformation of the Central Nervous System Associated with Genital Type (Type 2) Herpes Virus. *J. Peds.* 75:13-18, 1969.
12. DESMOND, M. M.: Congenital Rubella Encephalitis, Course and Early Sequelae. *J. Peds.* 71:311-331, 1967.
13. MILLER, R. W.: Delayed Effects Occurring Within the First Decade After Exposure of Young Individuals to the Hiroshima Atomic Bomb. *Pediatrics.* 18:1, 1956.
14. WOOD, JAMES W., JOHNSON, KENNETH G., & OMORI, Y.: In Utero Exposure to the Hiroshima Atomic Bomb: An Evaluation of Head Size and Mental Retardation: 20 Years Later. *Pediatrics* 39, March 1967.
15. YAMAZAKI, J. N.: A Review of the Literature on the Radiation Dosage Required to Cause Manifest Central Nervous System Disturbances from in Utero and Postnatal Exposure. *Pediatrics* 37:877, 1966.
16. HARREL, R. F., WOODYARD, E., GATES, A. I.: The Effects of Mothers' Diets on the Intelligence of Offspring. Bureau of Publications, Teachers College, New York, 1955.
17. COWLEY, J. J. & GUESEL. R. D.: *J. Genet. Psychology* 203:233, 1963.
18. EICHENWALD, H. F. & FRY, P. C.: Nutrition and Learning. *Science,* 163:644-648, 1969.
19. DRILLIEN, C. M.: *Journal Obstet. Gyn.,* British Commonwealth. 64:161, 1957.
20. KNOBLOCH, H., RIDER, R., HARPER, P.: Neuropsychiatric Sequelae of Prematurity. *J.A.M.A.* 161:581, 1956.
21. DANN, M., LEVINE, S. Z., NEW, E. V.: A Long Term Follow-up Study of Small Premature Infants. *Pediatrics* 33:945, 1964.
22. DRILLIEN, C. M.: The Incidence of Mental and Physical Handicaps in School Age Children of Very Low Birth Weight. *Pediatrics* 39:238, 1967.
23. BABSON, S. G. ,HENDERSON, N., CLARK, W. M., JR.: The Preschool Intelligence of Oversized Newborns. *Pediatrics* 44:   , 1969.
24. KAWI, A. & PASAMANICK, B.: Association of Factors of Pregnancy with Reading Disorders in Childhood. *J.A.M.A.* 166:1420, 1958.
25. PASAMANICK, B. & KNOBLOCH, H.: Brain and Behavior: Session 2: Symposium 1959 2: Brain Damage and Reproductive Casualty. *Amer. J. Orthopsychiatry* 30:298, 1960.
26. HONZIK, M. P., HUTCHINGS, J. J. & BURNIP, S. R.: Birth Record Assessments and Test Performance at Eight Months. *Amer. J. Dis. Child.* 109:416, 1965.
27. SCHACTER, F. F. & APGAR, V.: Perinatal Asphyxia and Psychologic Signs of Brain Damage in Childhood. *Pediatrics,* 24:1016, 1959.
28. GRAHAM, F. K., ERNHART, C. B., THURSTON, D. & CRAFT, M.: Development Three Years after Perinatal Anoxia and Other Potentially Damaging Newborn Experiences. *Psychol. Monograph.* 76:1, 1962.
29. CABAK, V. & NAJDANVIC, R.: Archives Dis. Children, 40:532, 1965.
30. DYGGVE, H.: Prognosis in Meningitis Neonatorum. *Acta Paediatrics,* 51:303-312, 1962.
31. YU, J. S. & GRANANG, A.: Purulent Meningitis in the Neonatal Period. *Arch. Dis. Childhood,* 38:391, 1963.
32. PICKLES, M. M.: Haemolytic Disease of the Newborn. Charles C. Thomas, Publisher, 1949.
33. DAY, R. & HAINES, M. S.: Intelligence Quotients of Children Recovered from Erythrobastosis Fetalis since the Introduction of Exchange Transfusion. *Pediatrics,* 13:333-337, 1954.
34. BJURE, J., LIDER, G., REINAND, T. & VESTBY, A.: A Follow-up Study of Hyperbilirubinemia in Full-Term Infants without Iso-immunization. *Acta Paediatrica,* 50:437-443, 1961.
35. HOLMES, G. E., MILLER, J. B., SMITH, E. E.: Neonatal Bilirubinemia in Production of Long Term Neurological Deficits. *Amer. J. Dis. Child.* 116:37, 1968.

36. SHILLER, J. G., SILVERMAN, W. A.: "Uncomplicated" Hyperbilirubinemia of Prematurity. *Amer. J. Dis. Child.* 101:587-592, 1961.
37. CORNBLATH, M., JOASSIN, G., WEISSKOPF, B., SWIATIK, K.: Hypoglycemia in the Newborn. *Ped. Clinics N. Amer.* 13:3, 1966.
38. EEG-OLOFSSON, GENTZ, J., JOKAL, U., NILSON, L. R., ZETTERSTROM, R.: Neonatal Symptomatic Hypoglycemia. *Acta Paediatrica Scandinavica.* Suppl. 171, p. 85, 1967.
39. HAWORTH, J. C. & McRAE, K. N.: Neurological and Developmental Effects of Neonatal Hypoglycemia. *Canad. Med. Ass. J.* 92:861, 1965.

9

INDIVIDUAL DIFFERENCES IN THE MEASUREMENT OF EARLY COGNITIVE GROWTH

Michael Lewis, Ph.D.

Educational Testing Service (Princeton, N. J.)

"Attention is the first and fundamental thing in volition"
WILLIAM JAMES

Before proceeding to the text itself it would be helpful to preview what is to follow; this would allow the reader to arrange the subsequent material into the pattern intended by the writer. The chapter is divided into several sections which have the function of moving from the more general to the highly specific. The first section deals with some broad issues surrounding the topic of attention. The second section, as a consequence of this earlier discussion, proposes some models for viewing the attentional process itself. The third section deals with the more specific issue of the relationships between normal intellectual functioning and attention while the last, and most specific section, deals with CNS dysfunction in infants and children and attention. This section is concerned therefore with the more specific consequences of some of the broader, more theoretically oriented sections. The summary section integrates the entire chapter.

STUDYING ATTENTION

The study of attention, like much investigation in psychology, is not new, and often recurs as a theme. The terminology changes. Technology provides new instruments and more sensitive measures. But many of the problems remain the same (Lewis, 1967a). Preyer's work in the late 1880's (Preyer, 1888) serves as an example. As are an increasing number

This research was supported by the National Science Foundation, under Grant GB-8590, and by the National Institute of Child Health and Human Development, under Research Grant 1 PO1 HD01762.

of contemporary researchers, he was deeply curious about infant behavior, specifically, as his book title suggests, the *Mind of the Child*. Careful reading of his work reveals a great interest in and study of attention as a means of investigating the development of the infant's mind. His observations were among the first descriptions of eye-hand regard, for example. Another example of early observations related to contemporary issues of attention are Darwin's (1897) writings on infancy. In a biographical sketch of an infant, Darwin observed that the infant's eyes became fixed and the movement of his arms ceased when he saw a brightly colored tassel. This observation antedates energetic and technological studies of attention in the infant by approximately 70 years. Neither for that matter is the general study of attention an innovation. William James (1890) devoted much energy to exploring the various properties of attention, and perhaps nowhere else can one find as lucid an exposition of the subject as in his *Principles of Psychology*.

It is not, however, until the last decade that the study of attention in infants produced much interest in this country. Fantz's (1956, 1958, 1961) early and exciting experiments provided the crucial impetus. The sensory physiologist had misled the psychologist, fostering the belief that because the sensory apparatus was immature, the organism was an insensate being. This together with James's statement about the blooming grey mass of confusion, which was the sensate condition of the newborn, succeeded in convincing the researcher not to waste his efforts on an uninteresting organism. Fantz's (Fantz, 1963; Fantz, Ordy, & Udelf, 1962) work dispelled this belief, and together with the Russian work which was beginning to become available (Razran, 1961), rekindled interest in the infant and the problems of attention. Most exciting, Fantz's pioneering led the investigator to a rich and unmarked field to map.

For all the work that has been and continues to be generated, attention is not easily definable. In its general sense, it seems to be the process by which an organism directs his sensory and elaborating (cognitive) systems. This direction is in the service of all subsequent action, thought or affect. Researchers have attempted to define it more carefully through such physiological and behavioral observations as receptor orientation (Fantz, 1956; Lewis, Kagan, & Kalafat, 1967); decreases in ongoing activity such as moving (Kagan & Lewis, 1965; Lewis & Goldberg, 1969a); decreases in talking, vocalization (Dodd & Lewis, 1969; Lewis & Goldberg, 1969a) and sucking (Dubignon & Campbell, 1968a, 1968b; Haith, Kessen, & Collins, 1969; Kaye, 1966); several specific autonomic nervous system changes such as heart rate decreases (Graham & Clifton, 1966; Lacey, 1967; Lewis, Kagan, Kalafat, & Campbell, 1966; Lewis & Spaulding, 1967); galvanic skin resistance change (Crowell, Davis, Chun &

Spellacy, 1965) ; vaso-dilation in the head and vaso-constriction in the extremities (Sokolov, 1960, 1963a) ; changes in breathing rate (Stein-schneider, 1968) and, finally, cortical changes (Sharpless & Jasper, 1956). These changes usually indicate attention to external events and enable the organism subsequently to act, think or feel. It seems clear, therefore, that attending is a central process in the ongoing functions of life.

The recent intensification and broadening of research on infant attention is being carried out in the belief that the study of attention will provide important data on the anlagen of intellectual development and the growth of mental structure. In order to understand the various research efforts, one must clarify an essential distinction. This distinction was proposed by William James in 1890. James discusses two kinds of attention: "passive immediate sensorial attention" and "associational attention." In passive immediate sensorial attention, the organism is forced to attend regardless of his intention. A loud explosion outside his window forces the student to hear it, direct his attention, and even to explore it by looking out the window, even when he is engrossed in his reading. Usually this type of attention is elicited by stimulus intensity and carries the organism, often without desire, to attend. Moreover, some sensory experiences are more apt to produce this passive attending than others. Those stimuli which can act on the receptors independent of the organism's cooperation or intention are more apt to produce this passive attending. Sound, for example, reaches the auditory receptors whether or not we are oriented toward the source of the sound, while visual stimulation requires orientation of the receptors. This distinction between sensory experiences is worth investigating; however, I know of no work that has been done.

In the study of this type of attention the nature of the organism plays a small role. Bright lights, within a nonpainful range, elicit more attending than dull ones (Doris & Cooper, 1966) , loud sounds more than soft ones. Indeed, except for determining what is too intense for an infant, a scale of attention-producing events can be constructed. Such a scale would require only a quantitative description of the stimuli. In studies of this type of attention distribution, intensity, number, variation and complexity are the dimensions that are most commonly explored (Ames, 1966; Berlyne, Ogilvie & Parham, 1968; Brennan, Ames & Moore, 1966; Faw & Nunnally, 1968; Haith et al., 1969; Hershenson, Munsinger & Kessen, 1965; Silfen & Ames, 1964) .

In the case of associational attending, the organism attends because of the relationship of the stimulation to his ongoing functions. It is the relationship between the event and the organism's mental structure that is crucial. Thus the student attends to the attractive coed because of a certain motive or affect system. The nature of the stimulus has relevance only as the organism chooses it to. Scales of interest or relevance must take the organism into account, for they have no meaning without him. This type of attending is voluntary and under the control of the subject. While passive studies of immediate attending usually have focused on the dimensions of intensity, number, variation and complexity, studies of associational or voluntary attending explore surprise, familiarity, novelty and incongruity (for diverse examples across ages and methods see Berlyne, 1950, 1966; Charlesworth, 1964; Gullickson, 1966; Lewis & Goldberg, 1969a; Lewis, Goldberg & Rausch, 1967; Maddi, Propst & Feldinger, 1965; McCall & Kagan, 1967; Meyers & Cantor, 1967). Observation of these constructs makes the comparison between the types of attending immediately obvious. How can one define familiarity or novelty along scaling dimensions which are independent of the organism? Unlike intensity or complexity, novelty and familiarity are completely dependent on the subject. Indeed they are defined by the organism, his past experiences and his mental structures.

An extremely important corollary to the investigation of this type of attending is that by observing what causes attending behavior one may determine the associational value of the event to the organism. It is by means of this corollary that the study of attending behavior, specifically associational attending, becomes meaningful. The researcher is provided with a channel through which he is able to observe the organism's internal processes. Moreover, by studying these attentional differences over age, he can come to understand the growth and development of mental structures themselves. Lastly, by studying these attentional differences as indices of intelligence we avoid the pitfall of substituting motor for intellectual behavior. Try as we may they don't appear to be synonymous.

It is clear that both approaches to the study of attention are needed. Both types contribute to our understanding of the organism's response to its environment. With this distinction in mind, however, let us focus on somewhat more specific issues in the study of attention—the issues of attention as an instrument for exploring mental structure, as well as attention as a measure of mental structure. The first alternative brings us to a discussion of schema development, while the second brings us to a discussion of attention as a measure of cognitive processes.

Schema Development

A schema can be defined as a relatively persistent organized classification of information, a model which the organism uses in arranging information. At any given time, an organism has schemata at different points of development which, with time, will codify and then alter toward or be rejected for new schemata (Lewis, 1969). This analysis is most applicable to schema development in infants and young children who by necessity have fewer schemata, and the ones they have are in greater flux. To explore these schemata, and through them the developing organism's mental structure, investigators adopt this assumption: When the input from the environment matches a recently or nearly formed schema, the infant will spend long periods of time looking or attending to this input. After the schema is well developed, the infant will lose interest in stimuli which too well approximate it. Thus, if a stimulus array partially violates an existing schema, the violation will elicit attention. However, if the infant cannot perceive his schema within it, he will not spend time looking at the stimulus (Berlyne, 1960; Fiske & Maddi, 1961; Piaget, 1954; Sokolov, 1963b). It is the distribution of the infant's attention that provides the clue to the nature of his mental structure. Much work has been conducted on the development of face schema using this type of model to explore infant mental structure (Haaf & Bell, 1967; Kagan, Henker, Hen-Tov, Levine & Lewis, 1966; Lewis, 1969). In these studies using human faces and distortion of faces as stimuli, the results indicated that for the first half year of life, before the face schema is fully formed, realistic faces elicited most attention (Haaf & Bell, 1967; Kagan et al., 1966). However, in the only longitudinal study to date, Lewis (1969) was able to show that over the first year of life there was a corresponding increase in attention to distortion as interest in or attention to realism decreased. The results were interpreted in terms of schema development with the growth and codification of the human face schema resulting first in attention, then in disinterest.

With the exception of two studies (Kagan, 1969; Lewis, Dodd & Harwitz, 1969), the exploration of other schema growth has not been undertaken. The two studies in question deal with the growth of the body schema. While not fully in agreement, both studies suggest that the body schema is formed after the face schema. In passing, however, it should be mentioned that the study of these schemata represent the exploration of long-term schemata and their growth—that is, schemata that occur over long periods of time in the "natural" occurrence of the infant. In addition it must be pointed out that since little attention can be caused by either a well formed schema or no schema at all, it is often necessary to employ a longitudinal design in order to determine an individual's stage of schema development. It might be possible to explore schema growth that is short term and experimentally induced. Such an attempt has been made by McCall and Kagan (1967). Under the assumption that divergent inputs—in terms of the infant's schema— elicit less attention than a slight violation, these experimenters attempted to show an inverted V function such that inputs which too closely matched or were too divergent would elicit equal amounts of attention. To date, the results fail to support this theoretical function. However, this work is a good example of how experimentally to induce a short-term schema. McCall and Kagan placed a visual pattern in the infant's home and instructed the parents to display the pattern over the crib for 15 or so minutes a day. They hoped to build up a schema of this design which could be manipulated in terms of divergence from it. While the experiment failed to show an inverted V function of attention, it does point up an interesting question concerning short- and long-term schema growth. This will be dealt with in subsequent sections.

Attention as a Measure of Cognitive Capacity

An alternative view of the study of attention is that attention itself is a measure of mental processes and, as such, a core process vital for the subject's intellectual growth. One view of attention and its distribution is as an information processing operation wherein the amount of attention is directly proportionate to rate of processing. Under this system, attention can be viewed as a measure of cognitive functioning.

Concurrently, individual differences in ability to sustain or distribute attention can be viewed as indicative of important and central differences in intellectual growth and capacity. Alternatively, attention may be related to other central cognitive functioning by its relationship to other learning phenomena. For example, the infant who is able to attend well will have an advantage in subsequent learning over another infant less capable of attending. That is, attention is most necessary for any subsequent intellectual functioning and individual differences in it will be predictive of differences in other learning phenomena. It is possible to observe at least three attributes of attending in which subjects differ: length of attending, i.e., the ability to sustain attention over relatively long periods of time; attention differentiation, or the ease with which an organism can differentiate between similar but different events, i.e., an infant's ability to draw more fine discriminations; attention distribution, i.e., habituation or response decrement to redundant information.

Individual differences in any of these attributes directly indicate differences in cognitive capacity, or may affect capacity—or both. For example, observe the infant who shows longer fixations at a visual stimulus than another infant. Is this not indicative of the first infant's ability to sustain his attention and take in more of the environment? Stechler (1964) showed that in the newborn this difference in amount of attending was directly related to the amount and type of medication given to the infant's mother during labor. Infants whose mothers had less or no medication showed longer fixation times than did infants whose mothers received heavy medication. This attentional process was clearly influenced by medication affecting CNS function. Whether this type of individual difference reflects basic cognitive differences, or whether these differences lead to cognitive differences via differential ability to process information—or both—remains to be investigated.

Still another individual difference related to some type of CNS function appears to be the number of fixations. That is, given a stimulus event of X seconds, some infants exhibit more discrete turning from and towards the event than do others (Cohen, 1969a; Lewis et al., 1966). In some sense they are able to spend less time each time they attend. This type of data suggest that there may well be important individual differences in ability to sustain attention, some infants being better able to maintain longer periods of alertness and attending. The relation of this type of individual difference to CNS function has been suggested by the work showing number of fixations to be related to birth condition. Lewis, Bartels, Campbell and Goldberg (1967) showed birth condition as measured by the Apgar Score to be related to the number of fixations on a stimulus in 3-month-old and 9- to 13-month-old infants, the infants with poorer scores showing more fixations per trial of presentation.

The consequences of these individual differences for subsequent learning are not hard to project. Imagine two children, one having a single attention span of 10 minutes while the other has only a 5-minute span. The lesson they are listening to is 10 minutes long. The first child listens for all that time and learns the material. The second child after the first 5 minutes loses contact with the material and the second half of the lesson is gone. Their learning experience is quite different. Notice that there may be no difference in the learning capacity—as measured by some independent test—of the two children, but the only difference is in their differential ability to attend. Perhaps the future will bring not only curricula tailored to individual needs, but tests of individual attending ability which will allow the teacher to determine how long a child can remain focused before he tunes out. It is clear that adults who have difficulties attending for long periods often derive a system whereby additional time is allotted to a task—reading a paper or text— so that many "breaks" may be taken. This same concept could be formalized and introduced on an individual basis among the young.

Habituation or response decrement, the last attribute under discussion, is the most interesting and the most investigated of the three. Habituation simply refers to the decrease in response strength as a function of repeated stimulation. Various alternative hypotheses, ranging from receptor fatigue to CNS functioning, have been proposed. A leading theorist on habituation, Sokolov (1963b), has proposed that habituation is related to information processing in which a "neuronal model" is built of the external event. We have tried (Lewis, 1967b; Lewis, 1969; Lewis et al., 1969; Lewis & Goldberg, 1969a) in several recent papers to demonstrate that the rate of response decrement is related to CNS functioning and is under cognitive control. Those infants and young children who show faster response decrement are those subjects with a more efficient CNS function. In the sections below we will explore this aspect of attention in greater detail.

To recapitulate, the study of attention can be used (1) as a measure of the development of mental structures, called schemata; or (2) as a way of observing individual differences related to or predictive of subsequent cognitive development. The following discussion will attempt to deal with attending from the point of view of attention distribution as an indication of individual differences in cognitive capacity. To do this it will be necessary, however, to explore the general notions of the relationship of attending to internal representations, be they short or long term in nature. Before going on to the next section, however, it should be pointed out that the study of the development of mental structures and the study of attentional differences as differences in cognitive capacity are not exclusive categories. They differ chiefly in terms of their concern for individual differences and their differential emphasis on long- and short-term mental structures. The subsequent sections will make it abundantly clear that it is an emphasis rather than substance which distinguishes these approaches.

INTERNAL REPRESENTATIONS OF EXTERNAL EVENTS: A MODEL OF ATTENDING

A major aspect of psychological thought and inquiry should deal with the internal representations of external events. More often, however, it has been philosophy and linguistics which have been involved in this domain. Perhaps the first to offer a coherent exposition on the subject, at least in Western thought, was Plato. In his often cited image of the cave, man sees only the shadows cast by true reality, the ideal representation. The relationship of representations (especially the Ideal) to reality has continued to engage the effort of many Western philosophers, including such men as Spinoza, Descartes, Locke, Berkeley and Hume. More recently Russell and Chomsky have also chosen to pursue the study of knowing (or learning) by invoking the relationship between reality and man's representation of that reality.

Whether or not we choose to accept the notion of the Ideal falls to philosophical discourse; however, psychologists are concerned with how internal representations of external events are formed and the nature of these representations. While in the past, occupation with these questions has not been great in psychology, the resurgence of interest in cognition and thinking has renewed interest in these questions as well. Until recently, only the psychophysicists were directly concerned with such issues. The psychophysicists' job was to relate an external event—

usually some simple aspect of a stimulus event such as intensity—to an internal representation. Another group of investigators, following a task different from the psychophysicists', has also been concerned with internal representations. Using the term "meaning," these theorists have been searching for just such representations. Osgood and his co-workers (Osgood, Suci & Tannenbaum, 1957), by exploring the meaning of a word (itself a representation), are able to describe the representation itself. For example, by finding that "father" also means big, powerful and angular, Osgood is attempting to map out the internal representation of the external event—the word "father." This technique, as is well known, is called the semantic differential and has wide application as the semantic study of meaning.

One reason why psychology in general is reluctant to deal with the issue of representations is its failure to deal with inference and subjective evaluation and report. This is the legacy of behaviorism. For those who seek an alternative to subjective evaluation and report, the study of attending offers one.

External events—signs, symbols or stimuli—acquire internal representations. They may be long-term representations, called schemata, or short-term. It is the study of short-term representations, their rate of acquisition, as well as their nature that is of concern to us here. Two general classes of internal representations can be identified—experimentally produced representations and environmentally established representations which have already been or are in the process of being developed. Such representations could include face schema as well as phenomena such as Piaget (1954) describes as conservation of substance. The internal representations which are built up over long periods are determined by the experience of the organism in concert with maturation. In the experimental production of internal representations, the experimenter assumes the representation is short-lived. While the duration or strength of the internal representation may be different, it is believed that the experimentally induced representations are developed in much the same manner and are governed by the same processes as the naturally developed ones. Therefore, it may be possible through experimental manipulation to gain some understanding of the infant's thought processes, and his representations in particular, by exploring the short-term acquisition of internal representations.

According to many theorists, one way to measure the strength of the representation is to observe whether the presentation of an external event elicits attentive behavior (Berlyne, 1960; Sokolov, 1963b). As internal representations are acquired, external events which match that representation elicit little attention and lead to habituation. External events which do not match the internal representation elicit attention.

Thus, the study of attention can provide an important methodology for the exploration of internal representations.

Before turning to experimental manipulation of internal representations, take note of the relationship between attention, language (at least labeling) and internal representations. It might be argued that both the use of language and attention differences are processes which allow one to explore internal representations. We have stated that when a subject shows relatively concentrated attention to a particular stimulus, he has not yet acquired a highly articulated internal representation, whereas if he exhibits minimal attention, we assume the reverse.

The same indications can be provided by a child's acquisition of the lexicon. If he has a word for an object, let us say horse, we can assume that he has a well-defined schema or representation, while if he has no label, he has a relatively weak internal representation. While it is true that internal representations are possible without labels, most psychologists would agree that labeling provides or is indicative of a more articulate representation. Moreover, not only is labeling relevant to representation but the speed of label production should reflect, to some degree, the ease of retrieving that representation in the memory system. Ease of retrieving should be related to articulation of internal representations. Thus, fast retrieval of the word should reflect a well-formed representation, while slow retrieval, a minimally formed one. In a recent study (Lewis, 1970) on attention and verbal labeling, children three to five years of age were shown a series of pictures which could be classified as familiar, discrepant and novel. A variety of attention measures was obtained. Subsequently, the children were asked to name the pictures. These responses, along with their latency, were tape recorded. The data reveal that the children's speed and accuracy of labeling were related to their attentive behavior, with familiar stimuli producing mostly correct labels with short latencies while incongruous or novel stimuli produced mostly incorrect or no labels with long latencies. The results data support the belief that poorly defined and difficult to locate internal representations have corresponding incorrect or no labels which are produced with long latencies whereas highly available and articulated internal representations have corresponding correct labels which are easily retrieved in memory storage. The data suggest that language production and retrieval, and attention distribution both can be used to map internal representations, especially those that are long term. It is to be noted however that this procedure requires the organism to label, a task obviously impossible for the young infant. This, plus the fact that there are not many known long-term representations (aside from face and body schemata, psychologists have been at a loss to describe others), requires the study of short-term experimentally induced internal representations.

In order to accomplish this, we must turn to the study of habituation. Habituation is response decrement to repeated stimulation which is not accounted for by peripheral mechanisms such as receptor or effector fatigue. Recently, it has been discussed as an aspect of learning (the building up of internal representations) by Lewis (1967b), Thompson and Spencer (1966), and by Razran (1961). The most comprehensive discussion of response decrement as a learning process is to be found in the Russian work on the orienting reflex or attending response (Pavlov, 1949; Sokolov, 1963b). Indeed, Sokolov has offered an elaborate information processing system in which a "neuronal model" (internal representation) is acquired as a function of repeated stimulus encounter. This model or internal representation he defines as an organization of neuronal cells in the cortex which retain and process such information as intensity, duration, and quality of stimuli. Such a model is developed by the repetition of the same stimulus. In the process of model building, if the presented stimulus corresponds to the model, some type of negative feedback occurs, resulting in the decrease or absence of a response. However, if the presented stimulus does not correspond with the neuronal model or the model is not yet fully developed, central excitation takes place and an orienting reflex occurs.

Model acquisition can be viewed in the following way. Each presentation is compared to any memory trace or model created by the preceding presentations. Memory trace is reinforced, that is, the model made stronger, by some process such as increasing the number of neuronal cells involved, or perhaps by more permanent biochemical changes.

This postulated model and process of testing may involve many cells and their interaction or even possibly single cell memory. Sokolov's model, then, provides a method for investigating short-term acquisition of internal representations and makes the assumption that long-term representations are developed in a like manner.

It is important to note that internal representations of external events are characterized by two attentional responses. First, attention decreases with repeated presentation. That is, as the representation is built up, positive match between it and the internal representation leads to inattention; in Sokolov's terms it leads to inhibition and inattention. Secondly, when the repeatedly experienced event is changed (that is the external event does not match the representation) then attention recovers; Sokolov has termed the recovery an "orienting response" (OR). Both of these attentive responses are indicative of the internal representation acquisition.

Before applying Sokolov's formulation to the study of attention there remain several important issues. When these issues are discussed, the problem of individual differences in representation acquisition can be explored. To begin, it is necessary to bring into focus the entire process by which information is processed and attention elicited. There are two general issues: the nature of the internal representation, and the type of process by which the external event is matched against the internal representation.

Nature and Definition of an External Event

The first issue in the discussion of an attending response as suggested by Sokolov is the nature and definition of an external event and its correspondence to an internal representation. This problem, namely the nature of an external event or stimulus, has been neglected by psychology. In the contemporary literature only Gibson's (1960) lucid discussion is known to bear on this issue. It is clear that representations of external events are more than mere mirror images of the external world. This in itself adds an important dimension to Sokolov's formulation, and indeed, somewhat confounds it, because it forces the subject's cognitive aspects into the discussion of perception, and leads to a serious criticism of the match-inattention, mismatch-attention hypothesis described above.

For example, an organism has seen a repeated presentation of a box from one angle and thus has built up an internal representation of the box. If now the same box is presented from a slightly different angle, will attending occur? In a broad sense, does any change represent a "new" box and elicit attending and will this attention be as great as the attention associated with an entirely different, "new" event? Intuitively, this seems highly unlikely. If it were the case, organisms would constantly attend to every alteration and slight change in the same event—clearly an inefficient process. What probably occurs outside the controlled setting of the laboratory is that the organism sees the box from a variety of angles and constructs an internal representation of the box which is a composite of his total experience with it. The total experience includes more than mere sensation, that is, it may include some type of cognitive manipulation. The subject's experience may thus be an idealization of the box—something greater than all his sensory experiences. In this way he is able to maintain invariance of the object over many different alterations of view.

In light of the preceding discussion, it seems clear that some external changes are less important than others. Indeed, some changes are not changes in the stimulus itself—various views of the same animal do not constitute a different ideated stimulus or animal, but only an altered sensation (Gibson, 1960). This consistency across some sensory changes is an important developmental principle. Older organisms are more able to hold object constancy over sensory change than are younger ones. In fact, constancy, regardless of sensory change, is essential to Piaget's notions of knowledge and his system of epistemology (Elkind, 1967; Kohlberg, 1966).

We must infer, then, that the nature of the external event is also influenced by the developing mental structure of the organism and is capable of altering over time, an element which must be taken into account when discussing an external event.

Problems in a Matching Process Hypothesis

Another difficulty in Sokolov's theory and therefore in our discussion of the function of attention to internal representations is the time the organism requires to search for the representations that match external events. It is obvious that if all representations had to be scanned in order to find a match, the attending response would be a slow response indeed and not at all the rapid phenomenon we observe. It is necessary, therefore, that some additional processes facilitating the search procedure be hypothesized. One solution to this difficulty is to propose that internal representations may be composites of specific stimulus events. These representations may produce or facilitate simultaneous scanning of multidimensional models. Moreover, branching procedures, where certain aspects of an external event can be monitored first, are possible. Such a branching procedure would reduce the number of representations scanned and therefore reduce the time required for the matching process and resulting attentive behavior. Alternatively, a process which reduces some of the time and effort in the search for match may make use of previously constructed plans or strategies. That is, the organism constructs these plans or strategies for attending prior to the presentation of the sensory event itself. Such examples are to be found in the literature under the terms "expectations," "anticipation" or "response set." By the use of such procedures, an organism-determined continuum could be constructed along which the internal representations are placed. Thus, search procedures move along this predetermined continuum and the organism has to match the external event against only a selected few internal representations. An example of this selective attending as a function of some plan or strategy is best provided by the mother who sleeps through a loud noise caused by traffic, but wakes to her baby's cry, a sound of equal or lesser intensity. In any case, various aspects of an external event would have greater or lesser importance in matching the representation.

Some important issues have been raised here regarding the definition of both a "new" external event and the matching process. We have suggested that some type of hierarchy, probably under cognitive control, of either perceiving, searching or processing external events with internal representations is present in the organism. Sokolov's matching and mismatching theory becomes further stressed when stimuli with past meaning are presented. Remember, Sokolov states that it is only mismatch between an external event and an internal representation which produces attention, not match. Below it is shown that for signal stimuli (stimuli with past meaning), match as well as mismatch elicits attending behavior.

Signal stimuli or events may vary in the magnitude of attention because of differences in motivational content. That is, some events have previously been associated with a rewarding condition. A dinner bell would produce a greater attending response than a bell of equal intensity but of different pitch. Obviously, the difference could be explained in terms of differential reward value associated with the dinner bell. Moreover, this example points out that attending elicited by a signal stimulus may vary as a function of the organism's state. Thus, when hunger is decreased or increased, the dinner bell may elicit less or more attending behavior.

Still another reason for differential attending to various signal events may be biological. The perceiving of a target stimulus for an innate releasing mechanism (IRM) (Tinbergen, 1951) might elicit greater attention than an event of equal or greater complexity but unrelated to the IRM. Alternatively, the physiological structure of the organism must be considered. Color events, for example, would elicit no attending in early human experience because the retinal cones are still relatively poorly defined. However, in the older infant and young child, color stimulus events might become more relevant and therefore elicit attention.

A final factor which might affect differential degrees of attending is the change in mental structure as a function of maturational processes and in maturational processes and experiential interactions. Implied is that mental structures, independent of such peripheral variables as sensory maturation, have altered and thus produced differential attending. The development or change in detecting salient environmental dimensions (often referred to as concepts), such as color, size, shape, etc., could provide an example here.

Before going on to offer our own model of attending, it is important to repeat that in Sokolov's neuronal model theory, mismatch between external nonsignal events and internal representations elicits attention whereas for signal events it is the match between external and internal representations which elicits attention. A simple mismatching theory appears to become strained in explaining this difference.

General Model of Attending

An attempt to incorporate the above mentioned considerations into a model of attending follows. Alternative models have been presented;

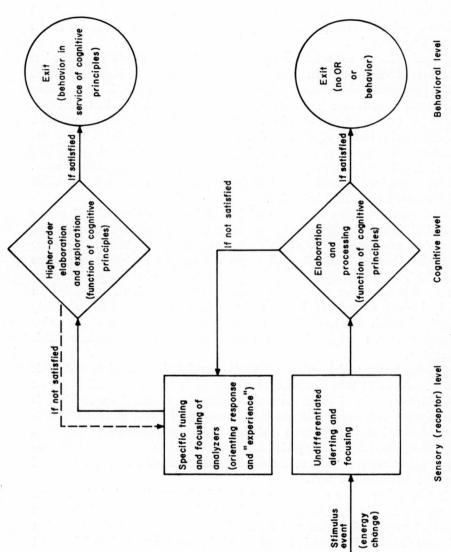

Fig. 1. A schematic representation of the process of attending to external events by comparison with internal representations.

however, most fail to consider the need for including cognitive rules acting upon external events. In a recent attempt to construct a model of attention and memory, Norman (1968) deals with one aspect of these cognitive rules. Figure 1 presents a diagram outlining a model which can account for some of the problems encountered earlier.

In the figure the energy qualities of the stimulus event, or the alterations in energy qualities caused by an event, are the initiators of the attentional process. These alterations produce a general state of arousal or alerting whose function it is to effect the change from totally unprepared, undifferentiated behavior to organized behavior—either internally organized as in thoughts, etc., or externally as in some motor response. Concomitant with this alerting phase is the start of the analyzer tuning, stimulated by the energy change itself. This alerting-arousing function may be subcortical, located at the reticular level, and occurs in short time spans.

At the next point in the information processing, the first type of elaboration operation occurs. Its outcome will determine whether the organism focuses on the stimulus event. This first elaboration operation could be either cortical or subcortical and may be in the service of any number of cognitive principles. These cognitive principles are yet undefined but might consist of certain expectations or rules, innate releasing mechanisms, or specific mental structures. Moreover, these principles may be programmed by the subject for specific events (as in the example of the mother programming herself to wake only when the infant cries), or be a more general, longer lasting program (such as response set in a learning problem). More importantly this principle will determine if it is match or mismatch which is to produce attention. Two outcomes of this first elaboration are possible. In some cases, the elaboration will determine that the alerting event is unimportant and no further tuning or focusing will occur. On the other hand, the operation may indicate that the information is relevant to some cognitive principle and it therefore becomes necessary to completely tune and/or focus the analyzers for the next operation. One might picture the function of this first elaboration as the initial cognitive attempt of the organism to monitor the relevance of the information. In some sense, it could be thought of as a screen omitting from consideration only those sensory events which are irrelevant to the various cognitive principles. However, it is recognized that there are some classes of sensory events which impose themselves regardless of the desire or intent of the organism.

It is important to note that the review/analysis of the initial elaboration phase makes no statement regarding either the match or mismatch of the external event to any internal representation. Both may be involved and may depend on the nature of the external event and the particular cognitive principle involved. Thus, for signaled events, a matching process may be important, while for nonsignaled events, mismatching would provide the significant operation.

If the information is unimportant, inhibition occurs, alerting ceases and the analyzers stop focusing and turn to alternative events. This is a flowing process rather than one with a series of discrete actions. Relevant information (always defined by the organism's cognitive principles) causes excitation and the full tuning of the analyzers so that a second state of elaboration, exploration and processing may occur. Typically, it is at this point, that is, the point of the signal to proceed tuning, that what has been called an attending response becomes visible. Thus, at each of these operations general information (meaningless information) is becoming either differentiated and acted upon (becoming meaningful) or rejected, depending on the nature of the various cognitive principles.

After full tuning of the analyzers, the second elaboration operation is performed. Again this elaboration operation is in the service of cognitive principles, for example, the reduction of stimulus uncertainty (Lewis & Goldberg, 1969a; Pribram, 1967). It might be necessary, given that the information supplied by the analyzers is not sufficient to satisfy the cognitive principles at work during the second elaboration state, to refocus or utilize an alternative set of analyzers and then reconsider the elaboration step. Thus, some type of oscillation could take place until the particular cognitive principle was satisfied.

The model proposes two levels of sensory analyzers and two levels of elaboration, all in the service of a set of cognitive principles. This model differs from most attentional models in that it contains a feedback loop. Because of this feature it resembles Miller, Galanter and Pribram's (1960) TOTE system. That is, the attending response can be considered to be a tune-elaborate-tune-exit system. While certainly not answering many of the important questions (the nature of the various cognitive principles, for example), the model does account for the need to hypothesize both a tuning and elaborating process in the initial attentional interaction. Perhaps the model is best viewed not as containing a separate operation for each step, but rather an interactive process whereby both functions occur together, each necessary for the other. Thus, tuning and elaborating in an oscillating fashion moves the stimulus event from a general energy statement to a highly differentiated information statement sufficient for the organism to act upon.

We have argued for the possibility, indeed the necessity, of considering sensory and cognitive experiences together as inseparable. That is, experience, even sensory experience, has a cognitive component and cannot be considered alone. This being so, then by the manipulation of various stimulus events, it may be possible to explore the mental structure of the organism by determining stimulus salience hierarchies. Moreover, by observation of the change in these hierarchies, a developmental course in these saliences may be determined.

We have digressed so as to offer a cognitive model of attending rather than the simple match, mismatch model suggested by Sokolov. The rules governing the eliciting of attention are varied. It seems clear that one rule is related to the development of internal representations which can be measured by the speed or amount of response decrement to a redundant signal. Response decrement serves as an indication that the stimulus event is supplying no new information to the organism. The failure to supply new information may be one of the cognitive principles leading to inattention. Returning to a general model for investigating the short-term acquisition of internal representation, it is to be kept in mind that while this model is designed to investigate short-term representation acquisition, the same rules, expanded over time and trials, may account for long-term representation acquisition.

RESPONSE DECREMENT AS A MEASURE OF LEARNING: INDIVIDUAL DIFFERENCES
IN THE ACQUISITION OF INTERNAL REPRESENTATIONS

A simple experimental paradigm is all that is needed for investigating short-term representation acquisition. An event, S_1, is repeatedly presented for n trials, following which some new event, an alternation of S_1 —S_2—is presented on trial $n+1$. Response decrement having the form of a negative exponential function should occur to the repeated event, S_1 (Lewis & Goldberg, 1969a; Thompson & Spencer, 1966). The presentation of S_2 on trial $n+1$ should result in response recovery. Both the response decrement and recovery data should reflect internal representation acquisition, with greater rate or amount of decrement and greater amount of recovery reflecting faster acquisition.

Most learning situations, for example, instrumental learning and classical conditioning, are characterized by increases in frequency and/or strength of response as a function of increased subject-environment interaction. There are some learning phenomena, however, which are characterized by decrease in response strength or frequency but which nevertheless are included as learning. Extinction has been considered a process of learning not to respond as a result of the omission of reinforcement. Negative adaptation has been used to refer to decremental processes involving learning (Harris, 1943), although adaptation usually applies to processes of physiological fatigue. Habituation is response decrement to repeated stimulation which cannot be accounted for by peripheral mechanisms such as receptor or effector fatigue (Harris, 1943; Thompson & Spencer, 1966).

The explanation of response decrement is particularly germane to the question of whether or not the phenomenon under study is indeed a cognitive process. Response decrement can be attributed to receptor, effector, or general organism fatigue, and occurs because there is progressive physiological loss of the ability to respond. These phenomena are not related to what is considered cognitive processes. On the other hand Sokolov (1963b), Engen and Lipsitt (1965), and Thompson and Spencer (1966) all would argue that response decrement is indicative of a cognitive process. Razran (1961) in his review of the Russian work on attending states ". . . there is little doubt that if any (acquired) pattern is accorded cognitive status, the attending pattern is surely the most likely candidate" (p. 119).

Before going on to discuss the use of response decrement as a measure of individual differences in acquisition of internal representations, let us first consider some alternative causes of response decrement. According to one fatigue model, response decrement reflects a general condition of the organism and is unrelated to the stimulus. Thus, a change in the stimulus after n repetitions would not alter the pattern of decreasing attention. The Sokolovian model assumes response decrement is stimulus-specific and predicts response recovery to stimulus change. Indeed, an orienting reflex is defined as those responses which habituate (show response decrement) to repeated presentation of a stimulus (S_1) and which reappear when the stimulus is altered (S_2). The assumptions about S_2 in this model are limited to (1) S_2 is discriminable from S_1 and (2) S_2 is equal to or less intense than S_1. The intensity of S_2 must be less than S_1 in order to eliminate receptor fatigue (adaptation) and recovery as alternative hypotheses. Thus, both a fatigue and receptor adaptation hypothesis could be rejected by demonstrating response recovery to a stimulus change (S_2) after a period of response decrement produced by stimulus repetition. The recovery to S_2 has been demonstrated by many investigators using young children and infants as subjects (Bartoshuk, 1962a, 1962b; Engen & Lipsitt, 1965; Lewis, 1969; Lewis et al., 1967; Lewis & Goldberg, 1969a; Pancratz & Cohen, in press).

A similar fatigue model suggests that response decrement is caused by the organism's becoming physically restless. Cohen (1969b) investigated the effect of restlessness by starting some control subjects at the time equivalent to trial 21 of an experimental group. In this experiment, the control infants sat for the time equivalent to 21 trials in order to see whether their response to the first presentation corresponded to trial 1 or trial 21 of the experimental group. It corresponded to the first experimental trial and the restlessness hypothesis as an explanation of response decrement was rejected. For these reasons one would tend to reject a response decrement model based on general fatigue. In addition to the earlier extensive work (see Razran, 1961; Sokolov, 1963a, 1963b;

and Thompson & Spencer, 1966 for reviews), there is a growing body of neurophysiological data which strongly suggest that CNS changes such as negative slow potential change in the human cortex occur while the organism is acquiring expectations (that is, the memory, model or internal representation of some event) through repetitive stimulus presentation (Rebert, McAdam, Knott & Irwin, 1967; Walter, 1964; Walter, Cooper, Aldridge, McCallum & Winter, 1964). Moreover, visually evoked potentials are not solely determined by the physical qualities of the signal, but by such factors as reducing uncertainty, or the confirmation of an expectation (Sutton. Tueting, Zubin & John, 1967). These studies provide evidence for cortical changes as a function of the buildup of internal representations. Thus, the composite of the research effort to date supports the theory that response decrement is a cognitive process related to the growth of internal representations against which external events are compared. It then follows that if response decrement is a measure of the speed of model acquisition, then the amount or rate of this decrement should be associated with a more efficient system of forming representations, such that those infants who show more rapid response decrement are those who build internal representations faster.

In a series of experiments recently completed in our laboratory, as well as several others conducted elsewhere, just such a hypothesis has been tested. In the following discussion we will present this material, first describing those studies which observed variables characteristically associated with superior cognitive and/or CNS function and related them to response decrement differences. After presenting these, evidence of a more direct nature will follow.

Subject Variables Associated with Cognitive Function

Age differences in response decrement. Fantz in 1964 first demonstrated that there was an age-related relationship in response decrement for infants in the first months of life. Besides his work, there are several other studies with limited age ranges which have produced similar findings (Ames, 1966; Cohen, 1969b). These results were intriguing and we thought to continue to investigate this problem over a wide age range—the first three years.

To explore this problem, a visual event—a blinking light pattern—was presented to infants 3, 6, 9, 13, 18 and 44 months of age, a total of over 300 children. Initially, four repeated trials were presented, each trial 30 seconds long with a 30-second intertrial interval. Fixation time was scored and the results can be observed in Figure 2. Notice that there are two parameters of response decrement, amount of decrement and the percentage of subjects failing to show decrement. The amount of decrement score was a percent difference score achieved by subtracting

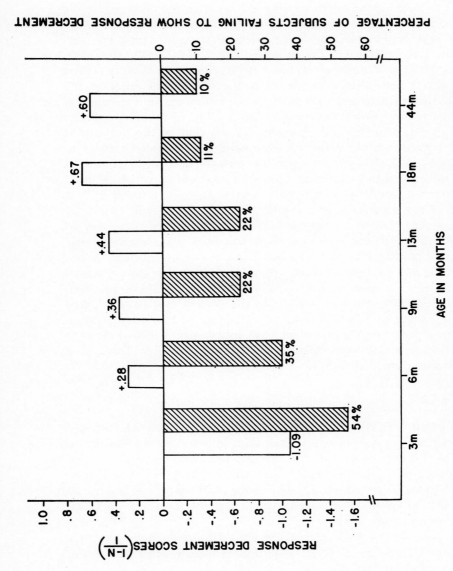

FIG. 2. Graphic presentation of the mean response decrement scores and the mean percentage of Ss failing to show response decrement for each age group over all experiments. The scale for the former is on the left side; the scale for the latter is on the right side of the graph. The data for the 44-month-olds are from only one experiment; the 18-month-old data are from two. All other age levels data are from the four experiments.

fixation on the last trial from fixation on the first and dividing the difference by the score on the first trial. This parameter shows a significant and monotonic function such that the older the child, the greater the response decrement. The second parameter, percentage of subjects failing to show decrement, was derived by observing what percentage of subjects had as high or higher scores on the last trial as on the first. The results are again a direct function of age. Clearly, response decrement increases with age in an orderly developmental pattern. In order to insure that these results were not a function of the specific stimuli used or determined by the number of trials, other experiments were conducted. In these the number of blinking light pattern trials was doubled and, on other occasions, visual stimuli other than blinking lights were used. Neither of these modifications altered the results. Nikitina and Novikova (1958) have also shown that the attending response is an age dependent function, relying more and more on cortical function as the animal ages. Finally, Vedyayev and Karmanova (1958) found that the higher the phylogenetic level, the faster the response decrement. Using carp fish, pigeons, polecats and rabbits they found the number of trials to extinction were 53-172, 15-40, 25, 6-15 respectively for the above animals. They use these results in support of their thesis.

Most striking in the infant data was the general lack of decrement for the 3-month-olds. In each of the experiments a 30-second intertrial interval was used, an interval which may have been too long for a very young infant's memory storage system (Watson, 1966). If this were the case, each repeated trial represented a new event for the young infant and thus no buildup of an internal representation could have been possible. Few experiments varying the intertrial interval have been performed using infants as Ss. Saayman, Ames, and Moffett (1964) produced response decrement in 3-month-olds by presenting one long trial of approximately four minutes. One could think of one long trial as having a 0-second intertrial interval length. Bridger (1961) using neonates and various intertrial intervals could best elicit response decrement to a repeated loud tone when the intertrial interval was shorter than five seconds. This result is supported by Bartoshuk's (1962a) failure to find differences between intertrial intervals of 60, 30, and 15 seconds. Moreover, the data for adult Ss clearly indicated marked response decrement as a function of shortening the intertrial interval (Geer, 1966; Glanzer, 1953; Welker, 1961).

In order to explore this possibility, a different group of 3-month-old infants was presented with the blinking light patterns for 30 seconds. For this experiment the intertrial intervals were 0, 5, or 15 seconds. Varying the intertrial interval did not enhance response decrement in the 3-month-old. This finding, together with the other decrement data, suggests that the 3-month-old infant's response to redundant stimuli may be qualitatively different from that of older age groups. While the data are not yet clear and there are some contradictory results, there is a growing body of literature to suggest that certain cerebral reorganization takes place around this age. For example, for the first 8 to 12 weeks, the amount of smiling and vocalization are relatively independent of environmental contingencies (Gewirtz, 1965; Lenneberg, Rebelsky & Nichols, 1965) and may be examples of responses whose emission is initially biologically determined and only subsequently influenced by environmental manipulations. While this appears true for these two responses, other environmental manipulations have been shown to be influential. That is, the early learning demonstrated by the Brown group, for example, would indicate that some environmental manipulations are effective (Lipsitt, 1967; Papousek, 1967; Siqueland & Lipsitt, 1966). Electroencephalographic work indicates a marked change in pattern of activity at around the 3-month period. These changes in both occipital rhythm (alpha wave) and evoked response to stimulation approximate, for the first time, that of an adult (Ellingson, 1967). Moreover, a number of primitive reflexes disappear or begin to disappear at this time. Their failure to disappear is usually a sign of neurological pathology or slow development (Peiper, 1963). Finally, additional and highly provocative data to support this view come from an unpublished study of South American children who died from respiratory diseases during the first six months of life and on whom autopsies were made. The DNA content in the brain showed a rapid increase reaching an asymptote at about three to four months of age (Winick, unpublished manuscript). These diverse facts argue for the possibility that infants around 12 weeks of age undergo a cerebral reorganization which enables them to show increasing rates of response decrement to attention-eliciting visual inputs.

There is a discrepancy between the 3-month data and those usually found for the neonate; that is, response decrement has been demonstrated in the neonate (Engen & Lipsitt, 1965). It is important to note that most of the reported neonatal work used auditory and olfactory stimulation, while the present experiments used visual stimulation. Moreover, the state of the newborn was not controlled, and as in the Engen, Lipsitt, and Kaye (1963) and Engen and Lipsitt (1965) work, the infants were asleep. In the present experiments, the infants were awake and alert. One might argue that the responses of the neonates elicited by the repeated stimulus appear to be related to startle-defensive reflexes. This startle-defensive reflex can be observed in the response of cardiac acceleration (Bartoshuk, 1962a, 1962b) and in the leg withdrawal and respiration responses (Engen & Lipsitt, 1965; Engen et al., 1963). Whether such responses elicited by a startle-defensive reflex have the same properties as responses elicited by an attentive or orienting reflex is still questionable, although Graham and Clifton (1966) have suggested that there are important differences between them. Moreover Lynn (1966) in a review of the literature presents ample evidence of the differences between them. The present discrepancy between the neonatal and older infant in terms of the amount of decrement they display might be a function of any number of variables and only further investigation can disengage them. One possible explanation offered by some of the Russian work is that the attending response in the newborn is subcortical and becomes cortical as the infant ages. Thus an OR can be exhibited by the newborn, but it is not the same as a more adult OR (Nikitina & Novikova, 1958).

Mother-infant interaction and its effect on response decrement. A second organism status variable has to do with the amount and contingency of stimulation provided the infant by the mother. Work from a variety of sources has demonstrated that the interaction between mother and infant appears to influence the infant's cognitive, social, and physical development (see Hunt, 1960, 1961, 1963; Provence & Lipton, 1962).

In a recent study conducted by Lewis and Goldberg (1969b), 20 12-week-olds and their mothers served in an experiment designed to investigate this problem. One hour before testing these infants, the mother and infant were left alone in a room which was filled with an assortment of furniture, cribs, and current popular magazines to read. The mother was told that the equipment was being warmed up. For 30 minutes a female observer, of whom the mother was unaware, recorded the mother-infant reaction by scoring a checklist.

During each 10-second period, the observer recorded—by checking off various behaviors—whether the mother looked at, smiled, vocalized or touched the infant. Also recorded was whether the infant's eyes were open or closed, whether he moved, cried or vocalized. Moreover, each time the infant exhibited large body movements, cried or vocalized, the observer recorded the latency of the mother's response as well as the nature of the response. Lewis and Goldberg found the more stimulation and the more contingent stimulation the mother provided the infant, the greater the response decrement to repeated visual stimulation. Furthermore, response decrement was related to the latency of the mother's response, such that the shorter the mother's latency of response to a child's behavior, the more response decrement the infant showed. Thus, greater response decrement was related to those maternal variables associated with the development of enhanced cognitive growth.

Social class, play behavior and response decrement differences. A third area of information is derived from a longitudinal study of infants (Lewis, 1967b). Data were available on socioeconomic level and although the data indicated a white, slightly skewed toward the middle class distribution, it was possible to divide the group into two levels. Socio-economic level was measured by the father's educational level and occupation. The response decrement data indicated that year-old infants from high SES families showed greater response decrement than infants from low SES families.

For this same group of infants, it was found that frequency of toy change in a free play situation at 13 months was related to response decrement. Infants with a high frequency of toy change showed rapid response decrement, while infants with low frequency of toy change showed less response decrement. This suggests that infants who process information rapidly (acquire internal representations rapidly) in one situation respond similarly to other tasks and situations. A partial replication of these results has been performed by Kagan (1969) who demonstrated the effect in one-year-old boys but not girls.

State differences in response decrement. Waking and sleeping states should also affect response decrement. One might hypothesize that be-cause there is a decrease in CNS functioning when the child or adult is asleep, behavior related to CNS function should decrease when the subject is asleep and be present when he is awake.

Johnson and Lubin (1966, 1967), Hord, Lubin and Johnson (1966) and McDonald, Johnson and Hord (1964) have found that cardiac response to a simple tone of short duration (approximately three sec-onds) does not produce response decrement when adult humans are asleep, but does produce decrement when the subjects are awake and not drowsy.

Concept formation, discrimination learning, IQ scores and response decrement. The agreement for CNS involvement in response decrement would be coalesced if more direct evidence could be found. We have recently completed two experiments with young children which provide strong indication of a link between decrement and CNS functioning by examining the relationship between decrement and more standard learn-ing problems (Lewis, 1967b; Lewis & Goldberg, 1969a).

In the first study, children 44 months of age were given a series of redundant visual stimuli and their decrement scores were obtained. Fol-lowing this procedure, each child was presented with a concept forma-tion task. The concept formation task involved six different concepts: (1) color with form constant; (2) color with form varied; (3) form with color constant; (4) form with color varied; (5) size with color varied, but form constant; (6) number with color varied, but form constant. Each of the six concept tasks had 20 trials. On each trial, a cardboard tray containing three items was presented. Two of the items were identical on the relevant dimension while the third was different. For the form and color concept tasks, the objects were two-dimensional colored papers of different shapes. The size and number concept tasks involved three-dimensional objects. The child was instructed to show which two of the three were exactly the same. If he was correct, he was given an M&M candy. However, if the child failed the first time, he was asked to try again. Thus, it was possible to make a maximum of 40 errors per concept or 240 over all six tasks. The procedure was similar to that used by Lee (1965) in her test of concept formation in preschool children. The results showed error differences across concepts but when the total number of errors was compared to the response decrement scores, a significant correlation (although relatively low) was observed.

In the second experiment, 32 children 44 months of age were just given repeated visual stimulation series from which a response decrement score was obtained. Following the presentation of the redundant signal, a standard learning task was presented. This was a two-choice visual discrimination task in which the discriminanda were a 20 curved line stimulus and a stimulus in which straight lines of the same color and length replaced the curved lines (see Lewis et al., 1967, for reproductions of both stimuli). The pictures were mounted on a sliding panel which enabled *E* to reverse the position of the stimuli. *S* was shown that each picture could occur in either position and that pressing the plexiglass window where the stimulus appeared could make a bell ring and lights go on. Then he was told, "Each time you make the lights and bells go on, you will win an M&M candy. . . . Now when I tell you, you can press *one* of the pictures. You'll know it's the right one when the light and bells go on and you get an M&M." Because of the concern for individual differences, the reinforcement was always associated with the curved lines. The position of the curved lines was varied according to a predetermined random ordering. The criterion for solving the problem was 10 consecutive correct responses. One hundred trials were presented and if *S* had not solved the problem, the test was terminated.

This problem was not easy for the 44-month-old child to solve and many subjects were not able to solve the task in 100 trials. Those children who did solve the two-choice discrimination problem showed significantly greater response decrement than those who failed. Finally, a correlation between the number of errors and response decrement revealed a significant relationship such that fewer errors were associated with greater decrement.

The last set of data are on the relationship between IQ as measured by a full scale Stanford-Binet and response decrement. For the longitudinal sample, discussed earlier, response decrement at one year and IQ scores at 44 months were available. The correlations between these were rho = .46 for girls and rho = .50 for boys. Thus, response decrement at an early age is positively correlated with a later measure of intelligence.

The results of all three standard measures of cognitive capacity are in agreement in that performance on each is positively related to response decrement to a redundant visual signal. Direct evidence relating cognitive function or capacity with response decrement has thus been provided.

To summarize, varying degrees of response decrement to repeated signals was found for infants within the first 44 months of life. Response decrement was directly related to the age of the infant, the younger infants showing less response decrement than the older ones. Response decrement was also shown to be related to other individual difference variables such as state of the subject, mother-infant interaction, measures of satiation, e.g., play behavior, and the socioeconomic status of the father. Finally, response decrement was directly predictive of performance on a two-choice discrimination learning task and IQ as measured by the Stanford-Binet Intelligence Scale, and correlated with performance on a concept formation task. The data are supportive, therefore, of the belief that response decrement represents a cognitive process whereby the organism learns not to attend to irrelevant information and supports the model of internal representation acquisition.

In the work reported in most of the studies from our laboratory, response decrement usually refers to the decrease in the amount of fixation time toward a repeated visual signal. Whether response decrement occurs for other receptor or processing systems or whether there is a developmental sequence, and further, whether response decrement for other systems is related to cognitive capacity, only further research can determine. Moreover, it is not known whether response decrement across different modalities is related. It does seem clear that response decrement of behaviors associated with the active taking in and processing of visual information, such as fixation and cardiac deceleration (Lewis et al., 1966; Lewis & Spaulding, 1967; Lewis & Wilson, 1970), is related to cognitive capacity and developmental organization. Further investigation may indicate that this decrement pattern applies to all behavior elicited in response to stimulus events designed to be attended. Moreover, experimentation is needed to explore the possibility that there are response decrement differences for stimulus events that vary in intensity and that elicit startle or fear rather than attention. A final consideration for subsequent investigation is the nature of response decrement. In general response decrement is a passive type of attentional activity. In order to map its developmental sequence over long periods of time—past the opening two or three years—it is important to consider the necessity of looking at more *active* modes of response: for example, looking at the rate of stimulus satiation in a free play period where the measure is the number of toy changes per unit time. In fact data already gathered have demonstrated a relationship between these modes of attending to the environment. This problem, namely response meaning and relevance change, has been presented before (Lewis, 1967a). It is important to keep in mind that response systems in the service of the same function may undergo important—and often unrecognizable—transformations and it is the function of the scientist interested in change to follow and map these transformations. To conclude—as is sometimes the case—that there are no consistencies across age for a particular function is to deny the possibility of these transformations.

That response decrement to a visual signal follows a lawful developmental pattern within the opening years of life and is related to perceptual-cognitive development implies several provoking consequences, one of the most interesting of which is the use of decrement score as an index of cognitive development. Such an index could provide a tool for evaluating the developmental organization of the very young, and equally important, for determining the effects of a variety of intervention programs—for example, the effects of a variety of environmental, pharmacological, or maternal behaviors. It might also be of use in measuring the perceptual-cognitive consequences of such adverse conditions in infancy as kwashiorkor (protein-calorie malnutrition), iodine insufficiency, birth trauma, or the effects of diverse socioeconomic variables.

RESPONSE DECREMENT AND CENTRAL NERVOUS SYSTEM DYSFUNCTION:
APPLICATION FOR THE STUDY OF INDIVIDUAL
DIFFERENCES IN CORTICAL FUNCTIONING

State differences in response decrement should immediately alert the student to the fact that there may be important cortical involvement in the process of response decrement. That waking infants, children and adults show response decrement, while sleeping subjects fail to exhibit this pattern, is strongly suggestive of this fact. Also it is clear that individual differences in rate of decrement might reflect CNS functions that are abnormal rather than normal as observed in the preceding discussion. Such abnormal differences in CNS function could be attributed to birth trauma, CNS injury or congenital problems. These abnormalities might be reflected in response decrement.

Research using animals as subjects strengthens this belief. In a review of response decrement (Thompson & Spencer, 1966) the authors cite numerous studies showing that decrement of attention differs markedly as a function of abnormal cortical involvement. There is reduced rate of response decrement after total decortication in dogs and chronic decerebration in cats. More specifically, in terms of located brain involvement, lesions in the auditory cortex in cats, frontal or temporal lesions in monkeys, cats, rats and man, and bilateral amygdalectomy all reduce the rate of decrement.

Turning from research with animals to research with humans, one finds that the Russians are responsible for most of the research in this area; this, of course, is due to the formulations of Pavlov and Sokolov on the subject. Reviewing the Russian work on attending reveals that cortical function has been strongly implicated in the role of response decrement. From the very first work on the OR, Pavlov (1949) demonstrated that response decrement was a cortical response and disruption of cortical function would affect the rate of decrement, as well as whether or not the organism showed response decrement at all. Because of the large amount of work done by the Russians, any review of response decrement and CNS dysfunction must therefore start with this body of work.

Bronstein, Itina, Kamenetskaia and Sytova (1958) report on the attending response in the newborn child. Using both auditory and tactile stimulation and normal and traumatized children (children with birth injury), the investigators found large differences in rate of response decrement to repeated stimulation. For normal children, the response to sound disappeared after one trial in almost 12 percent of the healthy children but in only 4 percent of the injured ones. Moreover, 50 percent of the injured children showed no decrement at all over all the given trials. Bronstein et al. also refer to the work of Itina who studied prematurely born babies. In these subjects, frequently it was not possible to produce response decrement and for two children, both hydrocephalics, no decrement was shown after "a great number of test trials."

Polikania and Probatova (1958) also investigated the attending response in premature infants who were 10-30 days old when the study was begun. Sound and light stimuli were used and approximately 60 infants were studied. Control Ss, as old postnatally as the premature infants, were obtained and the result indicated that for the premature Ss there was no tendency toward response decrement of the autonomic components of the OR. This was true for the very premature children, and remained so even when the children were older. The experimenters also report cases of "pathological conditions of the cortex, or where the cortex was underdeveloped or destroyed." In these conditions, the data all reveal that response decrement was most difficult—at times impossible—to obtain.

Adult subjects with more severe cortical involvement were studied by Briullova (1958). Significant differences between normals and experimental subjects in response decrement again were obtained. Finally, Gamburg (1958b) had similar findings for adult patients with long-standing effects of covert traumas (more than 5 years after trauma). Of the 60 or so subjects, most suffered from posttraumatic cerebrasthenia or encephalopathy, characterized by intellectual and emotional decline, among other symptoms. Once again, differences in response decrement both for auditory and electrodermal stimuli were reported.

It should be pointed out in passing that not only is there evidence of response decrement differences as a function of structural dysfunction (as in brain damage), but several studies have also found differences in response decrement as a function of the nature of the psychosis (simple versus paranoid schizophrenia) as well as between psychotics and normals (see Gamburg, 1958a; Israel, 1966).

Thus, there is a large and impressive quantity of literature linking CNS dysfunction and response decrement in animals as well as infants and adult humans. While much careful mapping of the particular areas of the cortex responsible for response decrement need be conducted, it is clear that there are important relationships between CNS function or dysfunction and response decrement. Vedyayev and Karmanova (1958) conclude from their study of the phylogenesis of the OR that the "characteristics of the higher nervous activity of various animals that have been well studied at present are reflected by such indicators as the speed of extinction of the OR." In other words, rate of response decrement varied as a function of higher nervous activity as seen in different animals along the phylogenetic scale. This idea was first expressed by Pavlov (1949) when he stated that the reflex arc of the OR is projected in the cortex as well as in the subcortical structures. For Pavlov, the speed of response decrement must be dependent "on the corticalization of the functions in the given animal on one hand, and on the relationship among the basic neural process on the other" (Vedyayev & Karmanova, 1958).

These facts, together with the earlier data on individual differences in response decrement, supply clear evidence for CNS involvement in decrement, and, moreover, indicate that the degree of response decrement can be used as an important indicator of CNS dysfunction as well as of cognitive development and learning. It is evident, then, that individual differences in response decrement have important implications for predicting the growth of cognitive capacity.

Recently, American psychology has begun to explore attending differences as they relate to differences in CNS functioning/dysfunctioning and cognitive development. For example, Cohen, Offner and Blatt (1965) have investigated the production and distribution of contingent negative variation (CNV) between normal and dyslexic children. Working under the assumption that the CNV is related to the buildup of a neuronal model, differences between these groups of children in terms of internal representation of external events, acquisition and therefore CNV would be predicted. Differences were obtained such that the E-waves of the dyslexic children's response, in anticipation of the stimulus, were of a lesser magnitude than those the normal subjects showed. Fenelon (1968) also found differences in normal and dyslexic children in their CNV production.

More directly related to CNS dysfunction and response decrement is the recent study by Hutt (1968). Hutt was interested in individual differences in the exploration of novelty and used both normal and brain damaged (general cerebral lesions) children 4 to 7 years of age. Her results agree with the earlier work indicating that an intact cortex is necessary for response decrement to occur. Hutt found that the proportion of time spent investigating a specific object, as opposed to other objects in the room, was longer for the brain lesioned subjects. After two weeks, the children were returned to the playroom and while the brain damaged subjects maintained their level of interest as before, the normal children's interest had fallen off. These more molar behaviors involving children's play, rather than some molecular behavior such as an autonomic response, are totally consistent with earlier findings using those molecular responses. Moreover, the play data conform to the work of Lewis (1967b) who found that children from higher socioeconomic levels—children who probably are more intelligent as measured by our standard tests—spent more time in varied play than playing with a single toy.

Another area of inquiry into individual differences has been the effects of medication (given to the mother in labor) on the development of the infant. Stechler (1964) in an early study demonstrated that attentional differences (in terms of amount of looking time) in the newborn could be affected by the level of medication given the mother. However, because the infants were seen 2-4 days after birth, it is not possible to talk about attention differences as produced by structural changes caused by the medication. The medication itself might still be in effect so short a time after birth.

Conway and Brackbill (1969) in a most recent study of attention and medication were able to show some very stable and long-lasting effects. These experimenters were interested in response decrement as an index of cortical integrity in the newborn.

Sound stimuli were presented and response decrement observed 2 and 5 days, and one month after birth. At 2 and 5 days, highly medicated infants showed 3 to 4 times as many trials to habituate as did the lightly or nonmedicated infant. Moreover, since the drugs themselves were no longer potent by a month (Moya & Thorndike, 1962), any differences observed would suggest that cortical structure and integrity might have been affected. Conway and Brackbill found that the significant difference between the medicated and nonmedicated groups still held one month after the medication, a strong indication of the potency of medication during labor and its long-term effects on cortical functioning and response decrement. In both studies—Stechler (1964) and Conway and Brackbill (1969) —attentional responses were used to demonstrate individual differences in cortical function as it relates to certain experimental variables. These studies suggest that response decrement as a measure of individual differences may be a valuable diagnostic device for evaluating differences in a variety of areas of pathology. Moreover, since the medicated groups showed no visible clinical trauma, response decrement seems to be a more sensitive measure capable of detecting individual differences in groups with subclinical deficits. Two recent studies support this contention.

Rather than study gross differences between children with severe cortical dysfunction and those with none, Lewis et al. (1967) chose to observe attention distribution of a sample in which all of the subjects were considered normal. If, as Knobloch and Pasamanick (1959) suggest, there is a continuum of casualty as a result of the birth process, then even within a normal sample, differences in degree of probable trauma should be available for observation. Successful observation of differences in this sample would provide evidence that response decrement can be used as a measure in samples with little pathology. Subclinical problems may be thereby investigated. Given that a relationship does exist between subclinical problems and subsequent difficulties in development, the diagnosis of these differences may be anticipated: evidence exists relating such problems as behavioral disorders in school with difficult deliveries (Knobloch & Pasamanick, 1959).

In the Lewis et al. study, the Apgar birth score was used as the measure of birth trauma continuum (Apgar, Holaday, James, Berrien, & Weisbrot, 1958; Apgar & James, 1962). This is a widely used and standardized test given 1 and 5 minutes after birth. There are 5 indications: heart rate, respiratory effort, muscle tone, reflex irritability and color. Each is rated on a scale of 0 to 2, 0 indicating no function; 1, function present but poor; and 2, function perfect. An infant in perfect condition would receive a score of 10. The Apgar score, although deficient in certain respects, has been found to be related to subsequent mental and motor performance (Edwards, 1968; Kangas & Butler, 1966). Approximately 40 infants were seen at 3 and 9-13 months after birth. Apgar scores, all of them in the normal range (see Drage & Berendes, 1966), were available as were measures of response decrement to a redundant visual stimulus. The children were divided on the basis of their Apgar scores into those with perfect scores and those with less than perfect scores but within the normal range. The results revealed that at 3 months response decrement was significantly different between the two groups and indicated greater decrement for the perfect scoring group. Parenthetically, it is to be noted that the group differences also supported Stechler's results. Total looking time, as in Stechler's (1964) study, was also available and indicated more looking for the perfect scoring group. In a replication of the Lewis et al. study still in progress, the results to date strongly support the earlier finding, the Ss with Apgar scores of

10 exhibiting greater response decrement than those with scores of 6 to 9.

The results of all the studies reviewed clearly indicate that rate of response decrement is affected by CNS dysfunction, medication, psychosis and other variables affecting cortical functioning. That some of these variables are subclinical suggests that the theoretical and technological advances are ready to offer a highly reliable and sensitive measure of cortical involvement and pathology. The use of response decrement as a diagnostic measure clearly is called for. Moreover, since measures of response decrement reflect more efficient CNS functioning, any intervention program, such as drug therapy or learning enrichment, can be evaluated by increases in rate of response decrement (as measured by both prior and subsequent performance) as well as by comparison with a control or healthy group of subjects. The practical considerations only await the investigator.

SUMMARY

Initially we discussed some of the broad issues surrounding the topic of attention. It was pointed out that attention could be used as a way of investigating internal representations—either long or short term, and/or could be used to observe basic attributes of cognitive ability. While both functions of attention are not exclusive, different research tactics are involved.

In the discussion of the relationship between attention and short- or long-term internal representation it has been assumed that a simple matching-mismatching process could account for attention distribution. Thus attention was elicited when there was a mismatch between internal representation and external event, and attention was inhibited when there was a match. By observing attentive behavior it was hypothesized that the researcher could map out some of the infant's internal representations. While this simple model has great appeal, it becomes obvious that a matching-mismatching model of attending is inadequate in accounting for the data. This is especially true when the external event has meaning prior to presentation. It is possible to demonstrate that both matching—as in finding something lost—and mismatching—as in violation of expectation—produce attention. To account for this it was necessary to construct a model of attending which utilized cognitive principles to determine whether an event was to elicit or inhibit attention.

Having suggested such a model, it was then possible to demonstrate that the rate/amount of response decrement, inferred as the rate of internal representation (model) acquisition for nonmeaningful stimuli, was related to and predictive of cognitive development and CNS efficiency. By exploring first subject status variables—variables associated with superior cognitive capacity—we were able to show that response decrement was positively correlated with the following: the age of the infant within the first three years of life, the state of the organism, the mother-infant interaction, and the socioeconomic status of the infant's parents. Moreover there was a positive relationship between amount of response decrement and other learning tasks—two-choice discrimination and concept formation. Finally IQ at 4 was related to response decrement at one year. The data strongly support the view that response decrement —a measure of internal representation formation—is a sensitive predictor of individual differences in a wide range of cognitive tasks and reflects efficient CNS functioning. Thus the more/faster the response decrement the more efficient the individual.

In the final section of the paper CNS dysfunction caused by such factors as prematurity, birth trauma, CNS injury and psychosis was explored. The hypothesis was that since response decrement was a useful predictor of efficient infant behavior its role in diagnosis and evaluating of pathology might be explored. Data from a wide variety of sources all seem to agree that response decrement is sensitive to gross differences among subjects in CNS dysfunction. More important, perhaps, was the strong suggestion that response decrement might be valuable as a diagnostic tool for investigating subclinical CNS dysfunction. The use of such a diagnostic tool would be invaluable given that only the grossest pathology has been demonstrable in infancy. This, together with the fact that it is a non-verbal task, makes it a most ideal test for infant pathology. Its role in evaluation of various types of intervention programs is not to be ignored either. Thus, before and after measures of response decrement can aid the clinician in his investigation of pathology and its correction.

Given that response decrement does measure CNS function and dysfunction we now have a most valuable research tool for the investigator of individual differences in the opening years of life. In addition it is not an age specific test, at least in the opening two or three years, which will enable us to explore developmentally many areas of inquiry and at the same time keep constant our experimental test. Past work on attention and response decrement should excite us to continue investigating this most interesting topic.

REFERENCES

AMES, E. W. Stimulus complexity and age of infants as determinants of the rate of habituation of visual fixation. Paper presented at the meeting of the Western Psychological Association, Long Beach, California, April 1966.

APGAR, V., HOLADAY, D. A., JAMES, L. S., BERRIEN, C., & WEISBROT, I. M. Evaluation of the newborn infant: Second report. *Journal of the American Medical Association*, 1958, 168, 1985-1988.

APGAR, V., JAMES, L. S. Further observations on the newborn scoring system. *American Journal of Diseases of Children*, 1962, 104, 419-428.

BARTOSHUK, A. K. Human neonatal cardiac acceleration to sound: Habituation and dishabituation. *Perceptual and Motor Skills*, 1962, 15, 15-27. (a)

BARTOSHUK, A. K. Response decrement with repeated elicitation of human neonatal cardiac acceleration to sound. *Journal of Comparative and Physiological Psychology*, 1962, 55, 9-13. (b)

BERLYNE, D. E. Novelty and curiosity as determinants of exploratory behavior. *British Journal of Psychology*, 1950, 41, 68-80.

BERLYNE, D. E. *Conflict, arousal, and curiosity.* New York: McGraw-Hill, 1960.

BERLYNE, D. E. Curiosity and exploration. *Science*, 1966, 153, 25-33.

BERLYNE, D. E., OGILVIE, J. C., & PARHAM, L. C. C. The dimensionality of visual complexity, interestingness, and pleasingness. *Canadian Journal of Psychology/Review of Canadian Psychology*, 1968, 22 (5), 376-387.

BRENNAN, W. M., AMES, E. W., & MOORE, R. W. Age differences in infants' attention to patterns of different complexities. *Science*, 1966, 151, 354-356.

BRIDGER, W. H. Sensory habituation and discrimination in the human neonate. *American Journal of Psychiatry*, 1961, 117, 991-996.

BRIULLOVA, S. V. On some aspects of the orienting reflex in persons having suffered a covert trauma of the brain and in neurotic persons. In L. G. Voronin, A. N. Leontiev, A. R. Luria, E. N. Sokolov, & O. S. Vinogradova (Eds.), *Orienting reflex and exploratory behavior.* Moscow: Academy of Pedagogical Sciences of RSFSR, 1958.

BRONSTEIN, A. I., ITINA, N. A., KAMENETSKAIA, A. G., & SYTOVA, V. A. The orienting reactions in newborn children. In L. G. Voronin, A. N. Leontiev, A. R. Luria, E. N. Sokolov, & O. S. Vinogradova (Eds.), *Orienting reflex and exploratory behavior.* Moscow: Academy of Pedagogical Sciences of RSFSR, 1958.

CHARLESWORTH, W. R. Instigation and maintenance of curiosity behavior as a function of surprise versus novel and familiar stimuli. *Child Development*, 1964, 35, 1169-1186.

COHEN, J., OFFNER, F., & BLATT, S. Psychological factors in the production and distribution of the contingent negative variation (CNV). Paper presented at the Sixth International Congress of Electroencephalography and Clinical Neurophysiology, Vienna, September 1965.

COHEN, L. B. Alternative measures of infant attention. Paper presented at The Society for Research in Child Development Symposium on *Determinants of Attention in Infants*, Santa Monica, California, March 1969. (a)

COHEN, L. B. Observing responses, visual preferences, and habituation to visual stimuli in infants. *Journal of Experimental Child Psychology*, 1969, 7, 419-433. (b)

CONWAY, E., & BRACKBILL, Y. Effects of obstetrical medication on infant sensorimotor behavior. Paper presented at the meeting of the Society for Research in Child Development, Santa Monica, California, 1969.

CROWELL, D. H., DAVIS, C. M., CHUN, B. J., & SPELLACY, F. J. Galvanic skin response in newborn humans. *Science*, 1965, 148, 1108-1111.

DARWIN, C. *The descent of man and selection in relation to sex.* (New ed.) New York: Appleton, 1897.

DODD, C., & LEWIS, M. The magnitude of the orienting response in children as a function of changes in color and contour. *Journal of Experimental Child Psychology*, 1969, 8, 296-305.

DORIS, J., & COOPER, L. Brightness discrimination in infancy. *Journal of Experimental Child Psychology*, 1966, 3, 31-39.

DRAGE, J. S., & BERENDES, H. Apgar scores and outcome of the newborn. *Pediatric Clinics of North America*, 1966, 13, 635-643.

DUBIGNON, J., & CAMPBELL, D. Intraoral stimulation and sucking in newborn. *Journal of Experimental Child Psychology*, 1968, 6, 154-166. (a)

DUBIGNON, J., & CAMPBELL, D. Sucking in the newborn in three conditions. Non-nutritive, nutritive and a feed. *Journal of Experimental Child Psychology*, 1968, 6, 335-350. (b)

EDWARDS, N. The relationship between physical condition immediately after birth and mental and motor performance at age four. *Genetic Psychology Monographs,* 1968, 78, 257-289.

ELKIND, D. Piaget's conservation problems. *Child Development,* 1967, 38, 15-27.

ELLINGSON, R. J. The study of brain electrical activity in infants. In L. P. Lipsitt & C. C. Spiker (Eds.), *Advances in child development and behavior,* Vol. III. New York: Academic Press, 1967. Pp. 53-97.

ENGEN, T., & LIPSITT, L. P. Decrement and recovery of responses to olfactory stimuli in the human neonate. *Journal of Comparative and Physiological Psychology,* 1965, 59, 312-316.

ENGEN, T., LIPSITT, L. P., & KAYE, H. Olfactory responses and adaptation in the human neonate. *Journal of Comparative and Physiological Psychology,* 1963, 56, 73-77.

FANTZ, R. L. A method for studying early visual development. *Perceptual and Motor Skills,* 1956, 6, 13-16.

FANTZ, R. L. Pattern vision in young infants. *Psychological Record,* 1958, 8, 43-48.

FANTZ, R. L. The origin of form perception. *Scientific American,* 1961, 204 (5), 66-72.

FANTZ, R. L. Pattern vision in newborn infants. *Science,* 1963, 140, 296-297.

FANTZ, R. L. Visual experience in infants: Decreased attention to familiar patterns relative to novel ones. *Science,* 1964, 146, 668-670.

FANTZ, R. L., ORDY, J. M., & UDELF, M. S. Maturation of pattern vision in infants during the first six months. *Journal of Comparative and Physiological Psychology,* 1962, 55, 907-917.

FAW, T. T., & NUNNALLY, J. C. A new methodology and finding related to visual stimulus selection in children. *Psychonomic Science,* 1968, 12, 47-48.

FENELON, B. Expectancy waves and other complex cerebral events in dyslexic and normal subjects. *Psychonomic Science,* 1968, 13, 253-254.

FISKE, D. W., & MADDI, S. R. *Functions of varied experience.* Homewood, Ill.: Dorsey, 1961.

GAMBURG, A. L. Orienting and defensive reactions in simple and paranoid forms of schizophrenia (first communication). In L. G. Voronin, A. N. Leontiev, A. R. Luria, E. N. Sokolov, & O. S. Vinogradova (Eds.), *Orienting reflex and exploratory behavior.* Moscow: Academy of Pedagogical Sciences of RSFSR, 1958. (a)

GAMBURG, A. L. Orienting and defensive reactions in post-traumatic cerebroasthenia and encephalopathy (second communication). In L. G. Voronin, A. N. Leontiev, A. R. Luria, E. N. Sokolov, & O. S. Vinogradova (Eds.), *Orienting reflex and exploratory behavior.* Moscow: Academy of Pedagogical Sciences of RSFSR, 1958. (b)

GEER, J. H. Effect of interstimulus intervals and rest-period length upon habituation of the orienting response. *Journal of Experimental Psychology,* 1966, 72, 617-619.

GEWIRTZ, J. L. The course of infant smiling in four child-rearing environments in Israel. In B. M. Foss (Ed.), *Determinants of infant behavior,* Vol. III. New York: Wiley, 1965. Pp. 205-248.

GIBSON, J. J. The concept of the stimulus in psychology. *American Psychologist,* 1960, 15, 694-703.

GLANZER, M. Stimulus satiation: An explanation of spontaneous alternation and related phenomena. *Psychological Review,* 1953, 60, 257-268.

GRAHAM, F. K., & CLIFTON, R. K. Heart rate change as a component of the orienting response. *Psychological Bulletin,* 1966, 65, 305-320.

GULLICKSON, G. R. A note on children's selection of novel auditory stimuli. *Journal of Experimental Child Psychology,* 1966, 4, 158-162.

HAAF, R. A., & BELL, R. Q. A facial dimension in visual discrimination by human infants. *Child Development,* 1967, 38, 893-899.

HAITH, M. M., KESSEN, W., & COLLINS, D. Response of the human infant to level of complexity of intermittent visual movement. *Journal of Experimental Child Psychology,* 1969, 7, 52-69.

HARRIS, J. D. Habituatory response decrement in the intact organism. *Psychological Bulletin,* 1943, 40, 385-422.

HERSHENSON, M., MUNSINGER, H., & KESSEN, W. Preference for shapes of intermediate variability in the newborn human. *Science,* 1965, 147, 630-631.

HORD, D. J., LUBIN, A., & JOHNSON, L. C. The evoked heart rate response during sleep. *Psychophysiology,* 1966, 3, 46-54.

HUNT, J. McV. Experience and the development of motivation: Some reinterpretations. *Child Development,* 1960, 31, 489-504.

HUNT, J. McV. *Intelligence and experience.* New York: Ronald Press, 1961.

HUNT, J. McV. Piaget's observations as a source of hypotheses concerning motivation. *Merrill-Palmer Quarterly,* 1963, 9, 263-275.

HUTT, C. Exploration of novelty in children with and without upper C.N.S. lesions and some effects of auditory and visual incentives. *Acta Psychologica,* 1968, 28, 150-160.

ISRAEL, N. Individual differences in G.S.R. orienting response and cognitive control. Paper presented at Eastern Psychological Association, 1966.

JAMES, W. *The principles of psychology.* New York: Henry Holt, 1890.

JOHNSON, L. C., & LUBIN, A. The orienting response during waking and sleeping. Paper presented at the Eighteenth International Congress of Psychology, Moscow, 1966.

JOHNSON, L. C., & LUBIN, A. The orienting reflex during waking and sleeping. *Encephalography and Clinical Neurophysiology,* 1967, 22, 11-21.

KAGAN, J. Continuity in cognitive development during the first year. *Merrill-Palmer Quarterly,* 1969, 15, 101-119.

KAGAN, J., HENKER, B., HEN-TOV, A., LEVINE, J., & LEWIS, M. Infants' differential reactions to familiar and distorted faces. *Child Development,* 1966, 37, 519-530.

KAGAN, J., & LEWIS, M. Studies of attention in the human infant. *Merrill-Palmer Quarterly,* 1965, 11, 95-127.

KANGAS, J., & BUTLER, B. Relationship between an index of neonatal delivery room conditions and pre-school intelligence. Paper presented at the meeting of the American Psychological Association, New York, 1966.

KAYE, H. The effects of feeding and tonal stimulation on non-nutritive sucking in the human newborn. *Journal of Experimental Child Psychology,* 1966, 3, 131-145.

KNOBLOCH, H., & PASAMANICK, B. Syndrome of minimal cerebral damage in infancy. *Journal of the American Medical Association,* 1959, 170, 1384-1387.

KOHLBERG, L. A cognitive-developmental analysis of children's sex-role concepts and attitudes. In E. E. Maccoby (Ed.), *The development of sex differences.* Stanford, Calif.: Stanford University Press, 1966. Pp. 82-173.

LACEY, J. I. Somatic response patterning and stress: Some revisions of activation theory. In M. H. Appley and R. Trumbull (Eds.), *Psychological stress: Issues in research.* New York: Appleton-Century-Crofts, 1967.

LEE, L. C. Concept utilization in preschool children. *Child Development,* 1965, 36, 221-228.

LENNEBERG, E. H., REBELSKY, F. G., & NICHOLS, I. A. The vocalizations of infants born to deaf and to hearing parents. *Human Development,* 1965, 8, 23-37.

LEWIS, M. The meaning of a response or why researchers in infant behavior should be oriental metaphysicians. *Merrill-Palmer Quarterly,* 1967, 13 (1), 7-18. (a)

LEWIS, M. Infant attention: Response decrement as a measure of cognitive processes, or what's new Baby Jane? Paper presented at the Society for Research in Child Development Symposium on *The Roles of Attention in Cognitive Development,* New York, March 1967. (b)

LEWIS, M. Infants' responses to facial stimuli during the first year of life. *Developmental Psychology,* 1969, 1, 75-86.

LEWIS, M. Attention and verbal labeling behavior: A study in the measurement of internal representations. Research Bulletin 70-56. Princeton, N. J.: Educational Testing Service, 1970.

LEWIS, M., BARTELS, B., CAMPBELL, H., & GOLDBERG, S. Individual differences in attention: The relation between infants' condition at birth and attention distribution within the first year. *American Journal of Diseases of Children,* 1967, 113, 461-465.

LEWIS, M., DODD, C., & HARWITZ, M. Attention distribution as a function of complexity and incongruity in the 24-month-old child. Paper presented at the Eastern Psychological Association Meetings, Philadelphia, April 1969.

LEWIS, M., & GOLDBERG, S. The acquisition and violation of expectancy: An experimental paradigm. *Journal of Experimental Child Psychology*, 1969, 7, 70-80. (a)

LEWIS, M., & GOLDBERG, S. Perceptual-cognitive development in infancy. A generalized expectancy model as a function of the mother-infant interaction. *Merrill-Palmer Quarterly*, 1969, 15, 81-100. (b)

LEWIS, M., GOLDBERG, S., & RAUSCH, M. Attention distribution as a function of novelty and familiarity. *Psychonomic Science*, 1967, 7 (6), 227-228.

LEWIS, M., KAGAN, J., & KALAFAT, J. Patterns of fixation in infants. In J. M. Seidman (Ed.), *The child: A book of readings*. New York: Holt, Rinehart & Winston, 1967.

LEWIS, M., KAGAN, J., KALAFAT, J., & CAMPBELL, H. The cardiac response as a correlate of attention in infants. *Child Development*, 1966, 37, 63-71.

LEWIS, M., & SPAULDING, S. J. Differential cardiac response to visual and auditory stimulation in the young child. *Psychophysiology*, 1967, 3, 229-237.

LEWIS, M., & WILSON, C. The cardiac response to a perceptual cognitive task in the young child. *Psychophysiology*, 1970, 6 (4).

LIPSITT, L. P. Learning the human infant. In H. W. Stevenson (Ed.), *Early behavior: Comparative and developmental approaches*. New York: Wiley, 1967.

LYNN, R. *Attention, arousal and the orientation reaction*. Oxford: Pergamon Press, 1966.

MADDI, S. R., PROPST, B. S., & FELDINGER, I. Three expressions of the need for variety. *Journal of Personality*, 1965, 33, 82-98.

McCALL, R., & KAGAN, J. Stimulus-schema discrepancy and attention in the infant. *Journal of Experimental Child Psychology*, 1967, 5, 381-390.

McDONALD, D. G., JOHNSON, L. C., & HORD, D. J. Habituation of the orienting response in alert and drowsy subjects. *Psychophysiology*, 1964, 1, 163-173.

MEYERS, W. J., & CANTOR, G. N. Observing and cardiac responses of human infants to visual stimuli. *Journal of Experimental Child Psychology*, 1967, 5, 16-25.

MILLER, G. R., GALANTER, E. H., & PRIBRAM, K. H. *Plans and the structure of behavior*. New York: Henry Holt, 1960.

MOYA, F., & THORNDIKE, V. Passage of drugs across the placenta. *American Journal of Obstetrics and Gynecology*, 1962, 84, 1778-1798.

NIKITINA, G. M., & NOVIKOVA, E. G. On the characteristics of the manifestation of the orienting reaction in animals during ontogenesis. In L. G. Voronin, A. N. Leontiev, A. R. Luria, E. N. Sokolov, & O. S. Vinogradova (Eds.), *Orienting reflex and exploratory behavior*. Moscow: Academy of Pedagogical Sciences of RSFSR, 1958.

NORMAN, D. A. Toward a theory of memory and attention. *Psychological Review*, 1968, 75, 522-536.

OSGOOD, C. E., SUCI, G. T., & TANNENBAUM, P. H. *The measurement of meaning*. Urbana, Ill.: University of Illinois Press, 1957.

PANCRATZ, C. N., & COHEN, L. B. Recovery of habituation in infants. *Journal of Experimental Child Psychology*, in press.

PAPOUSEK, H. Conditioning during early postnatal development. In Y. Brackbill & G. G. Thompson (Eds.), *Behavior in infancy and early childhood: A book of readings*. New York: Free Press, 1967. Pp. 259-274.

PAVLOV, I. P. *Complete works* (Poln. Sobr. Trud.). Moscow: U.S.S.R. Academy of Science Press, 1947-1949.

PEIPER, A. *Cerebral function in infancy and childhood*. (Trans. by B. Nagler & H. Nagler) New York: Consultants Bureau, 1963.

PIAGET, J. *The construction of reality in the child*. New York: Basic Books, 1954.

POLIKANIA, R. I., & PROBATOVA, L. E. On the problem of formation of the orienting reflex in prematurely born children. In L. G. Voronin, A. N. Leontiev, A. R. Luria, E. N. Sokolov, & O. S. Vinogradova (Eds.), *Orienting reflex and exploratory behavior*. Moscow: Academy of Pedagogical Sciences of RSFSR, 1958.

PREYER, W. *Mind of the child*. (Trans. by H. Brown) New York: Appleton, 1888.

PRIBRAM, K. H. The new neurology and the biology of emotion: A structural approach.

Paper presented at the meeting of the Eastern Psychological Association, Boston, April 1967.

PROVENCE, S., & LIPTON, R. C. *Infants in institutions.* New York: International University Press, 1962.

RAZRAN, G. The observable unconscious and the inferable conscious in current Soviet psychology: Interoceptive conditioning, semantic conditioning, and the orienting reflex. *Psychological Review,* 1961, 68, 81-147.

REBERT, C. S., McADAM, D. W., KNOTT, J. R., & IRWIN, D. A. Slow potential change in human brain related to level of motivation. *Journal of Comparative and Physiological Psychology,* 1967, 63, 20-23.

SAAYMAN, G., AMES, E. W., & MOFFETT, A. Response to novelty in the human infant. *Journal of Experimental Child Psychology,* 1964, 1, 189-198.

SHARPLESS, S., & JASPER, H. Habituation of the arousal reaction. *Brain,* 1956, 79, 655-680.

SILFEN, C. K., & AMES, E. W. Visual movement preference in the human infant. Revised version of paper presented at the meeting of the Eastern Psychological Association, Philadelphia, April 1964.

SIQUELAND, E. R., & LIPSITT, L. P. Conditioned head-turning in human newborns. *Journal of Experimental Child Psychology,* 1966, 3, 356-376.

SOKOLOV, E. N. Neuronal models and the orienting influence. In M. A. B. Brazier (Ed.), *The central nervous system and behavior:* III. New York: Macy Foundation, 1960.

SOKOLOV, E. N. Higher nervous functions: The orienting reflex. *Annual Review of Physiology,* 1963, 25, 545-580. (a)

SOKOLOV, E. N. *Perception and the conditioned reflex.* (Trans. by S. W. Wadenfeld) New York: Macmillan, 1963. (b)

STECHLER, G. Newborn attention as affected by medication during labor. *Science,* 1964, 144, 315-317.

STEINSCHNEIDER, A. Sound intensity and respiratory responses in the neonate: Comparison with cardiac rate responsiveness. *Psychosomatic Medicine,* 1968, 30, 534-541.

SUTTON, S., TUETING, P., ZUBIN, J., & JOHN, E. R. Information delivery and the sensory evoked potential. *Science,* 1967, 155, 1436-1439.

TINBERGEN, U. *The study of instinct.* Oxford: Oxford University Press, 1951.

THOMPSON, R. F., & SPENCER, W. A. Habituation: A model phenomenon for the study of neuronal substrates of behavior. *Psychological Review,* 1966, 173 (1), 16-43.

VEDYAYEV, F. P., & KARMANOVA, I. G. On the comparative physiology of the orienting reflex. In L. G. Voronin, A. N. Leontiev, A. R. Luria, E. N. Sokolov, & O. S. Vinogradova (Eds.), *Orienting reflex and exploratory behavior.* Moscow: Academy of Pedagogical Sciences of RSFSR, 1958.

WALTER, W. G. The convergence and interaction of visual, auditory, and tactual responses in human nonspecific cortex. In H. E. Whipple (Ed.), Sensory evoked response in man. *Annals of the New York Academy of Sciences,* 1964, 112, 320-361.

WALTER, W. G., COOPER, R., ALDRIDGE, V. J., McCALLUM, W. C., & WINTER, A. L. Contingent negative variation: An electric sign of sensorimotor association and expectancy in the human brain. *Nature,* 1964, 203, 380-384.

WATSON, J. S. The development and generalization of "contingency awareness" in early infancy: Some hypotheses. *Merrill-Palmer Quarterly,* 1966, 12, 123-135.

WELKER, W. I. An analysis of exploratory and play behavior in animals. In D. W. Fiske & S. R. Maddi (Eds.), *Functions of varied experience.* Homewood, Ill.: Dorsey, 1961. Pp. 175-226.

10

THE GENESIS AND PATHOGENESIS
OF SPEECH AND LANGUAGE

James F. Kavanagh, Ph.D.

Growth and Development Branch
National Institute of Child Health
and Human Development
National Institutes of Health (Bethesda, Maryland)

INTRODUCTION

The acquisition of spoken language, its development and those factors which may interfere with normal development have been the subject of philosophic speculation, naturalistic observation, clinical evaluation, empirical study, and rigorous experimental research. Unfortunately, some of those who have selected one approach to acquire and share their knowledge have tended to ignore the work of others who follow a different intellectual path. Their varied educational backgrounds and experiences, the variety and number of specialized journals and publishing firms, and perhaps a fair amount of academic discipline bias and inter-departmental snobbishness have contributed to the current diversity of information and understanding on this important subject.

In this Chapter an effort has been made to present an overview of the genesis and pathogenesis of speech and language drawing from a variety of different disciplines and information gathering methodologies. Accompanying the exposition of this information, certain specific unresolved problems are identified and suggestions for additional research are given. At the conclusion of the chapter these researchable questions are summarized and a statement concerning Federally supported research in this area is provided.

A brief comment should be made regarding the organization of material in this Chapter by way of explanation to the reader, if not in defense of the system. As Lewis (1951) has pointed out, "Anyone who attempts a survey of children's development is faced with a problem of presentation; whether to follow, one by one, particular strands through from beginning to end or, alternatively, to give a series of composite

211

pictures stage by stage (p. 9) ." This writer has elected to arrange his material roughly chronologically, i.e., what came before, the fetal and prelinguistic periods, and the time of emerging speech and language. The reader should not get the impression, however, that these topics representing chronological epochs are completely separable or distinct.

The writer has also elected to present his discussions of those possible pathogenic mechanisms which may interfere with the normal development processes, with the discussion of the developmental factors within each major period. The reader who has become accustomed to finding a separate discussion of the disorders of speech and language may find this arrangement disconcerting. It has been presented this way, however, because the author feels that the linguistic development of infants does pattern, in large measure, the development of the child organismically.

DEFINITIONS

Although speech and language have been the subjects of description and speculation since the dawn of art and science, the concepts remain difficult to define or to distinguish from each other. MacIntosh and Halliday (1967) have suggested that language is "organized noise used in social situations, or in other words 'contextualized systematic sounds (p. 3) .' "

J. B. Carroll (1953) has defined language as a "structured system of arbitrary vocal sounds and sequences of sound which is used, or can be used, in interpersonal communication by an aggregation of human beings and which rather exhaustively catalogues the things, events and processes in the human environment (p. 10) ." Winitz (1969) notes that Carroll's definition excludes non-vocal gestures and written codes or writing systems. Winitz states that physical gestures and other bodily acts are supplements to vocal acts and agrees with Carroll that printed and written systems are used as representatives of oral communication of a language, and, therefore, the two systems (oral and written) should not be used synonomously.

A recent publication of the National Institutes of Health attempts to distinguish between the terms. "Speech is a way of using the breath and certain muscles to make sounds in very precise patterns which other persons understand as words. Speech can be heard. Language means understanding sounds as words, thinking in words, clothing ideas in words. Language is silent." (Learning to Talk, 1969, p. 7)

Wood (1964) also makes a clear distinction between the two terms. She states that ". . . Language is the broader, more encompassing term, referring to a learned process of which speech is one part. By definition, language is an organized system of linguistic symbols (words) , used by human beings to communicate on an abstract level (p. 6) ." Speech, according to Wood, is the oral expression of language, beginning with the birth cry and continuing through many stages of development before it becomes a useful tool for communication.

While the distinction between speech and language presented above seem reasonable and are often used by speech scientists, it should be noted that some authors, particularly linguists and psychologists, use the terms "speech" and "language" interchangeably. This seems to have been particularly true in the earlier writings of the linguists. For example, Sapir's book *Language* (1921) is subtitled, *An Introduction to the Study of Speech.* In his introductory chapter he repeatedly uses the words "speech" and "language" as virtual synonyms. Similarly, de Laguna (1963), in her book *Speech, Its Function and Development,* which was first published in 1927, clearly uses the two terms interchangeably. In this linguistic text the author notes the common practice of regarding language, as distinguished from the act of speaking it, as a social phenomenon. But she quickly affirms that speaking is not just a phenomenon of individual life but is a social enterprise and therefore is related to group activity. She then proceeds to discuss speech as audible language.

And in Pei's *Glossary of Linguistic Terminology* (1966) language is defined as "a tool of communication by which human experience is analyzed differently in each community into units (monenes) each of which has semantic content and phonic expression: a system of communication by sound, operating through the organs of speech and hearing among members of a given community, and using vocal symbols possessing arbitrary, conventional meanings (p. 141)." This glossary defines speech as "The verbal expression of thought (p. 255)."

Zangwill, in his foreword to Luria and Yudovich's book (1966) states "Unfortunately psychologists in the West have tended—until very recently at least—to avoid the topic of speech, largely on account of the technical difficulties which its investigation presents. Soviet psychologists, on the other hand, have seen the study of language (it appears that these words are interchangeable for Zangwill) as the most fruitful approach to the general problem of mental development and as providing a bridge between studies of behavior in animals and man (p. 2)."

In this chapter the author has drawn upon the writings of representatives of many different disciplines concerned with the acquisition and development of speech and language as well as the basic process of human communication. As has been noted above, some of these writers make a clear distinction between the terms "speech" and "language" and others do not. When this author has been required to make a distinction between the production or reception of words as acoustically meaningful patterns and the silent generation or reception of words or groups of words symbolically representing ideas, then the appropriate terms "speech" or "language" are used differentially. However, frequently the author did not wish to make a distinction between the two terms. But, in an effort to avoid a misunderstanding in these instances, both words were usually used, e.g., the chapter title.

WHAT CAME BEFORE

A wide variety of investigators, including anthropologists, phoneticians, physicians, philosophers, psychologists, linguists, speech scientists, and biologists have been intrigued by the question "How does (did) man acquire the ability to learn to communicate with spoken language?" Several different approaches have been taken to solve this problem, affected in part by the knowledge base and discipline orientation, and in part by the fashion of the times.

During the 19th Century, it became quite popular, particularly among French linguists, to speculate about the first genetic ancestor of modern man to communicate with his fellow creatures. Did the "link" reproduce the sound of another animal to warn his family of pending danger (Bow-Wow or Onomatopoeic theories)? Did he convert the grunt made in the effort or pain of battle into a symbol of that battle (Pooh-pooh theory, Yo-he-yo theory)? Was it an accident which early man capitalized on or was he highly motivated by some unique circumstance? Or was Max Mueller correct when he propounded (and later rejected) his nativistic (ding-dong) theory which stated that language resulted from an instinct possessed by man alone, a faculty by which every impression from without received its vocal expression from within? According to Mueller this was because practically everything in nature which is struck rings; each substance has its own particular ring, and there is "a mystic harmony between sound and sense (Jespersen, 1964, p. 415)."

For those readers who join the author in enjoying the intellectual exercise and romantic fantasy of such speculations, they are referred to Jespersen's collection and discussions of the variety of such theories which have been offered as explanations of how the first ancestor of man used a spoken language.

Unfortunately, these theories cannot in most cases be tested and accepted or rejected because today language is omnipresent among all men, and difficult or impossible to observe in nonhuman animals. Today, scientists tend to avoid this sort of theorizing, not because of any lack of interest, but because they feel it falls far beyond legitimate scientific inference (Robins, 1964).

It is to be regretted that such a survey of the earlier literature fails to reveal factual information concerning the phylogenetic development of language nor does it help us to understand how today's child acquires the ability to use spoken language.

It is generally agreed among linguists that human language is unique in its ability to not only express motivation, but also to make reference to the environment. There is also agreement that ancient languages were not less complicated than the languages spoken by modern man, but rather were just as complex and efficient. Hoijer (1966) has stated that, "Despite current popular belief to the contrary, no language has yet been found which is primitive either in the same sense that anthropologists designate a Paleolithic culture as primitive or apply the term to a contemporary culture (p. 233)." This means that all languages, whether spoken by such peoples as the Australian aborigines or by cultivated Frenchmen, Englishmen or Germans, possess a fully developed system of distinctive sounds and equally well developed grammatical systems.

Moreover, while gesture language probably played a more dominant role in ancient man's social communication than it does in modern languages, there does not appear to be any strong evidence to indicate that a gesture language, as some have thought, preceded vocal language or speech, but rather it must be assumed that both gesture including general bodily activity and acoustically audible expression emerged simultaneously.

Anthropologic and linguistic studies of the communication systems of nonhuman primates have led us to believe that primate cries, gestures, rituals, and facial expressions used in social situations are, for the most part, expressive signals. That is, primates only evidence the ability to communicate certain information about their own motivational state. Thus, the mutual exchange of such signals between primates appears to have more in common with the signals used by most other animals than it has with the human language system.

Human language, however, appears to be different from nonhuman systems in that it not only has the ability to express motivation, but also to make reference to the environment (Lancaster, 1966). There is, in fact, a growing feeling among psychologists, linguists and anthropologists that human language may represent capacities not merely different in degree, but different in kind from the communication system employed in the rest of the animal kingdom.

One of the several possible explanations for the apparent quality difference between the communication systems employed by humans and all other animals seems to rest upon the particular changes that have evolved in the brain. Unlike all other living creatures, man is able to form associations between two sets of environmental stimuli, i.e., between the acoustic noise that we call a "word" and the sensory image representing the portion of the environment referred to by that word.

There is evidence that the size of the human brain more than doubled during the Pleistocene Era. It has been assumed that this expansion was disproportionately in favor of special areas of the cerebral cortex, particularly those areas which play a major role in behavior patterns which have become typical of the human species, more specifically those areas associated with communication by language.

Three areas of the human cortex have been identified as closely related to the development of speech and language. The first of these is Broca's Area which is located in the third frontal convolution of the left cortical hemisphere in right handed individuals. This area is noted for the controls which it permits through the motor cortex in the establishment and maintenance of speech. The second is Wernicke's Area which is located on the middle and posterior parts of the superior temporal gyrus. This area is a part of the auditory cortex and permits the association of sound patterns and acoustic memory.

A third speech-related area is located on the angular gyrus in the interior part of the parietal lobe, between the association areas for vision, audition and touch. It appears to be connected to all three sensory modalities by short association fibers and is structurally situated in such a position as to mediate between them and serve as an association area for the three sensory cortices. Geschwind (1965) indicates that the angular gyrus is particularly important in language development in that it permits language to be used and related to the outside world, not in respect to vocal speech and social interaction as in Broca's Area, but in respect to cognitive function, i.e., the recognition of relationships between words and their referents.

Lancaster (1966) has described the quality differences between man's cortex and the brain of lower animals. Of special importance is the fact that nonhuman primates have brains smaller than those of the human child when he is acquiring language. Anthropologists have reported that fossil records of the brain of Australopithecus do not differ from that of the apes, whereas the members of the species *Homo erectus* (Pithecanthropines) have much larger brains which are comparable in size to those of the speaking child.

Lancaster and others believe that the human child acquires language in a series of recognizable stages, and that his first words are not uttered until after his cranial capacity has exceeded that of primates and fossils belonging to the genus *Australopithecus*. It should be noted that there is general agreement that the basic features of English syntax are mastered by the age of 4. By this time the child's brain has usually grown to within ninety percent or even more of its total adult weight. Additional research is needed to determine the relationship between language and brain capacity.

Another argument has recently been given for the apparent quality difference between the communication systems of man and subhumans based on spectrographic and oscillographic studies of the vocalizations of the rhesus monkey, chimpanzee, and the gorilla (Lieberman, 1968). Lieberman, Klatt and Wilson (1969) have recently examined the vowel repertoire of the rhesus monkey by means of a computer program that calculated the formant frequencies from the area function of the animal's supralaryngeal vocal tract, which was systematically varied within the limits imposed by anatomical constraints. The investigators then compared the resulting vowels with those produced by humans and with nonhuman primates. Their findings indicate the acoustic "vowel space" (the full range of vowels a monkey could produce) of a rhesus is quite restricted compared to that of the human. They believe that this limitation is the result of a lack of a pharyngeal region that can change its cross-sectional area. They conclude that the animals thus lack the output mechanism necessary for the production of human speech.

They also assert that "some of man's recent ancestors also may have been unable to produce the full range of human speech; the skeletal evidence of human evolution shows a series of changes from the primate vocal tract that may have been, in part, necessary for the generation of speech. They concluded "The human speech-output mechanism thus should be viewed as part of man's species-specific linguistic endowment (p. 1187)."

While speculation about the linguistic skills of earlier man may prove fruitless, both the comparative studies of man and subhuman primates and modern anthropologic and archeologic investigations should be encouraged. We especially need more research in the biologic aspects of human evolution including man's possible genetic predisposition to acquire and develop language.

Representatives of the many different disciplines agree that the infant is conceived, develops embryonically and is born into an evironment filled with language. There is some evidence that language skill, as well as language inefficiency, tends to run in families. Some have speculated that there may be a physiological, perhaps genetic, predisposition for proficiency or lack of proficiency in language. Here we are referring to the clinical concept, dysphemia, a neurophysiological "weakness" which may set the stage for language disfluencies, errors of articulation or speech dysrhythmia (stuttering) (West, Ansberry, Carr, 1957, p. 269). Certainly, general motor coordination, intelligence and perception—both auditory and visual—will affect the infant's ability to provide a base with which he may later acquire language skills. Inasmuch as language and speech, as we measure these phenomena, are the outward manifestations—the reciprocal of the coordinated biological and cognitive activities of the infant—so all of those basic biological and psychological factors which permit him to develop as a normal infant also affect the development of his language.

218   *Exceptional Infant: Studies in Abnormalities*

THE EMBRYO AND FETUS

Even though all would agree the nine months of a child's life *in utero* play an important role in the establishment of the bases upon which language will develop, relatively little research has been conducted with the view to specifically relating fetal development to language.

There have been a few efforts to explore the ability of the fetus to perceive and react to accoustic stimulation. Sontag (1966) has indicated that in the 1920's a German investigator reported a number of instances in which expectant mothers were deterred from attending symphony concerts because the music and the applause of the audience greatly intensified the activity level of the fetus they were carrying. From his own research, Sontag (1966) reports that when a block of wood is placed over the abdomen of a woman eight months pregnant, and the block is struck by a doorbell clapper at the rate of 120 vibrations per second, there is, in the vast majority of instances, a convulsive response on the part of the fetus. Not only does he kick violently but also there is a noticeable movement of the entire fetus. Sontag has concluded that this bodily reflex is the same as the Moro reflex after birth.

Incidentally, Sontag has also shown that the more active an individual was as a fetus, the more likely he is at two-and-a-half years of age to avoid conflict and to show signs of social apprehension, such as being hesitant about joining a group of his peers. Furthermore, according to the Fels Research Institute studies of human development, this pattern of "aloneness" is likely to continue to adulthood. Could this social behavior affect language development and proficiency?

There have also been descriptive anatomical studies of the growth and development of fetal structures which, in the postnatal period, will have overlaid the production of oral speech and language upon their basic physiological function.

Sucking behavior involving the lips, tongue, palate, and pharynx has been reported at 24 weeks of gestational age (Shulejkina, Vainstein, Golubema, 1959). However, some of the physiological elements which are essential for sucking develop much earlier (Humphrey, 1968). Tongue movement has been identified at 14 weeks of gestational life, protrusion of the upper lip at 17 weeks, and of the lower lip at 20 weeks. Grooving of the tongue was achieved by lip and tongue stimulation through movement of the mandible at 15.5 weeks and lip pursing was observed at 20 weeks.

At the Second Symposium on Oral Sensation and Perception (Bosma, 1970), Humphrey reviewed the anatomical and neurophysiological development of the oral and pharyngeal cavities and the oral and facial reflex activity of the human fetus. Based on the monumental work of Davenport Hooker in the cinema studies of 159 fetuses, Humphrey reported that "the total pattern reflexes" which can be elicited from the maxillary and mandibular nerves at 7.5 weeks of gestation become progressively more discriminate and more varied in the period leading to the act of sucking and swallowing of amniotic fluid which appears at 24 weeks.

With four or more months of experience in coordinating mandibular, labial, lingual, palatal and pharyngeal activities, it is not surprising that a normal infant at birth is an efficient sucker. James Bosma, an investigator of oral and pharyngeal development states, "Suckling, maintaining the airway, and responding to tactual stimuli are 'mature' neonatal oral functions (1970, p. 270)." In fact, in contrast to many activities the child must later learn to perform, there is every reason to believe that the child does not learn to suck at birth for indeed he has already learned this complex act. The need at birth is only to apply this skill in a different environment.

Although the physiological bases for phonatory behavior has also developed during the fetal period, examination of its acoustic producing capabilities is usually delayed until the natal and postnatal period. McCarthy (Carmichael, 1954), has cited some evidence of vocalization by a fetus of five months, but very little descriptive research has been conducted on this topic.

While the oral, nasal, pharyngeal and laryngeal areas obviously play an important role in the production of oral speech and language the author does not, at this time, see a direct relationship between the motor development requisite for the basic biological functions of the fetus and later speech and language development. The search for a bridge between these functions separated by time and neurological sophistication must be continued.

THE NEONATE

Phonation

At birth, when the infant inhales his first breath of air, the vocal folds may vibrate with a resultant audible, complex sound. This noise is usually not identified as a cry. But after this initial inhalation with possible accompanying noise, the term "cry" is applied to the usually loud, vigorous acoustic product of vocal fold vibration and suprapharyngeal resonance that accompanies the expiration of the breath stream.

For the young mother and those in attendance during her delivery, there is perhaps no acoustic event that carries more listener anticipation than the newborn infant's first cry. The birth cry has also prompted a variety of mild anthropopathetic observations regarding the infant's emotional reaction to his change of environment. For example, after stating that there appears to be a neural-kinesthetic readiness for the birth cry, Boone (1965) then declares that the cry serves as an indication by the infant that he is ready to take his place as a separate entity in the human family. Similarly, according to Lewis (1963), the infant's initial expulsion of the breath of air is "an element of his violent reaction to his new environment . . . (p. 11)."

While this author is not disposed to the metaphysic or psychoanalytic philosophy suggested in the above and many similar statements found in the literature, there can be little doubt that the cry of the neonate is, indeed, a vivid announcement of his phonatory ability. Without question, at birth the infant is a very competent vocalizer. He can produce, through coordinated activity along the respiratory tract, those motions that produce acoustic phenomena identified as a cry, with a high degree of facility, regularity and individuality. Furthermore, this physiologic event provides immediate evidence of the infant's viability.

Lieberman, et al. (1968, 1969) recorded the cries of 20 normal newborn infants from birth to the fourth day of life. An analysis of the sound spectrograms made from these recordings showed that the cries were similar to the vocalizations of nonhuman primates insofar as the infants seemed to produce these sounds by means of a uniform cross-section, schwa-like, vocal tract configuration. The infants did not, however, produce the range of sounds typically found in adult speech.

These investigators believe that this inability seems to reflect, in part, certain limitations imposed by the neonate's vocal apparatus. This limitation resembles the nonhuman primate's vocal tract which also appears to be inherently incapable of producing the full range of human speech.

According to Lind (1965), human infant birth cries, while different from each other, are remarkably uniform for the same child and distinguishable from child to child. Moreover, if the general physiological similarity among normal infants tends to permit an acoustic end-product that contains certain sonic similarities, then infants with similar physiological or anatomical variations may have common characteristics which are distinguishable from those of the normal infant. Thus, some mothers, newborn nursery attendants, and neonatologists report they can distinguish one neonate from another, identify those in acute distress, and single out those who may have some abnormality of respiration, or of the upper respiratory pathway.

While there persists a strong suspicion that such babies with a variety of types of neurological and anatomical abnormality produce cry sounds which are different from normal infants, there is not, as yet, a body of scientific information about this possible diagnostic sign. However, clinicians continue to feel that a relatively high-pitched or weak cry is likely to be produced by an abnormal baby. They also distinguish as abnormal those cries which are labeled "whining" or sheep-like (Prechtl and Beintema, 1964).

Recent research has suggested that neonatal cry behavior may be under closed-loop auditory feedback control (Cullen, 1968). The cry sounds of 20 normal infants 24 to 168 hours old were recorded under two test conditions: synchronous auditory feedback and 200 msec delay in auditory feedback. The infants tended to reduce the average duration of their cry sounds by more than 100 msec during the delayed auditory feedback condition. The researchers noted this result was at variance with the increases in duration of connected speech which are consistently found in studies of children and adults. This study, while not providing conclusive proof that the cry behavior is under auditory feedback control, suggests that such a relationship may be established at birth. The technique may also provide an objective measure of the auditory capability of the neonate.

Whether or not this initial reflexive phenomena identified as the birth cry can be directly related to the genesis and pathogenesis of speech and language remains to be more fully explored through further research. A conservative answer would be that the child's ability to perform this complex sensory-motor activity is indicative of a measure of his preliminary readiness to orally produce communicative symbols, but does not necessarily indicate that the child will do so or will fail to do so. It must be noted that congenitally deaf or severely retarded children and those with gross neuro-motor dysfunction who survive gestation and delivery will produce cry sounds even though they may not develop speech and language in a normal manner or schedule.

However, while the cry of the normal hearing and the deaf neonate may be quite similar, there is some evidence that they soon can be distinguished from each other. For her doctoral dissertation at Northwestern University, Jones (1965) compared the acoustic features of crying vocalizations of young deaf and normally hearing children. Spectrographic measures of the crying vocalizations of the 40 deaf and 24 normal hearing children showed that:

1. The children with significant hearing impairment cried at higher pitches and demonstrated greater pitch variability in their cries than the normal hearing subjects.

2. Children with significant hearing impairment cried with similar intensity dynamics and duration, but demonstrated greater variability than the normals.

3. Differences occurred in the crying of the hearing impaired infants at the earliest age range (7 to 12 months). Similar differences remained through the upper age range (43 to 48 months).

Jones also concluded that the spectrogram appeared to have potential use as an aid in the early diagnosis of hearing impairment as well as serving as a useful tool for the study of infant vocalization.

Audition

There was for many years a controversy among physiologists, psychologists, and neonatologists regarding the auditory sensitivity of the newborn infant. In the first decade of the twentieth century, most European and American clinicians were convinced that otherwise normal infants were totally deaf at birth (Stern, 1924). Then, a few researchers reported some evidence the neonate could hear. Froeschls (1932) indicated that three-fourths of all the newborns studied by O. Kutvirt reacted to the tones C_1, C_2, and C_3 on the tuning fork within the first twenty-four hours postnatally. Also, according to Froeschls, Canestrini demonstrated in 1913 that infants show a change in the "brain pressure" caused by auditory stimulations. Canestrini placed over a fontanel an India rubber membrane of a calibrated capsule which graphically reflected changes in brain pressure.

Today there is general agreement that the normal infant has the capability of hearing acoustic signals which are audible to young healthy adults. For example, Stechler and Carpenter (1967) indicate that the newborn infant is able to selectively attend to stimuli under the dual control of the state of the organism (his internal environment) and the nature of the incoming information (the external environment).

Furthermore, Bortoshuk (1964), Bridges (1962), and Eisenberg (1967) have each reported that the neonate can discriminate auditory pitch and intensity differences of pure tones during the first few days and have suggested that more complex, melodic acoustic patterns may elicit from young infants a variety of reactions which are different from those prompted by pure tones.

From her behavioral and heart rate data of more than 700 infants, Eisenberg (1969) has reported, "There seems little doubt that attentive mechanisms are operant in earliest life (p. 42)." She is also convinced that the normal newborn infant discriminates sound on the basis of parameter variables and the organization of the stimulus envelope.

There is universal agreement that early detection of hearing loss is important because of the relationship between hearing and the development and maintenance of speech. Today when a hearing loss is suspected, it is common medical practice for the physician to informally produce some sort of noise in the immediate environment of the infant and observe his general reaction. When indicated, more formal assessments are then attempted with calibrated acoustic stimulation emanating from a signal generator such as an audiometer. The resultant gross bodily activity is evaluated as evidence of the ability to hear. The electroencephalograph, as used in early audiometric assessment, is still in its "infancy" but promises to be an important tool in the future (Goodhill, 1968).

A variety of different recorded sounds have also been used as stimuli for assessing the infant's auditory acuity. Mandel (1968) has recently reported a comparative study involving several of these commonly used stimuli. In this study, 36 infants ranging in age from 4 to 11 months were tested with five different recorded sounds that varied in band width and temporal configuration. The stimuli included a continuous band of white noise, the same band of noise interrupted twice per second, the wrinkling of onion skin paper, a narrow band of noise centered at 3000 Hz and warbled 3000 Hz tone. In this study with loudness and duration of the stimuli held constant, more responses occurred for sounds of a broad band spectrum than those of a limited band width.

Efforts have also been made to determine the effectiveness of measuring the infant's receptivity to acoustic stimulation by testing the effects of such stimulations on the child's feeding patterns. Kaye (1966) tested 120 newborn infants between the ages of 47 and 110 hours to determine the effect of the introduction of feeding and tonal stimulation of their sucking behavior. Infants received 10 second tonal stimulation at 30 second intervals and at three different intensity levels above the ambient noise level. Kaye determined that while there was no measurable effect the louder levels did increase responses over time.

Using an operant audiometric procedure developed for difficult-to-test retarded persons, Lloyd, et al. (1968) determined that children under two years could provide evidence of essentially normal hearing sensitivity as defined by thresholds of 20 dB or better (re: 1964 ISO) for the octave frequency range 250-8000 Hz.

We conclude that the newborn infant has the capacity for receiving acoustic stimuli and exhibiting evidence such stimuli have been received. We have shared some of the clinical research evidence that demonstrates that the infant can be tested for possible hearing loss. Much more research is needed in this area to provide even more reliable and feasible measures of auditory acuity with these difficult-to-test subjects.

It must be assumed that the reader will accept without documentation the long-observed fact that the untreated, congenitally deaf infant will not develop normal speech and language. However, Goetzinger (1965) has shown that even mild sensorineural hearing losses may result in delayed language development. It has also been suggested that a fluctuating hearing loss i.e., from 20 dB to 40 dB ISO for airborne sound with normal bone conduction which accompanies a chronic otitis media during the first two years of life will delay the acquisition of language skills (Holm and Kunze, 1969).

We continue to need more refined research data which can establish the relationships between the infant's acuity for sound throughout the speech frequencies and the acquisition and development of speech and language. Moreover, there is accumulative evidence that the newborn may be meaningfully studied at a fundamental level with regard to his perceptual strategy, his ability to match externally presented stimuli against an internal model and to store information in a short-term memory. As Stechler and Carpenter (1967) have pointed out, the infant will respond to a tone of one pitch which he has not recently heard, while he will not respond to a tone of another pitch which he has recently and repeatedly heard. These investigators believe this indicates that at some internal level the infant is able to discriminate the novel from the familiar because he has some memory of the habituated tone, even if the mechanism is no more than a temporary inhibition of receptivity at a given frequency.

From the work of Fantz and Nevis (1967), there appears to be strong evidence that perception precedes motor activity in the development of the young infant. This conclusion is in opposition to the frequent assumption that postnatal maturation and learning of sensory-motor responses is a prerequisite for perceptual-cognitive development.

Oral Sensation and Perception

The relationship between hearing and speech development, though not well understood, has long been referred to in the literature and accepted as positively correlated. Of much more recent investigative interest is the possible relationship between speech production, and somesthetic perception and motor function in the oral and pharyngeal area. This research interest in a large measure was prompted by a patient seen at the Clinical Center of the National Institutes of Health, who presented an unusual impairment of sensitivity in the oral cavity in apparent association with disabilities of speech and mature feeding patterns. This female patient and other patients with similar dysfunctions were the subject of a series of multi-disciplinary research conferences convened to explore a syndrome, which came to be called "oral asterognosis." Extensive descriptions of these impaired subjects have been presented in several publications (Bosma, Grossman, Kavanagh, 1967a; Kavanagh, Bosma, Grossman, 1968). The following is an abbreviated, illustrative case report and discussion of our first patient. For a more complete case report, the reader is referred to Bosma, Grossman, Kavanagh (1967b).

This female patient, E, was the second born of three pregnancies of her mother's only marriage. The mother recalled no episodes of infection during the pregnancy but reported recurring hemorrhages throughout the entire period. A severe hemorrhage at approximately the eighth gestational month demanded medical induction of labor of two-day duration, culminating in cervical dilation and high forceps delivery. At birth the infant weighed 5 lbs. 9 oz. She was notably pale and weak, but natal respiration was apparently spontaneous and subsequent respiration was without difficulty. Breast feeding was attempted for two or three weeks, but she sucked very poorly. At two weeks bottle feeding was attempted, but she continued to have extreme impairment of suckle feeding. While there was no evidence of choking, nasal regurgitation, or other respiratory problems associated with feeding, the parents noted her peculiar "lapping" motions and an odd "popping" sound during the tedious feeding process. When the spoon feeding of "Pablum" was initiated at nine or ten months, she experienced inordinate difficulty keeping the food in her mouth and on her tongue during swallow movements.

While other neurological development such as posture and gait was accomplished in early childhood, and on a normal schedule, E continued to have feeding difficulty and was unable to produce any intelligible speech.

At 7½ years of age, she was examined at a major university hospital. A tentative diagnosis of "ideational apraxia" was given after an extensive neurological and psychological evaluation failed to provide a more specific cause for the feeding problem and lack of speech. While academic progress was moderate and social development was surprisingly good, speech and oral language did not develop although extensive therapy was provided.

The patient was first brought to the Clinical Center at the age of 15 where numerous and exhaustive tests failed to reveal evidence of pathology of nasal ganglia, cerebellar systems, motor nerves, or skeletal muscles. Biopsies of finger tips and mucosa showed normal elements. Her acuity for pure tone, speech discrimination and general intellectual function was judged to be within normal limits. No indications of abnormalities of autonomic innervation were noted and the functions of olfaction and taste for salt, sweet and sour were grossly adequate.

The neurological examinations, however, demonstrated a number of abnormalities of perceived sensation. Pin prick was usually identified as a dull sensation and was never experienced as painful. This was generally true for the entire body surface, but particularly so in the oral cavity. While manual recognition of objects was impaired, she was completely unable to recognize by shape or size plastic geometric forms which were placed in her mouth.

Without visual feedback, the patient could not tell whether her tongue was extended in the midline or deviated to the right or left, nor could the tongue be voluntarily moved laterally.

Specialized techniques for the evaluation of sensation on the hard palate were employed, using electrodes placed within a prosthesis. At the midline, the threshold of perception was achieved at four times greater than normal intensity of electrical stimulation.

In contrast, subjective awareness of pain through stimulation of the teeth with a dental pulp tester was within normal limits.

The patient's speech articulation was grossly impaired and only rarely intelligible. Anteriorly produced sounds, such as the lingua-dentals, lingua-velars and the labials, were omitted or grossly distorted. Although fairly stable, the speech motor gestures, particularly the lingual motions, were slower and showed far less temporal and spatial differentiation than the corresponding gestures elaborated by normal subjects. Her efforts to produce speech sounds, in isolation or in sequence, rapidly evoked fatigue in marked contrast to her non-speech motor performance. She was inconsistently hypernasal, depending upon unidentified parameters of the subject's physical or mental state. Voicing was weak or absent.

This patient exemplifies those we have observed with near normalcy of physical form, hearing, intellect and adequacy of infantile oral, pharyngeal and respiratory functions but with a non-progressive, severe disability of speech production and mastication in association with a differential deficiency of sensory guidance of mature functions in the oral area. Clinicians who have worked with these subjects have noted their amiability, persistence in cooperative endeavor and general social maturity permitting communication in spite of their speech disabilities.

This syndrome gives indication by pathological deficit of a unique sensory perception system which is most critically distinguished by subjective indication at the mouth and less definitely in the hands. This apparently is a maturation-relevant system, which develops postnatally in relevance to the mature functions of speech, biting and chewing. These maturations probably are in correlation also with oral area awareness.

As we describe this syndrome, we are aware of our lack of adequate criteria and designations of sensation and perception in the oral region. In particular, we do not know which aspects of sensation and/or perception guide the motor elements of speech, but it is apparent that accurate non-acoustic afferent representation of movements of the speech producing mechanism are necessary for normal speech development.

The relationship and interdependencies of parallel acoustic and somesthetic sensory feedback of ongoing speech during the initial learning, and subsequent monitoring of speech motor activity remain an important issue for future research.

While study of these patients who exemplify an extreme form of neurological deficit helps us to elucidate the development of normal oral sensation and perception, detection of this disorder pattern should help to account for some of the failures in speech therapy which have been directed toward motor function and auditory discrimination. Early identification of these subjects and their accumulation in study centers may result in the development of effective sensory-oriented therapy, including the use of prosthetic sensory facilitation devices.

We must conclude, in addition to its more obvious motor functions, the mouth and its associated parts may play a sensory role in the development and/or maintenance of speech articulation as do the ear and the auditory feedback system.

Bosma (1970) states that ". . . the appropriate way to evaluate human oral functions is by observing and manipulating the sensory stimuli which elicit and guide those functions (p. 553)." He anticipates that as insights and skills in sensory elicitation of oral performances accumulate, we should be able to distinguish primary stimuli from the sensory cues which cause secondary or derivative modulations of motions, and with appropriately designed experiments and tests, we may discern the genesis of the maturing functions of biting, chewing and speaking. Bosma speculates that, "The definition of oral functions by their sensory elicitations may apply only to the functions in the nascent state. When they are stabilized in mature pattern they may acquire a motor autonomy, like that which mature speech seems to possess. At that point, they may be little affected by variations in oral sensations (p. 553)."

As reported during the Second Symposium on Oral Sensation and Perception, many other clinical observations have been made and empirical studies seported since the first patients of the type exemplified by the case report of subject E were seen at NIH. A variety of measures of tongue, lip, buccal mucosa and palate sensation and perception have been developed. Some investigators have continued to use the original "NIH 20" sets of plastic, geometric forms. Others have modified these forms or created new devices and mechanisms through which they may gain additional information concerning the sensitivity and discriminability of the oral region. It now appears that while oral functions such as those required in suckle are mature in early infancy, the ability to orally perceive forms in the mouth improves with age. It also appears that otherwise normal children vary widely in their ability to respond to the currently used tests of oral stereognosis.

At this writing, we are not certain about the relationship between the processes involved in oral, visual and manual form recognition. Moreover, it would now appear that the tests which have been used to assess oral stereognosis are yielding scores which have low correlations with speech and language development. Thus far, however, most of the research has involved groups of subjects divided and compared with gross clinical tools. Undoubtedly, the sensory-motor nature of the oral and pharyngeal region becomes an even greater and more complex research problem when visual and manual modalities compounded with intelligence and experience are studied as a single variable.

The Prelinguistic Period

The prelinguistic period, which begins with the birth cry and continues to the first true speech, is also a time of most dramatic change in the life of the infant. But while the total physical and mental growth and development of the infant during this critical period can, to some degree, be related to the emergence of speech and language, the material which follows has been, in general, restricted to vocal and closely associated behavior of the young child.

The vocal behavior of an infant, particularly during the first few months of postnatal life, has been identified by Sheppard and Lane (1968) as a "matrix of later language development (p. 64) ." Therefore, the differentiation and organization of infant vocalization as a function of maturational and environmental factors are of considerable interest.

The growth and development of the child during the prelinguistic stage, including his vocal behavior, have been the subject of study by representatives of many different disciplines applying a variety of descriptive and research methodologies. Some have focused on the mental and physiological development of the whole child and have described in some detail, as a part of their studies, the prelinguistic development. For example, Gesell and Amatruda (1964), in their classic studies of the development of the neonate and infant, describe the "average" child as he develops "language" and other behavior. Beginning at four weeks, the Gesell norms anticipate the infant will smile, "heed a bell," and make throaty noises. Similarly, language-related behavior is described as it appeared in their sample of children to the end of the fortieth week when single word utterances such as "mama" appeared.

From such developmental scales as the Gesell, other authors have prepared topical designations for certain landmarks or stages of prelinguistic development. Thus Berry and Eisenson (1956) in their chapter entitled "The Normal Development of Speech" describe four stages of prelinguistic development which precede true speech. They indicate that the early cry sounds of the newborn are entirely *reflexive vocalizations*. Then, at about six or seven weeks of age the infant begins to evidence his awareness of his own acoustic production. It appears at this time that the child definitely enjoys producing sound and that he produces it for his own pleasure. This cooing and gurgling and general vocal play is called *babbling*. Carroll (1961) suggests the term babbling should be applied to the infant's vocalizations when the "cooing" of the first several months gradually develops into a much more phonetically diversified type of random utterances, with both vowels and consonants. Carroll has also stated that, "The particular sound-types uttered by the babbling child have little relevance for later learning, for the types appear in more or less random sequences which bear little relation to the sequence observed after true language learning starts (p. 337)."

Van Riper (1963) indicates that a good deal of this type of vocal play is carried on when the child is alone and it seems to disappear when someone interrupts him. The infant's verbal behavior at this time is also characterized by stimulus generalization. Many different stimuli will evoke a rather singular response. Because the infant cannot differentiate among incoming stimuli and because he cannot vocalize differentially, he responds to incoming stimuli in a rather gross manner (Boone, 1965).

There appears to be general agreement that deaf babies begin to babble at a normal time, but because they are unable to hear the sounds they produce, they apparently lose interest and hence produce much fewer babbling sounds than the hearing child. If the babbling period is interrupted for any other reason such as a prolonged illness or gross physical anomaly, there may be a developmental delay or serious defect of speech or language. Berry and Eisenson and others have stated that the infant's babbling appears to contain the sounds of many different languages. Indeed, there appears to be widespread agreement that infants from a variety of racial and linguistic backgrounds all babble alike. The implication of this statement is that babbling is preparation for the later stages of prelinguistic development.

At around the fifth or sixth month when the child is beginning to visually fixate and grab at attractive objects, the babbling seems to change from the more reflexive beginning to a stage that has been termed *lalling*. According to those who have provided such labels to the naturalistic observations of infants in this period, the great significance of lallation is that hearing and sound production have now become associated. Indeed, the child appears to be using vocalization to attract attention of others and expressing his interests and needs. As in the babbling stage, there appears, according to such descriptions, to be more vowel-like sounds than consonants in his babbling utterances.

Two prelinguistic vocal behaviors appear to emerge at nine or ten months: "inflected vocal play" and "echolalia." Both of these features of the child's utterances in this stage of his development are worthy of note. During "inflected play" the child's pitch begins to rise and fall in patterns similar to that of his parents' language and appears to take on the general characteristics of the inflection and rhythm of adult speech. The rising pitch patterns typical of questions (in English) or the downward inflection of commands are often heard.

The term echolalia refers to the vocal behavior of the infant when he appears to imitate the sounds that others make and particularly those sounds which he has made during the lalling stage. Some parents are likely to think that this echoing of their speech is an example of true speech and declare that Junior has learned to talk. Actually, there may not yet be evidence of a complete association of the word with a particular item or part of the environment to make it worthy of the diagnosis, true speech. Finally, following this sequence, true speech will on the average emerge at around 12 to 18 months of age (Travis, 1957; Learning to Talk, 1969).

The more recently developed Bayley Scales of Mental Development and a variety of similar types of studies of the infant's mental and cognitive development as well as specific acoustic events in his prelinguistic vocalization have served as the bases for a variety of apparent divisions of the first year of life, elements which precede speech and language. While there is universal acceptance of the importance of this period in the child's life, so far as speech and language development is concerned, unfortunately, much of the research has consisted of descriptions by a single observer who has transcribed the utterances of a single infant or relatively small numbers of infants and often without full regard for sampling procedures.

There appear to be several reasons why research on the infant's prelinguistic vocalization has been so difficult. Many years ago in discussing her study of 25 babies, Shirley (1933) commented, "The two great drawbacks to the study of speech in infants are the difficulty of stimulating vocal responses and the difficulty of recording them (p. 47)." More recently, Sheppard and Lane (1968) have discussed some of the difficulties in obtaining reliable transcriptions of infant sounds from observations in naturalistic settings. There continues to be a host of difficult methodological problems that must be solved in obtaining high quality recordings of an infant's utterances: placement of the microphone, duration of the recorded sample, and determination of the specific stimulus for the recorded utterance. There are also many problems associated with obtaining valid and reliable transcriptions of the nonlinguistic acoustic products of a child with an immature phonological, articulatory and resonant system.

Analysis of nonlinguistic sonic phenomena has been accomplished, however, for several physiological activities, e.g., cardiovascular, respiratory, cough, masticatory, and gastrointestinal activity. Logan, Kavanagh and Wornall (1967) have reported their procedure for studying the recorded acoustic characteristics of deglutition through an analysis of spectrograms. While visual examination and comparison of the general characteristics of spectrograms has proved a reasonable clinical tool, a standardized quantifying procedure for classifying spectrograms is still needed by researchers. With such procedures, spectrographic recordings could become extremely useful tools in the armamentarium of those wishing to study the prelinguistic utterances of infants.

Until quite recently, most descriptions of infant prelinguistic vocalization have been based on qualitative analysis. Recently, however, there have been several attempts to increase the quantitative precision in the evaluation of infant utterances. Ringwall, Reese and Markel (1965) have been studying the behavioral correlates of infant vocalization. These investigators are recording infant utterances beginning a few days after birth and continuing until the children reach their second birthday. A research goal is to measure the relationship between infant vocalizations as predictors of later psychological development.

In the initial report of their research project, these investigators noted that previous phonetic and spectrographic analyses of the vocal behavior of infants in their prelinguistic stage have been either inappropriate, inordinately time consuming or limited in the number of relevant variables that could be attained.

Ringwall, et al., state that the major difficulties of a phonetic transcription of prelinguistic infant vocalizations is that the nonlinguistic characteristics of these vocalizations such as the length of the utterance, the direction of the airstream and the force of the airstream are not identified. They noted that Bullowa, Jones and Bever (1964) independently came to the same conclusion regarding the use of phonetic transcriptions in their study of prelinguistic infant vocalization. Ringwall, et al., believe the major difficulties of using the sound spectrograph alone to study prelinguistic vocalizations are the limitation in the size of the sample which can be analyzed at any one time, the lack of reliable evidence for measuring acoustic variables other than frequency, intensity and duration, and the inability to convert the spectrogram of infant prelinguistic utterances into meaningful linguistic data, such as the adult sounds the infant is attempting to approximate. Ringwall, et al., have, therefore, applied a method of coding infant vocalization which has been developed from the "distinctive features" concept of Jakobson, Fant and Halle (1952). These eight distinctive features are 1) vocalization (sound vs. silence), 2) length of sound (short vs. long), 3) length of silence between vocalization (short vs. long), 4) direction of air stream (egressive vs. ingressive), 5) air passage (oral vs. nasal), 6) muscular tension (lax vs. tense), 7) force of air stream (soft vs. loud), and 8) vocal cord vibration (voiced vs. voiceless).

In their initial study, Ringwall, et al., applied this distinctive feature method to the analysis of vocalizations of 40 three-day-old infants. The investigators concluded from their initial study that the distinctive features analysis has produced data that will be meaningful to the study of the relationships between infant vocalization and later linguistic and psychological development. The results thus far, according to Ringwall, appear to indicate that a distinctive feature's analysis is reliable, that it yields normative data on the quality and frequency of infant vocalizations and that it provides measures of individual differences between infants. They have reported that the application of both the spectrograph and the distinctive feature analysis will probably yield the maximum amount of information concerning prelinguistic infant vocalization.

Another investigation which is attempting to increase quantitative precision in the evaluation of infant utterances has been reported by Sheppard and Lane (1968). Motivated by their belief that an extension of our knowledge of vocal development requires new techniques, Sheppard and Lane made complete and continuous recordings of all the vocalizations of two infants during the first five months of life, beginning with the birth cry and continuing uninterrupted as the children were moved into plexiglass "air-cribs" at home. The prosodic features of a systematically selected sample of vocalizations were analyzed by extracting three acoustic parameters: fundamental frequency, amplitude and duration during each of the 108 samples.

The investigators reported that an examination of the developmental changes over the first 108 samples which represented 140 consecutive days showed that the average fundamental frequency at birth was approximately 450 cps., that it decreased to 370 cps. by sample number 33 (approximately 45 days), and that it then rose and stabilized at about 450 cps. for the duration of the study. The duration of vocalization ranged from 100 msec. to 800 msec. over the 108 samples. The authors have speculated about the developmental trends their data appear to show. They suggest these changes may be the result of chance fluctuations, or the infant's progressive physiological development, or a greater fundamental frequency of crying responses than those of non-crying responses. They indicate that both behavioral and physiological changes may enter into the final account of these observed developmental trends. The Sheppard-Lane procedure offers promising procedures for the evaluation of prelinguistic vocalization.

The Onset and Development of True Speech and Language

As in most other stages of child development, it is difficult to delineate clear-cut stages in the development of language. Not only do children vary one from another and from themselves day by day but also, as Carroll (1961) has pointed out, the criteria commonly used in observing such stages are somewhat arbitrary and are selected from the adult's point of view. This is particularly true with regard to the appearance of the infant's first word. Carroll has indicated that while this event is usually heralded as the start of true language development, it may simply represent a moment in the child's development where the voco-motor control catches up with a previously developed ability for voluntary symbolic communication. Therefore, it seems that children begin to speak no sooner than when they reach a given stage of physical maturation and an auditor, usually a parent, is willing to make the decision that the infant has produced his first word.

In spite of the possibilities for variation due to individual differences both in speaker and in auditors, there appears to be general agreement that the child will produce his first words at 11 or 12 months after birth with subsequent speech development proceeding rather slowly through the next year. In one of the most complete studies of this aspect of language development Morley (1965) indicates that the peak period for the appearance of true speech in her sample was from 9 to 12 months. During this period 66 percent of the children from 1000 families in Morley's study produced their first single words as distinct from the utterances of babbling. The average age for the use of first words in this group was 12 months, with a range of 6 to 30 months.

According to Morley, 73 percent of the children were using at least one word to "express their wants" by the time of their first birthday. Seven percent of this group were said to have done so before the age of eight months, and two percent were late in beginning to speak and did not attempt to use words until they were over two years of age. It is interesting to note that the appearance of the first true word is reportedly often preceded by a temporary period of silence, or at least a diminution of infant utterances. Although this phenomenon has been observed many times, no adequate explanation has thus far been offered.

The first words spoken by the infant are usually monosyllables or repetitions of monosyllables such as ma, pa, ma-ma, pa-pa. It has frequently been suggested that these are the first words because they are initiated with bi-labial sounds which are closely associated with nursing movements and represent the more gross controls required for opening and closing the mouth (Jakobson, 1960, Ferguson, 1964). It would seem just as probable that the words "mama" and "papa" have the most social meaning for the parents who await the onset of speech with breathless anticipation. It is common practice for parents to accept a variety of articulated sounds within and somewhat beyond the phoneme boundaries as representing a morpheme even though they may be only near approximations of the adult's pronunciation of that word.

Thus, "ma" is quite acceptable for mother, "dah" for dog, etc. The overzealous parent who demands perfect articulation is likely to be frustrated and may, by her eagerness, delay the child's language development. Of most importance is the fact that the child has for the first time associated a conventional, although distorted, symbol that represents an object of that environment, and that he uses this symbol to communicate with another person. Much to the dismay of many parents, the onset of the first word may be followed by a period of apparent no language learning, a period that may last for several months. This is particularly true when the child is, at the same time, learning to walk and is more intrigued with the variety of new visual stimulations that his increased mobility has provided than he is with mere words.

If the onset of his first word was approximately 12 months, the average child will have added only nine additional words when he is 18 months old (Gesell, 1964). But after the development of walking and other locomotor skills, vocabulary usually increases so that by the end of the second year the child will have approximately 270 words (Boone, 1965). Thereafter, the vocabulary makes rapid growth, in parallel with all of his linguistic competence. In five years the child increases his spoken vocabulary from one word to approximately 2500 words (Wellman, 1931). Moreover, from about 12 to 18 months, until the child reaches his fourth or fifth birthday, he develops virtually a complete adult grammar. Such a feat has prompted research scientists in a variety of disciplines to theorize extensively about the infant's ability to learn speech and language.

THEORIES OF SPEECH AND LANGUAGE DEVELOPMENT

Theories arise whenever a problem is recognized and no obvious or factual answer is available. We are still in the theorizing stage of our knowledge regarding language acquisition because all of the facts do not point to a single explanation. Some of the facts regarding language and speech development should, however, be kept in mind as our research continues in an effort to explain this phenomenon. The following are just a small sample of the "truths" which serve to haunt us whenever we attempt to understand how these communicative skills develop.

It is generally accepted that there are about 45 phonemes in spoken English. The sounds (allophones) which represent these phonemes, like snowflakes, are never repeated exactly the same way twice. Yet the almost infinitely variable allophone (or phone) is generated by the normal speaker and received by the normal ear at the rate of 20 per second. Moreover, the time which lapses between the production and the receiving of this sound apparently plays a significant role in the differentiation and comprehensibility of spoken language. But, unlike written text, the temporal arrangement does not follow so-called word boundaries. There may be larger pauses within a word than between words. Those scientists and engineers who have attempted to design computers capable of comprehending human speech indicate this is one of their most difficult problems and their chief reasons for failure. Even when pauses of substantial duration are provided between words, "listening machines" have great difficulty identifying particular groups of phonemes as morphemes (words). Thus far, it has been virtually impossible for them to recognize sequences of these words as meaningful sentences. Most young children experience no major difficulty with this task.

Another observation about language which must be accepted as fact and thus a part of the base for any acceptable theory about language development is the child's ability to obtain meaning from new sentences which have never been heard before. Unlike the computer that must be "taught" everything it gives back, the human not only can understand new sentences, but indeed apparently prefers them to cliches. In contrast, computers, even the most sophisticated, can only cope with the cliches (Davy, 1969). The human infant, on the other hand, easily recognizes the difference between language-like sequences of words, and non-language-like word sequences. And in spite of this apparently impossible teaching-learning situation, the child acquires the language of his environment in less than four years.

This phenomenal growth and development of child language has prompted a variety of speculations and theories from a variety of disciplines. Some have indicated that the acquisition of language by the child, though dependent upon maturation of the total organism, is essentially a learning process occurring with an interpersonal matrix of "mutual limitation" and "mutual feedback" between adult and child (Wyatt, 1965). It would then follow, as Wyatt suggests, that the optimum condition for successful language learning in early childhood is a continuous, undisrupted, and affectionate relationship between mother and child, demonstrated by frequent and appropriate communication between them, both non-verbal and verbal in nature. Such communication is appropriate for the child if the mother takes her cues from the child's behavior and verbalizations, and provides the child with a "corrective feedback." Similarly, Muriel Morley (1965) believes that the development of speech is not, as was once thought, an "instinctive process." She declares that, while it is dependent on neurological development, it is the result of imitation. But the imitation may be the result of an inborn urge of the child to be like those around him. The child develops the use of certain muscle groups during the gradual process of mental and neuro-muscular maturation for the imitation and use of the sounds of speech he hears around him in much the same way he learns to walk.

While no one would deny the importance of the mother-child relationship and the mutual feedback between the adult model and the child learner, some researchers have abandoned their earlier opinions regarding the type of learning involved in language acquisition. Eric Lenneberg (1964, 1969) has raised the question of whether there might be biological endowments in man which make human speech and language uniquely possible for our species. He stated that language is not acquired by imitation alone but, rather, "the child abstracts regularities or relations from the language he hears, which he then applies to building up language for himself as an apparatus of principles (1969, p. 638)." Children begin to speak no sooner and no later than when they reach a given state of physical maturation. While, on the average, children are likely to produce their first intelligent word shortly after their first birthday, Lenneberg suggests that speech and language development appear to correlate better with physical growth and the development of motor coordination than it does with the child's chronological age. To illustrate this point, he describes a number of observations of physically mature, mentally retarded children whose onset time for speech was similar to those children whose intellectual development was normal. Likewise children whose physical maturation was retarded also showed evidence of retarded speech development.

Other observers agree that children acquire language so readily that there must be some innate predisposition for this kind of learning, and that this, in turn, can only mean that evolution has prepared mankind in some very special way, for this unique human accomplishment. These persons are not necessarily convinced, however, of a "physiological" difference.

Some modern linguists have theorized the child is able to acquire language so efficiently because he can relate what he hears to his unconscious knowledge of the "deep structure" of all languages. This theory is not inconsistent with the fact that infants can learn any spoken language from Abyssinian to Zuni as their first language. This theory also helps to account for the often observed fact that children acquire the ability to speak a language in spite of linguistically barren home environments and a variety of physical and intellectual deficits. This is not to say that either the child's physiological condition or certain environmental conditions cannot or do not play a role in its speech and language development. It simply suggests that these are not the only factors which affect the growth of the child's language ability.

Of particular significance to this research problem area is the work of Noam Chomsky and the other linguists and psycholinguists at the Massachusetts Institute of Technology. In 1957, Chomsky published his now famous *Syntactic Structures,* a small book which has been described as a major breakthrough in the theoretical approaches previously taken by psychologists and linguists to explain language behavior. The book appears to have "sent shock waves among students of language and psychology and has generated a now rapidly rising tide of research and discussion (Davy, 1969, p. B4)."

Chomsky prompted many scholars to notice and re-examine older ideas concerning the ability of children to acquire language. As a result of

Chomsky's work, his colleagues have concluded the child's ability is much more extraordinary a phenomenon than had been apparently recognized previously. These investigators were once again drawn to the notion that language appeared to be unique to man, and that studying this ability would provide new insights into the mental capacity and development of children. Of even greater importance, they felt there was new evidence which might call for a re-examination and further exploration of brain function itself.

While many psychologists and linguists do not agree with Chomsky's theories, they would with one accord agree that he has made a considerable impact on the psycholinguistic research community. Chomsky has introduced two theoretical concepts which are the bases for considerable psycholinguistic research today: very young children are able to acquire (a) the rules of language grammar and (b) the rules for transforming the deep structure (underlying meaning) of the language to the surface structure (the spoken words). The following "sentences" have been created to demonstrate an individual's ability to recognize the grammar rules of his native language. Chomsky would ask the reader to compare "colorless green ideas sleep furiously" and "furiously sleep ideas green colorless." While it is not likely that the reader has encountered either of the two sequences of words, he is able to judge the first sentence as an English language-like sentence sequence, and the second as just randomly presented words. Thus, according to Chomsky and certain other psycholinguists, the human acquires, during the second and third years of life without being formally taught, the rules which govern the grammar of the language he will speak.

Chomsky also provides sentences which illustrate his theory of the "surface structure" and "deep structure" of language. On the surface, the sentences, "John is easy to please" and "John is eager to please" appear to have the same structure. We are aware, however, that John is the object of the first sentence and the subject in the second one, i.e., the deep structure is different. Many examples have also been provided to illustrate that sentences can have different surface structure but have the same meaning. A popular M.I.T. example is "John ate the orange" and "The orange was eaten by John." We know that the "deep structure" of these two sentences is the same, even though the "surface structure" has been altered. Thus, we know "the rule of grammar" which is not apparent on the surface, and we also "know" rules for transforming different kinds of deep structure. This ability makes it possible for us to produce and understand the very wide variety of sentences which we have not produced or heard before. Thus, Chomsky and his associates are sometimes referred to as "transformational grammarians."

There is a great deal of interest and some research now under way to explore the many possible ramifications of this set of hypotheses. For example, one might suggest that the differences between various foreign languages reside in the surface structure while the deep structure remains essentially the same. Perhaps all languages have the same deep structure, i.e. a universal grammar, and the differences between languages could be stated in terms of written rules which would transform the universal deep structure into an assortment of surface structures. Obviously, much more research in this area is required.

RESEARCH FINDINGS

Prompted by these theories, there have been several important studies of children's language made through an analysis of recordings of their speech and language in naturalistic and structured settings (Weir, 1962; Brown, Fraser, Bellugi, 1964). From such studies, psycholinguists have concluded that young children indeed "generate" their own grammar to form their own language and apparently do not just produce carbon copies of adult speech. Thus, while many parents continue to diagnose the speech and language of the two and three year old child as babyish or immature, it may be more appropriate to identify it only as reasonably different as a result of the child applying a rule to the surface structure of the language which in a particular instance is not in common usage. For example, a two year old might say "me did go" for "I went."

Evidence is now available that the two-word sentences produced by young children during their second year of life are not composed of randomly selected words from the adult's vocabulary. Nor are these words necessarily the words which have been stressed in the child's presence or presented in the order that the child uses them. Of course, this does not mean that children completely ignore the speech of adults. Their speech efforts are affected by adult speech, but their "copy" is significantly altered. It is not a perfect reflection of the adult pattern.

Brown et al. (1964) analyzed the relationship between the speech of the child and the adult. She found that when the child "imitates" an adult speaker, he reduces the length of the adult utterance, but tends to preserve the word order. Apparently, if a child has been producing two-word sentences spontaneously, then his response to adult speech, which is composed of longer sentences, will continue to be about the same, i.e., two words. The child tends to reduce the length of the adult utterance by dropping out the nonessential words and retaining the words that communicate the central idea. In this regard, the child's speech sounds much like the abbreviated notes one might take at a lecture.

Of particular interest is the composition and arrangement of these two and three-word sentences. It would appear according to Brown

(1964) and others that children store their vocabulary in two mental lists or files, a large one and a smaller one. The child assembles word strings (they may not be sentences in the formal sense of the word) by selecting a morpheme (word) from one file and then selecting a second word from the other list. While each child will have a different set of words, a particular child will be highly consistent in his own language strings. Thus, it appears there is research evidence that young children have acquired rules which govern their selection of words to be learned, and used.

The child is not, however, bound by these rules. Slobin (1965) has described the changes in the child's speech which his parents can effect during this stage of language development. In this study, when the parent lengthened the sentence used by the child, in about one half of the instances the child expanded his utterance. Thus, he concluded that his studies provide evidence that children "imitate" and that such an expansion procedure could be used to help children learn the language of adults. It also appears that the adult's speech, which presumably serves as the model, may be affected by the child's vocal behavior. There is currently under way, at Johns Hopkins University, (Phillips) a graduate research study of the speech directed towards children by their mothers. This project appears to indicate that mothers significantly alter and broaden their inflectional excursions when they direct their speech toward a child who responds vocally to that speech.

One of the several research topics which have been a subject of serious debate in the last several years is the effect of the environment on the acquisition and development of speech and language. Some authorities believe there is strong evidence to support the general notion that the child's early linguistic environment is the most important factor affecting the rate of language development (Carroll, 1961), while others believe maturation is more important. Templin (1957) has reported that language development is faster in upper socioeconomic groups than in lower groups and concludes the environment is the most important factor affecting this development.

Indeed, a wide variety of child rearing practices seem to be related to language development and language disorders in childhood. There is, for example, ample evidence that orphans living in residential schools develop language more slowly than children living in non-institutional environments. And all would agree that the model or example of speech and language which is provided for the young child, whether it be for a "surface structure" or "deep structure" learning, will be provided by the adults (or siblings) in the child's immediate environment and those models will to some degree affect the child's language.

An extreme example of environmental effect on language development is reported by Powell, et al. (1967), as a syndrome of psychosocial dwarfism. Such children are shy, introvertive, solitary and extremely retarded in their speech development. They also tend to overeat, and throw violent temper tantrums. Investigators at Johns Hopkins University have seen such children who have been inappropriately diagnosed "hypopituitary dwarfs" because they were inordinately small for their age. When these children were taken from their homes and placed in different environments, however, their apparent endocrine dysfunction disappeared and they grew from five to ten inches in a single year. Furthermore, their speech and language growth was considerable. When these children were returned to their homes, they immediately stopped growing in stature and language. Powell has indicated that this retardation of growth is apparently related to the child's lack of parental love and attention rather than a specific physiological dysfunction.

On the other hand, Lenneberg (1969) has argued that it is not particularly surprising that language deficits will occur in children who have a hearing loss or that children will have deficient language if they can hear only the discourse of uneducated persons. What interests Lenneberg and many others is the child's underlying capacity for language. He has observed that normal hearing children of deaf parents eventually learned not one but two languages and two sound systems, those of their deaf parents as well as those of the rest of the community. Lenneberg concludes that impoverished environments are not conducive to good language development, but good language development is not contingent on specific training measures. Further research is needed to determine the relative importance and inter-relationships between the child's physical maturation and social environment in his language development.

This portion of the Chapter would not be complete without a comment or two about the attitude toward communication that is frequently transmitted by the parent to the child at an early age. Undoubtedly, even this attitude is partly affected by the child's innate ability or early successes in the acquisition of language. Yet the parent who requests or demands articulatory excellence or grammatical or syntactical perfection of a child who is just beginning to learn the rules and patterns of his language may be seriously delayed or may develop feelings of self doubt and impotence regarding his skill in oral speech. Indeed, such attitudes may remain with him throughout his life. While the mysterious phenomena of stuttering is well beyond the scope of this chapter, there is some evidence that perfectionistic parents who require "good" speech of their young child may in some instances teach their children to be concerned about and try to avoid inevitable "errors."

It is also beyond the scope of this Chapter to discuss at any length or depth the nature of and the causes for the development of so called "effeminate" speech in the male or masculine speech patterns in the female. Much research must be continued to fully elucidate the development of sexual identity. It would appear, however, that these speech problems are closely associated with general personality development. It must be noted, however, that effeminate speech patterns in young boys are quite distinguishable from the speech of girls of comparable age. In other words, "effeminate" is not an appropriate label for such differences in tonal pattern and emphasis.

It seems appropriate to conclude this Chapter with a few remarks about bilingualism, and the effect of a bilingual environment upon the development of speech and linguistic competence in the young child. It is obvious that true bilingual experience would require the child to acquire with equal force two different phonemic codes, including the suprasegmental features such as inflectional patterns, and two sets of morphemes. Under such conditions the child would also be required to learn the rules of each language which control the distribution of these elements.

Most often, however, particularly in the United States, the child is reared in a cultural environment in which one of the languages predominates and, as such, is the primary language (Kinzel, 1964). The secondary language then seems to interfere with the development of the primary language, although the interference is actually reciprocal. The child appears to have misapplied the recently acquired phonological system and linguistic rules and temporarily to have fulfilled the functions of the primary language with the elements of the secondary.

Language clinicians have frequently reported examples of delayed language and of dialect problems of the bilingual child. Less has been reported concerning the language learning conditions under which a bilingual experience does not interfere with phonological or linguistic development. Nor has there been much study of the benefits of such experience during the first years of life, i.e., the critical period for learning language, on the overall cognitive and intellectual growth and development of the child.

It would appear that much valuable information concerning the language learning and general cognitive processes in children would be gained through more comprehensively controlled experiments in which the quantity and content of two (or more) different languages are systematically provided to the child's environment.

SUMMARY OF RESEARCH NEEDS

Throughout this Chapter frequent reference has been made to the need for further research into the several aspects of language acquisition and development in children and into the variety of biological and environmental conditions which may adversely affect this important human process. While the list of questions which follows will serve to draw together these recommendations for further investigation as well as summarize the principal areas of the genesis and pathogenesis of speech and language contained in this Chapter, it is by no means an all inclusive list of possible research questions.

1. Can a theory of the origin of speech in man be developed that can be scientifically tested? Would such a theory help us to understand the acquisition and development of speech and language in the infant?

2. What is the relationship between the size, capacity and function of the brain of nonhumans and the brain function of infants during the emergence of spoken language?

3. Is man biologically predisposed to language?

4. What aspects of prenatal life may affect speech and language development?

5. What is the relationship between prenatal development of such complex neuro-muscular acts as sucking with subsequent speech and language performance?

6. What is the relationship between the cry of the neonate and his later speech production?

7. Can a more reliable and practical clinical procedure for determining the auditory acuity of the neonate be devised?

8. What is the relationship between the infant's auditory acuity and his acquisition and development of speech and language?

9. What are the relationships and interdependencies of acoustic and oral sensory feedback in the acquisition and development of speech?

10. Can more valid and reliable procedures be devised to record and analyze the prelinguistic utterances of infants?

11. What is the significance of the silent period which often precedes the first true speech?

12. Why is it more difficult to build a "listening" machine than one which can "read?" Why can most children learn to perceive aural language easier than visual language?

13. What is the relationship between the child's early linguistic environment, his motivation and the development of speech and language?

14. What new insights might be gained regarding a child's language and cognitive development from a rigidly controlled study of bilingual experience?

"In a very important sense one of the most critical needs for further research concerning pathologies of the speech production system is for more comprehensive understanding of the normal speech producing mechanism. It is an obvious, but sometimes overlooked, fact that information concerning pathological conditions and their effects can only be interpreted and understood by appropriate comparison to data concerning the normal system—there are numerous gaps in our understanding of the normal speech production processes (Human Communication and Its Disorders, 1969, p. 164) ."

Furthermore, while there are many unresolved problems concerning speech and language which will require studies of older children and adults, we believe that the early childhood years are particularly important for future research. This appears true not only because they are, as has been stated in this Chapter, critical to later growth and development of the child, but also because the early, preschool years have been relatively neglected by researchers.

It is noteworthy that during the fiscal year of 1969 the Federal agencies primarily concerned with support of research with children's speech and language expended less than two percent of their extramural funds on projects related to the acquisition of first language.

Agency	No. of Projects	FY 1969 Funds	Percent of Total Extramural Funds
Natl. Inst. Child			
Health & Human Dev.	17	$646,000	1.7
Office of Education	11	330,000	1.5
Natl. Science Foundation*	9	442,000	1.0
Natl. Inst. Neurol.			
Diseases & Stroke	7	379,000	0.8
Natl. Inst. Mental Health	2	47,000	0.06
Children's Bureau	——	——	——

* NSF awards are for two years, so these funds are for FY 68 and FY 69 combined.

The relatively small amount of research supported during this period reflects in a large part the reluctance of the scientific community to request support to conduct research in this area. As the importance of the area is more fully appreciated and methodological problems are solved, it is to be hoped that an increased amount of research will be extended into the early and perhaps the most important years of life.

REFERENCES

1. Berry, M. F., Eisenson, J. *Speech Disorders, Principles and Practices of Therapy*, Appleton-Century-Crofts, Inc., New York, 1956.
1a. Boone, D. R. Infant Speech and Language Development, Report No. 839, The Alexander Graham Bell Association for the Deaf, Inc., 1965.
2. Bortoshuk, A. K. Human Neonatal Cardiac Response to Sound: A Power Function, *Psychon. Science*, 1:151-2, 1964.
3. Bosma, J. (Ed.) Second Symposium on Oral Sensation and Perception, C. C. Thomas: Springfield, 1970.
4. Bosma, J., Grossman, R., Kavanagh, J. Impairment of Somesthetic Perception and Motor Function in the Oral and Pharyngeal Area, *Neurology*, 17:7, July, 1967a.

5. Bosma, J., Grossman, R., Kavanagh, J. Chapter 18—A Syndrome of Impairment of Oral Perception: Symposium on Oral Sensation and Perception. C. C. Thomas: Springfield, 1967b.
6. Bridges, W. H. W. H. Bridges Sensory Discrimination and Autonomic Function in the Newborn, *J. Amer. Acad. Child Psychiat.*, 67-82, 1962.
7. Brown, R., Fraser, C., Bellugi, U. Explanations in Grammar Evolution: Acquisition of Language, *Soc. for Res. in Child Develop.*, 1964.
8. Bullowa, M., Jones, L. G., Bever, T. G. The Development from Vocal to Verbal Behavior in Children: Acquisition of Language, Monog. for the Soc. for Research in Child Devel., Bellugi, U., Brown, R. (Eds.) Society for Res. in Child Devel., 1964.
9. Carmichael, L. The Early Growth of Language Capacity in the Individual: New Directions in the Study of Language, E. Lenneberg (Ed.) Cambridge: The M.I.T. Press, 1964.
10. Carmichael, L. Manual of Child's Psychology. 2nd Edition, 505, New York: Wiley, 1954.
11. Carroll, J. B. Language Development in Children: Psycholinguistics, S. Saporta (Ed.), Holt, Rinehart and Winston, New York, 1961.
12. Carroll, J. B. The Study of Language, Cambridge: Harvard University Press, 1953.
13. Chomsky, N. Syntactic Structures. The Hague: Morton, 1957.
14. Cullen, J. K., Fargo, N., Chase, R. A., Baker, P. The Development of Auditory Feedback Monitoring: I. Delayed Auditory Feedback Studies on Infant Cry, *J. Speech and Hearing Res.* 11:1, March 1968.
15. Davy, J. Using Language as an Avenue into the Mind. *The London Observer*, Aug. 1969.
16. de Laguna, G. A. Speech: Its Function and Development. Bloomington: University Press, 1963. (First published in 1927)
17. Eisenberg, R. B. Stimulus Significance as a Determinant of Newborn Responses to Sound. Paper read at Society for Research in Child Development, New York, 1967.
18. Eisenberg, R. B. Auditory Behavior in the Human Neonate: Functional Properties of Sound and Their Ontogenetic Implications. *International Audiology*, Vol. VIII, No. 1, pp. 34-45, Feb. 1969.
19. Fairbanks, G. An Acoustical Study of the Pitch of Infant Hunger Wails. *Child Devel.* 13:227-232, 1942.
20. Fantz, R., Nevis, S. The Predictive Value of Changes in Visual Preferences in Early Infancy: Exceptional Infant, Vol. 1, The Normal Infant. Brunner/Mazel, Inc., New York, 1967.
21. Ferguson, C. A. Baby Talk in Six Languages. *American Anthropologist*, Vol. 66, No. 6, Part 2, pp. 103-114, Dec. 1964.
22. Fisher, M. S. Language Patterns of Preschool Children. *Child Devel. Monograph* No. 15, 1934.
22a. Froeschls, E. *Psychological Elements in Speech*, Boston Expression Co., Boston, 1932.
23. Fulton, R. T., Lloyd, L. L. Audiometry for the Retarded. Baltimore: The Williams & Wilkins Co., 1969.
24. Geschwind, N. Disconnection Syndromes in Animals and Man. *Brain*, 88:237-294, 1965.
25. Gesell, A., Amatruda, C. S. Developmental Diagnosis. Paul B. Hoeber Med. Div. of Harper & Row, 1964.
26. Goetzinger, C. P. Effects of Small Perceptual Losses on Language and on Speech Discrimination. *Volta Rev.* 64:68, 1965.
26a. Goodhill, V. Deafness research: Where are we? *Volta Review*, Vol. 70, No. 8: 620-629, 1968.
27. Golumba, E. L., Shulejkina, K. V., Vainstein, I. I. The Development of Reflex and Spontaneous Activity of the Human Foetus During Embryogenesis. *Obstet. & Gynecol.* (USSR) 3:59-62, 1959.

28. HOIJER, H. The Problem of Primitive Language: in Carterette, E.C. (Ed.) Brain Function, Vol. III, Speech, Language and Communication, UCLA Forum, *Med. Sci.,* No. 4, Los Angeles: Univ. of California Press, 1966.

29. HOLM, V., KUNZE, L. Effect of Chronic Otitis Media on Language and Speech Development. *Pediatrics,* 43:5, May 1969.

30. HUMPHREY, T. The Development of Mouth Opening and Related Reflexes Involving the Oral Area of Human Foetuses. *Alabama J. Med. Sci.,* 5:2, April 1968.

31. Human Communication and Its Disorders—an Overview and Report of the Subcommittee on Human Communication and Its Disorders, National Advisory Neurological Diseases and Stroke Council, National Institute of Neurological Diseases and Stroke. *Nat. Inst. of Health, P.H.S., H.E.W.,* 1969.

32. IRWIN, O. C. Phonetical Description of Speech Development in Childhood: In L. Kaisen (Ed.) *Manual of Phonetics,* North Holland Publ., Amsterdam, 403-4 25, 1957.

33. JAKOBSON, R. Why Mama and Papa? in B. Kaplan and S. Wopner (Eds.) *Perspectives in Psychological Theory,* 124-134, New York, 1960.

34. JAKOBSON, R., FANT, C. G. M., HALLE, M. Preliminaries to Speech Analysis, M.I.T. Press, Cambridge, Mass. 1952.

35. JESPERSON, O. Language: Its Nature, Development and Origin, W. W. Norton & Company, Inc., New York, 1964. (written in 1921)

36. JONES, M. C. An Investigation of Certain Acoustic Parameters of the Crying Vocalization of Young Deaf Children, Univ. Microfilms, Ann Arbor, Mich. 1965.

37. KAVANAGH, J. F., BOSMA, J. F., GROSSMAN, R. C. Disabilities of Mature Feeding and Speech Associated with Defects of Oral Sensation and Perception. Presented at the 45th Annual Meeting of the International Association for Dental Research, Washington Hilton Hotel, Washington, D.C., March 16-19, 1967.

38. KAVANAGH, J. F., BOSMA, J. F., GROSSMAN, R. C. Troubles de L'Alimentation et de la Parole Associés à des Defectuosités de la Sensation et de la Perception Buccales, *Médecine et Hygiene,* Genève, Février, 1968.

39. KAYE, H. The Effects of Feeding and Tonal Stimulation on Nonnutritive Sucking in a Human Newborn, *J. Exper. Child Psych.,* 3:131-134, 1966.

40. KINZEL, P.F. Lexical and Grammatical Interference in the Speech of a Bilingual Child, Vol. 1, Univ. of Washington, Seattle, 1964.

41. LANCASTER, J. B. The Biology of Language, paper presented to the Am. Anthropol. Assoc. meeting, Nov. 1966.

42. Learning to Talk. Speech, Hearing and Language Problems in the Preschool Child. U.S. Dept. of HEW, Public Health Service, N.I.H., 1969.

43. LENNEBERG, E. H. On Explaining Language, *Science,* May 9, Vol. 164, pp. 635-643, 1969.

44. LENNEBERG, E. H. A Biological Perspective of Language. New Directions in the Study of Language. Lenneberg (Ed.) M.I.T. Press, Cambridge, Mass. 1964.

45. LEWIS, M. M. Language, Thought and Personality in Infancy and Childhood, Basic Books, Inc., New York, 1963.

46. LEWIS, M. M. Infant Speech: A Study of the Beginnings of Language, Humanities Press, New York, 1951. (2nd Revised Edition).

47. LIBERMAN, P., HARRIS, K., WOLFF, P., RUSSELL, L. H. Newborn Infant Cry and Non-Human-Primate Vocalization, Speech Research, Haskins Laboratories, New York, 1969. SR-17/18.

48. LIEBERMAN, P. H. Primate Vocalization and Human Linguistic Ability, *J. Acoust. Soc. Amer.,* 44, 1575, 1968.

49. LIEBERMAN, P. H., KLATT, D. H., WILSON, W. Vocal Repertoires of Rhesus Monkey and Other Non-Human Primates, *Science,* 164:1185-1187, June 6, 1969.

50. LIND, J. (Ed.) Newborn Infant Cry, Uppsala, Almquist & Wiksells, 1965.

51. LLOYD, L. L., SPRODLIN, J. E., REID, M. J. An Operant Audiometric Procedure for Difficult-to-Test Patients, *J. Speech and Hearing Disorders,* Vol. 33, #3, 236-245, Aug. 1968.

52. LOGAN, W. J., KAVANAGH, J. F., WORNALL, A. W. Sonic Correlates of Human Deglutition, *J. Applied Physiol.,* Vol. 23, No. 2, Aug. 1967.

53. Luria, A. R., Yudovich, F. Speech and the Development of Mental Processes in the Child, Staples Press, London, 1966.
54. MacIntosh & Halliday, Patterns of Language, Longman's Green & Co., Ltd., London, 1967.
54a. Mandel, M. I. Infant responses to recorded sounds, *J. Speech and Hearing Res.,* Vol. 11, No. 4:811-816, Dec., 1968.
55. McCarthy, D. Organismic Interpretation of Infant Vocalizations, Child Development, Vol. 23, No. 4, Dec. 1952.
56. Morley, M. E. The Development and Disorders of Speech in Childhood, The Williams and Wilkins Co., Baltimore, 1965.
57. Pei, M. Glossary of Linguistic Terminology, Columbia Univ. Press, New York, 1966.
58. Phillips, J. Personal communication to the author from Malcolm S. Preston, the Johns Hopkins University, February 1970.
59. Powell, G. F., Brasel, J. A., Blizzard, R. M. Emotional Deprivation and Growth Retardation Simulating Idiopathic Hypopituitarism: Part I, Clinical Evaluation of the Syndrome, Vol. 276, *The New England J. Med.,* 23:1271-1278, June 8, 1967.
60. Powell, G. F., Brasel, J. A., Raiti, S., Blizzard, R. M. Emotional Deprivation and Growth Retardation Simulating Idiopathic Hypopituitarism: Part II, Endocrinologic Evaluation of the Syndrome, *The New England J. Med.* Vol. 276, 23:1279-1283, June 8, 1967.
61. Prechtl, H., Beintema, D. The Neurological Examination of the Full Term Newborn Infant, William Heineman, Medical Books, Ltd., London, 1964.
62. Ringwall, E. A., Reese, H. W., Markel, N. N. A Descriptive Features Analysis of Pre-linguistic Infant Vocalization. *The Development of Language Functions,* Klaus F. Riegel (Ed.). Report No. 8, Nov. 1965.
63. Robins, R. H. General Linguistics, an Introductory Survey, Indiana Univ. Press, Bloomington, Indiana. 1964.
64. Sapir, E. Language, Harcourt, Brace & World, Inc., New York, 1921.
65. Sheppard, W. C., Lane, H. L. Development of the Prosodic Features of Infant Vocalization. *J. Speech and Hearing Res.,* Vol. II, No. 1:94-108, March 1968.
66. Shirley, M. M. Chapter IV, The Beginnings of Speech: Intellectual Development: The first Two Years of Life, Vol. II, The Univ. of Minnesota Press, Minnesota, 1933.
66a. Shulejkina, K. V., Vainstein, I. I., Golubema, E. L. The Development of reflex and spontaneous activity of the human fetus during embryogenesis. *Obstet. & Gynecol.* (U.S.S.R.) Vol. 3: pp. 59-62, 1959.
67. Slobin, D. I. The Role of Initiation in Early Language Learning: A paper presented to the Society for Research in Child Development, 1965.
68. Sontag, L. Implications of Fetal Behavior and Environment for Adult Personality, *Annals of New York Academy of Sciences,* 134:782-6, Feb. 1966.
69. Stechler, G., Carpenter, G. A Viewpoint on Early Affective Development, *Exceptional Infant, Vol. 1, The Normal Infant,* Brunner/Mazel, Inc., New York, 1967.
69a. Stern, W. *Psychology of Early Childhood,* H. Holt and Company, New York, 1924.
70. Templin, M. C. Certain Language Skills in Children, The Univ. of Minn. Press, Minneapolis, 1957.
70a. Travis, L. E. (Ed.) *Handbook of Speech Pathology,* Appleton-Century-Crofts, Inc., New York, 1957.
70b. Van Riper, C. Speech Correction: *Principles and Methods* (rev. ed.), Prentice-Hall, Inc., Englewood Cliffs, N. J., 1963.
71. Weir, R. Language in the Crib, Mouton and Co., 1962.
72. Wellman, B. L., Case, I. M., Mengert, I. G., Bradbury, D. E. Speech Sounds of Young Children, Univ. of Iowa Studies in Child Welfare, Univ. of Iowa, 1931.
73. West, R., Ansberry, M., Carr, A. The Rehabilitation of Speech (Third Edition), be secured from the author.

74. WINITZ, H. The Development of Speech and Language in the Normal Child, *Speech Pathology,* (eds.) Rieber, R. W. and Brubaker, R. S., North Holland Publishing Co., 3:44, Amsterdam, 1969.
75. WOOD, N. E. Delayed Speech and Language Development, Foundations of Speech Pathology Series, Prentice-Hall, Inc., Englewood Cliffs, N. J., 1964.
76. WYATT, G. L. Speech and Language Disorders in Pre-school Children: a Preventive Approach, *Pediatrics,* 36:4, Oct. 1965.

11

LISTENING, LANGUAGE, AND THE AUDITORY ENVIRONMENT:

Automated Evaluation and Intervention

Bernard Z. Friedlander, Ph.D.

Professor, Department of Psychology, University of Hartford (Conn.)

Practical problems, if they are good ones, have a way of generating general questions that extend beyond the immediate issues from which they arise. We recently set out to investigate some clinical problems of language listening in hearing-impaired infants and young children. Our goal was to develop improved ways to evaluate and enrich the subjective language experience of very young children with moderate and severe hearing losses and receptive language disabilities. We are quite sure that the more we can learn about evaluating and expanding these children's receptive language skills the easier it will be to help them progress in the improvement of their speech and general language competence. Before we had gone very far we found ourselves deeply embedded in some very provocative and paradoxical observations about children's listening and their adaptation to their natural environment. In this presentation I will deal mainly with the practical aspects of these problems, but I think there are a number of important theoretical issues lying very close to the surface of the phenomena I will discuss.

Preparation of this report was supported in part by Grant C-278 from the Maternal and Child Health Service, Health Services and Mental Health Administration, U.S.-P.H.S., Department of Health, Education, and Welfare. I wish to acknowledge the valuable assistance of Antoinette Cyrulik, Barbara Bergman Davis, Carol Harris, Robert Putzer, Thomas Schuyler, and Sara Wisdom.

Portions of the text were presented in a symposium paper entitled, "Identifying and Investigating Major Variables of Receptive Language Development," at the 1969 meeting of the Society for Research in Child Development, Santa Monica, California. Some of the concepts of receptive language development referred to in this article are dealt with at substantially greater length in the paper, "Receptive Language Development in Infancy: Issues and Problems," presented at the 1969 Merrill-Palmer Conference on Infant Development, and published in the *Merrill-Palmer Quarterly*, 1970, vol. 16, no. 1.

Clinical and research needs

Three major generalizations set the framework within which new studies of receptive language development in very young children gain their importance: the *impact* of receptive language handicaps on other growth functions; the *incidence* of receptive handicaps; and the *cumulative* nature of receptive handicaps in early experience.

Little that is new can be said about the severity and impact of receptive language disabilities on other aspects of growth, except possibly to paint the picture with a darker brush. Specialists in different disciplines may quibble as to which type of disability is more catastrophic for a child to endure. But there can be no question that any inhibition in the growth of language strikes very close to the central path of mental development. This is so largely because of the critical role of speech and language in the growth of higher level intelligence and adaptive competence. It is difficult to overestimate the seriousness of the barriers to language learning when a child cannot effectively hear and organize the sounds of speech. Also, the child who is cut off from effective language communication with parents, siblings, and peers is vulnerable to secondary disorders of socialization and emotional development, in addition to the obvious disruptions in the cognitive sphere. But even in the absence of secondary complications, impaired hearing and/or associated language input disabilities at any stage of infancy and early childhood put severe limitations on most children's opportunities for the kinds of school-oriented development now virtually essential for achieving independence and self-fulfillment as an adult.

With respect to incidence, language disabilities in which receptive dysfunctions cannot properly be ruled out are probably far more prevalent than is generally recognized. Deafness and gross hearing impairments are the disabilities that gain the most attention, but they may be only the tip of a much larger iceberg. Provocative statistics can be found in the records of public school systems with aggressive programs for case-finding and special services. (Direct population information on language-related disorders in infancy and early childhood is extremely difficult to collect and assess, because extensive, serious concern with these age levels is largely a development of only the last decade.)

For example, in 1968-69 the Special Education Section of the Madison, Wisconsin, public schools provided services for 2,436 children, out of a total school population of 33,000. Of the total cases in all services, 1,335 (about 55%) received special services for speech and language therapy, language disabilities, and for hearing impairments. In other words, *more than half* of the total caseload (which includes the "big name" disabilities such as mental retardation, emotional disturbance, and physical handicap) involved substantial language dysfunction.

Further complicating the situation is the fact that of the 1,335 children who required language services *fewer than 10% had problems of deafness and hearing impairment,* and a negligible number required merely supportive therapy for superficial disorders of articulation (Gruenwald, 1970) . The largest proportion of these children suffered relatively poorly defined disorders of communication in which receptive and expressive language processes were almost inextricably bound together, and they were loosely labelled as being delayed or disordered in their patterns of development and function.

(This number of approximately 1,200 children out of a total school population of 33,000 is probably a non-typical *underestimation* of the prevalence of language disorders with receptive involvement in the general population. This is so for several reasons. The number does not include children with reading disabilities as the primary presenting complaint by which the school system categorizes its cases. It is highly probable that a significant proportion of the children requiring remedial reading could be described as having problems traceable to language disorders of input coding. The number does not include the children with language disabilities who, rightly or wrongly, may have been categorized according to some other primary complaint. And it does not include children with language disabilities for whom socio-cultural isolation in ethnic ghettos produces major problems of linguistic alienation when these children encounter the dominant middle-class stream of the public school value structure. Madison escapes this problem to a considerable extent by virtue of its relatively homogeneous socio-cultural mix and the relative absence of socio-economic and ethnic ghettos.)

With or without these added numbers, we can see that the problems of language disability in which receptive decoding difficulties may have significant involvement encompasses, both relatively and absolutely, large numbers of children in ways that are far from adequately known and understood. Taken all together, without any numerical legerdemain, it is possible that this general category of disability affects more children than any other.

As for the cumulative nature of childhood language disabilities, one of the most universal characteristics of these disorders is that of *insidious onset.* There are occasional cases of children whose normal language development is suddenly and conspicuously halted by the consequences of infection or trauma, but these cases are rare. It is far more common for the disability to emerge or become recognized gradually, over an extended period of time, with little clear indication of the cause of the developmental failure. Weeks, months, or even years may pass during which the problem becomes progressively more serious as the child drifts further and further below the lower limits of very broad, poorly defined developmental norms. Under these circumstances, events conspire against the child. The initial disorder, however, mild, moderate or severe it may be, is compounded by the secondary deprivation of cumulative language learning experiences which in normal growth occur in dozens or hundreds of incidental language learning opportunities every day.

The impoverished vocalizations of two and three-year old children with severe hearing loss and no voice production disability is a conspicuous example of the progressive, cumulative dysfunction that can occur when one critical link in the language learning chain is broken or missing. In almost every case these are children who began to vocalize and babble in normal fashion. But expressive language patterns become dissipated toward the end of the first year in the absence of auditory experience and self-reinforcement, even when there is no productive language disorder. Intervention in the form of hearing aid amplification appears to bring substantial restoration of vocalizing, especially if it is begun early enough. Some observers are optimistic about the possible outcome of language development for children in whom the opportunity for language listening is even partially restored (Ling, 1970). However, the work done so far touches very few children and involves, to a great extent, an element of personal interaction between child and therapist in which the actual operating variables remain obscure.

If we consider the indefinitely large number of subtle ways that auditory perception can be distorted other than simply by loss of hearing sensitivity, the problem of cumulative deficit takes on a new dimension. Historically, the psychological complexities of auditory perception have not been studied as extensively as visual perception but the intricacies and vulnerabilities of the auditory modality are probably just as great—if not greater. The signal properties of distinctive language signs are marked by extremely fine-grained differences in acoustical energy. The distinctions of meaning and reference conveyed by expressive shadings of intonation are just as subtle as the distinctive features that characterize words and their phonemic constituents. If he is to begin to participate successfully in the perilously balanced linguistic consensus between himself and his communication partners, the infant and young child must recognize, organize, and decode these features, plus the delicate signal information of auditory signal/noise relationships, of sound localization and of the temporal ordering of words that make up the acoustical properties of the stream of speech.

The incredible delicacy of these information-handling processes is matched by the delicacy of the central nervous system structures and functions by which they operate, and their delicacy renders them exceptionally vulnerable to dysfunction due to a host of causes. It is known that the physiological and psychological foundations for language processing can be irreversibly disrupted by multiple causations, ranging from the relatively uncommon insult of prenatal maternal rubella to the relatively common insult of an infant's sustained high fever. It is simply unknown how many other accidents of genetics and growth can blunt and disrupt the young child's ability to recognize and organize the sounds of speech. But where this ability is blunted or disrupted week after week and month after month with or without overt evidence that critical growth processes have gone awry, it becomes almost inevitable that a young child's perception of the intricate web of sounds that form the fabric of language will become distorted—perhaps beyond recognition.

I.   INFANT LANGUAGE LISTENING

Objectives

Our immediate practical objective is to try to identify and reduce to measurement some of the specific constitutents of infants' listening experience that serve as the foundations for language acquisition. A number of converging arguments prompt us to focus our investigation on receptive processes. Not the least persuasive of these arguments is the fact that input functions in children's language development have been very seriously neglected, if not almost totally ignored, despite nearly universal agreement that adequate receptive organization is the prime prerequisite for all other language growth. As a notable exception, the field of audiology has come to appreciate the importance of evaluating acoustical sensitivity in infants. Major progress is being made in clinical and experimental audiological studies from the neonatal period on up, but there are large gaps in the kinds of infant audiometric information that can be secured, and between infant hearing as an audiological function and infant listening as a psycholinguistic function. These gaps are only very slowly being narrowed.

Virtually all investigators of language acquisition agree in one fashion or another with Myklebust's simple statement that "output follows input" (1960). This principle holds that the organization of effective receptive listening is indispensable for the development of speech and language competence. There is ample room for disagreement as to the relative weights that ought to be assigned to different kinds of input and output experience in the attainment of language competence, but few would disagree with the general rule and observation that inputs must and do precede outputs.

Even the most rigidly Stalinist Skinnerian, and perhaps even Skinner himself, would recognize that it is in the nature of our species for infants to engage in a great deal of listening behavior before they engage in any reasonable approximation of truly verbal behavior. It would be vain to ignore the probability, or fact, that this period of relatively passive listening includes a great deal of very important passive learning. And one hopes that even the most doctrinaire cognitivist tenant on the other side of Harvard Yard will acknowledge that happy babies with happy supportive parents gain a great deal of joyous reinforcement in the reciprocal babbling, baby talk, and telegraphic speech of their earliest years. But present knowledge of how the input processes actually function in language development—and the critical stimulus material on which they operate—is little more than a suggestive outline on an otherwise blank slate.

Our second goal was to learn more than is now known about the constituent experiences of receptive language development during the critical months and years of infancy and early childhood when normally endowed babies seem to learn so much about language from an optimum environment. It is our intention to put this knowledge to work in providing enriched supplementary language learning opportunities for children who have access to only a seriously degraded range of language stimuli during these same periods. Important bodies of clinical data and observation (Fry, 1966) indicate that children with moderate and severe hearing losses may gain an advantage in acquiring speech if they are fitted with hearing aids at the earliest possible age. Eighteen months or even younger is not deemed too early, if the hearing loss is clearly ascertained. These observations are consistent with the "new look" emphasis on the importance of early experience in all domains of perceptual learning.

But merely prescribing early application of hearing aids does not really solve the clinical problem. Many hearing-impaired infants are not identified as such until well into the preschool years. Others have hearing impairments at perceptual levels with or without simple losses of auditory sensitivity. Hearing aids may help solve the sensitivity problem, but they leave the child's perceptual and schema-organizing disability unaffected—just as eyeglasses or brighter illumination do little for the child with visual disturbances in figure-ground relationship, distortion of shape constancy, and the like. Still other hearing-impaired children are mentally retarded to one degree or another, and amplification by itself is not a solution for their language learning problem. In short, no matter which way one looks at this problem of early language experience for hearing-impaired children, one finds new domains in which our hard knowledge about the organizational processes on the input side of language development, for deaf, perceptually disabled, and normal youngsters, is hopelessly inadequate.

Techniques

Fortunately we were not obliged to start from scratch in trying to work out the practical problems of what ought to be included in a perceptive language evaluation and enrichment program. In addition to the general conceptual apparatus of perceptual learning, we had two types of automatic equipment that have already proved useful in helping to identify significant elements of young children's listening environments and listening behavior. One of these aids is the time-sampling voice-activated tape recorder. With one of these recorders placed in the home of a cooperative family, and moved from room to room with the baby, one quickly accumulates an embarrassment of riches in the form of voluminous records of normal language interactions in the home. Careful listening and re-listening to these tapes produces an almost inexhaustible supply of hypotheses about aspects of the language environment that may have the greatest impact in shaping infants' listening behavior and listening development. This phase of the work will be described later.

Another aid is the PLAYTEST System (1). PLAYTEST is nothing more than an automated two-channel audio-visual feedback toy with which one can conduct experimental investigations of children's listening preferences in the ordinary environment of the home and school. The type of PLAYTEST that gives only audio feedback from a stereo tape player attaches to a baby's crib (in somewhat the same fashion as the Busybox one can buy in a toystore). The child is free to play with it whenever he is in the crib. A second type gives visual feedback from a closed circuit video tape recorder, as well as audio feedback. [Because of the expense of video tape playing equipment this type of PLAYTEST is presently used only in schools where a considerable number of children can be tested each day. As the price comes down and various minor technical problems are solved, it will become feasible to use the audio-video PLAYTEST systems in babies' homes just as the audio systems are presently employed. Rosenbloom and Aronson recently demonstrated experimentally (Bruner, 1969) that normal babies as young as 3 to 8 weeks can detect incongruities of audio-visual intermodal integration. This finding suggests that it may be necessary as well as possible to evaluate these functions far more systematically than has ever been done before with babies in whom some developmental deficit is suspected. Formal studies of sound level discrimination by normal and language impaired preschool children which employ the audio-video system are described elsewhere (Friedlander, 1969; Friedlander & Putzer, in preparation).]

---

1. Information about the use of PLAYTEST systems in research and evaluation may
   New York, Harper & Brothers, 1957.

In both the audio and video-audio PLAYTEST systems a response register records the frequency and duration of the children's feedback-producing responses to select between various pairs of pre-programmed feedbacks. With suitably selected pairs of stimulus feedbacks, with routine experimental controls, and with statistical analysis of the children's response data, it becomes possible to determine with considerable refinement just what properties of complex auditory and language stimuli the infants and preschool children can actually discriminate.

Early research

Studies already completed and some presently in progress indicate the kinds of linguistic and acoustical variables that can be programmed for tests of babies' ability to make selective discriminations based on listening alone. In early experiments with single babies in the 8-15 month age range, it became evident that normal infants could successfully discriminate between forward and backward speech, between voices of their mothers and of strangers, between familiar and unfamiliar speakers using flat and bright intonations, and between short, highly redundant story segments and long story segments with far less redundancy and greater "information" (Friedlander & Kessler, 1965; Friedlander, 1968). Recent studies with groups of babies have very handsomely upheld the original findings about infants' recognition of linguistic redundancy (Friedlander and Wisdom, in preparation), and initial results of studies now in progress show that normal babies are equally astute in discriminating the basic acoustical property of loudness level, and possibly of filtered frequencies as well.

Figure 1 illustrates the performance of an exemplary 15-month boy who had a PLAYTEST audio unit on his crib at home for 16 days in a two-phase study. These data represent how the procedure works with any pair of audio stimuli that may be programmed on the instrument. In the first six days the audio feedback was programmed so the baby's responses on one of the two knob switches mounted in the crib produced only an uninteresting electronic hum through the loudspeaker. His responses on the other knob turned on a program of attractive lullabies. The sounds continued only as long as the baby continued to press the toy-like switches, and the response register recorded the number of seconds of responses.

(As in all these studies, the position of the toy associated with each feedback is inverted periodically as a correction for position habit—which is often extremely persistent with babies. The investigator visits the home periodically to adjust these inversions, to record the response data, and to change from one stimulus program to another as required. On days when the investigator does not visit the home, the mother

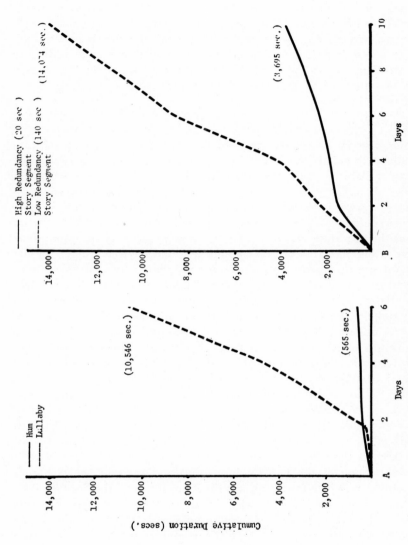

Fig. 1. Significant listening selection by a bright 15-mo. boy with feedback stimuli at two levels of auditory complexity. This boy's rapid discrimination between lullabies and a monotonous electronic hum (A) was followed by equally rapid discrimination of different levels of redundancy in selections from the same story (B).

reports the data to the investigator by telephone according to a stand-ardized procedure.)

The purpose of this phase was simply to establish without question that the baby could and would play with the PLAYTEST at a high enough level of activity to produce worthwhile data, and to demon-strate discriminative preference between two feedbacks that were ob-viously very different in interest level. This baby's performance showed that he had no difficulty or uncertainty in making this discrimination, inasmuch as he made more than 10,000 seconds of responses in a six-day period to listen to the lullabies and less than 600 seconds of responses to hear the electronic hum. In other words, he listened to the songs for nearly three hours and to the hum for less than 10 minutes during the periods when his mother put him in his crib for his naps, at bed time, and upon awakening in the morning. (An automatic time clock on the PLAYTEST turns the unit on in the morning about 15 minutes before the infant normally awakens so the baby can play with the toy as soon as he wakes up. Most babies seem to enjoy this early morning listening, and the mothers seem equally pleased to have an extra 15 minutes or so in bed before the babies cry for food or to be changed.)

The second phase in Figure 1 shows an almost equally dramatic dis-crimination, but of a far more subtle difference in stimulus properties. In this phase both audio channels gave feedback from the same children's story, narrated in dialogue form with a male and female voice speaking alternate passages. However, the two channels of the PLAYTEST toy gave selections from the story edited to different lengths. One channel repeated itself after 20 seconds, and the other repeated itself after 140 seconds. The second channel obviously contained a much greater amount of narrative information (about a bunny and a duck), while both channels were identical with respect to the distribution of the two voices, the narrative style, the intonation patterns, and the type of vocabulary.

The data show how decisively this baby selected the long, low redun-dancy story segment in preference to the short, high redundancy story segment—to the extent of about 14,000 seconds of listening response time for the long story segment to about 3,700 seconds of listening response time for the short story segment. This very subtle discrimina-tion in infant listening has been replicated with seven babies (mean age, 14.6 months) as part of a larger study that examined factors of age, sex, and patterns of selective responding (Friedlander and Wisdom) .

Several aspects of the response patterns suggest that the listening indicated by the selective responding is part of a complicated set of psychological processes involving attention to and appraisal of the language feedbacks at a rather high level of sophistication. Six of the babies showed a very conspicuous "cross-over" effect. They first selected

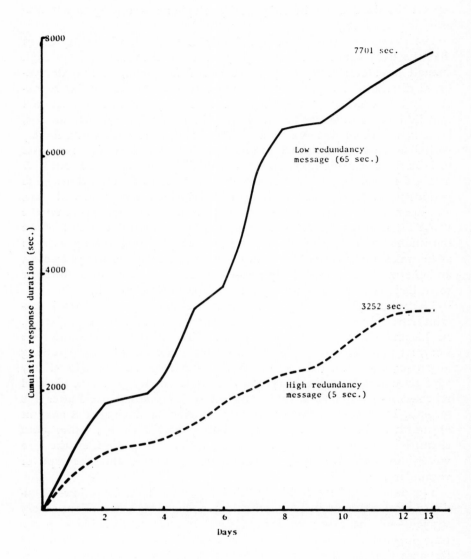

TB-67-CNC

Fig. 2. Discriminative selection between high and low redundancy messages by a 2.5-year-old institutionalized Down's Syndrome boy.

the short, high redundancy story as the preferred feedback to listen to, and then switched to the long, low redundancy story segment, with its richer informational content. This response pattern lends itself to the interpretation that the babies first prefer the simpler material they can more easily assimilate and then reorganize their preference in favor of the longer, more complicated story segment—showing a kind of psychological appetite for more nourishing fare.

Another fragment of data, based on the listening responses of a 2.5-year-old severely retarded Down's Syndrome boy in an institution suggests that the redundancy discrimination effect may be a rather general one that characterizes selective reception at various stages of development. Figure 2 shows the response record of a boy who was tested over a period of 13 days in a very noisy infant ward in a large, hospital-type institution. This boy's expressive language was limited to occasional grunts that seemed to indicate only the most urgent wishes or distress, and cooing gurgles when he appeared to be content. Virtually nothing could be ascertained about his receptive language, except that he gave no evidence of being deaf. He engaged in mutual social play with the ward aides, who were demonstratively fond of him, but it was not possible to determine to what extent these encounters involved specifically linguistic interaction.

One aide was especially voluble and affectionate in caring for this boy and her voice was used on the PLAYTEST tape recordings. The low redundancy message was 65 seconds long and the high redundancy message was 5 seconds in length. In both messages the aide's voice through the loudspeaker spoke a series of personal friendly greetings and statements to the boy whenever he pressed either knob. This boy was given a simpler redundancy problem to solve than the ones customarily offered to normal infants. It was thought that he probably would not be able to recognize the difference in length between alternate listening selections in which the shorter message was too long for him to be able to assimilate all its distinctive linguistic features.

Two things are especially noteworthy about the Figure 2 data. First, there was the obvious discrimination of the language feedbacks at the different levels of redundancy. It is apparent that he made the distinction right from the start, and ended by making more than twice as many seconds of listening time for the low than for the high redundancy message. Second, it seems rather remarkable that the boy listened so much at all considering the very low level of his apparent linguistic competence. The data suggest that receptive language experience constituted some active psychological function that played a significant role in his environmental adaptation, even though he was unable to show this the way most young children do, i.e. in reciprocal linguistic interaction in play and conversation. His clear discrimination of the two types of feedback rules out the possibility that his active responding was simply a matter of free operant manipulation with a new toy.

It would have been extremely desirable to test this child on audio samples with different levels of message redundancy, in order to pinpoint the level at which his discriminative ability would cease to function. Unfortunately the study had to be suspended when the child had one of his recurrent bouts of pneumonia. By the time he recovered it had become necessary to assign the PLAYTEST instrument to another project.

It is challenging to anticipate that these discriminative response patterns for such slightly differentiated linguistic features might lead to an orderly scaling of preverbal infants' capacity to differentiate language inputs at graded levels of complexity with increasing psychological development. Far more extensive data than are yet available must be examined in support of preliminary hypotheses before such a major analysis of language development could be undertaken, and these anticipations must wait the outcome of further investigations that are as yet barely under way.

PLAYTEST techniques also show promise for examining infants' sensitivity to acoustical properties of sound and language stimuli, such as intensity and frequency spectrum, in addition to evaluating discrimination of the linguistic and communication variables already mentioned. This application is illustrated in Figure 3, which is the record of a normal 12-month boy's discrimination of gross differences in loudness level and filtered frequencies—as measured in his crib in his room at home.

In the first phase of the study, shown at the left, the baby could choose between a program of nursery songs in the 70-73 dB range and exactly the same songs at detection threshold level (44-46 dB). The detection threshold level was barely audible—unmeasurably louder than the ambient noise level of the room—but it could be clearly heard by a number of adults who were asked to listen for it attentively. (All sound intensity measurements were made on the linear scale of a B & K type 2203 sound level meter, with the microphone placed on the axis of the speaker 20″ away from it at the opposite side of the crib from where the speaker was mounted.) The baby's four day record of 5,914 seconds of responses for the higher loudness level was overwhelmingly greater than his 1,427 seconds of responding for the lower loudness level, indicating clear discrimination.

In the second phase, another double program of nursery songs was presented at the same measured loudness level of 70-73 dB, but one of the two programs was passed through a Kron-Hite model 3550 low pass filter which nominally filtered out frequences above 500 Hz. Thus the baby had a choice between the full frequency spectrum of the music

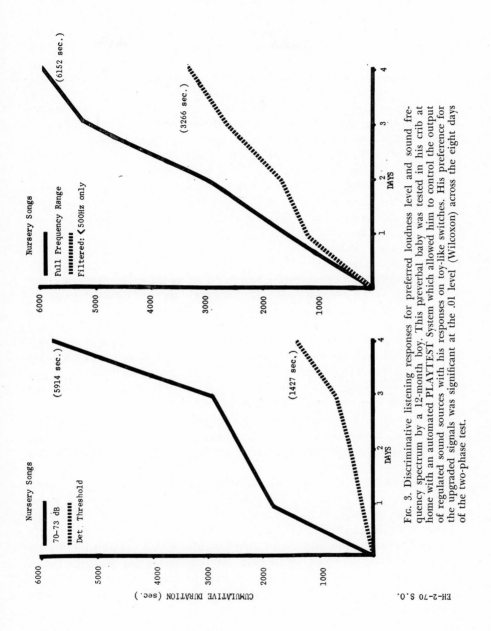

FIG. 3. Discriminative listening responses for preferred loudness level and sound frequency spectrum by a 12-month boy. This preverbal baby was tested in his crib at home with an automated PLAYTEST System which allowed him to control the output of regulated sound sources with his responses on toy-like switches. His preference for the upgraded signals was significant at the .01 level (Wilcoxon) across the eight days of the two-phase test.

when he played with one PLAYTEST knob and a very severely truncated low frequency spectrum when he responded on the other.

(Those not familiar with the effects of frequency filtering at different levels might think of the sound properties of this treatment as being an extreme form of playing a hi-fi system with the bass adjustment turned all the way up and the treble adjustment turned all the way down, and the volume somewhat reduced. Even though the sound intensity of the two programs was carefully equated with the sound measuring instrument, the filtered program sounded slightly less loud to all the adults who were asked to make subjective loudness judgments. Readers not acquainted with this basic acoustical information may not be aware that effective processing of auditory inputs is just as dependent upon discrimination of sound frequency characteristics as upon sound intensity characteristics. Sensory acuity for loudness and frequency are of approximately equal concern in evaluating the integrity of a person's hearing sensitivity, and both capabilities are equally vulnerable to deficits.)

The data for phase two show that the baby discriminated the difference in frequency spectrum somewhat less decisively than he discriminated the difference in loudness, with 6,152 seconds of listening responses for the full range program and 3,266 seconds for the filtered program. Though he listened to the filtered program in phase two considerably more than he listened to the detection threshold program in phase one, the selective preference was decisive for each day. The phase two record shows that the baby listened to the two selections almost equally on the first day. He seemed to be comparing them critically in a pattern that did not appear in the first phase, but after that the discriminative preference was quite unmistakable.

When the preferences for all eight days are combined, the baby's selection of the upgraded auditory stimulus in preference to the degraded stimulus was statistically significant at the .01 level by a two-tailed Wilcoxon matched-pairs test.

These results suggest that this technique offers substantial promise of meeting the need for a method with which to conduct more analytical evaluations of babies' discrimination of properties of natural sounds than have thus far been possible.

However, while the promise of meeting this need is substantial, limitations on present knowledge should be thoroughly recognized. Fewer than 50 normal babies have been tested thus far with the PLAYTEST technique. The very great advantages of testing babies when they are at ease in their normal environments, over extended periods, and with naturalistic sound stimuli bears the compensating disadvantage of being slower and possibly more expensive than procedures in which a child is tested in the clinic. Because of the expense, the utilization of new techniques, and the time required for each child, amassing a sizable pool of baseline data is a slow process—though an essential prerequisite for evaluating suspected deficits. The crisply discriminative data reported here in Figure 3 record the performance of one of the first infants tested in a baseline study concerned specifically with measurement of infants' discrimination of acoustical variables, and the study was far from complete when this article was written. The other babies tested thus far in the loudness discrimination phase give approximately equivalent records of clear selective preference for the louder program, but the sound frequency discrimination data contain some puzzling inconsistencies. It remains unknown at present whether these inconsistencies are due to unsolved methodological problems, to some infants' relative indifference to gross degradation of frequency values that nevertheless allow transmission of substantial acoustical information, or to the possibility that some infants in the initial study who were believed to have normal hearing did. in fact, suffer high frequency hearing losses that would make both the full range and the filtered selections sound substantially alike.

These are the kinds of problems that must be solved before this extremely promising method can take its place as a fully validated technique for measuring babies' auditory and receptive language capabilities. In the domain of auditory sensitivity it is essential to test larger numbers of babies at many different levels of sound intensity and frequency filtration, with many types of sound selections. In the domain of auditory perception, it is necessary to establish parameters of infants' selection of such fundamental organizing properties of the sound environment as signal/noise ratios and temporal ordering. And in the domain of language and communication, baselines must be established for infants' discriminative recognition of differences in speech and non-speech stimuli, values of intonation and stress, distinctive phonemic and morphological features, repetition and redundancy, relationships between speech sounds and environmental events, and other properties that have major determining influences in the organization of language listening competence.

Pursuing new information on these topics involves procedural and conceptual difficulties of bewildering complexity. But every intermediate step in the acquisition of reliable descriptions of infant performance offers the prospect of improved methods for establishing normal baselines of language growth, for identifying and confirming hearing and listening deficits, for evaluating the nature of hearing disabilities, and for programming effective intervention where it may be required.

It is important to keep this work in perspective. Receptive language development is too intricate a process to yield its secrets easily. It would be presumptuous to think that the relatively simple procedures described thus far will suffice to determine the critical variables that operate as children progress toward orientation to and organization of the world of sound and spoken language. However, despite its acknowledged simplicity in the face of an intricate phenomenon, this general method has one extremely important advantage. PLAYTEST studies of children's actual language listening force an investigator to keep directly and firmly in contact with the fundamental, primary data of infants' language learning experiences on a daily basis in their actual, natural setting. All our speculations on how the process of receptive language functioning takes shape in normal growth and how it takes mis-shape in abnormal growth are forced into almost daily confrontations with numerical data of infants' actual listening experience. It is not possible to take refuge from taxing problems in overly simplified abstractions. These confrontations have a disciplining effect on the tendency to speculate in theoretical flyers.

II. LANGUAGE ENVIRONMENTS IN INFANCY

Tape recordings of family language interactions in the natural environment of the home provide another body of data that has a chastening effect on the tendency to seek simple explanations for complex phenomena. In this section I will try to describe and discuss some exemplary tapes of spontaneous family language in homes with infants and young children at important stages of language learning. These recordings give a reasonably faithful representation of the actual sound environment within which a baby lays down the foundations of his primary language learning experience. Unfortunately, the mechanics of publishing make it impossible to accompany this text with the tape recordings selected for discussion.* The only way to gain a fully realized sense of the important acoustical and linguistic elements in these samples is actually to listen to them.

Careful analysis of home language interactions, well recorded on quality audio equipment, tends to breed an enhanced respect for the awesome intricacy of the language learning process in its natural habitat. As one listens to such recordings, it seems altogether inexplicable how so delicate a fabric as language can be woven from such crude, chaotically tangled, poorly organized, and seemingly random raw materials as the natural sounds that surround an infant in a bustling household.

Perhaps the very first problem that must be considered in studying variables that affect receptive language processes and development is

---

* A limited number of copies of these tape recordings are available on loan. Interested persons are welcome to borrow these tapes and copy them for their own use, returning the borrowed tapes to the author. The tapes are standard ¼-inch audio tapes and may be copied by mating any two standard audio tape recorders. Inquiries should be directed to the author, Department of Psychology, University of Hartford, West Hartford, Connecticut.

that most speech a young child hears in his natural environment is extremely difficult to analyze with respect to basic stimulus properties. A baby faces a monumentally difficult task in shaping up the language signals he hears into relatively stable and consistent categories. Among the American families we have studied, speech articulation in adult and sibling conversation is almost uniformly poor. (Some of the foreign born parents who have participated in our studies speak English with far more precise articulation of consonants than native American speakers.) Speech messages and language signals are deeply embedded in background noise; sound intensity levels are often inaudibly low or assaultively high; the speech stream flows with great rapidity; two or more people are often speaking at one time; and grammatical structures are often incomplete or very distorted. In such a mess, what is the stimulus?

Informal recording

These characteristics of degraded language stimuli are exemplified in one family recording of a father and mother conversing in the presence of their six-month-old daughter. The baby can be heard occasionally reacting to parent utterances, and it is evident from the content of the parents' speech that the baby is eliciting some of it. A fourth participant in this conversation is the family cat. (Almost as many utterances are directed toward the cat as to the baby. The context of the conversation does not help us determine to whom the cat's utterances are directed.) The pace of the conversation is relatively rapid; the intermittent sounds of a music box repeatedly intrude into the parents' dialogue in a way that is far more distracting than one would expect from a sound source usually thought of as being simple and non-abrasive.

Though a motivated listener can follow most of the dialogue without extreme effort, the level of intelligibility is very low. Just how low is suggested by one startling phrase which sounds as if this perfectly proper young mother is recommending that her husband caress the cat in an unusually intimate fashion. It takes very close analytical listening to discover that she is simply suggesting that he should be nice to the cat and "scratch his *bald spot.*" Only with such close analysis does it become apparent that the mother's falling intonation at the conclusion of the phrase, with a sharp drop in articulatory precision and sound intensity, is the cause of the confusion between what the mother seemed to say and what she actually did say. The reason this misunderstanding is so salient is that the erroneous first impression has a substantial element of startle value in terms of the content of the misapprehension. Upon re-listening to the tape repeatedly, one discovers that many phrases in the mother's speech are equally indistinct, but they pass unnoticed because context and redundancy make her meanings perfectly clear to an adult with a substantial amount of listening experience.

But we are left with the uncomfortable question of wondering how an infant listener with little experience in utilizing context and redundancy factors in connected discourse learns to discriminate and correctly categorize ambiguous utterances that are on the borderline between changes of intonation and actual differences in message content. As far as I am aware, there are no answers to this question, except the rather obvious and unhelpful ones that a) infants and young children are extremely vulnerable to linguistic confusion, and b) most of them learn language adequately in spite of this vulnerability.

Then one is reminded of the indications cited in the preceding section that substantial numbers of children *don't* learn language adequately. Other questions begin to percolate through the layers of possibility that language learning disabilities may represent some combination of interactions between the infant and young child's listening experiences in a sub-optimal environment, and marginal dysfunctions of auditory acuity and auditory perception. These questions sound a theme that recurs repeatedly when one brings an analytic attitude to the evaluation of linguistic interactions in infants' normal listening environments.

But returning to the tape recording already partially described, the most provocative aspect of this baby's language environment is that the home is bilingual. The mother always speaks English in the child's presence. The father, a native of Milwaukee and a Wisconsin graduate student in Spanish, always speaks Spanish in the child's presence. This is not simply for the sake of his own language exercise, but with the calculated intention that his daughter grow up with command of both languages. (The father's hopes were amply fulfilled. Two years after the original recordings in this home, little Tena can converse in English and Spanish with equal fluency.)

This family setting gives an excellent opportunity to confront an infant's major signal recognition problem—a problem to which the associated problems of articulation, embeddedness, and so forth are merely subsidiary. At six months, the baby was not a fluent speaker of Spanish. She was not even a fluent speaker of English. Because we are fluent speakers of English, our perceptual mechanisms help us fill in the organization framework as well as the missing stimulus signals of the mother's speech. Our highly developed knowledge of English allows us to divide her speech stream into appropriate phonological, lexical, suprasegmental, and grammatical units, and decode the stream despite its stimulus deficiencies. But without an existing scheme for categorizing these properties of the signal in the father's Spanish, it is extremely difficult for most of us even to *hear* them as they speed by and quickly fade. Non-Spanish speakers simply do not have the categories to identify the signal stimuli, irrespective of meaning.

We must assume that this baby had the same trouble perceiving the sound signals of the mother's English we have in perceiving the sound signals of the father's Spanish—and possibly even more. We are experienced in at least one language, and this experience has taught us that unfamiliar languages have an ultimately decipherable structure. But this is knowledge the baby did not have. That ignorance puts her in the position of having to construct appropriate organizational categories of speech sounds, intonations, referential correlatives, and grammar— and she must do so using a basic raw material which is defective in its signal clarity in the first place. This is not an enviable position to be in. Yet it is obvious that most children learn language without fuss or bother, despite what seem to us to be almost unimaginable complexities —just as the normal bumblebee manages to fly despite the aeronautical engineers' inability to figure out how his wings manage to create enough lift to raise and propel his bulk.

When we are aware of the problem of recognizing the constituent elements of language for the untrained ear, we gain a clearer insight of another dimension of language learning difficulty for children whose language acquisition does not run a smooth course. Not only must they cope with the problems of "poor performance" in the speech articulation of most of the people to whom they listen. They must also manage somehow to discover organizational components and regularities and relate them to meaning, in a code whose systematicity is deeply buried in a mass of surface irregularities. It should come as no surprise that so many children have language learning disabilities, even though most do not. Perhaps the real surprise is that so *few* children have language learning disabilities.

Additional informal tape recordings of the natural sound environment in other homes illustrated factors that might be assumed either to facilitate or to inhibit language learning in infancy and early childhood. Recordings in the homes of single children contained occasional episodes of richly intimate vocal and verbal interactions between parent and child in which the course of the infants' increasing language mastery could be more or less easily recognized. In some of these episodes it was apparent that the parents were modifying their normal inter-adult speech patterns in order to accommodate the infants' limited comprehension. Some were frankly tuitional, with the parents adopting what appeared to be an intentional teaching role. In others, the parents' verbal style seemed to make no concession to the baby's linguistic status. As long as the infant's utterances came at a suitable time to give the appearance of dialogue reciprocality, the parents seemed to accept even the most limited utterance from the infant as a signal to go on with other utterances of their own. One mother often became involved in rather long and complicated dialogues with her baby in which the baby's only participation consisted of occasional coos, babbles, or grunts. This observation does not necessarily imply that the mother was indifferent to the probability that the baby did not understand the meaning content of her speech and that the dialogues were essentially non-reciprocal. Perhaps a more suitable interpretation would be that she appeared to regard the baby as a perfectly satisfactory conversational companion who did not need to speak at length in order to be regarded as a peer. (In *David Copperfield*, Dickens doesn't suggest that Aunt Betsey regarded Mr. Dick as anything less than her trusted and valued friend, even though he seldom spoke to her in anything other than monosyllables. It is only because he confesses his apprehension to David that we suspect Mr. Dick is "simple.")

Recordings from homes with single infants produced environmental records in which the presumptively facilitory and inhibitory language influences seemed in some approximate balance. But the language environments in which there were active, voluble older siblings in addition to the infant and parents were often so tumultuous the words *pandemonium* and *chaos* hardly seem adequate for description. We secured one series of tapes from a home with a baby girl about a year old, two brothers aged four and six, a father whose voice was usually calm, and a mother whose voice was often strident. When this family had a boisterous and rollicking dinner table conversation—often with the radio or TV going in a nearby room—the tape recording was so good humoredly volcanic it sounded more overpowering than the Moscow Philharmonic playing Tchaikovsky's *1812 Overture* with a full battery of cannon in the finale. Yet despite the clamor, which accompanied virtually all family activities when the older brothers were present, the baby's language development appeared to proceed on or ahead of schedule. Before she was 18 months old this child was able to form simple two and three word utterances, and act correctly on moderately complex verbal instructions that required a substantial element of verbal comprehension.

It is probable that this baby had occasional private dialogue time with her mother when the brothers were out of the house and that the structure of her developmental language organization may have formed as a result of these experiences. However, her language environment as a whole must be regarded as having been categorically different from the environment that surrounds an infant whose family activities are conducted at a calmer level, and where there are no older siblings. The complexity of this child's language environment seemed not to interfere with her linguistic development. But one wonders if all babies who are surrounded by linguistic chaos are so fortunate. The question again arises, what the effects might have been if this baby had brought some degree of receptive disability with her into this especially demanding environment. It is hard to imagine that language learning could have followed a smooth course if she had.

Systematic recording

The initial set of tape recordings of infants' and young children's language environments in their homes raised so many provocative questions it soon became evident that the work had to be conducted in a more systematic fashion. Though the raw recordings contained a wealth of observational information, means had to be found to convert these observations to orderly categories and numerical data in order to begin to assess specific variables that might have greater or lesser influence in shaping language growth. In the absence of systematic data collection, it was not possible to ascertain to what extent individual recordings were truly representative of a given language environment. Except in the grossest terms, observational narratives could not give details on ways in which language environments were the same or different for babies in different families. In terms of fine details, linguistic properties of the form and content of infants' language environments could not be identified without itemizing and enumerating types of language inputs to which infants are exposed in different families and at different stages of development.

Two techniques for collecting and analyzing home recorded tapes have proved instrumental in dealing with these methodological problems. These techniques are described elsewhere (Friedlander, Cyrulik & Davis). It is sufficient here simply to note them briefly, indicating the types of data that can be obtained, and suggest ways they may prove useful in evaluating environmental factors in cases involving babies and young children with known or suspected language disabilities.

In the recording procedure tapes are collected with a time-sampling voice activated tape recorder system that compiles periodic records of sound and language environments in the home according to uniform pre-selected schedules. The tape recorder is regulated by an automatic clock that turns the system on and off on a pre-set duty cycle. Sampling is usually conducted for five minutes out of every 20 minutes, giving a potential total record of 15 minutes of tape for every hour of elapsed time during the day. This schedule can be varied from one to 60 minutes of each hour, according to any time distribution that may be desired for various sampling purposes. During the system's "on" times, the recorder operates whenever there is a sound loud enough to activate the adjustable monitor circuit in the microphone. A second clock circuit shuts down the whole system during the night when the infant is asleep.

(To avoid connotations of surreptitious snooping, no effort is made to conceal the microphones or the case that contains the tape recorder. A clearly visible red light on the side of the case indicates when the microphone circuit is on, and the mother and father are shown how to operate a safety switch that allows them to disconnect the microphone during conversations they may wish not to have recorded. Showing respect for the families' options to preserve their privacy is an important requirement for gaining their confidence in the integrity of a research program which might otherwise be looked upon as an unwelcome intrusion. As a further step to preserve privacy, family names are coded and indicators of family identity are edited out of tapes that are used for demonstration purposes.)

Studies completed thus far have been carried out with families in small apartments. A single microphone is placed at a central location, usually between the living-diningroom and the kitchen, where the infants and parents spend most of their time together. Studies can just as well be conducted in larger homes with microphones placed wherever they are needed.

Collecting the tape recordings is a relatively simple part of the job of studying infants' language environments in the home. Reducing the raw recordings to quantifications within reliable categories is far more demanding. It is a task that taxes the judgment, skill, and patience of a person trained to discriminate fine differences in the acoustical and linguistic properties of spontaneous speech in the unstructured settings of family interaction. It usually takes between two and three hours to codify one hour of tape when making more or less routine analyses, and it can take as long as four or five hours to analyze each hour of raw tape when the work calls for detailed specification of the linguistic properties of utterances. The task is especially challenging with tapes from households in which the radio, TV, or a phonograph runs as a frequent obbligato to other motifs or communication.

(The presence of the mass media is pervasive in many American homes. Media sources account for very large percentages of some children's total language exposure—as is indicated below. It would hardly seem realistic to try to explain language acquisition without reference to these major sources of influence. Yet surprisingly, one hardly ever finds mass media factors discussed in the contemporary professional literature on language development.)

The most important kinds of data collected thus far with these techniques include 1) distribution of all sampled utterances made by individual members of the family—including the baby—and by other speech sources such as guests, radio, and TV; 2) distribution of sampled utterances directed toward the infant; 3) distribution of infant-directed utterances classified in linguistic categories, e.g. reflective expansion, imitation, mimicry elicitation, direct reinforcement, tuitional modeling.

These data provide numerical estimates of who speaks to whom in the household, how much of the sampled language in a home is directed toward the baby, and the types of language interactions in which the baby is included as a participant.

Perhaps the principal value of these kinds of data lies in the information they give about the quantity and quality of home language interactions. These data can be especially worthwhile in assessing the developmental language opportunities of infants and young children with known or suspected language disabilities. Elonen (1970) comments that hearing-impaired babies may be the victims of unintentional linguistic neglect, especially in families in which other children occupy much of the parents' and others' linguistic attention. Some families fall into a pattern of acquiescing to the affected child's hearing disability and his inability to "demand" verbal interaction. These families tend to shape their communication with him in non-linguistic modes as a kind of detour around the dysfunction. Elonen says this pattern may be especially damaging to the child's language growth if it persists after hearing aids are provided. The child may then be denied the maximum language experience most observers view as an essential accompaniment to the potential benefits that hearing aids may confer.

The home language sampling technique offers the opportunity to make on site evaluations of family language patterns. These evaluations can then be used in advising parents on ways in which the family language environment might be restructured to meet the child's needs more appropriately. Such restructuring may be as simple as urging the parents to restrict the use of a continuously running radio, which the mother might "tune out" when it conveys no needed information, but which might monopolize the auditory environment of a child with a hearing aid. Efforts to restructure the auditory environment on the basis of systematically collected tape recordings have already been attempted in an institution for young children. Upon listening to these tapes, members of the institution's senior staff identified a number of factors that were deemed counterproductive to the children's language development (St. John, 1970).

The data sample in Table 1 illustrates ways in which two separate families can be very different and very similar with respect to the language environments within which infants develop. This table also illustrates one simple type of quantification made possible with the time-sampling tape recorder method. Both the Smith and the Jones families had 12-month old babies, both were of the same socio-economic status, and both fathers were graduate students at the University of Wisconsin.

Inspection of the upper section of the table shows that the families were radically different in terms of the infants' exposure to TV (the principal element of the "Other" category); in the comparison between

TABLE 1

PERCENTAGES OF SYSTEMATICALLY SAMPLED UTTERANCES IN THE HOMES
OF TWO 12-MONTH INFANTS, SHOWING THE SOURCE OF ALL
UTTERANCES AND THE SOURCES OF INFANT-DIRECTED
UTTERANCES

Source of Utterance	Smith Family	Jones Family
All Utterances		
Mother	22%	11%
Father	18	4
Baby	35	15
Other (guests, radio, TV)	25	70
Infant-directed Utterances		
Mother	67%	73%
Father	30	24
Guests	3	3

the mothers' and fathers' utterances; and in the productivity of the infants' own utterances. It is hard to say which of these observations is most meaningful in characterizing the difference in the babies' total language environments. Non-family voices constituted almost three-quarters of the speech in the Jones sample but only one-quarter in the Smith sample; the percentage of the Jones father's utterances were only one-fourth as numerous as for the Smith father; the Smith baby's utterances account for more than twice as great a portion of the whole sample as the Jones'.

What seem to be enormous differences in the family language patterns in terms of the sampling of all utterances take on an altogether different appearance when we compare the two families in terms of sampled utterances *directed toward the infant,* as indicated in the lower section of Table 1. By this indicator, the remarkable thing about these data is how very much the two families were alike. They are different by only a few percentage points in each category.

Perhaps the most outstanding reversal in this shift from difference to similarity is suggested in the role of the Jones baby's father. The all-utterance data, giving him only four percent of the sample, create the impression that the father is merely a shadow figure in the family constellation. But the measure of infant-directed utterances shows that he is responsible for almost a quarter of the personal utterances to which the Jones baby was exposed—almost exactly the same as the father's role in the Smith baby's language environment. In other words, the Jones father played a major role in the baby's *personal* language environment, though he played only a minor role in the *total* language environment.

This difference between the personal and the total language environments is important in practice as well as in theory. It happens that the Jones father was the father cited above who set out to teach his baby Spanish by speaking only Spanish in her presence. According to the sampling information on infant-directed utterances, the baby heard about one-third as much Spanish from the father as she heard English from the mother. Though there are no formal tests on which such judgments can be made, observation by tape recorder and by visits to the home when the child was 22 months old suggest that she was almost as fluent in her use of and response to Spanish as she was in English.

It is certainly noteworthy that the father obtained this actualization of his bilingual objectives *while occupying so small a percentage (only 4%) of the infant's total language environment samples* when she was 12 months old.

With respect to language acquisition theory, these kinds of observations offer the potential for casting considerable light on a basic question, which in turn casts significant reflection on problems of aiding infants and young children with known and suspected language difficulties. The question is, to what extent are infants and young children dependent on their environment in learning language, and what are the essential features of the language environment from which they attain language competence? Shipley, et al., summarize two opposed prevailing views that can be reduced, without too much danger of oversimplification, to a variant form of the nurture-nature controversy (Shipley, Smith & Gleitman, 1968).

This summary notes that psychologists tend to consider young children as having very general abilities for forming inductive generalizations, which allow them to induce linguistic regularities from the speech they hear. Their acquisition of linguistic regularities is viewed as essentially a learning process, which is highly dependent upon the environment and the linguistic corpus in which the child is embedded. Linguists, however, argue that the corpus is so overwhelmingly complex that a child is unable to sort out its chaotic irregularities well enough to formulate inductive generalizations successfully. In place of a learning paradigm based on inductions derived from experience, linguists claim the child utilizes innate mechanisms for deducing semantic and syntactic structures from a given corpus of natural speech. The nativist position of the linguists elevates the importance of the comprehensive corpus, including the entire set of language inputs to which the child is exposed, with relatively little concern for the child's task of learning to formulate linguistic categories based on speech sounds and grammatical structures —formulations with which he is deemed to be innately endowed. Psychologists, on the other hand, are inclined to elevate the importance of factors of selectivity in determining the effective learning corpus that is presumably limited to sets of inputs that attain special salience in terms of the infant's overall adaptation to his external and internal environment. (See Friedlander, 1970, for an extended discussion of variables affecting salience.)

Mr. Jones' success in teaching his daughter Spanish would appear to support the selectivist position, because so much was accomplished in the child's language learning by such a small portion of her total language exposure. But this appearance might be deceptive because we have only fragmentary information on which to estimate the language learning impact of the TV, which occupied so much of this family's non-personal linguistic "life space." One informational fragment is extremely provocative. Mrs. Jones reported that at the age of 22 months the little girl was learning to count, without parental tuition, solely by watching the *Sesame Street* TV program.

This report proved to be more than just a fond maternal fantasy. A visit to the home by two critical observers confirmed that the child could, in fact, recite the numbers one to seven without error, and that she was gaining fast on 8, 9 and 10 in self-generated practice sessions. There was no reason to suppose that she attained the numerical concepts along with the verbal trick, but it was apparent that she had learned at least this much speech by watching and listening to TV. How much else she may have learned that did not lend itself to easy recitation was anybody's guess—just as it is still probably a matter of guesswork whether the comprehensivist or the selectivist view most appropriately describes the influence of the environment on a child's language learning.

(It is not unlikely that future research might show this plausible polarity to be inappropriate as a description of general language learning processes. For example, infants and young children with rich natural intellectual and environmental endowments might be able to learn language rapidly and easily as a consequence of broad, incidental contact with a comprehensive corpus. Less well endowed children, on the other hand, might be restricted to learning from a narrower, selective corpus of language inputs more heavily saturated with personal involvement.)

Returning, finally, to the problems of language-impaired infants and young children, there may be an important lesson to be learned from the fact that the Jones baby learned Spanish, and that she did so despite the fact that her father's speech to her in Spanish occupied so small a portion of her total language environment. This lesson suggests that a little language learning *if it is of the right sort and comes at the right time* can have a disproportionately large impact on the growth of language competence. For all its bewildering complexities, perhaps the language learning process has some underlying simple framework that can be built upon in promoting the development of communicative skills. The setting in which the Jones baby learned two languages with ease and fluency may have some important constituents that can be adapted to the needs of children who experience unusual difficulty in learning just one language.

The problem is to identify what language learning experiences are of the right sort and when is the right time to cultivate them. These, of course, are the overarching questions for further research and they open up virtually endless possibilities for further study. Ling's work (1970) in teaching fluent speech to the extremely deaf by a combination of psychological, linguistic, and instructional techniques demonstrates that highly effective interventions can be devised for language disabilities previously looked upon as virtually hopeless.

To the extent that the research techniques described in this report can help to specify listening disabilities, to increase our presently limited knowledge of normal receptive language processes, and to learn more about how language environments affect the emergence or inhibition of language communication, these methods may assist in meeting the needs of that substantial number of infants and young children for whom language learning is a difficult, often unrewarded struggle instead of a natural consequence of growth.

REFERENCES

BRUNER, J. S. Annual Report, Center for Cognitive Studies. Harvard University, 1969.

ELONEN, ANNA. Personal Communication, 1970.

FRIEDLANDER, B. Z. The effects of speaker identity, voice inflection, vocabulary, and message redundancy on infants' selection of vocal reinforcement. *J. Exp. Child Psychol.*, 1968, 6, 3, pp. 443-459.

FRIEDLANDER, B. Z. Preschool children's self-measurement of listening discrimination of four loudness levels of natural sounds with an automated videotape free-play game. American Speech and Hearing Assn., Chicago, 1969.

FRIEDLANDER, B. Z. Receptive Language development in infancy: Issues and problems, *Merrill-Palmer Quarterly*, vol. 16, No. 1, 1970.

FRIEDLANDER, B. Z. & KESSLER, J. W. Longterm monitoring of an infant's selective play for perceptual rewards. Society for Research in Child Development, Minneapolis, 1965.

FRIEDLANDER, B. Z., CYRULIK, ANTOINETTE, & DAVIS, BARBARA BERGMAN. Time-sampling analysis of infants' natural language environments in the home. In preparation.

FRIEDLANDER, B. Z. & PUTZER, R. K. Automated testing of the effect of sound intensity level on preschool children's self-selection of video reinforcement. In preparation.

FRIEDLANDER, B. Z. & WISDOM, SARA. The effect of message redundancy on language listening preference in the home among infants at two age levels. In preparation.

FRY, D. B. The development of the phonological system in the normal and the deaf child. In Smith, F. & Miller, G. A. (Eds.), *The Genesis of Language*. Cambridge, Mass., M.I.T. Press, 1966.

GRUENWALD, L. Personal Communication, 1970.

LING, D. Personal Communication, 1970. (Ling has done pioneering work in teaching fluent speech to persons who are profoundly deaf. His work is documented in tape recordings. Inquiries should be directed to Daniel Ling, Ph.D., McGill University Project for Deaf Children, Beatty Hall, 1266 Pine Avenue West, Montreal, Quebec.)

MYKLEBUST, J. R. *The Psychology of Deafness*. New York, Grune & Stratton, 1960.

SHIPLEY, ELIZABETH F., SMITH, CARLOTA S. & GLEITMAN, LITA R. Technical Report VIII: A Study in the Acquisition of Language: Free Response to Commands. Eastern Pennsylvania Psychiatric Institute, 1968.

ST. JOHN, R. Personal Communication, 1970.

12

THE THEORETICAL AND RESEARCH BASE FOR A PROGRAM OF EARLY STIMULATION CARE AND TRAINING OF PREMATURE INFANTS

Logan Wright, Ph.D.

Department of Pediatrics
Childrens Memorial Hospital
The University of Oklahoma Medical Center

INTRODUCTION

The purpose of this chapter is to make several points concerning the development of premature infants, and to present certain techniques which show promise for influencing their development. These include the following:

(1) Premature children are a high risk group, being vulnerable to deficits in almost every area of development.

(2) The vulnerability of prematures is increased significantly if, during infancy, they are reared in an environment providing minimal sensory-motor stimulation.

(3) Lower socioeconomic environments tend to provide infants with a minimum of sensory stimulation, leaving prematures from such settings in dire need of some type of intervention which will increase their rate of development as well as extend the upper limits of development.

(4) Early stimulation techniques offer an effective means of developmental intervention which can produce increments in the rate of development as well as extend the upper limits of development.

The following material will describe the theoretical and research bases, as well as the specific design, for a program of research to provide premature children from lower socioeconomic environments with extensive amounts of stimulus enrichment during the early months of life. The details of the stimulation provided and the measures obtained to quan-

276

tify and otherwise assess the impact of stimulus enrichment will be explained, and data from an initial pilot study will be reported.

THE PREMATURE INFANT

As additional emphasis is placed on discriminating between term infants of low birth weight and those of shortened gestational age, it has become increasingly important to define what is meant by the term "prematurity." Yerushalmy (1968) has emphasized the importance of such distinctions and designated 36 gestational weeks or less as the definition of "true" prematurity. Work by Hodgman (1969) supports the importance of distinguishing between small term babies and true prematures. In a study of 12,000 live born infants, she reports that approximately 50% of the prematures weighed more than 2,500 grams at birth, and that these large premature babies may account for as much as 8% of the total neonatal population. It is estimated that an additional 8% of the population has a birthweight below 2,500 grams (Sinclair, 1968). While the developmental prognosis for both large and small prematures appears similar (the developmental characteristics of prematures will be discussed on the following pages), the term infant of less than 2,500 grams presents a significantly more bleak prognostic picture. Hodgman lists seven indicators which she feels can validly differentiate the true premature child from a small term infant. These are lower weight and less fat, more gelatinous and less flaky skin, less stiffness and cartilage of the external ear, "fuzzier" hair, less breast tissue, "floppier" posture, and more poorly developed reflexes. Bone x-rays were not found to be helpful.

Although prematurity as defined in our research involves both a gestational age of 36 weeks or less and birth weight below 2,500 grams, most research on premature children has relied on a criterion involving only birth weight. In general these data indicate a vulnerability to developmental deficit in almost every area. Five extensive reviews of literature have been conducted (Benton, 1940; Alm, 1953; Dunham, 1955; Wiener, 1962 and Braine, Heimer, Wortis & Freedman, 1966). These reviews have generally been critical of studies of premature children, particularly because of their failure to employ adequate control groups and quantifiable (as opposed to impressionistic) measures. Some criticisms have also been leveled at various studies for failing to deal with important control variables, such as the effect of socioeconomic status, neonatal insult variables, etc., which often accompany prematurity and which might account for the major portion of developmental impairment. For instance, Braine, et al (1966) have indicated that the neonatal insult variables of hypoxia and neonatal weight loss may account for the major portion of developmental impairment during the first 15 months of life. Studies by Drillien (1959) and Wortis and Freedman (1965) suggest that the magnitude of developmental impairment is greater if the premie is raised in a lower socioeconomic setting. Along this line, Dann, Levine and New (1958) found that premature children born into families receiving private medical care have higher IQ's than those whose families could not. This also suggests that socioeconomic variables rather than simply prematurity itself might be involved.

In spite of numerous criticisms of studies investigating the effects of prematurity on subsequent development, the results of such studies tend to be quite similar, and indicate that premature children experience developmental retardation during at least the first two years of life (Brandt, 1924; Forschner-Boke, 1924; Gesell, 1925, 1928; Korthauer, 1929; Levy, 1928; Looft, 1921; Mohr & Bartelme, 1934; Wall, 1913; Baedorf, 1938; Drillien, 1958; and Knoblock, Rider, Harper & Pasamanick, 1956). Surveys of the premature literature also suggest that, following the first two years of life, a majority of prematurely born infants begin a "catching up" process wherein a majority (though certainly not all) eventually reach developmental levels which are within normal limits (Looft, 1921; Ziechen, 1926; Comberg, 1927; Melcher, 1937; and Drillien, 1959). Although most premature children eventually attain developmental levels which are within normal limits, they continue *as a group* to function at significantly lower levels than normal children in almost every area. The review by Braine, et al (1966) suggests, however, that the degree of prematurity (usually defined a lower birth weight) is a definite factor in determining the degree of developmental retardation, and the extent to which "catching up" occurs.

Stature—The low birth weight of premature children quite obviously raises the possibility of a corresponding deficit in later physical structure. Lubchenko, Horner, Reed, Hix, Metcalf, Cohig, Elliott and Bourg (1963) attempted to study the size of 197, 10-year olds with a birth weight below 1,500 grams. Of the 94 children from this population who survived the first year of life, 41% were below the 10th percentile for their age group on weight and 47% were below the 10th percentile on height. These authors speculated that undernutrition during the first few weeks of life might possibly be the mechanism underlying retarded growth.

Vision—Eames (1945), in a study of 155 prematures and 439 full-term infants, found a significantly higher percentage of prematures with vision below 20/30 than normals. In a later study of 25 prematures and 25 controls Eames (1946) also found that prematures showed poorer visual acuity on Snellen chart tests. Lubchenko, et al (1963) reported that 38 subjects (60%) from a group of 63 prematures under investigation possessed moderate to severe visual problems. Many researchers

(Patz, Hoech & De La Cruz, 1952; Kinsey, Jacobus & Hemphill, 1956) feel that much of the visual difficulty of prematures, particularly as reported in older studies, comes from excessive exposure to oxygen during the neonatal period, and the resulting retrolental fiberoplasia.

Audition—Although there are no studies indicating a high incidence of auditory *impairment* in premature children, Shirley (1938) found hypersensitivity to auditory stimuli in a group of 50 premature children as compared to 50 full-term infants. This finding was replicated with another group of 50 prematures and 50 full-term children (Shirley, 1939).

Neurological development—Dann, et al (1958) and Drillien (1959) have both concluded that the prognosis for central nervous system development of the premature child is poor. Alm (1953) reported a "high proportion" of brain damaged individuals among a sample of 999 prematures. Mohr and Bartelme (1930) found 35 brain injured patients in a study of 113 premature children. Lubchenko et al (1963) have noted a high incidence of mongolism among prematures. They also report that prematures were inferior to controls in possessing hyperactive deep tendon reflexes as well as sustained and unsustained ankle clonus. Mohr and Bartelme (1930) report a higher incidence of spasticity. Harper, Fischer and Rider (1959) investigated 460 prematures and 440 controls between three and five years of age, and found significantly fewer neuromotor deviations among controls. Rossier (1962) in studying 125 infants four to seven years of age with birth weights of less than 1,500 grams found 20% of his sample to have abnormal motor development and 7% to show serious motor deficit. Studies by Baedorf (1938), Schoberlein (1938), Shirley (1938, 1939), Beskow (1949) and Lilienfeld, Pasamanick and Rogers (1955) have all concluded that premature children are both more distractible and hyperactive than normals. Only two studies (Davis, 1951 and Lezine, 1958) report no differences between prematures and controls in neurological and motor development. In general, it would appear that premature children *are* more likely to encounter neurological difficulties, and that they may exhibit symptomatology which is associated with minimal celebral dysfunction and learning disability.

Speech and language development—There is a difference of opinion among researchers regarding the effect of prematurity on speech and language development. Drillien (1959) has concluded that speech development is the *most* likely area of impairment among premature children. This is based primarily on a finding of limited verbal ability in prematures at two years of age by comparison to controls. Lezine (1958) found that prematures make fewer vocalizations prior to eight months of age, but found no differences between prematures and normals at the age at which first words and first sentences were uttered. Mohr and

Bartelme (1930) also found no delay in the age of talking if allowances are made for the actual period of prematurity.

Development of general intelligence—Asher (1946) administered an intelligence test to 217 premature children and obtained a significant negative correlation between birth weight and IQ. Hess & Lundeen (1949) examined 212 premature children between three and 17 years of age whose birth weight had been 1,250 grams of below. Of this group, only 126 possessed normal intelligence. Dann et al. (1958), in comparing 34 prematures to their siblings, obtained significantly lower IQ scores for the premature group. Lubchencko et al. (1963) report that 25 of 60 prematures to whom they administered the (WISC) *Wechsler Intelligence Scale for Children* scored below 90 on full scale IQ. Davis (1951) reports that the premature children in his sample performed more poorly than controls on performance IQ, verbal IQ and full scale IQ on the WISC. Douglas (1956) also found prematures to perform more poorly than controls on vocabularly tests.

Severe intellectual impairment—Barlow (1945) compared 514 six- to eight-year-old prematures with 501 full-term controls. He found that three times (34%) as many prematures possessed some degree of mental retardation as controls (11%). Pasamanick and Lilienfeld (1955) investigated the birthweight of 276 retarded children (IQ's less than 80) and 232 controls. The percentage of prematures was significantly higher among retardates than controls. Similarly, Levine and Dann (1957) report that 30 subjects in a sample of 68 children with birth weights of approximately 1,000 grams had IQ's below 90.

School performance—Asher and Roberts (1949) investigated the birth weight and IQ of 4,800 grammar school children in Great Britain. The 877 children possessing some learning problem possessed a significantly lower birth weight than the remainder of the sample. Douglas (1960) reports that fewer prematures (10%) than controls (22%) passed examinations for admittance into British Grammar School. However, Davis (1951) and Blegan (1952) report no significant academic impairment among prematures as a group.

Reading—Uddenberg (1955) compared 64 prematures and 64 controls at 10 years of age, and found prematures to perform significantly lower than controls on an unspecified reading test. Douglas (1956) investigated 407 pairs of eight-year-old prematures and controls matched on age, sex, ordinal position in the family, mother's age and social class. The prematures were significantly more impaired in reading ability. These findings were replicated with a comparison of 355 pairs of 11-year-old prematures and controls (Douglas 1960).

Although fraught with methodological problems such as the frequent absence of quantifiable measures, the inadequate utilization of control groups as well as other controls, and varying definitions of prematurity, the research literature in this area yields a reasonably consistent picture of the premature child as one who is more susceptible to retardation in both physical and cognitive development. As such, he stands in greater need of some effective means of intervention which is capable of accelerating his rate of development, and hopefully increasing the upper limits of his development.

EARLY STIMULATION AS A MEANS OF ACCELERATING DEVELOPMENT

In recent years, data have emerged which indicate the beneficial effects of early stimulation on development. Although most of the research has been carried out on infrahuman subjects, a few studies have begun the difficult task of assessing the effect of early stimulation on humans. The primary theoretical bases for this research is found in Hebb's (1949) neuropsychological theory and Piaget's (1947) theory of development.

Theoretical bases—Piaget's work is more descriptive than explanatory in that he is primarily interested in identifying a hierarchal system of stages and milestones through which the child passes in the process of cognitive development, than in questions of *why* one child might develop more rapidly than another. Piaget places his greatest theoretical emphasis on the first two years of life which he calls the "sensorimotor period." Hunt (1961) interprets Piaget's description of development during this stage as the emergence of "a hierarchal organization or symbolic representations and information processing strategies deriving to a considerable degree from past experience" (page 109). If Hunt's interpretation of Piaget's work is accurate, then the statement, "resulting to a large extent from past experience," would indicate a bias on Piaget's part toward the importance of early stimulation. The details of Piaget's theory can be examined in detail in the works of Hunt (1961) and Flavell (1963).

Hebb: Hebb (1949) first became concerned with intellectual development as the result of two puzzling observations. One concerned the differential effects of early (e.g. first two years of life) and late (e.g. post adolescent) brain damage. He was struck by the extensive impact on learning and intelligence of relatively minor insults and ablations during the first two years in comparison to the relatively inconsequential effects of more extensive brain damage later in life. Secondly, Hebb was puzzled by the long period of intellectual immaturity in humans by comparison to lower animals (e.g. the fact that many vertebrates are capable of greater learning than humans during the first two years of life).

To begin his theorizing, Hebb distinguished two types of brain tissue. The function of the first is to manage nerve impulses associated with sensory input and motor output. This he called "committed tissue" because its functions (reflexes, etc.) were predetermined at birth. A second type of tissue was called "associative tissue" because the functions of this tissue are not determined at birth, but must be "established." Presumably, associative tissue is involved when new learning or new associations take place.

Hebb makes another important distinction between association tissue and sensory-motor tissue. Sensory-motor tissue must be activated by external stimuli, while it is felt that the human organism (through the use of association tissue) is capable of "autonomous central processes," involving behaviors which are initiated within the organism. In other words, association tissue and autonomous central processes are the means by which the human organism can incite itself to action. Hebb labeled the ratio of association tissue to sensory-motor tissue the A/S ratio, and theorized that the limits of intelligence are determined by this ratio. The larger the proportion of association tissue to sensory-motor tissue, the greater the organism's potential for cognitive complexity. It is obvious that the A/S ratio would differ from speci to speci, and thus (at least according to Hebb) explain the difference in intelligence between organisms at various points on the phylogenic scale. However our concern is with differences in intelligence within a single speci (humans). Hebb's theory allows for two means by which humans might differ in intelligence. One would involve inherited differences in the A/S ratio. The other would result from the differential extent to which the functions of association tissue were acquired or established.

This brings us to the most crucial aspect of Hebb's theory (at least as it pertains to early stimulation research) : the manner in which the associative tissue, which underlies higher cognitive functions, is established. Hebb's view on this point is that associative tissue, as well as the autonomous central processes, are established by virtue of *a wealth of sensory-motor experience during the first two years of life.* During these early months, the majority of the organism's behavior is less complex and presumably supported by sensory-motor tissue. However, associative tissue and autonomous central functions are being established, even though they are not particularly active. Therefore, differences in intelligence within species (particularly humans) are explained primarily by the differential extent to which the associative tissue and autonomous central processes are established. Again, it is important to note that the extent of establishment is dependent upon the amount of sensory-motor experience received during the critical period (first 18 to 24 months of life) .

From the above account, it is possible to see how Hebb's theory is capable of accounting for the two observations which puzzled him and which caused him to theorize in the first place. The lengthy period of intellectual immaturity in human beings is explained by the fact that humans possess extensive amounts of association tissue which must be established. Therefore, the first few months of life are spent primarily in sensory-motor activity while the more advanced processes (involving association tissue) are being established. Other organisms possessing greater amounts of committed tissue can use this to perform a variety of more unconscious or reflexive functions. Also, the lesser amount of association tissue in animals requires a shorter period of time for their functions to be established. The fact that humans possess more association tissue not only requires a longer period of immaturity during which time the associative tissue is being established, but the fact that more associative tissue *is* established enables human organisms to exceed, by far, the intellectual attainments of other species, once these processes are initiated.

Hebb's theory is also capable of explaining the differential effects of early and late brain damage, the second question which brought about his theorizing. Early brain damage is felt to interfere with the processes of establishing association tissue and autonomous functioning. Thus, the impairment is extensive because a great deal of the association tissue is never established. However, later brain damage, occurring after the majority of associative tissue and intellectual functions have been established, would not be expected to have as extensive an impact.

It should be fairly obvious from the above paragraphs that hypotheses concerning early stimulation derive naturally from Hebb's writings. It follows directly from his theory that any organism deprived of sensory-motor experience during the early months of life (e.g. prior to weaning in infra-human subjects or the first 24 months in humans) would experience a resulting and proportional *decrement* in the rate of cognitive development. This is because the associative tissue and accompanying functions would be less completely established. By the same token, any organism experiencing an environment enriched in sensory stimulation should experience an accompanying and proportional *increment* in cognitive development.

Hebb's emphasis on providing a wealth of sensory-motor experience during the early months of life places its emphasis on the *quantitative* aspects of such stimulation, with the *manner* in which the organism is stimulated being less important than the *amount* of stimulation provided through some sense modality. It also suggests that the modality to be developed need not be stimulated directly. For instance, motor functioning might be accelerated through visual stimulation or vice versa. The fact that such "indirect" forms of stimulation are possible during the early critical periods of cognitive development is supported by several works (Danzinger & Frankl, 1934; Dennis & Dennis, 1941; and Thompson & Heron, 1954). However, as has been pointed out earlier (Wright

1968), there is no evidence for the benefit of indirect stimulation (such as improving a child's reading through such things as having him walk a balance beam, etc.) following the first two years of life as is suggested by Kephart (1960) and Doman, Spitz, Zucman, Delacato, and Doman (1960).

The fact that the quantative aspects of stimulation seem most important during the first two years of life does not appear to generalize beyond that point. There is, in fact, theoretical as well as research evidence (Gray & Klaus 1965) to suggest that for human subjects the *qualitative* aspects of stimulation become primary by four years of age. Therefore, sensory-motor stimulation provided in a rather gross fashion may be beneficial in accelerating development during the first two years of life, but direct stimulation, remediation and practice (in other words, working directly with the behavior one wishes to accelerate) seem not only desirable but necessary after this time.

Another important variable which must be considered in programs providing stimulus enrichment involves constancy versus variability of stimulation. Several authors (Pratt, 1934; Irwin & Weiss, 1934a, 1934b, 1934c; Brackbill, Adams, Crowell & Gray, 1966; Denenberg, 1966) have demonstrated the diluting or passifying effect of *continuous* stimulation. Presumably, the organism "adapts" to such stimulation in a way which causes it to lose many of its stimulating properties. The same stimulation provided in a more variable or random manner would apparently produce greater reactivity and otherwise possess greater potential for accelerating development.

RESEARCH EVIDENCE CONCERNING THE EFFECTS OF EARLY STIMULATION

Infrahuman research in stimulus deprivation—There are numerous studies showing the detrimental effects of early stimulus deprivation on infrahuman subjects such as rats, rabbits, dogs and chimps. These include Hebb's (1937, 1947) own studies, investigations by Riesen (1947), Brattgard (1952), Guaron and Becker (1959) Forgays and Forgays (1952) Forgus (1954, 1955a, 1955b) as well as Thompson and Heron (1954).

Stimulus deprivation research with humans—The literature on early stimulus deprivation of human subjects is conspicuously vague, and fraught with methodological problems. Most of these studies involved investigations of "isolates" such as children chained in dark rooms with food slipped under the door to them (e.g. Mason, 1942) and ferals, children presumably reared by animal parents (e.g. Gesell, 1941). Reports of the initial functioning of feral and isolate children suggest that their early upbringing possessed extreme consequences as far as subsequent development is concerned. However, the doubtful accuracy of these accounts, as well as some very real questions as to whether or not some of the reported cases ever existed, prohibits much confidence being placed in them. Studies of the deprivation associated with children reared in orphanages and other institutions, while generally providing more easily substantiated data, have also been attacked on methodological grounds. An excellent critical review of this area with accompanying research suggestions is presented by Yarrow (1961). His major conclusions are: (1) There is a definite effect operating in cases of maternally deprived infants which produces a developmental decrement. (2) This effect (presumably involving some form of stimulus deprivation) needs to be clarified and researched. (3) Research in this area needs to be planned in a manner which is more systematic and rigorous and where the question asked has at least some chance of being answered.

Infrahuman studies of stimulus enrichment. Studies involving stimulus deprivation have been succeeded in more recent years by investigations of the effects of stimulus enrichment. The most significant work with infrahuman subjects has come primarily from the laboratories of Levine, Denenberg, and Kretch. The means of providing increased stimulation have included everything from handling and provision of play objects, to mild shock. These investigations have shown that increased stimulation in rats produces variability in plasma corticosterone response, an earlier adrenal absorbic acid response, earlier opening of eyes, earlier onset of estrus, greater weaning weight, greater adult weight and greater resistance to disease (Denenberg & Karas, 1961); Levine, 1962; Levine, Haltmeyer, Karas & Denenberg, 1967; Haltmeyer, Denenberg & Zarrow, 1967). Greater problem solving ability, increased exploratory behavior, less "emotionality" have been demonstrated by Denenberg and Morton (1962), Schaeffer (1963), Denenberg and Karas, (1961), Levine and Wetzel, 1963), and Denenberg, (1967). Krech (1966; Krech et al. 1962) has shown that early stimulation can affect not only learning, but chemistry and anatomical structure of the brain as determined by post mortem analysis.

Stimulus enrichment of human subjects—Recent years have produced an upsurge in the number of psychological studies involving human infants. A few investigators (Rheingold, Gewirtz & Ross, 1959; Kagan & Lewis, 1965; Lipsitt, Pederson & De Lucia, 1966), have provided impressive demonstrations of early learning and conditioning. They have shown that infants can learn, vocalize and emit social responses at a much earlier age than was previously thought possible. Such results provide clear evidence that infants' rates of development are being accelerated. However, parceling out whether this effect results from early cognitive stimulation which is concomitant with the conditioning experience and which increases development, or whether it can be explained solely on the basis of conditioning principles, is difficult if not impossible to ascertain.

Although most early stimulation studies have been conducted in just the past few years, work of this general nature can be traced back as far as that of Pratt (1934). His investigations concerned the effect of repeated auditory stimulation on the general activity of newborn infants. He found that gross total activity was increased during periods in which subjects were provided auditory stimulation. Although Pratt did not generalize beyond the fact that auditory stimulation increased activity among newborns, present day scholars might speculate that any variable increasing the activity rate of the newborn organism would have some potential for increasing the rate of development.

Recent studies of the effects of early stimulation can be divided into at least two general classes. One involves an investigation (usually post hoc) of the amount of stimulation provided in the normal course of upbringing. These studies usually involve questionnaires obtained from mothers, or naturalistic observations of mothers, which are designed to assess their childrearing activities, and particularly the amount of sensory-motor and other forms of stimulation which they provide. Mothers are usually divided into high and low stimulators, and measures of offspring development are then sampled in an attempt to relate maternal stimulation to some parameter of development.

Hopper and Pinneau (1957) unsuccessfully attempted to decrease the frequency of regurgitation in 21 experimental newborns (as compared to 21 controls) by having their mothers provide them with 10 minutes of special stimulation (defined as handling, rocking, swinging, rolling, fondling, tickling, bouncing, etc.) prior to each feeding. Their data *did* indicate that frequency of regurgitation decreased in both groups with age over the five-week period encompassed by the study. This indicates some relationship between the frequency of regurgitation and development, i.e. the older the child, the less he regurgitates. Had this study been successful in decreasing the rate of regurgitation through stimulation, it would have constituted one of the earliest examples of the successful application of early stimulation methods in accelerating the rate of development. As the results turned out, the study is mainly significant in representing an early attempt to test the early stimulation hypothesis.

Moss and Kagan (1958) investigated a sample of 19 boys and 25 girls from their population of subjects at the Felds Institute in Yellow Springs, Ohio. A Parent Behavioral Rating Instrument was administered in order to assess the rate at which parents "pushed" or otherwise showed concern over the rate at which their child learned to walk, talk, roll over, etc. The results (which were identical in both an initial and replication study) indicated a significant correlation between parental stimulation and IQ scores for boys at age three, but not at age six. No correlation between maternal acceleration and IQ scores for girls was found at either age three or age six. It should be noted that the type of "stimulation" employed was a nonspecific class of behaviors, presumably associated with maternal concern. It is probably not very similar to the usual forms of sensory-motor stimulation provided in laboratory studies where stimulation is experimentally manipulated. However, the results of this investigation do raise some interesting questions with regard to early stimulation work. Can we expect sex differences in the stimulus enrichment for male as opposed to female subjects? It is likely that stimulation is capable of increasing the immediate *rate* of development, but is incapable of extending the upper limits of development. The effects of stimulation, at least in this study, appear to differentially affect males and females, and to wash out by age six.

Rubenstein (1967) conducted a similar investigation to that of Moss and Kagan. She time-sampled the maternal attentiveness (defined as the number of times the mother was observed to look at, touch, hold or talk to her baby) provided for 44 five-month-old infants, and attempted to relate this to exploratory behavior at age 11 months. Babies were divided into those receiving high, low, and medium attentiveness. Samples were obtained in two separate three-hour periods at the time the child reached five months of age. The high attentiveness group exceeded the low attentiveness group in looking at, tactile manipulation of, and vocalizing to a novel stimulus when the novel stimulus was presented alone. The high attentiveness group exceeded both other groups in looking at and manipulating novel stimuli in preference to familiar ones. It was concluded that early stimulation, in the form of maternal attentiveness, is capable of facilitating exploratory behavior (an important early indicator of cognitive development in infants).

Irwin (1960), who 35 years ago (Irwin & Weiss, 1934a, 1934b, 1934c) was conducting research on the effect of stimulation on infants, has carried out an intriguing study of the effects of naturalistic, or mother-provided, stimulation. He investigated the effect of 15-20 minutes of auditory stimulation offered daily over an 18 month period. The stimulation consisted of mothers reading to their children. Subjects were 24 experimental and 10 control children between 13 and 30 months of age. For a criterion measure, he simply calculated the number of spontaneous vocalizations made by the child during visits to the home which occurred once every two months throughout the entire period of the experiment. Although little difference was found between the two groups on mean scores for frequency of vocalization prior to the 17th month, from that time on the difference increased consistently, with the experimental group having higher scores than controls.

The work of Schaffer and Emerson (1968) constitutes something of a bridge between studies involving naturalistic stimulation and a second type of stimulus enrichment program for human subjects: experimentally induced stimulation provided in a laboratory setting. Their interests concerned the relationship between environmental stimulation and performance on developmental tests. Subjects were 20 infants between five and six months of age. These were divided into two equal groups and given the *Griffith Developmental Scale* on three successive days. One group was tested after a brief no-stimulation period on all three days, while the other group received the no stimulation on only the first day and a stimulation period on the second and third days. Stimulus enrichment consisted of an adult's interacting with the child by standing over his cot, smiling and talking to him for three minutes; providing tactile stimulation by stroking his face and hands for three minutes; picking him up and setting him on the knee for three minutes; then returning him to his cot and providing three additional minutes of the same type of stimulation provided during the first three minutes. Mean developmental quotient on the *Griffith Developmental Scale* for all nonstimulated subjects (including the experimental group on test one) was 103. The mean score for experimental subjects on testing two and three (where stimulation was provided) was 113. There were no significant differences between the first, second and third testings for control subjects who received no stimulation. However, there was a significant difference between the developmental quotients of experimental subjects between the first (no-stimulation) and the second and third (stimulation) testings.

The closeness in time of the stimulation to the testing period in the above study, combined with the similarity of stimulation experiences to behaviors being measured by the developmental test, makes the procedure appear as something of a test "coaching" activity. This raises an important, though possibly disconcerting issue. Is early stimulation purely a means of increasing the rate of development of experimental subjects, or does it include components which serve primarily to increase subjects' ability to respond more effectively to criterion measures designed to assess their development? If so, what proportion of the total gain reported in various studies can be attributed to "coaching" versus more bonafide increments in development? The fact that the answer to this question is so difficult to parcel out may mean that its shadow will lurk over early stimulation work for some time. However, care in temporally separating stimulation and testing periods as well as providing stimulation which does not constitute overt practice for criterion testing can help to reduce fear of this type of contamination. A study of Sayegh and Dennis (1965) also bares upon this question. Although their manipulations do not appear as likely to constitute practice or coaching as did that of Schaffer and Emerson, the design leaves some doubt as to whether the experimental manipulations affected the subjects' development or simply their test taking ability.

Specifically, Sayegh and Dennis examined five experimental and eight control infants in The Creche, an institution for infants in Beirut, Lebanon. Their hypothesis was that the retardation experienced almost uniformly by infants raised in this facility could be attributed largely to the poverty of their experiences which were relevant to testing situations. The average developmental quotient as measured by the *Cattell Scale* for the 31 children between four and 12 months of age, who resided in this facility, was 60. Subjects were 13 infants between seven and 18 months of age, who were unable to sit alone. They were divided into groups of five experimental and eight control subjects possessing equivalent means with respect to chronological and developmental age. Experimental subjects were given one hour of increased stimulation on 15 different days. These experiences included attempts to accustom them to sitting upright, encouraging interest in objects, and assistance in developing skill in object manipulation. When all subjects were post-tested after a one month interval, the increase in developmental age for experimental subjects was four times the rate maintained prior to pre-testing. Control subjects gained significantly less than the experimental group but at a more rapid rate than they had exhibited during the pre-experimental period. The authors concluded that the increase in rate of growth in developmental age for controls could be explained by supplementary experiences inherent in the experimental procedures which had not been anticipated by the researchers. It is important to note that when supplementary experiences for experimental subjects stopped, both groups displayed very little gain in developmental age over the ensuing six-week period.

Although criterion measures were not obtained at approximately the same time that stimulation was provided, anyone familiar with the content of tests such as the *Cattell* will recognize some similarity between Sayegh and Dennis' experimental manipulations (encouraging sitting, manipulation of objects, etc.), and the performance required by developmental scales. The possibility, then, remains that a portion of their results can be attributed to coaching or practice.

White and Castle (1964) were among the first experimenters to investigate the effects of experimentally induced stimulation on human infants in this country. They, too, investigated children who had been born and raised in an institution. Their subjects were 10 experimental and 18 control children who were provided with 20 minutes of extra handling daily from the sixth to the 30th day of life. The effects of handling on visual attention, visually directed reaching, weight gain, performance on the Gesell developmental schedules and incidence of illness were assessed. No differences were found with regard to visually directed reaching, weight gain, general health, or performance on the Gesell schedules. However, a significant difference was obtained between the two groups on visual attention to the environment. Subsequent studies (White & Held, 1964; White, 1967) have demonstrated the beneficial effects of increased handling on visually monitored hitting and tactile exploration of nearby objects during the second and third months of life. And, White (1967) has demonstrated that handling can accelerate the age at which viewing an object and bringing it to the mouth (a behavior of important developmental significance according to Piaget) is observed in institutionalized infants. In the latter study, experimental subjects were able to perform this function in a period of time ranging from 89 to 98 days of age, while the same behavior in control subjects occurred between 100 and 147 days of age, a highly significant difference.

Another significant study in the field of early stimulation of human infants was performed by Casler (1965a). Eleven experimental infants from an orphanage were provided with 1,000 minutes of increased tactile stimulation over a ten-week period (10 minutes each morning, 10 minutes each afternoon, five days per week). The effects of this procedure on performance of the 11 experimental infants (as compared to 11 controls), on the *Gesell Developmental Schedules,* was assessed. Significant differences were obtained favoring the experimental group. However, a similar study (Casler 1965b), which attempted to assess the effects of 1,000 extra minutes of supplementary *verbal* stimulation, failed to produce significant differences between experimentals and controls on the *Gesell Schedules.*

The work of Ottinger, Blatchley, and Denenberg (1969) represents an example of recent and more carefully specified investigations of the effects of early stimulation. Like White and his associates, they were interested in the effects of early stimulation on visual attentiveness. The study involved the performance of 14 experimental and 14 control children on a visual fixation task similar to that described by Frantz (1958). Experimental subjects were provided with 140 minutes of primarily tactile and kinestic stimulation during the first three days of life. On the fourth day, experimental subjects performed better than controls on both variables of the Frantz task, in that they spent more time with their eyes open and more time fixated on the visual target. The Ottinger et al. data clearly did not involve what is generally called coaching or practice, since the majority of stimulation provided was either tactile or kinestic in nature, and the criterion measure involved visual functioning. However, the molecular nature of this investigation raises other questions. Is there any means by which to determine how long lasting are the effects of this type of stimulation? The fact that visual development is significantly accelerated at four days of age gives minimal hope of lasting benefit to the development of vision or other forms of cognition. This investigation *does,* however, demonstrate that significantly detectable differences in rate of development can be produced in *very young children* and as a result of only 140 minutes of extra stimulation.

Greenberg, Uzgiris and Hunt (1968) have performed one of the most recent investigations of the effects of early stimulation. They also chose the development of visual functions (age at which a blinking response appeared) for measuring the effects of early stimulation. Ten experimental infants were provided with a visual object which was attached to their crib within view, and in the line of vision for an eight-week period beginning at five weeks of age. Control subjects had no such devices attached to their crib. Significant differences between experimental and control subjects were obtained on the age at which a blinking response appeared.

RESEARCH—INTRODUCTION

Although the actual number of investigations has been few, the above studies do serve to reinforce hypotheses concerning the facilitating effects of early stimulation and the debilitating effects of early stimulus deprivation, as they effect the development of both human and infrahuman subjects. From the standpoint of our work at the University of Oklahoma Medical Center, it seemed reasonable to assume that an extensive program of early stimulation provided for premature infants contained a legitimate hope for increasing their rate of development as well as extending the upper limits of development. It was at this point, that we decided to launch a series of investigations of our own.

At any time a decision is reached to engage in an early stimulation project, several strategy decisions must be made. Among these is the issue of whether the research will attempt to influence some aspect of development with is very microscopic (such as the age at which a child obtains a blinking response), or more general aspects of development (such as are measured by performance on a developmental scale). In some ways this is a question of *relevance* versus *rigor*. If the experimental manipulations are quite specific, then a high degree of rigor can be employed, and the question asked has a stronger chance of being definitively answered. However, the molecular nature of the question, which contributes to experimental rigor, may distract from the relevancy of the question for clinical purposes. Clinicians and parents are interested in what can be done to accelerate a child's overall rate of development more than how to precipitate an earlier blink reflex.

A second issue comes into play if several different means of stimulation are provided in research of this type. When only one form of stimulation is provided, then any consequences of this manipulation can be attributed to this variable. However, if an experimental manipulation providing many forms and differing amounts of stimulation produces an effect, it still remains for future studies to parcel out which of the possible sources of gain are actually responsible for what proportion of the obtained effect. Our investigation, unlike most of those discussed on previous pages, elected a strategy of providing extensive amounts of varying kinds of stimulation over a prolonged period of time in an attempt to produce an extensive impact on the development of premature children. If the experiment is successful in producing a major effect, then something should be known immediately about the application of these results to the clinical problems of premature children from lower socioeconomic environments. However, additional work would be required in order to refine those aspects of the experimental manipulation which are responsible for gain.

RESEARCH PLAN

Objectives: The specific aims of our research can be outlined as follows:

1. To determine if early stimulation can counteract the combined effects of premature birth and socioeconomic environment.

2. To minimize the chances of detecting the possible effects of early stimulation by investigating several stimulation methods and by assessing their impact on a variety of developmental processes.

3. To determine the course and "holding power" of experimental effects by assessing development longitudinally over a period of years.

4. To further determine the duration of any experimental effects by assessing development at various intervals following the termination of the stimulus enrichment procedures.

5. To determine if self initiated stimulation is possibly more beneficial than stimulation over which subjects have no control.

6. To develop and evaluate the utility of mechanical home-stimulator devices as well as certain forms of "parents-provided" stimulation.

7. To obtain further information on the usefulness of criterion measures (such as the *Cattell Scale, Hunt-Uzgiris Scale, Bayley Scale*; infant conditioning tasks; neurological evaluations; plasma cortisone chemistries; weight gain; crying behavior; cardiac deceleration; etc.) for assessing infant development.

8. To obtain information on the ordinary home care practices for premature children in lower socioeconomic families.

9. To hopefully develop stimulation regimen which might be incorporated in pediatric care and management prescriptions for prematures and/or lower class infants.

Subjects—The subjects in the initial phase of our investigations are children admitted into the premature nursery at the University of Oklahoma Medical Center weighing less than 2,500 grams, and the product of a gestational period of 36 weeks of less. These patients must weigh 2,000 grams or more, and not require temperature control, oxygen or otherwise need to be confined to an isolette. All subjects are under the care of a staff pediatrician who assumes medical responsibility, and who excludes from the study any child who he feels would be adversely affected by the experimental procedures.

Parents of subjects are from the lower socioeconomic level which is defined as a family income of less than $3,000 per year plus $500 for each dependent. Parents of all potential subjects sign a common consent form indicating their willingness to cooperate in the study by having their children provided with supplementary stimulation and also to provide the necessary data for criterion measures. Parents are told that not all children accepted into the study will receive increased stimulation, but will only be evaluated on the criterion measures. After receiving parental consent, subjects are assigned to either the control group or one of three experimental groups.

Procedure—All experimental subjects receive the same experience during the first 21 days of the study. This involves eight daily periods of the following:

   1. Kinestetic stimulation provided by a rocking bassinet following a head to toe motion completing one cycle every five seconds. The subject's head is 15° above a level plane at the beginning and end of the cycle, and 40° above a level plane at the middle of the cycle. Rocking begins one hour prior to each of the subject's eight daily feedings, and occurs for random periods of five to 10 minutes of rocking punctuated by five to ten minutes during which the infant does not rock. This process is controlled by an automatic timer, and yields approximately 30 minutes of actual rocking during each of the three-hour cycles.
   2. Auditory stimulation of approximately 50 db consisting of music and talk from a 24-hour FM radio station. To increase stimulus variability, an automatic timer activates and deactivates the radio at random intervals of between five and 10 minutes. This produces approximately 90 minutes of auditory stimulation during each of the day's eight, three-hour cycles.
   3. Tactile, kinestetic and visual stimulation provided by a nurse who picks the subject up and carries him about the room, exposing him to a wide variety of visual cues for approximately 10 minutes before and 10 minutes following each of the eight daily feedings. Visual stimulation is also increased by providing striped sheets for the beds of all experimental subjects.

On completion of the 21-day hospital-based stimulation program, certain criterion measures are obtained from all subjects. Those in the

experimental groups are then provided with one of three types of home
stimulator cribs. Study parents have previously agreed to use nothing
in addition to the stimulator crib for the child's bed until nine months
following the cessation of the hospital-based stimulation program. Visits
to these families by a public health nurse and research assistant insure
proper use of stimulator crib, and a rapid correction of any parental
deviation from the prescribed program as well as any mechanical breakdown of the apparatus.

Piaget's third stage of development, "secondary circular reactions,"
occurs in a period from roughly three to eight months of age, a time
corresponding to the period time of which our experimental subjects
spend in their home stimulator cribs. This is the time, according to Piaget, during which the child first begins to deliberately *cause* events to occur. He cites an example (Piaget, 1952) of such behavior in his daughter
Lucienne at three months of age. It was at this point that she first
discovered that shaking her legs would cause a joy producing experience
(movement of a doll suspended above her crib). As a result, the child
would frequently shake her legs vigorously in order to move the crib
and the doll, and then smile broadly when the desired event would
occur (page 157). According to Piaget's observation, this is a typical
example of the first occurrence of a child's exercising control over his
environment. However, the importance of one's manipulating his environment may be difficult to overstate. It is clear from observing adults that
some exercise a high degree of control, while others seem to remain
at the mercy of their environment, allowing it to control them. Present
social concerns in America relating to apathy in the culturally deprived
child, welfare among the lower classes, etc., dramatize the importance
of an individual's exercising deliberate control over his environment
rather than assuming a passive dependency on the environment and
whatever it may provide for him. It is possible that experiences between
three and eight months of age when, according to Piaget, the individual
is first beginning to control his environment, are crucial in regard to
subsequent adult behaviors such as apathy, dependency, or various forms
of coping in the area of cognition. It seems possible that if a child has
the opportunity for successful environmental manipulation during this
period, then such behavior may be gotten off to an all important "good
start" during what may be a true critical period of its development.
If, on the other hand, there is little opportunity at this age to manipulate one's environment, than a process of apathy or disinclination
to engage the environment and manipulate it may be set in motion.
For these reasons, we decided to incorporate into our investigations some
forms of stimulation over which subjects could exercise control.

Stimulation group I: The stimulator crib for this group is activated
by a timer for 10 hours daily. The exact period varies according to the

living pattern of the family, but generally lasts from approximately 8:00 a.m. until 6:00 p.m. The stimulator crib is capable of vibrating, providing music and talk from a radio, and displaying a variety of multicolored geometrically designed light patterns. Each of these three types of stimulation is activated for 15 minutes every hour and a half and is followed by a 15-minute "no stimulation" period. Thus, the subject receives alternating 15-minute periods of stimulation and no stimulation, with the type of stimulation varying in order between each of the three types. Each subject is thus guaranteed a standardized stimulation experience during the time he spends in the stimulator crib. Variation in the stimulation experience which results from different subjects being kept by their parents in the stimulator cribs for different lengths of time should randomize itself across groups and thus not bias group comparisons.

Stimulation group II: The stimulator crib for this group is also activated for a 10-hour period daily. This 10-hour period also varies according to the living pattern of the family, but generally begins at approximately 8:00 a.m. and lasts until 6:00 p.m. At the beginning of each 10-hour period the apparatus automatically provides 45 minutes of stimulation involving 15 minutes of vibrating 15 minutes of music and talk, and 15 minutes of visual stimulation from the multicolored, geographically designed light patterns. This apparatus also automatically provides stimulation, identical to that described above, during the last 45 minutes of the daily 10-hour stimulation period. During the eight and a half hour interim between the two automatically provided stimulation periods, the apparatus can be activated only by movements of the subject within his crib. The crib is constructed so that one minute of one type of stimulation can be set off by a subject's movement which is equal to or greater than a 40° rotation the entire body, a 60° extension or flexion of either an arm or leg, or a 90° rotation of the head. Head movement activates the auditory stimulation, arm and leg movement activates the visual stimulation, and rotation of the entire body activates vibrating stimulation. Automatic counters tally the number and type of one-minute stimulation periods which each subject activates over a given period of time.

Stimulation group III: The stimulator crib for this group operates in a manner similar to that of stimulator group II. However, the one-minute stimulation periods are activated by subject vocalizations at a magnitude less than the crying level. This is accomplished by means of a vocal key, operating on the principle of telemetry, and attached to each subject's neck just above the vocal cords. Any appropriate vocalization alternately activates the vibrating, auditory, and visual phases of stimulation. However, only one form of stimulation is activated at a time.

At the end of the nine months of stimulation provided by the home stimulator cribs, a logistic decision must be made. One choice will be to discontinue stimulation at this point, while continuing to measure the effects of earlier stimulation over the next several months. A second alternative would be to provide parents of experimental subjects with training on the provision of naturalistic (parent provided) stimulation. Criterion measures obtained at one year of age and beyond would then provide data concerning the impact of the total stimulation program, but would prohibit a parceling out of the lasting effects of the stimulation which was offered during the first ten months. Also, at the end of the present 36-month experimental period, the investigators will be required to make an additional logistic decision about whether or not to provide the same infants with additional stimulation at this point. If the decision is made to continue to provide stimulation, it would no doubt take the form of more direct forms of stimulation and tutoring, rather than the more indirect forms of stimulation such as were provided during the first 10 months of life.

Criterion measures—Physical maturation is assessed by measures of height and weight at the time of discharge from the hospital (at the end of the initial 21-day stimulation program) and at three, six, nine, 12, 24, and 36 months of age). A quantifiable neurological examination similar to that suggested by Beintema and Prechtl (1968) is obtained at the beginning and end of the initial 21-day stimulation period and at six, 12, 24 and 36 months of age. This examination is administered by a pediatric neurologist who is unaware of the group (experimental or control) to which the subject belongs. The *Hunt-Uzgiris Scale, Cattell Infant Intelligence Scale,* and the *Bayley Scale of Infant Development* are administered to all subjects at six, nine, 12, and 18 months of age. A combination of the *Cattell Scale* and the revised *Stanford-Binet* (Form L-M) is administered at 24 and 36 months. The ability of subjects to perform on a neonatal conditioning task devised by Siqueland and Lipsitt (1966) will be tested at the end of the initial 21-day stimulation period. Performance of subjects on a conditioning task requiring them to press a panel for reinforcement will be measured at 12, 24, and 36 months of age. Lipsitt, Pederson and De Lucia (1966) have demonstrated that 12-month-old infants can be conditioned by means of this apparatus. An acoustical analysis will be made of subjects' crying behavior at the end of the initial 21-day stimulation period as well as at the end of the ensuing nine-month home stimulator experience and at 12, 24, and 36 months of age. This analysis involves snapping the patient's foot with a rubber band and recording the ensuing cry on an apparatus which permits these vocalizations to be broken down into components such as duration, frequency, and variability of cry phonations. Previous research by Karelitz and Fisichelli (1962) has related cry phonations to central nervous system integrity. Caldwell and Woodcock (unpublished data) have demonstrated the sensitivity of cry phonations to developmental changes associated with early stimulation. Heart rate response to the rubber band stimulus is also obtained at the same time as cry recordings, since Woodcock (1969) has demonstrated a relationship between development and heart rate response to such stimulation. Two studies (Haltmeyer, Denenberg & Zorrow, 1967; Levine, Haltmeyer, Karas & Denenberg, 1967) have shown that plasma corticosterone chemistries in rats is related to early stimulation. This finding has produced some speculation that adrenal cortical functions such as corticosterone or other glucocorticoids may represent an underlying mechanism explaining the beneficial effects of early stimulation on development. For this reason, glucocorticoid chemistries were included in our investigations as a criterion measure. These counts are obtained by awakening subjects from a sleeping state during a nonstimulation period on the first, tenth, and twentieth days of the initial 21-day stimulation day period. They are also obtained along with the cry and heart rate measures in response to the rubber band stimulus. Obtaining glucocorticoid chemistries under the two conditions of no stimulation and rubber band snap carries with it the maximum possibility of measuring subjects' response under conditions of both maximum and minimum stimulation.

Although the above investigation is currently underway, insufficient data has been obtained for any statistical manipulations to be performed or reported. However, the results of an initial pilot study, performed in order to iron out procedures and to obtain some idea about the effects of the initial 21-day stimulation period, have been secured. These results are reported below.

PILOT STUDY

The initial pilot study involved subjecting five experimental and five matched control premies to the initial 21-day stimulation program. Criterion measures included pre and post neurological examinations, weight gain, glucocorticoid chemistries, and response on the head turning conditioning task described by Siqueland and Lipsitt (1966). There were two male and three female subjects in both the experimental and control groups. No differences existed between the two groups in weight at the beginning of the study, and all subjects were free from any significant illness or disability.

No differences were obtained between groups as measured by pre and post neurological examinations.

Weight gains for experimentals and controls are shown in Table 1. While not statistically significant, there is some suggestion that experimental subjects may in fact gain less weight than controls.

Glucocorticoid chemistries (unlike the design reported above) were

TABLE 1

PERFORMANCE OF EXPERIMENTAL AND CONTROL SUBJECTS
ON THREE CRITERION MEASURES

Subject		Weight gain —grams	17-OH corticosteroids: on 5th day	on 10th day	on 15th day	Number of rooting responses out of 30 trials
Experimental	I	580	24.1	21.9	13.1	21
"	II	700	25.5	21.2	13.4	20
"	III	560	27.9	19.8	11.4	17
"	IV	730	20.9	11.4	11.2	22
"	V	580	27.7	11.7	11.4	16
Control	I	800	63.5	52.4	34.0	4
"	II	660	45.5	41.4	53.8	10
"	III	740	55.5	44.1	39.4	5
"	IV	700	51.4	45.8	54.3	6
"	V	685	55.1	51.4	41.4	7

obtained on a fifth, tenth, and fifteenth day of the investigation. Table 1 shows the number of micrograms percent of plasma 17-OH cortico-steroids. From Table 1, it can be seen that stimulated infants produced much less glucocorticoid material than did their matched controls. The most plausible explanation for this finding seems to be that obtaining the blood necessary to assess glucocorticoid chemistries is in itself stressful or stimulating experience which involves awakening the child, tieing of a rubber band about his arm, inserting a needle into the ante-cubital vein and extracting 1 cc. of blood. It would appear that the stimulated infants are more resistant, at least less reactive, to this form of stress.

An attempt was made to assess the performance of five experimental and five control infants on the neonatal conditioning task described by Siqueland and Lipsitt (1966). This task involves a classical conditioning procedure whereby the infant "learns" to emit a rooting reflex (head turning in search of a nipple) to the sound of a buzzer. Conditioning is accomplished by stimulating the infant's cheek with a nipple or piece of cotton (unconditioned stimulus) so as to evoke the rooting reflex (unconditioned response). A buzzer (condition stimulus) is sounded at the same time that the conditioned stimulus (touching the subject's cheek) is presented. The conditioned response involves a turning of the head when only the bell is sounded. Contrary to our expectation, none of the premature subjects (in either the experimental or control group) possessed a fully developed rooting reflex at the end of the 21-day period. It was, therefore, impossible to condition subjects to emit this reflex to a conditioned stimulus. As a result of these circum-stances, the measure obtained on this task was not a measure of the number of conditioned responses as had been anticipated, but rather the number of times that a rooting reflex was emitted in response to a stimulus on the subject's cheek. Subjects were allowed to respond to 30 trials of having a nipple pressed against their cheek approximately three centimeters from the edge of the mouth. A head-turning response was reinforced with an opportunity to suck on the nipple stimulus for three seconds and thereby obtained a sweet tasting glucose solution. Table 1 shows the number of head-turning responses (out of a possible 30) which were emitted by experimental and control subjects.

There was one very striking but *un*quantifiable source of data which emerged out of our pilot study. It involved the reaction of the nursing staff to stimulated and control infants. During the period of time in which the first control and experimental subjects were being run, members of the nursing staff expressed concern about "what was being done to the experimental subjects." The basis for their concern, as it turned out, was that stimulated subjects stayed awake more, cried more, and were generally both more responsive and more demanding. Control subjects seemed content to lie quietly (almost vegetatively it seemed) in their cribs which in turn caused nursing staff not only less work, but considerably less concern. The fears of nurses were resolved by explaining that higher levels of demand and responsivity on the part of premies was likely a good rather than a bad sign. However, it was not until some nurses were able to observe the improved performance of experimental subjects on the head-turning task at the end of the 21-day program that they were able to feel completely comfortable with this procedure.

SUMMARY AND CONCLUSIONS

The preceding pages have described the research and theoretical bases for a program of early stimulus enrichment for premature children. The likelihood is that children born prematurely and/or reared in lower class socio-economic environments, are extremely vulnerable to developmental delay and deficit. Data supporting this vulnerability is presented. The experimental design for a longitudinal investigation of the effects of early stimulation is outlined, and the results of an intial pilot study are reported. The pilot investigation produced marked differences between experimentals and controls on glucocorticoid chemistries and neurological development (as measured by subjects' rooting reflex), but did not produce significant differences in weight gain or over-all neurological development. The theoretical and research bases, as well as our initial pilot data, serve to reinforce the hypothesis that an early stimulation program can produce detectable increments in the rate of development and extend the upper limits of development for premature children.

REFERENCES

ALM, I.: The long-term prognosis for prematurely born children: follow-up study of 999 premature boys born in wedlock and 1002 controls. *Acta Paediat.* (Stockholm) 42 (suppl. 94): 1953.

ASHER, C.: The prognosis of immaturity. *Brit. Med. J.* 1: 793-796, 1946.

ASHER, C., & ROBERTS, J. A. F.: A study of birth weight and intelligence. *Brit. J. Prev. Soc. Med.* 3: 56-68, 1949.

BAEDORF, K.: The mental development of children with birth weight below 1,700 grams. *Z. Kinderheilk.* 59: 218-235, 1938.

BARLOW, A.: Prognosis in prematurity. *Arch. Dis. Child.* 20:184-185, 1945.

BEINTEMA, D. J. & PRECHTL, H. F. R. *A neurological study of newborn infants.* Lavenham, England, William Heinemann Medical Books, Ltd., 1968.

BENTON, A. L.: Mental development of prematurely born children: Critical review of literature. *Amer. J. Orthopsychiat.* 10: 719-746, 1940.

BESKOW, B.: Mental disturbance in premature children of school age. *Acta Paediat.* 37: 125-145, 1949.

BLEGAN, S. D.: The premature child. *Acta Paediat.* 42: (No. 88) 1952.

BRACKBILL, Y., ADAMS, G., CROWELL, D. H., GRAY, M. L.: Arousal level in neonates and preschool children under continuous auditory stimulation. *J. Exp. Child Psychol.* 4: 178-188, 1966.

BRAINE, M. D. S., HEIMER, C. B., WORTIS, H., FREEDMAN, A. M.: Factors associated with impairment of the early development of prematures. *Monogr. Soc. Res. Child Develop.* 31 (Serial No. 106): 1966.

BRANDT, P.: The destiny of prematures. *Mschr. Kinderheilk.* 27: 209-221, 1924.

BRATTGARD, S. O.: The importance of adequate stimulation for the chemical composition of retinal ganglion cells during early postnatal development. *Acta Radiol.* (Stockholm) (suppl. 96): 1952.

CASLER, L.: The effects of extra tactile stimulation on a group of institutionalized infants. *Genet. Psychol. Monogr.* 71: 137-175, 1965a.

CASLER, L.: The effects of supplementary verbal stimulation on a group of institutionalized infants. *J. Child Psychol. Psychiat.* 6: 19-27, 1965b.

CHOW, K. L., & NISSEN, H. W.: Interocular transfer of learning in visually naive and experienced infant chimpanzees. *J. Comp. Physiol. Psychol.* 48: 229-237, 1955.

COMBERG, M.: The fate and development of premature infants up to early school age. *Z. Kinderheilk.* 43: 462, 1927.

DANN, M., LEVINE, S. Z., & NEW, E.: The development of prematurely born children with birth weights or minimal postnatal weights of 1,000 grams or less. *Pediatrics* 22: 1037-1053, 1958.

DANZINGER, L., & FRANKL, L.: On the problem of functional maturity. *Z. Kinderforschung* 43: 219-54, 1934.

DAVIS, D. C.: Comparative study of the growth and development of premature and full term children with special reference to oral communication. Unpublished doctoral dissertation, Northwestern University, Evanston, Illinois, 1951.

DENENBERG, V. H.: "Animal studies on developmental determinants of behavioral adaptability," in Harvey, O. J. (ed.): *Determinants of behavioral adaptability,* New York: Springer Publishing, 1966.

DENENBERG, V. H.: "Stimulation in infancy, emotional reactivity, and exploratory behavior," in Glass, D. C. (ed.): *Neurophysiology and emotion.* New York: Rockerfeller University Press, 1967.

DENENBERG, V. H., & KARAS, G. G.: Interactive effects of infantile and adult experiences upon weight gain and mortality in the rat. *J. Comp. Physiol. Psychol.* 54: 685-689, 1961.

DENENBERG, V. H., & MORTON, J. R. C.: Effects of preweaning and postweaning manipulations upon problem-solving behavior. *J. Comp. Physiol. Psychol.* 55: 1096-1098, 1962.

DENNIS, W., & DENNIS, M. G.: Infant development under conditions of restricted practice and minimum social stimulation. *Genet. Psychol. Monogr.* 23: 149-55, 1941.

DOMAN, R. J., SPITZ, E. B., ZUCMAN, E., DELACATO, C. H., & DOMAN, G.: Children with severe brain injuries. *JAMA*. 174: 257-62, 1960.

DOUGLAS, J. W. B.: Mental ability and school achievement of premature children at eight years of age. *Brit. Med. J.* 1: 1210-1214, 1956.

DOUGLAS, J. W. B.: "Premature" children at primary school. *Brit. Med. J.* 1: 1008-1013, 1960.

DRILLIEN, C. M.: Growth & development in a group of children of very low birth weight. *Arch. Dis. Child.* 33: 10-18, 1958.

DRILLIEN, C. M.: A longitudinal study of growth & development of prematurely and maturely born children. Part III: Mental development. *Arch. Dis. Child.* 34: 487-494, 1959.

DUNHAM, E. C.: *Premature infants.* New York: Harper, 1955.

EAMES, T. H.: Comparison of children of premature and full term birth who fail in reading. *J. Educ. Res.* 38: 506-508, 1945.

EAMES, T. H. Comparison of the eye conditions of hypermature, premature and full term school children. *Eye, Ear, Nose & Throat Monthly,* 1946, 43, 36-41.

FLAVELL, J. H.: *The developmental psychology of Jean Piaget.* Princeton, N. J.: Van Nostrand, 1963.

FORGAYS, D. G., & FORGAYS, J. W.: The nature of the effect of free environmental experience in the rat. *J. Comp. Physiol. Psychol.* 45: 322-328, 1952.

FORGUS, R. H.: The effect of early perceptual learning on the behavioral organization of adult rats. *J. Comp. Physiol. Psychol.* 47: 331-336, 1954.

FORGUS, R. H.: Influence of early experience on maze-learning with and without visual cues. *Canad. J. Psychol.* 9: 207-214, 1955a.

FORGUS, R. H.: Early visual and motor experience as determiners of complex maze-learning ability under rich and reduced stimulation. *J. Comp. Physiol. Psychol.* 48: 215-220, 1955b.

FORSCHNER-BOKE, H.: A description of prematures from the Children's Hospital. *Arch. Kinderheilk.* 75: 20-35, 1924.

FRANTZ, R. L.: Pattern vision in young infants. *Psychol. Record* 8: 43-47, 1958.

GESELL, A.: *The mental growth of the pre-school child.* New York: Macmillan, 1925.

GESELL, A.: *Infancy and human growth.* New York: Macmillan, 1928.

GESELL, A.: *Wolf child and human child.* New York: Harper and Bros., 1941.

GRAY, S. W., & KLAUS, R.: An experimental program for culturally deprived children. *Child. Develop.* 36: 887-98, 1965.

GREENBERG, D., UZGIRIS, I. C., & HUNT, J. McV.: Hastening the development of the blink-response with looking. *J. Gen. Psychol.* 113: 167-176, 1968.

GAURON, E. F., & BECKER, W. C.: The effects of early sensory deprivation on adult rat behavior under competition stress: an attempt at replication of a study by Alexander Wolf. *J. Comp. Physiol. Psychol.* 52: 689-693, 1959.

HALTMEYER, G. C., DENENBERG, V. H., & ZARROW, M. X.: Modification of the plasma corticosterone response as a function of infantile stimulation and electric shock parameters. *Physiol. Beh.* 2: 61-63, 1967.

HARPER, P. A., FISCHER, K., & RIDER, R. V.: Neurological and intellectual status of prematures at 3 to 5 years of age. *J. Pediat.* 55: 679-690, 1959.

HEBB, D. O.: The innate organization of visual activity: II. Transfer of response in the discrimination of brightness and size by rats reared in total darkness. *J. Comp. Psychol.* 24: 277-299, 1937.

HEBB, D. O.: The effects of early experience on problem-solving at maturity. *Amer. Psychologist* 2: 306-307, 1947.

HEBB, D. O.: *The organization of behavior.* New York: Wiley, 1949.

HESS, J. M., & LUNDEEN, E. C.: *The premature infant,* ed 2, Philadelphia: Lippincott, 1949, pp. 318-323.

HODGMAN, J. E.: Clinical evaluation of the newborn infant. *Hospital Practice* pp. 70-85, (May) 1969.

HOPPER, H. E., & PINNEAU, S. R.: Frequency of regurgitation in infancy as related to the amount of stimulation received from the mother. *Child Develop.* 28: 228-235 (No. 2), 1957.

HUNT, J. McV.: *Intelligence and experience.* New York: The Ronald Press Company, 1961.

IRWIN, O. C.: Infant speech: Effect of systematic reading of stories. *J. Speech Hearing Res.* 3: 187-190 (No. 2), 1960.

IRWIN, O. C., & WEISS, L. A.: Differential variations in the activity and crying of the newborn infant under different intensities of light: A comparison of observational with polygraph findings. *Univer. Iowa Stud. Child Welf.* 9: 139-147, 1934a.

IRWIN, O. C., & WEISS, L. A.: The effect of clothing on the general and vocal activity of the newborn infant. *Univer. Iowa Stud. Child Welf.* 9: 151-162, 1934b.

IRWIN, O. C., & WEISS, L. A.: The effect of darkness on the activity of newborn infants. *Univer. Iowa Stud. Child Welf.* 9: 165-175, 1934c.

KAGAN, J., & LEWIS, M.: Studies in attention in the human infant. *Merrill-Palmer Quarterly* 11: 95-127, 1965.

KARELITZ, S., & FISICHELLI, V. R.: The cry thresholds of normal infants and those with brain damage. An aid in the early diagnosis of severe brain damage. *J. Pediat.* 61: 679-685, 1962.

KEPHART, N. C.: *The slow learner in the classroom.* Merrill Books, 1960.

KINSEY, V. E., JACOBUS, J. T., & HEMPHILL, F. M.: Retrolental fibroplasia: Cooperative study of retrolental fibroplasia and the use of oxygen. *AMA Arch. Ophthal.* 56: 481-543, 1956.

KNOBLOCK, H., RIDER, R., HARPER, P., & PASAMANICK, B.: Neuropsychiatric sequelae of prematurity. *JAMA* 161: 581-585, 1956.

KORTHAUER, O.: What do we achieve with institutional care of the very small premature? *Z. Geburtsh. Gynerkol.* 94: 104-122, 1929.

KRECH, D.: Environment, heredity, brain and intelligence, read before Southwestern Psychological Association, Arlington, Texas, 1966.

KRECH, D., ROSENZWEIG, M. R., & BENNETT, E. L.: Relations between brain chemistry and problem-solving among rats raised in enriched and impoverished environments. *J. Comp. Physiol. Psychol.* 55: 801-807 (No. 5), 1962.

LEVINE, S. "Psychophysiological effects of infantile stimulation," in E. L. Bliss (ed.): *Roots of behavior,* New York, Harper, 1962.

LEVINE, S., HALTMEYER, G. C., KARAS, G. G., & DENENBERG, V. M.: Psychological and behavioral effects of infantile stimulation. *Physiol. Beh.* 2: 55-59, 1967.

LEVINE, S., & WETZEL, A.: Infantile experiences, strain differences, and avoidance learning. *J. Comp. Physiol. Psychol.* 56: 879-881, 1963.

LEVINE, S. J., & DANN, M.: Survival rates and weight gains in premature infants weighing 1000 grams or less. *Ann. Paediat. Fenn.* 3: 185-192, 1957.

LEVY, S.: About physical and mental development of premature babies. *Kinderheilk* 121: 41-84, 1928.

LEZINE, I.: The psychomotor development of young prematures. *Etudes Neo-Natales* 7: 1-50, 1958.

LILIENFELD, A. M., PASAMANICK, B., & ROGERS, M.: Relationships between pregnancy experience and the development of certain neuropsychiatric disorders in children. *Amer. J. Public Health* 45: 637-643, 1955.

LIPSITT, L. P., PEDERSON, L. J., & DELUCIA, C. A.: Conjugate reinforcement of operant responding in infants. *Psychology Science* 4: 67-68, 1966.

LOOFT, C.: The small brain and the development of intelligence. *Acta Pediat.* 1: 282-297, 1921.

LUBCHENKO, L. O., HORNER, F. A., REED, L. H., HIX, I. E., METCALF, D., COHIG, R., ELLIOTT, H. C., & BOURG, M.: Sequelae of premature birth. *Amer. J. Dis. Child.* 106: 101-115, 1963.

MASON, M. K.: Learning to speak after six and one-half years of silence. *J. of Speech Disorders,* 7: 295-304, 1942.

MELCHER, R. T.: Development within the first 2 years of infants prematurely born. *Child. Develop.* 8: 1-14, 1937.

MOHR, G. J., & BARTELME, P.: Mental and physical development of children prematurely born. *Amer. J. Dis. Child.* 40: 1000-1015, 1930.

MOHR, G. J., & BARTELME, P.: "Development studies of prematurely born children," in Hess, J. H., Mohr, G. J. and Bartelme, P. (eds.): *The physical and mental growth of prematurely born children,* Chicago: University of Chicago Press, 1934, pp. 57-217.

Moss, H. A., & Kagan, J.: Maternal influences on early IQ scores. *Psychol. Rep.* 4: 655-661, 1958.

Ottinger, D. R., Blatchley, M. E., & Denenberg, V.: Stimulation of human neonates and visual attentiveness, read before APA, Washington, D.C., 1969.

Pasamanick, B., & Lilienfeld, A. M.: Association of maternal and fetal factors with development of mental deficiency; abnormalities in prenatal and paranatal periods. *JAMA,* 159: 155-160, 1955.

Patz, A., Hoech, L. D., & De La Cruz, E.: Studies on the effect of high oxygen administration in retrolental fibroplasia: I Nursery observations. *Amer. J. Ophthal.* 35: 1248, 1952.

Piaget, J.: *The psychology of intelligence.* London: Routledge & Kegan Paul, 1947.

Piaget, J.: *The origins of intelligence in children.* New York: International Universities Press, 1952.

Pratt, K. C.: The effects of repeated auditory stimulation upon the general activity of newborn infants. *J. Genet. Psychol.* 44: 96-114, 1934.

Riesen, A. H.: The development of visual perception in man and chimpanzee. *Science,* 106: 107-108, 1947.

Rheingold, H. L., Gewirtz, J. L., & Ross, H. W.: Social conditioning of vocalizations in the infant. *J. Comp. Physiol. Psychol.* 52 :68-73, 1959.

Rossier, A.: The future of the premature infant. *Develop. Med. Child. Neurol.* 4: 483-487, 1962.

Rubenstein, J.: Maternal attentiveness and subsequent exploratory behavior in the infant. *Child Develop.* 38: 1088-1100, 1967.

Sayegh, Y., & Dennis, W.: The effect of supplementary experiences upon the behavioral development of infants in institutions. *Child Develop.* 36: 82-90 (No. 1), 1965.

Schaeffer, T., Jr.: Early "experience" and its effects on later behavioral processes in rats: II. A critical factor in the early handling phenomenon. *Trans. N.Y. Acad. Sci.* 25: 871-889, 1963.

Schaffer, H. R., & Emerson, P. E.: The effects of experimentally administered stimulation on developmental quotients of infants. *Brit. J. Soc. Clin. Psychol.* 7: 61-67, 1968.

Schoberlein, W.: Zur Frage der Entwicklung der Unreifgeborenen. *Monatschr. Kinderheilk,* 1938, 76, 80, 106 In Benton (1940).

Shirley, M.: Development of immature babies during their first two years of life. *Child Develop.* 9: 347, 1938.

Shirley, M.: A behavior syndrome characterizing prematurely born children. *Child Develop.* 10: 115-128, 1939.

Sinclair, J. C.: Low birth weight infants: Physiological considerations, in Barnett, H. L. (ed.): *Pediatrics,* New York: Appleton Century-Crofts, 1968, pp. 78-90.

Siqueland, E. R., & Lipsitt, L. P.: Conditioned head-turning in human newborns. *J. Exp. Child Psychol.* 3: 356-376, 1966.

Thompson, W. R., & Heron, W.: The effects of restricting early experience on the problem-solving capacity of dogs. *Canad. J. Psychol.,* 1954.

Uddenberg, G.: Diagnostic studies of prematures. *Acta Psychiat. Scand.,* suppl. 104, 1955.

Wall, M.: On the subsequent development of premature children with special reference to later nervous, psychiatric and intellectual disturbances. *Mschr. Geburtsh. Gynakol.* 37: 456-486, 1913.

White, B. L.: An experimental approach to the effects of experience on early human behavior, read before the Minnesota Symposium on Child Psychology, Minneapolis, 1967.

White, B. L., & Castle, P. W.: Visual exploratory behavior following postnatal handling of human infants. *Percept. Motor Skills* 18: 497-502, 1964.

WHITE, B. L., & HELD, R. M.: Observations on the development of visually-directed reaching. *Child Develop.* 35: 349-364, 1964.

WIENER, G.: Psychological correlates of premature birth: A review. *J. Nerv. Ment. Dis.* 134: 129-144, 1962.

WORTIS, H., & FREEDMAN, A.: The contribution of social environment to the development of premature children. *Amer. J. Orthopsychiat.* 35: 57-68, 1965.

WOODCOCK, J. M.: The effect of rocking stimulation on neonatal reactivity. Unpublished doctoral dissertation. Purdue University, 1969.

WRIGHT, L.: "Highlights of human development, birth to age eleven," in Sloan, M. R. (ed.): *Perceptual-Motor Foundations: A Multidisciplinary Concern,* Wash., D.C.: Amer. Assoc. Health, Physical Educ. & Rec., pp. 1-18, 1968.

YARROW, L.: Maternal deprivation: Toward an empirical and conceptual reevaluation. *Psychol. Bull.* 58: 459-490, 1961.

YERUAHALMY, J.: The low-birthweight baby. *Hospital Practice.* 3: 62-69, 1968.

ZIECHEN, T.: *Mental disorders including mental deficiency and psychopathology in childhood.* Berlin: Rewther and Reichard, 1926.

13

CHANGES OVER TIME IN THE INCIDENCE AND PREVALENCE OF MENTAL RETARDATION

Zena A. Stein, M.A., M.B., B.Ch.

Associate Professor and Director, Epidemiology Research Unit,
N. Y. State Department of Mental Hygiene, Division of Epidemiology,
Columbia University

and

Mervyn W. Susser, M.B., B.Ch., F.R.C.P.(E.)

Chairman, Division of Epidemiology, Columbia University

Historical changes in disease are a stock-in-trade for the epidemiologist. Change in disease implies change in its causes. Thus the search for causes is advanced by the analysis of trends and the factors associated with the trends. These associations bring targets for the preventive attacks of public health into better focus. With chronic disorders that are not preventable, analyses of trends establish an informed basis for the planning of treatment and care.

Mental retardation tends to be seen as a rather stable phenomenon, whether in individuals or in populations, but it is unlikely that the present rate of social change leaves any health disorder unaffected. In this chapter we first mention some of the difficulties of the epidemiologist peculiar to the analysis of time trends in mental retardation. Next, we discuss ways in which technical and social developments may have affected these trends. Finally, we consider the implications for public health.

ANALYSIS OF TRENDS

Statements about trends in time, like all statements about the distribution of health disorders in populations, depend on incidence and prevalence rates. Neither of these measures is free from problems.

Incidence describes the frequency with which disorders arise in a popu-

305

lation during a defined period of time. The search for causes of the trends and distributions of health disorders is best pursued by studies of incidence. Time order is an essential criterion in establishing causal relations, and incidence relates disorders to circumstances that exist at the time of onset of a disorder or that are antecedent to it. Most incidence rates must take data from service agencies, however, and entry to services may not coincide with the onset of disorders, and may not represent all those in the population who suffer the disorders. Incidence is a better indicator of demand than of need. Only when the disorder is severe and the services adequate do demand and need converge.

Since prevalence describes the amount of disorder existing in a population at a particular time, regardless of time of onset, it affords a useful measure of the existing load of disorder to be provided for. Prevalence studies have the advantage that investigators can go out to discover and enumerate existing illnesses in representative samples of defined populations; they need not wait for what turns up. But prevalence is less useful in the search for the causes of the existing disturbances of disorder; it gives a cross-sectional view of a population's experience at one time, and cannot establish with precision the circumstances in which disorders of long and variable duration arise.

Moreover, a problem of sampling inheres in a cross-sectional view of health disorders. A sample of illnesses prevalent at any one point in time is not an unbiased sample of all illnesses experienced by the defined population. An influenza epidemic could be missed altogether, and so too could congenital anomalies that cause fetal and perinatal deaths, whereas disorders of long duration have a good chance of appearing in a census. In severe mental retardation there is no recovery, and duration is synonymous with survival. Thus some who contribute to incidence do not live long enough to enter a count of prevalence; the long-lived swell and bias the numbers of the subnormal population who contribute to prevalence. Hence prevalence and incidence are not interchangeable terms for measuring frequencies. The divergence between incidence and prevalence is exaggerated where duration varies widely and where it changes through time. Both these circumstances hold for the duration of severe mental retardation.

The relation between prevalence and incidence can be simply stated: The prevalence of a condition is a product of its incidence and its duration. It follows that an analysis of time trends in mental retardation can be made if there is knowledge of two of the three terms, incidence, duration and prevalence. When either incidence or duration is known, inferences about the other term can be drawn from prevalence studies. The paucity of information on the incidence and duration of mental retardation makes historical inferences somewhat tenuous. We shall attempt them nonetheless.

A special problem in the epidemiology of mental retardation is the definition of the case. Cases, to be counted, must be distinguished from non-cases, but the lines of demarcation are blurred by confused definition. Recognized mental retardation is a social attribute. Recognition is a consequence of failures to perform the social roles demanded of individuals at each stage of life. The order of society determines how taxing these roles shall be. What is expected in particular social roles, therefore, varies with time and among societies, and among the classes of a single society (161).

The manifestation of mental retardation as a social attribute encompasses at least three components: organic, functional and social. A primary organic component we may term *impairment*. Impairment of the brain or of its metabolism is diagnosed by the methods of clinical medicine. A functional component, which we may term *disability,* arises from the limitation imposed on individual function by the impairment, and by the individual's psychological reaction to it. In mental retardation, functional disability is expressed in intellectual deficit, and is diagnosed by the methods of psychology. The social component of mental retardation is defined by the special social roles assigned to the individual. This social limitation we may term mental *handicap;* it describes the manner and degree in which primary impairment and functional disability alter the expected performance of social roles. Handicap is diagnosed by the methods of sociology and social medicine.

Organic, psychological, and social criteria yield different frequencies of mental retardation and make quite different contributions to our understanding of the condition. The components of mental retardation measured by each criterion do not have a one-to-one relationship with each other, and they are made apparent by different circumstances. Impairments that can be recognized at birth and for which a one-to-one relationship with functional disability and mental handicap can be predicted, as in Down's syndrome, are not common. Cerebral palsy is an impairment recognized by the signs of brain damage. Not all cases of cerebral palsy suffer the functional disability of intellectual deficit, or are assigned the special social role of the handicapped person. Hydrocephalus is an anatomical deformity that may or may not be accompanied by cerebral impairment, or functional disability, or social handicap. Phenylketonuria is an inherited impairment of metabolism that does not always lead to functional disability, and when it does treatment may avert or reduce the disability and handicap.

Conversely, recognized functional disability cannot always be related to definitive organic lesions. In a large proportion of cases of mental retardation even with severe intellectual deficits, a specific clinical diagnosis cannot be made. In these cases, the presence of organic impairment is merely assumed.* Severe mental retardation of unspecified diagnosis thus describes a residual class, a dump-heap of cases that is heterogeneous in terms of organic impairment. Yet it is a homogeneous class in terms of functional disability and social handicap.

In mild mental retardation, on the other hand, the intellectual deficit and functional disability of the "cultural-familial" syndrome is not preceded by detectable organic impairment, and is not always accompanied by the social role of mental handicap. Sometimes the social role of mental handicap is assigned to individuals who have neither impairment of the brain nor intellectual disability. Their social roles are inadvertently acquired by their admission to 'treatment' because of a combination of behavior disorders and lack of social support. Thus a proportion of the inmates of many institutions for mental deficiency have neither detectable clinical lesions nor I.Q. scores below the normal range.

In studies of incidence, the order of usefulness of each criterion descends from organic, through psychological to social. The practical reasons for this order emerge from the information each criterion yields when analyzed by age. To take first the social dimension of mental handicap in early life, incidence is a difficult measure to apply, or even to conceptualize. Failures in role performance emerge gradually without a sharp point of onset. In the dependent state of infancy, role failures may go unrecognized, or may even be denied by some parents, and they become apparent only at school ages, when social roles are better defined. The incidence of functional disability is also difficult to measure at young ages. Since psychometric measures are not reliable in early life, they do not point unequivocally to the onset of new cases.

By contrast, some impairing conditions, for instance Down's syndrome, are the clearcut entities that epidemiologists most desire for population surveys. Yet even these conditions are not without measurement problems. The life of a unique individual begins with the formation of a zygote. Some aberrant chromosomal arrangements preclude zygote formation altogether; some permit the zygote to divide but are incompatible with fetal survival; others permit a bare few days of extra-uterine life; and the trisomy 21 of Down's syndrome is compatible with survival in spite of a high risk of death from fertilization onwards. Indeed, most of the impairments of severe mental retardation have their onset in intra-uterine life. At best, therefore, counts are based on the emergence of impairment at birth, and unknown numbers are aborted early in fetal life.

In a strict sense, these counts of impairment at birth are measures of the age-specific prevalence of impairment, and not measures of its

---

* In uncontrolled studies, brain lesions have been found in 90 per cent or more at autopsy.

incidence. It is an uncertain assumption that the impaired survivors fairly represent impairments among all conceptions. The true incidence of impairments among age-peers, and the time relations between hypothetical causal factors and the actual onset of the condition, can therefore only be inferred from impairment at birth. Where impairment is not immediately apparent, this knowledge must be inferred from functional disability and social handicap at later ages. Epidemiologic inference, however, has enabled the age of inception of impairment to be determined within reasonable limits for several conditions. In Down's syndrome and phenylketonuria, and in retardation due to intra-uterine irradiation and rubella infection, an approximate age of inception can be given.

In studies of prevalence, the order of usefulness of the social, psychological and organic criteria is reversed. We have noted that prevalence best establishes current needs for treatment and care. In mental retardation these needs rest on the social component of the condition, which embraces all the other components. The prevalence of the social role of mental retardation is more easily established than is the prevalence of disability and impairment. The individuals among children and adults who are socially defined as mentally retarded by their backwardness at school or their failures in occupational roles can often be identified from records and interviews. To determine levels of functional disability requires psychometric testing. For school-children test scores may be no more difficult to come by than their educational performance, but for adults tests will usually have to be specially undertaken among a reluctant population. To determine organic impairment requires still more elaborate clinical examinations and more laborious surveys.

The remainder of this paper will weave together evidence about processes that influence the development and survival of mentally retarded individuals. In order to clarify the issues, it is essential to bear in mind the meaning of each index of retardation, and the meaning of the incidence and prevalence rates to which the indexes contribute the numerator. We shall first consider the factors that may have altered incidence and then the factors that may have altered prevalence. We shall suggest that changes have occurred in both rates, in the main in opposite directions. The changes have implications for public health and medical policies.

CHANGES IN INCIDENCE

A. *Chemical Factors*

Technological development has added to the possible causes and perhaps to the incidence of mental retardation. The side-effects of medical treatments, industrial processes, and of warfare, expose people to pervasive chemical and physical agents.

Drugs like LSD* can affect the chromosomes (77, 35, 36). Because chromosomal abnormalities underlie some types of mental retardation, notably Down's syndrome, such drugs attract suspicion as possible causes of mental retardation. Drugs like thalidomide, and perhaps LSD (193, 73, 157), affect later fetal development (92, 104), and thereby also attract suspicion as causes of mental retardation. Proof that drugs cause mental retardation is still lacking. Studies of meclozide, which is teratogenic in rats (82), failed to show an association with congenital abnormalities (89, 191) and by implication with organic impairments underlying mental retardation. In Birmingham, England, during the years 1957 to 1963, variations in the rise of incidence of congenital anomalies did not suggest a relationship with the use of drugs during pregnancy, excepting thalidomide (88, 89, 90).

The heavy metals, mercury and lead, are proved causes of mental retardation. These metals continue to reach and affect individuals by a variety of routes, including pollution of water, food and air. In Minamata Bay in Japan, mercury discharged from an industrial plant was concentrated by shellfish in the bay. Over a period of several years, children born to women who habitually ate these shellfish during pregnancy were afflicted by cerebral palsy and mental retardation (72, 109, 163). Control of the mercury contamination reduced the incidence of the condition. In the United States recently, at least one family suffered severe mental effects from mercurial poisoning. The family had eaten the meat of pigs fed on mercury-treated grain. The treatment was intended to protect the planted grain from pests (177, 178).

Lead poisoning has long been known to produce encephalopathy and retardation (24, 17). In recent years, this cause of mental retardation has been increasingly recognized in infants from areas where the peeling wall paint of old slum houses contained lead. The increase could reflect a true rise in incidence (111). Lead has also been suspected as a cause of mild mental retardation, because evidence of lead is found in slum areas where mild mental retardation is common (183, 62, 65). One growing source of lead in the environment, and of body burdens (115, 125), is the exhaust fumes from the gasoline used by automobiles (166). Areas with heavy motor traffic could thus be hazardous for infants and young children.

Defoliants have been shown to cause congenital anomalies in experiments with rats (181). The policy of the United States government under Presidents Kennedy, Johnson and Nixon has been to expose the Vietnamese people to heavy and promiscuous distribution of these substances.

---

* Lysergic Acid Diethylamide

In the rivers, defoliants are concentrated by shellfish, and shellfish comprise a regular part of the diet of children and pregnant women. No studies of effects on humans have been reported. The hazard cannot be assessed; neither can it be dismissed.

Mental retardation might be associated in intricate ways with some other chemical causes. Infants of low birth weight have a raised risk of death and of mental retardation (12, 60, 182). Chemical causes of low birth weight, therefore, may contribute to the incidence of mental retardation. Smoking during pregnancy reduces mean birth weight. The several possible mechanisms are all ultimately biochemical. According to one large study (59, 22), if not some others (149, 190), smoking also increases perinatal mortality in the proportion expected from the lowered birth weight, but no data on the association of smoking with mental retardation are available.

Multiple birth is often a cause of low birth weight, and the known association of twinning with mental retardation (98, 16) is possibly mediated through retarded growth and low birth weight (3, 32, 79). A new biochemical cause of multiple births is the use of sex hormones to induce fertility. Another growing cause of low birth weight is the habitual use of opiates by the mother (80).

In these several instances, women have been increasingly exposed to causes of low birth weight, although as yet no causal associations with mental retardation have been established. National trends may not be inconsistent with the increased exposure of mothers to factors that induce low birth weight. In the United States, the frequency of low birth weight has risen among black mothers and remained steady among whites (31), in contrast with a decline in Britain (2) and probably Japan (68).

Smoking is on the decline in most subgroups of the population of the United States (71). The main risk of a rise in the incidence of mental retardation from chemical causes lies in the uncontrolled exposure of pregnant women to drugs and medication, and to the promiscuous pollution of the environment.

B. *Physical Factors*

Among known physical agents that can cause mental retardation, by far the most serious is ionising radiation. The sources studied have been first, therapeutic and diagnostic irradiation; and second, the atomic bombs exploded over the populous cities of Hiroshima and Nagasaki, at the order of President Truman, as Japanese resistance was collapsing in 1945 at the end of World War II.

Pelvic irradiation early in gestation can lead to cerebral damage. Clinical observations date from 1929 (116). Epidemiological observations date from the Hiroshima bomb, August 6, 1945. The effects of the bomb included mental retardation, microcephaly, and leukemia. The susceptibility of the fetus at different ages, and its response to varying doses of radiation, varied with each of these conditions. Where mental retardation was the outcome, there seemed to be a critical fetal age for radiosensitivity, but a continuous dose-response effect. By contrast, where microcephaly was the outcome, there seemed to be sensitivity throughout gestation and no critical fetal age, but there did seem to be a critical or threshold dose below which there was no effect (108). Where leukemia was the outcome, sensitivity extended throughout life, and there seemed to be a continuous dose-response effect (110).

In the case of mental retardation, the most severe effects occurred among eight women who were in the seventh to fifteenth week of pregnancy, and who were within 1200 meters of the "hypocenter" of the explosion. All their eight infants were mentally retarded. Outside this period of pregnancy, the frequency of mental retardation hardly exceeded the normal expectation (Figure 1). A review of 26 case-reports of fetal injury that followed diagnostic or therapeutic X-ray also showed the fetus to be most vulnerable at seven to fifteen weeks (50).

To explain the lack of effect in the first six weeks of gestation, one hypothesis with a basis in experimental work (133, 74) is that embryos before six weeks of age are radio-insensitive. A directly opposite hypothesis is that irradiation of embryos before six weeks of age is frequently lethal, but does not maim those that may survive. A retrospective study at Nagasaki supports the possibility that radiation is sometimes lethal to the young embryo (188).

Thus mothers who had had severe exposure to irradiation reported fewer pregnancies as well as an excess fetal loss when compared with controls. At Hiroshima, few infants in the sample were exposed to irradiation in the first six weeks of gestation, according to the available reports. The expected number is not given, and cannot be calculated by us because of an inconsistency in the published reports on the actual composition of the sample (132, 108).

A follow-up after 17 years suggested that the effects on intellectual function of nuclear irradiation during the sensitive period of gestation varied directly with the dose. The risk of intellectual disability was raised in the offspring of mothers who were seven to fifteen weeks pregnant and more than 1200 meters away from the "hypocenter," but not to the same order of risk as among those who were within 1200 meters (185).

Microcephaly proved to be a manifestation of nuclear irradiation which was to some degree independent of mental retardation. Many microcephalic children grew up without intellectual disability, and the condition occurred only with exposure within a distance of 1500 meters

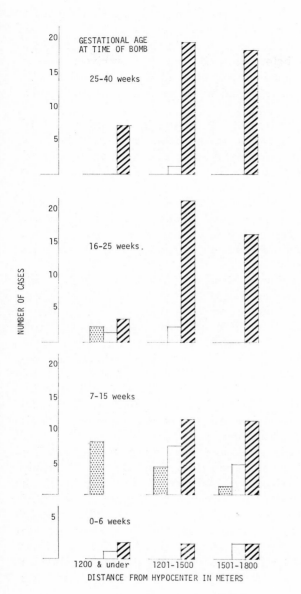

Adapted from 108

FIG. 1.
MR & microcephaly in children exposed *in utero* to the atomic bomb at Hiroshima.

from the hypocenter. On the other hand, it seemed to follow exposure at any stage of gestation (and even postnatally).

Effects of irradiation have also been sought in children whose mothers or fathers were irradiated before the children were conceived. To test this possibility, a study was made of the cohort of Japanese children who were born between 1948 and 1959, and whose parents had been exposed to the atomic explosions.

After 1/1/48, some 90 per cent of all mothers in the fifth month of pregnancy registered for free supplementary food rations. At the same time they were drawn into the study. A series of infants was examined at birth, and a proportion of the series was examined again a few months later. Effects of pre-conception exposure were not detected either in the incidence of congenital abnormalities or of mental retardation. In Down's syndrome, the cases found among 5,582 exposed mothers proved to be only half the expected number (143). One suggested effect, that the sex ratio had been altered in favor of females (142), was later set aside (144).

The question of the relationship between irradiation of the gonads before conception and subsequent retardation has lately been reopened. In a case-history study, Sigler et al. compared the radiation experience of mothers and fathers of 216 cases of Down's syndrome and 216 controls matched for maternal age (148). Mothers exposed to fluoroscopy or to therapeutic radiation had a relative risk of a birth with Down's syndrome of 2.3 to 1. Mothers exposed to diagnostic, fluoroscopic and therapeutic radiation combined had a relative risk of 7 to 1. The information about irradiation was derived from family reports. The validation of these reports from clinical records was not extensive, and on this ground the result awaits confirmation.

The finding of Sigler et al. gets support from a prospective Canadian enquiry by Uchida and her colleagues (174). The cases in the study were the 972 children conceived by 2,200 women after they had been subjected to abdominal irradiation. This sample of mothers comprised those among 6,062 irradiated women of reproductive age who could be located for interview. The 972 controls were mainly children born to the same 2,200 women before they were irradiated, and matched for maternal age. The control sample was supplemented from the children of mothers irradiated before or after the period during which the mothers of cases were irradiated.

There was an increased number of cases of Down's syndrome among older mothers irradiated before the child's birth. Five infants with Down's syndrome were born to 81 mothers 40 years and over, a relative risk of 2½ to 1 compared with the generality of mothers of the same age. The complex presentation of this study leaves doubts about the exact method used.

Temperature, weather, and season of birth are other factors of the physical environment that have been studied in relation to the incidence of mental retardation. The results are somewhat inconsistent (124, 86, 45) and in any case, season and weather do not produce measurable secular trends, which are here our chief interest.

The major physical factor in the trends of mental retardation is thus irradiation. The chief sources have been military weapons and medical care. In future, it is conceivable that power plants may add to these sources. In mental retardation, as in cancer, exposure to irradiation cannot be regarded as entirely safe at any level, because the risk seems to have a linear relationship to dose (119, 63, 75). Low dosage has not been shown to lead to mental retardation, but there is no evidence to suggest a threshold dose below which irradiation is harmless.

C. *Infections*

The infections that influence the incidence of mental retardation are a mixed bag (179). For the most part, changes in infectious diseases have led to a fall in incidence of impairment, and of mental retardation generally. In some infectious diseases, there has been no discernible change. In other diseases, survival of once-fatal attacks has led to a rise in the prevalence of impairments, and to a consequent rise in the incidence of subsequent functional disability and mental handicap.

Known infections have never been responsible for more than a small minority of cases of mental retardation (107, 23, 15), and the fall in overall incidence from this cause is probably slight. Changes have come about with alterations in the virulence of organisms or in the resistance of the host, and with the use of new measures for prevention and treatment.

Changes in the virulence of organisms, occurring independently of the health status of the population, are not amenable to forecast. Epidemics of rubella, influenza, mumps and measles vary in severity, and each of these diseases is responsible for a small number of cases of mental retardation. Epidemics continue to occur that are more severe than some observed in the past.

It is often difficult to determine whether the variation in the effects of infection is produced by changes in the virulence of the organism, or by changes in the vulnerability of the host population. Rubella during pregnancy was apparently more damaging in 1964 in New York (42) than it was in the 1950's in England (101, 147). Despite the severe effect of congenital rubella on the fetus in the New York epidemic, however, the infection did not often cause mental retardation. When mental retardation did occur, it accompanied a lesion of the sense organs. In the English epidemics, congenital rubella also did not lead to uncomplicated mental retardation, and the mean I.Q. of children followed over 10 years was not lowered (147).

Influenza viruses are notoriously changeable. The strains are unstable, and at different times they vary markedly in virulence. Infection during pregnancy has appeared on occasion to increase the incidence of oesophageal tube lesions, of cleft palate, and of oesophageal atresia (91) as well as anencephaly, but there is no known direct association with mental retardation.

Mumps encephalitis, too, as reported across the United States, shows some variation in case fatality rate from year to year (175):

	Cases	Deaths	% Fatality
1963	671	6	0.89
1964	932	18	1.93
1965	634	4	0.63
1966	628	10	1.6
1967	849	8	1.14
1968	408	2	.49

Where cases and fatalities are so few, however, either variation in case-reporting or misclassification of deaths might both contribute to fluctuation of this magnitude.

Measles varies in severity according to the characteristics of the host population (122). Measles is a more frequent cause of death among infants in developing than in developed countries, and in developing countries it is a more frequent cause of death among the malnourished than among the better fed (113, 114). Serious complications like encephalitis and mental retardation probably march with the fatality rates. A small reduction in mental retardation might therefore follow improvement in social conditions. In the United States between 1960 and 1966, about 250 cases of measles encephalitis were reported each year. These would have resulted in an estimated annual average of 22 cases of mental retardation.*

Even uncomplicated measles may have mental sequelae (6). These postulated effects, too, may depend on the interaction of infection and host characteristics. In one series of studies, reading readiness at school entry was used as an index of intellectual disability (19, 20, 57, 58). Children with a history of measles from better-off communities showed no effects as compared with controls. Children from poor communities did show some retardation compared with controls.

Viral encephalitides contribute sporadically a small number of cases to the pool of mentally retarded persons. In epidemics, the rate of fatali-

---

* About one-third of the 80 per cent who survived measles encephalitis were under two years old, and one-third of these children can be expected to be retarded.

ties and of brain damage with subsequent mental retardation among infants is high (13). Rare primary encephalitides show no promise of a decline either in incidence or in the mental sequelae they cause.

The immunization program that controls measles is itself a rare cause of mental retardation. Encephalitis with resulting mental retardation can also follow immunization against pertussis (102, 14). There is little doubt, however, that with regard to mental retardation more is to be gained than lost by widespread immunization against these diseases.

Effective treatment as well as primary prevention has changed the relationship of some infectious diseases to the incidence of mental retardation. Congenital syphilis is an example of an undoubted infectious cause of mental retardation. The disease has virtually been eliminated in some European countries, and has declined in the United States, but even in this instance the overall gain has been small.

The size of the decline in incidence of mental retardation that followed the decline of congenital syphilis is somewhat difficult to assess, because the incidence attributable to it in the past is uncertain (169). In Europe and the United States 30 to 60 years ago, cross-sectional prevalence surveys of mentally retarded persons in institutions yielded positive serological tests for syphilis in 10% or more (70). These rates cannot be taken to reflect the actual mental retardation caused by congenital syphilis. Positive tests are not sufficient evidence for the diagnosis of neurological impairment, and until the mid-1950's most tests used were not highly specific for syphilis (151). Moreover, cases with positive tests came from families that were also likely to generate "cultural-familial" retardation. Controlled comparisons are therefore needed to assess the meaning of the distribution of positive tests. In 1908, before serological tests were available, Tredgold assigned congenital syphilis as a cause in only 5 of 1000 "aments" (170). He commented on the paucity of mental retardation among patients with congenital syphilis in hospital practice (171). In the interwar period also, after the advent of serological tests, some estimates of the frequency of mental retardation attributable to syphilis were lower than 1% (48, 11). In the early 1930's, Penrose estimated four per cent, or three per cent excluding cases without collateral signs of syphilis (126). In 1959, Berg and Kirman estimated 0.6% (15).

The example of tuberculous meningitis illustrates that the effects of treatment on incidence have not always been in one direction. During the first decade after World War II, new treatments changed tuberculous meningitis from a uniformly fatal condition to one that permitted survival. Because a proportion of the early survivors had impairments of the brain, they added to the incidence of disability and handicap from mental retardation (84). In the 1960's the incidence of primary tuberculosis and its complications continued to decline and treatment became more effective, and few new cases of mental retardation due to tuberculous meningitis appeared (99, 169).

Interaction between treatment, survival and the prevalence of impairment may partly explain the absence of a visible trend in other meningitides. Bacterial meningitis (apart from the tuberculous forms) caused about one-third of the cases of mental retardation due to infection in a series of cases reported from the Walter E. Fernald Hospital, Massachusetts (134). In this series, the divergence from each other of the age-specific prevalence for congenital syphilis, tuberculous meningitis and other forms of bacterial meningitis can be interpreted as due to generation effects particular to certain birth cohorts (Table 1). The data sug-

TABLE 1*

AGE DISTRIBUTION OF PATIENTS AT THE WALTER E. FERNALD SCHOOL
WITH SELECTED CAUSES OF RETARDATION—1966

Age	Congenital Neuro-Syphilis	Tuberculous Meningitis	Other Bacterial Meningitis
0-9		7	6
10-19		7	11
20-29	2	2	11
30-39	9	1	1
40-49	17	1	8
50-59	14		8
60-69	12		5
70-79	1		2

* Adapted from 134

gest to us that there has been a decline over time for congenital syphilis; a clustering in a short period of time for tuberculous meningitis and a steady rate for bacterial meningitis.

Bacterial meningitis, over the past half century in the United States, has had epidemic periods with no long term trend in the reported incidence. Thirty years ago, after the introduction of sulphonamides, there was a sharp decline in the case-fatality rate (47). Although the proportion with mental sequelae may also have declined at that time, the larger number of survivors in subsequent years could have generated a number of cases of mental retardation as large as before (52, 150). Interaction between infection and treatment continues to evolve. Meningitis organisms have grown resistant to chemotherapy and antibiotics, but recently antibacterial agents have been developed to counter some of the resistant infections (49).

Certain infections that occur at and around birth have recently attracted suspicion as neurologic pathogens. Cytomegalovirus has been implicated as a cause of mental retardation (9, 156). It is also associated with infantile spasms and fits, and possibly with microcephaly, both common in mentally retarded populations. Mycoplasma infections, virus-like agents identified only in recent years, have also been suspect as a cause of mental retardation, but firm evidence is still lacking (29, 30). Congenital toxoplasmosis is a rare but well documented protozoal cause of mental retardation (55, 165, 187). In a large series of pregnancies studied longitudinally in the cities of the Eastern United States, antibodies to toxoplasma at the third and fourth months of pregnancy developed in 2 per 1000 (146). Congenital toxoplasmosis was observed in one-quarter of the offspring, an incidence of 0.5 per 1000 in all. Prevention of this cause of mental retardation may be technically within our grasp. There is no evidence that any of these infections have had changing effects on the incidence of mental retardation.

We conclude that the incidence of mental retardation due to known infections has declined with time, although these infections comprise but a small proportion of all causes of impairment. Social change has improved host resistance and immunity, effected environmental control, and provided the techniques to prevent and treat such infectious diseases as syphilis, bacterial meningitis, pertussis, measles, mumps, and rubella. Further gains from the control of infectious diseases seem to be within reach. A reduction in incidence of uncertain magnitude may follow better understanding of the encephalitides, toxoplasmosis and cytomegalovirus. Even taken together, however, these gains are likely to be modest.

D. *Social*

Social factors are intimately linked with the distribution of mental retardation. Here we shall mention only three broad factors. One relates to obstetric care, a second to poverty, and a third to demographic change.

Obstetric care. Obstetric care has some clear effects, and some uncertain ones, on the complications of pregnancy and childbirth. These complications include toxemia of pregnancy, precipitate labor, premature separation of the placenta, prolonged labor, cerebral anoxia, and prematurity. The relation of each of these complications to mental retardation has been evaluated many times (46, 45, 123, 94, 67, 136, 7). Whether the perspective is that of epidemiology or pathology, the results are not consistent.

Obstetric and neonatal pediatric care can undoubtedly alter the incidence of mishap in childbirth, and the chances of survival. In developed countries, more of the total infants born survive than before, and fewer of the total born are exposed to brain-damaging experiences. The smaller proportion of infants thus exposed to brain-damaging experiences, however, share in the better chance of survival of the total, and may even do so disproportionately. The selective factors in these survivals vary in environments separated by time, place and social class. Hence the chances of impairment, disability and mental handicap from birth injury are unlikely to remain constant across different environments.

Gross cerebral injury at birth was reported as a cause of mental retardation in about 1.8 per cent of admissions in a recent study of a Connecticut institution (189). The room for observing improvement in such retrospective analyses is therefore not great. Sixty years ago, Tredgold wrote: "of abnormalities of labour as a cause of amentia . . . the total number of cases which are the immediate consequence of these conditions is relatively very small, being probably not more than one or two per cent of all aments."* Thirty years ago, Penrose reported a prevalence of about one per cent among 1280 patients living in an English mental deficiency institution (127). In prospective studies of the consequences of difficulties in labor, an association with mental retardation has not always been found (10, 56, 8). In all these prevalence data, the relative contributions of the incidence of impairment and of changing survival cannot be disentangled. We can only observe that their resultant shows little change. Conflicting results also emerge in studies of other complications of pregnancy.

In many conditions obstetric care must be prenatal if it is to modify the outcome of pregnancy. Methods devised to prevent kernicterus due to Rh incompatibility in the newborn have had dramatic success (186, 66), and should virtually eliminate kernicterus as a cause of mental retardation. According to one recent follow-up study of survivors, about one-half to one per cent of cases of severe neonatal jaundice (more than 15 mgms. bilirubin) have been followed by mental retardation (76). Current prevalence studies in institutions for mental retardation attribute about one per cent of cases to this cause (189).

In several conditions the accepted forms of prenatal care await adequate tests of their value. Prenatal care can detect and apparently control toxemia of pregnancy, and toxemia probably contributes to a continuum of cerebral impairment (21). Prenatal care has no proved means to raise birth weight and prevent prematurity. Better nutrition amongst the poorest classes and the reduction of smoking offer the present best hopes (18).

Thus obstetric care can reduce gross brain damage at birth, prevent kernicterus, control toxemia, and cure syphilis. Obstetric care has yet to prove itself against other potential prenatal causes of mental retardation.

---

* Tredgold excluded cases with a history of some obstetric abnormality where he thought the primary cause of retardation was a "neuropathic diathesis." Some 17% in all gave a history of obstetric abnormalities. No control data for obstetric abnormalities are available (172).

Poverty. An association between mental retardation and poverty has been recognized at least since the beginning of the century. Observers have been in doubt about which was the antecedent variable. As the selective racial theories of social Darwinism lost force, so poverty of the environment has been given greater prominence as a causal antecedent rather than a consequence of mental retardation. The "cultural-familial" syndrome associated with poverty is a form of mild intellectual disability without detectable clinical lesions, and is by far the commonest type of mild mental retardation. The syndrome is virtually specific to children of the "demotic" families of the lowest social strata. It can be inferred from this distribution, considered together with known patterns of marriage and mobility, and from the recoveries that occur in adult life, that this form of retardation is a consequence of the social environment during growth and development (158, 153).

Although the "cultural-familial" syndrome is a characteristic of certain types of family, this does not imply that the causes of the condition reside within the families alone. Demotic families share the same harsh social and physical environment and impoverished educational experience. What factors mediate the relationship between poor environment and retardation is not precisely understood. One factor could be nutrition of the developing fetus and newborn child, although the evidence is by no means complete (44, 43, 184, 154). The ancient story of famine and starvation has two new twists that impinge on this hypothetical causal relationship. First, in some societies malnutrition may be affecting the balance between survival and mental retardation in a manner analogous to obstetric care. Where medical institutions dispense effective modern treatment for infants and reduce case fatality from acute nutritional failure, there are more survivors, but the increase in survivors creates a larger class at risk of impairment.

The second new element in the pattern of infant malnutrition is the decline in breast-feeding among families too poor and too unschooled to provide suitable substitute foods. In developing countries, and possibly in the United States, this nutritional impoverishment of infants is a consequence of the need for mothers of newly urbanized migrant families to go out and earn fulltime wages.

Many other factors may contribute to the association of mild mental retardation and poverty. Compared with the better-off, the poor have experienced more infectious diseases with less treatment and more severe effects, enjoyed less enduring family ties, and been burdened with a greater frequency of all kinds of functional disabilities and physical handicaps. They have been poorly schooled, have suffered discrimination in social and public life, and have had a high liability to conviction for crime. All these elements could contribute to intellectual disability, and to the assignment of the role of mental handicap.

If these elements do contribute to "cultural-familial" retardation, the incidence of intellectual disability should have declined. In Europe and North America, the poor of today are measurably better situated with regard to nutrition, health care, morbidity and education than they were fifty years ago and less. Such poverty-linked health disorders as tuberculosis, pellagra, rickets, infant deaths, and stunted growth have declined sharply.

Factors that influence the trend of the social component of mental retardation, however, might not all act in the same direction as they do for disability and impairment. Social roles are more complex than before, and present-day societies demand higher levels of education for them. Individuals are labeled mentally handicapped when they fail to meet the demands of these social roles, as in school, in the armed forces, and at work. Yet despite the rise in standards for role performance, there is no evidence of an increase in the incidence of either intellectual deficit or mental handicap, but rather the reverse.

The only available population data on time trends are in terms of age-specific prevalence. With "cultural-familial" retardation, prevalence in childhood may be a fairly constant function of incidence. The condition most often manifests in the primary school years: measured intelligence appears to decline with age in response to marked environmental disadvantage, until it crosses a threshold of functional disability and is translated into recognized social handicap (53, 105, 162). Individuals with "cultural-familial" retardation are often able to discard the role of mental handicap in the third decade of life, especially if they are not incarcerated in the role, as it were, by custodial care. With the decline in custodial care, the duration of handicap may have shortened. Fortunately, age-specific rates are available for age groups too young to be much affected by such a decline. Among them the equation of prevalence with incidence retains its usefulness.

Table 2 suggests that in British schoolchildren there was a fall in the age-specific prevalence of mild mental retardation during the past half century. The decline is evident in intellectual disability, as measured by low scores on the same nation-wide intelligence tests given 15 years apart to Scottish schoolchildren (145). It is even more evident in mental handicap, although here the data from the two time periods do not have the same high order of comparability (153). The rate of admission to institutions for mild mental retardation has also declined.*

Swedish workers also have noted an apparent decline in the age-specific prevalence of mental retardation. Rejection of young men drafted for military service, by a constant criterion of mental deficiency,

* Admissions are a crude measure of the trend in incidence of retardation; admission policies alone, by reducing the proportion of cases admitted, could explain the change.

TABLE 2[a]

A. PREVALENCE OF MILD MENTAL RETARDATION AT SCHOOL IN ENGLAND 1925-27 AND 1955-59 (EXCLUDING SEVERE SUBNORMALITY)

Year of testing	locale	age	criterion	no. tested	rate 1/000
1925-27	6 sample areas, England	7-10 yrs.	<70 I.Q.	36,692	20.7
1955-59	Salford, England	10 yrs.	<80 I.Q.	19,500	13.3[b]

B. LOW SCORERS IN SCOTTISH INTELLIGENCE SURVEYS— 1932 AND 1947

Year of testing	locale	age	criterion	no. tested	rate 1/000
1932	Scotland	11 yrs.	<19 on the Mental Survey Group Test	87,498	188
1947	Scotland	11 yrs.	<19 on the Mental Survey Group Test	70,805	165

[a] Adopted from 153 and 145.
[b] Point prevalence (i.e. the number of identified cases compared with the population at risk at one point in time) was estimated for age ten from incidence data. See (153, 155).

declined in the period after World War II (135). The decline was particularly marked in one isolated village, and the researchers attributed the decline, not to social improvement, but to the shuffling of genes brought about by the breakdown of marriage isolates. In their view, mental retardation is in the main genetically determined, and inbreeding within isolates maintains or increases prevalence. This brings us to the consideration of demographic factors.

Demography. Inbreeding occurs under two broad conditions of mating. First, where mating is more or less random, or prohibited between cognates, a small breeding population should increase homozygosity, and raise the chance that heterozygous and recessive genes will be expressed. Akesson's finding that sparsely populated rural villages in Sweden contributed more than their expected share of cases to institutions for the retarded is consistent with such a process (1). The Swedish military data referred to above, however, show that the rejection rate for low intelligence had declined not only in the isolated village, but throughout the region and, to a smaller degree, throughout Sweden. These trends do not fit a genetic hypothesis based on breeding in isolates, nor does the short time span of the studies allow for marked genetic change. In Sweden, as elsewhere, there is no doubt about the extent of social change over the period of study. Data on marriage and social mobility in a sample of retarded individuals from the north of England also give no indication that random inbreeding is a significant factor in the syndrome of cultural retardation (161).

The second condition for inbreeding occurs with mating between relatives, as in incest and in cousin marriages. Among humans, the results of two small studies suggest that incest affects offspring adversely; reproductive loss, severe mental deficiency, and some congenital anomalies were more frequent (141, 27). Mating between sibs seemed to occur in less socially aberrant circumstances than mating between parent and child, but the offspring seemed at an equal disadvantage in terms of severe mental deficiency and some congenital anomalies. These are plausible genetic consequences of inbreeding. Although satisfactory controls are difficult to find, since incest can hardly be thought of as representative in any population, the effects have seemed worse than would be expected in any social group.

Incest is an extreme form of consanguineous union. Studies of other forms of consanguinity, which yield larger numbers, have not conclusively shown adverse effects. Extraneous social factors are difficult to exclude in studies of consanguinity; marriage behavior is characteristic of particular social groups. Thus in Japan, consanguineous marriage is common but it increases with declining social class, and so too do such measures of the possible outcome of consanguinity as child mortality and mental deficiency. On the other hand, where consanguinity has been studied in homogeneous social groups, measures of the outcome variables have usually been unsatisfactory. In the tiny island isolate of Tristan da Cunha in the South Atlantic, for instance, the total genealogy has been traced since its founding in 1817. Although estimates of intelligence levels associated with inbreeding were low, the estimates depended on the subjective judgment of a single physician (140).

If inbreeding is a factor in the incidence of mental retardation, then it is probable that its contribution is declining. Marriage isolates are certainly breaking down, and simultaneously the kinship structures and social immobility that facilitate consanguinity are less common than before (162).

The demographic factor of maternal age is of quite a different kind from inbreeding. This factor contributes to major changes in the incidence of the most prevalent form of severe mental retardation, namely, Down's syndrome. The chances of bearing a child with Down's syndrome increase sharply with the age of the mother at conception (Figure II). Paternal age and parity are closely linked with maternal age but they have no added effect (131, 96).

The incidence rates at birth of Down's syndrome at each maternal age exhibit a high degree of stability at different times and places (130, 103, 95). The proportionate contribution of older women to total prevalence therefore depends on three main trends: the age-structure of the

Figure II

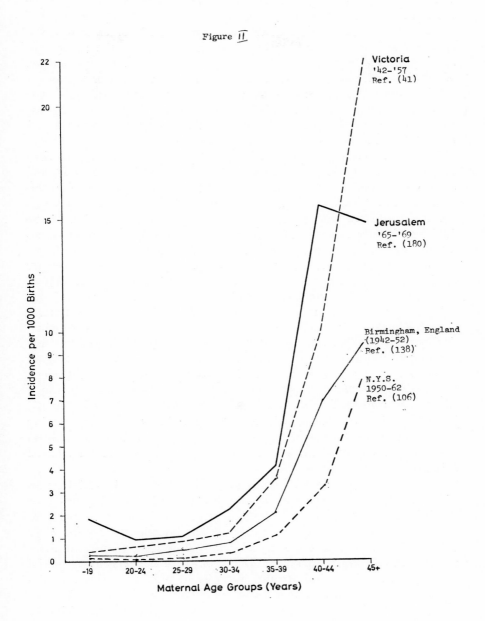

child-bearing population; the age-specific fertility rates of this population; and the expectation of life of individuals with the syndrome. The
frequency of all births depends on the proportion of women of different
ages comprising the child-bearing population, and on the age-specific
fertility rates among them, and is highly variable (41). The proportion
of all births with Down's syndrome is therefore also variable.

We have calculated the expected number of cases of Down's syndrome
born to women in New York City over the last 15 years. Using the
expected age-specific rates given by Collman and Stoller (39), we estimate that the number born has fallen from about 203 in 1953 to about
165 in 1967. Over the same period, the total number of live births born
to all women fell from 161,455 to 145,708. The crude rate of Down's
syndrome probably declined from 1.25 per 1,000 to 1.13 per 1,000, because of a relative increase in the number of babies born to younger
mothers compared with older mothers. There was no reduction in the
fertility of older mothers. If the incidence of Down's syndrome at all
maternal ages can be kept as low as the incidence among young women,
the present rate at birth would be cut by about one-third. Since Down's
syndrome at the present time accounts for 15-25% of all known cases of
severe mental retardation surviving infancy (64, 164), a reduction of one-
third in live births with the syndrome would be of major importance.

The natural variation in child-bearing points to the possibility of reducing the frequency of retardation by voluntary restriction of fertility.
This possibility is open primarily to older women and also to a small
number of women at special risk of bearing affected children. Genetic
counselling, to inform couples of the probability of their bearing a
genetically abnormal child, can have but a small role in reducing the
incidence of mental retardation. Edwards estimates that counselling
could prevent a few cases of Down's syndrome (54); in phenylketonuria
it could prevent only the births occurring subsequent to an affected
child.

To sum up this review of trends in incidence, the main social causes
of mental retardation seem to be on the decline. In this they resemble
the infections, although the impact of general social forces is likely to
be greater than that of the control of specific infections. Only the physical and chemical causes of mental retardation seem to present more
widespread dangers than before. Many of these dangers are potential
rather than manifest, and are not likely to be reduced without considerable and sophisticated attempts at surveillance and control. On the
whole, when all causes are taken into account, the overall incidence
rates of impairment, functional disability, and mental handicap are
probably declining. The decline is of uncertain scale but could be
considerable, a point to which we shall return in the discussion of
prevalence.

CHANGES IN PREVALENCE

Like most other populations, the mentally retarded population is both dynamic and unstable. It is dynamic in that there is continual recruitment of new individuals and loss of old ones. It is unstable in that the balance between losses and recruitment is changing.

Rising Longevity and Prevalence

Losses to the mentally retarded population are occurring at a slower rate than before because the death rate is declining and survival is improving. For evidence we turn to Down's syndrome, an excellent epidemiological index. The diagnosis is one of the least equivocal in medicine, and the population is one of the most complete and representative within the whole class of mental retardation. Life tables constructed for cases of Down's syndrome show an undoubted increase in longevity over the last generation (26, 40). Prevalence at the age of ten years appears to have risen from 1 in 4,000 in 1929 (64), to 1 in 2,000 in 1949 (149), to 1 in 1,000 in 1960 (64).

Improvements in medical and surgical treatments, in public health and the techniques of immunization against infectious diseases, and in the physical environment and accident control, all reduce mortality in Down's syndrome. They prolong life without in any way modifying the accompanying mental retardation. The major cause of death in the past, respiratory infection (173), has been much reduced by antibiotic treatment. In most cases, death is now due to associated anomalies such as those of the heart or gut (121, 138). Leukemia kills a fraction (about 1 in 95) (110). Half of the infants born with Down's syndrome die before their fifth birthday, but those who survive beyond it tend to continue in reasonably good health for several decades, so that in later life, presenile symptoms and diabetes are coming to be recognized as common among them (7, 8). In industrial societies, Down's syndrome now makes the largest single contribution to the prevalence of severe mental retardation both in the community and in residential institutions.

Down's syndrome serves as a paradigm for all forms of severe mental retardation. The total number of handicapped persons for whom families and communities must now make provision has risen. Thus surgery prolongs the life of children with spina bifida and hydrocephalus, conditions accompanied often by severe physical handicap and sometimes by mental handicap (87, 100, 139). During the decade 1950 to 1960 the peak rate for deaths attributed to all congenital anomalies shifted from the under five-year age group to the five to fourteen-year age group (112).

Survival is reflected in the prevalence of all forms of mental retardation. In Salford, England, data compiled from community registers point

TABLE 3

REGISTERED SEVERELY SUBNORMAL POPULATION IN SALFORD IN
1948 AND 1963 COMPARED

A. PERCENTAGE OF TOTAL ON REGISTER BY 10-YEAR AGE GROUPS

AGE GROUPS

	N	0-9	10-19	20-29	30-39	40-49	50-59	60-69	Unknown	
Jan. 1, 1948	147	8.0	25.2	27.5	22.9	9.5	3.8	2.3	0.8	100
Jan. 1. 1963	238	15.5	21.4	15.1	16.4	16.0	10.1	3.8	0.9	100

B. AGE-SPECIFIC RATES PER 100,000 BY 10-YEAR AGE GROUPS*

AGE GROUPS

	0-9	10-19	20-29	30-39	40-49	50-59	60-69	All
Jan. 1, 1948	70	290	270	221	96	49	39	150
Jan. 1, 1963	152	209	182	198	180	113	61	220

* Much of the increased rate in the 0-9 year age group is the result of an active case-finding
program instituted about five years before 1963. Improved registration had small effect on the
older age groups.
Adapted from 151

to a longer life span for severely subnormal people in 1963 than in
1948 (151). In the interval there was an average increase in the rate
of the registered population of 4.75 per 100,000 per year. Table 3 shows
that this increase in the population has been accompanied by aging.
The most notable increment was to the older age groups. Migration and
registration occurring unevenly among the age groups distort these
patterns, but with due caution we can conclude that within fifteen years
a longer lifespan had increased the prevalence of severe subnormality.

Prevalence studies at successive points in time provide evidence of a
changing trend in recruitment to the mentally retarded population. The
trends suggest a fall in incidence as well as a rise in longevity in developed countries. New cases of Down's syndrome are probably occurring
less frequently than before because older mothers have curtailed their
child bearing period. New cases of other types of severe mental retardation have probably declined even more dramatically. But the survivors
live longer.

In 1960 in England, the prevalence of Down's syndrome at ten years
of age observed by Goodman and Tizard was higher than that observed
by Lewis 35 years previously, while the prevalence of other kinds of
severe subnormality at the same age was only two-thirds as high (64,
168). In the face of prolonged survival for all kinds of severe subnormality, a decline in the prevalence of mental retardation other than
Down's syndrome could come about only through a considerable decline
in incidence (Table 4).

Advances in public health, medicine and surgery, and social change
generally, have evidently reduced the incidence of impairment and

TABLE 4

ESTIMATES OF TRENDS IN INCIDENCE OF OTHER FORMS OF SEVERE MENTAL
RETARDATION DERIVED FROM THE PREVALENCE OF DOWN'S SYNDROME
IN 1931 AND 1968

	1931	1961	% change	Refs.
(i) Prevalence of severe mental retardation (0/00) 7-14 yrs. (Middlesex).	3.88	3.54	—9	64,168
(ii) Estimated rate 0/00 of Down's Syndrome at birth.	1.3	1.15	—12	138,130
(iii) Estimated % survivors at age 10.	25	50	+100	129,26,40
(iv) Estimated prevalence (0/00) of Down's Syndrome 7-14 yrs.	0.325	0.575	+77	
(v) Observed prevalence (0/00) of Down's Syndrome 7-14 yrs. (Middlesex).	0.34	1.14	+235	64,168
(vi) Estimated prevalence (0/00) 7-14 yrs. of severe mental retardation other than Down's Syndrome.	3.55	2.875a	—19	
(vii) Estimated incidence (0/00) of severe mental retardation other than Down's Syndrome.				
(1) assuming no fall in death rate.	3.55 (k)	2.875 (k)	—19	
(2) assuming death rate falls as in Down's Syndrome.	14.20	5.75	—59.5	

a The observed rate of Down's Syndrome in Middlesex in 1961 (v) seems too high. The much
more conservative estimate (iv), based on (ii) and (iii), is used in the calculation.
k is a factor representing a constant relationship between incidence and prevalence.

intellectual disability, but at a slower rate than they have increased
survival and prevalence.

The Reduction of Prevalence

Two approaches to reducing prevalence seem promising. One possibility is to curtail development of the embryo when unequivocal impairment can be identified. The other is to limit functional disability
and social handicap in impaired persons, and to cultivate the maximum
intellectual and social potential of those affected.

For the purpose of reducing the prevalence of impairments, pregnant
women provide a productive target population. They are readily recognized and conveniently reached through the health services they use.

Moreover, the outcome at birth is registered by law, and seldom escapes notice and professional observation. Obstetric services serve as epidemiological check points at which to identify vulnerable groups.

We have discussed the degree to which the attribute of advanced maternal age identifies a substantial group of women at risk of bearing a child with Down's syndrome. Primary prevention reduces incidence; it would aim to concentrate conceptions in younger women by making known the risk to older women and preventing pregnancies among them (97). If older women should conceive by intent or mischance, however, it is possible to identify those among them who have conceived an embryo with chromosomal impairment. At 14 to 16 weeks after conception, Down's syndrome can be diagnosed with sensitivity, specificity and apparent safety (117, 97). In one series of 19 cases aspirated before 20 weeks gestation, cells were cultivated in 17. Well over 8,000 amniocenteses have been reported, including more than 200 between 8 and 20 weeks gestation. No complications in the mothers were encountered in these 200, nor in the 50 infants in that series allowed to continue till term.

The reduction of the prevalence of intellectual disability and mental handicap can be approached in two main ways. In metabolic disorders such as phenylketonuria and cretinism, treatment of the underlying impairments can control their impact on intellectual function and role performance. In other conditions, the direct improvement of intellectual function and role performance can be attempted.

The effect of controlling underlying impairment on intellectual disability has been best elaborated, if still imprecisely, in phenylketonuria. Even in untreated cases impairment and disability do not have a one to one relationship. Changing prevalence and altered processes of selection, treatment services and hospital admissions further complicate the picture. In all probability, individuals with phenylketonuria have shared the rising expectation of life of others with mental retardation. In the mid-1930's, Penrose searched for phenylketonuria among 1280 cases of mental retardation in Colchester, and found only one in 1,000 (128). In the 1960's, the prevalence in similar institutions was about ten in 1,000 (28). New case-finding methods as well as increased survival may have contributed to this ten-fold rise. The extension of screening from institution populations to the relatives of affected persons added cases. The new avenues of selection brought into the clinical spectrum biochemically impaired individuals without intellectual disabilities. Later, the routine screening of newborn infants revealed still other disorders of phenylalanine metabolism that caused only temporary biochemical impairment and no known intellectual disability.

Selection by screening at birth may have added to the prevalence of actual impairment, and not only to the known prevalence of disability and mental handicap; the recognized biochemical impairment was likely to stimulate increased medical attention, with consequent prolongation of life. On the other hand, dietary treatment in infancy and childhood has probably reduced the degree of intellectual disability, and perhaps its prevalence, in the cohorts of phenylketonuric infants identified at birth (192).

That the prevalence of intellectual disability can be reduced by means that develop intellectual function is indicated by several studies among the mildly retarded (155). First, longitudinal data on adolescents admitted to an institution for the mentally deficient showed that they continued to make I.Q. gains into their late twenties (33, 34). Second, in a cohort study of subjects labeled "educationally subnormal" at school, I.Q. gains were found in young adulthood among those with "cultural-familial" retardation (152). Third, a special education program, begun in the pre-school years and maintained for about three years, improved the performance of mildly retarded children (83). Thus improvement in the intellectual function of mildly retarded individuals is known to occur, and the application of pedagogic and social techniques offers promise of accelerating it. Widespread use of these methods would be necessary to induce changes in the prevalence or in the distribution of the degree of disability.

The severity of mental handicap can be reduced by developing the full social potential of mentally retarded individuals. The age-specific prevalence of mild retardation declines sharply from the mid-20's (160). The decline coincides with the somewhat delayed adoption of adult roles by mildly retarded persons. The young man who marries, or who acquires economic independence through working, no longer occupies the social role of a "retarded" person. In follow-up studies of mildly retarded men and women, two-thirds to three-quarters have settled well in the extramural environment (135, 81, 167, 168, 38, 37, 6). The treatment of mild mental retardation by socialization to adult roles can be expected to accelerate recoveries, and thereby to reduce the prevalence of handicap.

The concept of socialization can equally well be applied to severely retarded individuals. Severely retarded children living in a large institution improved both mental scores and their social skills compared with matched controls, when they were removed to a smaller home and given more individual attention (168). Among adults, when "moderately" retarded people are encouraged to achieve semi-independence by living in residential hostels and taking up supervised work, their level of "dependency" declines accordingly (25). Programs aimed at pedagogic, social and residential improvements have thus contributed to some reduction in the severity of mental handicap. These programs, being recent, can be expected to do more in the future (85).

Public health policy must choose which of the findings outlined above should be applied. An ecological approach is centered on the priorities of the total environment. A community approach is centered on the priorities of social units, from the national to the family level. A humane approach is centered on the priorities of individuals. Each approach may be intellectually acceptable, but each poses moral and ethical choices.

Planning must be concerned with reducing both incidence and prevalence. The greatest gains will come from a reduction in incidence. We must therefore aim to forestall each of the many causes outlined above. At the same time we must reduce disability and handicap in those who are impaired or disabled. A number of approaches are suggested by the preceding analysis.

1. Surveillance systems need extensive and sophisticated development. The environment must be monitored for new physical and chemical hazards introduced by war, industry, and by therapeutic practices. The need for vigilance in pretesting drugs and food substances, and in controlling and inspecting their distribution, is recognized and beginning to be put into effect in the United States. The need for a rapid feedback surveillance system that can detect the harmful effects of substances to which the population is exposed is given less attention. The cause of the gross abnormalities of ectomyelia induced by thalidomide was not identified and stopped in Europe until thousands of maimed infants had been born. Insidious effects pose an even greater hazard. Public health must be equipped with efficient systems of recording the incidence and prevalence of abnormalities in infants and children. Canada already has such a system (120). In a rapidly changing environment, this essential safeguard needs to be maintained continuously and nationwide, and where feasible, across nations as well.

2. The effort to control infections must continue. The successes of the past raise the hope of eliminating many of these causes of mental retardation one by one.

3. The role of war and of poverty among the causes of mental retardation should be recognized. World War II brought famine to Russia, Germany and Holland, and atomic bombs to Japan; more recently wars have brought famine to Biafra, and defoliants to Vietnam. Even in peacetime, preparations for nuclear attacks and for biological and chemical warfare have added demonstrably to the hazards of the environment. Peace, on the other hand, makes possible the use of world resources for the reduction of poverty. The manifold contributions of poverty to mental retardation have been emphasized in the preceding pages.

4. The potential of family planning in reducing the frequency of

mental retardation, especially Down's syndrome, should be made real. Primary prevention can be provided through health education and birth control, and secondary prevention through diagnostic amniocentesis centers associated with facilities for terminating selected pregnancies.

5. Adequate facilities should be provided for the care and training of mentally retarded persons. We can predict that the numbers of retarded people will continue to increase for some time. By "adequate" we mean facilities capable of realizing to the full each individual's potential for adjustment in family and community. Besides medical services, social training and pedagogic programs are needed to avert or overcome disability. Community and social services are needed to reduce handicap and dependency.

6. New knowledge must be sought to reduce incidence, which is the most productive area of action. Public funds for the relevant research in the health, behavioral and social sciences are essential to this activity.

BIBLIOGRAPHY

1. AKESSON, H. O.: *Epidemiology and Genetics of Mental Deficiency in a Southern Swedish Population.* Sweden, the Institute for Medical Genetics of the University of Uppsala, 1961, p. 74.
2. ASHFORD, J. R., FRYER, J. G. & BRIMBLECOMBE, F. S. W.: Secular trends in late foetal deaths, neonatal mortality, and birthweight in England and Wales, 1956-65 *Brit. J. Prev. Soc. Med.* 23:154, 1969.
3. BABSON, S. G., KANGAS, J., YOUNG, N. & BRAMHALL, J. L.: Growth and development of twins of dissimilar size at birth. *Pediatrics* 33:327, 1964.
4. BAILAR, J. C. & GURIAN, J.: Congenital malformations and season of birth; a brief review. *Eugen Quart.* 12:146, 1965.
5. BAILAR, J. C. & GURIAN, J.: The medical significance of date of birth. *Eugen Quart.* 14:89, 1967.
6. BALLER, W. R., CHARLES, D. C. & MILLER, E. L.: Mid-life attainment of the mentally retarded: a longitudinal study. *Genet. Psychol. Monogr.* 75:235, 1967.
7. BARKER, D. J. P.: Low intelligence and obstetric complications. *Brit. J. Prev. Soc. Med.* 20:15, 1966.
8. BARKER, D. J. P. & EDWARDS, J. H.: Obstetric complications and school performance. *Brit. Med. J.* 2:695, 1967.
9. BARON, J., YOUNGBLOOD, L., SIEWERS, C. M. F. & MEDEARIS, D. N.: The incidence of cytomegalovirus, herpes simplex, rubella, and toxoplasma antibodies in the microcephalic, mentally retarded, and normocephalic children. *Pediatrics.* 44:932, 1969.
10. BENARON, H. B. W., BROWN, M., TUCKER, B. E., WENTZ, V., & YACORZYNSKI, G. K.: The remote effects of prolonged labor with forceps delivery, precipitate labor with spontaneous delivery, and natural labor with spontaneous delivery on the child. *Amer. J. Obstet. Gynec.* 66:551, 1953.
11. BENDA, C. E.: Congenital syphilis in mental deficiency. *Amer. J. Ment. Defic.* 47:40, 1942.
12. BENTON, A. L.: Mental development of prematurely born children: a critical review of the literature. *Amer. J. Orthopsychiat.* 10:719, 1940.
13. BERENDES, H. W.: The role of infectious diseases in the causation of mental subnormality: a brief overview. *In* U.S. Department of Health, Education, and Welfare: *The Prevention of Mental Retardation through Control of Infectious Diseases.* Washington, D.C., Public Health Service Publication no. 1692.

14. BERG, J. M.: Neurological complications of pertussis immunization. *Brit. Med. J.* 2:24, 1958.
15. BERG, J. M. & KIRMAN, B. H.: Syphilis as a Cause of Mental Deficiency. *Brit. Med. J.* 2:400-404, 1959.
16. BERG, J. M. & KIRMAN, B. H.: The mentally defective twin. *Brit. Med. J.* 1:1911, 1960.
17. BERG, J. M. & ZAPELLA, M.: Lead poisoning in childhood with particular reference to pica and mental sequelae. *J. Ment. Defic. Res.* 8:44, 1964.
18. BERGNER, L. & SUSSER, M. W.: Prenatal nutrition and low birthweight: an epidemiological analysis. *Pediatrics.* 46:946, 1970.
19. BLACK, F. L., FOX, J. P., ELVEBACK, L. & KOGON, A.: Measles and readiness for reading and learning: 1. Background, purpose, and general methodology. *Amer. J. Epidem.* 88: 333, 1968.
20. BLACK, F. L. & DAVIS, D. E. M.: Measles and readiness for reading and learning: 2. New Haven study. *Amer. J. Epidem.* 88:337, 1968.
21. BUCK, C., GREGG, R., STAVRAKY, K., SUBRAHMANIAM, K. & BROWN, J.: The effect of single prenatal and natal complications upon the development of children of mature birthweight. *Pediatrics.* 43:942, 1969.
22. BUTLER, N. R. & ALBERMAN, E. D. (Eds.): *Perinatal Problems: The Second Report of the 1958 British Perinatal Mortality Survey.* Edinburgh and London, E. and S. Livingstone Ltd., 1969, pp. 72-84.
23. BYERS, R. K., RIZZO, N. D.: A follow-up study of pertussis in infancy. *New Engl. J. Med.* 242:887, 1950.
24. BYERS, R. K.: Lead poisoning: review of the literature and report on 45 cases. *Pediatrics.* 23:585, 1959.
25. CAMPBELL, A. C.: Comparison of family and community contacts of mentally subnormal adults in hospital and in local authority hostels. *Brit. J. Prev. Soc. Med.* 22:165, 1968.
26. CARTER, C. O.: A life-table for mongols with the causes of death. *J. Ment. Defic. Res.* 2:64, 1958.
27. CARTER, C. O.: Risk to offspring of incest. *Lancet.* 1:436, 1967.
28. CENTERWALL, W. R. & CHINNOCK, R. F.: Phenylketonuria: Replies from a letter to institutions for the mentally retarded. *In* U.S. Department of Health, Education, and Welfare: *Four Surveys of Phenylketonuria High Risk Groups.*
29. CHANOCK, R. M.: Mycoplasma infections of man. *New Engl. J. Med.* 273:1199, 1965.
30. CHANOCK, R. M.: Mycoplasma infections of man (concluded). *New Engl. J. Med.* 273:1257, 1965.
31. CHASE, H.: Infant mortality and weight at birth: 1960 United States birth cohort. *Amer. J. Public Health.* 59:1618, 1969.
32. CHURCHILL, J. A.: The relationship between intelligence and birthweight in twins. *Neurology* (Minneap.) 15:341, 1965.
33. CLARKE, A. B. D. & CLARKE, A. M.: Recovery from the effects of depriavtion. *J. Midland Ment. Defic. Soc.* 4:58, 1957.
34. CLARKE, A. B. D., CLARKE, A. M. & REIMAN, S.: Cognitive and social changes in the feebleminded: three further studies. *Brit. J. Psychol.* 49:144, 1958.
35. COHEN, M. M., MARINELLO, M. J. & BACK, N.: Chromosomal damage in human leukocytes induced by lysergic acid diethylamide. *Science.* 155:1417, 1967.
36. COHEN, M. M. & MUKHERJEE, A. B.: Meiotic chromosome damage induced by LSD-25 *Nature.* 219:1072, 1968.
37. COLLINS, J. E. & SPEAKE, J. G.: Success in employment of educationally subnormal children. *Med. Officer.* 101:167, 1959.
38. COLLMANN, R. D. & NEWLYN, D.: Employment success of educationally sub-normal ex-pupils in England. *Amer. J. Ment. Defic.* 60:733, 1956.
39. COLLMANN, R. D. & STOLLER, A.: A survey of mongoloid births in Victoria, Australia, 1942-1957. *Amer. J. Public Health.* 52:813, 1962.
40. COLLMANN, R. D. & STOLLER, A.: A life table for mongols in Victoria, Australia. *J. Ment. Defic. Res.* 7:53, 1963.

41. COLLMANN, R. D. & STOLLER, A.: Shift of childbirth to younger mothers, and its effect on the incidence of mongolism in Victoria, Australia, 1939-1964. *J. Ment. Defic. Res.* 13:13, 1969.

42. COOPER, L. Z.: German measles. *Sci. Amer.* 215 (1):30, 1966.

43. COURSIN, D. B.: Relationship of nutrition to central nervous system development and development. *Fed. Proc.* 26:134, 1967.

44. CRAVIOTO, J., DE LICARDIE, M. S. & BIRCH, H. G.: Nutrition, growth, and neuro-integrative development: an experimental and ecologic study. *Pediatrics Suppl.* 38:319, 1966.

45. CREAMER, B.: Toxaemia of pregnancy and the child. *J. Obstet. Gynaec. Brit. Comm.* 62:914, 1955.

46. DARKE, R. A.: Late effects of severe asphyxia neonatorum: a preliminary report. *J. Pediat.* 24:148, 1944.

47. DAUER, C. C., KORMS, R. F. & SCHUMAN, L. M.: *Infectious Diseases.* Cambridge, Mass., Harvard University Press, 1968, p. 48.

48. DAYTON, N. A.: Congenital syphilis as a cause of mental deficiency. *Boston Med. Surg. J.* 193:668, 1925.

49. DEAL, W. B. & SANDERS, E.: Efficacy of rifampin in treatment of menigococcal carriers. *New Engl. J. Med.* 281:641, 1969.

50. DEKABAN, A. S.: Abnormalities in children exposed to x-radiation during various stages of gestation: tentative timetable of radiation injury to the human fetus, part 1. *J. Nucl. Med.* 9, suppl. 1:471, 1968.

51. DENNIE, C. C.: *A History of Syphilis.* Springfield, Ill., Charles C. Thomas, 1962, p. 33.

52. DESMIT, E. M.: A follow-up study of 110 patients treated for purulent meningitis. *Arch. Dis. Child.* 30:415, 1958.

53. DEXTER, L. A.: *The Tyranny of Schooling: An Inquiry into the Problem of "Stupidity."* New York, Basic Books, 1964.

54. EDWARDS, J. H.: Experience in Birmingham. Paper presented at New York Academy of Sciences' and National Foundation—March of Dimes' conference on Down's Syndrome (Mongolism), 1969.

55. EICHENWALD, H. F.: Congenital toxoplasmosis: a study of one hundred fifty cases. *Amer. J. Dis. Child.* 94:411, 1957.

56. FAIRWEATHER, D. V. I. & ILLSLEY, R.: Obstetric and social origins of mentally handicapped children. *Brit. J. Prev. Soc. Med.* 14:149, 1960.

57. FOX, J. P., BLACK, F. L., ELVEBACK, L., KOGON, A., HALL, C. E., TURGEON, L. & ABRUZZI, W.: Measles and readiness for reading and learning: 3. Wappingers Central School District study. *Amer. J. Epidem.* 88:345, 1968.

58. FOX, J. P., BLACK, F. L. & KOGON, A.: Measles and readiness for reading and learning: 5. Evaluative comparison of the studies and overall conclusions. *Amer. J. Epidem.* 88:359, 1968.

59. FRAZIER, T. M., DAVIS, G. H., GOLDSTEIN, H. & GOLDBERG, I. D.: Cigarette smoking and prematurity: a prospective study. *Amer. J. Obstet. Gynec.* 81:988, 1961.

60. FREEDMAN, A. M. & WILSON, E. A.: Mental retardation associated with conditions due to trauma or physical agents. *In* Carter, C. H. (Ed.): *Medical Aspects of Mental Retardation.* Springfield, Ill., C. C. Thomas, 1965.

61. GIBBS, F. A., GIBBS, E. L., CARPENTER, P. R. & SPIES, H. W.: Electroencephalographic abnormality in "uncomplicated" childhood diseases. *J.A.M.A.* 171:1050, 1959.

62. GIBSON, S. L., LAM, C. N., McCRAE, W. M. & GOLDBERG, A.: Blood lead levels in normal and mentally deficient children. *Arch. Dis. Child* 42:573, 1967.

63. GOFMAN, J. W. & TAMPLIN, A. R.: *Federal Radiation Guidelines for Radiation Exposure of Population-at-large-Protection or Disaster?* testimony presented before the Sub-Committee on Air and Water Pollution of the Committee on Public Works of the U.S. Senate, 1969.

64. GOODMAN, N. & TIZARD, T.: Prevalence of imbecility and idiocy among children. *Brit. Med. J.* 1:216, 1962.

65. GORDON, N., KING, E. & MACKAY, R. I.: Lead absorption in children. *Brit. Med. J.* 2:480, 1967.

66. GORMAN, J. G., FREDA, V. J. & POLLACK, W.: Intramuscular injection of new experimental gammaglobulin preparation containing high levels of anti-Rh antibody as means of preventing sensitization to Rh. *Proc. IXth Congr. Int. Soc. Hemat.* 2:545, 1962.

67. GRAHAM, F. K., PENNOYER, M. M., CALDWELL, B. M., GREENMAN, M. & HARTMANN, A. F.: Relationship between clinical status and behavior test performance in a newborn group with histories suggesting anoxia. *J. Pediat.* 50:177, 1957.

68. GRUENWALD, P., FUNAKAWA, H., MITANI, S., NISHIMURA, T. & TAKEUCHI, S.: Influence of environmental factors on the foetal growth in man. *Lancet.* 1:1026, 1967.

69. HALLGREN, B. & HOLLSTROEM, E.: Congenital syphilis: a follow-up study with reference to mental abnormalities. *Acta Psychiat et Neurolog*, suppl. 93: 1954, p. 17.

70. *Ibid.*, pp. 9-17.

71. HAMMOND, E. C. & GARFINKEL, L.: Changes in Cigarette Smoking 1959-1965. *Amer. J. Public Health.* 58:30, 1968.

72. HARADA, Y., ARAKI, Y., SUDAH, H. & MIYAMOTO, Y.: Minamata disease in children. *Bulletin Kumamoto Domon Kaishi.* :6, 1965.

73. HECHT, F., BEAKS, R., LEES, M. H., JOLLY, H. & ROBERTS, P.: Lysergic-Acid-Diethylamide and cannabis as possible teratogens in man (letter). *Lancet.* 2:1087, 1968.

74. HICKS, S. P.: Developmental malformations produced by radiation. *Amer. J. Roentgen.* 69:272, 1953.

75. HOLCOMB, R. W.: Radiation risk: a scientific problem? *Science.* 167:853, 1970.

76. HYMAN, C. B., KEASTER, J., HANSON, V., HARRIS, I., SEDGWICK, R., WURSTEN, H. & WRIGHT, A. R.: CNS abnormalities after neonatal hemolytic disease or hyperbilirubinemia. *Amer. J. Dis. Child.* 117:395, 1969.

77. IRWIN, S. & EGOZCUE, J.: Chromosomal abnormalities in leukocytes from LSD-25 users. *Science.* 157:313, 1967.

78. JERVIS, G. A.: Premature aging of the mongoloid. Paper presented at the N.Y. Academy of Sciences' and National Foundation-March of Dimes' conference on Down's Syndrome (Mongolism), 1969.

79. KAELBER, C. T. & PUGH, T. F.: The influence of intrauterine relations on the intelligence of twins. *New Eng. J. Med.* 280:1030, 1969.

80. KAHN, E. J., NEUMANN, L. L. & POLK, G. A.: The course of the heroin withdrawal syndrome in newborn infants treated with phenobarbital or chlorpromazine. *J. Pediat.* 75:495, 1969.

81. KENNEDY, R. J. R.: *The Social Adjustment of Morons in a Connecticut City.* Hartford, Conn., Mansfield-Southbury Social Service, 1948.

82. KING, C. T. G.: Teratogenic effects of meclizine hydrochloride on a rat. *Science.* 141:353, 1963.

83. KIRK, S.: *Early Education of the Mentally Retarded.* Chicago, University of Illinois Press, 1958.

84. KIRMAN, B. H.: Tuberculous meningitis as a cause of mental deficiency (letter). *Brit. Med. J.* 2:1515, 1958.

85. KUSHLICK, A.: A Method for Evaluating the Effectiveness of Pediatric Care for the Severely Subnormal. In *56th Ross Conference on Pediatric Research*, pp. 54-61, Columbus, O., Ross Laboratories, 1967.

86. LANDER, E., FORSSMAN, H., AKESSON, H. O.: Season of birth and mental deficiency. *Acta. Genet.* (Basel). 14:265, 1964.

87. LAURENCE, K. M.: The survival of untreated spina bifida cystica. *Develop. Med. Child. Neurol.* suppl. 11:10, 1966.

88. LECK, I. & MILLER, E. L. M.: Short term changes in the incidence of malformations. *Brit. J. Prev. Soc. Med.* 17:1, 1963.

89. LECK, I.: Examination of the incidence of malformations for evidence of drug teratogenesis. *Brit. J. Prev. Soc. Med.* 18:196, 1964.

90. Leck, I., Record, R. G., McKeown, T. & Edwards, J. H.: The incidence of malformations in Birmingham, England, 1950-1959. *Teratology.* 1:263, 1969.

91. Leck, I., Hay, S.. Witte, J. J. & Greene, J. C.: Malformations recorded on birth certificates following A2 influenza epidemics. *Public Health Rep.* 84:971, 1969.

92. Lenz, W. & Knapp, K.: Fetal malformations due to thalidomide. *Ger. Med. Month.* 7:253, 1962.

93. Lewis, E. O.: *The Report of the Mental Deficiency Committee, part 4.* London, His Majesty's Stationery Office, 1929, p. 191.

94. Lilienfeld, A. M. & Pasamanick, B.: The association of maternal and fetal factors with the development of mental deficiency: 2. Relation to maternal age, birth order, previous reproductive loss and degree of mental deficiency. *Amer. J. Ment. Defic.* 60:557, 1956.

95. Lilienfeld, A. M. & Benesch, C. H.: *Epidemiology of Mongolism.* Baltimore, Md., the Johns Hopkins Press, 1969, pp. 27-38.

96. *Ibid.,* pp. 38-41.

97. Littlefield, J. W.: The pregnancy at risk for a genetic disorder. *New Engl. J. Med.* 282:627, 1970.

98. Looft, C.: L'évolution de l'intelligence des jumeaus. *Acta. Paediat.* (Stockholm). 12:41, 1931.

99. Lorber, J.: Long-term follow-up of 100 children who recovered from tuberculous meningitis. *Pediatrics.* 28:778, 1961.

100. Macnab, G. H.: The development of the knowledge and treatment of hydrocephalus. *Develop. Med. Child. Neurol.* suppl. 11:1, 1966.

101. Manson, M. M., Logan, W. P. D. & Loy, R. M.: Rubella and other virus infections during pregnancy. *Rep. on Public Health and Med. Subjects.* 101:1960.

102. Masden, T.: Vaccination against whooping cough. *J.A.M.A.* 101:187, 1933.

103. Matsunaga, E.: Parental age, live-birth order and pregnancy-free interval in Down's syndrome in Japan. *In* Wolstenholme, G. E. W. (Ed.): *Mongolism.* Boston, Little, Brown, and Co., 1967.

104. McBride, W. G.: Thalidomide and congenital abnormalities (letter). *Lancet.* 2:1358, 1961.

105. Mercer, J.: Social system perspective and clinical perspective: frames of reference for understanding career patterns of persons labelled as mentally retarded. *Soc. Prob.* 13:19, 1965.

106. Milham, S. & Gittlesohn, A. M.: Parental age and malformations. *Hum. Biol.* 37:13, 1965.

107. Miller, H. G., Stanton, J. B. & Gibbons, J. L.: Para-infectious encephalomyelitis and related syndromes: a critical review of the neurological complications of certain specific fevers. *Quart. J. Med.* 25:427, 1956.

108. Miller, R. W.: Delayed effects occurring within the first decade after exposure of young individuals to the Hiroshima atom bomb. *Pediatrics.* 18:1, 1956.

109. Miller, R. W.: Prenatal origins of mental retardation: epidemiological approach. *J. Pediat.* 71:455, 1967.

110. Miller, R. W.: Delayed radiation effects in atomic-bomb survivors. *Science.* 166:569, 1969.

111. Moncrieff, A. A., Koumides, O. P., Clayton, B. A., Patrick, A. D., Renwick, A. G. C. & Roberts, G. E.: Lead poisoning in children *Arch. Dis. Child.* 34:1, 1964.

112. Moriyama, I. M.: *The Change in Mortality Trend in the U.S.* Washington, D.C., National Center for Health Statistics, series 3, no. 1., Government Printing Office, 1964.

113. Morley, D.: Severe measles in the tropics—1. *Brit. Med. J.* 1:297, 1969.

114. Morley, D.: Severe measles in the tropics—2. *Brit. Med. J.* 1:363, 1969.

115. Murozumi, M., Chow. T. J. & Patterson, C.: Chemical concentrations of pollutant lead aerosols, terrestrial dusts, and sea salts in Greenland and Antarctic snow strata. *Geochimica et Cosmochimica Acta.* 33:1247, 1969.

116. Murphy, D. P.: The outcome of 625 pregnancies in women subjected to pelvic or roentgen irradiation. *Amer. J. Obstet. Gynec.* 18:179, 1929.

117. NADLER, H. L. & GERBIE, A. B.: Amniocentesis in the intrauterine detection of genetic disorders. *New Engl. J. Med.* 282:596, 1970.

118. NEEL, J. V. & SCHULL, W. J.: *The Effect of Exposure to the Atomic Bombs on Pregnancy Termination in Hiroshima and Nagasaki.* Washington, D.C., National Academy of Sciences—National Research Council Publication, 461, 1956.

119. NEWCOMBE, H. B.: Radiation protection in Canada part VI, problems in the assessment of genetic damage from exposure of individuals and populations to radiation. *Canad. Med. Ass. J.* 92:171, 1965.

120. NEWCOMBE, H. B.: Pooled records from multiple sources for monitoring congenital anomalies. *Brit. J. Prev. Soc. Med.* 23:226, 1969.

121. OSTER, J., MIKKLESON, M. & NIELSON, A.: The mortality and causes of death in patients with Down's syndrome. *Int. Copenhagen Congr. Sci. Study Ment. Retard.* 1:231, 1964.

122. PANUM, P. L.: *Observations Made During the Epidemic of Measles on the Faroe Islands in the Year 1846.* Cleveland, Delta Omega Society, 1940.

123. PASAMANICK, B. & LILIENFELD, A. M.: Association of maternal and fetal factors with the development of mental deficiency: 1. Abnormalities in the prenatal and paranatal periods. *J.A.M.A.* 159:155, 1955.

124. PASAMANICK, B. & KNOBLOCH, H.: Seasonal variations in complications of pregnancy. *Obstet. Gynec.* 12:110, 1958.

125. PATTERSON, C.: Contaminated and natural lead environments of man. *Arch. Environ. Health.* 11:344, 1965.

126. PENROSE, L. S.: *A Clinical and Genetic Study of 1280 Cases of Mental Defect.* London, His Majesty's Stationery Office, 1938, p. 38.

127. *Ibid.,* p. 41.

128. *Ibid.,* p. 49.

129. PENROSE, L. S.: The incidence of mongolism in the general population. *J. Ment. Sci.* 95:685, 1949.

130. PENROSE, L. S. & SMITH, G. F.: *Down's Anomaly.* Boston, Little, Brown. and Co., 1966, pp. 155-158.

131. *Ibid.,* pp. 157-158.

132. PLUMMER, G.: Anomalies occurring in children exposed *in utero* to the atomic bomb in Nagasaki, *Pediatrics.* 10:684, 1952.

133. PLUMMER, G. Anomalies occurring in children exposed *in utero* to the atomic bomb in Hiroshima. *Pediatrics.* 10:687, 1952.

134. POSKANZER, D. C., SALAM, M. Z.: Mental retardation related to infectious diseases in patients at Walter E. Fernald State School. In *The Prevention of Mental Retardation through Control of Infectious Diseases.* Wash., D.C. Public Health Service Publication No. 1692.

135. RAMER, T. The prognosis of mentally retarded children. *Acta. Psychiat. et Neurology.* suppl. 41: 1946.

136. RAURAMO, L., GRONROOS, M. & KIVIKOSKI, A.: A comparative study of the obstetrical history of pupils in schools for backward children and elementary school pupils. *Acta. Obstet. et. Gynec. Scandinav.* 40:321, 1961.

137. RAYNER, S.: An investigation of the change in prevalence of mental deficiency in Sweden. *Hereditas.* 51:297, 1964.

138. RECORD, R. G. & SMITH, A.: Incidence, mortality, and sex distribution of mongoloid defectives. *Brit. J. Prev. Soc. Med.* 9:10, 1955.

139. RICKHAM, P. P. & MAWDSLEY, T.: The effect of early operations on the survival of spina bifida cystica. In *Hydrocephalus and Spina Bifida. Developmental Medicine & Child Neurology,* Supplement 11, 1966, 20-26.

140. ROBERTS, D. F.: Incest, inbreeding, and mental abilities. *Brit. Med. J.* 4:336, 1967.

141. SCHULL, W. J.: Empirical risks in consanguineous marriages: sex ratio, malformations. and viability. *Amer. J. Hum. Genet.* 10:294, 1958.

142. SCHULL, W. J. & NEEL, J. V.: Radiation and the sex ratio in man. *Science.* 128: 343, 1958.

143. SCHULL, W. J. & NEEL, J. V.: Maternal radiation and mongolism. *Lancet.* 1:537, 1962.

144. SCHULL, W. J., NEEL, J. V. & HASHIZUME, A.: Some further observations on the sex ratio among infants born to survivors of the atomic bombings of Hiroshima and Nagasaki. *Amer. J. Hum. Genet.* 18:328, 1966.
145. Scottish Council for Research in Education: *The Trend of Scottish Intelligence: A Comparison of the 1947 and 1932 Surveys of Intelligence of Eleven-Year Old Pupils.* London, University of London Press, 1949.
146. SEVER, J. L.: Perinatal infections affecting the developing fetus and newborn. In *The Prevention of Mental Retardation through the Control of Infectious Diseases.* Wash., D.C. Public Health Service Publication No. 1692.
147. SHERIDAN, M. D.: Final report of a prospective study of children whose mothers had rubella in early pregnancy. *Brit. Med. J.* 2:536, 1964.
148. SIGLER, A. T., LILIENFELD, A. M., COHEN, B. H. & WESTLAKE, J. E.: Radiation exposure in parents of children with mongolism (Down's syndrome). *Bull. Johns Hopkins Hosp.* 117:374, 1965.
149. SIMPSON, W. J.: A preliminary report of cigarette smoking and the incidence of prematurity. *Amer. J. Obstet. Gynec.* 73:807, 1957.
150. SMITH. E. S.: Purulent meningitis in infants and children: a review of 409 cases. *J. Pediat.* 45:425, 1954.
151. SMITH, A. & RECORD, R. G.: Maternal age and birth rank in the aetiology of mongolism. *Brit. J. Prev. Soc. Med.* 9:51, 1955.
152. STEIN, Z. A. & SUSSER, M.: Families of dull children, part 4, increments in intelligence. *J. Ment. Sci.* 106:1311, 1960.
153. STEIN, Z. A. & SUSSER, M.: Mild mental subnormality: social and epidemiological studies. *In* Redlich, F. (Ed.). *Social Psychiatry.* U.S.A., Research Publication of the Association for Research in Nervous and Mental Disease, vol. 47, 1969.
154. STEIN, U. A. & KASSAB, H. J.: Malnutrition and mental retardation. In Wortis, J. (Ed.). *Mental Retardation: An Annual Review, vol. 2.* New York, Grune and Stratton, Inc., 1970.
155. STEIN, Z. A. & SUSSER, M.: Mutability of Intelligence and Epidemiology of Mild Mental Retardation. *Review of Educational Research.* 40:29, 1970.
156. STERN, H., BOOTH, J. C., ELEK, S. D. & FLECK, D. G.: Microbial causes of mental retardation: the role of prenatal infections with cytomegalovirus, rubella virus, and toxoplasma. *Lancet.* 2:443, 1969.
157. STUBBS, V. & JACOBSON, C. B.: LSD and genetic damage. *George Washington Magazine*: 26, 1968.
158. SUSSER, M.: *Community Psychiatry: Epidemiologic and Social Themes.* New York, Random House, 1968, pp. 299-321.
159. *Ibid.*, p. 287.
160. *Ibid.*, p. 281.
161. *Ibid.*, p. 386.
162. SUSSER, M. & WATSON, W.: *Sociology and Medicine* (ed. 2). London, Oxford University Press, 1971.
163. TAKEUCHI, T. & MATSUMOTO, H.: Minamata disease of human fetuses. In Nishimura, H., Miller, J. R., and Yasuda, M. (Eds.): *Methods for Teratological Studies in Experimental Animals and Man: Proceedings of the Second International Workshop in Teratology, Kyoto, 1968.* Tokyo, Igaku Shoin, Ltd., 1969.
164. TARJAN, G., EYMAN, R. K. & MILLER, C. R.: Natural history of mental retardation in a state hospital, revisited. *Amer. J. Dis. Child.* 117:609, 1969.
165. THALHAMMER, O.: Congenital toxoplasmosis. *Lancet.* 1:23, 1962.
166. THOMAS, H. V., MILMORE, B. K., HEIDBREDER, G. A. & KAGAN, B. A.: Blood lead of persons living near expressways. *Arch. Environ. Health.* 15:695, 1967.
167. TIZARD, J. & O'CONNOR, N.: The employability of high-grade mental defectives. 1. *Amer. J. Ment. Defic.* 54:563, 1950.
168. TIZARD, J.: *Community Services for the Mentally Handicapped.* London, Oxford 1964.
169. TODD, R. M. & NEVILLE, J. G.: The sequelae of tuberculous meningitis. *Arch. Dis. Childh.* 39:213, 1964.

170. TREDGOLD, A. F.: *Mental Deficiency (Amentia)*. London, Bailliere, Tindall and Cox, 1908, p. 21.
171. *Ibid.,* pp. 21-22.
172. *Ibid.,* p. 28.
173. *Ibid.,* p. 188.
174. UCHIDA, I. A., HOLUNGA, R. & LAWLEY, C.: Maternal radiation and chromosomal aberrations. *Lancet.* 2:1045, 1968.
175. U. S. Department of Health, Education, and Welfare: *National Communicable Disease Center Annual Encephalitis Summary* 1963, 1964, 1965. 1966, 1967, and 1968.
176. U. S. Department of Health, Education, and Welfare: *National Communicable Disease Center. Weekly Report Annual Supplement.* 17, no. 53:1969, p. 24.
177. U. S. Department of Health, Education, and Welfare: *National Communicable Disease Center Weekly Report.* 19, no. 3, 1970, pp. 24-25.
178. U. S. Department of Health, Education, and Welfare: *National Communicable Disease Center Weekly Report.* 19, no. 4, 1970, p. 40.
179. U. S. Department of Health, Education, and Welfare: *The Prevention of Mental Retardation through the Control of Infectious Diseases.* Washington, D.C., Public Health Service Publication No. 1692.
180. WAHRMAN, J. & FRIED, K.: The Jerusalem prospective newborn survey of mongolism. Paper presented at the N. Y. Academy of Sciences' and National Foundation—March of Dimes' conference on Down's Syndrome (Mongolism), 1969.
181. WHITESIDE, T.: Defoliation. *New Yorker* : 32, Feb. 2, 1970.
182. WIENER, G.: Psychologic correlates of premature birth. *J. Nerv. Ment. Dis.* 134:129, 1962.
183. WIENER, G.: Varying psychological sequelae of lead ingestions in children. *Public Health Rep.* 85:19, 1970.
184. WINICK, M.: Malnutrition and brain development, *J. Pediat.* 74:667, 1969.
185. WOOD, J. W., JOHNSON, K. G., YOSHIAKI, O., KAWAMOTO, S. & KEEHN, R. J.: *Mental Retardation in Children Exposed in Utero to the Atomic Bomb—Hiroshima and Nagasaki.* Atomic Bomb Casualty Commission technical report 10-66, 1966.
186. WOODROW, J. C., CLARKE, C. A., DONOHOE, W. T. A., FINN, R., McCONNELL, R. B., SHEPPARD, P. J., RUSSELL, S. H., LEHANE, D., KULKE, W. & DURKIN, C. M.: Prevention of RH hemolytic disease: third report. *Brit. Med. J.* 1:279, 1965.
187. World Health Organization : *Toxoplasmosis: Report of a WHO Meeting of Investigators.* Geneva, World Health Organization technical report 431, 1969.
188. YAMAZAKI, J. N., WRIGHT, S. W. & WRIGHT, P. M.: Outcome of pregnancy in women exposed to the atomic bomb in Nagasaki. *Amer. J. Dis. Child.* 87:448.
189. YANNET, H.: "Discussion" of Poskanzer, D. C. and Salam, M. Z.: Mental retardation related to infectious disease in patients at Walter E. Fernald State School. In *The Prevention of Mental Retardation through Control of Infectious Diseases,* p. 28. Wash., D.C., Public Health Service Publication No. 1692.
190. YERUSHALMY, J.: Mother's cigarette smoking and survival of infant. *Amer. J. Obstet. Gynec.* 88:505, 1964.
191. YERUSHALMY, J. & MILKOVICH, L.: Evaluation of the teratogenic effects of meclizine in man. *Amer. J. Obstet. Gynec.* 93:553, 1965.
192. YI-YUNG HSIA, D.: The role of phenylalanine in mental development. Paper presented at the N. Y. Academy of Medicine's third International Conference, "The Future of the Brain Sciences," 1968.
193. ZELLWEGER, H., McDONALD, J. S. & ABBO, G.: Is Lysergic-Acid diethylamide a teratogen? *Lancet.* 2:1066, 1967.

Part III
Behavior Disorders
and
Psychopathology

14

MINOR PHYSICAL ANOMALIES AND HYPERACTIVE BEHAVIOR IN YOUNG CHILDREN

Mary Ford Waldrop, M.A.

and

Charles F. Halverson, Jr., Ph.D.

Child Research Branch
National Institute of Mental Health

EVIDENCE OF CONGENITAL CONTRIBUTORS TO BEHAVIOR

In five separate studies we have found evidence of possible congenital contributors to individual differences in impulse control. This evidence is based on our finding that relatively uncontrolled, fast moving, hyperactive behavior is related to the presence of certain minor physical anomalies in young children. We found that "normal" boys with a high incidence of minor physical anomalies (which either are present at birth or are part of the child's developmental pattern) were apt to be the frenetic, impatient, intractable children in a nursery school setting and the hyperactive, "troublesome" children in an elementary school. In all likelihood the same factors operating in the first weeks of pregnancy influenced the occurrence of *both* the morphological aberrations and the predisposition for impulsive, fast moving behavior. When we saw hyperactive play behavior we frequently found that the boys involved also had minor physical anomalies such as head circumference out of normal range, epicanthus, widely spaced eyes, curved fifth finger, adherent ear lobes, and a wide gap between first and second toes. We also found that for girls the behavioral concomitants of the anomaly score were inconsistent: while in one study the results for boys and girls were similar, in another study they were not. That is, in one study we found that normal preschool children of both sexes who tended to be uncontrolled, impulsive, and intractable were also likely to have more than an average number of minor physical anomalies. In another

343

study, however, we found that normal preschool girls who were over-controlled, inhibited, and intractable were likely to have more of these anomalies. In both these studies girls with high anomaly scores were stubborn and had difficulty with control, too much control in one study, too little control in the other.

Because these minor anomalies as a group are typically associated with Down's Syndrome and with other major congenital defects, they have been thought to result from chromosomal irregularities or some kind of insult affecting embryological development.

This chapter will review five separate and completed studies that have focused on behavioral and developmental differences between children having many minor physical anomalies and children having few of these anomalies. In addition, three studies currently underway will be discussed briefly.

Three of the five completed studies were a part of the ongoing longitudinal research program of the Child Research Branch, National Institute of Mental Health. First, the Original Study (Waldrop, Pederson, & Bell, 1968) was done on a sample of two-and-a-half-year-olds attending a research nursery school. Second, the Replication Study (Waldrop & Halversen, 1971) was done on another sample of two-and-a-half-year-olds attending the same research nursery school. The purpose of this second study was to check on the validity of the findings from the original investigation. Third, a follow-up study, called the Stability Study (Waldrop & Halversen, 1971), was done on the original sample when the children were seven-and-a-half-years old. The aim of this study was to assess the stability of the anomalies and their relation to behavior. The fourth and fifth studies were done on samples of children who were not participating subjects in the longitudinal research. The fourth, called the Easter Seal Study (Waldrop & Halversen, 1971), was done on children congenitally deficient in speech and/or hearing to see if those children with more major congenital defects also had more anomalies. The fifth, the Elementary School Study (Waldrop & Goering, 1971), was done on a sample of children attending a public elementary school. The purpose here was to see if the anomalies were related also to hyperactivity as defined in a school setting.

THE ANOMALIES: SCORING AND DESCRIPTIONS

The list of the minor anomalies used in our research was originally used by Goldfarb and Botstein (unpublished manuscript) to differentiate schizophrenic schildren from normal children. Using the results from this study we devised the following weighting system. For the nine minor anomalies that significantly differentiated the schizophrenics from the normal children, we gave weights of one or two depending on the degree to which the anomaly deviated from the normal characteristic. These nine anomalies are: fine electric hair, head circumference out of normal range, epicanthus, hyperteliorism, low-seated ears, adherent ear lobes, high steepled palate, curved fifth finger, and third toe $\geqq$ second toe. We assigned weights of one to the six anomalies that were more frequent, though not significantly so, among the schizophrenic children than among normal subjects. These six anomalies are: malformed ears, asymmetrical ears, furrowed tongue, single transverse palmar crease, partial syndactylia of the toes, big gap between first and second toes. In addition, the presence or absence of three additional anomalies was noted for a total score but was not counted in the weighted score. These three anomalies (more than one hair whorl, soft pliable ears, and smooth-rough spots on the tongue) showed either no incidence at all or a greater incidence—not significant—in the normal sample than in the schizophrenic one. Descriptions, illustrations, and scoring weights of all eighteen minor physical anomalies are given here. For varying reasons, not all of our studies have used exactly the same list of anomalies. The list now in use is given below. Variations from this list are explained with reference to the separate studies. The percentage of incidence of each anomaly in each sample studied is reported in the closing section of this chapter.

Anomalies in the Area of the Head

1. *Fine electric hair (weighted one or two)*
    Very fine (usually blonde) hair that simply will not comb down was given a weight of two. Below is a photograph of a child's hair that we weighted two. Fine hair that was soon awry after combing was rated one. In a few cases we had some doubt as to whether or not a child had fine electric hair that would rate a one; we never had any doubt about hair deserving a weight of two.

2. *Two or more hair whorls (weighted zero)*
    Most people have one spot near the crown of their head where their hair grows in a circular pattern. Hair whorls appear on either the right or the left hemisphere. A few people have more than one whorl and a few other people have a line, instead of a point, around which the hair grows. We considered an anomaly to be either two or more distinct whorls or a line an inch or more in length.

3. *Head circumference outside normal range (weighted one or two)*
    We considered an anomaly any head circumference that deviated from the mean of established norms by more than one standard deviation. Those that deviated between one and one-and-a-half standard deviations were weighted one, and those deviating more than one-and-a-half standard deviations were weighted two.
    Measurement of head circumference has proven to be one of the most difficult to assess. One simple difficulty was obtaining accurate and uniform tape measures. Another difficulty was judging just how tightly to pull the tape. We tried to apply the tape firmly over

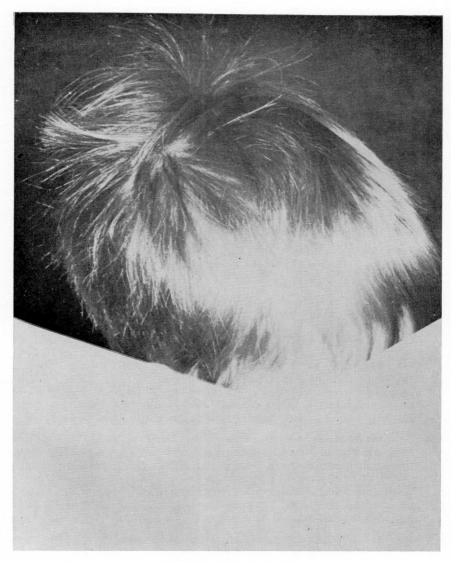

FIGURE 1.—Fine electric hair.

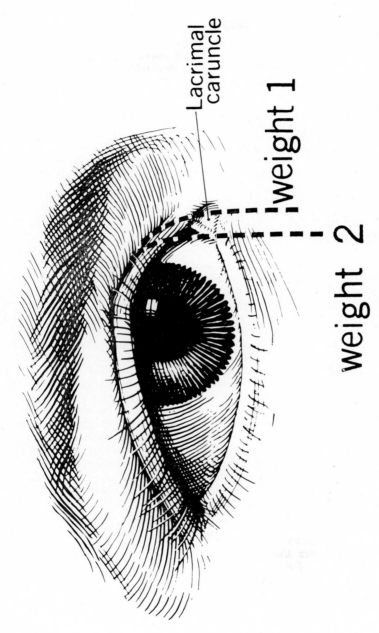

FIGURE 2.—Illustrations of different weights for epicanthus.

the globella and supraorbital ridges anteriorly and that part of the occiput posteriorly which gave the maximal circumference. This means that we positioned the tape over whatever points on the forehead and occiput that gave the maximal circumference. In each of the normal samples studied, we compared our means and standard deviations with the published norms (Vickers & Stuart, 1943). In the one study where standard deviations were equal to those of the norms but the means were different, we made the proper adjustments in each child's score. In the original study we considered as being out of normal range 27½ per cent of the cases. From a frequency distribution we selected the 27½ per cent that were most deviant from the mean. Empirically, among the 27½ per cent there was a cutoff point above and below which circumferences were weighted two. The problem with this method is that determining what is "out of normal range" depends on the total sample being measured.

Anomalies in the Area of the Eyes

1. *Epicanthus (weighted one or two)*
It is well known that epicanthus is more prevalent among infants and toddlers than among school-aged children (Gibson & Frank, 1961). In fact, in a sample of three-month-old children we observed that close to 75 per cent had epicanthus. It seems, therefore, that epicanthus should not be considered an anomaly unless it persists into early childhood. The presence of epicanthus was judged visually and weighted either one or two.

For making this judgment the examiner's and the child's eyes were at the same level. Epicanthus was considered present if, with the subject looking straight ahead, any vertical skin fold covered or partially covered the lacrimal caruncle on either eye. An epicanthic fold that partially covered the lacrimal caruncle on either eye was weighted one. Any epicanthus that covered as much as or more than the whole lacrimal caruncle was weighted two. We took note on which eye the epicanthus was found but did not differentiate in the scoring whether the fold occurred on one or both eyes. This method of judging epicanthus was similar to the method used by Taylor and Cameron (1963) who graded epicanthus on a 4-point scale. Figure 3 is a photograph of a child's eyes that were weighted two on epicanthus.

2. *Hyperteliorism (weighted one or two)*
Hyperteliorism means unusually wide-set eyes. Some writers prefer to speak of this in terms of the inner intercanthal distance being greater than normal (Pryor, 1969). It would have been far too difficult for us to obtain a precise measure of this distance on young children without restraining them. We settled on obtaining an estimate: holding a tape measure across the bridge of the child's nose, we sighted across the tape to gauge the distance between his eyes.

Pryor (1969) and Laestadius, Aase, and Smith (1969), as well as we ourselves, have found racial differences in this measure. Therefore, caution must be used in using any published norms.

For Caucasians we based our weights on the results of our Original Study. That is, those scores that were the highest (14 per cent, or one-half of 27½ per cent) were considered as indicating hyperteliorism. Again, a cutoff point was chosen above which a weight of two was given. Our way of measuring corresponded with norms obtained by Taylor and Cameron (1963), and by Pryor (1969). Taylor and Cameron measured Caucasian subjects, 681 males and 705 females from newborns to ninety-two years of age. Pryor's measures were made on thousands of subjects, including Caucasians, Mexicans, and Japanese from newborns to fifteen years of age.

FIGURE 3.—Epicanthus and hyperteliorism.

Even though there are reported sex differences in hyperteliorism, our measures were not precise enough to have different cut-off points for males as against females. Our cutoff points for various ages were:

	Weight 1 (in millimeters)	Weight 2 (in millimeters)
Newborns	$\geq 25 \leq 26$	≥ 27
3 months	$\geq 26 \leq 27$	≥ 28
2½ years	$\geq 29 \leq 30$	≥ 31
7 years	32	≥ 33
8 years	33	≥ 34
9 years	33	≥ 34
10 years	34	≥ 35
11 years	34	≥ 35
12 years	34	≥ 35

The child whose eyes are shown in Figure 3, above, had hyperteliorism weighted two.

Anomalies in the Area of the Ears

1. *Low-seated ears (weighted one or two)*

Low-seated ears are found among neonates with a variety of congenital malformations. For instance, Vincent, Ryan and Longennecker (1961) found a high percentage of infants born with major kidney defects had ears that were set unusually low on the head.

As was true for hyperteliorism, low-seated ears cannot be measured precisely on unrestrained young children. We did devise a way of placing a cloth tape measure so the lower edge went across the child's nose bridge, across the outer corner of the eye, and back across the top of the ear. When the line formed by the lower edge

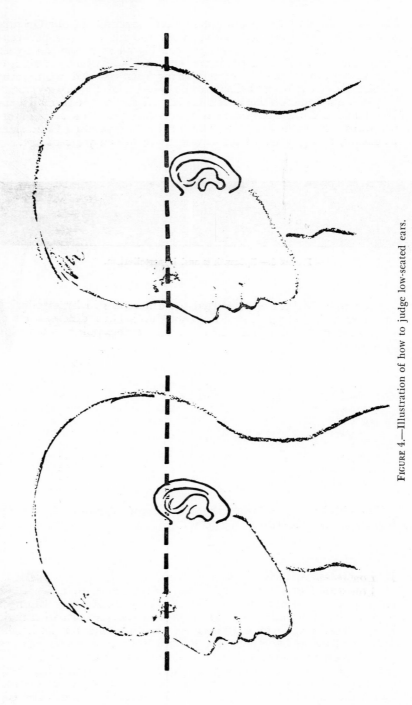

FIGURE 4.—Illustration of how to judge low-seated ears.

of the tape was above the top juncture of the ear by any distance up to or equal to .5 centimeters, a weight of one was given. When this distance was greater than .5 centimeters, a weight of two was given. Figure 4 shows how this measure was taken.

If the corner of the eye did not seem to be in line with the center of the eye orbit and the nose bridge, we would use what we judged to be the center of the orbit. In other words, in those few cases where it would seem that the outer corner of the eye was out of line, we would extend the tape from the bridge of the nose through the estimated center of the eye orbit past the top juncture of the ear with the head in order to judge whether or not the child had low-seated ears.

2. *Adherent ear lobes (weighted one or two)*

This anomaly was considered not present if any part of the lower edge of the ear extended below the lowest point of attachment to the head. When the lower edge of the ear extended toward the back of the head a weight of one was given. When the lower edge extended upward toward the crown of the head, a weight of two was given. These differences are shown in Figure 5.

3. *Malformed ears (weighted one)*

Very few ears were thought to be malformed. When we did see ears that were grossly misshapen, we would count this as an anomaly.

4. *Asymmetrical ears (weighted one)*

Ears that were obviously different from each other were called asymmetrical. That is, differences so minute they would have to be detected by measurement were not considered. Conditions we saw as examples of this anomaly are: one ear exceptionally small (or large), the other normal size; one ear protruding, the other lying close to the head; the shape of one ear different from the shape of the other ear. Moreover, when the ear on one side of the head was more low-seated than the ear on the other side, it was counted as being both low-seated and asymmetrical.

5. *Soft and pliable ears (weighted zero)*

Having this anomaly does not mean the ears are so lacking in cartilage that they are floppy instead of being able to stand upright. It does mean, however, that they are so soft they feel jellylike when the ear, held between thumb and first finger, is moved back and forth. Soft and pliable ears do not quickly spring back into place when flopped forward. In most ears the cartilage feels strong, but in soft pliable ears the cartilage feels weak.

Anomalies in the Area of the Mouth

1. *High-steepled palate (weighted one or two)*

Because the most common shape of the roof of the mouth is a rounded dome, a cross section through the highest point would be an arch. A cross section that was not an arch but an angle was considered an anomaly with a weight of two. A weight of one was given when there was a narrow flat part across the top of the

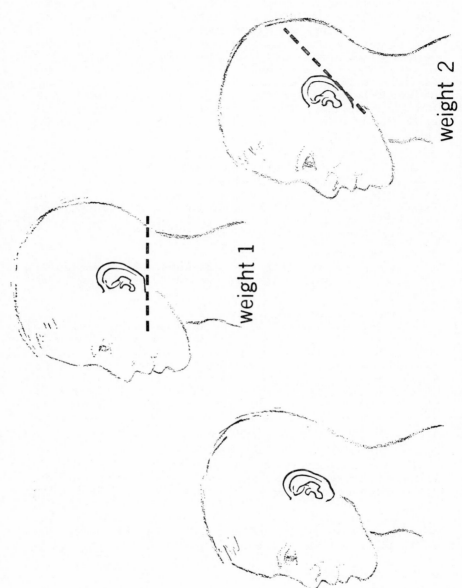

FIGURE 5.—Illustration of different weights for adherent ear lobes.

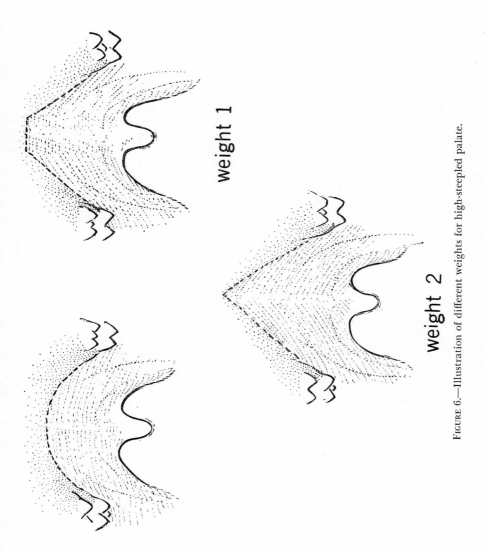

weight 1

weight 2

FIGURE 6.—Illustration of different weights for high-steepled palate.

two sides. The following drawings (Figure 6) illustrate these three shapes of palates.

Silman (1964) has pointed out that the shape of a palate does change during the first years of life. For those children two-and-a-half and older with high-steepled palates it is not known how their palates were shaped at birth. We have found, however, that there is a range in palate shape among newborns and also among three-month-old infants.

2. *Furrowed tongue (weighted one)*

In regard to tongue furrows or fissures, our findings substantiated those of Gibson and Frank (1961) who found this anomaly to be age related. That is, we found this anomaly more frequently among our sample of elementary school children than among our samples of infants and preschoolers. Tongues having one or more deep grooves, usually not along the center line, were weighted one.

3. *Tongue with smooth-rough spots (weighted one)*

A tongue with localized thickening of the epithelium is called a geographic tongue or a tongue with smooth-rough spots. It is important not to confuse this with a tongue on which papillae are outstanding because the exaggerated appearance of papillae can be a function of recent consumption of certain foods. Even though this "geographic tongue" condition was practically nonexistent among our samples, when one was seen a weight of one was given to it.

Anomalies in the Area of the Hand

1. *Curved fifth finger (weighted one or two)*

The tip of the fifth finger curving inward toward the other fingers was considered an anomaly. Clearly defining how to differentiate what was to be weighted one and what was to be weighted two has been difficult. Experience has made it possible, however, to establish rater reliability. Figure 7 is a photograph of a child's hand which we weighted as two. A curved finger with a smaller degree of curvature would be weighted one.

2. *Single transverse palmar crease (weighted one)*

A single transverse palmar crease, sometimes called a Simian Crease, is an unbroken line in the palm of the hand going more or less straight across the hand. Not only do those with Down's Syndrome have significantly more incidences of this anomaly than do normal people, but also those cases in which there was a known teratogenic agent (rubella) have this dermatoglyphic anomaly more frequently than do normal cases (Achs, Harper, & Siegel, 1966). A child having this anomaly on either or both hands would be given a weighted score of one. Figure 8 is a clear illustration of a single transverse palmar crease.

Anomalies in the Area of the Feet

1. *Third toe longer than second (weighted one or two)*

As can be seen in our report of the incidences of these anomalies we have observed that having a third toe longer than the second is partially a function of age. Relative to the other anomalies

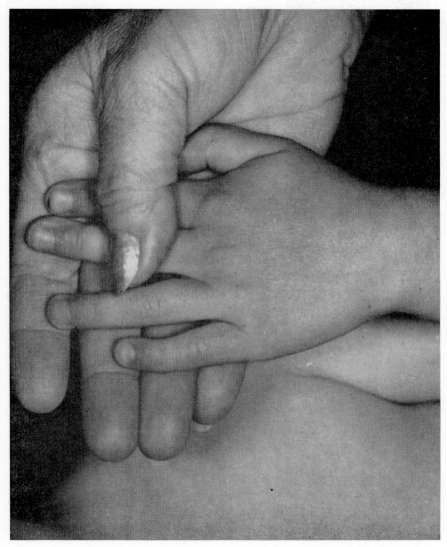

FIGURE 7.—Curved fifth finger.

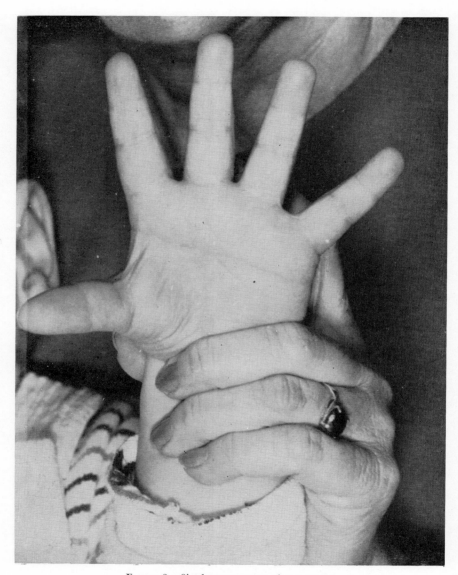

FIGURE 8.—Single transverse palmar crease.

considered, this one was quite common among the two-and-a-half-year-olds but quite rare among elementary school children. We checked for the presence of this anomaly when the child was sitting down and his foot was relaxed. With the toes held in an extended position, if the second and third toes appeared to be the same length, a weight of one was given. When the third toe was obviously longer than the second, a weight of two was given. The photograph in Figure 9 is an illustration of toes that were weighted two.

2. *Partial syndactylia of two middle toes (weighted one)*

Partial syndactylia (webbing) sometimes occurs between the second and third toes. In some few cases when this occurs between the second and third toes it also occurs between the third and fourth. Because almost everyone has some slight webbing of the toes, partial syndactylia is somewhat difficult to judge. We counted it as an anomaly when there were three indentations at the base of the toes instead of four. In addition, to be judged an anomaly, the webbing would have to extend to near the lower toe joints. Partial syndactylia of the two middle toes is also illustrated in Figure 9.

3. *Big gap between first and second toes (weighted one)*

Some children have such a big space between their first and second toes that it looks as if a toe is missing. For such a gap between the big toe and the second toe to be judged an anomaly, there had to exist a flat base across the gap of more than half the width of the second toe. This anomaly is also illustrated in Figure 9.

Table 1 (page 359) lists all eighteen anomalies with brief descriptions and scoring weights. A chart similar to this was used for recording the anomalies for each child we observed.

THE FIVE COMPLETED STUDIES

The Original Study

Data for the Original Study were collected over a two-year period when 74 normal two-and-a-half-year-olds (43 males and 31 females) attended our research nursery school in groups of five or six for periods of five weeks per group. These preschool children had been observed as newborns and had been considered free from complications of pregnancy and delivery. While attending the nursery school each child was examined for the presence of eighteen minor physical anomalies. Each child had two scores for anomalies: one score was a total count of all eighteen anomalies, and the other, a total of the weighted scores.

As originally published, this first study did not report one important anomaly (head circumference outside normal range) and did list one measure subsequently dropped. "Index finger longer than middle finger" was dropped from consideration in all future studies because it did not appear in our original sample of children or in the samples studied

FIGURE 9.—Third toe longer than second, partial syndactylia, and big gap between first and second toes.

TABLE 1

LIST OF ANOMALIES AND SCORING WEIGHTS

Anomaly	Weight
HEAD	

Fine electric hair:
Very fine hair that will not comb down	2
Fine hair that is soon awry after combing	1
Two or more hair whorls	0

Head circumference outside normal range:
$> 1.5\,\sigma$	2
$> 1.0\,\sigma \leqq 1.5\,\sigma$	1

EYES

Epicanthus:
Where upper and lower lids join the nose, point of union is:
Deeply covered	2
Partly covered	1

Hyperteliorism:
Approximate distance between tear ducts:
$> 1.5\,\sigma$	2
$> 1.0\,\sigma \leqq 1.5\,\sigma$	1

EARS

Low-seated ears:
Point where ear joins the head not in line with corner of eye and nose bridge:
Lower by > 0.5 cm	2
Lower by $\leqq 0.5$ cm	1

Adherent ear lobes:
Lower edge of ears extend:
Upward and back toward crown of head	2
Straight back toward rear of neck	1
Malformed ears	1
Asymmetrical ears	1
Soft and pliable ears	0

MOUTH

High-steepled palate:
Roof of mouth:
Definitely steepled	2
Flat and narrow at the top	1
Furrowed tongue (one with deep ridges)	1
Tongue with smooth-rough spots	0

HANDS

Curved fifth finger:
Markedly curved inward toward other fingers	2
Slightly curved inward toward other fingers	1
Single transverse palmar crease	1

FEET

Third toe longer than second:
Definitely longer than second toe	2
Appears equal in length to second toe	1
Partial syndactylia of two middle toes	1
Big gap between first and second toes	1

by Goldfarb and Botstein. "Head circumference outside normal range" was erroneously omitted from the original write-up, although the measure had been made along with the rest of the assessments. At a later time, therefore, the data of this original study were re-evaluated. This evaluation only served to slightly increase the magnitude of the reported significant correlations.

In the male sample of this first study the correlation between the total count of anomalies and weighted total score was .96; in the female sample this correlation was .90. With such high correlations only one of these measures needed to be used in the data analysis. We selected the weighted score because it showed somewhat greater range and yielded higher correlations with most of the behavioral measures.

Two examiners made independent judgments as to the existence and weights for each of the eighteen minor physical anomalies on 10 of the 74 subjects and on 14 children from a community nursery school. A reliability coefficient of .70 was obtained from these two independent judgments as to the existence and weight of these eighteen anomalies.

As a part of the nursery school phase of our ongoing longitudinal research program, 101 reliable observational, experimental, and rating measures were available on the male sample, and 96 such behavioral measures were available on the female sample. The behavioral measures (1) were obtained from two sources. One source, derived from observations of the children in the research nursery school, consisted essentially of cumulative time spent in various categories of activity (e.g., water play or manipulation of puzzles) or of frequency counts of specific types of behavior (e.g., aggressive acts against peers). These measures were obtained by cumulative stopwatches or by counters punched at intervals of two seconds. An observer followed the child's activity from one setting to another. Each of two observers contributed three full-morning observations on each child, thereby providing six complete observations per child. Split-half reliabilities of the observation categories were based on the correlation of two sums: one from the counts or times for observations 1, 3, and 5; the other from observations 2, 4, and 6. Only observer categories which showed high stability over the five-week period were retained in the analyses.

The second source of behavioral measures were ratings made by a male teacher and a female teacher. There were three groups of 11-point scales: those done on ten different days, those done on seven different

---

1. Definitions of the behavioral measures pertinent to this investigation and used in the larger longitudinal study have been deposited as Document No. 9862 with the American Documentation Institute Auxiliary Publications Project, Photoduplication Service, Library of Congress, Washington, D.C. 20540. A copy may be secured by citing the document number and by remitting $2.50 for photoprints or $1.75 for 35-mm. microfilm. Advance payment is required. Make checks or money orders payable to: Chief, Photoduplication Service, Library of Congress.

days, and those done only once after the termination of each five-week session. Reliabilities for the teacher ratings were based on independent ratings of 17 boys and 17 girls made by the male teacher and by the female teacher. In all cases, reliabilities shown in the material to follow are adjusted by the Spearman-Brown formula (McNemar, 1959, p. 157) to provide the best estimate of the reliability for actual scores used in the analysis, those based on all observations or on ratings by both teachers. Inter-observer reliability for behavior counts and cumulative times was checked periodically and always found to be greater than .90 for the measures listed.

The data analysis consisted essentially of examining the product-moment correlations between the physical anomaly weighted score and all behavioral measures. Because this procedure entails the risk of accepting chance relations, the males and the females were treated as independent samples. Relations were accepted only if similar in the two groups. Two intercorrelation matrixes (2), one for the male subjects and the other for the female subjects, are available for all behavioral variables found significantly related to the weighted scores for anomalies.

In each sample the number of measures showing significant correlations with the anomaly score was reduced in order to obtain a small enough number of variables for subsequent factor analyses. Two reduction methods were used: (a) one of any two measures correlating .75 or above was excluded, the one retained being the measure which had the higher correlation with anomalies; (b) variables were excluded which showed no more than one significant correlation coefficient with other measures in either the intercorrelational matrix for male subjects or the intercorrelational matrix for female subjects.

In this study, 21.4 per cent of the males and 32.3 per cent of the females had a weighted score of 0 for minor anomalies; 23.8 per cent of the males and 12.9 per cent of the females had a weighted score of 1; 54.8 per cent of the males and 54.8 per cent of the females had a weighted score of 2 or more. The mean for the males was 2.24 with a standard deviation of 1.98. The range was from 0 to 8 for males, 0 to 6 for females.

Eighteen out of the 101 behavioral measures in the male sample and 16 out of the 96 in the female sample related significantly to weighted scores for minor physical defects. Nine of these relations were the same in both samples.

Table 2 lists two Pearson product-moment correlation coefficients for each variable, one being the reliability of the measure and the other

---

2. Two intercorrelation matrices, one for the male sample and one for the female sample, of all behavioral variables significantly correlated with the weighted anomaly score in either sample, have been deposited as Document No. 9862 with the ADI Auxiliary Publications Project. See n. 1 for information about ordering copies.

TABLE 2

RELATION OF BEHAVIORAL VARIABLES WITH MINOR PHYSICAL ANOMALIES
(Original Study)

	Males*		Females**	
	Relia-bility	r with Anomalies	Relia-bility	r with Anomalies
Observations				
Free Play Inside				
Opposes peer	.88	*.34**	.91	*.32***
Watching peers	.93	—.31*	.71	—.26
Direct walking	.68	.44*	.74	.02
Free Play Outside				
Gross motor	.73	.30*	.25	NR***
Continuity of play	.65	—.11	.67	—.33**
Squeals	.75	.41*	.82	—.13
Sings	.74	.40*	.47	NR***
Stationary watching	.88	—.39*	.64	—.20
Rest				
Lying down	.88	—.02	.88	—.57**
Sitting up	.91	—.12	.88	.38**
Up and about	.89	.20	.81	.51**
Snack and Story				
Seating changes	.67	.23	.77	.34**
Ratings				
Ten Days				
Negative interaction	.89	*.36**	.93	*.52***
Involvement	.86	.09	.68	.39**
Vigor	.91	.20	.90	.33**
Seven Days				
Frenetic play	.77	*.42**	.95	*.58***
Induction intervention	.94	*.41**	.97	*.39***
Nomadic play	.94	*.38**	.92	*.41***
Spilling & throwing	.90	*.40**	.93	*.39***
Inability to delay	.84	*.50**	.92	*.46***
Emotional aggression	.75	.31*	.99	.17
Over-all Summary				
Perseveration	.59	*.55**	.73	*.60***
Tractability	.81	—.46*	.87	—.54**
Geographic orientation	.77	—.39*	.60	.04
Rhythm	.97	—.30*	.60	—.11

* $p < .05$ for $r = .30$ (two-tail), N = 43.
** $p < .05$ for $r = .30$ (one-tail), N = 31.
*** Not reliable for the sample indicated.

the relation of the variable to the weighted anomaly score. The nine measures found significantly related to anomalies in both samples are in italics.

The factor analysis for the male sample of 43 cases was based on 16 variables; the analysis for the female sample of 31 cases was based on 10 variables. Factor loadings for the first two principal components in each analysis are shown in Table 3 below, along with the amount of common variance accounted for by each factor. Again, measures replicated in the two analyses are indicated by italics.

TABLE 3

FACTOR LOADINGS FROM THE TWO ANALYSES
(Original Study)

Males Behavioral Variables	Factor I	Factor II	Females Behavioral Variables	Factor I	Factor II
Inability to delay	.85	—.18	*Inability to delay*	.85	.15
Nomadic play	.85	.35	Involvement	.78	—.29
Frenetic play	.84	—.24	*Frenetic play*	.77	—.11
Spilling & throwing	.83	—.04	*Nomadic play*	.77	—.39
Emotional aggression	.71	—.35	*Perseveration*	.74	.35
Squeals	.69	.28	*Opposes peer*	.71	.39
Opposes peer	.67	.09	*Spilling & throwing*	.66	—.09
Perseveration	.65	—.45	Up and about	.44	—.66
Negative interaction	.59	—.23	Continuity of play	—.56	.40
Gross motor	.54	.27	*Tractability*	—.66	—.56
Direct walking	.51	.43			
Rhythm	.06	.58			
Geographic orientation	—.32	.61			
Tractability	—.52	.57			
Stationary watching	—.52	—.53			
Watching peer	—.68	—.48			
Variance:	41.91%	15.52%		48.66%	12.42%

Two of the nine behavioral measures showing significant correlations with the weighted anomaly score in both samples were eliminated in the process of reducing the number of variables in order to use factor analysis. "Introduction of intervention" was excluded from both analyses because in the male sample this measure correlated .77, .78, and .88 with the measures "Frenetic play," "Inability to delay gratification," and "Emotional aggression," respectively; in the female sample "Introduction of intervention" correlated .79 with the measure "Opposes peer." "Negative interaction" was eliminated from the analysis of females because it correlated .86 with "Opposes peer." The remaining seven variables that showed significant correlations with the anomaly score in both samples also had significant loadings on the first factor for each of the samples. Because these two first factors account for 42 per cent and 49 per cent of the common variance in the male and female samples, they are considered most meaningful. Further evidence that meaningfulness is concentrated in the two first factors is the fact that all but one variable had significant loadings on the first factors.

The seven variables replicated in the two analyses define the first factor for both males and females. Six of the seven had high positive loadings: Inability to delay gratification, Nomadic play, Frenetic play, Spilling and throwing, Opposes peer, and Perseveration. Tractability had a high negative loading on each of the first factors.

The behaviors which have been identified belong to a cluster which is often labeled "hyperactivity." The more minor anomalies a child evidenced, the more likely he would be aggressive, hyperkinetic, and intractable. The present findings indicate that the essential elements of hyperactivity can be detected without difficulty in a normal population. In fact, the present samples may be regarded as more "normal" than those usually used in psychological studies of preschool children, since cases were excluded whose records showed evidence of complications of pregnancy or delivery. In addition, the association has been confirmed at the level of directly observable behavior, and with children whose variations from the usual norms for appearance are not so striking as to lead one to suspect that their behaviors are substantially influenced by reactions of others to their appearance.

We found the results of this first study excitingly provoking of such questions as: Will these same results replicate on other samples of preschool children in the same nursery school?, Will the children in this study still have these anomalies at a later age and still be considered hyperactive when they are in elementary school?, Do newborns have a comparable range of incidence of these anomalies?, Would a group selected for the presence of some congenital defect, such as deficiency in speech and/or hearing, have more of these minor physical anomalies than our samples of normal preschool children?, Would elementary school children selected as being hyperactive have more of these anomalies than would a sample from the same school selected as being not hyperactive?, Do children with high anomaly scores have any observable chromosomal irregularities that children with low anomaly scores do not have?, Would high anomaly children have what can be considered congenital differences in their dermatoglyphics?

We found answers to some of these questions in our subsequent studies. Other answers may be found in studies that are underway.

Replication Study

The two-and-a-half-year-olds in the Replication Study were unlike the original subjects in that they were not selected as newborns having hospital records free from complications of pregnancy and delivery. Twenty-six of the children who participated in the Replication Study were selected because their parents, when newlyweds, had participated in another phase of the longitudinal research program at the Child Research Branch, National Institute of Mental Health. In addition, these 26 children had been observed as newborns. The other 32 children lived in neighborhoods near our research nursery school. The procedures and measures, however, that were used to evaluate the 33 boys and 25 girls as they attended our research nursery school in groups of five for five weeks were the same as those used in the Original Study. In the Original Study all preschool behavior measures relating significantly to the anomaly score were factor-analyzed for both males and females, with the result that measures reflecting fast acting, impulsive, uncontrolled behavior were loaded heavily on the first factor for males and the first factor for females. These two first factors, one for males and one for females, were labeled hyperactivity. The second factor for males represented a tractability factor, but the second factor for females represented intractability and inhibition.

The mean anomaly score for the replication sample of 33 males was 4.09, standard deviation was 2.08, and the range was from 1 to 9. Since the correlates of the anomaly score in this second sample of males were very similar to the correlates in the original sample, we obtained for each of the boys in the second sample a factor score based on the weights from the previous hyperactivity factor. (For this replication sample of males, the reliabilities for the ratings and observations ranged from .72 to .92.) This hyperactivity factor score was found to be significantly correlated with the anomaly score ($r = .49$, $p < .01$). That is, the boys in the Replication Study who had high anomaly scores tended to be high on the hyperactivity factor. Further substantiation of this relation was obtained by correlating the anomaly score with an objective count of times the child was restrained by the teachers during "resting" time ($r = .46$, $p < .01$). Frenetic, impulsive, poorly controlled behavior was again found to characterize preschool boys who had more than an average number of minor anomalies.

The mean anomaly score for the replication sample of 25 females was 3.56, standard deviation was 2.20, and the range was from 0 to 7. Relations to the cluster of variables making up the hyperactivity factor in the original sample of females did not replicate in the replication sample of females. Instead, variables making up the intractability-inhibition factor seemed to characterize the replication sample of females with the higher anomaly scores. A score for each girl based on the weighted measures from this previously obtained second factor was significantly related to the anomaly score ($r = .42$, $p < .05$). That is, girls with the greater number of minor anomalies tended to move about less, to oppose peers more, and to be more perseverative than did the girls with few such anomalies. For this replication sample of females the inter-rater and split-half reliabilities for the ratings and observations ranged from .53 to .92. Other correlates showed that during the five weeks of nursery school the girls with a high anomaly score were rated by the teachers as showing more fearfulness ($r = .48, p < .01$) and more vacant staring ($r = .63, p < .001$), and as staying closer to an adult ($r = .44, p < .01$), than those with low anomaly scores. These three measures were based on 11-point rating scales which had inter-rater reliabilities greater than .80. A child high on "Fearfulness" was described as characteristically appearing to be guarded, wary, defensive, apprehensive, frightened, or panicky. A child high on "Closeness to an adult base" was described as spending an unusually large amount of time clinging tightly to teacher, hiding her eyes, not exploring the situation either visually or otherwise. A child high on "Vacant staring" was described as being immobile and staring without apparent focus much more frequently than other children did. Since these three measures were significantly interrelated, a composite was formed by summing her standard scores on the three ratings. This composite was significantly related to the anomaly score ($r = .59, p < .01$). Thus, girls with high anomaly scores in this sample tended to be overcontrolled, inhibited, stubborn, and perseverative rather than hyperactive.

The higher incidence of these minor physical anomalies in the Replication Study when compared to the Original Study is due to having more precise norms which made it possible to set a smaller deviation from the normal as a criterion for an anomaly. Also, as mentioned earlier, we included in the Replication Study the anomaly "Head circumference outside normal range" that was not reported in the original study.

Stability Study

The stability data for the anomalies and hyperactive behavior were obtained from a follow-up study at age seven and a half of 35 males and 27 females who were among the two-and-a-half-year-olds studied in the original sample. A person who had not known the children at age two and a half, and had no knowledge of their previous anomaly score or their nursery school behavior, assessed each child for the presence of the minor physical anomalies. Intercoder agreement for this anomaly assessment was satisfactory ($r = .96$).

Impulsive, fast moving behavior at age seven and a half was evaluated by one objective measure and two reliable ratings made of the child in free play and testing situations. Two ratings, "Frenetic behavior" and "Inability to delay," were made with no previous knowledge of the child. A child rated high on "Frenetic behavior" was one who much more than others showed impulsive, fast moving, ineffective, incomplete, and hyperactive play. A child rated high on "Inability to delay" was one who when required to wait to take part in any activity seemed unusually unable to wait for gratification. The objective measure of hyperactive free play was the distance (in 9" x 9" square floor units) traversed during free play divided by time, for each shift in location during twenty minutes of free play. The setting was a nursery school playroom very similar to the one used when the children were age two and a half. Data were obtained from a continuous narrative spoken by an observer into a tape recorder and subsequently scored for number of shifts in location and rate of each shift. Reliabilities for the various codes were generally quite high (median agreement was 93 per cent).

In addition to being evaluated for minor physical anomalies and impulsive, fast moving behavior, each child was tested for IQ and motor coordination. The IQ measure (WISC) was part of a larger assessment package concerned with longitudinal correlates of cognitive behavior. We plan to report this aspect of the study elsewhere. Our thinking regarding individual differences in motor coordination was that "clumsiness" might be correlated with the anomaly score since poor gross and fine motor coordination has often been found associated with an aggregate of symptoms defining hyperactivity. Both "hyperactivity," or "acting out," and motoric involvements, such as athetoid movements and lack of balance, have been considered "soft signs" of some minimal cerebral dysfunction. In order to measure individual differences in both fine and gross motor coordination we constructed a scale which combined adaptations of the Lincoln Oseretsky test of motor development (Sloan, 1955) and a neurological examination developed by Ozer (unpublished manuscript; 1968). From the Oseretsky test we deleted a number of items that were either too easy or too difficult for our age range, and then added some of the tasks from the Ozer neurological examination.

The final version of the scale consisted of 34 items, most of which were scored on a simple pass-fail criterion. Typical tasks the child was asked to perform were balancing on each leg for at least ten seconds, touching each finger tip with the thumb in rapid succession, and sorting matchsticks into boxes as rapidly as possible. Intercoder agreement for the motor scale was quite high ($r = .97$).

The results of the Stability Study are summarized in Table 4. This table shows the correlation of the anomaly score at age seven and a half with the following: (a) the anomaly score at age two and a half, (b) the three measures of impulsive, fast moving behavior, (c) the motor coordination scale, (d) IQ measures, (e) a factor score based on the weighted measures included in the hyperactivity factor for males and hyperactivity factor for females from the Original Study, and (f) ratings for Frenetic play and Inability to delay when the children were

TABLE 4

CORRELATES OF THE ANOMALY SCORE AT AGE 7½
(Stability Study)

Variables	Males N = 35 X̄ = 4.91, σ = 2.66, Range: 1-11	Females N = 27 X̄ = 3.74, σ = 2.33, Range: 0-10
Anomaly score at 2½	.71***	.70***
Rate of shifts during free play at 7½	.30*	.36*
Inability to delay at 7½	.39**	.63***
Frenetic behavior at 7½	.34*	.52**
Motor coordination at 7½[a]	—.41**	—.48**
Full scale IQ at 7½[a]	—.34*	—.46**
Verbal IQ at 7½	—.35*	—.33*
Hyperactivity factor at 2½	.47**	.69***
Inability to delay at 2½	.49**	.41*
Frenetic behavior at 2½	.45**	.43*

a Correlates with IQ measures based on total anomaly scores and other correlates based on weighted anomaly scores.
* $p < .05$
** $p < .01$
*** $p < .001$

two and a half. Of interest, too, is the fact that "Frenetic play" at seven and a half correlated significantly with the same rating done independently at two and a half: males, .34 ($p < .05$) and females, .64 ($p < .001$). For "Inability to delay" the across-age correlates were: males, .50 ($p < .01$) and females, .40 ($p < .05$).

These data demonstrate that: (a) the weighted anomaly score tended to be stable over the five years, (b) children with high anomaly scores still tended to be more frenetic and have less behavioral control than children with few anomalies, (c) children at seven-and-a-half with high anomaly scores tended to be clumsy, (d) children at seven-and-a-half with more than an average number of minor physical anomalies tended to have lower than average IQ scores, (e) frenetic, fast moving behavior showed continuity over five years, and (f) the children at seven-and-a-half with high anomaly scores tended to have been hyperactive as two-and-a-half-year-olds. In other words, generally speaking both the anomaly score and the associated hyperactive behavior were stable over the five-year period. Also, children at seven-and-a-half with high anomaly scores were likely to be poorly coordinated and to have lower than average verbal ability.

Study of Children Deficient in Speech and/or Hearing

If minor anomalies do result from variations in embryological development, it would be reasonable to expect that there would be a higher incidence of the anomalies in a sample of children selected for congenital deficiencies than there would be in a sample of normal children. To test this hypothesis we examined 31 boys and 10 girls who had been referred by physicians to an Easter Seal Treatment Center Nursery School because of deficiencies in speech and/or hearing. Mothers of four of the thirty-one boys and seven of the ten girls were thought to have had rubella while they were pregnant with these children.

The mean anomaly score for the Easter Seal samples was compared with the mean anomaly score for the replication samples of boys and girls. The replication samples were chosen for this analysis because we used exactly the same method of scoring anomalies in these samples as in the Easter Seal samples. See Table 5.

A *t* value of 6.35 (*p* < .001) was obtained when the mean of the anomaly scores for males in the Easter Seal sample was compared with

TABLE 5

COMPARISON OF ANOMALIES IN EASTER SEAL AND REPLICATION SAMPLES

Sample	*Males*				*Females*			
	N	$\overline{X}$	σ	*Range*	N	$\overline{X}$	σ	*Range*
Replication Study	33	4.1	2.1	1- 9	25	3.6	2.2	0- 7
Easter Seal	31	7.6	2.3	3-12	10	8.3	2.3	4-11
Rubella Subsample	4	7.2	2.3	5-11	7	9.0	1.8	6-11

the mean for males in the Replication Study. For females this *t* value was 5.39 (*p* < .001).

In the small subsample of four boys and seven girls from the Easter Seal sample where there was evidence of a teratogenic agent (rubella) present during early prenatal development, the mean anomaly scores were also significantly higher than the mean anomaly scores in the replication samples. For males the *t* was 2.32 (*p* < .05), for females the *t* was 6.48 (*p* < .001), and for the combined sample the *t* was 5.96 (*p* < .001).

From Table 7 (p. 377) we can make interesting comparisons across the male samples of the percentage of children having each of the observed anomalies. Indeed, it was surprising to find that close to three-fourths of the boys in the Easter Seal Center sample had curved fifth fingers, high steepled palates, and partial syndactylia of the second and third toes.

No behavior measures were collected on the Easter Seal children. Their teachers, however, characterized at least 32 of the 41 children as hyperactive, and used phrases such as "destructive," "overactive," "management problem," "unable to wait," "constantly demanding attention," "jumpy," "very aggressive," "a behavior problem," "swings from the rafters" to describe them.

The results from the Easter Seal sample are evidence that there is a higher incidence of these *minor* physical anomalies among children with *major* congenital problems. This finding, plus the well known fact that an even higher incidence of these minor anomalies is found among children with gross chromosomal defects (Down's Syndrome), argues for the congenital etiology of the anomalies. Thus it would seem that the higher the incidence of multiple minor physical anomalies the greater the severity of a congenital problem.

Elementary School Study

In our studies just described the cumulative incidence of certain minor physical anomalies was consistently related to hyperactive play behavior in small selected samples of children and relatively circumscribed samples of behavior.

We felt the need for expanding our explorations to a larger, more heterogenous population. We also were interested in seeing if the concept of "hyperactivity" in the school situation related to the anomaly score in the same way as hyperactive play behavior had related to the anomaly score in the nursery school setting. Too, we wanted an opportunity to assess the anomalies independently of the assessment of hyperactivity. Although presumably these anomalies are either present or absent, there is a degree of judgment called for, and a knowledge of both the child and the expected results could create some bias on the part of the examiner. This possible source of bias was controlled in some, but not all of our previous studies.

If the index of anomalies is related to a rather fundamental behavioral disposition, it would be expected that, among elementary school boys, those judged by their teachers to be "hyperactive" would have significantly more minor physical anomalies than those boys judged by their teachers to be nonhyperactive. In addition, it would be expected that among the hyperactive boys, those judged to be the most hyperactive would have significantly more minor physical anomalies than boys judged to be least hyperactive. On the basis of our past results we had no clear indication as to whether girls with high anomaly scores would or would not tend to be among the hyperactives. We were, therefore, eager to see what the results would be but were unable to make predictions.

The sample for this study was drawn from an elementary school with an enrollment of approximately 775 pupils in a city with a total population of about 23,000. The community is relatively stable. The principal had been at this same school for 10 years and consequently knew all the children rather well.

At the meeting with the faculty, without mentioning the hypotheses to be tested, each teacher was asked to list the three children in her class whom she judged to be most hyperactive. These made up our experimental group. On a separate card each teacher was asked to list three additional children who, in her opinion, would fall in the normal range of behavior being neither hyperactive nor lethargic. These made up our control group. We found that the teachers had little difficulty in identifying the most hyperactive children in their classrooms. Children who are least able to "sit still and pay attention," being incessantly "on the move," are generally quite easily distinguished in classroom situations. Teachers know those children who are most fatiguing to them. The principal added two more names to the hyperactive list, and then ranked the entire list of designated hyperactives in order of severity. On the day we examined the children for anomalies, some from the experimental group and some from the control group were absent, resulting in a total of 46 hyperactive children, 34 males and 12 females, and a total of 44 nonhyperactive children, 18 males and 26 females.

Using the same scoring procedure we had used in our past studies, we computed for each child a total anomaly score and a weighted anomaly score. When we found that the weighted score correlated .86 with the total score, we used only the weighted score in analyzing these data.

Having fine electric hair was eliminated from the list of anomalies in this study because some of the subjects were Negroes. Of all the anomalies observed in this study, only the measure used to gauge hyperteliorism (intercanthal distance) showed a significant difference of means $(t = 2.54)$ between Negroes and Caucasians. (For Negroes, $\bar{x} = 3.31$ cm and $\sigma = .29$; for Caucasians, $\bar{x} = 3.13$ cm, $\sigma = .27$.) Therefore, .2 cm was subtracted from each Negro child's measure of intercanthal distance to equate the scores of hyperteliorism for racial differences.

The examiner in this study had no knowledge of whether or not a child was hyperactive nor had she ever seen any of the children before they were brought to the examining room. All the children were seen in random order at about five-minute intervals. In scoring the presence of these minor physical anomalies, adequate reliability had been established in the previously reported studies $(r = .70$ and $r = .96)$.

Since Negroes constituted 24.5 per cent of the total population in this elementary school, 30 per cent of our hyperactive sample, and 18 per cent of our nonhyperactive sample, t tests were run to see if there were any significant racial differences in the mean number of anomalies. Because no significant differences were found $(t = .13)$ there is no racial breakdown in the analysis of the data. (For Negroes, $N = 22$, $\bar{x} = 4.14$, $\sigma = 2.42$; for Caucasians, $N = 68$, $\bar{x} = 4.22$, $\sigma = 2.34$.)

In checking for sex differences, we found there was a significant mean difference in anomaly scores for males and females, $t = 3.16$, $p < .01$. (For males, N $= 52$, $\bar{x} = 4.69$, $\sigma = 2.38$; for females, N $= 38$, $\bar{x} = 3.53$, $\sigma = 2.16$.)

As a total group the hyperactive children had significantly more anomalies than did the children who were not hyperactive. Table 6 shows, however, that these significant differences were true only for the males.

Table 6 also shows that out of the 46 hyperactive children, 34 were male and only 12 were female or about three fourths of the hyperactives were male. When the anomalies were compared with the principal's rank ordering of all the children selected as hyperactive, a rank order correlation for males of .39 ($p < .05$) was found. The more hyperactive a boy was, the more minor physical anomalies he was likely to have.

TABLE 6

MEANS AND MEAN DIFFERENCES IN ANOMALY SCORES
(Elementary School Study)

	Hyperactive			Nonhyperactive					
	N	$\overline{X}$	σ	N	$\overline{X}$	σ	t	p	Pt. Biserial r
Males	34	5.59	2.03	18	3.00	2.06	4.20	<.001	.50
Females	12	3.50	2.22	26	3.54	2.13	.05		

For the boys in this sample we have found that hyperactive behavior was again associated with the presence of minor physical anomalies. As in one of our previous studies, this relation was not true for girls. This sex difference is probably related to there being three times as many boys as girls chosen as being hyperactive. This is quite consistent with others who report very few females among the clinically hyperactive, and with there being almost no females in the congenitally deviant sample we studied. We are again led to consider (along with many others) the probability that genetic and teratogenetic stresses affect males and females differently, males being more vulnerable (Singer, Westphal, & Niswander, 1968).

We now see that the relation of hyperactivity to physical characteristics is true for boys from a large elementary school as well as for boys from the smaller and relatively more select samples reported here. This fact enhances the meaning and generality of the findings. It is also important that in this study the assessment of hyperactivity and the assessment of the anomalies were completely independent. Children were selected as being hyperactive or nonhyperactive by teachers who had no knowledge of the hypotheses being tested, but who did have intimate knowledge about the child's classroom behavior during at least one school year. The person checking the children for the presence of the minor anomalies had no previous knowledge of any of the children, and had very little chance, if any, of seeing spontaneous behavior on the part of any child being examined since each child was visible to her for only a few minutes.

From the data obtained we can conclude that teachers in this elementary school thought there was no difference in the proportional representation among the hyperactives between Negroes and Caucasians. Also of significance is the finding that after adjustment for racial differences in hyperteliorism there was no difference in the anomaly score for Negroes and the anomaly score for Caucasians.

STUDIES CURRENTLY UNDERWAY

Newborns

A major part of the longitudinal research currently underway at the Child Research Branch is the study of the first newborns whose parents were subjects in a study of early marriage. From a sample of approximately 100 infants, 32 boys and 27 girls have been examined for the presence of 17 of the 18 anomalies. Obviously we could not check for fine electric hair in newborns. It pleased us to find that there is a range from zero to nine on the weighted score and a range from zero to eight on the total score. Eventually we will know if there is any relation between the presence of multiple anomalies and a wide variety of both physiological and behavioral measures. We are particularly eager to see if there will be a replication of a finding which was obtained prospectively (the anomaly score obtained when the child was seven-and-a-half-years-old with a measure obtained at the neonatal period). This finding for males was a correlation of .45 ($p < .01$) between the anomaly score and latency of response to tactile stimulation. That is, the higher the anomaly score the slower the response of the baby to tactile stimulation.

Three-Month-Old Infants

Another major project in the longitudinal research program underway at the Child Research Branch is the study of three-month-old infants and their interactions with their mothers. From this sample of approximately 120 infants, 40 males and 37 females have so far been examined for the presence of 17 minor physical anomalies. Again it was not appropriate to include fine electric hair. Out of the 77 infants examined at three months, 37 had also been examined as newborns. This gave us an opportunity to test for the stability of these anomalies from birth to three months. The total anomaly score at birth correlated

.72 with the total anomaly score at three months. The weighted anomaly score at birth correlated .52 with the weighted anomaly score at three months. These correlational coefficients indicate that the total anomaly score tends to be more stable from birth to three months than does the weighted anomaly score.

Because this study is currently underway no definite results from these data can be reported at this time. Some preliminary findings, however, may be of interest. For example, there was a higher incidence of epicanthus when the children were three months old than when they had been newborns. This is similar to the findings reported by Taylor and Cameron (1963) and Mustardé (1963). Also, there were more instances of the third toe's being longer than the second toe among the three-month-olds than among the newborns. Instances of soft pliable ears decreased from birth to three months. It should be emphasized that at this time nothing can be said about the significance of these changes in incidence of these three anomalies. If they do prove to be significant, these changes would seem to be a function of the developmental processes. Therefore, it might be better to call these three physical characteristics anomalies only when they persist into early childhood. For most of the anomalies there does seem to be stability between newborn and three months.

At a future time we plan to report not only on the stability of the anomalies from birth to three months but also on the relations of the anomalies with various behaviors measured when the infant was three months old.

Chromosome, Dermatoglyphic, and Blood Study

An adjunct study to the major longitudinal study is being done with the cooperation of Dr. Matti Al-Aish, a research geneticist in the field of chromosomal analysis and Mr. Christopher Plato, a research geneticist in the field of dermatoglyphics and blood groupings. We were able to obtain blood samples and palm prints on most of the 62 subjects in the Stability Study. Specifically, we have dermatoglyphic data on 45 children (28 males, 17 females), we have blood grouping data on 38 children (22 males, 16 females), and we have the karyotypes of 60 children (33 males, 27 females).

One preliminary finding we will mention briefly is in regard to the atd angle. This angle is measured from palm prints by the straight line passing through triradius "a" near the base of the index finger and triradius "t" usually found near the wrist in the themar area of the palm, and the straight line through triradius "t" and triradius "d" found near the base of the fifth finger. This is a standard way of measuring how far up into the palm triradius "t" is located. Children with major congenital defects are likely to have triradius "t" located closer to the base of the fingers than normal children, and thus have a larger atd angle. The early results from this present study seem to show that, particularly for females, the atd angle is a measure showing an unusually large number of interesting correlates which indicate possible associations between having a high atd angle, having a high anomaly score, being clumsy, and displaying fast moving, impulsive behavior.

Collaborative Study with Harvard University

In cooperation with Dr. Jerome Kagan of Harvard, we found that the presence of multiple minor physical anomalies was related to behavioral tempo and style in a small sample of 17 male and 15 female subjects when they were 13 months old and later when they were 27 months old. For boys at both ages it was found that a rapid rate of habituation time to visual forms was strongly correlated with high anomaly scores. Boys with high anomaly scores grew bored with the stimuli at a faster rate. These relations did not hold for girls. Data on additional subjects will be needed to substantiate these early findings.

A Special Follow-up Study of Two-and-a-Half-Year Olds

We have conducted a one-day study of 30 two-and-a-half-year-olds with their mothers. Investigators in another study (Moss, Robson, & Pedersen, 1969) had collected data on these children when they were eight months old and again when they were nine months old. When we studied them at two and a half years of age, we found that the children from this sample with high anomaly scores were likely to be explorative, vigorous, unable to wait, frenetic, and excitable. Also, they paid little attention to their mothers, not involving them in their play and not following them when they went into an adjoining room. At eight months old and at nine months old these same children had shown little separation anxiety or gaze aversion. These tentative findings plus the tentative finding in the study of newborns, that high anomaly scores are related to low tactile sensitivity, make us wonder if children with high anomaly scores are the insensitive "tough little kids."

INCIDENCE OF THE ANOMALIES

We want to emphasize that it is the child with *multiple* minor physical anomalities who is apt to be hyperactive. It is the *cumulative* incidence of the anomalies that is important. Except for single transverse palmar crease we found examples of each of the anomalies among the children who could wait, who were not impulsive and not frenetic. Because it is having several anomalies and not merely one that is important, any statistical analysis based on considering each anomaly separately would be misleading.

Percentage of Children with Each Anomaly

Table 7 is a report of the percentage of children in each sample having each anomaly. From the information in Table 7 we can see the prevalence of each anomaly in each of our "normal" samples as well as in our congenitally deviant sample. For instance, it is much more common to see children with highsteepled palates than children with asymmetrical ears. Also, from this table we can get some indication about which of the anomalies may be age related. Big gap between first and second toes was seen more frequently among school-aged children than among the preschoolers.

Comparing Frequency Distributions of the Anomaly Score

We compared the frequency distribution of the anomaly scores of the hyperactive boys with the frequency distribution of the anomaly scores of the nonhyperactive boys (See Figure 10). To do this, the anomaly scores for each sample were standardized, $\bar{x} = 50$ and $\sigma = 10$.

Boys in the Original Study and the Replication Study were considered high on hyperactivity if they scored above the mean on the hyperactivity factor score as defined in the Original Study. Boys in the Stability Study were high on hyperactivity if they scored above the mean on a measure made up of the sum of their standard scores on "Frenetic play," "Inability to delay," and rate of shifts during free play. In the Elementary School Study this division between hyperactive and nonhyperactive children was made by the teachers. Since we had no behavior measures on the children in the Easter Seal Study, we could not include them in this analysis. Data on girls were not included in the analysis because the relation of physical anomalies to hyperactive behavior was not consistent across female samples.

For the hyperactive boys, $\bar{x} = 54.1$, $\sigma = 9.69$; for the nonhyperactive boys, $\bar{x} = 45.0$, $\sigma = 7.62$. As expected, the mean anomaly standard score for the hyperactive boys was significantly higher than the mean anomaly standard score for the nonhyperactive boys ($t = 6.7$, $p < .0001$).

Obviously some overlap existed in the frequency distribution of the anomaly scores for the hyperactive boys and the frequency distribution of the anomaly scores for the nonhyperactive boys. There were, however, very few boys with high anomaly scores who were not hyperactive. In fact, only 12 nonhyperactive boys out of 73 had anomaly standard scores above 50; only 6 were above 55. Individual case studies of these "exceptions" would be interesting.

There were more instances of boys with low anomaly scores being

TABLE 7

PER CENT OF INCIDENCE OF EACH ANOMALY

Anomalies	Original Study Males N=43	Original Study Females N=31	Replication Study Males N=33	Replication Study Females N=25	Stability Study Males N=35	Stability Study Females N=27	Elementary School Study Males N=52	Elementary School Study Females N=38	Easter Seal Study Males N=31	Easter Seal Study Females N=10
Fine electric hair	14	16	12	12	11	7	—	—	16	40
> 1 hair whorl	26	42	27	24	43	26	23	18	44	50
Head circumference outside normal range	26	29	30	28	23	19	50	34	56	40
Epicanthus	23	16	42	32	40	26	31	16	68	80
Hyperteliorism	5	0	15	0	37	30	27	18	56	30
Low-seated ears	2	3	21	4	11	4	17	5	28	30
Adherent ear lobes	16	19	27	20	29	41	19	24	12	30
Malformed ears	0	0	6	0	0	4	2	3	16	20
Asymmetrical ears	14	10	27	8	17	4	21	13	64	30
Soft & pliable ears	26	23	21	24	17	15	38	13	48	40
High-steepled palate	44	26	55	52	49	33	42	37	72	70
Furrowed tongue	0	0	9	0	6	4	17	16	—	—
Smooth-rough tongue	0	3	0	4	9	0	29	26	—	—
Curved 5th finger	14	6	21	24	63	56	37	39	88	60
Single transverse palmar crease	2	3	12	8	6	4	12	3	4	20
3rd toe ≧ 2nd toe	16	45	39	40	3	7	6	5	32	40
Partial syndactylia of two middle toes	7	0	30	16	40	37	52	50	68	100
Big gap between 1st & 2nd toes	5	0	9	36	69	37	44	32	48	60

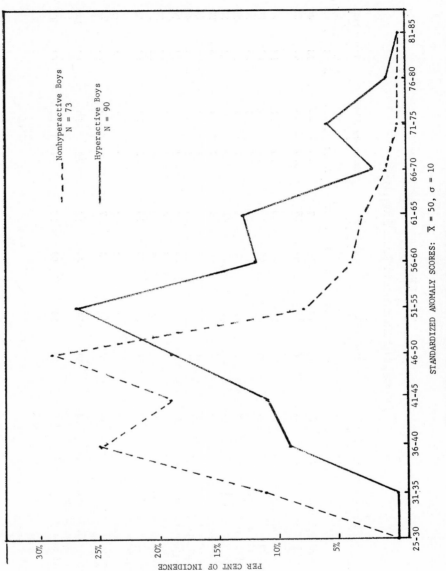

FIGURE 10.—Frequency distributions of the anomaly score.

hyperactive than of boys with high anomaly scores being nonhyperactive. Out of 90 hyperactive boys, 34 had anomaly standard scores of less than 45. The finding that some hyperactive boys do have low anomaly scores indicates that hyperactivity may be the effect of experiential as well as congenital factors. In other words, there are contributors to hyperactivity other than congenital differences.

CONCLUSION

Obviously, knowledge that hyperactive behavior seems to be linked to some congenital variables will do nothing to diminish the amount of hyperactivity. Yet it does seem reasonable to think that knowing a child may be unable to exert wished for controls might reduce emotions frequently associated with hyperactivity, such as hostility, blame, and self-hate. The knowledge that the cumulative incidence of certain minor physical anomalies is associated with hyperactivity for boys provides us with the tool to identify a potentially hyperactive boy before his behavior becomes stressful to everyone around him. If our subsequent research on these high anomaly children "identified at birth" continues to show these relations to hyperactivity (from our longitudinal work), clinically it might be extremely valuable to make the anomaly assessment a routine pediatric procedure very early in life. Parents and professionals alike could be made alert to potential behavior problems. Appropriate therapy could be instituted before parents and children have suffered several years of agony and disruption.

REFERENCES

ACHS, R., HARPER, R., & SIEGEL, M. Unusual dermatoglyphic findings associated with rubella embryopathy. *New England Journal of Medicine*, 1966, 274, 148-150.
AREY, L. B. *Developmental anatomy.* (6th ed.) Philadelphia: Saunders, 1954.
BENDA, C. E. *The child with mongolism.* New York: Grune & Stratton, 1960.
DOWN, J. L. H. Observations on an ethnic classification of idiots. *London Hospital Clinical Lectures Reports*, 1866, 3, 259-262.
GIBSON, D., & FRANK, H. F. Dimensions of mongolism; I. Age limits for cardinal mongol stigmata. *American Journal of Mental Deficiency*, 1961, 66, 30-34.
GOLDFARB, W., & BOTSTEIN, A. Physical stigmata in schizophrenic children. Unpublished manuscript, Henry Ittelson Center for Child Research, Brooklyn, N. Y.
GUSTAVSON, K. *Down's syndrome: a clinical and cytogenetical investigation.* Uppsala: Institute for Medical Genetics of the University of Uppsala, 1964.
LAESTADIUS, N. D., AASE, J. M., & SMITH, D. W. Normal inner canthal and outer orbital dimensions. *The Journal of Pediatrics*, 1969, 74, 465-468.
McNEMAR, Q. *Psychological statistics.* (2nd ed.) New York: Wiley, 1959.
MOSS, H. A., ROBSON, K. S., & PEDERSEN, F. A. Determinants of maternal stimulation of infants and consequences of treatment for later reactions to strangers. *Developmental Psychology*, 1969, 1, 239-246.
MUSTARDE, J. Epicanthal folds and the problem of telecanthus. *Transactions of the Ophthalmological Societies of the United Kingdom*, 1963, 83, 397-411.
OSTER, J. *Mongolism.* Copenhagen: Danish Science Press, 1953.

OZER, M. N. The neurological evaluation of school-age children. *Journal of Learning Disabilities,* 1968, 1, 84-87.

OZER, M. N., & MILGRAM, N. A. The effects of neurological and environmental factors on the language development of Head Start Children: an evaluation of the Head Start Program. Unpublished manuscript.

PENROSE, L. S. *The biology of mental defect.* (Rev. ed.) London: Sidgwick & Jackson, 1963.

PRYOR, H. B. Objective measurement of interpupillary distance. *Pediatrics,* 1969, 44, 973-977.

SILMAN, J. H. Dimensional changes of the dental arches: longitudinal study from birth to twenty-five years. *American Journal of Orthodontics,* 1964, 50, 824-842.

SINGER, J. E., WESTPHAL, M., & NISWANDER, K. R. Sex differences in the incidence of neonatal abnormalities and abnormal performance in early childhood. *Child Development,* 1968, 39, 103-112.

SLOAN, W .The Lincoln-Oseretsky motor development scale. *Genetic Psychology Monographs,* 1955, 51, 183-252.

TAYLOR, W. O. G., & CAMERON, J. H. Epicanthus and the inter-canthal distance. *Transactions of the Ophthalmological Societies of the United Kingdom,* 1963, 83, 371-396.

VICKERS, V. S., & STUART, H. C. Anthropometry in the pediatrician's office. Norms for selected body measurements based on studies of children of North European stock. *Journal of Pediatrics,* 1943, 22, 155-170.

VINCENT, R. W., RYAN, R. F.. & LONGENNECKER, C. G. Malformation of ear associated with urogenital anomalies. *Plastic Reconstructive Surgery,* 1961, 28, 214-220.

WALDROP, M. F., PEDERSEN, F. A., & BELL, R. Q. Minor physical anomalies and behavior in preschool children. *Child Development,* 1968, 39, 391-400.

WALDROP, M. F., & HALVERSON, C. F., JR. Minor physical anomalies: their incidence and relation to behavior in a normal and a deviant sample. *Readings in Development and Relationships,* Ed. Russell C. Smart and Mollie S. Smart. New York: Macmillan Co., 1971.

WALDROP, M .F., & GOERING, J. D. Hyperactivity and minor physical anomalies in Elementary School children. *American Journal of Orthopsychiatry,* 1971, 41 (in press).

15

PATHOLOGY IN THE BRAIN AND ANTI-SOCIAL DISORDER

Philip J. Graham, M.D.

Director, Department of Psychological Medicine
Hospital for Sick Children, London (England)

INTRODUCTION

Among the many factors important in the development of childhood behavioral and emotional difficulties, the role of disorders of the brain might be expected to be a large one. Yet the precise contribution of the organic sub-strate in the genesis of psychiatric disorder is usually difficult to evaluate in the individual child, and even in the study of large groups of disturbed and non-disturbed children, its relevance is indeterminate.

One reason for this difficulty may lie in the confusion of terms and concepts current in the field of brain disorder. Terms such as cerebral damage, dysfunction, and immaturity are sometimes used as alternatives where, more properly, they should be regarded as referring to different aspects or levels of organization and disorganization (Bax and Mackeith 1963) (Richman 1968). Anatomical damage, neurophysiological dysfunction and psychological disability may co-exist in the same child, but the presence of each type of disorganization reflects pathology at a different level and requires separate evidence. It is not usually possible to make assumptions about the existence of one type of disorganization or disease from the existence of another type. This is especially the case in considering the individual child. In the study of populations of children it is somewhat easier at least to consider statistical relationships between groups of children suffering from disorders at different levels of organization.

Brain damage implies the presence of injury to or disease of anatomical structures which can be confirmed either by macroscopic or microscopic means. As well as the clinical neurological examination, a number of other ancillary investigations may provide information as to the presence of brain damage. EEG and neuro-radiological procedures are amongst

381

the most widely used. The evidence provided by these procedures is, in fact, often equivocal, but occasionally they can furnish definite positive evidence. Cerebral palsy is the most common clinical manifestation of brain damage, but there are numerous other less common disorders in childhood occurring as a result of disease or damage to the brain. The term "brain damage" has however been used in a number of other contexts, and in particular it has unfortunately been employed (e.g. by Strauss and Lehtinen 1947) to describe children showing characteristic *behavioral* patterns.

Brain dysfunction can be said to occur when there is a neurophysiological change leading to distortion of normal development patterns or impaired function of already acquired skills. Neurophysiological dysfunction is often, but by no means necessarily, associated with brain damage. Epilepsy, for example, the most common and least arguable example of brain dysfunction, may arise from disease of the brain such as a tumor or cyst but usually it occurs in the absence of a lesion demonstrable even at autopsy. In practice it is often difficult to ascertain in the individual child whether dysfunction is or is not accompanied by damage. The term "brain dysfunction" has also been used to describe a behavioral syndrome (e.g. Clements and Peters 1962), the features of which are the same as the "brain damage" or "brain injury" syndromes.

Developmental delay implies failure to acquire skills by the usual age. Such delays may be specific, as in the case of developmental language disorders, or they may be more general, as with global intellectual retardation. "Delay" in this context expresses a psychological concept, although sometimes those using it clearly mean to imply that there is an underlying cerebral immaturity. In fact our knowledge of the relationship between cerebral maturation and the acquisition of skills is still so limited that it is not usually possible to make this assumption. Failure to acquire a particular ability is often just as likely to arise from some form of environmental deprivation as from biological immaturity. Most commonly the reasons underlying a developmental lag are unknown, and the use of the adjective "Developmental" is descriptive and not explanatory.

Finally, it is necessary to consider critically other even more circumstantial evidence which is often put forward in a clinical setting to substantiate an organic causation for a psychiatric condition.

Some writers (e.g. Rogers et al. 1955) have purported to show causal links between, on the one hand, complications of pregnancy and delivery and the neo-natal period and, on the other hand (amongst other disabilities), behavioral and intellectual inadequacies later in life. It is important to remember, however, that the presence of a history of birth trauma or neo-natal illness does not provide evidence for current brain damage, brain dysfunction, or developmental delay. The plasticity and resilience of the infant brain in recovery even from severe injury is well known. It is true that in some cases there is clear evidence of damage at birth leading to the development of, for example, cerebral palsy, but we should not be tempted to generalize from these cases to others where current evidence of brain damage is lacking, and a link between events at birth and behavior in later life is highly speculative.

Problems have also arisen where unwarranted aetiological or diagnostic assumptions have been made in the interpretation of results of psychological tests. It is unfortunate, for example, that the presence of a significantly higher verbal than performance score on the Wechsler Intelligence Scale for Children (WISC) has become so widely recognized as providing evidence for the presence of brain damage, for this is a mistaken view (Herbert 1964). Similarly the suggestion that brain damaged children make characteristic errors in the Bender-Gestalt test involving the copying of designs is erroneous, for once corrections are made for general intellectual level, correlations between the presence of such errors and signs of neurological disorder become extremely low (Wiener 1966).

The results of tests such as the WISC and the Bender-Gestalt provide excellent evidence for the presence of psychological ability and disability in defined areas of intellectual functioning. Standardized psychological tests are often the best, and in some cases, the only means we have of isolating disorders of spatial perception, motor co-ordination, verbal comprehension and expression, speed of intellectual functioning, persistence, inter and intra-sensory integration, etc. etc. By their nature they cannot provide definite evidence for or against the existence of brain damage or dysfunction, and survey results suggest that they fail to provide even a tentative indication as to the presence of such aetiology in most cases. What they can provide is a statement of the child's performance in a number of different areas in relation to other children of his age. By taking arbitrary cut-off points one can therefore delineate groups of children characterized, for example, by their clumsiness, impersistence or language retardation.

Similarly if one considers psychiatric (as opposed to psychological) examination from this point of view (if one excludes the rare cases of delirium and dementia), the evidence suggests that the presence of particular behavioral or emotional syndromes can carry no implications for organic aetiology. Projective tests, such as the CAT and the Rorschach, may provide insight into the psychological mechanisms associated with the disturbance, but they too can provide no exidence for or against organic aetiology.

Clarity in the use of these concepts becomes especially important when one attempts to relate disorder at one level of organization with disorder at another level. It is, of course, likely that pathology at one level determines pathology at another, although the causal mechanism where-by this occurs often remains obscure even after an association has been established.

One illustration of this fact lies in the interpretation of the Isle of Wight survey of neurological disorders in childhood (Rutter et al. 1970b). Here the central positive finding relates to the highly significant association between handicapping psychiatric disorder (behavioral or emotional disturbance) and brain damage/dysfunction.

Whereas in the general population the rate of psychiatric abnormality was found to be 6.6%, in the group with uncomplicated epilepsy (epi-

TABLE 1

PREVALENCE OF PSYCHIATRIC DISORDER IN NEURO-EPILEPTIC
CHILDREN AGED 5-14 YEARS ATTENDING SCHOOL

| | With psychiatric disorder | | TOTAL |
	No.	%	
General population (10 and 11 year old children)	144	6.6	2,189
Physical disorders not involving brain	16	11.5	135
Blind only	1	16.6	6
Deaf only	2	15.4	13
Lesion at or below brain-stem	2	13.3	15
Miscellaneous other physical disorders	11	10.3	107
Brain disorder	34	34.3	99
Uncomplicated epilepsy	18	28.6	63
Lesion above brain-stem (but no fits)	9	37.5	24
Lesion above brain-stem (with fits)	7	58.3	12

lepsy associated with other evidence of brain damage), the rate was over four times this figure (28.6%). In children with non-epileptic lesions in the brain the rate was 37.5% and, where there was both epilepsy and brain damage, the rate of psychiatric abnormality was 58.3%. Because this rate of psychiatric abnormality was significantly higher than that in a group of children suffering from physical disorders other than those affecting the brain (e.g. post-poliomyelitis paralysis, heart disease, asthma), it was assumed that the high rate of psychiatric disorder is, at least in part, due to the presence of cerebral abnormality, rather than occurring as a secondary consequence of having a physical handicap.

It was notable that the types and manifestations of psychiatric disorder did not differ from those seen in the general population. In particular, both anti-social and emotional disorders occurred with roughly equal frequency. Further, although amongst the brain damage/dysfunction group there was a high rate of overactivity, fidgetiness, distractibility, poor concentration, and social disinhibition, these items of behavior were much more common in that group of brain damaged children who, in addition, showed marked evidence of anti-social and emotional disorder.

The presence of psychiatric disorder in the "neuro-epileptic" children was associated with physical, social, familial factors as well as with the level of intelligence of the child. Thus the presence of a psychomotor pattern to the fit, a low occupational level of the father, the presence of poor emotional health in the mother, and low intelligence in the child were all positively associated with the existence of behavior or emotional disorder in this group. It would seem then that, although physiological factors are important in the development of psychiatric disorders in this age group, the causal mechanisms underlying this process are extremely complex.

The high rate of psychiatric disorder in children with obvious brain damage/dysfunction should make one look carefully for evidence for such organic factors in children not obviously neurologically impaired. Electroencephalographic (EEG) studies by other workers do provide such evidence. Jasper et al. (1938) were the first to note high rates of EEG abnormality in psychiatrically disturbed children. Since that time, despite the fact that for clinical purposes in the individual child with a psychiatric disorder the EEG retains only very limited value, numerous other studies have confirmed and elaborated upon these initial findings. Ellingson (1954) reviewed 18 similar studies that had been carried out at that time. There was a surprisingly consistent rate of EEG abnormality varying between 5% and 15% in the six studies where normal children had been examined, compared with a much higher rate (in all but one of the studies) in psychiatrically abnormal children—the rates here varying between 33% and 92%. Most of these studies appeared to have been carried out with severely disturbed children. Since Ellingson's review these findings have received further confirmation, especially by the controlled study carried out by Stevens et al. (1968) where boys with aggressive, anti-social and overactive behavior were found to show similarly high rates of EEG abnormality. An earlier study by Cattell and Pacella (1950) had also shown differences between rates of EEG abnormalities in children with neurotic traits (5%) and conduct disorders (56%)—a difference of particular relevance in the light of the Isle of Wight findings. It should be emphasized that as far as most of these studies are concerned the term "EEG abnormality" often reflects a failure of maturation rather than a neurophysiological disorder. Nevertheless, important physiological differences clearly exist between normal children and groups of children with anti-social problems.

It seems, therefore, that amongst the totality of children with psychiatric disorder, physiological factors are important in this particular group. It is possible that such factors operate to account for a small degree of the variance in the production of disorders in a large group of children, or that they have a more significant role in a small number of children. Evidence is lacking to support either alternative, but again the Isle of Wight study provides relevant information.

In the 10 and 11 year age group an attempt was made by these workers (Rutter et al. 1970a) to identify all children with psychiatric disorders (including anti-social disorder) as well as all those with severe educational problems. The study of a randomly selected control group in the same age range allowed useful comparisons to be made with the deviant groups.

Here the central finding related to the strong positive association between anti-social or conduct disorders and severe retardation in reading. Now reading retardation was related in this study as in many others to the presence of a large number of other more fundamental developmental cognitive and other disabilities. Imperfect ability to differentiate right from left, a delayed start to speech, clumsiness, constructional difficulties and motor impersistence were all positively associated.

About a third of the children with severe reading retardation were also showing serious anti-social disorder. The children with both reading disorder and anti-social disorder had just as many of the developmental cognitive disabilities described above as did reading retardation children without anti-social disorder. This suggests that the aetiology of the reading problem did not differ according to whether the child in addition showed an anti-social disorder.

On the other hand, when examining family background variables in anti-social children with severe reading problems and anti-social children without severe reading problems, it was shown that the latter came from larger families and had a higher rate of "broken homes." This suggests that less extraneous or domestic stress is necessary in the production of anti-social behavior amongst children already handicapped by serious reading difficulties.

Reading problems were not the only evidence of cognitive incapacity shown by Isle of Wight anti-social children. Compared with normal controls they were noted by their teachers to show poor concentration as well as motor problems such as restlessness and fidgetiness. In many of these comparisons, the anti-social children were significantly different from neurotic children. Further, at psychiatric interview, the anti-social children were found to be significantly more distractible and impersistent than control children, and to be more socially disinhibited than either control or neurotic children. It is of importance to note that these characteristics occurred in by no means all anti-social children, and it is of interest, for example, that within the groups those anti-social children who were good readers were rated by their teachers as showing "very poor concentration" significantly less than those who were poor readers.

Particular cognitive and motor difficulties therefore frequently accompany anti-social behavior and in an important group of cases seem to antedate the conduct disorder and perhaps play a role in its genesis. This is no evidence in favor of the organicity of such behavior, although it does provide evidence *against* an emotional basis for the reading problems. It therefore seems reasonable to look for other causation for the generality of these severe educational difficulties, some of which seem to lead on to anti-social problems or at least to share common underlying features.

Again the question is posed whether when biological factors exert an influence they do so to a greater or lesser extent in a large number of children or whether their main importance lies in their role in the production of disorder in a relatively small number of children. The only way to resolve this problem would be to study a large population of children over a long period of time. In the past such research has been relatively unrewarding in its results, and it is likely that for some time to come we will have to rely on cross-sectional and short-term prospective studies.

In the meantime, examination of the already published evidence, mainly from clinical studies, makes it seem likely to the present writer that there does exist an important, although possibly uncommon developmental syndrome, which is determined very early in life and which, if not biologically produced, at least has singular neurophysiological associations. It is postulated that this syndrome is first manifest in infancy, and in a proportion of sufferers persists at least into early adult life, showing itself in the same people in different ways in infancy, childhood, adolescence and early adulthood.

The studies of infantile temperamental characteristics by Thomas and his co-workers (1968) suggest that such a syndrome may first be identified in infancy when poor adaptability and frequent intense negative moods lead on in the absence, and sometimes even in the presence of sympathetic parental handling to behavior disorders in the immediate pre-school period. The 37 children aged 5-11 years described by Stewart et al. (1966) with overactivity and short attention span seem to have much in common in their earlier lives with those described by Thomas. They had had many early feeding and sleeping problems. Quite a number of these overactive children described by Stewart had begun to show anti-social disorders—nearly half were said to show undue defiance and lying. (It is of interest that amongst this group complication of pregnancy and delivery were not especially common). The group of somewhat older anti-social Isle of Wight children with severe reading retardation, and other cognitive and motor disabilities, may arise from the same stock as those described by Stewart and Thomas.

Later, in adolescence and early adult life, the follow up studies of Menkes et al. (1967) suggest that, at any rate in the severely disturbed hyperkinetic child, the outcome is poor in terms of social adjustment and later criminality. The electroencephalographic evidence of Hill and Watterson (1942) and the 30-year follow-up studies of anti-social children by Robins (1966) point to the same conclusions.

Many writers have suggested that the cause of such disorders may be modified by favorable environmental circumstances, so that it should not be assumed that the outcome is necessarily so disastrous. The degree of organicity may indeed itself be unrelated to outcome. The work of Pond and Landucci (1954), for example, suggests that the presence and extent of EEG abnormalities in a psychiatrically disturbed group bear no relation to psychiatric outcome.

Others, and in particular Werry (1968), in a comprehensive and helpful review, have of course postulated earlier the existence of such a syndrome as that described here. The title of Werry's paper "developmental hyperactivity," derived from Bakwin, however, although acknowledging the probable existence of maturational factors in its course, seems to highlight unnecessarily and perhaps even misleadingly one particular feature of the condition. The overactivity may, after all, only be present after infancy and before adolescence, whereas the handicapping nature of the syndrome may cover the whole life span. The term "impulse control problem" suggested by Lucas et al. (1965) seems preferable, although if this also is prefaced by "developmental" it becomes long-winded. Alternatively the term "developmental disinhibition" is proposed as perhaps best describing the low threshold to discomfort in infancy, the basic motor, cognitive and social disabilities of middle childhood, and the aggressive behavior disorder of later life. The use of the term "disinhibition" would not imply any particular neurophysiological or neuropsychological (Pavlovian) mechanism.

Whichever of these titles for this hypothetical clinical entity is preferred, it should be accepted that to describe the syndrome in terms of "brain damage" or even "brain dysfunction" would be even more misleading.

CONCLUSIONS

In considering possible organic aetiology of psychiatric disorder in children, it is important to distinguish anatomical from physiological and psychological concepts. In the individual disturbed child it is usually extremely difficult to gauge the contribution of biological factors with any precision. Findings from epidemiological surveys suggest that when brain damage/dysfunction is present, the child is much more likely to be suffering from a psychiatric disorder. The contribution of organic factors to the production of psychiatric disturbance which is unaccompanied by obvious brain damage/dysfunction is more problematic. There may be a small group of children difficult in infancy and anti-social in later life, whose disturbances are primarily biologically determined, and whose behavior disorder presents in characteristic fashion at different ages in childhood and early adulthood. The term "developmental disinhibition" is proposed to describe the disorder from which these individuals suffer.

I am grateful to Dr. Naomi Richman for a helpful discussion of a draft of this paper.

REFERENCES

Bax, M. C. O. & Mackeith, R. (1963), Minimal Brain Dysfunction, Heinnemans, London.

Cattell, J. P. & Pacella, B. L. (1950), An electroencephalographic and clinical study of children with primary behaviour disorders. *Amer. J. Psychiat.*, 107, 25.

Clements, S. B. & Peters, J. E. (1962), Minimal brain dysfunction in the school-age child. *Arch. Gen. Psychiat.*, 6, 185-197.

Ellingson, R. J. (1954), Incidences of EEG abnormalities among patients with mental disorder of apparently non-organic origin: critical review. *Amer. J. Psychiat.*, 111, 263.

Herbert, M. (1964), The concept and testing of brain-damage in children: a review. *J. Child Psychol. Psychiat.*, 5, 197-216.

Hill, D. & Watterson, D. J. (1942), Electroencephalographic studies of psychopathic personalities. *J. Neurol. Psychiat.*, 5, 47-65.

Jasper, H. H., Solomon, P. & Bradley, C. (1938), Electroencephalographic analyses of behaviour problem children. *Am. J. Psychiat.*, 95, 641.

Menkes, M. M., Rowe, J. S. & Menkes, J. H. (1967), A twenty-five year follow-up study on the hyperkinetic child with minimal brain dysfunction. *Pediatrics*, 30, 393-399.

Pond, D. A. & Landucci, L. (1954), L'elettroencefalografia in psichitria infantile. *Minerva Med.*, 45, 1-19.

Richman, N. (1968), The Ideology of Mental Health. American Orthopsychiatry Annual Meeting Symposium, Chicago.

Robins, L. N. (1966), Deviant Children Grown Up. Baltimore. Williams and Wilkins Co.

Rogers, M. E., Lilienfeld, A. M. & Pasamanick, B. (1955), Pre-natal and para-natal factors in development of childhood behaviour disorders. *Acta psychiat. et neurol. Scandinav.*, Suppl. 102, pp. 1-157.

Rutter, M., Tizard, J. & Whitmore, K. (eds.) (1970a), Education, Health and Behaviour, London: Longmans.

Rutter, M., Graham, P. & Yule, W. (1970b), A neuropsychiatric study in childhood, London: Heinnemans.

Stevens, J. R., Sachdev, K. & Milstein, V. (1968), Behaviour Disorders and the Electroencephalogram. *Arch. Neurol.*, 18, 160-177.

Stewart, M. A., Pitts, F. N., Craig, A. G. & Dieruf, W. (1966), The Hyperactive Child Syndrome. *Amer. J. Orthopsychiat.*, 36, 861-867.

Strauss, A. A. & Lehtinen, L. E. (1947), Psychopathology and Education of the Brain Injured Child. New York.

Thomas, A., Chess, S. & Birch, H. (1968), Temperament and Behaviour Disorders in Children. New York Univ. Press, New York.

Werry, J. S. (1968), Developmental Hyperactivity. Pediatric Clinics of North America, 15, 581-599.

16

A COMPARISON OF INFANT-MOTHER INTERACTIONAL BEHAVIOR IN INFANTS WITH ATYPICAL BEHAVIOR AND NORMAL INFANTS

Nahman H. Greenberg, M.D.

Associate Professor of Psychiatry
Child Development Clinical and Research Unit
Department of Psychiatry, College of Medicine
of the University of Illinois at the Medical Center

I. INTRODUCTION

This is a report of findings of an investigation of behavioral interaction between mothers and infants without atypical behavior, the mother-control infant (*M-CI*) *S*s, and infants with atypical behavior, the mother-atypical infant (*M-AI*) *S*s. The information which is presented was derived from the mother in her descriptions of interaction with her infant being reported during tape-recorded interviews. The infant subject was always present at these interviews and this permitted a look at interactions between the mother and infant by an observer who recorded what he saw as *narrative descriptions*. Motion films were

Supported in part by Project 1723, "Psychosomatic Differentiation During Infancy," Psychiatric Training and Research Authority, Department of Mental Health, State of Illinois, and in part by Project 502 "Growth and Development of High-Risk Infants," Maternal and Child Care Projects, City of Chicago Board of Health and the Childrens Bureau, Department of Health, Education, and Welfare.

Also supported in part by a Research Scientist Development Award MH 13,984 from the National Institute of Mental Health, Department of Health, Education, and Welfare.

Acknowledgments: Specific studies contributed to this report and were carried out with the help of a number of colleagues. I am especially grateful for the contributions of John G. Loesch, M.D., Mr. Norman Bartley (photographer), and to Mr. Joel B. Heineman and Mr. Charles L. Ririe for their technical contributions in film data reduction and statistical processing. Other contributors include, Marcia Loer, Ph.D., Steven Gold, Ph.D., Cynthia Krol, M.A., Joan Klonowski, M.D., and Mrs. Johnnie Williams.

made of infant-mother pairs in a sequence of set situations and the films were another important source of information on infant-mother interaction.

A.   *Behavioral Differentiation and Stimulation*

In planning these studies and in designing the techniques of data collection and methods of statistical treatment, we were guided by certain concepts of early infant development. Our studies of infant development attempt to delineate and describe behavior patterns and functions emerging in the course of behavioral differentiations. The appearance of differentiated and organized behavior gives evidence of developmental progress and of gains in adaptational levels. These processes are assumed to be significantly influenced by environmental stimulation such as occurs during care and stimulation to satisfy biological needs, to regulate behavior state and to soothe infants.

The emergence of a range of more discrete, varied, and complex behavior subserves motoric, perceptual, cognitive and other psychosocial functions and is evidence of ongoing developmental processes involving sequential differentiations of neural, neurophysiological, and neuroendocrine apparatus and mechanisms. The developmental achievement of major importance is the build-up, in the infant, of a capacity for more and varied options in selecting behavioral responses (behavioral plasticity), an increasing capacity to benignly tolerate and assimilate more complex and intense somatic visceral stimulation without behavioral and inner disruption (stimulation tolerance), and an increasing capacity for more ordered and regulated behavior (behavioral regulation). The acquisition of these characteristics constitutes gains in levels of adaptation.

The characteristics of inner (visceral) and external (somatic) stimulation and the functional uses of neural mechanisms significantly influence the extent and quality of the neural and neurophysiological differentiations, the individuation, syntheses and ordering of neural matrices, and the development of sensory thresholds. Since the developmental processes of differentiation are affected by stimulation, consequences of the early stimulation characteristics can be looked for in the quality and subsequent course of adaptation.

B.   *Stimulation, Maternal Behavior, and Infant Development*

Our knowledge of the dimensions of sensory stimulation essential for optimum development of the infant, and of mediating physiological mechanisms and processes is rather scanty. In studies involving animals raised in restricted environments, reduced stimulus input had disruptive effects and impaired such functions as perception, learning, and socialization. It is relatively easy to design environments in which to rear experimental animals who will develop a susceptibility to extreme and unusual behavior or who will fail to differentiate the special behavior necessary for the development of cognitive, perceptual, and social functions. An impoverished sensory environment arrests behavioral development, retards biological development, and causes change in the central nervous system. Thus, even neural, neurophysiological, and neurochemical structures and functions are vulnerable to the stresses created by altering the natural stimulus environment in which experimental animals are reared. Changes in RNA concentration or in some measure of enzyme utilization show prompt effects of increased stimulation levels and, with prolonged differential rates of stimulation, protein levels change. Even the "traditional" timetable of behavioral maturations can be hastened, slowed down, or even aborted by environmental events.

Infant care is ordinarily provided by the mother and, as the one most directly involved with her baby, the mother exercises a sizeable influence on the amount and variety of infant stimulation especially in the actual behavior of infant care and stimulation. The effectiveness of such endeavors depends on maternal interactions with components of the infant's sensorimotor systems e.g., sucking apparatus, visual and auditory systems and senses to touch, pain, pressure, position and movement. The infant-care and stimulation characteristics and functional uses of infant sensorimotor equipment during infant-mother interactions significantly influence the characteristics of behavioral differentiation and organization, foster the build-up of sensory thresholds and, consequently, nurture early adaptational development.

In summary, maternal behavior is a major contributor of infant stimulation through the following uses of stimulation:

1. selection of specific stimulations that the infant receives, thus, helping to shape the sensory environment;
2. to activate and maintain differentiation and to sustain the functional integrity of neurosensory and neuromotor apparatus;
3. by raising and lowering of sensory thresholds;
4. to change behavior state, regulate arousal, and foster attentional and alerting behavior;
5. to carry out the specific infant care techniques, such as feeding.

The appearance of atypical behavior among infants free of congenital neural defects, or of other major birth abnormalities, is taken as evidence of a disruption in development, and a consequence of inadequate, insufficient, faulty, or extreme and abusive infant care and stimulation. The consequences of such disturbances in the care, rearing, and stimulation of infants and young children are made known in the appearance of atypical or unusual behavior in infants which indicates faulty development, a vulnerability to stress, and a greater probability for later development of abnormalities in cognitive, sensorimotor, social, and emotional functions. Atypical behavior includes disturbed feeding and elimination, rhythmic hypermotility patterns, a variety of focal habits, exaggerations of behavior state, and the faulty or retarded development of major areas of behavior. Specific changes occur in feeding behavior, in motor patterns and in physical, sensorimotor, language, social, and adaptive development. Previous studies (Greenberg, 1970) suggest four groups of atypical behavior:

1. *failure-to-thrive syndrome*: a variety of behavioral abnormalities center around a retarded rate of weight gain, retardation and abuse.
2. *pica* accompanied by lead poisoning.
3. *patterned hypermotility syndrome* consisting of body-rocking and head-banging.
4. *syndrome of generalized atypicality*.

III.   A CRITIQUE ON PARENT-CHILD RELATIONSHIPS AND
INFANT-MOTHER INTERACTIONAL RESEARCH

A.   *Introduction*

The broad assumption that environment influences mental, social and emotional development during childhood underlies the idea that essential environmental factors affecting development are to be found in the personality and behavior of the parents of children. It is also generally believed that parental influences are inordinate during the earliest years of development and in particular during infancy when the baby's contact is mostly with the mother. These broad assumptions have contributed to the prevailing view that maternal influences on infants produce significant lasting change and that long-term influences of "normal" maternal behavior during infancy may insure against major emotional disturbances, while insufficient, distorted or faulty maternal behavior may lay the foundations for severe psychopathology in older children and in adults. Since maternal behavior can, at least according to these ideas, modify the course of early development, especially during the first year of life, studies of environmental influences on infant development usually involve examinations of infant-mother or of infant-mother surrogate relationships. While such broad assumptions provide a general rationale and indicate the need for intra-familial, parent-child and infant-mother interactional research, they lack the detailed conceptualization necessary for a research design.

B.   *The Direct Study of Infant-Mother Interaction*

The aim of most research on parent-child interaction has been to learn about influences of parent behavior on the behavior and development of children. The direct study of interaction has been approached with assorted techniques for recording observations that are carried out in a variety of circumstances. Naturalistic observations have been recorded in the form of descriptive summaries, detailed narratives, anecdotes and impressions or have been used as protocols from which various measures were derived. Other studies have used preselected categories of observable behavior, such as specific sequences of interactions or interactive dyads of parent and child behavior rated during the observations or soon afterwards (Hatfield, Ferguson, and Alpert, 1967; Baumrind, 1967). Sequential interactions have been studied by time-sampling scaled observations (Zunich, 1962). Continuous recordings of interactions have become feasible in recent years by means of electronic and electromechanical monitoring of acts and events that generate indirect but important measures of interaction (Matarazzo, Saslow, and Matarazzo, 1956).

C.   *The Indirect Study of Infant-Mother Interaction*

Interviews and questionnaires have been used to assess infant-mother interaction, parental motivations, traits and attitudes, and to learn of the current practices or, by retrospection, of past practices and child care routines. In fact, the majority of studies that relate parental behavior and development rely on questionnaires, interviews, and retrospective data (Freeberg and Payne, 1967). However, reports concerning mother-child interaction that are obtained from questionnaires or interviews have been considered to be highly subjective (Kogan and Wimberger, 1966). In retrospective reports, discrepancies, which tend to underestimate the age of the infant, are found to occur (Haggard, Brekstad, and Skard, 1960).

These procedures have had substantial and widespread use in studies of infant-mother interaction carried out to learn about the influences of mothers' stimulations, rearing and care of infants on their infants' early development. A perusal of published research on infant-mother interaction and a review of findings and observations from a quite wide variety of studies suggest that there has been only limited progress in achieving the aim of understanding how maternal behavior influences early development.

D.   *Methodological Issues*

Major stumbling blocks in the achievement of these research goals appear to be some fairly severe flaws in methodology, both theoretical and technical or procedural. From a *theoretical and methodological view-point* these important problems can be seen.

First, there is a general lack of carefully specified and logically for-mulated and detailed conceptualizations of how the mother and infant actually go about influencing each other, and, especially in empirical terms, of what maternal behavior influences what aspects or sectors of infant development. The formulation of propositions that connect con-cepts of early development with observable interactions has been lack-ing and the use of developmental theories, conceptualizations and de-rivative constructs to guide the selection of *what to look for in maternal behavior* as well as *in infant behavior* has therefore been sparse. The untoward effects of such methodological deficits are often found in the conceptual remoteness of parent data from the child and infant data used to assess parental influences on early development. Related to these problems is the general tendency to rate traits or attitudes of parents, rather than that which is actually observed. The observer is called upon to use impressions and inferences to rate scales that lack behavioral correlates, operational definitions or attributes that are observable.

Second, given two sets of data that appear conceptually remote from each other, most investigators fail to report the ideas or to propose a conceptualization bridging parent and infant sets of data. Such formula-tions or speculations, however, tentative, should be provided. Simple correlational findings or the presence of parent and infant data that were simultaneously collected do not in themselves reveal obvious relationships.

Third, there have been serious sampling problems. A typical flaw in sampling is observed in the procedures for recruiting mothers as sub-jects. Recruitment has most often proceeded on the rather shaky and tenuous scientific premise that public clinic registrants are available and willing. This may satisfy desires for convenience, but, unfortunately, may also seriously interfere with the selection of subjects that satisfy characteristics pertinent to the research problem. Another sampling error often occurs when subject selection is based on broad and gen-eral sociocultural information, such as socioeconomic status, age, parity, and marital status. This information is usually obtained by self-report techniques rarely if ever deliberately checked for reliability. Subjects selected on the basis of such information are very often not much better known by the investigators. The background, personality, problems and life situations of these subjects are all too often unknown. Since much research pertaining to the influence of maternal behavior on infant development hopes to include maternal personality variables, it is im-portant to note that such variables in fact do not ordinarily enter into subject selection. Very gross psychological assessments may be carried out, such as to exclude "psychotic" mothers from the sample, but not much more is done. Another issue in sampling is whether infant-mother interactions observed under "identical circumstances" can be considered to be representational. They may well be for some, but not for other, infant-mother pairs. It is uncommon to find research that includes systematically observed and recorded interactions of mother and infant pairs carried out in at least two different situations—for example, in the home as well as in the nursery school, in the home as well as in the laboratory, in the presence of as well as in the absence of the baby's father.

From a *technical and procedural viewpoint,* there are serious observer limitations with unselected naturalistic observations, as well as major problems in the analyses of such data. The use of pre-selected categories of behavior fosters systematic and reliable observation and lessens some of the analytic difficulties of data reduction. Unfortunately, efforts to increase reliability usually lead to categories of behavior that are too general. On the other hand, attempts to get more detailed and specific observational data can seriously affect reliability or impose severe restrictions on the variety or on the number of specific behaviors that can be rated. From our own experience (Greenberg, 1964, 1965; Loesch and Greenberg, 1964), we are well aware that it is a most difficult task to clearly identify or to agree upon "meaningful," specific or important events occurring at a moment of interaction. If observers are asked to record or to list or to rate from memory events they observed to transpire between an infant and mother only a few minutes earlier, it is highly improbable that adequate interrater agreements will be obtained on specific bits of interaction. In our own experience interrater agreement at an adequate statistical level depends on using rather general scales. This makes the possibility of documenting specific infant-mother interactions, by using direct observation, highly unlikely. In rating infant-nurse interaction in a Foundling Nursery, and in spite of limiting the number of items to be rated, we discovered that two observers frequently focused on, selected and rated quite different events that were occurring in the same time interval. The observers were unable to recall or to focus and rate observations on the same items unless the number of items were reduced to but a very small number. There are other technical issues which pertain to validity. One example of this problem is the small but often cited literature on mother-infant visual contact. The specific question raised is whether such observations are possible, given the techniques as reported. Our own efforts to study such interactions have been rather futile without film, and even with filmed interactions to work with, such assessments can be carried out only by indirect methods and measures, and a generous dose of inference.

In summary, evaluating the rationale of methodology guiding parent-child and particularly infant-mother interactional research requires special attention to assessing the techniques of variables employed to describe and quantify mother-child or mother-infant interaction and to the concepts underlying their selection. Three major questions might be considered, namely:

1. What are the concepts of early development guiding the selection of observable infant and maternal behavioral interactions?
2. Do the assessment techniques obtain interactional information that is pertinent to concepts of early development?
3. Were the interactional variables stated as empirical observables, i.e., containing descriptions of actual (physical) maternal actions or behavior; were the nonempirical variables recognized as abstractions, e.g. did the infant-mother interaction variables contain descriptions requiring interpretation and subjectivity or were they closer to empirical descriptions?

IV. METHOD

A. *Subjects*

1. *Selection*

Mother and infant *S*s were referrals from the Department of Pediatrics Clinics at the University of Illinois Hospitals. Subjects were referred on the basis of infant criteria including:

i. *age:* less than 30 months;
ii. *atypical behavior:* one or more of the atypical forms of behavior listed in the tables of atypical behavior (Tables 1a, 1b, and 1c);

TABLE 1a. ATYPICAL BEHAVIOR OF INFANCY

DISORDERS OF FEEDING AND OF THE GASTROINTESTINAL TRACT

1. Disturbances of sucking (e.g., weak sucking response, uncoordinated sucking)
2. Body hypertonicity, overstimulated by sucking
3. Regurgitation and vomiting
4. Avoidance of or refusal to feed from a bottle and/or breast
5. Refusal of specific foods
6. Refusal to chew
7. Nonacceptance of new diets or changes in diets
8. Anorexia
9. "Bottle-fixation" accompanied by an exclusion of other foods (nutritional anemia)
10. Food fads (other than bottle fixation)
11. Excessive eating (overeating. bulimia, hyperphagia)
12. Rumination
13. Pica. including coprophagia and trichphagia
14. Celiac disease
15. Malnutrition (underfeeding)

DISORDERS OF ELIMINATION

1. Diarrhea
2. Constipation
3. Psychogenic megacolon
4. Encopresis
5. Withholding stools

RHYTHMIC (STEREOTYPICAL) PATTERNS OF BODY MOTILITY

1. Head-rolling and head-nodding accompanied nystagmus (spasmus nutans)
2. Body-swaying (body-rocking)
    i. Normative
    ii. Repetitious
    iii. Excitatory
3. Head-banging
    i. Repetitious
    ii. Agitated

TABLE 1b. ATYPICAL BEHAVIOR OF INFANCY

DISORDERS OF HABIT FORMATION (HABIT PATTERNS, FOCAL ATYPICAL BEHAVIOR)

1. Disturbances of sleep
   i. Resistances to sleep
   ii. Drowsiness
   iii. Fitful sleep
   iv. Hypersomnia
   v. Hyposomnia and insomnia
2. Breath holding
3. Aerophagia
4. Biting and chewing of self (e.g., of lips, tongue, nails and other body parts)
5. Biting and chewing of others
6. Grinding of teeth (bruxism)
7. Sucking habits (e.g., of thumb, finger, lips, and inanimate objects)
8. Spitting
9. Pulling and picking of self (e.g., of lips, nose, and other body parts)
10. Trichotillomania (pulling out of hair, e.g., scalp and eyebrows)
11. Rubbing or stroking of self
    i. Masturbation
    ii. Of body parts other than genitalia
    iii. Stroking of self with inanimate objects

EXAGGERATIONS OF BEHAVIOR STATE OR AROUSAL

1. Overactivity
2. Excessive crying of early infancy (so-called "colic")
3. Hypersensitivity associated with a hyperalertness
4. Hypertonicity
5. Fussiness and restlessness
6. Lethargy, weakness, hypoactivity (energy impoverishment)
7. Excessive drowsiness
8. Hypotonicity

TABLE 1c. ATYPICAL BEHAVIOR OF INFANCY

1. Chronic, excessive or uncontrollable crying with screaming
2. Marasmus

DISORDERS OF MANIFEST AFFECT

3. Depression
4. Prolonged and undue infantile stranger reaction
5. Prolonged and undue infantile separation reaction

ATYPICAL DEVELOPMENTAL PATTERNS

General or in specific areas, e.g., motor, social, language, adaptive

1. Physical
   i. Accelerated
   ii. Retarded (failure to grow, failure to thrive)
   iii. Uneven
2. Maturational patterns (specify area and type)
   i. Accelerated
   ii. Regression (e.g., loss of walking, talking)
   iii. Lag in cerebral integration
   iv. Retarded (environmental, hospitalism, delayed laterality)
   v. Uneven (includes pseudomature patterns)

DISORDERS OF EARLY OBJECT RELATIONS

1. Avoidance responses (e.g., head-turning, crawling away)
2. Fetishism of infancy—attachment to inanimate objects
3. Absence of maternal separation response (atypical if not observed by the 9th or 10th months)
4. Prolonged and undue infantile stranger reaction
5. Prolonged and undue infantile separation reaction accompanied or replaced by atypical behavior (e.g., silent body-rocking and total withdrawal)

OTHER BODILY (VISCERAL) DISTURBANCES

1. Skin complaints
2. Respiratory complaints

iii. *physical health:* no major medical disease including congenital neural defects and other serious birth abnormalities;

iv. *hospitalizations:* no prior hospitalization or institutional experience longer than two weeks duration;

v. *maternal separation:* no maternal separations longer than two weeks.

Control Ss satisfied all of the above criterion except item ii., atypical behavior. They were without evidence of atypical behavior but were being followed in the Pediatrics Clinic for inguinal hernias. At the time of referral, each infant had been scheduled for hospitalization to enable surgical repair of the hernia. There were sixteen male infants in the *M-CI* group of subjects. Individual mothers of these sixteen Ss were matched for socioeconomic and marital factors with individual mothers of the atypical infants and thirteen infants were matched for ordinal position.

2. Size of Sample

There were forty-two infants with atypical behavior and sixteen male infants without atypical behavior. Each infant-mother pair was studied according to the data collection procedures listed below. The motion filming of infant-mother interaction in set situations was accomplished in eleven of the *M-CI* paired Ss and in eleven of the *M-AI* paired Ss.

3. Other characteristics of the sample.

The mothers of the control Ss and of the atypical Ss were comparable for age, marital status, ethnic background, and an estimate of socioeconomic class. They differed in that the mothers of the control infants had more years of schooling (11.2 versus 8.7) * and a fewer number of siblings (2.8 versus 5.8) *.

The selection criterion succeeded in generating a sample of atypical infant Ss without major medical disease, congenital or birth abnormality. The average age of infants at the time of referral was 13.5 months. The average birth weight of the atypical behavior Ss was 6.9 pounds (SD = ± 1.3) which is at the 25th percentile value. The average weight at the time of referral was 16.3 pounds which is at less than the 1st percentile value for 13.5 months. The group of atypical behavior infants appeared to have begun life with a reasonable expectation of thriving but one year later were serious developmental problems.

B. Data Collection Procedures

1. For each infant

    a. *Medical data:* all available prenatal, paranatal and pediatric data including information on physical growth and observations pertinent to assessing overall development.

    b. *Infant Behavior Inventory* (IBI): This is a two part questionnaire designed to discover and record specific forms of atypical behavior, to trace their chronology, and to determine patterns or combinations of behavior.

---

* These differences were of statistical significance, p value = <.05.

2. *For assessing maternal attitudes and personality*

    a. *Clinical Interviews:* tape-recorded semi-structured interviews are designed to learn about the mother's history and family background and to obtain data to permit objectified evaluations of some broad dimensions of personality and maternal attitudes.

    b. *Projective Psychological Tests:* Rorschach, Thematic Apperception and Draw-A-Person tests are administered to each mother. The data are used to make independent assessments of mothers' motivations, and personality structure.

    c. *Personal History Questionnaire* (Parent Information Form II) : Each mother completes a self-administered questionnaire of more than 100 items which cover several different areas including self, family, medical data, education, interests and occupational history.

    d. *Parent-Child Relations (PCR) Questionnaire*

3. *For assessing maternal behavior*

    a. *Maternal Behavior Anecdotal Descriptions:* Descriptions of interaction between the infant and mother as reported by the mother during interviews.

    b. *Anecdotal Descriptions of Infant-Mother Interactional Behavior* between infant and mother as observed and recorded by independent observer during the interviews.

    c. *Motion Film-Recorded Infant-Mother Interaction in Set Situations:* Each infant and mother are filmed together following a standard protocol during which a sequence of settings and events occur including:

        i. undirected spontaneous interaction, 10 minutes;

        ii. feeding of infant by the mother, 10 minutes;

        iii. a "stranger" joins the infant and mother, 5 minutes;

        iv. mother leaves the room and the "stranger" is alone with the infant, 5 minutes;

        v. "stranger" leaves the room and the infant is alone, 5 minutes;

        vi. mother returns and reunites with the infant, 5 minutes.

V. MATERNAL ATTITUDES

A comparison of maternal attitudes was carried out by analyzing the data* collected by the Personal History Questionnaire (Parent Information Form II) and the findings are summarized.

A. *Attitudes and Adjustment to Pregnancy*

During their pregnancy with the infant subjects, the M-AI mothers had a greater number of complaints, they had fewer slight symptoms,

---

* Analysis of data included identifying variables, coding procedures, categorizing responses, and placing response frequencies in the form of two by two contingency tables. These tables were statistically tested for discrepancy by means of Fischer's test for exact probabilities.

but many severe symptoms (p $<$.01). With one exception, none of these mothers admitted to a planned pregnancy. They all greeted pregnancy with a note of unhappiness and some mothers incriminated pregnancy for their infants' problem.

B. *Perception of the Infant's Problem and Awareness of the Infant*

The M-CI mothers seemed to be more aware of their infants' problem (p $<$.02). Mothers of atypical infants spoke of their infants' future with striking inappropriateness. "He can be a big businessman and have lots of factories" was the expectation of one mother. The height of incredibility is the instance of an infant girl almost two years old, who appeared neglected, was unable to walk, dragged herself around the floor throughout the interview, and received no attention from her mother, who said:

> I don't know. She might be a very selfish child because we pet her so much.

C. *The Role of Mother*

Many more of the control mothers indicated "being needed" as a source of satisfaction in the mother role (p $<$.01), while the mothers of atypical infants focused on activities as a source of satisfaction (p $<$.05).

A much higher percentage of the M-AI mothers seemed contradictory in their concerns about being a mother (p $<$.02) and more than the control mothers; their concerns were oriented toward the present (p $<$.05). Similar percentages in both groups indicated that they did not desire any more children.

The majority of the M-AI mothers were among the younger members of their families (p $<$.05) and probably had fewer opportunities to care for small children. These mothers also have more young children than the control mothers, therefore less experience in infant care with their own infants and more demands in terms of child care. The combination of possible lack of experience in child care, immature age, and, in some cases, heavy demands because of a number of small children may be operative in some of atypical infants' mothers' dissatisfactions with their mother role.

D. *Perception of Family Roles*

A much higher percentage of control mothers saw the father as emotionally tied to the family (p $<$.05), saw their own primary function as giving affection to their children (p $<$.01) and realized the emotional ties between husband and wife. Less than half of the M-AI mothers saw that husband wife ties were emotional. More of the M-AI mothers failed to discriminate between husband and father roles and between wife and mother roles.

VI. MATERNAL BEHAVIOR AND INFANT-MOTHER INTERACTIONS

A study based on descriptions given by the mothers during tape-recorded interviews and an observer's narrative anecdotes of infant-mother interaction during these interviews.

A. *Introduction*

Descriptions of infant-mother interaction in the home were obtained from the mothers during tape-recorded interviews. These descriptions were compared with narratives of infant-mother interaction viewed by an observer during the interviews. Interactional data which show agreement are reported as the findings of this study.

B. *Maternal Interaction with Specific Sensorimotor Modalities and Behavior States*

1. *Rationale*

These descriptions of interaction are based on the reports of the mothers' use of specific sensorimotor modalities of the infant for pacification, behavior state regulation, and in infant care, for example, feeding, and on the reports of mothers' responses to various infant behavior states, for example, to crying.

The mother-infant stimulation equilibrium can be described by the infants' general behavior, its level of arousal, and the specific sensorimotor modalities infant employed by the mother to maintain or change these levels. To explore early behavior from this viewpoint is not artificial. Young infants tend to be observable in behavior states which follow a continuum of general arousal levels; sleep, drowsy, awake-inactive, fussy, and crying and each state has been shown to have specific psychophysiological response characteristics (Greenberg, 1965). The infant's sensorimotor mechanisms are used by the mother to regulate behavior state. The mechanisms include nutritive and non-nutritive sucking, holding, movement, and sound and visual stimulation including the smiling mechanism. Observations of these various infant sensorimotor-maternal interactions used to regulate and distribute behavior states can describe infant events in terms of arousal increases and reductions. Thus, the mother-infant equilibrium can be thought of as two systems which interact through specific mechanisms of stimulation and pacification, and with corresponding shifts of arousal levels. These behavior states are reacted to differentially by the mother and by different mothers. Due to the relative simplicity of early mental structures these interactions can be approximately described by the infant's observable behavior and its sensorimotor interactions with the mother.

With further development, the behavior states and sensorimotor functions undergo differentiation and complex organization, the processes become more complex and more complex explanatory descriptions are required.

2. *The Use of Anecdotal (Interview) Data*

One purpose of the clinical interviews is to inquire about the earliest months of infancy and specifically to obtain mothers' descriptions of early infant care practices, stimulation patterns and special or unusual interactions with their babies. Retrospective data ordinarily suffer from poor reliability especially if the past is examined for specifics and detail. Maternal descriptions are used in these studies for a specific purpose of learning about predominant patterns of interaction used with the infant. The reliability of this type of information appears to be adequate. The results indicate that patterns of mothering which occupy disproportionate amounts of mothers' time and which are of unique emotional meaning are reliably recalled. These findings pertain to those broad areas of infant-mother involvement and interaction where the descriptions contained in the interview data were judged to be reliable.

C. *Sensorimotor Patterns of Infant-Mother Interaction: Assessing Their Use in Infant Care*

Six patterns or foci of infant-mother interaction were compared in sixteen mothers of the *M-AI* group and sixteen matched mothers of the control *M-CI* group. The categories are:

1. the overall response of mothers during the neonatal period at home, including feeding;
2. mothers' initial and subsequent reactions to infant crying;
3. infant pacification versus frustration;
4. holding;
5. use of a nipple pacifier;
6. playing with and the overall enjoyment of the infant.

D. *The Overall Response of Mothers During the Neonatal Period at Home, Including Feeding*

1. *First-born*

Of the sixteen *M-CI* infants, eight Ss in each group were first born. The mothers of both groups experienced intense apprehension, uncertainty, helplessness and inadequacy. These reactions were out of all proportion to the realities of the circumstances and centered around three major areas: the need to cope with a crying infant, mastering the feeding situation and apprehension about handling the infant ordinarily thought to be fragile, delicate and easily damaged.

In seven of the eight *M-AI* mothers, these reactions persisted for greater lengths of time (three to seven months) than the *M-CI* (a few days to a few weeks). The *M-CI* mothers responded to the initial distress with total withdrawal and the turning over the infant care to another adult, the constant use of a nipple pacifier to reduce infant crying and a relative paucity of holding the infant except during feeding.

The *M-AI* mothers reported much distress during the initial months and were especially preoccupied with controlling their infants' crying. Holding was predominantly used to control crying. The babies of the *M-AI* mothers were frequently held for inordinate periods of time as the following excerpts illustrate:

M-AI Infant *S* 1.

> in the first three months I would hold her all the time, I was so afraid she wasn't going to make it . . . and she would sleep good and I would just sit up and hold her and she would sleep, and I would say I am not doing anything but ruining her let me lay her down and I would catch myself holding her more than I did the others . . . sometime I would hold her about an hour and a half at a time . . . until she was about three months that's when she was alright . . . after she was three months old I didn't give her too much attention, I didn't hold her a lot.

M-AI Infant *S* 2.

> it worried me about her crying . . . when she was small I really enjoyed holding her for probably a month or two, maybe after I got more used to her you know, I used to like to sit and hold her . . . well then I wanted to put her down, I had all these things to do and at that time she had gotten used to it and then she didn't want to, she didn't want to be left alone . . . she wanted me to hold her all the time, just sit and hold her. I would put her on the floor and she would cry when I put her down, she acted as if she was afraid I was going to leave her then she would cry after that so I would sit and hold her . . . I couldn't leave her with my husband because I really didn't trust him to keep her, I wouldn't let him keep her . . . because I felt that he would go to sleep, or she might get strangled or anything because he wasn't easy to wake up, because I am always listening to hear her, even when I am sleep, you know if she whines, I'll be up . . . I'll be angry a lot of times, but not enough to hit her, because my nerves are real bad and she used to cry all the time and it would just make me so nervous to the point where I would holler at her or spank her or anything. Most of the times I would try to do what she wanted me to do.

M-AI Infant *S* 3.

> she didn't eat in the hospital or anything either, not well . . . she just wouldn't swallow . . . she would keep it in her mouth or else it would dribble out all over her . . . half of the day at least, I carried her around; at night time I would hold her and rock her, I was rocking her all night . . . would have her in my arms all night long each night, I held her from the time she was born. At first I thought that she was just stubborn and wanted more attention than she was getting.

M-AI Infant *S* 4.

> she hollered quite a bit at first, for the first month and a half. Then after that she didn't cry too much . . . it didn't bother me any that I had to get up with her at night, it didn't bother me at all, it didn't make me angry or anything like that you know, So I got up with her and would sit up with her and feed her and sit and hold her for awhile, walk with her, burp her and things like that through the night or most of the night until she got where she would sleep through the night or most of the night and wake up early in the morning . . . I didn't reject her because she was crying.

2. *Second-born*

Seven of the remaining eight infant *S*s of both the M-AI and *M-CI* groups are the second of two children. The period of distress and the feelings of inadequacy were transient or non-existent in the mothers of the control infants. The mothers of infants with atypical behavior reported essentially the same responses as described with first-born *M-AI* infant *S*s.

E. *Feeding*

The high incidence of feeding problems among the *M-AI* infant *S*s differentiated them from the control infants. Aside from maternal contributions to the onset or perpetuation of infant feeding problems, the mothers of atypical infants were usually confronted with disturbed feeding which included vomiting, regurgitation, refusal to accept food, retention of food in the mouth, weak sucking, and rumination. Additional efforts were exerted by the mothers to get the infants to feed and retain their food.

Although some of the *M-CI* mothers feared their infants were not getting enough to eat, the *M-AI* infants were certain since retarded rates of weight gain were evident within the first three months after birth.

The *M-CI* mothers readily used feeding and sucking to soothe. Nipple pacifiers were placed into service early and were frequently used. This was quite rare in the *M-AI* group where feeding and non-nutritive sucking for soothing was rarely described. The disinclination of *M-AI* mothers to use feeding to soothe their babies when distressed seemed understandable in the light of the infants' propensity for feeding disturbances. The rare use of nipple-pacifiers is less understandable especially since independent testing of these infants proved the nipple pacifier to be an effective pacifier for all Ss younger than seven months of age.

F. *Mother's Initial and Subsequent Reaction to Infant Crying*

Most mothers spoke of initial distress and an imperative urge to somehow stop their infant from crying—to somehow do something. Both groups of mothers retrospectively observed that early failures to handle the infants' crying were experienced as threatening. They recalled feeling helpless, inadequate, and feared doing harm to the infant.

The *M-CI* mothers recalled becoming flexible. The sense of urgency decreased and some effort was made to first evaluate the nature of the cry. Initial fear and irritation yielded to the emergence of concern, curiosity, and efforts to protect the infant from excesses of distress. Attempts to alleviate possible causes were accompanied by the offer of a nipple-pacifier.

Two distinct patterns of response evolved among the *M-AI* mothers. *One* pattern was that of keeping the infant constantly pacified or quiet and without exception the technique was to hold the infant for protracted periods of time. Relief for the mother came when the infant slept. In the older *M-AI* infant Ss, there were frequent reports of sleep disturbances with intense crying relieved only when the infant was allowed to sleep with the mother in the same bed. A *second M-AI* pattern involved the mother's disregard of and apparent aloofness to the infant's crying. Indifference and detachment seemed to be the posture which some of these mothers described in an accommodation to the crying of their babies. These mothers also admitted to spanking their infants, a practice employed with increasing frequency from about the seventh month. Two *M-AI* mothers admitted to spanking when their babies were as young as two and three months of age.

Thus, mothers of infants with atypical behavior occasionally lost control of their anger, which they feared would happen. They would hold and rock their babies for inordinate periods of time and rarely used feeding or a nipple-pacifier to pacify.

G. *Infant Pacification Versus Frustration*

Crying took on two meanings for most mothers, i.e., a sign of distress and a demand for gratification. Considerable conflict developed in some mothers over "spoiling" the infant; i.e., the idea that if the infant was usually pacified, he would continue to expect and demand it. Many

M-CI mothers had conscious conflicts over pacification but on inquiry confessed to allowing positive feelings to determine interactions with the infant. Most *M-CI* mothers did not carry into action their own ideas of it being "bad" to always satisfy the infant.

Two general patterns of response to crying were observed in the *M-AI* group of mothers. One group of mothers seemed determined to never interpret crying as evidence of frustration. Crying became prevalent when the infant was no longer held. The second *M-AI* group of mothers were insensitive or indifferent to these issues as they appeared to hold to the notion of early toughening up and the abolition of demandingness.

H. *Holding*

It was very surprising to learn of the strong negative evaluation of holding which characterized both mother groups. Holding was the same as "spoiling," causing infant demandingness and "getting his own way." In actual behavior, the two groups of mothers differed on holding. The *M-CI* mothers engaged in holding during play and while feeding their babies, but rationed the amount of holding time. The *M-AI* mothers voiced similar opposition to holding as the cause of spoiling, however in actual interaction, an inordinate amount of time was devoted to holding, often to prevent crying even as the mother engaged in cooking, cleaning and washing.

I. *Use of a Nipple-Pacifier*

Bottle feeding and nipple pacifiers were readily utilized by most *M-CI* mothers and most extensively by those who had a strong need to minimize the amount of time spent crying. The nipple pacifier was an alternative to holding the infant. The mothers who played with or held their infants a great deal used the nipple pacifier less frequently. Nipple pacifiers were rarely used by the *M-AI* mothers.

J. *Playing with and the Overall Enjoyment of the Infant*

M-CI mothers gave spontaneous accounts of enjoyment of and family participation with the infant—holding, smiling, playing, and talking. This was practically non-existent among the *M-AI* mothers who described interaction in terms of the mechanics of care. The *M-CI* mothers often spoke of their enjoyment in feeding; the *M-AI* mothers reported the ordeals of feeding. Playing, smiling, and talking were prominent features of the interaction of the *M-CI* mothers even before the advent of the smiling response. These mothers felt that talking or personal presence would soothe irritable babies. It was common view of *M-CI* mothers that a baby's irritableness, as opposed to crying, expressed a longing for closeness and what baby needed when fussy was to be nearby, to be talked with and only occasional play or holding is needed. These attitudes and behaviors were reinforced by the infants' response of quieting and smiling. Sound and sight were emphasized as means of contact and for maintaining a baby's quiescence.

The *M-AI* mothers did not spontaneously or on direct inquiry recall talking, singing, or playfully exciting their babies.

VII. PATTERNS OF INFANT-MOTHER INTERACTION AND STIMULATION CHARACTERISTICS

Assessments of behavioral interaction in set situations
using motion filmed observations.

A. *Background*

After using a variety of procedures to assess maternal behavior including direct observation guided by preselected categories of stimulation variables, it was not yet possible to generate the quality and form of information needed in a study of influences of maternal stimulation on early infant behavioral and psychophysiological differentiation. The need was for rather varied and detailed interactional data including rather specific and quantifiable stimulation data. To obtain this information would require repeated observations of the same one or group of interactions and this depended on the availability of a permanent record of the interaction. This might allow assessments of stimulation patterns, the number and variety of stimulation, the amount of stimulation in terms of numbers, intensity, and the amount of stimulation time.

Filmed observations allow for improved interrater reliability and for review and re-examination and facilitates increasing accuracy and precision in observation.

B. *Filming Protocol*

Motion-filmed observations of infant-mother interaction are used in studying normally developing babies as well as atypical behavior babies. In bringing her infant to be filmed, mothers are asked not to feed their babies for one hour prior to coming and to bring a bottle or food. A special room is used for filming (Illustration 1.) and appears not too unlike an ordinary living room.

A 16 mm single system, sound-recording Auricon camera with a zoom lens was operated by a professional photographer, and located behind a one-way mirror. The entire film sequence usually lasted 40 minutes.

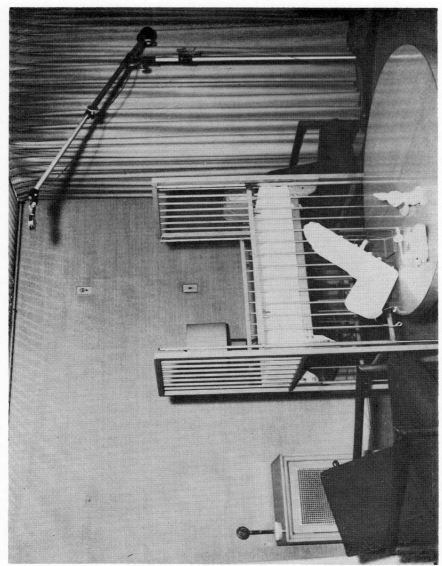

ILLUSTRATION 1. Room for the filming of infant-mother interaction.

C. *Patterns of Infant-Mother Interaction: Narrative Descriptions*

1. *Introduction*

The films are viewed a number of times and the behavior of the infant-mother pairs is carefully observed. During the repeated viewing of each film, detailed descriptions of overt behavior are narrated by two independent observers. Transcribed narrative descriptions are checked against additional viewing of the same film and revised as indicated.

2. *Sequence of undirected infant-mother interaction*

a. *Play*

Differences in the behavior of the two groups of mothers were consistently described during the initial ten minutes of interaction, an undirected and unstructured situation. Although the mothers of both groups tended to rely on the various toys and dolls available in the room to occupy the ten minutes time, the quality of play interaction was obviously different between the *M-AI* and *M-CI* pairs of *S*s.

The play of *M-CI S*s was organized, the mothers were matter-of-fact and although some of the play objects were unfamiliar, play itself was not. Chatter or other vocalizations from the mother were frequent with occasional cheerfulness. The mothers had no difficulty in maintaining an interest in the situation while attending to the baby. There was an organized quality to the play behavior and time was spent on specific activities.

The interactions of *M-AI* pairs of *S*s were described differently from the *M-CI S*s. The *M-AI* mothers were described as very busy or they were described as very inactive and not interactive. A few *M-AI* mothers alternated between the two, between vigorous activity and calm apathy. Four *M-AI* mothers remained completely inactive and unresponsive during the initial ten minutes of filming. Other *M-AI* mothers spent the time in sporadic, inconsistent and poorly organized play. Toys and dolls were not selected from the toybox. Instead, they were gone through in rapid succession, something to keep busy. Attention shifted quickly from one thing to another and changes were greeted by excessive expressions of short-lived interest.

b. *Facial and other expressive behavior*

Facial expressions of *M-AI* mothers were frequently described as stereotypical and fixed. Two of these mothers had extraordinarily masked expressions and appeared to never move any part of a blank face, and were never observed to smile. This was in contrast to those *M-AI* mothers who always possessed a standardized cheerful smile, even as they talked angrily to their babies.

The voices of these *M-AI* mothers were usually subdued, at times inaudible, and usually flat—except when their ire was directed at the infants. When anger was directly expressed at their babies, their expressionless posture was temporarily lifted.

Gross body movements were restrained even when they appeared busy. They frequently seemed immobile if not rigid. Animated behavior was not observed. Occasional intense expressions were directed toward the babies with words and phrases such as "no-no," "you're bad," and "are you getting mad." Although restricted in gross movements, these mothers engaged in an inordinate number of small bodily acts; hands busily manipulated small objects, nails were bitten and lip smacking flourished.

c. *Some attributes of stimulation*

A striking feature of seven *M-AI* mothers was their undisguised and repetitious physical overstimulations. These included moderate slapping, playful biting, mild hitting, vigorous rubbing of the baby's body with toys, harsh stroking, tight grasps, poking, nibbling, and an inordinate amount of time spent grooming various parts of the infants' body.

3. *Feeding*

Descriptions of the filmed feeding were quite similar to the mothers' self-report. On film, the older *M-AI* infants seemed enveloped by an array of simultaneously occurring events or stimulations introduced by the mother and which the infant could not avoid. The following excerpts are from narrative descriptions and illustrate the situation.

   i. The mother offers the baby a bag of potato chips . . . mother and baby take some chips out and hold them . . . the mother offers one and the infant bites the chip . . . mother loudly tells the baby to take out the chip from the bag but holds the bag out of the baby's reach and then teases the baby again.
   ii. The infant is given a bottle and she puts it into her mouth and sucks. Mother caresses the baby, takes the bottle out, kisses the bottle, puts the bottle back . . . mother takes the bottle out and nibbles on the bottle making loud sucking noises.
   iii. The baby is given a bottle of milk which she sucks while held by her mother . . . the mother removes, reinserts, again removes and again returns the bottle to the baby's mouth . . . this is repeated six or seven times . . . the baby continues to suck on her bottle now and the mother is changing her diaper all the while her baby continues to suck on bottle of milk.

4. *Stranger, separation and reunion sequences*

Six *M-CI* and seven *M-AI* infant *S*s were nine months of age or older. All six *M-CI* infant *S*s responded to the appearance of the stranger with a look of apprehension and they crept closer to their mother; all six

M-CI infants cried when their mother left the room and they continued to cry for the five minutes of separation. They looked at the door of the room through which their mother exited but made no real effort to go to the door. Their mother's return was greeted with diminution or cessation of crying.

The responses of the *M-AI* infants were less uniform and included no response, withdrawal, avoidance behavior, body-rocking, ordinary crying, and severe crying to the extent of shrieking during maternal separation. Reunion with the mothers also produced a variety of responses. The infants who were most distressed demonstrated relief. The two infants who appeared to have no reaction to their mothers leaving were equally casual to their return and the body-rocking of the baby begun when the mother left stopped on her return.

D. *Patterns of Infant-Mother Interaction: Characteristics of Maternal Stimulation*

1. *Stimulation Variables*

A set of ten descriptions was selected to characterize both qualitative and quantitative aspects of maternal stimulation. Specification of the behaviors comprising each of the categories was stressed to minimize rater inference and speculation. The ten sets of descriptions are subsumed under four categories of sensory modes (Table 2).

TABLE 2

MATERNAL STIMULATION VARIABLES

A. *Kinesthetic*
1. Mother handles infant, i.e., position of baby's body is changed in space, tossed up and down, swung, held overhead.
2. Mother manipulates baby's limbs or head, i.e., baby's position does not change.

B. *Tactile*
3. Mother shakes, kisses, tickles, pets infant with part of her body or with an object (involves only active touching—do not score if mother simply holds infant's hand, leg, etc.).
4. Mother places object in infant's hand or infant reaches and touches object which mother has just introduced.
5. Mother inserts bottle or pacifier in infant's mouth.
6. Mother grooms or cleans, e.g., adjusts or changes clothing, wipes mouth, combs hair, picks at nose or ears.

C. *Auditory*
7. Mother vocalizes to infant in any form, i.e., coos, talks, sings, shouts, etc.
8. Mother uses an instrument to make sounds—e.g., rattle, music box, radio.

D. *Visual*: To score any visual stimulation the observer must be able to see infant's eyes focused or fixated in the direction of mother's face or the object being presented.
9. Mother presents objects which are visually fixated or followed.
10. Mother makes faces at, imitates infant's expressions, smiles at infant, or maintains eye contact.

2. *Film Rating Procedures and Apparatus*

a. *Rating procedure*

For each film, ten maternal stimulation variables and six infant behavior states were rated continuously through the use of three stimuli indicating boxes, and simultaneously recorded. Each box had four buttons which could be pressed to signal the presence of four different types of maternal stimulation. Above each button was located a thumbwheel switch for the selection of any of twelve types of maternal stimulation to be indicated by the adjacent button. Three out of the six trained raters were required in the rating of each film. As a behavior was observed, a corresponding button was depressed, and remained down ("on position") for the duration of the activity. The electrical signals from four buttons in each of three groups (stimuli 1-4, 5-8, 9-12) were added using binary weights so as to produce a composite signal whose value was proportional to:

$$1x \ (E_1) + 2X \ (E_2) + 4x \ (E_3) + 8x \ (E_4)$$

$$Ep = 0 \text{ when stimulus not present}$$
$$Ep = 1 \text{ when stimulus present}$$
$$p = 1 \text{ through 4; 5 through 8; 9 through 12}$$

It can be seen that the values of the resultant signal ranged (in steps of 1) from 0 (no stimuli present) to 15 (all 4 stimuli in the group present).

One of the boxes had six additional buttons to indicate six levels of infant behavior state. The electrical signal level from these buttons was proportional to behavior state.

b. *Analog recording*

The three composite stimuli and behavior state signals were fed to a Beckman Dynagraph strip chart recorded to produce a four-channel visual record. A back-up recording was made on a Precision Instrument FM magnetic tape recorder.

c. *Digital record*

The four signals were digitized by Raytheon multiverter at a rate of 10 scans (of the four signals) per second. The resultant digital information was recorded on magnetic computer tape by a Precision Instrument incremental tape recorder and subsequently transferred to Magnetic disk for high speed computer processing.

d. *Inter-rater reliability*

Inter-rater reliability was determined by using three pairs of judges and three filmed mother-infant pairs. All three infants filmed were the second-born (two males and one female) and ranged in age from six to twelve weeks.

Inter-rater reliability was measured in two ways. The first was an interjudge comparison of the total amount of time each of the ten maternal variables was recorded "on." For each of the ten stimulation variables, the total amount of time it was recorded as "on" was tabulated. The Pearson product-moment correlations between judges' ratings for the three films ranged from .84—.99, with median, mode and mean of .91.

Though the correlations based on each variable summed across time were high, it was possible that they were arrived at by recordings at different times. The total time for each variable should be made up of behaviors recorded at the same point in time. The second measure of inter-rater reliability was a partial check on this. Each variable was divided into 60 twenty-second segments and the judges' ratings were compared in pairs in each segment to see if both had an instance of that behavior recorded. Thus, there were three alternatives: both judges had a behavior recorded (both "on"); both had nothing recorded, (both "off"); and one had a behavior recorded while the other did not (one "on" and one "off"). The latter was taken as a measure of error. Three interjudge comparisons were carried out for each of three films. The interjudge percent of agreement ranging from 90.9 to 95.9. Both measures of inter-rater reliability indicated that substantial agreement existed among the judges.

e. *Computation of maternal stimulation variables ratings*

The continuous and simultaneous rating of ten stimulation variables in addition to the six infant behavior state variables permits a wide range of questions to be posed and statistical procedures applied. An example of the information made available is given with Illustration 2, a photograph of a computer print-out. The amount of stimulation versus no stimulation time, the amount of time per stimulation variable, the use of single variables, combinations of stimulations, and by comparing such data with other infants' data, it becomes apparent that a wide range of measures become available which may help in differentiating individuals, groups of babies, and age effects in the light of the quality of stimulation.

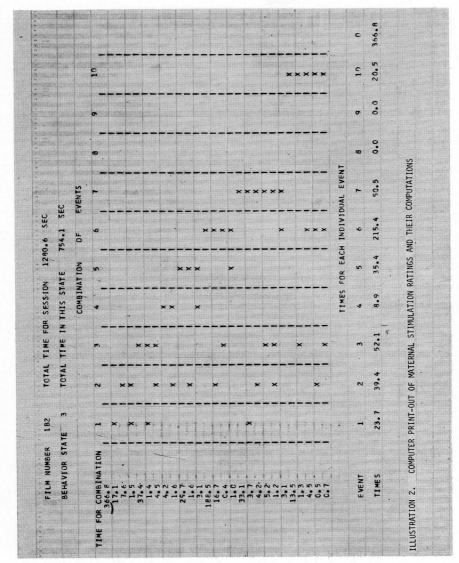

ILLUSTRATION 2.   COMPUTER PRINT-OUT OF MATERNAL STIMULATION RATINGS AND THEIR COMPUTATIONS

ILLUSTRATION 2. Computer print-out of maternal stimulation ratings
and their computations.

3. *The Amount of Maternal Stimulation*: A summary of findings
   from an analysis of the undirected interaction sequence.

Ratings of maternal stimulation were carried out on seven *S*s from
each of the two infant groups. Determinations were made of the amounts
of total stimulation time, of distinct stimulation time and of mixed
stimulation time. These were converted to percents of time in each of
three infant behavior states to control for the differing time spent by
infants in sleep, wakefulness, and in crying. This was done since the
amounts of stimulation in any of the behavior states depend, in part,
on the amount of time of the specific behavior state (rho = 0.89). In
addition, the two infant *S*s groups were compared on each of the four
major modes of stimulation.

The average ($\bar{x}$) percent of total film time spent in stimulation was
not significantly different between the two *S*s groups; 65.3% for the
M-AI infants and 61.2% for the M-CI group. The percent stimulation
time during wakefulness-inactivity and during infant crying did not differ significantly between the two infant groups. Differences occurred in
the use of combined stimulations and in the use of distinct stimulations
and in the group of M-AI infants there were two subgroups in which their
combined stimulation times averaged 61.2% total stimulation time. Four
of the M-AI infant *S*s clustered together around the low average ($\bar{x}$)
stimulation time of 42.1% and the other three clustered together around
a high average of 87.0% stimulation time.

An analysis of the specific modes reveals group differences particularly
in the auditory and kinesthetic modes. In the M-AI group, the amount
of auditory stimulation measured as amount of time (in seconds) of
auditory stimulation was decidedly less ($<.02$) and the amount of kinesthetic stimulation (variable i) was significantly greater. In the M-AI
infants there was a typical pattern of minimal mix among the four
major modes of stimulation. If an M-AI infant is high in kinesthetic-
vestibular stimulation, then auditory, visual and tactual stimulations are
down in amount of stimulation time. In the group of M-CI infants,
a mix of two or three major modes of stimulation was characteristic.
This did not increase the percent of total stimulation time but rather
gave the periods of stimulation a quality of enrichment.

VIII. DISCUSSION

This report contains selected findings on the infant-mother interactional behavior of infants who have atypical behavior and of infants
who are without atypical behavior. There are rather clear differences
in the interaction patterns of the two groups of infant-mother pairs.
From other data collected in these studies there are further supports
to a linking of atypical behavior, atypical development, disturbed and

often withdrawn mothers, negligence and abuse in the care and treatment of babies and a variety of other personal, familial and life situational difficulties.

It seems reasonable to conclude that atypical behavior and atypical development can be induced and maintained by insufficient, faulty, or extreme stimulation. It seems also reasonable to conclude that in an environment favorable to the progress of normal differentiation and adaptation, enriching stimulation is provided; that is, repeated stimulation of mild or moderate intensity, varied in type with perhaps some balance between constancy and novelty and presented appropriate to the infant's state and needs. The levels of stimulation need to vary but clearly not to include excesses on the high or low side of overstimulation and stimulus deprivation.

BIBLIOGRAPHY

1. AINSWORTH, M. Reversible and Irreversible Effects of Maternal Deprivation on Intellectual Development. Child Welfare League of America, 1962, 42-62.
2. BALDWIN, A. L., KALHORN, J. & BREESE, F. H. Patterns of Parent Behavior. *Psychol. Monogr.*, 1945, 58 (3): Whole No. 268.
3. BALDWIN, A. L., KALHORN, J. & BREESE, F. H. The Appraisal of Parent Behavior. *Psychol. Monogr.*, 1949, 63 (4): Whole No. 299.
4. BAUMRIND, D. Child Care Practices Anteceding Three Patterns of Preschool Behavior. *Genet. Psychol. Monogr.*, 1967, 75, 43-88.
5. BAYLEY, N. & SCHAEFER, E. S. Relationship between Socioeconomic Variables and Behavior of Mothers Toward Young Children. *J. Genet. Psychol.*, 1960, 96, 61.
6. BEACH, F. A. & JAYNES, J. Effects of Early Experiences upon Behavior of Animals. *Psychol. Bull.*, 1954, 51, 239.
7. BISHOP, M. Mother-child Interaction and the Social Behavior of Children. *Psychol. Monogr.*, 1951, 65:11 Whole No. 328.
8. BLOOM, B. S. Stability and Change in Human Characteristics. New York, Wiley, 1964.
9. BRONFENBRENNER, U. Toward a Theoretical Analysis of Parent-child Relationships in a Social Context. In Parental Attitudes and Child Behavior, Glidewell, (Ed.). Springfield, Thomas, 1961.
10. CALDWELL, M. Mother-Infant Interaction During First Year of Life. *Merrill-Palmer Quart.*, 1964, X (2), 119-28.
11. CALDWELL, B. M. The Effects of Infant Care. In Review of Child Development Research, M. L. Hoffman and L. W. Hoffman, (Eds.). New York, Russell Sage Foundation, 1964, Vol. 1, 4-87.
12. CASLER, L. Maternal Deprivation: A Critical Review of the Literature. *Monogr. Soc. Res. Child Develpm.*, 1961, 26.
13. CLAUSEN, J. A. Family Structure, Socialization, and Personality. In Review of Child Development Research, M. L. Hoffman and L. W. Hoffman, (Eds.). New York, Russell Sage Foundation, 1966, Vol. 2, 1-53.
14. DRECHSLER, R. J. & SHAPIRO, M. Two Methods of Analysis of Family Diagnostic Data. *Family Process*, 1963, 2, 367-370.
15. DYK, R. B. & WITKIN, H. A. Family Experiences Related to the Development of Differentiation in Children. *Child Develpm.*, 1955, 36, 21-55.
16. FARINA, A. & BUNHAM, R. M. Measurement of Family Relationships and Their Effects. *Arch. Gen. Psychiat.*, 1963, 9, 64-73.
17. FERREIRA, A. J., WINTER, W. D. & POINDEXTER, E. Some Interactional Variables in Normal and Abnormal Families. *Family Process*, 1966, 5, 60-75.

18. FRANK, L. K. On the Importance of Infancy. New York, Random House, 1967.
19. FREEBERG, N. E. & PAYNE, D. T. Parental Influence on Cognitive Development in Early Childhood: A Review. *Child Develpm.*, 1967, 38, 65-87.
20. GREENBERG, N. H. Studies in Psychosomatic Differentiation During Infancy. *Arch. Gen. Psychiat.*, 1962, 7, 17.
21. GREENBERG, N. H. Origins of Head-Rolling (Spasmus Nutans) During Early Infancy. *Psychosomatic Med.*, 1964, 26, 162.
22. GREENBERG, N. H. Developmental Effects of Stimulation During Early Infancy: Some Conceptual and Methodological Considerations. *Annals of The New York Academy of Sciences*, 1965, 118, 831-859.
23. GREENBERG, N. H. Atypical Behavior During Infancy: Infant Development in Relation to the Behavior and Personality of the Mother. In The Child in His Family. *The International Yearbook for Child Psychiatry and Allied Disciplines*, Volume 1, New York, Wiley, 1970.
24. HAGGARD, E. A., BREKSTAD, A. & SKARD, A. On the Reliability of the Anamnestic Interview. *J. of Abn. and Soc. Psychol.*, 1960, 61, 311-318.
25. HATFIELD, S., FERGUSON, L. & ALPERT, R. Mother-Child Interaction and the Socialization Process. *Child Develpm.*, 1967, 38, 365-414.
26. HESS, R. & SHIPMAN, V. Early Experience and the Socialization of Cognitive Modes in Children. *Child Develpm.*, 1965, 36 (4), 869-886.
27. KRECH, S., ROSENZWEIG, N. R. & BENNETT, E. L. Relations between Brain Chemistry and Problem Solving Among Rats Raised in Enriched and Impoverished Environments. *J. Comp. Physiol. Psychol.*, 1962, 55, 801-807.
28. KOGAN, K. L. & WIMBERGER. An Approach to Defining Mother-Child Interaction Styles. *Percept. & Mot. Skills*, 1966, 23, 1171-1177.
29. LOESCH, J. G. & GREENBERG, N. H. Patterns of Maternal Behavior During Early Infancy. Presented at the Annual Meetings, Amer. Psychiat. Assoc., Los Angeles, Calif., 1964.
30. LOVELAND, N. T. The Relation Rorschach: A Technique for Studying Interaction. *J. Nerv. Ment. Dis.*, 1967, 145, 93-105.
31. LUBIN, B., LEVITT, E. E. & ZUCKERMAN, M. Some Personality Differences between Responders and Non-responders to a Survey Questionnaire. *J. Consulting Psychol.*, 1962, 26, 192.
32. MATARAZZO, J. D., SASLOW, G. & MATARAZZO, R. G. The Interaction Chronograph as an Instrument for Objective Measurement of Interaction Patterns During Interviews. *J. of Psychol.*, 1956, 41, 347-367.
33. MOUSTAKAS, C. E., SIEGEL, I. E. & SCHALOCK, H. D. An Objective Method for the Measurement and Analysis of Child-Adult Interaction. *Child Develpm.*, 1956, 27, 109-134.
34. OURTH, L. & BROW, K. B. Inadequate Mothering and Disturbance in the Neonatal Period. *Child Develpm.*, 1961, 32, 287-295.
35. RABKIN, L. Y. The Patient's Family: Research Methods. *Family Process*, 1965, 4, 105-132.
37. SACKETT, G. P. Effects of Rearing Conditions upon the Behavior of Rhesus Monkeys (Macaca Mulatta). *Child Develpm.*, 1965, 36, 855-868.
38. STOLZ, L. M. Influences on Parent Behavior. Stanford, Calif., Stanford University Press, 1967.
39. WHITE, B. L. & HELD, R. Plasticity of Sensorimotor Development in the Human Infant. In The Causes of Behavior: Readings in Child Development and Educational Psychology, Rosenblith, J. F. and Allinsmith, W. (Eds.). Boston, Allyn & Bacon, 1966.
40. YARROW, L. J. Maternal Deprivation: Toward an Empirical and Conceptual Reevaluation. *Psychol. Bull.*, 1961, 58, 459-490.
41. YARROW, L. J. Research in Dimensions of Early Maternal Care. *Merrill-Palmer Quart.*, 1963, 9. 101-114.
42. ZUNICH, M. Relationship between Maternal Behavior and Attitudes Toward Children. *J. Genet. Psychol.*, 1962, 100, 155-165.

17

INFLUENCE OF PERINATAL DRUGS ON THE BEHAVIOR OF THE NEONATE

T. Berry Brazelton, M.D.

Clinical Assistant Professor, Harvard Medical School and
Childrens Hospital Medical Center
Boston, Massachusetts

Neonatal behavior has a potent influence on the development of his mother's reaction to the newborn infant, and may shape his future. Since his behavior at birth may be a reflection of his intrauterine and perinatal experiences, it seems important to try to define their effect. The psychoanalytic approach to child development has relied heavily on the environmental shaping of the child. I have found three aspects of the evolution of individual differences in behavior at birth which need further underlining:

1) the determining limitations of the structure of the genotype,
2) the influence of the first nine months of prenatal life in its shaping of the expression of the genotype—viz. the intrauterine experiences of the burgeoning fetus,
3) the kind of behavior which the neonate demonstrates in the first "imprinting" period of the mother-infant interaction as it determines their future course together. This alone can establish the importance of the intrauterine experience on the eventual outcome of the infant's personality potential.

THE GENOTYPE AND INTRAUTERINE INFLUENCES

The biological or hereditary structure of the individual is expressed by genes, which constitute the limits of his potentiality for development. We are becoming more aware of some of the fascinating variations in racial heredity which may be evidence of subtle differences in such genotypes (cf. Geber in Africa (1), Mexican Indian infants (2), Freedman's

Reprinted in part from *American Journal of Psychiatry,* 126, pp. 1261-1266, 1970. Copyright 1970, the American Psychiatric Association.

Japanese babies (3)). Whether or not the maintenance of individual characteristics in these cultures is based on the genotype or its environment is a fascinating question. Perhaps the kind of infant that she produces shapes the mother's reaction in a way that makes her mother her child the way she does; he evolves as a result of this interaction into a particular phenotype, and the culture is perpetuated.

But, there are recent studies which show that the expression of the genotype is heavily influenced by prenatal factors which affect the cellular structures of the fetus in a lasting fashion, and produce effects which later environmental influences cannot overcome. There seem to be "critical periods" for influencing cellular development and its potential for expression in the developing fetus. The formula for behavioral phenotype at birth becomes genotype X environment, and the first important environment is intrauterine.

Examples from recent literature of intrauterine influences which stir the imagination are:

1) Money *et al.* (4), studied ten patients who had the typical XY chromosomes of a male, but who had the external appearance of females at birth, and developed as females into adulthood. When they presented themselves for sterility studies, blind vaginal pouches, no uterus or ovaries, and abdominal undeveloped testicles proved their potential maleness. As adults, functioning as females, they were studied for female gender roles and identity. Other than an inability to reproduce or lactate, they were healthy normal females in their adjustment to life—sex life, mothering of adopted children, etc. This condition is known as fetal feminization of a male. It has been brought about by an insensitivity of the fetus to androgen at a cellular level. This lack of response to male hormones left the fetus sensitive to female hormones circulating from his mother. In early fetal life, neural organization was set in motion at a hypothalamic level which produced female genitalia, breast development at puberty, adult female sexual behavior, and female cycling after puberty, as well. Androgens have not reversed this when administered after puberty. Thus, the intrauterine conditioning of female hormones has essentially changed *for life* the male genotype into a female phenotype—behavior and all.

Another example of this can be demonstrated in rats. Androgens given to mothers during pregnancy have masculinized the infants even though they are female in genotype (5). In this vein, a commonly used female hormone, progesterone, which is used to prevent abortion in the female, is reported by Russell (6) to "over"-masculinize male infants, with mild to moderate hypertrophy of the penis and scrotum, exceptional muscularity and accelerated neuromuscular development with observable hyperkinesis. He reports that they are tense, irritable infants who demonstrated gastro-intestinal difficulties. Female infants may have an enlarged clitoris, and a pseudomasculine increase in neuromuscular mass, accompanied by behavior more vigorous than their control counterparts.

2) Zamenhof *et al.* (7) fed pregnant rats an 8% protein-insufficient diet, and the control group a normal diet. At birth, the offspring of the hypoproteinemic group had fewer brain cells (as demonstrated by DNA content of the brains), twice as little protein as expected for the size of the brain, as well as decreased birth weights. This decrease in brain cell number *and* in qualitative protein content of each cell confirms the hypothesis for CNS underdevelopment which has been raised in human groups beset with malnutrition in pregnant women. These quantitatively and qualitatively deficient brains are poorly adapted to normal development and must be more susceptible to any insult, however mild, of hypoxia, maternal depressant drugs and other paranatal events. So here is a double potential for change of the genotype's development—the numerically inadequate, undernourished brain cells coupled with hypersensitivity to insult.

3) Paradoxically, growth hormone given pregnant rats by Block *et al.* (8) seemed to increase the number of brain cells, as well as their problem-solving capacities.

4) Hurley (9) reports the results on the mouse fetus of manganese deficient maternal diets during pregnancy. The offspring had a congenital ataxia which was severe and irreversible—demonstrated by poor coordination and muscle balance, inability to right themselves from supine or in swimming, and constantly poor balancing as they walked. Since this syndrome mirrored the congenital ataxia which exists genotypically as a mutant in an albino strain of mice, these abnormal mice were fed large doses of manganese during their pregnancy. With an extra supply of this element, the offspring reverted to normal behavior. In this series of experiments, she demonstrates some of the phenotypic effects of dietary lack of a single element on the genotype. When the mutant genotype is unusual in its demand for nutrients, as in the albino mutant strain, supplying it in adequate amounts for the mutant gene results in a reversal of the abnormal phenotype. Such control of intrauterine effects on genetic cellular material suggests many new avenues for investigation if we are to understand abnormalities of the neonate.

5) The area of drug abuse in the adult and adolescent public raises issues about influencing fetal development which must be documented. The clinical defect which thalidomide babies demonstrated paved the way for more extensive investigation of maternal drugs' effect on the susceptible fetus. Again, critical periods of cellular development need to be taken into account if we are to understand such drug effects. Maternal ingestion of LSD resulted in infants with persisting chromosomal defects of their own which tended to repair incompletely, according to Dr. Cheston Berlin (10). No permanent structural or central nervous system defects were demonstrated in the sixteen neonates, but no analysis of their behavior other than a gross neurological examination was done. Future sterility and reproduction of congenital defects in next generation offspring may result from such

unrepaired chromosomal defects. Jacobsen (11) found a strik-
ingly high incidence of abortion (50%) in 75 LSD users with
major abnormalities of the fetuses demonstrated. He also confirmed the chromosomal flaws in mother and infant.

6)) Cases of narcotic addiction (morphine, heroin) in mothers are
reported resulting in withdrawal symptoms in their neonates of
restlessness, irritability, tremors, convulsions, sleeplessness, fever,
gastroenteritis, yawning and sneezing in the first week and until
the appropriate drug is given to counteract these symptoms (12,
13). Codeine withdrawal symptoms have been reported by Van
Leewen (14). Acute alcohol withdrawal in infants in this country (15) and in a Yukon Indian baby (16) led to fever, alternating twitching and lethargy, and hyperbilirubinemia in the
neonatal period.

7) Aspirin in large doses given the mother just prior to delivery
has been demonstrated to cause a decrease in albumin binding
capacity and to increase the danger of brain damage from hyperbilirubinemia in the infant (17).

8) Tranquilizers such as reserpine, meprobamate, and chlorpromazine given to pregnant animals have been demonstrated by
Hoffeld *et al.* (18) to affect both the birth weight and response
to learning tasks of their infants. The time in pregnancy of
administration of the drugs had an important influence—controls
> mid > late > early. Young (19) showed that these animals
were markedly susceptible to stress in the neonatal period. Any
stress added to their environment in the first 30 days (another
critical period) resulted in animals who had permanent and
more severe learning defects. Ordy *et al.* (20) showed a decrease
in liver glycogen as a result of prenatal chlorpromazine which
might result in an impaired response of the organism to stress
reaction and mobilization of glycogen stores. Too few of these
investigations have been applied to human pregnancy and
offspring.

9) The influence of pesticides on the fetus and neonate is being
investigated in birds and animals by Khera and Clegg (21).
They find teratologic effects from high doses, which result from
1. direct neurotoxicity and, 2. an interference with maternal fetal
membrane function and resultant intracellular damage in the
developing fetus. Since maternal and fetal tissues store these
pesticides and their metabolities, and there is a concentrating
increase in maternal milk in the human, we may suspect subclinical damage in the human infant similar to that reported in
birds and animals.

PERINATAL MEDICATION

My interest in medication effects on the neonate was initiated by the
observation of neonates who had scored excellent Apgars (22) in the
delivery room, and remained clinically responsive for half an hour (long
enough to be sent to the nursery downstairs). After this initial period
of responsiveness (which I postulate is largely due to the neonate's

ability to mobilize his resources to respond to the stimulation of labor, delivery, and the onslaught of new environmental stimuli), these newborns went rapidly into a state of relative unresponsiveness. They became unresponsive to any but very disturbing stimuli with little motor activity, and slowed heart and respiratory rates. They demonstrated poor circulatory responses to the relative hypoxia which was present in their circulatory and central nervous systems, and their responses to oxygen-threatening events such as mucus in their airways became impaired. This depressed behavior lasted for a few hours to a day, and then not-so-gradually tapered off; subclinical behavior manifestations could be demonstrated for as much as a week in many infants (23).

Now that there is evidence in pediatric literature for a beneficial decrease of total serum bilirubin concentration in newborn infants after phenobarbitone is given perinatally to the mothers (24), there is a trend to ignore other side effects and to recommend higher doses of sedative drugs even in complicated deliveries (25). Wilson (26) has urged caution in acceptance of pediatric routine use of barbiturates in treatment of anticipated hyperbilirubinemia. He points to the other side effects on cellular metabolism which may be subtler and overlooked in our zeal to avoid exchange transfusions. For example, toxic effects on the liver may result in:

1. an increase in liver enzymes which render other drugs ineffective, (e.g. digitoxin, dilantin),
2. an increase in sterol production and hormone metabolism which may produce undesirable androgenic and estrogenic supereffects (comparable to the overmasculizing or feminizing effects mentioned earlier) may bring about subclinical results in many infants which we cannot detect.

Since the exact mechanism of the barbiturate's action on the neonate is still unclear, he urges caution and a continued search for drugs which are more specific in treatment of such neonatal conditions as bilirubinemia.

The ready transmission of barbiturates to the fetus from the mother is well-known. When the cord is cut, his circulating level is 70% of hers (27), but his liver, kidneys, and tissue storage differs markedly from hers. His immature kidneys excrete drugs poorly and his liver is taken up with deconjugation of bilirubin and maternal hormones for which barbiturates must compete for detoxification (28, 29). Ploman and Persson (30) found that the selective tissue storage of depressant drugs such as barbiturates was many times higher in the midbrain than in the circulating blood. And last of all, this selective storage lasted for as much as a week in the immature brain and affected the CNS reactions and the midbrain-mediated behavior of the neonate all of that time.

But, since these infants survive and there are no clinical evidences of CNS damage demonstrable with grossly inadequate neurological techniques in these neonates, premedication of mothers in labor is an accepted obstetrical practice. Little is done to change it.

Recent studies conclusively demonstrate subtle but transient effects of medication on the neonate. Borgstedt and Rosen (31) found meperidine (50-100 mgm.) and promethazine (25-50 mgm.) in accepted premedicating doses caused impairment of behavioral states (on Prechtl and Beintema's scale (32)) in 29 of 33 babies of medicated mothers versus 1 of 8 nonmedicated at 1-2 days of age. EEG alterations were

	MEDICATED MOTHERS	NON-MEDICATED MOTHERS
BEHAVIORAL STATE		
IMPAIRED:	29	1
NOT IMPAIRED:	4	7
NEWBORN EEG		
ALTERED:	28	1
NOT ALTERED:	5	7
BOTH BEHAVIOR AND EEG		
ALTERED:	24	1
NOT ALTERED:	1	7

from BORGSTEDT and ROSEN

FIGURE 1.—EEG and behavioral effects of medication (from Borgstedt and Rosen 31, copyright 1968: American Medical Association.)

present in 28 of these versus 1 of the 8 controls. Behavioral impairment disappeared in all but 3, two days later, but EEG alterations persisted for a week in 10 of them. All of these infants had excellent Apgars at delivery, and all were normal later in a neurological evaluation (Figure 1).

Kron *et al.* (33) demonstrated that newborn sucking behavior was depressed for 4 days after delivery by routine maternal medication—depressed in sucking rate, pressure, and in amount of consumption.

I found a 24-48 hour lag in the neonate's ability to adapt to the breast feeding situation from maternal medication, as reported by 41 multiparous mothers who had nursed before (14 were low, 27 high medication—scopolamine $>.04$, barbiturates >150 mgm. 1-6 hours prior to delivery (34). A 24-hour delay in weight gain confirmed this (Figure 2).

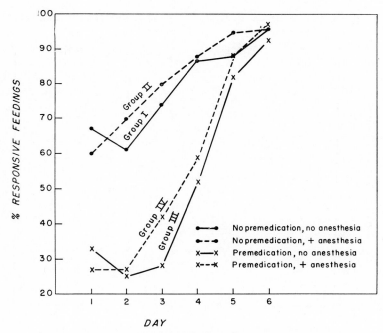

FIGURE 2.—Effects of premedication and anesthesia on breast
feeding responsiveness (from Brazelton 34)

The inhalant anesthesia given mothers affected the infant relatively little,
and Figure 3 summarizes the barbiturate effect. Mothers were asked to
score them for 1) initial alertness, 2) difficulty in rousing them to institute active nursing, 3) how long they could maintain a state appropriate
for feeding, with the usual stimulation. All these infants were normal
neurologically on subsequent follow-up.

"The data for the first day in Figure 3 are based on a single feeding, and it must be recognized that there may be many variables
in addition to the barbiturate premedication given the mother
which can influence the results obtained. In this group of babies,
the reports show a wide divergence in responsiveness to the feeding situation on the first day. Sixty-five% of the feedings in Groups
I and II were effective; but in Groups III and IV only thirty%
were effective. There is an early significant difference between the
responsiveness of babies whose mothers were given little or no
barbiturate premedication according to these data (reliability of
the difference between the two groups is equal to 0.03).
On the second day, the data are based on two feedings, hence it
has more significance in denoting a difference in responsiveness
of the two combined groups of babies. In the group whose mothers
had little premedication, feedings were sixty-five% effective. Only

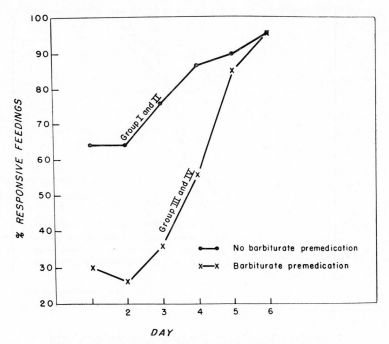

FIGURE 3.—Barbiturate effect on breast feeding responses
(from Brazelton 34)

twenty-five% of the feedings were successful in the more heavily
medicated group. This difference of sixty-five% versus twenty-five%
shows a reliable significance of p = .002.

On the third day, the two groups varied considerably in their
responsiveness to feedings—seventy-five% were successful in the
group with little medication, in contrast to thirty-five% in the
more heavily medicated group. Since there were three feedings per
day, the significant difference shows a reliability of p = .001.

On the fourth day, the infants in the group with little premedication responded to eighty-seven% of the feeding situations, whereas those in the more heavily medicated group showed responsiveness
to fifty-five%. Based on five feedings in each group, there was a
significant difference with a reliability of p = .001.

By the fifth and sixth days, the infants in each group were reported to be awake and alert in most of the feeding situations (over
eighty-five%), and there was no significant difference in their
ability to nurse.

In the two groups of babies, whose mothers received little or no
barbiturates, the number of effective feedings increased from sixty%
on the first two days to more than seventy-five% on the third day,
and to eighty-seven% by the fourth day.

In the groups of babies whose mothers received large doses of barbiturates prior to delivery, there was a five-day interval before eighty-five% of their daily feedings were successful.

Thus there seems to be a marked difference in the effectiveness of the early postnatal feedings in the two groups, and a difference of forty-eight hours between the two groups in attaining effective feedings in seventy-five% of the daily trials.

Figure 4 shows the twenty-four hour difference between the two groups (p significance beyond the .001 level) in the beginning of effective weight gain of the babies.

Several conjectures may be made for this significant difference in the beginning of weight gain in these babies. They include: 1) a difference in the mother's ability to awaken the baby because of effects of medication on her, 2) less effective stimulation of the breast by the sleepy baby so that milk production is delayed, 3) a delaying effect of medication on the production of milk, and, 4) a delay due to medication of the neonate's physiologic ability to utilize breast milk." (From Brazelton [34])

My concern is for subtler effects on the early mother-infant relationship, and how much it may be affected by depressant drugs at a critical time in their interaction when such processes as "imprinting" or sets of mind may be involved. This was demonstrated by two mothers and their infants that we studied in detail over the first week for a longitudinal study (23). Marked differences in their recovery rates were noted despite similar doses of premedication given the mothers (seconal: 200 mgm. at 3 hours, demerol; 125 mgm. in one, and thorazine; 25 mgm. in the other: phenergan; 25 mgm I.M. 1½ hours prior to delivery in the alert mother) (Figure 5). Evaluation consisted of three kinds of observations:

"1. For a half hour the infant was observed in a quiet room without any scheduled presentation of stimuli. We concentrated on movement and state changes in response to:
   1) internal stimuli (where possible to assess, such as gastro-intestinal activity, mucus, etc.) ;
   2) random external stimuli, such as environmental noise, light changes etc.
   3) certain more structured stimuli which were part of the mother's care and handling of her infant:
      a) tactile—stroking around the mouth, on the belly and extremities, restraint, and uncovering;
      b) kinesthetic—handling and changing the infant's position in the crib, holding, rocking, cuddling;
      c) auditory—reaction to voice, rattle, bell;
      d) visual—human face, red ball, flashlight, and room light changes;
      e) sucking—on a finger cot, pacifier, and sugar water.

   We were particularly interested in the quality of the infant's responses. His ability to attend to each stimulus, to focus all or part of his attention, and to damp out or modulate repeated

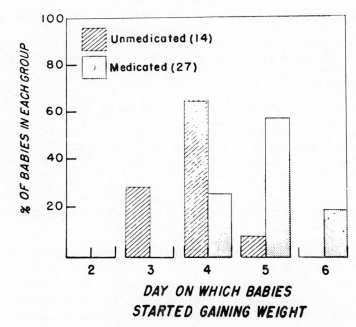

FIGURE 4.—From Brazelton 34.

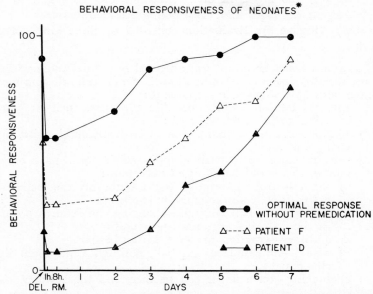

FIGURE 5.—From Brazelton & Robey 23.

responses was assessed. The build up of tension with repeated stimulation and the changes in the state of consciousness as he roused or slept, as well as the mode of state changes, were all of major interest in these "unstructured" periods of observation. The stimuli were not presented by predetermined schedule either in timing or in frequency of presentation. They were offered when it seemed most possible to produce the infant's optimal response to the stimulus within the limitations of his state of consciousness. We attempted to evaluate each stimulus response within several different states.

2. Structured behavioral neurological evaluation—This aspect of the infant's daily evaluation included a classical neurological examination (Andre-Thomas and Sainte-Anne, 1960; Paine, 1960) plus a series of behavioral tests designed by Graham et al. (1956). The structure of presentation was flexible and again, attempted to bring out the infant's optimal response. Initial state of responsiveness was determined as a base line for further observation. Spontaneous movements were observed and recorded, e.g., quantity, tempo, freedom and fluidity of movement, tremulousness, jerkiness, predominant or repeated patterns, frequency and type of startles, and preferred positions.

   In addition to the detection of abnormalities, we were concerned with the *quality* of the infant's responses, i.e., his capacity to attend and focus on them, to modulate or to damp out repeated responses along with changes in states of consciousness as the test situation continued. His irritability, vigor or apathy, over-all maturity, and organization were assessed on each daily examination.

3. Evaluation of autonomic responsiveness—In three days, a series of photic stimuli were presented in a structured electro-physiological observation period. A three-second light stimulus at intervals of sixty seconds was presented for twenty times. This period was designed to record the heart rate, respiratory rate, EEG, and behavioral responses to repeated stimulation.* The observations were made on successive days giving us an opportunity to evaluate the effect of maturation on the systems.

   Of interest in our evaluation of these infants were differences between them in cardiac and respiratory base rates, responsiveness to stimulation as reflected in these various parameters, and the infant's ability to suppress repeated responses." (From Brazelton [38], Copyright 1970, the American Psychiatric Association.)

The mothers had a paradoxical reaction to that of their infants, the more "depressed" infant delivered by a wide awake mother and vice versa. This paradoxical action of drugs suggests many things—difference in tissue storage and receptivity, both in mother and infant, storage by the mother protecting the infant, etc. There was little doubt but

---

* These observations are comparable to the data collected for a larger group of infants studied at the Boston Lying-In-Hospital, as part of Grant ♯BP2372, "Perinatal Factors in the Origin of Cerebral Palsy and Mental Retardation."

that the drugs affected the imprinting responses in both of these mothers and infants.

I would like to refer to Bowlby's (35) concept of imprinting as it affects maternal behavior and the early mother-infant attachment. Animal experiments suggest the importance of this critical neonatal period in making their relationship. Hess (36) has demonstrated a delayed latency of acquisition of initial imprinting performance of chicks by meprobamate given the neonatal chick. Kovach (37) found that sympathetic drugs given early (amphetamine and epinephrine) facilitated initial following behavior and increased the strength and duration of the imprinting. They postulated that any agent which produced general activation of the CNS would lead to the same results, and conversely that any depressant drug might delay and reduce the strength of the imprinting behavior.

The importance of re-evaluating "routine" use of drugs prenatally and perinatally must be stressed. The subtle subclinical effects on developing embryonic tissue and on sensitive neural organization in the fetus and neonate may be of lasting importance to future development. Watching a drugged mother and a depressed infant who must make a go with each other should make us re-evaluate the "routine" use of premedication and anesthesia at delivery, in the light of its effect on the early mother-infant interaction, as well as its lasting effect on the subsequent outcome of their lives together.

REFERENCES

1. GEBER, M. & DEAN, R. A. F.: The state of development of newborn African children. *Lancet,* 1, 1216 (1957).
2. BRAZELTON, T. B., ROBEY, J. S., & COLLIER, G. A.: Infant development in the Zinacanteco Indians of southern Mexico. *Pediatrics,* 44, 274 (1969).
3. FREEDMAN, D. G., WASHBURN, S. L., & JAY, P. C.: *Perspectives in Human Evolution.* Holt, Rinehart, Chicago (1968).
4. MONEY, J., EHRDARDT, A. A., & MASICA, D. N.: Fetal femininization induced by androgen insensitivity in the testicular feminizing syndrome: Effect on marriage and maternalism. *Johns Hopkins Med. J.,* 123, 105 (1968).
5. FEDER, H. C., PHOENIX, C. H., & YOUNG, W. C.: Suppression of feminine behavior by administration of testosterone propionate to neonatal rats. *J. Endocrinol.,* 34, 131 (1966).
6. RUSSELL, A.: Progesterone is harmful to male fetus; report in *Pediatric News,* p. 1, January, 1969.
7. ZAMENHOFF, S., VAN MARTHENS, E., & MARGOLIS, F. L.: DNA (cell number) and protein in neonatal brain: Alteration by maternal dietary restriction. *Science,* 160, 322 (1968).
8. BLOCK, J. B. & ESSMAN, W. B.: Growth hormone administration during pregnancy; a behavioral difference in offspring rats. *Nature,* 205, 1136 (1965).
9. HURLEY, L. S.: Maternal Zinc and Manganese Deficiency and Fetus Development. Symposium on Fetal Malnutrition, Foundation March of Dimes, New York, Jan. 28, 1970.
10. BERLIN, C. M.: Effects of LSD taken by pregnant women on chromosomal abnormalities of offspring; report in *Pediatric Herald,* p. 1, January and February, 1969.

11. JACOBSEN, C. S.: Association between LSD in pregnancy and fetal defects. Personal communication (1969).

12. COBRINIK, R. W., HOOD, R. T., JR., & CHUSID, E.: Effect of maternal narcotic addiction on the newborn infant. *Pediatrics, 24,* 288 (1959).

13. HENLEY, W. L., & FITCH, G. R.: Newborn narcotic withdrawal associated with regional enteritis in pregnancy. *N. Y. J. Med., 66,* 2565 (1966).

14. VAN LEEWEN, G., GUTHRIE, R., & STANGE, F.: Narcotic withdrawal reaction in a newborn infant due to codeine. *Pediatrics, 36,* 635 (1965).

15. NICHOLS, M. M.: Acute alcohol withdrawal syndrome in a newborn. *Am. J. Dis. Child., 113,* 714 (1967).

16. SCHAEFFER, D.: Alcohol withdrawal syndrome in a newborn of a Yukon Indian mother. *Canad. Med. Assoc. J., 87,* 1333 (1962).

17. PALMISANO, P. & CASSIDY, G.: Aspirin linked to diminished binding capacity in neonates; report in *Pediatric Herald,* p. 1, January 10, 1969.

18. HOFFELD, D. R., McNEW, J., & WEBSTER, R. L.: Effect of tranquilizing drugs during pregnancy on activity of offspring. *Nature, 218,* 357 (1968).

19. YOUNG, R. D.: Effects of differential early experiences and neonatal tranquilization on later behavior. *Psychol. Rep., 17,* 675 (1965).

20. ORDY, J. M., SAMARAJSKI, T., & COLLINS, R. L.: Prenatal chlorpromazine effects on liver, survival, and behavior of mice offspring. *J. Pharmacol. Exp. Ther., 151,* 110 (1966).

21. KHERA, K. S. & CLEGG, D. J.: Perinatal toxicity of pesticides. *Canad. Med. Assn. J., 100,* 167 (1969).

22. APGAR, V.: A proposal for a new method of evaluation of the newborn infant. *Curr. Research Anesthesia Analgesia, 32,* 260 (1960).

23. BRAZELTON, T. B. & ROBEY, J. S.: Observations of neonatal behavior. The effects of perinatal variables, in particular that of maternal medication. *J. Ch. Psychiat., 4,* 613 (1965).

24. TROLLE, D.: Decrease of total serum bilirubin concentration in newborn infants after phenobarbitone treatment. *Lancet, 2,* 705 (1968).

25. TROLLE, D.: A possible drop in first week mortality rate for low birthweight infants after phenobarbitone treatment. *Lancet, 2,* 1123 (1968).

26. WILSON, J. T.: Phenobarbital in the perinatal period. *Pediatrics, 43,* 324 (1969).

27. BAKER, J. B. E.: The effects of drugs on the fetus. *Pharmacol. Revue, 12,* 37 (1960).

28. FOUTS, J. R. & ADAMSON, R. H.: Drug metabolism in the newborn rabbit. *Science, 129,* 897 (1959).

29. JONDORF, W. R., MAICKEL, R. P., & BRODIE, B. B.: Inability of newborn mice and guinea pigs to metabolize drugs. *Biochem. Pharm., 1,* 352 (1958).

30. PLOMAN, L. & PERSSON, B.: On the transfer of barbiturates to the human fetus and their accumulation in some of its vital organs. *J. Obst. and Gynecol. Brit. Emp., 64,* 714 (1957).

31. BORGSTEDT, A. D. & ROSEN, M. G.: Medication during labor correlated with behavior and EEG of the newborn. *Am. J. Dis. Child., 115,* 21 (1968).

32. PRECHTL, H. & BEINTEMA, D.: *The Neurological Examination of the Full Term Normal Infant.* Little Club Clinics in Developmental Medicine, No. 12, Heineman, London (1964).

33. KRON, R. E., STEIN, M., & GODDARD, K. E.: Newborn sucking behavior affected by obstetric sedation. *Pediatrics, 37,* 1012 (1966).

34. BRAZELTON, T. B.: Psychophysiologic reactions in the neonate: II. Effect of maternal medication on the neonate and his behavior. *J. Pediat., 58,* 513-518 (1961).

35. BOWLBY, J.: *Attachment and Loss.* Vol. I: Attachment. Basic Books, New York (1969).

36. HESS, E. H.: Effects of meprobamate on imprinting in waterfowl. *Ann. N. Y. Acad. Sci., 67,* 724 (1957).

37. KOVACH, J.: Effects of autonomic drugs on imprinting. *J. Comp. Physiol. Psychol., 57,* 183 (1964).

38. BRAZELTON, T. B.: Effect of Prenatal Drugs on the Behavior of the Neonate, *Am. J. Psych., 126,* 1261-66 (1970).

18

FURTHER CONSIDERATIONS RE-GARDING MATERNAL PERCEPTION OF THE FIRST BORN

Elsie R. Broussard, M.D., Dr.P.H.

Associate Professor of Public Health Psychiatry and Head of the Community Mental Health Program, Graduate School of Public Health; Assistant Professor of Child Psychiatry, School of Medicine, and Adjunct-Member of the Staff of Western Psychiatric Institute and Clinic, University of Pittsburgh

and

Miriam Sergay Sturgeon Hartner, M.D.

Adjunct Assistant Professor of the Community Mental Health Program, Graduate School of Public Health, and Clinical Instructor of Child Psychiatry, School of Medicine, University of Pittsburgh

When a woman becomes a mother she has certain expectations as to what kind of mother she will be and what kind of child she will have. After delivery the mother-child relationship develops into a cyclical system. The mother provides the environment critical to the child's survival. Her sensitivity to the infant's needs enables her to provide an optimum environment to foster a healthy development. The way the mother relates to the child will be modified by her perception of his appearance and behavior. His behavior will, in turn, be affected by her handling of him.

These assumptions have led us to focus on the mother's perception of her infant. This paper will review the development of our longitudinal study of mothers and their first-borns, and discuss the implication of changes in maternal perception.

Historically many have felt that the time just before and following

The authors wish to express their gratitude to Sara Arnaud, Ph.D., Naomi Ragins, M.D., Lucy Zabarenko, Ph.D., Mrs. Fredricka Latshaw, Mr. Ted Grice, and Mrs. Karen Picard for their generous assistance.

432

birth is significant in setting patterns of the interaction between mother and child which may continue for long afterwards (1, 2, 3). The phase of relative undifferentiation of the early neonatal period has drawn the attention of many persons concerned both with general problems of development, including behavioral and physiological activities and with the more limited area of ego development during infancy.

In order to study the psychosomatic differentiation during infancy, Greenberg divided the infant's gross behavioral states into four categories: 1) sleeping, 2) minimal random activity, 3) moderate random activity, 4) extreme random activity (4). He then measured the cardiac rate in a group of neonates, during the first five neonatal days and again at the late neonatal period, seven to twenty-one days.

During the first five days, cardiac rate failed to differentiate the two behavioral states of sleep and minimal random activity. This was seen as reflecting a level of organization in which observed arousal states are not adequately influential in altering certain physiological activities. During the late neonatal phase, seven to twenty one days, however, Greenberg noted significant differences in the cardiac rate during sleep and states of minimal and extreme random activity.

In another study, he compared behavioral reactions and cardiac rate changes and responses to pacification in two groups of infants. One group lived in a nursery; the other lived within a family unit. No differences existed between the groups for each of the pacification techniques in the early neonatal period. Distinction could be observed in the late neonatal phase, however. In addition, the "family" infants established significant intermodality differences at an earlier age than did the "nursery" infants, indicating earlier differentiation of these behavioral responses. The finding that the organization of response patterns appeared earlier in the family infants lends testimony to the integrative aspects of mothering.

In developing his theory of the parent-infant relationship, Winnicott (5) said:

> "One half of the theory of the parent-infant relationship concerns the infant and is the theory of the infant's journey from absolute dependence, through relative dependence, to independence and in parallel the infant's journey from the pleasure principle to the reality principle and from autoeroticism to object relationships. The other half of the theory of the parent-infant relationship concerns maternal care. That is to say the qualities and changes in the mother that meet the specific and developing needs of the infant toward whom she orientates."

He also stated: (1) that the infant and maternal care together form a unit, (2) that whenever one finds an infant one finds maternal care, and (3) that without maternal care there would be no infant (5).

Brody has postulated that the mother's unconscious attitude to her child is expressed by the way in which she responds to the child's successive stages of maturation (6). She also states that the primary autonomous ego functions can only come into being if there is facilitation from the environment. In the film, "Mother-Infant Interaction" she presents vignettes of seven patterns of mothering which center around feeding. The ratings were based upon clinical observations in regard to categories of Empathy, Efficiency, and Control. In this film she illustrates examples of mother-infant interaction which she suggests are reflected in the child's behavior at one year of age.

Coleman, Kris and Provence have described variations in parental attitude to the child, continuously influenced by the child's growth and development (7). They suggest that the adaptability of the parents may "gain importance in early diagnosis of expected difficulties."

Our longitudinal study provides evidence that the mother's early perception of her first-born is in fluid state. Before presenting a more detailed comment of these early changes, we will describe some of the thinking which went into the development of the instruments of measurement.

In our culture, great emphasis is placed on "being better than average." Therefore, it seemed logical to assume that mothers, delivering healthy, full-term first born infants, would expect their babies to be better than average. Using the mother's concept of the average baby as an anchor for comparison of her own infant's behavior, Broussard devised the Neonatal Perception Inventories. These represented a measure of the mother's perception of the average baby and her own baby. (See Appendix I). The behavioral items included in these Inventories were: crying, spitting, feeding, elimination, sleeping, and predictability. These items were selected on the basis of past clinical experience with the concerns young mothers expressed about their babies.

These inventories were completed by 318 primiparae on the first or second postpartum day (Time I) while they were still in the hospital. Of these, 46.5% rated their infants as better than average. The Perception Inventories were again administered when the infants were approximately one month of age (Time II).* At this time 61.2% of the women rated their infants as better than average. Thus, we were able to compare data collected at two points in time.

One of our hypotheses was that mothers who originally rated their babies as not being better than average at Time I would experience

---

* At the end of the neonatal period home visits were made by trained interviewers. None were made by the investigators. The average age of the infants at the time of this interview (Time II) was 32.3 days. The median age was 29.9 days and the standard deviation was 2.59. At this time the mothers completed the Neonatal Perception Inventory II, the Degree of Bother Inventory, and Schaefer's Postnatal Research Inventory to assess maternal attitudes, e.g. Depression, Irritability.

a dissonance between their expectations of the average baby and perception of their babies immediately after delivery. One could further expect that these mothers would attempt to reduce the dissonance.** Those who were successful in doing so were expected to have low problem scores at Time II. On the other hand, if mothers were unable to reduce the dissonance or if they experienced an increase in dissonance, the problem score would be expected to be high.

Since the threshold of parental annoyance varies widely in accordance with a parent's emotional orientation to the child, the ultimate decision as to what constitutes a problem for a specific mother varies among mothers. In order to measure problems in infant behavior, a Degree of Bother Inventory was designed. (See Appendix II). This assessed the degree to which mothers were bothered by their infants' behavior in regard to the same six behavioral items, and was administered when the infants were one month old.

Relation of Maternal Perception of the Neonate to Problems in Infant Behavior

The maternal perception of her infant at Time I was not correlated with problems in infant behavior at one month of age. However, the perception of her infant at Time II was correlated with the problems in infant behavior at one month of age. Those mothers who rated their infants as better than average were less bothered by their infants' behavior than those mothers who did not view their infants as better than average (X^2 sig. at $P<.001$).

Relationship of Other Maternal Attitudes to Maternal Perception

Schaefer's Postnatal Research Inventory was completed by the mothers when the infants were one month old (Time II) (8). Data were analyzed for the six scales having the highest internal consistency reliabilities.* Dichotomizing at the mean score of each scale, the values were allocated to high or low attitude scale scores. These were then analyzed to see if a relation existed to the maternal perception of her infant at Time I and Time II. None of the six scales were correlated with the mother's perception of her infant at Time I. However, at Time II the maternal perception of her infant was associated with the Depression, Negative Aspects of Child Rearing and Irritability Scales. The X^2 values were 8.58 $P<.01$; 7.25 $P<.01$; 21.45 $P<.001$ respectively. The Mother's

---

** See Festinger, Leon. *A Theory of Cognitive Dissonance.* Evanston, Ill., Row Peterson, 1957.

* These were the Depression, Negative Aspects of Child Rearing, Irritability, Need for Reassurance, Fear or Concern for the Baby and the Mother's Psychosomatic Symptom Anxiety scales.

Psychosomatic Symptom Anxiety Scale approached significance at the $P < .05$ level with a X^2 of 3.30 (significant value is 3.88). Mothers who had not rated their babies as better than average scored higher on these attitude scales than mothers who did view their babies as better than average.

Stimulus for Further Research

The findings: 1) that changes occur in the maternal perception of the first-born during the first month of life; 2) that 40% of the mothers did not view their one-month old infants positively; 3) that the Degree of Bother Inventory and several of Schaefer's maternal attitude scales were correlated with maternal perception at Time II but not at Time I suggested that the maternal perception of her infant at Time II could serve as a predictive instrument to identify a group of primiparae whose infants would be at High-Risk for subsequent emotional disorder (9, 10).

Infants were categorized as High-Risk if their mothers did not perceive their behavior as better than average at Time II. Infants whose mothers had rated their behavior as better than average at Time II were identified as Low-Risk. All data were coded and handled in a blind manner by research assistants. The senior author had no knowledge of the risk ratings assigned to individual cases. Thus it was possible to conduct a blind follow-up study to test the hypothesis that measurement of the mother's perception of the neonate at one month of age could serve as an instrument to identify those children at High-Risk for subsequent emotional and developmental deviations. The results of this research and the details of the study design have been reported elsewhere (11). Only a brief resumé of data will be presented here in order that the reader can follow the subsequent discussion.

Relationship of Maternal Perception of the Neonate to Later Development

When the children were between four years and six months and four years and ten months, the authors completed clinical evaluations on 85 of the original study population of first-borns. These evaluations were conducted in a blind manner. Neither of the investigators had prior knowledge of the risk categories of the children. The classification proposed by the G.A.P. Committee on Child Psychiatry was used as a frame of reference to formulate the diagnoses.*

---

* The major diagnostic categories of the primary diagnosis assigned to the 85 children were as follows: 60.0% had Healthy Responses; 30.6% had Developmental Deviations; 3.5% were diagnosed as Psychotic Disorders (mild). The remaining 5.9% were divided among the Psychoneurotic, Psychophysiologic, Personality, and Reactive Disorders.

The children were then divided into categories according to an apparent need for therapeutic intervention. A X^2 test for association was done to determine the relation of the Probability of Risk rating of the child established at one month of age and the need for intervention. A statistically significant association was evident between the prediction and outcome. $X^2 = 16.432$ P$<$.001. More infants in the High-Risk group needed therapeutic intervention at age $4\frac{1}{2}$ than did those in the low-Risk group.

The mother's perception of her infant as measured by the Perception Inventories on the first or second postpartum day did not prove to be related to the subsequent development of the child at age $4\frac{1}{2}$.

When both the ratings attained at the immediate postpartum period (Time I) and one month of age (Time II) are used as a predictive instrument, their combined predictive ability is somewhat greater than when Time II is used alone.

These data are shown in Table 1.

TABLE 1

PERCENTAGE DISTRIBUTION OF THE NEED FOR INTERVENTION
AT AGE $4\frac{1}{2}$ ACCORDING TO MATERNAL PERCEPTION

Maternal Perception - Time I		Need for Intervention	
		Yes	No
Positive	N = 31	N = 12 / 38.7%	N = 19 / 61.3%
Negative	N = 54	N = 22 / 40.8%	N = 32 / 59.8%

Maternal Perception - Time II			
Positive	N = 49	N = 10 / 20.4%	N = 39 / 79.6%
Negative	N = 36	N = 24 / 66%	N = 12 / 34%

Combined Maternal Perception Time I Time II			
Positive Positive N = 17		N = 3 / 17.6%	N = 14 / 82.4%
Negative Positive N = 32		N = 7 / 21.9%	N = 25 / 78.1%
Positive Negative N = 14		N = 9 / 64.2%	N = 5 / 35.8%
Negative Negative N = 22		N = 15 / 68.2%	N = 7 / 31.8%

438   *Exceptional Infant: Studies in Abnormalities*

If the mother has a positive perception of her infant at either Time I or II, her child is less likely to need intervention than if she consistently maintains a negative perception of her infant at both times. Of the infants who were viewed as better than average at both Time I and Time II by their mothers, 82.4% were diagnosed as healthy at age 4½. This is in marked contrast to those infants who were not viewed as better than average by their mothers at either Time I or Time II. Of this group, only 31.8% were classified as healthy at age 4½.

Fifty-four percent of the primiparae shifted the perception of their infants from Time I to Time II. Of the 31 mothers who had a positive perception of their infants at Time I, 17 (54.8%) maintained this positive perception. Of the 54 mothers who did not see their babies as better than average at Time I, 32 (59.3%) did view them as better than average at Time II. These data are shown in Table 2.

TABLE 2

CHANGE IN THE MOTHER'S PERCEPTION OF HER BABY FROM
TIME I TO TIME II

Maternal Perception at Time I	No.	%	Maternal Perception at Time II			
			No. Postive	%	No. Negative	%
Positive	31	36.5%	17	54.8%	14	45.2%
Negative	54	63.5%	32	59.3%	22	40.7%
Total	85	100.0%	49	57.6%	36	42.4%

Relation of Schaefer's Postnatal Research Inventory to the Need for Intervention at 4½

High maternal scores on the Psychosomatic Anxiety Symptom, Depression, and Negative Aspects of Child Rearing Scales were associated with the need for intervention at age 4½ years. X^2 values were 6.85 $P<.01$; 6.31 $P<.02$; 4.43 $P<.05$ respectively. The X^2 value for Irritability was 3.80 approaching significance at the $P<.05$ level (significant value is 3.88).

Other Selected Variables

The need for intervention and the probability of risk were not related to the educational level of mother or father, the father's occupation, changes in income since delivery, prenatal or postpartum complications, type of delivery, age of mother at delivery, religious preference of the mother, moves, or sex of the child.

Health History of the Child Since Birth

Each mother rated her child's health at 4½ years on a 5-point scale designated excellent, very good, average, fair, and poor. A greater proportion of mothers whose infants were at Low-Risk viewed their preschool children as having had "Excellent" health than those whose neonates had been considered at High-Risk. (Sig. $P<.001$). The specific illnesses experienced by the children did not differ between the High and Low-Risk groups.

Health of Mother Since Delivery

Mothers rated their own health since delivery on a similar 5-point scale. Again there were differences between the groups in the way the mothers perceived their health. More mothers with Low-Risk infants viewed their own health as "Excellent" than did mothers of High-Risk infants. (Sig. $P<.05$). There was no difference in the nature, severity or frequency of occurrence of the illnesses between the groups to account for this. One can postulate that the psychic reality for mothers of High-Risk infants may be generally less positive and less optimistic. For whatever reason, the mothers of infants at High-Risk lacked the sense of well-being required to view their health or the health of their children as "Excellent." Their perception of health appears quite subjective and not based on the absolute frequency of occurrence or nature of the illnesses.

Among the population studied, the critical variable associated with need for intervention appears to be the mother's perception of her infant at one month of age.

SUMMARY DISCUSSION

The primipara's perception of her infant as compared to the average infant on the first or second postpartum day did not serve as a predictor of the child's subsequent development. This suggests that her earliest perceptions of her infant are based on fantasy. The nature of the fantasy is a highly individual matter which may reflect her sense of self or her identification with other objects in her life.

At this point in time, some of the infant's physiological measurements are unreliable. These inconsistencies may be such that a reliable feedback system is not possible. During this period of relative undifferentiation of the infant, the mother needs to be able to identify with the infant's primitive needs and yet be able to maintain her own reality orientation. Winnicott describes a state of heightened sensitivity to the infant's needs as "primary maternal preoccupation" (12). He believes that if a mother is to permit the infant to come into being she must be able to successfully enter into and complete this state of "normal illness."

The primipara's perception of her infant at one month of age was related to the child's subsequent development. There was less psychopathology evident at age $4\frac{1}{2}$ among the children viewed as better than average by their mothers at one month of age than among those not viewed as better than average. Apparently the processes for successful mother-child interaction have been set in motion by the time the child is one month old. Something appears to have been established that is predictive of subsequent development. Our data indicate how early a certain "set" is made. Many things happen to children (and their mothers) between the time of delivery and age $4\frac{1}{2}$. A mother who has good coping ability can see the child through most of them. Admittedly there are thresholds of tolerance to life stresses; however there was no relation between the frequency of occurrence of acts of fate during the pregnancy and the first month post partum and the mother's perception of her child at one month of age. Nor was there an association between the need for intervention at $4\frac{1}{2}$ and factors such as surgery, moves, or changes in finances.

Mothers who perceived their one-month old babies as better than average tended to score lower on the Depression, Irritability, Negative Aspects of Child Rearing and the Psychosomatic Anxiety Symptom scales than those who did not see their babies as better than average. A greater proportion of them considered their infant's health to be "Excellent." This was in contrast to the mothers who did not see their infants as better than average although no differences existed between the groups with regard to the reported actual occurrence of illnesses among the children or their nuclear families. These mothers also tended to lack the little bit of extra enthusiasm needed to rate their own health as having been "Excellent."

The establishment of a maternal perception that is predictive seems to come about after the mother has had a real, albeit short, experience in living with her baby. Our measurement of the mother's perception of her one-month old infant seems to have tapped a kind of "Coping Combo"—a mother-infant team that seems to be a going concern. If a mother has succeeded in early coping, she is more likely to have a sense of accomplishment and see her baby as a "pretty good baby," i.e. "better than average." The outcome of the child's development and ability to master the successive life tasks may be dependent for a large part on the mother's positive hopefulness, a sense that things will work out. (This does not imply a pathologic denial).

That the mother's perception of her one-month old infant proved to be a predictor of the child's subsequent development may reflect:

1) the relatedness of maternal perception to mother-child interaction (if the mother is satisfied with her interaction with her infant and feels rewarded, she is more likely to respond with a positive perception of her infant.)
2) a relationship between maternal perception and the mother's ongoing ego capabilities which will foster and maintain the development of a "true" object relationship with her child throughout succeeding levels of the child's development.

That the early maternal perception of her infant is fluid and the "set" so early established indicate the need to emphasize support systems for mothers during the early postpartum period. The present system of postnatal and pediatric care often does not provide professional support for the mother during the critical interim between discharge from the hospital and the next "routine" contact with the physician at four to six weeks. Further institution and evaluation of programs aimed at fostering support for the new mother by husband, family, caring professionals, and society appear to be indicated.

The Neonatal Perception Inventory provides an easily administered screening instrument to aid in identifying a population of infants at high risk for subsequent emotional difficulty. Early identification will allow maximum opportunity for therapeutic intervention. (*See next page.*)

APPENDIX I

This appendix consists of:
1) The Neonatal Perception Inventory I completed on the first or second postpartum day (Time I).
2) The Neonatal Perception Inventory II completed when the infants are one month of age (Time II).
3) Instructions for administering the Inventories.
4) Method of Scoring the Inventories.

Code No. ......

NEONATAL PERCEPTION INVENTORY I

AVERAGE BABY

Although this is your first baby, you probably have some ideas of what most little babies are like. Please check the blank you think best describes the AVERAGE baby.

How much crying do you think the average baby does?

a great deal	a good bit	moderate amount	very little	none

How much trouble do you think the average baby has in feeding?

a great deal	a good bit	moderate amount	very little	none

How much spitting up or vomiting do you think the average baby does?

a great deal	a good bit	moderate amount	very little	none

How much difficulty do you think the average baby has in sleeping?

a great deal	a good bit	moderate amount	very little	none

How much difficulty does the average baby have with bowel movements?

a great deal	a good bit	moderate amount	very little	none

How much trouble do you think the average baby has in settling down to a predictable pattern of eating and sleeping?

a great deal	a good bit	moderate amount	very little	none

NEONATAL PERCEPTION INVENTORY I

YOUR BABY

While it is not possible to know for certain what your baby will be like, you probably have some ideas of what your baby will be like. Please check the blank that you *think* best describes what *your* baby will be like.

How much crying do you think your baby will do?

| a great deal | a good bit | moderate amount | very little | none |

How much trouble do you think your baby will have feeding?

| a great deal | a good bit | moderate amount | very little | none |

How much spitting up or vomiting do you think your baby will do?

| a great deal | a good bit | moderate amount | very little | none |

How much difficulty do you think your baby will have sleeping?

| a great deal | a good bit | moderate amount | very little | none |

How much difficulty do you expect your baby to have with bowel movements?

| a great deal | a good bit | moderate amount | very little | none |

How much trouble do you think that your baby will have settling down to a predictable pattern of eating and sleeping?

| a great deal | a good bit | moderate amount | very little | none |

Code No. ......

NEONATAL PERCEPTION INVENTORY II

AVERAGE BABY

Although this is your first baby, you probably have some ideas of what most little babies are like. Please check the blank you think best describes the AVERAGE baby.

How much crying do you think the average baby does?

| a great deal | a good bit | moderate amount | very little | none |

How much trouble do you think the average baby has in feeding?

| a great deal | a good bit | moderate amount | very little | none |

How much spitting up or vomiting do you think the average baby does?

| a great deal | a good bit | moderate amount | very little | none |

How much difficulty do you think the average baby has in sleeping?

| a great deal | a good bit | moderate amount | very little | none |

How much difficulty does the average baby have with bowel movements?

| a great deal | a good bit | moderate amount | very little | none |

How much trouble do you think the average baby has in settling down to a predictable pattern of eating and sleeping?

| a great deal | a good bit | moderate amount | very little | none |

Code No. . . . . . .

NEONATAL PERCEPTION INVENTORY II

YOUR BABY

You have had a chance to live with your baby for a month now. Please check the blank you think best describes your baby.

How much crying has your baby done?

a great deal	a good bit	moderate amount	very little	none

How much trouble has your baby had feeding?

a great deal	a good bit	moderate amount	very little	none

How much spitting up or vomiting has your baby done?

a great deal	a good bit	moderate amount	very little	none

How much difficulty has your baby had in sleeping?

a great deal	a good bit	moderate amount	very little	none

How much difficulty has your baby had with bowel movements?

a great deal	a good bit	moderate amount	very little	none

How much trouble has your baby had in settling down to a predictable pattern of eating and sleeping?

a great deal	a good bit	moderate amount	very little	none

The Neonatal Perception Inventory is easily and quickly administered by telling the mother:

> "We are interested in learning more about the experiences of mothers and their babies during the first few weeks after delivery. The more we can learn about mothers and their babies, the better we will be able to help other mothers with their babies. We would appreciate it if you would help us to help other mothers by answering a few questions."

The procedures are identical for administering the Average Baby form of the NPI on the first or second postpartum day and the NPI at one month of age. The mother is handed the Average Baby form while the individual administering the Inventory says,

> "Although this is your first baby, you probably have some ideas of what most little babies are like. Will you please check the blank you *think* best describes what *most* little babies are like."

The tester waits until the mother has completed the Average Baby form and takes it from the mother and then hands the mother the Your Baby form.*

The procedure for administering the Your Baby forms of the NPI is the same at Time I and Time II. However, the instructions given to the mother vary slightly to take into account the time factor. At Time I the tester tells the mother:

> "While it is not possible to know for certain what your baby will be like, you probably have some ideas of what your baby will be like. Please check the blank that you *think* best describes what *your* baby will be like."

At Time II, she says:

> "You have had a chance to live with your baby for a month now. Please check the blank you think best describes your baby."

The Average Baby Perception form elicits the mother's concept of the average baby's behavior. The Your Baby Perception form elicits her rating of her own baby. Each of these instruments consists of six single item scales. Values of 1-5 are assigned to each of these scales for each

---

* The tester remains with the mother during the entire administration procedure.

of the inventories. The blank signified *none* is valued as *1* and *a great deal* has a value of *5*. The lower values on the scale represent the more desirable behavior.

The six scales are totaled with no attempt at weighting the scales for each of the inventories separately. Thus, a total score is obtained for the Average Baby and a total score is obtained for the Your Baby.*

The total score of the Your Baby Perception form is then subtracted from the Average Baby Perception form. The discrepancy constitutes the Neonatal Perception Inventory score.**

The inventories have shown both construct and criterion validity.

---

* On the basis of 318 primiparae delivering normal, full-term, single births, the total scores range from 7 to 23 out of a possible score of 6 to 30, the differences between the scores range between +9 to —9.

** Example: Given a total Average Baby score of 17 and a total Your Baby score of 19, the Neonatal Perception Inventory score is —2. One month old infants rated by their mothers as better than average (+ score) are considered at Low-Risk. Those infants not rated better than average (— or 0 score) are at High-Risk for subsequent development of emotional difficulty.

APPENDIX II

Code No. ......

DEGREE OF BOTHER INVENTORY

Listed below are some of the things that have sometimes bothered other mothers in caring for their babies. We would like to know if you were bothered about any of these. Please place a check in the blank that best describes how much you were bothered by your baby's behavior in regard to these.

Crying	a great deal	somewhat	very little	none
Spitting up or Vomiting	a great deal	somewhat	very little	none
Sleeping	a great deal	somewhat	very little	none
Feeding	a great deal	somewhat	very little	none
Elimination	a great deal	somewhat	very little	none
Lack of a predictable schedule	a great deal	somewhat	very little	none
Other: (Specify)	a great deal	somewhat	very little	none
....	a great deal	somewhat	very little	none
....	a great deal	somewhat	very little	none
....	a great deal	somewhat	very little	none

The Degree of Bother Inventory to assess problems of infant behavior is administered when the infant is one month old. The total problem score is calculated by assigning values of 1-4 to each of the six items on the inventory. These are totaled with no attempt in weighting the items. The range in scores was from 6-23 out of a possible range of 6-24. The Degree of Bother Inventory had high face validity.

BIBLIOGRAPHY

1. ESCALONA, SYBILLE, K. The psychological situation of mother and child upon return from the hospital. In *Problems of Infancy and Childhood; Transactions of the Third Conference of the Joshua Macy Jr. Foundation.* March 7-8, 1949, pp. 30-51, New York, 1950.
2. SONTAG, L. W. The significance of fetal environmental differences, *Am. J. Obst. and Gyn.,* 42:996-1003, 1941.
3. JOSSELYN, IRENE M. *Psychosocial Development of Children.* New York; Family Service Assn. of America, 1948.
4. GREENBERG, NAHMAN H. Studies in psychosomatic differentiation during infancy. *Arch. Gen. Psych.,* 7:389-406, 1962.
5. WINNICOTT, D. W. The theory of the parent-infant relationship. *Int. J. of Psycho-Analysis,* XLI:585-595, 1960.
6. BRODY, SYLVIA. *Patterns of Mothering,* International University Press, Inc., New York, New York, 1966.
7. COLEMAN, KRIS & PROVENCE. The study of variations of early parental attitudes. *The Psychoanalytic Study of the Child,* VIII:20-47, 1953.
8. SCHAEFER, EARL & MANHEIMER, HELEN. Dimensions of perinatal adjustment. Unpublished paper (mimeographed) presented at the Eastern Psychological Assn. Meeting, New York, April 16, 1960.
9. BROUSSARD, E. R. Unpublished Doctoral Thesis: A study to determine the effectiveness of television as a medium for counseling groups of primiparous women during the immediate postpartum period. University of Pittsburgh, Library of the Graduate School of Public Health, Pittsburgh, Pennsylvania.
10. ————. Evaluation of anticipatory counseling to primiparae using the medium of television. Mimeographed paper presented at the American Public Health Association meeting, San Francisco, California, 1966. Abstracted in *Public Health Reports,* Vol. 82, No. 3, March 1967, p. 225.
11. ——, & HARTNER, M. S. Maternal perception of the neonate as related to development. Accepted for publication in *Child Psychiatry and Human Development,* 1970, Vol. 1, No. 1 (in press).
12. WINNICOTT, D. W. Primary maternal preoccupation. *Collected Papers: Through Paediatrics to Psycho-Analysis,* No. 20, Vol. IX, 1958.

19

ENVIRONMENTAL FACTORS IN THE DEVELOPMENT OF INSTITU-TIONALIZED CHILDREN

Nancy Bayley, Ph.D.

Institute of Human Development, University of California at Berkeley and Sonoma State Hospital

Leanne Rhodes, M.A.

Research Assistant, Sonoma State Hospital

Bill Gooch

Research Analyst, Sonoma State Hospital

and

Marilyn Marcus, Ph.D.

Research Psychologist, Sonoma State Hospital

In evaluating the competency of institutionalized retarded children, both the original determinants of the retardation and the institutional environment must be taken into account. This kind of evaluation can now be made through the first eight years of life of ten children with Down's Syndrome who have been in a special program at a State hospital for the mentally retarded since early infancy (Dameron, 1963). Stedman and Eichorn (1964) first approached this problem by comparing mental, motor and social maturity scores of these children with scores of a matched group of ten home-reared mongoloids when both groups of children were about two years old. In their study Stedman and Eichorn

Supported by the California State Department of Mental Hygiene, Project No. 63-16-23, 64-16-23, 66-16-23, 67-16-23, 68-16-34.

The institutional infants are members of a longitudinal study, originally directed by Dr. Lawrence Dameron, being conducted at Sonoma State Hospital. Subsequently, under the general direction of Dr. Charles McKean, the program has been continued by Dorothy H. Eichorn (1960), Donald Stedman (1961), Nancy Bayley (1964), and Marilyn M. Marcus (1968). We wish to thank Dr. Eichorn and Dr. Charles McKean for their valuable support and editorial advice.

450

found that the institutional environment of the hospital-reared infants, even though it was somewhat enriched (in that the staff-child ratio was higher than existed elsewhere in the institution), was less adequate than the environments of the home-reared children. The home-reared group was significantly superior in both mental test and Vineland Social Maturity scores. In their discussion, Stedman and Eichorn pointed out that the hospital group was most retarded in two kinds of functions: language and skill in manipulating small objects. They concluded that these areas of deficiency appeared to result from the children's lack of opportunities to practice these behaviors rather than from a lack of basic potential (Stedman and Eichorn, p. 396).

Several years after the Stedman and Eichorn study, it became possible to repeat the program of tests on the home-reared children. Retests were done when they were approximately five years old, and again a year later. Subsequently the testing schedule was changed to an individual chronological age basis, with the fourth round of comparative tests occurring at eight years.

The small hospital sample is perhaps unique in several ways. Their environment has been controlled and well documented, and their development has been assessed at frequent intervals throughout their lives, the tests extending from approximately three months to the current ages of eight to nine and one-half years.

Both groups attended school, and the institutionalized group has had a period of intensive language training. Thus, the effects of an institutional environment can be examined through a series of comparisons with a matched sample of home-reared children both before and after specified changes in the environment were instituted.

SUBJECTS

Hospital-Reared Children

These are ten mongoloid children (AAMD, Class VI), who were admitted to the Special Projects' Unit of Sonoma State Hospital when they were between one month and four and one-half months of age. For the purposes of the research project, the subjects (born between February, 1959, and June, 1960) were selected from referrals of healthy mongoloids which had been requested of county and community agencies. Ordinarily the Hospital does not accept healthy children with Down's Syndrome under six years of age. Selection was based on a confirmed diagnosis and freedom from other severe problems (Stedman and Eichorn, p. 393). As noted in previous publications (Dameron, 1963; Stedman and Eichorn, 1964), the original purpose of the project was not to study institutionalization, but rather to explore the course of mental, motor, and physical development of a sample of healthy mongoloid infants.

The children's mental and motor development was assessed and body size was measured at frequent pre-established intervals in order to obtain developmental reference points for use in a variety of studies.

The 1969 physical environment of the hospitalized children differs little from that described in the Stedman and Eichorn (1964) report. The children's housing consists of two dormitory rooms, a dining room, and a large playroom. The effective adult-child ratio continues to be one to five. As infants, the children may also have had above average institutional stimulation because they served as subjects in psychophysiological studies before the age of two years as well as undergoing frequent developmental examinations. Aside from these experiences, the environment was characteristic of an efficiently run institution.

Home-Reared Children

The selection in 1961 of a comparative sample of 10 mongoloid children living with their own families was made from the same geographic region (the greater San Francisco Bay Area), through comparable community agencies and on the basis of the same diagnostic criteria as were the experimental or hospital-reared children. Because the hospital children's ages spread over a 16-month range, each home-reared subject was matched by age to a hospital child. In most instances it was also possible to match by sex. Age pairing increased the likelihood of comparability for such purposes as length of experience in institution or home, and it also permitted direct analysis of within-pair differences in performance on tests given at varying ages. In the fourth comparison, all subjects were tested at eight years of age.

By the time of the second comparison at five years, three of the home-reared subjects, two boys and one girl, were unavailable for study and had to be replaced. The replacements were selected by the same procedures as the original group.

The socioeconomic status of the families of both samples is Class III (middle class) on the Hollingshead Index of Social Position. The general adequacy of the hospital sample on admission is reflected in their initial IQs; the mean IQ on the first test (Bayley Scales, rescored on revised standards,* given between 2 and 6 months of age, was 67, with a range of 60 to 72.

---

* The standards used here are those of the revised Bayley Scales of Infant Development, 1969. These scales have been shown to be reliable (Werner and Bayley, 1966), and to show no evidences of sample bias. The scales do not use "IQs" but indices (Mental Development Indices and Psychomotor Development Indices) based on standard deviations from mean raw scores. However, the indices do not go below 50, and thus can not be used for severely retarded children. In this study, where it is necessary to compare scores of children differing in age, the ratio IQ $\left(\dfrac{MA}{CA}\right)$ is used. Individual increments in scores are presented as mental ages and motor ages.

For purposes of comparison with the earlier study, succeeding examinations involved the same testing instruments, procedures and analyses to the extent that they were relevant.

The hospital children were tested on a schedule which shifted, after twenty-one months, from one-month to three-month intervals. Tests of the home sample at the 5-year and 6-year comparisons were administered within three-month periods (each child close to a test-age of his hospital match), thus replicating the procedure of Stedman and Eichorn. For the second comparison, the mean age at testing was, for the hospital sample, 61 months 18.6 days, and for the home sample, 61 months 12.2 days. The ages ranged from 54 to 71 months, and the mean intrapair age difference at testing was 6.6 days (range 0 to 40). At the third comparison the mean ages were 74 months 6 days (hospital) and 74 months 4.3 days (home), with ranges from 66 to 81 months; the mean intrapair age difference was 2.1 days. For the fourth comparison both samples were tested at eight years (96 months). The hospital sample is composed of seven males and three females, the home sample of five males and five females.

For the second and later tests, the home-reared children were brought to the Harold E. Jones Child Study Center in Berkeley, California, for evaluation. The first comparison tests, at twenty-eight months, were conducted in the children's own homes. The Special Projects' children were tested, as usual, in the project's laboratory.

The scales used in all testings were the revised Bayley Scales of Infant Development: Mental and Motor (Bayley, 1965, 1969; Werner and Bayley, 1966), and the Vineland Social Maturity Scale (Doll, 1957). Stanford-Binet Mental Tests (Form L-M) were also administered at the five-year tests (second comparison) whenever suitable and to all twenty children at the six and eight year tests (third and fourth comparisons). In the five-year and later testing sessions, the unpublished research form of Bayley's Infant Behavior Record* (Bayley, 1969; Honzik, Hutchings, and Burnip, 1965; Freedman and Keller, 1963) was completed for each child after the testing session. On this profile, thirty-three items are rated, the majority of them on a nine-point scale. Ward nursing personnel and the mother served as informants for the Vineland Scale; many items for this scale could also be scored directly or at least verified from observations made at the time of testing or on the ward.

Because the second hospital-home comparison at five years revealed an increasing difference between the two groups of children in mental development, and because the striking contribution to the difference

---

* The third section of the Bayley Scales of Infant Development, published as the Infant Behavior Record, Bayley, 1969.

was again found to be a relative deficit in language function in the hospital as compared with the home group, a program of language stimulation for the hospital children was instituted. This program, which began in July, 1965, and in 1969 was still in effect, may be characterized as providing on a broad base and with language as the primary tool an institutional living situation in which meaningful interpersonal interactions are pervasive and relevant to all aspects of the children's lives. The program involves not only the utilization of specific procedures and teaching aids that have been developed for the purpose, it also includes the participation in these procedures of both school and ward personnel.*

RESULTS

The Comparative Studies

The first two comparisons at 2 and 5 years between the home-reared children show the effects on the experimental group of continued institutionalization; the third and fourth comparison at 6 and 8 years (Figures 1, 2 and 3) demonstrate the counteracting effects of the language-based enrichment program. Table I includes the means, ranges, t ratios and probability levels from the four comparisons (the Stedman and Eichorn data have been recalculated on the 1969 norms of the Bayley Scales of Infant Development). This table includes the data for the full sample of ten pairs of cases (the hospital members are the same at all tests; three home members were replaced after the 2-year comparison). Although the data for the constant sample of seven pairs who were included in all four testings are not differentiated in the table, analysis shows the three replacements in the home sample to have earned scores very similar to those of the constant sample of seven.

Table II reports the results of the item analyses of the mental, motor and social scales and the Infant Behavior Record for the 5-year comparison. Table III gives the same information for the 6-year comparison. Table IV gives the same information for the 8-year comparison. Table V reports within group correlations for the results of the mental, motor, and social scales.

Mental Scales

As was the case with the first comparison results reported by Stedman and Eichorn, for the Bayley Mental Scale, second comparison differences at five years between the hospital and home-reared groups of children were significant, the respective mean IQs being 29.2 and 40.3. Indeed, the t ratio had increased.

---

*A paper by Rhodes et. al. (1969) describes in detail this language oriented enrichment program, the evaluation techniques employed, results of tester validation studies, and the program results.

TABLE 1

MEANS, RANGES, *t* RATIOS, AND PROBABILITY LEVELS FOR ALL FOUR
COMPARATIVE STUDIES

Mental	Hospital		Home			
	Mean IQ*	Range	Mean IQ	Range	t	P (2 tailed)
Test 1	35.4	24-56	50.3	39-61	4.036	<.005
Test 2	29.2	13-36	40.3	34-55	4.570	<.005
Test 3	39.2	16-51	45.3	32-61	1.391	<.20
Test 3 (N=9) (Stanford Binet)	40.1	31-48	44.9	36-58	1.409	<.20
Test 4	39.5	14-56	41.1	31-51	0.392	>.50
Test 4 (N=9) (Stanford Binet)	42.3	34-56	41.1	31-51	0.393	>.50
Motor	Mean MQ	Range	Mean MQ	Range	t	P
Test 1	42.6	30-55	49.5	34-57	2.213	<.10
Test 2	34.5	23-45	41.6	32-54	2.242	<.10
Test 3	40.9	23-53	43.5	33-57	0.672	>.50
Test 4	40.0	18-55	42.4	34-57	0.580	>.50
Social	Mean SQ	Range	Mean SQ	Range	t	P
Test 1	61.8	45-83	75.0	62-90	3.127	<.025
Test 2	38.1	20-47	57.4	45-78	4.038	<.005
Test 3	43.7	24-53	59.0	44-75	2.997	<.025
Test 4	44.4	18-54	59.8	46-80	3.241	<.005

* Ratio quotients $\frac{\text{Mental Age}}{\text{Chronological Age}}$ and $\frac{\text{Motor Age}}{\text{Chronological Age}}$ are used throughout this paper instead of the deviation indices (MDI and PDI) used in the Standard tests. The indices do not apply meaningfully to children who score below an index of 50.

In the second comparison, as in the first, there were fifteen items on the mental scale which differentiated the two groups. They are, as before, primarily items involving language use and comprehension.

At the 6-year tests (after the training program had been in effect for several months) the group differences in mean IQ on both the Bayley Mental Scale and on the Stanford-Binet L-M were not significant.

Because on this round of tests both the Bayley Scale and the Stanford-Binet were given, it was possible to compare the groups on a scale (the Binet) which was new to all the children (the Bayley Scale had been new to the home-reared children at the two-year or first comparison). The hospital group has experienced the Bayley tests at frequent intervals since early infancy, while the Stanford-Binet was (except for two or three items) new to them. If there were any practice effect specifically related to familiarity with the Bayley Scales, the experimental group should have done relatively better on it than on the Binet Tests.

To test this possibility, the Stanford-Binet scores of the two groups were compared for the number of items passed, mental ages, and ratio IQs (the deviation IQ tables do not accommodate this level of mental

TABLE 2

Items Favoring Home-Reared Children—Mental, Motor, and
Social Scales and the Infant Behavior Profile
Second Comparative Study (5 years)

Mental Scale	
Item	P
	(one-tail)
Joins two words	<.005
Names two objects	<.005
Names three pictures	<.005
Names three objects	<.005
Names five pictures	<.005
Imitates stroke, vertical and horizontal	<.005
Uses words to make wants known	<.01
Mends broken doll, marginally	<.01
Points to five pictures	<.01
Pink formboards: Reversed	<.01
Shows shoes, or other clothing or own toy	<.025
Tower of 3 cubes	<.05
Names one picture	<.05
Points to three pictures	<.05
Points to seven pictures	<.05

Motor Scale	
Tries to stand on walking board	<.025
Stands on left foot alone	<.025
Walks on tiptoe a few steps	<.025

Social Scale	
Talks in short sentences	<.005
Asks to go to toilet	<.005
Helps at household tasks	<.005
Unwraps candy	<.01
Eats with fork	<.05
Cuts with scissors	<.05
Cares for self at toilet	<.05
Washes face unassisted	<.05
Uses table knife for spreading	<.05

Infant Behavior Profile	U	P
		(two-tailed)
Banging*	14.5	<.02
Goal Directedness	21.5	<.05
Attention Span	21.5	<.05

* The hospital group did more banging than did the home group.

TABLE 3

ITEMS FAVORING HOME-REARED CHILDREN—MENTAL, MOTOR, AND SOCIAL
SCALES AND THE INFANT BEHAVIOR RECORD

Third Comparative Study (6 years)

Item	Bayley Mental Scale	P (one-tail)
Discriminates two: (cup, plate, and box)		<.01
Mends broken doll, exactly		<.05
Discriminates three: (cup, plate, and box)		<.05
Stanford-Binet L-M		
Picture Vocabulary 8+		<.01
Naming Objects		<.05
Picture Vocabulary 3+		<.05
Motor Scale		
Catches Ball in Arms		<.025
Social Scale		
Uses table knife for spreading		<.025
Bathes self assisted		<.025
Relates experiences		<.05
Uses skates, sled wagon		<.05

Infant Behavior Record	U	P (two-tailed)
Fearfulness*	19.0	<.02
Banging Toys**	19.5	<.05

* This item favored hospital-reared; they were less fearful.
** The hospital group exhibited more banging activity.

functioning). If a child did not attain a Binet basal age by passing all
six items at the two-year level, a mental age was calculated from a basal
age of 18 months (all but one hospital case had achieved at least this
level on the Bayley Scale) by adding to 18 one month for each item
passed (Sternlicht, 1965). The legitimacy of combining items from these
two scales is supported by data from a group of 120 normal California
children (Bayley, 1969) tested on both scales. For groups aged 24, 27,
or 30 months the mean difference in mental age was 1.1 month, with the
Binet yielding a higher score.

The hospital children passed a mean of 11.6 Binet items, the home
children a mean of 15.2 items. The resulting Binet ratio IQ means are
40.1 and 44.9 for the hospital and home cases, respectively. This difference of 4.8 IQ points on the Binet with an N of 9 pairs is similar to
the 6.1 point difference for the Bayley Scale with an N of 10 (p =
< .10). Thus there is no indication of practice effect on scores of the
hospital children, or of any handicap to the home children.

TABLE 4

ITEMS FAVORING HOME-REARED CHILDREN—MENTAL, MOTOR, AND SOCIAL
SCALES AND THE INFANT BEHAVIOR RECORD

Fourth Comparative Study (8 years)

Stanford-Binet L-M

No single items

Motor Scale

	P
	(one-tail)
Hops on one foot Less than 6½ feet	<.05

Social Scale

Relates experiences	<.01
Plays competitive exercises games	<.05
Uses skates. sled, wagon	<.01
Prints simple words	<.05
Plays simple table games	<.025
Goes to school unattended	<.025
Uses table knife for spreading	<.01
Bathes self assisted	<.01

Infant Behavior Record

	U	P
		(two-tail)
Fearfulness*	15	<.01
Initial response**	25	<.05

* This item favored hospital-reared; they were less fearful.
** This item favored hospital-reared; they were less shy in their initial response to the testing situation.

The extent to which the pre-existing gap has been closed is also evident from the reduced number of significantly differentiating items. On the Bayley Mental Scale and on the Stanford-Binet there were only three differentiating items each for a total of six (as contrasted with fifteen on the Bayley Mental Scale alone at each of the earlier comparisons).

The 8-year Mental Scale scores of the two groups were almost identical. All of the home-reared children achieved true basal scores on the Binet. Their mean IQ was 41.1 and the range 31 to 51. Nine of the hospital-reared earned valid Binet IQs, with a mean of 42.3 and a range of 34 to 56. The tenth hospital-reared child obtained a ratio IQ of 14 on the Bayley Mental Scale, and the resulting group mean (nine Stanford-Binet L-M IQs and one Bayley IQ) was 39.5.

Because the environmental enrichment program is a language-oriented program, the Binets at the 6-year and 8-year comparisons were analyzed to determine if the hospital-reared children were performing better on the verbal than on the non-verbal items. This does not seem to be the case. At the 6-year comparison the hospital-reared passed 34% of the verbal and 60% of the non-verbal items; the home-reared passed 55% of the verbal and 75% of the non-verbal items. The 8-year comparison showed that the hospital-reared passed 41% of the verbal and 62% of the non-verbal items. The home-reared passed 43% of the verbal and 68% of the non-verbal items.

To summarize the mental test results for these four testings, the differences are markedly reduced by the 6-year comparison and are least at the 8-year comparison. This generalization holds both for total scores (whether IQ or MA) and for the number of differentiating items. At the last or 8-year tests the children in both groups were attending school, the length of attendance for the home children ranging from 18 to 36 months. The principal change in the experimental (hospital) group was their experience in the intensive language-training program. Training began about three months before the 6-year tests which took three months to complete.

MOTOR SCALE

At no time have the motor scale total scores reflected significant differences between the functional levels of the two groups. However, at five years there were three items (see Table 2) on which the home-reared scored significantly higher: tries to stand on the walking board, stands on left foot alone, and walks tiptoe a few steps. Significant differences in favor of the home-reared were found for only one item on each of the subsequent tests—catches ball in arms at six years and distance hopped on one foot.

Comparisons of mean motor quotients within groups show that between the 2 and 5-year tests the hospital children lost an average of 8.1 MQ points $(p = < .01)$, and the home-reared group lost an average of 7.9 points $(p = < .02)$. Between the 5 and 6-year comparisons, the hospital group gained an average of 6.4 points $(p = < .001)$, and the home-reared group gained an average of 1.9 MQ points $(p = < .05)$. Between the 6 and 8-year comparisons, the hospital group lost an average of 0.9 points $(p = N/S)$, and the home-reared group lost an average of 1.1 MQ points $(p = N/S)$.

SOCIAL SCALE

Between-group differences on the social scale are significant at all four comparisons (see Table 1). The number of items on the social scale which differentiated at a significant level between the two groups increased from two at 2 years to nine at 5 years (see Table 2). At 6 years the hospital group continued to be at a disadvantage, with a mean SQ of 43.7 as compared to the home group's SQ of 59.0 $(p = < .025)$. An item analysis showed four items to differentiate at significant levels. At the 8-year test the mean social quotients remained about the same (44.4 and 59.8 respectively), but the number of significant items had increased to eight (see Table 4).

Within-group differences showed that the hospital-reared group lost an average of 23.7 SQ points (p = < .001) between the first and second studies at two and five years but gained an average of 5.6 points (p = .001) between the second and third at five and six years. There was a slight although insignificant gain (0.7 SQ points) from the third to fourth test. The home-reared group lost an average of 17.6 SQ points (p = < .01) between the first and second (two and five year) comparisons and gained an average of 1.6 points (p = N/S) between the second and third at five and six years. Between the third and fourth tests at six and eight years the home-reared also made only a slight and insignificant gain (0.8 SQ points). Except for the six and eight-year tests, differences between all possible pairs of means are significant for the hospital sample. In the home-reared group, only the mean of the first and second (two and five year), first and third (two and six year), and first and fourth (two and eight year) tests differ significantly.

Within-Group Correlations

When within-group correlations are computed for each administration of the mental, motor, and social scales, 18 of the possible 22 correlations in the hospital group (see Table 5) are significant. For the home-reared group, only 10 of the 22 are significant. These 10 correlations (with one exception) were between the 2 and 6-year and the 6 and 8-year mental, motor, and social tests. The magnitude of the rs for both groups indicates, in general, high stability over short intervals at the older ages. The high stability of the hospital children may reflect their relatively constant physical environment, but is attributable in part to one child who consistently had exceptionally low scores.

Infant Behavior Record

The Infant Behavior Record was not used in the 2-year comparison. In Table 2 are listed the three items of the Record which differentiated between the two groups on the 5-year comparison. One additional item, thumbsucking (on the part of the hospital children) approached significance (p = < .10).

At 6 years only two items differentiated the groups (see Table 3). Two additional items, attention span and initial response to strangers, approached significance (p = < .10) with the home youngsters tending to exhibit a longer attention span and a shyer initial response than the hospital youngsters. The banging activity of the hospital group is the one item on this scale which differentiated the two groups at both five

TABLE 5

INTERTEST CORRELATIONS: HOSPITAL AT UPPER RIGHT, HOME
AT LOWER LEFT IN ITALICS

A. MENTAL QUOTIENT

HOSPITAL

	Bay 1	Bay 2	Bay 3	Bi 3	Bi 4
Bayley 1 (2.5 yrs.)		.526	.645*	.790*+	.896+
Bayley 2 (5 yr.)	*.441+*		.797*	.490+	.607+
Bayley 3 (6 yr.)	*.522+*	*.578*		.839**+	.555+
Binet 3 (6 yr.)	*.648+*	*.833***	*.651* *		.764*+
Binet 4 (8 yr.)	*.760*+*	*.665* *	*.590*	*.842** *	

HOME

B. MOTOR QUOTIENT

	1	2	3	4
1 (2½ yr.)		.702*	.885**	.802**
2 (5 yr.)	*.397+*		.827**	.823**
3 (6 yr.)	*.277+*	*.949** *		.936**
4 (8 yr.)	*.607+*	*.831** *	*.734* *	

C. SOCIAL QUOTIENT

	1	2	3	4
1 (2.5 yr.)		.832**	.763*	.759*
2 (5 yr.)	*.339+*		.950**	.962**
3 (6 yr.)	*.193+*	*.804** *		.979**
4 (8 yr.)	*.180+*	*.609*	*.859** *	

+ Correlations with Binet tests for Hospital sample are computed for an N of 9 because one child did not achieve a valid score on the Binet. The *r*s involving first test for Home cases are computed with N of 7 because 3 cases were replaced at test 2.
* P = <.05
** P = <.01

and six years. Fearfulness (the home-reared youngsters exhibited a more fearful reaction to the new or strange), was the only item that reached significance on the eight-year tests (see Table 4). One other item, initial response (shy versus not shy) to the testing situation, approached significance (p = < .10). The home-reared children were more likely to be shy. However, the scales for responsiveness (either positive or negative) to persons and responsiveness to toys did not differentiate the groups. Also of interest are other items on which the two groups did not differ at any time: cooperation, activity, reactivity, tension, emotional tone and endurance.

Individual Patterns of Development

As the two samples were retested, the importance of changes within groups became evident. If their IQs are taken at face value, the hospital group lost an average of 6.2 IQ points between the 2-year and

5-year comparisons, while the home group lost an average of 10.0 points. These decrements are significant at the .05 and .025 levels of confidence, even for the 7 pairs who were included in all 4 testings.

Because of the 16-month spread in the children's chronological ages, the comparison in growth rates for the two samples may be most clearly presented in the form of mental age and motor age growth curves. The individual mental age curves are shown in Figure I (parts a, b, and c). The hospital children's curves give their Bayley Scale mental ages (age equivalents on the BSID norms [Bayley, 1969]) for all tests through about 36 months mental age, and, as a separate curve, their Stanford-Binet mental ages for all scorable tests. Each hospital case is compared with his or her age-mate from the home sample.

These curves show periods of faster and slower growth in the often-tested hospital children, as well as changing status in comparison to the home-reared children. With the exception of one very slow child, the individual curves of the hospital children indicate that the rate of growth picked up moderately at about 4 to 5 years and at mental age 12 to 14 months. This slight acceleration occurred although the children had little or no language. It appears to be explained in part by the fact that the children were now better able to cooperate for a more pro-longed period. After the children's entrance into preschool, their rate of mental growth again appears in most instances to increase somewhat. The real spurt in mental age occurs, however, after the initiation of the language training program. There is also some indication that, after a slow start, the accelerated growth in competence is at the stage of maturity (that is, a mental age of about 12 to 14 months) at which normal children are starting to use words.

In these individual mental age curves, as in the first comparative set of IQs, it is clear that the home-reared children are definitely superior to the hospital children at around two years of age. Their relative superiority is even more evident in the curves at the 5-year comparative testing. By the third, or six-year, comparison the differences are greatly reduced, whether the scores compared are the Bayley or the Stanford-Binet mental ages. As of the eight-year tests, the hospital-reared are maintaining a high rate of mental growth while the home-reared tend to be slowing, with the result that the IQs of the two groups are becoming equal.

Mental vs. Motor Development

The rates of motor as contrasted with mental growth in the hospital children may be seen most clearly when the age curves of the means for motor age and mental age are compared, as in Figure 4. Growth rates on the two scales are closely similar over the first 21 months. After this age,

GROWTH IN MENTAL AGE

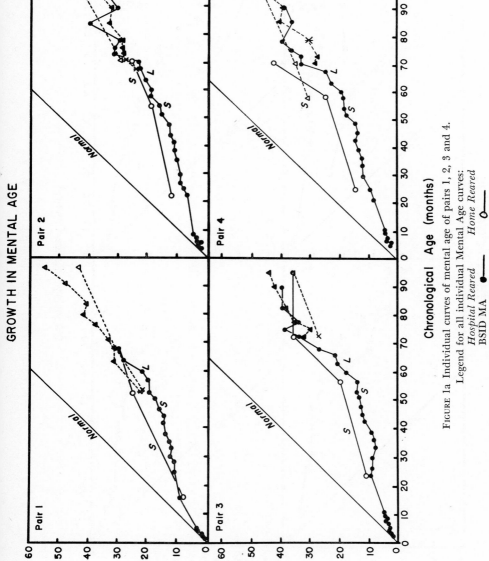

Chronological Age (months)

FIGURE 1a Individual curves of mental age of pairs 1, 2, 3 and 4.
Legend for all individual Mental Age curves:

Hospital Reared   Home Reared
BSID MA   ●   ○
Binet MA   ▲   △
Estimated Binet *
S = start of School
L = start of Language training

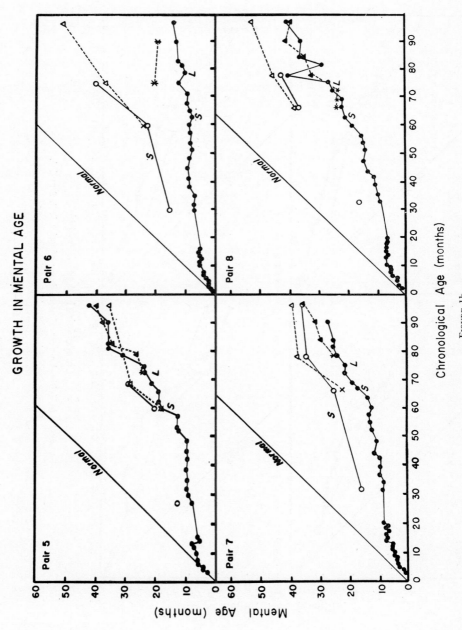

Individual curve of mental age of pairs 5, 6, 7 and 8.

GROWTH IN MENTAL AGE

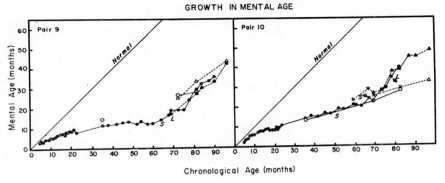

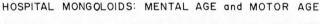

Chronological Age (months)

FIGURE 1c
Individual curve of mental age of pairs 9 and 10.

HOSPITAL MONGOLOIDS: MENTAL AGE and MOTOR AGE

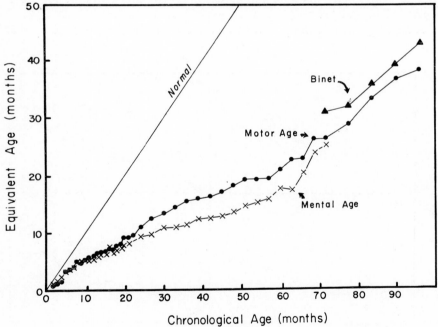

FIGURE 2
Chronological age curves of mean age equivalents of scores on the Bayley Mental and Motor Scales of Infant Development, for 10 hospital-reared mongoloids. Not all cases were tested at each age. For tests missed between 10 and 69 months interpolated age-equivalents were used in computations of means at each age. The curve of means for Stanford Binet, Form L-M, mental ages are for the 9 cases who achieved a basal mental age of 2 years on this test, for five tests at chronological ages 6 through 8 years.

mental growth lags behind and does not catch up until the children are six years old. The greatest difference is found at about four years of age, before the environment of these children was enriched, first by school attendance and then by language training. It is interesting to note that by 6½ years the mental ages are above the motor ages. This later mental acceleration is more evident if Case 6 is omitted from the means after 15 months, when his mental growth first drops far behind the others. For the sample of nine children whose mental ages at 16 months ranged from 6.0 to 9.0 (mean of 7.2), mean mental age equalled mean motor age by the time the children were 69 months old. Their mean Stanford-Binet mental age at eight years (96 months) was 2.2 months advanced over their motor age. Our records on the home-reared are not sufficient to make as complete a comparison. However, at 6 years the mean mental and motor ages were 33.4 and 32.2 respectively, and at 8 years the age equivalents were 42.4 for the mental scale and 40.9 for the motor.

Motor Development

The individual curves of motor development are given in Figure 3 (parts a, b, and c).

Rate of growth in body control and coordination as measured by this

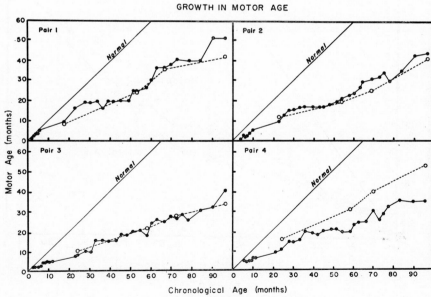

GROWTH IN MOTOR AGE

FIGURE 3a
Individual curves of motor ages of pairs 1, 2, 3 and 4.
Legend for all individual Motor Age curves:
Hospital Reared   Home Reared

GROWTH IN MOTOR AGE

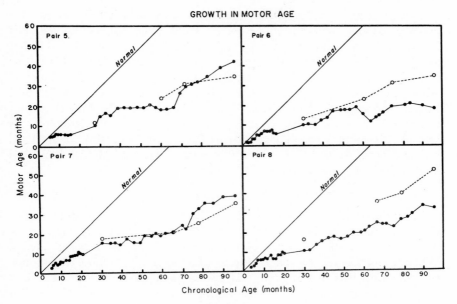

FIGURE 3b
Individual curves of motor ages of pairs 5, 6, 7 and 8.

GROWTH IN MOTOR AGE

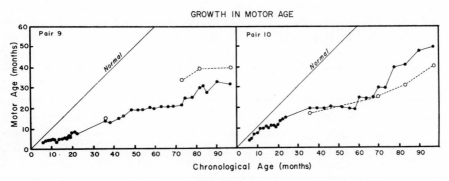

FIGURE 3c
Individual curves of motor ages of pairs 9 and 10.

scale shows less extreme individual differences than were found for mental growth. The slowest child, Case 6, is also the one who shows extremely slow mental growth. Nevertheless, his motor retardation is not as pronounced as his mental retardation. At eight years his mental age was 13.0 months; his motor age was 17.3 months. Because of his restricted proficiency in comprehending and following instructions, this latter score is probably lower than actual motor ability warrants. The most advanced in motor scores of the hospital children is Case 1. This child had a motor age of 40 months at 6 years, when his Stanford-Binet mental age was 39 months. Between 20 and 66 months (characteristic for this group) his mental scores lagged (usually 5 to 6 months) behind his motor scores. At eight years his motor age was 52.4 months and his Stanford-Binet mental age was 56 months.

DISCUSSION

In any discussion of these results, it is necessary to take into account the performance of the one child (Case 6) whose scores over time on all measures fall well below the range of the rest of the hospital group. When the selection of the children who were to compose the home-reared group was made, great effort was taken, as in the original hospital sample, to avoid the selection of any child who might exhibit defects (such as epilepsy or severe heart damage) other than those specifically relevant to the diagnosis of mongolism. There were several children who were evaluated for inclusion in the home-reared comparison group whose potential would seem to have been comparable to that of the one profoundly retarded youngster in the hospital-reared group. Because there was some question, even though slight, of the presence of complicating factors other than mongolism, none of these children was included in the home-reared sample. As a consequence, there is no child in the comparison group who is so severely handicapped as this one hospital-reared subject. In order that research results not be biased in favor of one group or the other the criteria for the selection of groups were kept comparable (Stedman and Eichorn, 1964). Unfortunately, complicating defects cannot be detected as readily in very young infants as in older children, so the effort to select only "healthy" subjects was less successful for the hospital sample than the home-reared.

There are several aspects of this study that may pertain to the general course of early development in mongoloids as well as to the specific effects of institutional life on their development.

First, because the same children from two differently reared groups have been tested repeatedly over all or most of their first 8 years, we can observe trends in mental growth under two sets of circumstances. The home-reared children are growing up in above-average environments, which include attendance in special nursery schools for retarded children. The hospital-reared children, although they experienced to some degree the impersonal environment of an institution, also attended nursery school, and later had intensive training in a comprehensive program centered around language development. It is worthy of note that, although the general expectation for mongoloids is that their IQs decrease with age, for these groups, all three of the developmental quotients (mental, motor, and social) either were stable or increased between the 5 and 6-year tests. However, at the 8-year tests the home-reared had lost an average of 3.8 IQ points, while the hospital-reared had gained an average of 0.3 IQ points. The increase in age equivalents (mental and motor) for individual cases is illustrated in Figures 1, 2, and 3. The moderate increases of the home-children may be attributed in part to their attendance in nursery schools that are specifically concerned with improving the competence of the mentally retarded. It is also possible that the very fact of their participation in this research tended to make both their parents and their teachers more attentive to the children and their potentials for growth. It remains for investigation, perhaps on other longitudinal samples, whether there is inherent in the Down Syndrome a period at around 5 to 6 years when the developmental process, as measured in age equivalents, accelerates over rates exhibited at younger ages. Whatever the cause, we have found these home-reared children at 6 years to be capable of more adequate function than had been anticipated from their earlier performance.

The hospital children's greater increments in scores at the 6 and 8-year comparisons appear to be clearly related to the program of intensive stimulation. There was some acceleration in rate of change following school attendance. However, school occupies only two and a half hours a day. The language training program was extended beyond school to afford meaningful interpersonal communication and learning experiences in ways which approach in richness those of home-reared children. Whether or not these changes in mental test scores between the 5 and 6-year tests for both groups, (and between the 6 and 8-year tests for the hospital group) represent true gains, the most relevant finding for this study is the fact that the hospital children's gains were significantly greater, and the differences between the two samples have been reduced. Indeed, at the 8-year comparison the scores on the mental and motor scales are essentially the same for both groups.

On the Vineland Social Maturity Scale, a large number of the items that discriminate between the two groups involve behaviors which the hospitalized youngsters, because of the nature of institutional settings, are not given the opportunity to learn. Three such items which favored the home-reared at the 6 and 8-year test ages were: "uses table knife for spreading," "bathes self assisted," and "uses skates, sled or wagon unsupervised outside of their yard." With one exception (relates experiences), the remaining items which differentiated between the two groups at eight years also appear to tap behaviors which reflect the essence of the difference between institutional and home care. Although the Vineland manual provides a method of scoring such "no opportunity" items where full credit can be given, in this instance the number of items which must be scored "no opportunity," as well as their placement in the scale, drastically reduces the number of remaining items which can be meaningfully used to compare the two groups. As Dr. Doll himself points out in the scoring instructions, the "net effect of such (compromise) scores will not affect the total score materially in most instances (except in some institutional environments)" (Doll, 1957, p. 14). It is the feeling of these authors that the phrase "except in some institutional environments" is descriptive of our situation, and that the hospital-reared children are being penalized if the differences in opportunity are not taken into account in any interpretation of the differences in SQ which we are reporting.

The same cannot be said, however, about item number 44, Relates Experiences, which requires that the child give "simple accounts of experiences . . . with sequential and coherent content and relevant detail . . ." (Doll, p. 27). There is no doubt in the authors' minds that this item discriminates in a valid manner a relevant and telling difference in language behavior in favor of the home group.

Scores on the Infant Behavior Record at the time of the 5-year comparative study (see Table 2) indicated that the hospital-reared children exhibited more banging behavior (banging of hands and test materials on the table), a lesser degree of goal-directed activity, and a shorter attention span than did the home-reared children. The hospital-reared children also tended to do more thumbsucking ($p = < .10$). At the 6-year comparison, one item, banging behavior, retained its significance. It may be that the greater amount of banging was originally a stimulus-seeking activity which became strongly habituated in the understimulated hospital babies. In addition, as they grew older, the hospital children continued to show a tendency toward a shorter attention span ($p = < .10$). Like other institutional children accustomed to many caretakers (e.g., Rheingold and Bayley, 1959), their initial response to the testing situation was less shy than was that of the home-reared group ($p = < .10$), and they were significantly less fearful throughout. Although this difference might be enhanced by the fact that the examiner was familiar to the hospital children, it is common knowledge that institutional children characteristically approach strangers readily. Also, these children gave no evidence of fearfulness toward an outside examiner who administered the mental tests once to each child when they were between 6½ and 8 years old. Among the (300) normal home-reared children of similar mental ages (C.A. 18 to 30 months) in our 1964-68 California sample, 59% evidenced some fearful reactions (slight to strong) in the testing situation. At the 8-year comparison the initial response and fearfulness items maintained the same significance levels, but the banging behavior of the hospital children had disappeared.

For those who have worked with and observed these children, the overall improvement of the hospital children at the time of the 6 and 8-year comparisons is very impressive.

Prior to July, 1965, they had little or no expressive speech. Their expressive vocabularies averaged about four words per child; some children relied entirely on non-verbal avenues of communication, and the most verbal child of the group had a vocabulary of about 10 to 12 words. They could not tell their own or each other's names, nor could they be trusted not to run away in the corridors or on the grounds if their hands were not held. None could be relied upon to go to the bathroom unattended. To enter the dayhall with the children was to subject one's person to a thorough mauling with little hands, reaching, tugging, pawing, pulling, and grabbing everywhere.

With the exception of the one profoundly retarded youngster, the children's expressive and receptive vocabularies have grown impressively. Currently (at mean age of eight and one-half years), these nine children are speaking in sentences. There is no longer a run-away problem. Most of the children have become so trustworthy that they can be given a dime, allowed to walk to the candy machine, get a candy bar and return to the ward unattended. The candy machine is located approximately fifty yards and two corners down the corridor from the ward; there are several doors along the way, including two which open directly to the outside, through which these youngsters could pass if they so wished. These nine children can be trusted to leave their classroom, use the bathroom facilities, and return to the classroom unattended and without incident. The amount of socially undesirable behavior when research personnel or strangers join the children has been appreciably reduced. A reading program was developed for the children in the winter of 1966-1967 and as of this writing the nine children are reading (with comprehension) an average of 250 words each.

REFERENCES

BAYLEY, N. Comparisons of mental and motor test scores for ages 1-15 months by sex, birth order, race, geographical location, and education of parents. *Child Development*, 1965, 36, 379-411.

BAYLEY, N. Scales of Infant Development, The Psychological Corporation, New York, 1969.

DAMERON, L. E. Development of intelligence of infants with mongolism, *Child Development*, 1963, 34, 733-738.

DOLL, E. A. Vineland Social Maturity Scale, Nashville: Educational Test Bureau, 1957.

FREEDMAN, D. J. & KELLER, BARBARA Inheritance of Behavior in Infants, *Science,* 1963, 140, 196-198.

HONZIK, M. P., HUTCHINGS, J. J., & BURNIP, S. R. Birth record assessments and test performance at eight months, *Amer. J. Dis. Child.,* 1965, 109, 416-426.

RHEINGOLD, H. L. & BAYLEY, N. The later effects of an experimental modification of mothering, *Child Development,* 1959, 30, 363-372.

RHODES, L. J., GOOCH, B., SIEGELMAN, E. Y., BEHRNS, C. A., & METZGER, R. B. Descriptive Report: A language stimulation and reading program for severely retarded mongoloid children. State of California Department of Mental Hygiene, Bureau of Research Publications. Research and Demonstration Monograph No. 11, pp. 102, 1969.

STEDMAN, D. J. & EICHORN, D. A comparison of the growth and development of institutionalized and home-reared mongoloids during infancy and early childhood, *Amer. J. Ment. Def.,* 1964, 69, 391-401.

STERNLICHT, M. A downward application of the 1960 revised Stanford-Binet with retardates, *J. Clin. Psychol.,* 1965, 21, p. 79.

WERNER, E. E. & BAYLEY, N. The reliability of Bayley's revised scales of mental and motor development during the first year of life, *Child Development,* 1966, 37, 39-50.

20

CONTRIBUTIONS OF DEVELOPMENTAL RESEARCH TO A THEORY OF SCHIZOPHRENIA

Barbara Fish, M.D.

*Professor of Child Psychiatry and Director, Child Psychiatry,
New York University Medical Center*

ABSTRACT

Since 1952 the author has been studying abnormalities in the development of infants who later became childhood schizophrenics. The material summarized here is drawn from six separate studies involving 213 children, of whom 89 are schizophrenic. The neurological features of schizophrenia in infants and young children bridge the gap between the neurophysiological and the psychological studies of this disorder. In infancy, the inadequate central nervous system integration disturbs the growing organization of alertness, activity, muscle tone, vestibular function, proprioception and autonomic stability, and produces a fluctuating and erratic pattern of development. It is suggested that this fluctuating level of integration in schizophrenia is itself part of a basic integrative disorder of central nervous system functioning and that it is related to the fluctuating states of attention and arousal which can be observed.

Since 1952 the author has been studying abnormalities in the development of infants who later became childhood schizophrenics. In adult schizophrenics it is not possible to determine which biochemical and psychophysiological dysfunctions are manifestations of the disease itself and which are secondary to prolonged anxiety, social isolation or other conditions secondary to hospitalization (Kety, 1959; Richter, 1957; Shakow, 1962).

From the infant studies, one can report on the developing manifestations of disorder in the first months of life in those children who have now been independently diagnosed as schizophrenic. Transient neurological deviations have been observed even in the first month of life, which confirm Bender's descriptions of the characteristically disorgan-

473

ized development in the histories of schizophrenic children (Bender, 1947; Bender and Freedman, 1952).

The neurological features of schizophrenia in infants and young children bridge the gap between the neurophysiological and the psychological studies of this disorder. The data permit us to hypothesize a model for schizophrenia that relates disturbances in more primitive central nervous system functions to the more complex psychological symptoms which occur later and which are more generally recognized. The infant data also suggest in what ways the disorder may be related to altered brain function.

SCOPE OF DATA AND METHODS

The material to be summarized here is drawn from six separate studies involving 213 children, of whom 89 are schizophrenic.* All of them were examined originally by the author and have been followed for four to eighteen years. Most were brought because of suspected psychiatric disorder. Of these, 12 schizophrenic children were first seen between six months and two years of age and are now in their teens (Fish, 1960a), 32 schizophrenic children were first seen between one and one-half and five years of age and are now five to fifteen years of age (Fish, et al., 1968), and 44 schizophrenic children were first seen between three to twelve years of age and are now in their teens and early 20's (Fish, 1961, 1964; Fish and Shapiro, 1965).

In two of the studies, the neurological, physical and psychological development of 32 infants was followed for signs considered by the author to be predictive of childhood schizophrenia. In the first prospective study, three out of sixteen infants examined at one month of age in a well baby clinic were judged to be "vulnerable" to schizophrenia on the basis of their abnormally uneven development (Fish, 1957, 1959). At 10 years of age the one with the most abnormal early development was independently diagnosed as a childhood schizophrenic and all three were independently evaluated as grossly pathological on psychological testing, compared to the other children (Fish, et al., 1966b, 1965).

In the second prospective study the development of 16 infants born to hospitalized schizophrenic mothers was followed from the first day of life. The maturation of vestibular function and arousal were followed in this group, in addition to the methods of the earlier study. Four infants showed marked deviations in the direction of excessive apathy or irritability, but only one of these showed grossly maladaptive behavior at two years of age (Fish, 1963; Fish and Alpert, 1962, 1963).

* Portions of this work were supported in part by Public Health Service Grant MH-04665 from the National Institute of Mental Health and by a grant from the Harriett Ames Charitable Trust.

Despite the many technical problems in studying infants (Fish, 1963) there are unique opportunities for anyone who is interested in brain-behavior relationships. It is a period when the behavioral repertoire and personality organization are relatively simple compared to adults'. However, the children require intensive study over long periods of time and results cannot be evaluated until years or even decades later. Histories even one and two years later miss many important details and must be limited to the few variables that can be checked (Fish, 1961; Fish et al., 1968).

The rapidity of maturation provides quantitative landmarks for many functions under the control of the central nervous system, so that one can measure the rates of development of many different functions and compare them to established norms. In these studies Gesell's standards (Gesell and Amatruda, 1947) were used for postural and locomotor development, fine coordination and visual-motor functioning, and language development (Fish, 1957, 1959, 1960a, 1961, 1963; Fish et al., 1968, 1965). Height, weight and head growth were measured on the Wetzel Baby Grid (Fish, 1957). The maturation of arousal, the responsiveness to the stimuli and the maturation of the vestibular responses to caloric stimulation were defined according to the group trends under standard conditions (Fish, 1963; Fish and Alpert, 1962, 1963).

One can therefore study the quantitative relationships between the rates of different aspects of development at any given age and their longitudinal patterns in time. In this way it is possible to measure disorders of patterning and organization in developing central nervous system functioning and to study the relationships of such disorganization to the presence of clinical symptoms and the appearance of later clinical disorder.

RESULTS

1. *Disturbance of the timing and integration of neurological maturation in infancy*

Studies of the development during infancy of children who are now known to be schizophrenic reveal that disorders of neurological maturation may occur as early as the first month of life. There does not appear to be a fixed neurological defect. Rather, there seems to be a disorder of the timing and integration of neurological maturation. This may affect any of the functions controlled by the central nervous system but it can be measured most readily in the first year of life, when it affects postural and locomotor development, and in the next few years in visual-motor and language development.

There may be unusual fluctuations in the rates of various aspects of development, with periods of marked acceleration and retardation succeeding one another, sometimes with the transient loss of a previously acquired ability. There may be a disruption in the normal cephalo-caudad gradient of postural development, so that progressive control of muscular segments does not proceed in the usual orderly fashion from head to toe. A child may be able to stand even precociously but be unable to roll over, or be able to roll over but be unable to sit (Fish, 1960a).

These irregularities in the rates of development lead to peculiar sequences and also to unusual juxtapositions of retardation and precocity. The spread in a child's abilities at any one time may range from severely defective to normal, or even precocious functioning. This may produce discrepancies between different functions (locomotion, visual-motor, language and so on) or among several aspects of any one of them.

An analogous "scatter" in the psychological performance of older schizophrenic children and adults is sometimes attributed to anxiety or disturbed motivation. When it is seen under two years of age, and particularly in the first month of life, it is obvious that poor integration of central nervous system functioning can occur in schizophrenic children long before complex motivational and defensive behavior have developed.

2. *Disorders of arousal, vestibular and autonomic functioning and somatic growth*

The clinical disorders of arousal and vegetative functioning in very young schizophrenic children suggest some possible relationships to underlying alterations in brain function. At an age when normal waking infants cry and thrash vigorously, there may be an abnormally quiet, inactive state, with little or no crying, flaccid muscle tone, and minimal responses to proprioceptive stimuli (Fish, 1957, 1960a; Fish and Alpert, 1953). Unlike infants with peripheral neuromuscular disorder (Walton, 1957) this hypotonia is associated with 2+ to 3+ loose, pendular, deep tendon reflexes, and is apparently of central origin. It may be associated with increased somnolence and a diminished response to auditory and visual stimuli and a slow, feeble, athetoid motility, like that of premature infants (Fish, 1957, 1960a; Fish and Alpert, 1963). Or there may be a dissociation between the motor and sensory aspects of arousal with an infant who is flaccid and inert showing normal or precocious visual following and attention (Fish and Alpert, 1963). In the latter infants, this "quiet" state clinically resembles the "adynamia" which Hess produced in cats by electrical stimulation of the lateral anterior hypothalamus (Hess, 1957).

Three of the infants born to schizophrenic mothers who showed this hypoactive state had persistent "immature" responses of tonic deviation without nystagmus on vestibular stimulation (Fish and Alpert, 1963). Adults show tonic deviation when anaesthetized or in semi-coma. Lorente de No's experimental studies indicate that the rapid eye movement component depends upon the function of the reticular formation (Lorente de No, 1933). Fish suggested that the persistent tonic response in these deviant infants was related to a dysfunction in the developing reticular system (Fish and Alpert, 1963).

This abnormally quiet and lethargic state was observed as early as the first day of life (Fish, 1963; Fish and Alpert, 1962, 1963) and has persisted in some from one month of age to 18 months (Fish, 1957, 1960a). It has been observed before any clinical irritability or hyperactivity appeared (Fish, 1957, 1960a; Fish and Alpert, 1963). Other schizophrenic infants were initially alert and active, but became inactive, toneless and apathetic at 8 to 30 months of age, at the same time their development lagged or regressed and they became withdrawn, with decreased and psychotic speech (Fish, 1961).

Physiological disturbances may coincide with the lags and regressions in neurological development of schizophrenic children during their first two years. The vasomotor disturbances are similar to those of adult schizophrenics (Shattock, 1950) and include pallor, peripheral cyanosis, cutis marmorata, and dermatographia. Gastro-intestinal disturbances include spastic constipation, no outward expression of hunger, difficulty in swallowing solid foods and even inability to suck (Fish, 1960a). In the schizophrenic infant seen from one month of age, body growth and growth in head circumference slowed down and accelerated parallel with the course of neurological maturation (Fish, 1957, 1959).

In 1960 Fish suggested that in schizophrenics whose disease is manifested in infancy, a disruption in the normal functioning of the reticular activating system (Lindsley, 1952; Magoun, 1952) and the hypothalamus (Hess, 1957) might account for the parallel disturbances in somatic growth, autonomic control, muscle tone, activity and alertness (Fish, 1960a). There is also a continuing dysfunction of whatever central nervous system mechanisms normally regulate the rate, sequence and spatial pattern of postural and other aspects of maturation.

3.   *Relationship between developmental disorder and clinical severity*

The clinical picture can be related to the time of life when development is disorganized. A different pattern of assets and handicaps is produced, depending on which function was emerging, or was due to emerge, at the time development became disorganized. In the first year of life, deviations in arousal, homeostasis, and motor development are most prominent. Disorders in visual-motor functioning and social responsiveness are very subtle, even if present in the first year (Fish, 1957, 1960a) and may only become obvious in the second year, along with distortions of speech, comprehension and concept formation (Fish et al., 1968).

The severity of the lags and disorganization in development also varies. In general, when the early transient neurological disturbances are the most severe, there is greater interference with later intellectual and social adaptive functioning and less capacity for defense formation. The most severe early impairments are less modifiable by pharmacologic or nonpharmacologic treatment (Fish, 1960b; 1964; Fish et al., 1966a, 1968) and appear, so far, to have a worse long-term prognosis whether or not there has been good mothering (Fish et al., 1968). Some of these children resemble chronic simple or hebephrenic adult schizophrenics even at three to four years of age, in their fragmented and stereotyped thought-disorder and behavior and in their responses to treatment (Fish, 1964; Fish et al., 1968).

Infants with only minimal to moderate deviations may develop paranoid manifestations at 10 to 11 years of age or later. Others may show only latent schizophrenic symptoms, neurotic or characterological manifestations that are much more responsive to the impact of their environment and to treatment (Fish, 1961; Fish et al., 1966b, 1965). The subgroups of young schizophrenic children appear to be part of a spectrum of developmental disorders related to prognosis as well as to initial onset and severity. The different types of early childhood schizophrenia do not appear to be discrete and unrelated syndromes but arrests and deviations of developmental sequences along a continuum of disturbed functioning (Fish, 1961; Fish and Shapiro, 1965; Fish et al., 1968, 1965).

These children have not been followed long enough to know whether there is any relation between early deviations in development and later acute eruptions of psychosis. The latter might well occur in the absence of any early manifestations of disorder which could be detected by our present methods.

4. *Relationships between neurological and psychological manifestations*

Observing the unfolding of symptoms in very young schizophrenic children provides clues as to some possible relationships between the neurological and psychological manifestations. These may simply be concomitant variations in more primitive and in higher integrative functions but they pose questions for future research.

The infants with lagging postural control and hypotonia showed marked anxiety in relation to gravity and an increased need for physical support and guidance in body skills in infancy. Often the psychological symptoms persisted even after they achieved independent locomotion.

There was sometimes a delay in the organization of proprioceptive impulses as early as four months of age, with hand-regard lagging relatively behind the perception of objects in space. This primitive form of deficient self-awareness was sometimes followed by more complex body image disturbances, reflected in apractic difficulty, confusion about spatial relationships and difficulty in learning visual-motor tasks (Fish, 1960a). Such early disturbances in proprioceptive organization and in imitation could contribute to the schizophrenic child's later problems in perception, identification, and in the learning of everyday behavior.

When development proceeded disharmoniously, there were problems not seen in children with normal or with uniformly retarded development. If a child was attempting to master problems of manipulation and spatial relationships at a seven to nine month level when he was unable to sit at a four month level, his inability to maintain erect posture limited his ability to explore his environment at the critical time when manual dexterity was nascent, unless he was supported by an adult (Fish 1960a, 1963). It appeared that the unattended "quiet," floppy infant may suffer from secondary sensory deprivation when he does not get sufficient support and vertical experience. One can also postulate that his experience of his own body and of his surroundings, which depend upon the integration of visual, tactile and kinesthetic impressions (Schilder. 1950), will be distorted when these aspects of development are "out of phase" and are learned in the context of marked anxiety in relation to gravity.

Poor integration of many of the functions, biological and psychological, which are under control of the central nervous system has long been recognized as the basic disturbance which underlies the many disparate phenomena of schizophrenia. The same basic defect in integrative functioning is seen in the fragmented behavior of schizophrenics in infancy and early childhood.

One can demonstrate ability in isolated problem-solving, such as puzzles, or in rote vocabulary and memory for associations, but these abilities do not become integrated into useful, goal-directed activity. They remain nonadaptive, haphazard, or stereotyped fragments of behavior. Many of these children begin to say words by one to one-and-a half years of age and speak in sentences by two to two-and-a-half years of age, but from the start their comprehension is poor and their speech is echolalic, fragmented, and is rarely, if ever, used for communication.

These difficulties may be exaggerated by the infantile "anhedonia," anergy and apathy. An infant's early lack of energy, "drive," attention and affective responsiveness often confuses and distresses the mother. It disrupts the early social-affective interaction which should occur between mother and infant. In some homes the overly quiet infant is left alone except for the rare times when he cries, which only increases his apathy and social isolation (Fish, 1957, 1963).

The apathy may affect other aspects of learned behavior which depend upon reinforcement through the infant's pleasure and the mother's responses and approval. Normal infants and children show great delight in their newly acquired achievements and repeat them ad infinitum. Both the pleasure and the repetition may play an important part in the learning process. Young schizophrenic children frequently show less "drive," attention, interest and perseverance. They often ignore or appear apathetic following their successes in problem-solving and do not "practise" and exploit their abilities as the normal infant does. Performance may deteriorate rather than improve with repetition. Words may be acquired briefly and then be dropped for months or years.

The slow and delayed responsiveness of many of these children appears to add to their confusion. While they are apparently still dreamily responding to an earlier word or phrase, those around them chatter at conversational speed and events continue to move on at a normal pace. The original word the child is "learning" becomes misidentified with subsequent and unrelated words and events. I believe that his disturbed arousal and responsiveness keep the schizophrenic child's experience of events out of phase with the normal experience of time and reality and add to his confusion of causality. In treatment, some of these children are able to learn the correct associations if one simplifies and slows down the presentation of words and stimuli to the pace of their apparent comprehension.

Even in infancy there are many concomitant disturbances, any one of which could "explain" much of the clinical picture. At this point we cannot judge how much any of these disturbances contribute to the phenomenology of schizophrenia or whether they are all coincidental manifestations of the central nervous system disorder.

CONCLUSION

The different clinical manifestations of childhood schizophrenia can be viewed as variations on the common theme of a basic disturbance in neurological development. These early neurological disturbances may merely be more primitive manifestations of the same underlying disorder of integration that is manifested in adult schizophrenia by the disorganization of complex psychological functions. In infancy, the inadequate central nervous system integration disturbs the growing organization of alertness, activity, muscle tone, vestibular function, proprioception and autonomic stability. The usual orderly progression of development gives way to unusual sequences of retardation and acceleration, producing associations of immaturity and precocity during critical periods of early life.

The different patterns of early neurological disturbance result in a variety of clinical pictures, with different patterns of assets and handicaps and a spectrum of severity. The pattern of maternal and environmental care may exaggerate the child's developmental disturbances, or may help him to compensate, depending on the quality of the interaction and the severity of the child's disorder.

In addition to the effects of the central integrative disorder, the discrepancies in neurological development may in themselves interfere with the schizophrenic child's developing an adequate image of his own body, disturb his perception of form and space and disrupt his identification with others. The early disturbances in arousal, ranging from under-responsiveness, with an inability to sustain attention, to over-excitability and the inability to screen out irrelevant internal or external stimuli, may add to the early fragmentation and confusion in establishing patterns of learned meanings and behavior. Delayed responsiveness keeps his experiences out of phase with the normal experience of time and reality.

The fluctuating and erratic patterning of development distinguishes the longitudinal course of the schizophrenic child from those with chronic brain damage. The same erratic functioning occurs in the microcosm of the minutes and hours of a single examination, resulting in a profile of successes and failures not readily explained by chronic organic impairment. The schizophrenic child may stand erect one instant and then wobble on rubbery legs, may perceive objects, form and space in the usual way and then suddenly appear disorganized about these relationships. A fluctuating awareness of himself and the environment and an erratic and unpredictable ability to function seem to be more disorganizing for the developing personality of the schizophrenic child than is a stable neurological defect in functioning of comparable degree. It is certainly more baffling to his parents and teachers.

It is this unusual variability in function which makes us characterize the schizophrenic's performance as "peculiar" and "deviant," rather than the result of any known organic impairment. I suggest that this fluctuating level of integration in schizophrenia is itself part of a basic integrative disorder of central nervous system functioning and that it is related to the fluctuating states of attention and arousal which can be observed in infancy and childhood, as well as in some adult patients.

REFERENCES

1. BENDER, L. (1947). Childhood schizophrenia: Clinical study of 100 schizophrenic children. *Am. J. Orthopsychiat.* 17:40.
2. BENDER, L. & FREEDMAN, A. M. (1952). A study of the first three years in the maturation of schizophrenic children. *Quart. J. Child Behav.* 1:245.

3. FISH, B. (1957). The detection of schizophrenia in infancy. *J. Nerv. Ment. Dis.* 125:1.

4. FISH, B. (1959). Longitudinal observations of biological deviations in a schizophrenic infant. *Amer. J. Psychiat.* 116:25.

5. FISH, B. (1960a). Involvement of the central nervous system in infants with schizophrenia. *Arch. Neurol.* 2:115.

6. FISH, B. (1960b). Drug therapy in child psychiatry: Pharmacological aspects. *Compr. Psychiat.* 1:212.

7. FISH, B. (1961). The study of motor development in infancy and its relationship to psychological functioning. *Amer. J. Psychiat.* 117:1113.

8. FISH, B. (1963). The maturation of arousal and attention in the first months of life: A study of variations in ego development. *J. Amer. Acad. Child Psychiat.* 2:253.

9. FISH, B. (1964). "Evaluation of psychiatric therapies in children," in Hoch, P., and Zubin, J., (eds.), *The Evaluation of Psychiatric Treatment.* Grune & Stratton, New York, pp. 202-220.

10. FISH, B. & ALPERT, M. (1962). Abnormal states of consciousness and muscle tone in infants born to schizophrenic mothers. *Amer. J. Psychiat.* 119:439.

11. FISH, B. & ALPERT, M. (1963). "Patterns of neurological development in infants born to schizophrenic mothers," in *Recent Advances in Biological Psychiatry,* Vol. 5, Plenum Press, New York, pp. 24-37.

12. FISH, B. & SHAPIRO, T. (1965). A typology of children's psychiatric disorders: I. Its application to a controlled evaluation of treatment. *J. Amer. Acad. Child Psychiat.* 4:32.

13. FISH, B., SHAPIRO, T. & CAMPBELL, M. (1966a). Long-term prognosis and the response of schizophrenic children to drug therapy: A controlled study of trifluoperazine. *Amer. J. Psychiat.* 123:32.

14. FISH, B., SHAPIRO, T., CAMPBELL, M. & WILE, R. (1968). A Classification of schizophrenic children under five years. *Amer. J. Psychiat.* 124:1415.

15. FISH, B., SHAPIRO, T., HALPERN, F. & WILE, R. (1965). The prediction of schizophrenia in infancy: III. A ten-year follow-up report of neurological and psychological development. *Amer. J. Psychiat.* 121:768.

16. FISH, B., SHAPIRO, T., HALPERN, F. & WILE, R. (1966b). The prediction of schizophrenia in infancy: II. A ten-year follow-up of predictions made at one month of age, in Hoch, P. and Zubin, J., (eds.), *Psychopathology of Schizophrenia,* Grune & Stratton, New York, pp. 335-353.

17. GESELL, A. & AMATRUDA, C. S. (1947). *Developmental Diagnosis: Normal & Abnormal Child Development, Clinical Methods and Pediatric Applications,* Ed. 2, Paul B. Hoeber, Inc., New York.

18. HESS, W. R. (1957). *The Functional Organization of the Diencephalon,* Hughes, J. R. (ed.), Grune & Stratton, Inc., New York.

19. KETY, S. S. (1959). Biochemical theories of schizophrenia. *Science* 129:1528, 1950.

20. LINDSLEY, D. B. (1952). Brain stem influences on spinal motor activity. *A. Res. Nerv. & Ment. Dis., Proc.* (1950) 30:174.

21. LORENTE DE NO, R. (1933). Vestibular-ocular reflex arc. *A.M.A. Arch. Neurol. Psychiat.* 30:245.

22. MAGOUN, H. W. (1952). The ascending reticular activating system. *A. Res. Nerv. & Ment. Dis., Proc.* (1950) 30:480.

23. RICHTER, D. (1957). Biochemical aspects of schizophrenia in *Schizophrenia: Somatic Aspects,* Richter, D. (ed.), Macmillan Co., New York, pp. 53-75.

24. SCHILDER, P. (1950). *The Image and Appearance of the Human Body.* International Universities Press, New York.

25. SHAKOW, D. (1962). Segmental set. *Arch. Gen. Psychiat.* 6:1.

26. SHATTOCK, F. M. (1950). The somatic manifestations of schizophrenia: clinical study of their significance. *J. Ment. Sc.* 96:32.

27. WALTON, J. N. (1957). The limp child. *J. Neurol. Neurosurg. Psychiat.* 20:144.

21

ABNORMAL SOCIAL BEHAVIOR IN YOUNG MONKEYS

Stephen J. Suomi and Harry F. Harlow

University of Wisconsin

INTRODUCTION

Investigators of human development face numerous obstacles in their attempts to discover meaningful psychological relationships by controlled experimental research. The mere use of human children as subjects dictates to a very large extent certain restraints which must characterize empirical study in this area. Quite bluntly, a student of development is free to neither manipulate nor control all variables central to his specific problem if his research involves human neonates, infants, or young children. This lack of freedom results from ethical and practical considerations and extends across the traditional approaches to child research, be they controlled experiments or semi-controlled observations within a laboratory situation (Bandura & Huston, 1961), semi-controlled experiments or uncontrolled observations in the child's "natural environment" (Schaffer & Emerson, 1964), or information gleaned from retrospective reports of child subjects, peers, parents, and teachers (Sears, Maccoby, & Levin, 1957).

These problems pose a particular dilemma to the child developmental worker whose field of speciality is abnormal social behavior. He is typically presented with young subjects who exhibit affective disorders, and he is typically asked not only to deduce the genesis of such behavior but also to formulate means to alleviate it. Practical experimental and proper ethical restrictions render this task formidable. Society frowns

This research was supported by United States Public Health Service Grants RR-0167 and MH-11894 from the National Institutes of Health to the University of Wisconsin Regional Primate Research Center and Department of Psychology Primate Laboratory, respectively. At time of writing the senior author was being supported by a predoctoral fellowship from the National Institute of Health, no. 1 FOI NH47025-01. The authors would like to express their appreciation to Mrs. Helen Lauersdorf for her helpful comments concerning the manuscript and to Mr. Robert Dodsworth and his staff for assistance in collection and preparation of the figures.

on those who would deliberately attempt to induce psychopathological behavior in child subjects in order to test hypotheses relating to potential causes of affective disorders. Except for rare cases, practical matters such as an investigator's time, a parent's willingness, and a child's availability render continuous monitoring of the etiology of any observed disorder difficult if not impossible. Finally, there invariably exists a considerable discrepancy between an investigator's ability to conceive an effective therapeutic procedure and his ability to administer it. It is not surprising that with respect to study of child behavioral abnormality numerous questions remain uninvestigated and unanswered.

Contrast the predicament faced by investigators of human primate development, both normal and abnormal, with the situation encountered by those who study the psychological development of nonhuman primates. Virtually all primate species, particularly the Old World monkeys and the apes, possess highly complex social structures within their living groups. The processes by which an infant develops into a functioning member of its social unit are neither easy to observe nor easy to understand.

The investigator who wishes to study such development in the species' natural habitat faces methodological difficulties probably as challenging as those existing for the study of human development. Field observers, while not hampered by ethical restraints, cannot easily maintain strict control over variables such as social history of individual group members, dominance patterns, or predatorial threat when observing existing situations, although Japanese researchers have recently approached this goal (Imanishi, 1963). Provision of auxiliary food supplies, introduction of novel objects into the subject's home range, and release of nonmembers in proximity of the group under observation represent feasible manipulations of environmental factors, but these are often limited by the field investigator's unwillingness to alter the environment beyond the range of naturally occurring fluctuations. Data are usually restricted to observational records, since monitoring of physiological measures in a field situation is difficult and, unlike the case with human subjects, use of verbal interviews with or written questionnaires from the subjects presents irreconcilable methodological problems. Finally, the mere act of physically observing the subjects often tries both the ingenuity and patience of field researchers. Social obstacles of parents, teachers, PTA groups, and hospital personnel may seem trivial to an investigator more familiar with the impenetrable terrain, roaming predators, and weather best described as inclement and unfriendly.

With respect to the development of psychologically abnormal members of any primate group, a final word concerning field studies should be mentioned. Field observers are not apt to see prolonged psychopathological behavior in their subjects for a most elementary reason: such subjects are not apt to survive very long (Berkson, 1970; Kling, Lancaster, & Benitone, 1970). Whereas Man provides hospitals, clinics, asylums, and prisons for physiologically and psychologically disabled members of his species, Nature does not. Perhaps this is why some psychiatrists feel that Man is the only species who can afford the privilege of prolonged psychopathological disability (Kubie, 1953). As will be subsequently shown, we do not share this view.

Within a well-established primate laboratory the experimental situation is entirely different. Here an experimenter's ability to manipulate variables relevant to his research and to control variables not relevant to his research is at a maximum. Within limits he can dictate the social and nonsocial history of any subject at his disposal. Moreover, the laboratory affords the primate researcher the opportunity to measure a wider range of variables with far greater precision and reliability than could ever be envisioned within a field situation. With subjects available and observable 24 hours a day every day, an experimenter's choice of collectable data is limited only by his ingenuity, sophistication with methodology and instrumentation, and the size of his budget. Finally, the ethical considerations a laboratory observer of nonhuman primates faces are certainly real but relatively modest in comparison to those encountered by observers of human children. Theoretical problems such as possible effects of total social isolation from birth on an organism's subsequent social development can be considered only hypothetically with respect to human subjects. With nonhuman primate subjects these problems can be attacked empirically. A manipulation employed with monkeys that could make a man famous might well make the same man a menace to society if instead he used human subjects.

There is an additional factor—one intimately tied to the subject matter of this volume—which must be considered when evaluating the relative merits of field *vs.* laboratory study of nonhuman primate development. Whereas in an undisturbed field environment developmental abnormality is the exception and is rarely observed, it has been strongly argued by some (e.g., Jay, 1965) that no subject born and reared in a laboratory experiences truly "normal" social development. In one sense, this point is virtually indisputable. No laboratory in the world can provide an infant monkey with an environment identical to that encountered by its feral-born and raised counterparts, at least in terms of duplicity of factors such as weather and seasonal changes, and presence of predators.

But in another sense this may be merely a moot point. For the rhesus monkey, the species from which most of the data presented in this chapter have been taken, there is no "standard" feral environment. Free-ranging rhesus monkeys are found both in the jungle forests and cities of India, and certain social aspects of the behavior exhibited by city monkeys differ considerably from those of forest-living monkeys (Singh, 1969). In contrast, intellectual performance of rhesus monkeys, as assessed by WGTA learning test batteries, are essentially the same regardless of whether the monkeys came from the forest or cities of India or from an American laboratory (Singh, 1969; Harlow, Schiltz, & Harlow, 1968). In other words, defining a "normal rearing environment" for the rhesus monkey makes as little sense as defining a normal rearing environment for the human species. Which is more normal, the deserts inhabited by Australian aborigines or the apartment complexes inhabited by Manhattan savages? More meaningful, we feel, is instead to define normality in terms of consistent behavior which emerges in subjects across all feral environments rather than in terms of any environmental factors preceding these behaviors.

By development of normal behavior, we mean development of certain behavioral patterns, to be described shortly, which have been identified in field observations of rhesus monkeys. Not all laboratory born and reared rhesus monkeys are abnormal by this criterion. In the past ten years researchers at the Wisconsin Primate Laboratories have devised rearing paradigms under which infant monkeys do exhibit social behavioral development essentially identical to that seen in feral-raised infants. Modifications and fragmentations of these paradigms, on the other hand, produce monkeys whose social development deviates from this normative pattern. The forms that these deviations take, i.e., the behavioral abnormalities exhibited by monkey subjects reared in carefully chosen, controlled social environments, will constitute the body of this paper.

The remainder of this chapter is divided into four sections. The first section will deal with behaviors exhibited by all rhesus monkey infants regardless of rearing experience, and with the "normal" social development that has been observed for monkeys given extensive opportunity to interact with mothers and peers in a laboratory environment. The second section will deal with the behavioral consequences of removing or modifying certain elements of the mother-peer rearing paradigm. The rationale underlying the experiments whose data are reported in these first two sections was primarily investigation of parameters which purportedly lead to formation of species-normative affectional systems (Harlow & Harlow, 1965). This is not the case for findings reported in the third section of this chapter. Here, data will be presented from studies whose designated purpose was to deliberately induce a specific form of psychopathological behavior, namely depression, in rhesus monkey subjects. The final section will deal with ongoing efforts to rehabilitate monkey subjects who, owing to inadequate or incomplete early social experience, exhibit abnormal or nonexistent social behaviors.

At this point it may be wise to express a certain caution to the reader. What follows will be data, generated by laboratory study of rhesus monkeys, which address themselves to normal social development, abnormal social development, and reversal of psychopathological behavior patterns. As will soon be obvious, practical experimental considerations essentially prohibit replication of many of these studies using rhesus monkeys in a feral environment, and both practical and ethical considerations certainly prohibit replication of some of these studies using human subjects in any environment. Cross-species reasoning, e.g., taking conclusions derived from laboratory studies of nonhuman primates and drawing analogies to human behavior, is often very compelling. In some cases these analogies may be quite justified, and in other cases they may not. Nonhuman primate subjects can be viewed from theoretically biased positions ranging from "rhesus monkeys are subjects who exhibit their own species-specific behaviors interesting from ethological and psychological points of view" to "rhesus monkeys are essentially furry little men with tails." While we have our own definite biases, we do not feel this is the appropriate place to present a case for or against any analogical reasoning. We will only present the data, and any analogies to be drawn will be left strictly up to the reader's discretion.

I. *Prepotent Behaviors and "Normal" Social Development*

Like most primates, rhesus monkeys are relatively helpless creatures at birth and continue to require extensive care for several months following entry into the world. In the rhesus monkey, it is believed that environmental influences have their maximal effect, in terms of subsequent behavior patterns, during the first year of life. The behavioral consequences of living in a variety of social environments for the first postnatal year will presently be discussed at length.

However, it is becoming increasingly evident that rhesus monkeys are not proverbial Lockean tabulae rasae at birth. Rather, it appears that they enter the postnatal environment with a wealth of prepotent behavior patterns and response biases. Those which have been empirically identified fall into three general classes: (a) reflex-type behaviors exhibited at or shortly following birth and relatively independent of motivational factors, (b) consistent social preferences expressed when a neonate is placed in a free-choice situation, and (c) latent behavior patterns which, while not exhibited at birth, emerge later in the infant's life, at a time relatively uncorrelated with preceding or existing environmental stimulation, but in a form apparently quite dependent upon these factors.

These patterns constitute what some have termed fixed action patterns (FAPS) or instinctive behaviors. We prefer to call them unlearned or prepotent behavior patterns. Whether they arise from genetic factors, prenatal factors, or, more likely, an interaction of the two, is irrelevant to this discussion. Those prepotent behavior patterns already identified probably represent only a small fraction of the unlearned potentiality within the species, and we feel that their role in the process of social development has probably been underestimated by theoreticians concerned with attachment formation by primates, both human and non-human (Sackett, 1971). However, we will limit our discussion to those prepotent patterns which have been identified for the neonatal rhesus monkey and which apparently have important consequences for interpretation of abnormal social development in this species.

A. *Reflex Behaviors*

Two important reflex behaviors exhibited by a rhesus neonate at or shortly following birth are clinging reflexes and rooting and sucking reflexes, behaviors which help the infant to maintain intimate physical contact with its mother and to obtain nourishment from her. Stimulation of the palmar surface of the hand or the plantar surface of the foot of a neonate elicits a clinging response in the form of a grasp reflex capable of supporting the entire weight of the infant's body (Mowbray & Cadell, 1962). A similar reflex of comparable strength has been observed in human neonates (Fulton, 1955). The power of the clinging reflexes can be illustrated by placing an infant on its back on any flat, solid surface. The infant immediately will shift into a prone position (basic righting reflex) unless it is clinging to a soft-covered object, in which case it will continue to lie on its back (Mowbray & Cadell, 1962). This demonstrates a prepotency of clinging over the righting reflex, a reflex system considered the most primary and universal of all reflex systems in vertebrates (Hamburger, 1963).

Fundamental reflexes associated with nursing are rooting and sucking responses. Stimulation of the neonate's face, particularly near the mouth, will cause the infant to rotate its head sideways or vertically until oral contact is made with the source of stimulation; sucking immediately follows (Figure 1) (Harlow & Harlow, 1965).

These reflex behaviors do not come under full voluntary control until the rhesus neonate is approximately 20 days of age, the transition being gradual rather than sharply delineated (Harlow, 1962a). Subsequent to this period, prolonged and extensive exhibition of these behaviors may represent inappropriate response patterns. But all rhesus monkeys, both those that develop normal social behaviors and those that do not, show clinging and sucking responses at or shortly following birth.

B. *Social Preference Patterns*

A second class of prepotent responses includes unlearned social preference patterns. A rhesus infant, when given the choice, exhibits a preference for an adult rhesus female over an adult female pigtail macaque or stumptail macaque, two species closely related to the rhesus, even if it has not been previously exposed to any adults of any species (Sackett, Suomi, & Grady, 1968; Sackett, 1970). Also, a rhesus infant prefers a rhesus adult female to a rhesus adult male, again in the absence of any prior exposure (Suomi, Sackett, & Harlow, 1970). The adaptive nature of these preferences should be obvious. In addition, their exhibition has an important implication. To consistently exhibit these preferences, rhesus infants must be capable of distinguishing among the stim-

Fig. 1.—Sucking responses by a 3-day-old rhesus neonate.

ulus animals with which they are presented, even if they have never seen those types of stimulus animal previously. Hence, even at a very early age, the infants must be extremely sensitive to certain cues within the social environment. This sensitivity is evidenced by the observation that naive rhesus infants can discriminate between nulliparous and multiparous rhesus females, a task difficult for an experienced human observer.* The finding that social experiences within the first month of life can alter these unlearned preferences (Sackett, Porter, & Holmes, 1965) has important implications for consideration of factors appearing early in life which may lead to normal or abnormal social behavior later in life.

---

* Allyn C. Deets, personal communication, 1970.

C. *Latent Behavior Patterns*

A third class of prepotent responses includes behaviors which are not exhibited at birth but which emerge at a relatively consistent chronological period later in life, apparently independent of preceding or existing environmental conditions. Two such behaviors relevant to this chapter are fear and aggressive responses.

Fear responses, e.g., grimaces and associated vocalizations for the rhesus species (Altman, 1962), emerge at between 70 and 110 days of

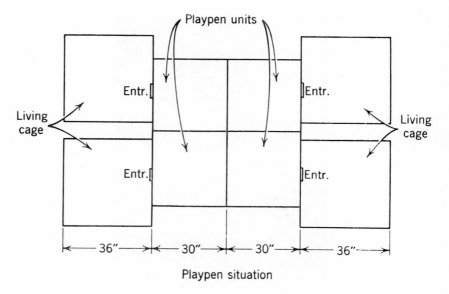

Fig. 2.—The playpen apparatus.

age, regardless of whether the subject has been reared in total social isolation (Sackett, 1966) or with mother and peers (Harlow, Harlow, & Hansen, 1963). Aggressive responses, e.g., both "threats" and actual biting which can inflict wounds upon the recipient, first appear at about 6 months of age, but are exhibited in relatively moderate form among well-socialized infants until the end of the first year of life (Rosenblum, 1961).

Although the time of emergence of each of these two response systems is relatively independent of rearing condition, the *forms* that these responses take upon emergence, we believe, are intimately tied to both prior and existing social environments of individual monkeys. Moreover, the manner in which each of these two emerging response systems is integrated into the infant's existing behavioral repertoire appears to be crucial for subsequent development. Our premise is that integration of the fear response into species-appropriate social development is facilitated by the presence of a mother or mother substitute, that integration of aggression into species-appropriate social activity is facilitated by social play with age-mates, and that an infant monkey reared in a social environment lacking a mother or mother substitute and/or the opportunity for peer interaction will exhibit subsequent abnormal social behavior of a predictable nature. In other words, for species-normative social development the minimal social requirements of an infant monkey's environment appear to be a form of mother and presence of peers.

FIG. 3.—Mother-infant cradling.

Over the past 10 years a wealth of data relevant to this position has been accumulated. Most of these data were generated from studies where mothers and infants were housed in "playpen units" for the infants' first year of life (Hansen, 1966; Alexander, 1966; Joslyn, 1967; Rosevear, 1970). A standard playpen unit is illustrated in Figure 2; basically it consists of four outer cages or living units and an inner cage or play unit which itself may be partitioned into halves or quarters. A small opening in each living cage allows each infant, but not its mother, access to the entire play unit or the particular segment of the play area adjacent to the infant's living unit. A more detailed description of the apparatus may be found in Hansen (1966).

In this situation a rhesus infant spends most of its first month of life in physical contact with its mother, usually cradled in her arms (Fig. 3).

During this period it gradually achieves voluntary control over many behaviors previously exhibited primarily by reflex action. By the end of the first month the infant begins to explore the world about it, leaving the mother for short periods of time. The degree to which an infant leaves its mother's protective grasp seems to be primarily a function of the mother's permissiveness. Her attitudes invariably change with time— whereas at 2 months her infant retrieval responses are at a maximum, by 4 months she frequently rejects the infant, in effect forcing it into the outside world. Consequently the amount of time the infant spends in contact with its mother decreases sharply after the second month, due undoubtedly to an interaction between the infant's increasing eagerness to explore and the mother's decreasing eagerness to cradle and nurse her offspring. Figures 4-6 summarize these trends.

The developing infant's exploratory behavior begins to increase rapidly during the second month. Using its mother as a base it makes brief forays into the play unit to investigate both inanimate play objects and animate playmates. At the slightest provocation, however, the infant scurries back to its mother. It appears that the mother provides a base for security, an exceedingly important role at the time infant fear responses emerge. Stimuli which would terrify a 3-month-old infant separated from its mother fail to elicit similar fear responses when infant and mother are together.

By the end of the second month crude infant-infant interactions begin to emerge. At first the infants do not appear to differentiate between inanimate objects and animate peers in their exploratory behavior. True play with other infants appears by the third or fourth month and rapidly increases in frequency and sophistication with age. By 4 months sex differences are readily apparent in play behavior, with males exhibiting greater activity and generally rougher play, while females are more passive and initiate play interactions less frequently. At 6 months of age elementary sex posturing is exhibited by both sexes, and aggressive biting appears, particularly in males.

Play dominates the monkey's behavioral repertoire by 8-10 months of age, becoming increasingly more aggressive and sexual in nature as the subjects grow older. By this age, interactions have become sex-segregated. Tested in an independent situation 8-month males prefer male peers to female peers while 8-month females exhibit a preference for females (Suomi, Sackett, & Harlow, 1970). In the playpen situation males are more likely to play with males, and their play is of an aggressive, rough-and-tumble nature. Eight-month females rarely initiate play with a male, and what play they do exhibit is primarily of noncontact form. The development of play and associated behaviors is illustrated in Figures 7-10.

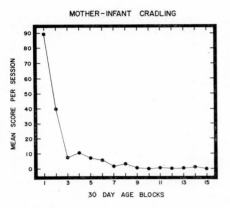

FIG. 4.—Decline of mother-infant cradling.

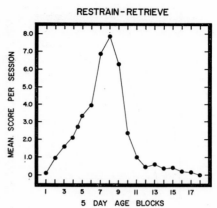

FIG. 5.—Maternal restrain-retrieve behaviors.

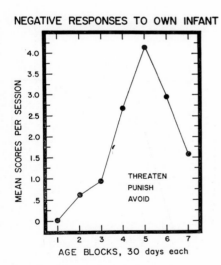

FIG. 6.—Maternal negative responses to own infant.

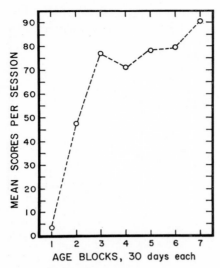

FIG. 7.—Infant time spent outside of home cage containing mother.

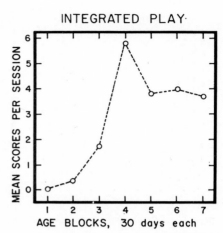

FIG. 8.—Development of integrated play.

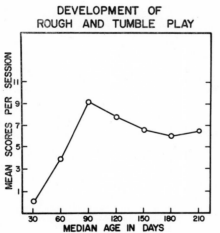

FIG. 9.—Development of rough-and-tumble play.

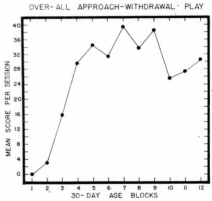

FIG. 10.—Development of approach-avoidance play.

By the end of the first year aggressive and sexual behaviors are well integrated into the play interactions of mother-peer reared infants. Play continues to dominate the infants' activity, mother-directed behaviors continue to decline, and disturbance behaviors such as self-orality, self-clasping, and stereotypic rocking are virtually nonexistent.

Monkeys reared with mothers and peers for the first year of life continue to exhibit adequate social behavior when given the opportunity later in life to interact with others of their species. Housed together, such animals rapidly establish exceedingly stable dominance hierarchies, with social order primarily maintained by subtle gestures such as threats, grimaces, and presents rather than by overt aggression. When sexually mature these monkeys display both eagerness and sophistication in their sexual advances (Senko, 1966) and, contrary to most laboratory-born primates, reproduce readily. Mother-peer reared monkey females are generally excellent monkey mothers (Harlow, Harlow, Dodsworth, & Arling, 1966). Finally, regardless of subsequent social history, rhesus monkeys given extensive maternal and peer experience during the first year of life seldom exhibit the profound behavioral abnormalities so characteristic of laboratory-born primates given less extensive early social experience. Excessive self-orality, self-aggression, self-clasping, compulsive rocking and huddling, and stereotypic limb movements are rarely seen in these animals.

Monkey subjects raised in more socially complex laboratory environments, i.e., in pens containing adult females, juveniles, and other infants (Rosenblum & Kaufman, 1967) or in a nuclear family situation which includes adult males (Harlow, Harlow, Schiltz, & Mohr, 1971), are not noticeably superior in the above respects to mother-peer playpen-reared subjects. More importantly, mother-peer reared monkeys, by these criteria, are quite comparable to monkeys observed in feral environments (Altman, 1962; Imanishi, 1963; Koford, 1963; Southwick, Beg, & Siddiqi, 1965). Moreover, those investigators who have followed the social development of infant rhesus in field habitats report behavioral trends chronologically similar to those observed for infants growing up in a mother-peer playpen situation. For these reasons we have concluded that monkeys raised from birth in mother-peer social environments are capable of developing behavioral patterns which fall within acceptable limits of what we would call species-normative social behavior.

II. *Abnormal Behavior Resulting from Rearing in Socially Deprived Environments*

The previous section discussed certain elements of behavior which emerge in developing rhesus infants, regardless of rearing experience, and described a laboratory procedure for rearing infants who subsequently exhibited normal social development. In efforts to investigate parameters affecting social development of rhesus monkeys, experimenters at the Wisconsin Laboratories have altered the mother-peer rearing environments by systematic substitution and/or deletion of social elements in this environment. Although the designated purpose of these studies was not the production of abnormal behavior patterns, certain social abnormalities were observed. A discussion of these abnormalities and their relationship to a specific rearing situation comprises the body of this section.

A. *Developmental Consequences of Surrogate-Peer Rearing*

One modification of the mother-peer rearing environment involves substituting cloth surrogate mothers (Harlow, 1958; Harlow & Suomi, 1970c) for real monkey mothers. Though inanimate and, in most cases, nonnutritive, cloth surrogates have been shown to be surprisingly effective in eliciting clinging responses from infants raised in their presence and in alleviating infant fear responses to a strange situation (Harlow & Zimmermann, 1959). Unlike real monkey mothers they neither reject nor punish their maturing infants. However, several studies have demonstrated that monkeys reared in a surrogate-peer environment show adequate, though somewhat delayed, social development and, with a few exceptions, exhibit relatively normal social, sexual, and maternal behavior upon maturation.

Hansen (1966) reared two groups of infant monkeys in a playpen situation, one group with surrogate mothers and the other with real monkey mothers. Throughout the first year of life the surrogate-peer reared infants exhibited higher levels of self-orality and "maternal" contact and lower levels of all forms of play than the mother-peer reared infants. These observed differences may have been enhanced by the fact that the surrogate-group was sex-balanced while the infants reared with real mothers were all males. Even so, with the exception of self-orality, group differences converged subsequent to the first year. In most other respects, Hansen's surrogate-peer reared infants became socially competent adults.

Rosenblum (1961) reared infants in individual cages with surrogates but allowed them brief (18-minute) daily periods of social interaction in groups of four in a social playroom, illustrated in Figure 11 and further described in Harlow (1962b). Like Hansen's infants these surrogate-peer monkeys exhibited normative patterns of social development, except for consistently high levels of self-orality, a slight acceleration in the appearance of approach-avoidance play, and retardation of the appearance of aggressive play (Harlow & Harlow, 1968).

More recently, groups of four infants have been reared in individual quadrants of a living-experimental quad cage, illustrated in Figure 12 (Suomi & Harlow, 1969), each containing a simplified cloth surrogate (Harlow & Suomi, 1970c). They have been permitted 2 hours of social interaction per day, both in pairs within the quad cages and as groups of four in a playroom. With the exception of high levels of self-orality, these monkeys appear to be socially normal. It is our conclusion that surrogate-peer rearing produces few behavioral abnormalities in monkeys

PLAYROOM III

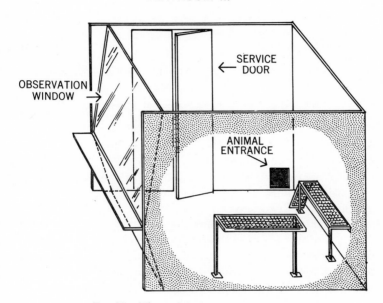

Fig. 11.—The social playroom apparatus.

other than heightened self-orality and occasional displays of self-clasping and stereotypic rocking. Social, sexual, and maternal behaviors appear relatively well-developed in these monkeys by adulthood.

B. *Developmental Consequences of Peer-Only Rearing*

Several groups of monkeys have been reared in the continuous presence of peers only, i.e., without either surrogate or real mothers. This rearing condition has been called the "together-together" situation. Although the number of members comprising together-together groups has ranged from two to six, certain behavioral abnormalities have emerged in these monkeys regardless of group size.

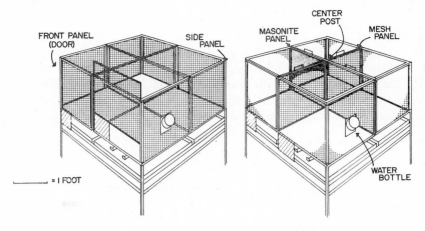

COMBINED LIVING EXPERIMENTAL
CAGE

FIG. 12.—The living-experimental (quad) cage.

With no mother, real or artificial, to cling to, together-together reared monkeys soon learn to cling to each other in what has been denoted as a "choo-choo" pattern (Figure 13). This clinging pattern persists far longer than does maternal clinging for mother-peer reared infants, probably attributable to two factors. First, infants do not actively reject a clinging partner with the frequency or severity of a monkey mother. Second, in a mother-peer situation infants are often enticed from ventral maternal contact by the presence of an exploring, nonclinging peer. In a together-together situation, if all group members are clinging to each other no exploring peer exists to break the cling pattern.

FIG. 13.—Choo-choo cling pattern of together-together reared infants.

In addition to intensive and prolonged clinging, together-together reared monkeys exhibit excessive self-orality, abnormally low levels of locomotion and exploration, and retardation in the appearance of play behavior and sexual posturing. They are also hypersensitive to minimal stress situations, quite possibly resulting from lack of a protective maternal object within their social environment.

Nevertheless, clinging eventually disappears in together-together reared monkeys, usually beginning at about the 5th month, and correspondingly normal play patterns do emerge although their frequency and intensity seldom approach the levels achieved by comparable-aged mother-

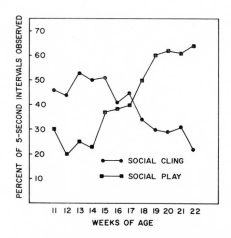

F‍ɪɢ. 14.—Development of cling and play responses for two groups of together-together reared monkeys.

peer reared monkeys (Figure 14). Aggressive play is rarely exhibited. Self-orality persists in these monkeys to adulthood, as does sensitivity to fear stimuli and lack of aggressive behavior. Together-together reared monkeys are timid animals, at least by monkey standards. Yet their sexual behavior eventually becomes relatively normal, and the females usually make good mothers. In summary, most behavioral abnormalities observed in together-together reared monkeys disappear by the end of the 2nd year of life, and those that remain apparently have only cursory effects upon subsequent social, sexual, and maternal behavior (Harlow & Harlow, 1968).

C. *Developmental Consequences of Mother-Only Rearing*

The consequences of deprivation of peer experience for infants provided normal mothering from birth have been studied by Alexander

(1966) in a playpen situation so structured that subject infants could see and interact with only their mothers. Four mother-reared infants were peer-deprived for the first 4 months of life, while members of a second group of four interacted with only their mothers for the first 8 months. The 4-month mother-only infants, when finally permitted peer interactions with each other, rapidly developed adequate, typical monkey play patterns. They appeared to be socially and sexually competent except for somewhat lower levels of contact peer interaction and heightened aggression when compared with a control mother-peer playpen group. The 8-month group showed similar, though exaggerated, differences when compared to their controls. These monkeys were separated from their mother at 12 months of age.

Subsequent testing of these animals 2 months later with 6-month-old stranger stimulus monkeys yielded similar findings. The 8-month mother-only subjects were hyperaggressive to the stimulus animals, the 4-month mother-only monkeys were mildly aggressive, while control subjects showed little aggressive behavior toward the 6-month-old strangers. Peer deprivation appears to produce contact-shy, hyperaggressive monkeys, and the longer the period of deprivation, the more exaggerated the syndrome. Nevertheless, the monkeys reared with mothers only in the above study were, generally speaking, not grossly abnormal in their subsequent social and sexual behavior. Had the peer deprivation been more extended, the findings may have been different.

The three rearing situations presented thus far have produced monkeys that, except for a few specific abnormalities, exhibit play, sexual, and maternal behaviors within the limits of what we would term as normal. However, the form of the exhibited abnormalities specific to each rearing condition are of more than passing interest. While we are not Freudians in any sense of the word, we cannot ignore the consistent finding that monkeys denied real mothers possessing functional breasts show excessive and prolonged self-orality regardless of presence of peers and/or breastless surrogate mothers.

Probably more important is the finding that monkeys reared only with peers react abnormally to mildly stressful situations, while monkeys reared only with mothers are hyperaggressive in a social situation. These data are absolutely consistent with the idea that presence of a mother or mother substitute facilitates integration of the prepotent fear response into an infant's behavioral repertoire, while opportunity for peer interaction facilitates socialization of the prepotent aggressive response when it emerges.

D. *Developmental Consequences of Partial Social Isolation Rearing*

In contrast to the above rearing environments which permit physical interaction with social stimuli is a rearing condition termed partial social isolation (Cross & Harlow, 1965). Here monkeys are individually housed in bare wire cages that permit them to see and hear but not physically contact other members of their own species. The developmental consequences of such early experience are most profound.

Partial isolate neonates cling and suck just like all rhesus neonates. However, in the absence of real mothers, surrogates, or peers, they cling to themselves and suck their own digits (Figure 15). These two patterns dominate their behavior for at least the first 6 months of life. Correspondingly, partial isolates locomote and explore less than age-mates liv-

FIG. 15.—Self-mouth and self-clasp behavior by monkey reared in partial social isolation.

FIG. 16.—Self-aggression in partial isolate monkey.

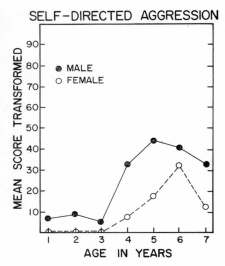

FIG. 17.—Maturation of self-aggression in partial isolate monkeys.

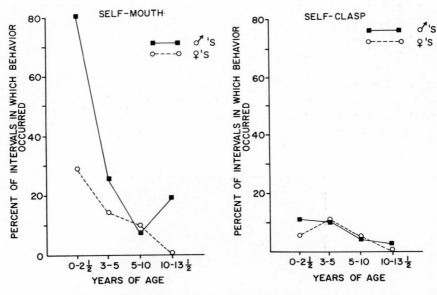

Fig. 18.—Self-mouthing in partial isolate monkeys (home cage).

Fig. 19.—Self-clasping in partial isolate monkeys (home cage).

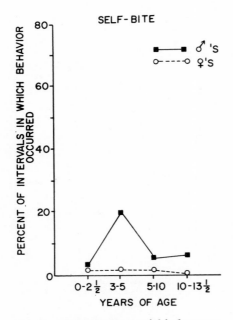

Fig. 20.—Self-biting in partial isolate monkeys (home cage).

ing in more socially enriched environments, and instead develop repetitive stereotypic behavior patterns such as rocking or cage-swinging. As partial isolate monkeys grow older aggressive responses emerge, but in the absence of a social target the animals turn upon themselves and self-aggress (Figures 16 and 17) (Cross & Harlow, 1965).

In time many of the partial isolates' overtly abnormal behavior patterns diminish or disappear (Figures 18, 19, and 20). However, adaptive behaviors such as locomotion and exploration also diminish as the

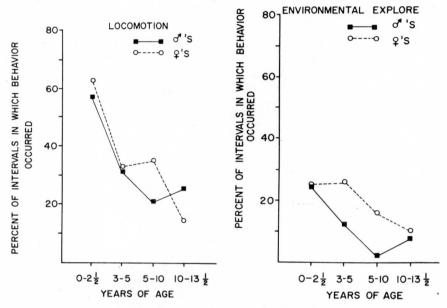

FIG. 21.—Locomotion in partial isolate monkeys (home cage).

FIG. 22.—Exploration in partial isolate monkeys (home cage).

subjects grow older (Figures 21 and 22). Ten-year-old partial social isolates spend the overwhelming majority of their time doing essentially nothing other than sitting at the front of their cages staring vacantly outward (Suomi, Harlow, & Kimball, 1971). However, if stressed by external stimulation they often break into repeated episodes of extreme self-aggression or bizarre individual stereotypic activity (Cross & Harlow, 1965).

Monkeys reared in partial social isolation for the first year of life show serious deficits in their social, sexual, and maternal behaviors. In social situations they rarely initiate interactions but instead usually exhibit avoidance and disturbance behavior patterns (Pratt, 1967, 1969). If repeated social interactions are permitted partial isolates eventually show unsophisticated rudiments of play activity. Their sexual behavior is best described as incompetent. Although desire may be evident, proper posturing and technique, even in the presence of a willing and sophisticated partner, are not (Figure 23). Few female partial isolates have become pregnant by natural means, and instances of successful intromission by partial isolate males are exceedingly rare (Senko, 1966). Those females who have become pregnant have turned out to be, for the most part, inadequate mothers (Harlow *et al.,* 1966). A large percentage of them are indifferent or brutal, often to the point of lethality, to their offspring (Figure 24).

Fig. 23.—Abnormal sexual behavior by mature male partial isolate.

Fig. 24.—Abusive partial isolate mother crushing her infant.

In summary, partial social isolation rearing has severe debilitating effects upon development of species-appropriate behaviors of rhesus monkeys. Partial isolates' social repertoires are limited and primitive, and are superceded by behaviors of excessive self-orality, self-clasping, and somewhat later chronologically, self-aggression and stereotypy, behaviors seldom exhibited by monkeys given adequate maternal and peer experience early in life.

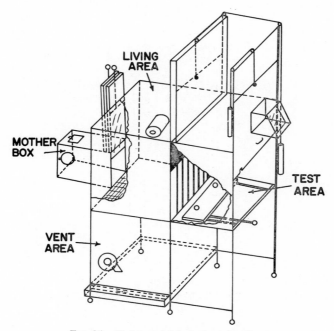

Fig. 25.—Total social isolation chamber.

E. *Developmental Consequences of Total Social Isolation Rearing*

The behavioral abnormalities exhibited by monkeys reared in partial social isolation seem relatively mild in comparison to those displayed by monkeys reared from birth for prolonged periods of time in total social isolation. Total social isolation denies infants both physical and visual (Rowland, 1964) and in some cases auditory (Sackett, 1965) contact with members of any primate species. A typical social isolation chamber is illustrated in Figure 25.

Monkeys reared for the first 3 months of life in total social isolation exhibit, upon emergence, extreme depression, but this is a transient effect and these subjects, if given the opportunity for social interaction, subsequently show normal social development (Boelkins, 1963; Griffin &

Harlow, 1966) . However, 6 or more months of social isolation from birth has drastically more devastating behavioral consequences. Six-month total isolates, when placed in pairs in a playroom with pairs of same-aged socially reared controls, exhibit absolutely minimal social responses (Figure 26) . Even after months of playroom experience isolate play behavior is most infrequent and directed solely toward other isolates, never toward controls (Rowland, 1964; Harlow, Dodsworth, & Harlow, 1965) . Total isolates exhibit even less exploratory and locomotive behavior than partial isolates, while their stereotypy is more pronounced and bizarre.

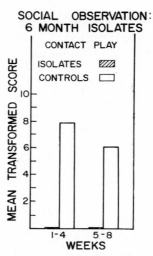

FIG. 26.—Play in 6-month to-tal isolates and controls.

As in all monkeys aggressive behavior develops in 6-month total isolates, but it is either self-directed or, in social situations, inappropriately directed. Mature social isolates readily attack a neonate, something a socially normal monkey will never do, or they may try to attack a dominant adult male, something few socially-sophisticated monkeys are foolish enough to attempt.

Like partial isolates, monkeys subjected to 6 or more months of total isolation are sexually inept as adults, and the females are maternally incompetent. In summary, total social isolation has a devastating permanent effect upon the development of appropriate monkey social behavior. Furthermore, the adverse effects of total social isolation are apparently proportional to the duration of isolation. Whereas 6-month isolates are social misfits, monkeys isolated for the first year of life seem to be little more than semi-animated vegetables, incapable of defending themselves in any social situation (Harlow & Harlow, 1968).

On the basis of the above parametric researches it becomes painfully obvious that the nature of an infant monkey's social environment early in life has profound consequences for subsequent social development. Early denial of either maternal or peer exposure produces subtle but significant aberrations in otherwise normal social development. Denial of all social exposure produces profound and permanent social debilitation.

It is interesting to note that isolation manipulations which effectively destroy an infant's social capability when initiated at or shortly following birth have far less severe consequences when employed with older subjects. Feral-born rhesus monkeys can be individually housed for years without damaging their reproductive or maternal capabilities. Monkeys reared in a social environment for the first 6 months of life, then subjected to 6 months of total social isolation, subsequently exhibit hyper-aggressive social behavior but nevertheless do develop competent play and sexual responses to appropriate social stimuli (Clark, 1968; Mitchell & Clark, 1968). Both the quality and the chronological period of exposure to a given social environment appear to be crucial determinants of the effect of that environment on a specific monkey's social development.

III. *Experimentally Induced Depressive Responses in Young Monkeys*

The fallacy of attributing to man alone the potentiality for development of socially psychopathological behavior should now be apparent. In efforts to investigate parameters central to the development of affectional systems, numerous investigators of nonhuman primates have proved themselves remarkably successful in producing profound and prolonged social abnormalities in a surprising variety of forms.

Aided by the knowledge that monkeys possess the potential for psychopathology, we have recently initiated a comprehensive research program deliberately designed to experimentally induce, by behavioral manipulations, a specific psychopathological syndrome—depression—in monkeys. Although our proposed program involves monkey subjects of all ages, in keeping with the theme of this volume the description of researches involving depression-inducing manipulations will be limited to those employing monkey subjects under 2 years of age.

Interestingly enough, the motivation for initial efforts to produce depressive syndromes in infant monkeys came directly from the human psychiatric literature regarding observations of children who had been separated from their mothers for prolonged periods of time. The Swiss psychiatrist René Spitz was the first to term the children's reaction "anaclitic depression." He noted that some babies 6 to 12 months of age, when separated from their mothers via hospitalization, exhibited initial agitation, closely followed by symptoms of dejection, stupor, decreases in activity, and withdrawal. When reunited with their mothers these infants showed almost immediate and complete recovery from their depressive symptoms (Spitz, 1946).

Bowlby and his coworkers (Robertson & Bowlby, 1952; Bowlby, 1960) noted a similar reaction to maternal separation in children 2 to 5 years of age. He delineated three stages of the reaction: (a) initial "protest," characterized by increases in crying, screaming, and general activity, (b) "despair," which included withdrawal, mourning, and reduction of activity, and (c) following reunion with the mother, "detachment," where the children appeared to be indifferent, sometimes hostile, to their mothers. The inconsistency in reaction to reunion between Spitz's and Bowlby's original subjects may have been due to a factor as simple as age differences, although Bowlby presently does not feel that detachment represents an invariant phase of the reaction (Bowlby, 1969).

At any rate, it is an elementary matter to experimentally produce a monkey analogue to human mother-infant separation. One can simply rear mother and infant monkeys together for a specific period of time, separate them for a specific period of time, and then reunite them. This paradigm was first employed in a formal study by Seay, Hansen, and Harlow (1962), who reared a group of four infants with their mothers in a standard playpen situation for the first 6 months of life. The infants were then separated from their mothers by confinement to the play area while the mothers remained in the living units. Separation lasted 3 weeks during which time the infants could see and hear but not contact their mothers, although they could interact with each other. Following this period they were reunited with their mothers. The infants' reaction to separation was characterized by initial increases in activity and vocalization followed by a shift to activity levels below those prior to separation. Peer play was effectively obliterated throughout the entire period of separation (Figure 27).

Upon reunion, mother-directed behaviors were exhibited at levels above those of the preseparation period but these increases soon declined to preseparation baselines. In summary, the reaction to maternal separation exhibited by these monkeys was remarkably similar in the qualitative sense to the previously reported reactions of human infants experiencing maternal separation.

This study was replicated by Seay and Harlow (1965) with two groups of four mother-infant pairs, except that the period of separation was only 2 weeks and Masonite panels denied the infants visual access to their mothers during the separation period. The results were qualitatively identical to those of the previous study although, contrary to expectations, the overall infant reactions to separation appeared somewhat less severe. The mother-infant separation paradigm has since been employed at a number of laboratories (Jensen & Toleman, 1962; Hinde, Spencer-Booth, & Bruce, 1966; Kaufman & Rosenblum, 1967; Rosenblum & Kaufman, 1967), and despite variations in experimental procedures the results have been remarkably consistent from study to study. Upon separation the infant monkeys in every study have been reported to exhibit an initial period of extreme distress and agitation, characterized by marked increases in vocalization and activity. This behavior seldom persists longer than 48 hours, and if the separation continues, is usually followed by a period characterized by striking reduction in vocalization,

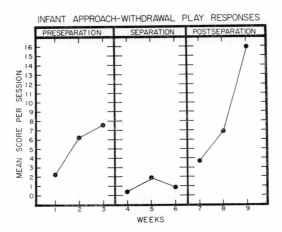

Fig. 27.—Infant approach-withdrawal play prior to, during, and following maternal separation.

locomotor, exploratory, and play activity, and in some cases, by autistic posturing (Figure 28). Some authors have called this behavior depression. Indeed, Kaufman and Rosenblum (1967) have postulated an adaptive mechanism to account for such a biphasic reaction. Upon reunion all authors have reported a temporary increase in mother-directed behavior which eventually drops to or below preseparation levels. Bowlby's detachment phase has not been observed in any of these studies.

We now possess data which provide convincing evidence that elicitation of this reaction in infant monkeys need not be limited to situations involving maternal separation. Rather, the protest-despair biphasic syndrome appears to be a generalized reaction to separation from any object or situation to which an infant has previously become sufficiently attached.

For example, if four monkeys are raised from birth as a together-

together group, then separated from each other when they are 3 months old, each infant will exhibit a protest-despair reaction during the period of separation. Upon reunion socially directed behaviors show a temporary increase over preseparation levels (Suomi, Harlow, & Domek, 1970). In other words, the reaction of infant rhesus monkeys when separated from other infant monkeys is practically identical qualitatively to the reactions of infant rhesus monkeys when separated from their mothers.

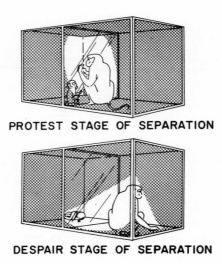

PROTEST STAGE OF SEPARATION

DESPAIR STAGE OF SEPARATION

Fig. 28.—Protest and despair phases of reaction to maternal separation.

A modification of the above paradigm demonstrates the power of this reaction. In a recent experiment (Suomi, Harlow & Domek, 1970) monkeys were reared from birth as a together-together group of four without mothers. When they were 3 months old, the subjects were separated from each other and placed individually in separate cages for 4 days, then returned to their home cage as a group for a 3-day period. They were again separated for 4 days then returned for 3 days. This 4-day separation, 3-day reunion cycle was repeated a total of 20 times, with one 6-week break between the 12th and 13th separations, during which time the subjects remained in their home cage as a group of four. After the 20th separation they were housed as an intact group for 6 more weeks.

Three clear-cut results emerged from this study. First, within each weekly separation and return, protest, despair, and recovery patterns were evident. This is illustrated in Figure 29 which shows the levels of behaviors observed during the first 24 hours and the last 48 hours of separation and the 72 hours of reunion each week, averaged over the first 12 separations. Clearly, high levels of locomotion and vocalization (protest) characterized the first 24 hours of each separation period. High levels of self-clasp and huddle (despair) characterized the last 48 hours of the separations, and high levels of infant-infant clinging (recovery) characterized the 72 hours per week of reunion. Second, the monkeys did not adapt to the multiple separation procedure. Their reaction to the 20th separation was virtually the same as their reaction to the first separation. A third, and most interesting, finding was that the multiple short-term separations produced a dramatic maturational arrest. Figure 30 shows the levels of behaviors prior to separation (age 3 months), during the 6-week together period following the 12th separation (age 6 months), and during the 6-week together period following the last separation (age 9 months). Clinging and self-orality remained at high levels at all ages, locomotion and exploration declined with age, and play was nonexistent. This is in sharp contrast to normal monkey development where clinging and self-orality decline with age and at 9 months are virtually nonexistent, where locomotion and exploration rise during this chronological period, and where play is at a maximum when the monkeys are 9 months of age. By the technique of repetitive short-term separations we had, in effect, produced 9-month monkeys that behaved like monkeys 3 months of age or younger.

This paradigm need not be limited to subjects reared in together-together groups. In a subsequent study (Suomi, Harlow, & Domek, 1970) four monkeys were reared with their mothers until 8 months of age, then placed together as a group of four until they were 13 months old. The subjects were then separated from each other for 4-day periods on a weekly basis, as described above, for a total of 6 times. Like the together-together reared subjects previously described, these monkeys exhibited the same protest-despair reaction to the weekly peer separations, despite the fact that they were older (13 months *vs.* 3-9 months) and had been reared with their mothers.

Another group of subjects were reared with their mothers until 6 months of age, then separated and placed together as a group of four. The maternal separation elicited the familiar protest-despair reaction. After a week of group housing the infants were separated from each other. The monkeys' individual reactions to separation from their peers were even more extreme than their reactions to separation from their mothers one week before. In particular, during the last 3 days of peer separation they spent less than 2% of the observation periods engaging in behaviors other than self-clasp, self-mouth, or huddle, certainly as profound a behavioral exhibition of monkey despair as one could envi-

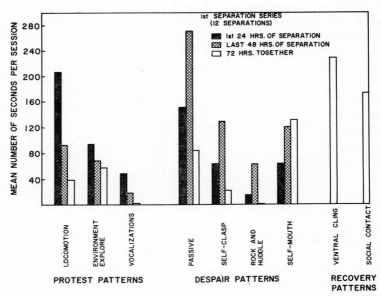

FIG. 29.—Protest, despair, and recovery from repetitive infant-infant separations.

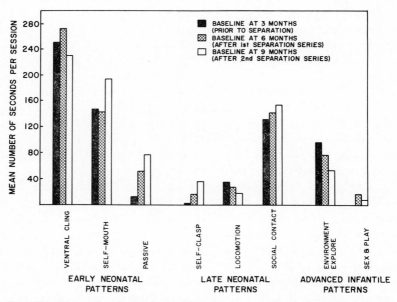

FIG. 30.—Maturational arrest resulting from repetitive infant-infant separations.

sion (Suomi. Harlow, & Domek, 1970). This experiment is presently being replicated using 2-week rather than 4-day separation periods. Preliminary data indicate that the above results are not likely to be artifactual.

In another ongoing study monkeys are being reared in a surrogate-peer situation where they are housed individually with simplified surrogates but given peer interaction with each other 2 hours daily, both within their home cages and in a playroom. When individual group members are removed from this situation and housed separately in another room for a 30-day period, they too exhibit a protest-despair form of reaction.

All in all, these data have convinced us that Spitz's "anaclitic depression," first observed in human infants separated from their mothers, most likely represents a general primate reaction to removal from a situation to which the subject has become attached. In line with Cairns' (1966) theoretical position, we feel the severity of the reaction is directly related to the strength of attachment, and the specific form in which it is exhibited is dependent upon the context of the situation prior to and during the period of separation.

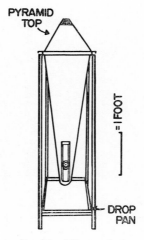

FIG. 31.—The vertical chamber.

A second approach to the production of depressive responses in young monkeys centers around an apparatus we term the "vertical chamber" (Harlow, Suomi, & McKinney, 1970). As can be seen in Figure 31 it is little more than a simple stainless steel trough with a mesh bottom, enclosed by a fine-mesh top, equipped with a food box and water bottle holder, and constructed to allow drainage of waste material and to provide for collection of urine.

These chambers were designed so that they would not produce physical discomfort or disability, since we feel it is pointless to study psychological abnormality if its appearance is irrevocably confounded with physical abnormality. Apparently for incarcerated subjects physical discomfort is not severe since while in the chambers they eat and drink adequately and show no abnormal loss of weight. This does not necessarily characterize these subjects once they have emerged from the chambers. On the other hand, depression has been characterized in human patients as embodying a state of "helplessness and hopelessness, sunken in a well of despair" (McKinney, Suomi, & Harlow, 1971), and so we designed our vertical chambers on an intuitive basis to reproduce such a state psychologically in our monkey subjects. Although in the chamber a monkey's visual and auditory input is only partially restricted and it is quite free to move about in three dimensions, it soon learns this has little effect, and subsequently the monkey spends the majority of its time huddled in a corner of the chamber (Figure 32).

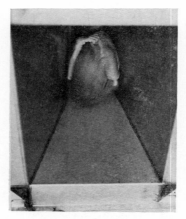

Fig. 32.—Typical subject posture within vertical chamber.

In an exploratory study we placed four individually reared subjects with an age range of 6-13 months in single chambers for a period of 30 days (Suomi & Harlow, 1969). Figure 33 illustrates some of the home-cage behaviors prior to incarceration and for 2 months following emergence from the chambers. It is obvious that the subjects' behavior patterns in their home cages had been drastically altered. More interesting

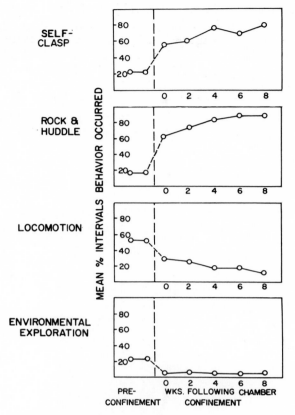

Fɪɢ. 33.—Effect of 30 days chamber confinement on selected rhesus monkey behaviors.

to us was the finding that the alterations were precisely in the direction of what we would call depressed.

A second study (Suomi, Harlow, Sprengel, & Gunderson, in preparation) illustrates how powerful the effects of chamber confinement early in life can be. As previously pointed out, while 6 months of total social isolation from birth is socially devastating, monkeys isolated for only the first 3 months quickly recover and develop normal social behaviors (Griffin & Harlow, 1966). In the present study we placed four 45-day-old monkeys in individual vertical chambers and confined them for 6 weeks so that upon emergence they were 3 months of age. Subsequently they were individually housed but given social experience 3 days per week in a playroom with equal-age stimulus monkeys, half reared individually and half reared with peers. Playroom testing continued until the subjects were 1 year of age.

Figure 34 shows the incarcerated subjects 4 days following removal from the vertical chambers. Long-term behavioral effects produced by chamber confinement are illustrated by the monkeys' home cage (Figure 35) and playroom (Figure 36) behaviors 8 months later when the subjects were almost a year old. The depressive behaviors of self-mouth, self-clasp, and huddle dominated the chambered monkeys' activity but were virtually nonexistent in both control groups. The reverse was true with regard to locomotive and exploratory behaviors. Most striking was the almost total absence of any form of social behavior by the cham-

Fig. 34.—Subjects 4 days after removal from vertical chambers.

bered monkeys despite the fact that they had been given extensive social experience beginning at 4 months of age. We have concluded from this study that chamber confinement produces more destructive behavioral effects in less time and with fewer individual differences among subjects than total social isolation, previously the most powerful psychopathology-producing technique employed with monkey subjects. Furthermore, the psychopathological behaviors produced were of a depressive nature.

A third study (Suomi, Domek, & Harlow, in preparation) has combined the manipulations of repetitive peer separation with vertical chamber confinement. Infants were reared with each other as a group of four from birth to 3 months, then separated from each other a total of 20 times, 4 days for each separation, in precisely the same sequence

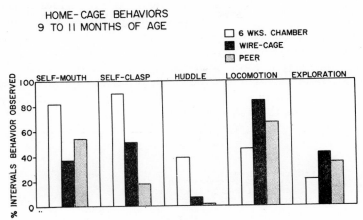

FIG. 35.—Home cage behavior from 9 to 11 months.

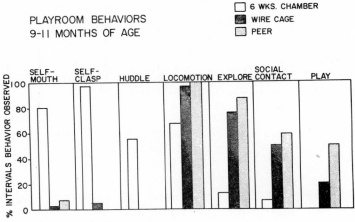

FIG. 36.—Playroom behavior from 9 to 11 months.

as for the previously reported repetitive infant-infant separation study. However, in this study the infants were confined to vertical chambers during the separation periods rather than housed in individual cages. As in the previous study, protest and despair reactions to the separations were noted and maturational arrest of development was clearly observed. For chamber-separated monkeys this arrest took a slightly but significantly different form from that of the cage-separated monkeys. Figure 37 illustrates that baseline behaviors following separation were typified by abnormally low levels of locomotion, exploration, and play, and high levels of self-orality, similar to findings of the previous study. However, upon reunion, the chambered monkeys showed significantly

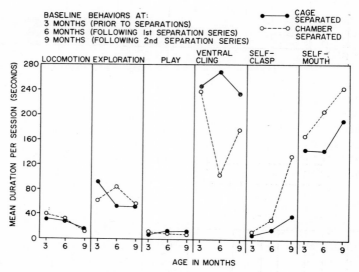

Fig. 37.—Effects of confinement in vertical chamber during repetitive peer separation *vs.* confinement in wire cage during separation period.

lower levels of social clinging and higher levels of self-clasping than the cage-separated monkeys. In other words, immature socially directed behaviors were "replaced" by immature self-directed behaviors. These and other data from the study lead us to suspect that we may have been observing Bowlby's detachment phase of reaction to separation, a phenomenon rarely seen in monkey subjects. It is apparent that chamber confinement coupled with separation produces depressive effects beyond those produced by the manipulation of separation alone.

These experiments have produced psychopathological behavior of a depressive nature in young monkeys. However, it is not clear that the subjects were entirely "normal" prior to our manipulations. The most powerful demonstration of the effectiveness of a given psychopathological behavior-producing manipulation must utilize subjects who are socially normal prior to any experimental manipulation. This is precisely what is being done in an ongoing study. Subjects are being reared in normal social groups with surrogates and peers, individually removed from the group and confined to vertical chambers for 30 days, then returned to the group. Preliminary data indicate that the once-normal subjects, upon return to their familiar social group, exhibit behaviors as depressive as those of any monkeys in previous studies, and that the form of the depression appears to be dependent upon age and social position within the established group at time of incarceration.

We have presented empirical evidence that depressive responses can be reliably induced in young monkey subjects regardless of prior rearing experience. The form, severity, and duration of the observed depressions are, we feel, directly related to the type of manipulations employed. In contrast to the controlled, long-term rearing environmental studies described in the previous section, these manipulations are relatively brief in duration, yet the psychopathology produced appears to be at least as severe as that resulting from total social isolation. On the basis of findings from both rearing condition experiments and the depression studies, it seems obvious that psychopathological social behavior is not an exclusive potentiality of the human primate. Given the appropriate time and situation, monkeys can be made as mad as men.

IV. *Rehabilitation of Aberrant Monkey Social Behavior*

Thus far our discussion has centered upon the experimental production, both deliberate and semi-deliberate, of abnormal social behavior in young rhesus monkey subjects. Justification of this research has been twofold: we have been interested in tracing the behavioral effects of controlled deviations from mother-peer rearing, and we have been interested in developing techniques for production of behavior patterns in young monkeys qualitatively similar to human depressive behavior. Yet, although our subjects have been monkeys and our methods scientific, we do have humanistic moments, and the very idea of developing techniques for production of psychopathology without devising techniques for alleviating this psychopathology strikes us as unfeeling and inhumane. Furthermore, there are scientific considerations involved. We strongly believe that the ultimate criterion of the ability to predict, understand, and control variables relevant to monkey psychopathology involves demonstration of the ability to produce experimentally a given psychopathology and subsequently to reverse the syndrome so that one retains socially adequate subjects.

With respect to the depression studies our venture into monkey psychiatry has been limited thus far to theoretical speculation. This is primarily because our major efforts have been concentrated on production of syndromes we can correctly call depressive, syndromes which are stable and prolonged with few individual differences between subjects. As pointed out in the preceding section this goal has largely been achieved with young monkey subjects. To consider rehabilitation prior to achieving this stage would have been relatively pointless. Just as it is less than totally acceptable to produce profound psychopathology in subjects who were less than psychologically normal prior to manipulation, it becomes no task of great difficulty to rehabilitate a depression in subjects who have not really been depressed. However, we are now in a position to begin significant rehabilitation of depressed monkeys.

If one believes the validity of cross-species analogies, then initial strategies for rehabilitation of depressed monkeys become readily apparent. One can merely employ therapeutic procedures which have been developed by psychiatrists dealing with human depressions. In the case of single mother-infant separation the analogy seems justified. Just as Spitz (1946) reported "immediate and complete recovery" of his anaclitically depressed human infants upon reunion with their mothers, virtually every monkey study utilizing mother-infant separation has found immediate recovery, apparently complete, when monkey mother and infant are reunited. An experimenter possessing a population of depressed nonhuman primates might well consider employing such drugs as imipramine and amitriptyline or procedures such as electroconvulsive therapy which have shown apparent success for relieving the depressions of some human patients. While an experimenter should by no means feel bound to such procedures, at least they provide a reasonable point of departure.

For other types of monkey psychopathology this may not be the case. The most extreme example is provided by the total social isolate. Human analogies to monkeys reared from birth in total social isolation for prolonged periods of time are practically nonexistent save for legends, such as that of Romulus and Remus, and preciously few documented cases, such as that of the Wild Boy of Itard. Yet it is possible to rear monkeys in isolation from birth and, as has been shown, the behavioral effects of at least 6 months of such confinement are devastating and apparently permanent. Possible rehabilitation of such subjects becomes interesting from both a practical and theoretical point of view.

It is obvious that 6 months of total isolation initiated at birth is debilitating for the rhesus monkey but it is not so obvious *why* this is the case. One theoretical explanation, embodied by critical period notions (Denenberg, 1964; Scott, 1962), suggests that during the first 6 months of life, probably between the 3rd and 6th month, the rhesus monkey passes through a *critical period* during which time social exposure is essential for subsequent social development. According to this position an animal denied social experience during the critical period will never exhibit normal social development, regardless of subsequent environmental conditions.

A second theoretical position (Fuller & Clark, 1966) maintains that the bizarre behavior patterns exhibited by monkeys removed from isolation is the result of *emergence trauma,* i.e., the shock of coming from an unstimulating environment into an environment of overwhelming complexity produces the isolate's inappropriate behaviors. Implications of this position for rehabilitative strategies point to gradual introduction of the isolate to the "normal" environment by exposure to successively more complex intermediate environments.

The idea of rehabilitation of isolates is not new. Attempts to reverse the syndromes caused by total social isolation have been initiated since the existence of an isolation syndrome was recognized. Most of these efforts have been summarily unsuccessful, a predicament readily predictable from the critical period interpretation of isolation effects.

For example, Sackett* attempted to increase initiation of social contacts by isolates with other animals by use of an adversive conditioning procedure. Social isolates were placed in a situation where their only recourse to avoid shock was to maintain contact with a trained stimulus animal. After several trials the isolates spent most of their time in this situation touching the stimulus animal. However, within this environment disturbance behavior by the isolates did not diminish appreciably, and there was virtually no generalization of increased social touching to other social situations.

Other experimenters (Clark, 1968; Pratt, 1969) attempted to alleviate the possible occurrence of "emergence trauma." Their rationale was to adapt subjects to the test situation prior to the actual social testing with stimulus animals. Their techniques involved removing individual subjects from their isolation chambers and placing them in an empty playroom several times during the subjects' 6-month tenure of social isolation. Any positive effects these adaptation periods had for alleviation of isolate disturbance in the actual social test situation following removal from isolation were not readily apparent, for "adapted" isolates exhibited social behavior essentially as incompetent as that of isolates who had not been given this prior experience.

Actually, the "standard" practice of exposing isolates to socially normal age-mates, generally in a playroom situation, might be conceptualized as a crude therapeutic attempt. The idea of employing normal subjects as therapists to socially damaged subjects has considerable value both

---

* Gene P. Sackett, unpublished data, 1968.

heuristically and theoretically. If one's goal is to change the behavior of an isolate from self-directed disturbance to socially-directed exploration and play, then it would seem obvious that exposure to socially normal monkeys at least some time during the rehabilitative process would be necessary. In practice, this has not worked well in the past. As has been pointed out, the usual reactions of socially adequate age-mates to 6- (and 9- and 12-) month social isolates are (a) aggression and/or (b) indifference. Such behavior by the control stimulus animals is not likely to elicit positive social responses from the isolates and, in fact, may increase the probability that the isolates will exhibit disturbance behavior.

However, evidence that isolates can be responsive to social stimulation of some sort has been accumulated in at least two independent situations. The first involved isolate females who became mothers. Their initial responses to their own infants were, in many cases, characterized by brutality and/or indifference. Some of the infants survived in the presence of, and in spite of, their mothers' behaviors, and this "survival" was marked by unceasing efforts by the infants to maintain body contact. From the fourth postnatal month onward the motherless mothers gradually gave up the struggle against their own babies, and the infants eventually achieved near-normative frequency of ventral and nipple contact (Harlow *et al.*, 1966). Some of these isolate mothers were impregnated again and, contrary to all predictions, exhibited normal monkey maternal behavior toward their subsequent infants. Clearly, for these once maternally inadequate isolate females, rehabilitation had transpired.

Further evidence for the potential of isolate rehabilitation came from a study utilizing heated surrogate mothers (Harlow & Suomi, 1970a). Six-month total isolates were individually housed following removal from isolation for a 2-week period during which time behavioral baselines were assessed. Surrogates were then introduced into the isolates' home cages. Within a few days the isolates began contacting the surrogates with increasing frequency and duration. Correspondingly, disturbance behavior decreased while locomotive and exploratory behavior rose above presurrogate levels. Following 2 weeks of individual housing with the surrogates, the isolates were housed in pairs. In this situation they exhibited, almost spontaneously, social play, sex, locomotive, and exploratory behavior, although the social behavior was clumsy at best and the isolates continued to exhibit disturbance behavior to some degree.

These studies convinced us that rehabilitation of isolates by employment of social stimuli was possible and that previous failures could probably be attributed at least in part to the type of responses directed toward the isolates by normal stimulus animals. Therefore, we designed an isolate rehabilitation study employing a judiciously chosen type of monkey "therapist" for the isolates. The therapists were essentially near-normal monkeys, having been reared in quad cages with heated surrogates and given 2 hours of peer interaction daily, both in pairs within their quad cages and as a group of four in a playroom. However, they were 3 months *younger* than the isolate subjects, i.e., their age when introduced to the isolates was approximately 3 months. Our prediction was that the therapist monkeys, at this age, when first introduced to the isolates would approach and cling to rather than aggress against the isolates, would initially play at an elementary rather than sophisticated level, and would exhibit minimal abnormal behavior themselves.

In this study (Harlow & Suomi, 1970b) four males, following 6 months of total social isolation from birth, were individually housed for a period

Fig. 38.—Disturbance behavior following removal from isolation.

of 2 weeks in order to assess postisolation baselines. Like typical 6-month isolates they showed little exploratory or locomotive behavior but instead exhibited high levels of self-clasping, self-mouthing, huddling, and stereotypic rocking disturbance behaviors (Figure 38). These subjects were then placed individually in quadrants of quad cages adjacent to four 3-month-old female therapist monkeys who themselves had had surrogate-peer rearing. The isolates were then allowed to interact with the therapist monkeys 2 hours per day, 3 days a week, as pairs (one isolate, one therapist) within the quad cages and 2 days a week in groups of four (two isolates, two therapists) in a playroom.

The isolates' initial response to both situations was to huddle in a corner, and the therapists' first response was approach and cling to the isolates (Figure 39). Within a week in the home cage and 2 weeks in the playroom, the isolates were reciprocating and clinging. Concurrently the therapists were exhibiting elementary play patterns among themselves and attempting to initiate such patterns with the isolates (Figure 40). Within 2 weeks in the home cage and a month in the playroom, the isolates were reciprocating these behaviors (Figure 41). Shortly after, three of the four isolates began to initiate play behaviors themselves, in addition to moving about and exploring the nonsocial environment. Correspondingly their disturbance activity, which initially had accounted for most of their behavioral repertoire, decreased to insignificant levels. The fourth isolate failed to respond in the above manner for $2\frac{1}{2}$ months, but subsequently emerged from its self-isolation

Fig. 39.—Therapist monkey clinging to huddled isolate.

Fig. 40.—Isolate (above) reciprocating social exploration by therapist (below).

Fig. 41.—Isolate (above) initiating play bout with therapist (below).

and eventually rose above the group means in its exploratory, locomotive, and play behaviors.

By 1 year of age the isolates were virtually indistinguishable from the therapist monkeys in amount of exploratory, locomotive, and play behaviors. To our surprise, the type of play appeared to be sex-specific to a large extent, i.e., the male isolates preferred rough-and-tumble play while the female therapists exhibited play almost exclusively of a non-contact form. The isolates could be identified by occasional lapses into self-clasping and huddling behaviors which the therapists did not exhibit. These disturbance patterns, however, were infrequent and of short duration. More significant were the intense, complex patterns of play among all subjects (Figure 42), as well as the appearance of elementary sexual behaviors in both the isolate and therapist monkeys.

Fig. 42.—Isolates (left, center) and therapist (right) interacting in rigorous play.

We will not consider these isolate subjects to have been completely rehabilitated until they exhibit mature adult rhesus monkey sexual behavior. For this we must wait until the subjects become physiologically mature adult rhesus monkeys. However, even at its present state this research has illuminating theoretical implications. The data to this point are absolutely inconsistent with a critical period interpretation of isolation effects. Moreover, they are not readily explicable by emergence-trauma notions, for the social stimuli were introduced to the subjects following isolation and after the subjects had exhibited typical isolate patterns of disturbance behavior. We feel alternative explanations of isolation effects are necessary to account for these data.

We plan to introduce similar techniques of utilizing social stimuli for social rehabilitation to 1-year isolates and to modify existing procedures to determine if the present techniques can be improved. Rehabilitation techniques practiced upon total social isolates can undoubtedly be utilized for other monkeys who exhibit psychopathological behavior, ranging from those reared in partial social isolation from birth to those subjected to depression-inducing manipulations. The extent to which these and other hypothesized therapeutic techniques can be employed to successfully reverse patterns of monkey psychopathology remains a subject for further research efforts.

CONCLUSION

This chapter has presented data generated from laboratory studies of rhesus monkeys. These studies have dealt with normative development of rhesus monkey social behavior, procedures by which aberrations in such normative development can be reliably induced, and procedures by which some of these aberrations can be reversed. It is obvious that these researches have far from exhausted the area of primate social development and that numerous important theoretical and empirical questions remain to be answered.

Yet, as investigators of nonhuman primate development we believe these researches have been illuminating in furthering our understanding of the potentiality of our subjects. As humans, we would like to believe that they, in some small way, have also furthered our understanding of the potentiality of our own species.

REFERENCES

ALEXANDER, B. K. The effects of early peer deprivation on juvenile behavior of rhesus monkeys. Unpublished doctoral dissertation, University of Wisconsin, 1966.

ALTMAN, S. A. A field study of the sociology of rhesus monkeys, *Macaca mulatta. Annals of the New York Academy of Science,* 1962, 102, 338-435.

BANDURA, A., & HUSTON, A. C. Identification as a process of incidental learning. *Journal of Abnormal and Social Psychology,* 1961, 63, 311-318.

BERKSON, G. Defective infants in a feral monkey group. *Folia Primatologica,* 1970, 12, 284-289.

BOELKINS, R. C. The development of social behavior in the infant rhesus monkey following a period of social isolation. Unpublished M.A. thesis, University of Wisconsin, 1963.

BOWLBY, J. Grief and mourning in infancy and early childhood. *Psychoanalytic Study of the Child,* 1960, 15, 9-52.

BOWLBY, J. *Attachment and loss, Volume I: Attachment.* New York: Basic Books, 1969.

CAIRNS, R. B. Attachment behavior of mammals. *Psychological Review,* 1966, 73, 409-426.

CLARK, D. L. Immediate and delayed effects of early, intermediate, and late social isolation in the rhesus monkey. Unpublished doctoral dissertation, University of Wisconsin, 1968.

CROSS, H. A., & HARLOW, H. F. Prolonged and progressive effects of partial isolation on the behavior of macaque monkeys. *Journal of Experimental Research in Personality,* 1965, 1, 39-49.

DENENBERG, V. H. Critical periods, stimulus input, and emotional reactivity: A theory of infantile stimulation. *Psychological Review,* 1964, 71, 335-351.

FULLER, J. L., & CLARK, L. D. Genetic and treatment factors modifying the postisolation syndrome in dogs. *Journal of Comparative and Physiological Psychology,* 1966, 61, 251-257.

FULTON, J. F. *A textbook of physiology.* Philadelphia: W. B. Saunders Co., 1955.

GRIFFIN, G. A., & HARLOW, H. F. Effects of three months of total social deprivation on social adjustment and learning in the rhesus monkey. *Child Development,* 1966, 37, 533-547.

HAMBURGER, V. Some aspects of the embryology of behavior. *Quarterly Review of Biology,* 1963, 38, 342-365.

HANSEN, E. W. The development of maternal and infant behavior in the rhesus monkey. *Behaviour,* 1966, 27, 107-149.

HARLOW, H. F. The nature of love. *American Psychologist,* 1958, 13, 673-685.

HARLOW, H. F. The development of affectional patterns in rhesus monkeys. In B. M. Foss (Ed.), *Determinants of infant behavior,* I. London: Methuen, 1962a. Pp. 75-88.

HARLOW, H. F. The heterosexual affectional system in monkeys. *American Psychologist,* 1962b, 17, 1-9.

HARLOW, H. F., DODSWORTH, R. O., & HARLOW, M. K. Total social isolation in monkeys. *Proceedings of the National Academy of Sciences,* 1965, 54, 90-96.

HARLOW, H. F., & HARLOW, M. K. The affectional systems. In A. M. Schrier, H. F. Harlow, & F. Stollnitz (Eds.), *Behavior of nonhuman primates,* Vol. 2. New York: Academic Press, 1965. Pp. 287-334.

HARLOW, H. F., & HARLOW, M. K. Effects of various mother-infant relationships on rhesus monkey behaviors. In B. M. Foss (Ed.), *Determinants of infant behavior,* IV. London: Methuen, 1968. Pp. 15-36.

HARLOW, H. F., HARLOW, M. K., DODSWORTH, R. O., & ARLING, G. L. Maternal behavior of rhesus monkeys deprived of mothering and peer associations in infancy. *Proceedings of the American Philosophical Society,* 1966, 110, 58-66.

HARLOW, H. F., HARLOW, M. K., & HANSEN, E. W. The maternal affectional system of rhesus monkeys. In H. L. Rheingold (Ed.), *Maternal behavior in mammals.* New York: Wiley, 1963. Pp. 354-381.

HARLOW, H. F., HARLOW, M. K., SCHILTZ, K. A., & MOHR, D. J. The effect of early adverse and enriched environments on the learning ability of rhesus monkeys. In L. E. Jarrard (Ed.), Carnegie-Mellon Symposium, in press, 1971.

HARLOW, H. F., SCHILTZ, K. A., & HARLOW, M. K. Effects of social isolation on the learning performance of rhesus monkeys. In C. R. Carpenter (Ed.), *Proceedings of the Second International Congress of Primatology,* Vol. 1. New York: Karger, 1968. Pp. 178-185.

HARLOW, H. F., & SUOMI, S. J. Induced psychopathology in monkeys. *Engineering and Science,* 1970a, 33, 8-14.

HARLOW, H. F., & SUOMI, S. J. Induction and treatment of psychiatric states in monkeys. *Proceedings of the National Academy of Sciences,* 1970b, 66, 241.

HARLOW, H. F., & SUOMI, S. J. The nature of love-simplified. *American Psychologist,* 1970c, 25, 161-168.

HARLOW, H. F., SUOMI, S. J., & McKINNEY, W. T. Experimental production of depression in monkeys. *Mainly Monkeys,* 1970, 1, 6-12.

HARLOW, H. F., & ZIMMERMANN, R. R. Affectional responses in the infant monkey. *Science,* 1959, 130, 421.

HINDE, R. A., SPENCER-BOOTH, Y., & BRUCE, M. Effects of 6-day maternal deprivation on rhesus monkey infants. *Nature,* 1966, 210, 1021.

IMANISHI, K. Social behavior in the Japanese monkey (*Macaca fuscata*). In C. H. Southwick (Ed.), *Primate social behavior.* Princeton, N. J.: Van Nostrand, 1963. Pp. 68-81.

JAY, P. Field studies. In A. M. Schrier, H. F. Harlow, & F. Stollnitz (Eds.), *Behavior of nonhuman primates,* Vol. 2. New York: Academic Press, 1965. Pp. 525-592.

JENSEN, G. D., & TOLEMAN, C. W. Mother-infant relationship in the monkey, *Macaca nemestrina:* The effect of brief separation and mother-infant specificity. *Journal of Comparative and Physiological Psychology,* 1962, 55, 131.

JOSLYN, W. D. Behavior of socially experienced juvenile rhesus monkeys after eight months of late social isolation and maternal-offspring relations and maternal separation in juvenile rhesus monkeys. Unpublished doctoral dissertation, University of Wisconsin, 1967.

KAUFMAN, I. C., & ROSENBLUM, L. A. The reaction to separation in infant monkeys: Anaclitic depression and conservation-withdrawal. *Psychosomatic Medicine,* 1967, 29, 648-675.

KLING, A., LANCASTER, J., & BENITONE, J. Amygdalectomy in the free-ranging vervet (*Cercopithecus aethiops*). *Journal of Psychiatric Research,* 1970, 7, 191-199.

KOFORD, C. B. Group relations in an island colony of rhesus monkeys. In C. H. Southwick (Ed.), *Primate social behavior.* Princeton, N. J.: Van Nostrand, 1963. Pp. 136-152.

KUBIE, L. S. The concept of normality and neurosis. In M. Heiman (Ed.), *Psychoanalysis and social work.* New York: International Universities Press, 1953. Pp. 3-14.

McKINNEY, W. T., SUOMI, S. J., & HARLOW, H. F. Depression in primates. *American Journal of Psychiatry,* 1971, in press.

MITCHELL, G. D., & CLARK, D. L. Long-term effects of social isolation in nonsocially adapted rhesus monkeys. *Journal of Genetic Psychology,* 1968, 113, 117-128.

MOWBRAY, J. B., & CADELL, T. E. Early behavior patterns in rhesus monkeys. *Journal of Comparative and Physiological Psychology,* 1962, 55, 350-357.

PRATT, C. L. Social behavior of rhesus monkeys reared with varying degrees of early peer experience. Unpublished M.A. thesis, University of Wisconsin, 1967.

PRATT, C. L. The developmental consequences of variations in early social stimulation. Unpublished doctoral dissertation, University of Wisconsin, 1969.

ROBERTSON, T., & BOWLBY, J. Responses of young children to separation from their mothers. *Cour du Centre International de l' Enfance,* 1952, 2, 131-142.

ROSENBLUM, L. A. The development of social behavior in the rhesus monkey. Unpublished doctoral dissertation, University of Wisconsin, 1961.

ROSENBLUM, L. A., & KAUFMAN, I. C. Interactions with group members and the effects of mother-infant separation in monkeqs. *American Journal of Orthopsychiatry,* 1967, 37, 300-301.

ROSEVEAR, J. Y. Early peer social development and diurnal variations in behavior in the rhesus monkey. Unpublished M.A. thesis, University of Wisconsin, 1970.

ROWLAND, G. L. The effects of total social isolation upon learning and social behavior of rhesus monkeys. Unpublished doctoral dissertation, University of Wisconsin, 1964.

SACKETT, G. P. Effect of rearing conditions upon the behavior of rhesus monkeys (*Macaca mulatta*). *Child Development,* 1965, 36, 855-868.

SACKETT, G. P. Monkeys reared in visual isolation with pictures as visual imput: Evidence for an innate releasing mechanism. *Science,* 1966, 154, 1468-1472.

SACKETT, G. P. Innate mechanisms, rearing conditions, and a theory of early experience effects in primates. In M. R. Jones (Ed.), *Miami symposium on the prediction of behavior,* 1968: *Early experience.* Coral Gables: University of Miami Press, 1970. Pp. 11-53.

SACKETT, G. P. Unlearned responses, differential rearing experiences, and the development of social attachments by rhesus monkeys. In L. A. Rosenblum (Ed.), *Primate behavior: Development in field and laboratory research,* Vol. 1. Academic Press, 1971, in press.

SACKETT, G. P., PORTER, M., & HOLMES, H. Choice behavior in rhesus monkeys: Effect of stimulation during the first month of life. *Science,* 1965, 147, 304-306.

SACKETT, G. P., SUOMI, S. J., & GRADY, S. Species preferences in macaque monkeys. Unpublished data, 1968.

SCHAFFER, H. R., & EMERSON, P. E. Development of social attachments in infancy. *Monographs of the Society for Research in Child Development,* 1964, 29, 1-77.

SCOTT, J. P. Critical periods in behavioral development. *Science,* 1962, 138, 949-958.

SEARS, R. R., MACCOBY, E. E., & LEVIN, H. Patterns of child-rearing. Evanston, Illinois: Row, Peterson, & Co., 1957.

SEAY, B., HANSEN, E. W., & HARLOW, H. F. Mother-infant separation in monkeys. *Journal of Child Psychology and Psychiatry,* 1962, 3, 123-132.

Seay, B., & Harlow, H. F. Maternal separation in the rhesus monkey. *Journal of Nervous and Mental Diseases*, 1965, 140, 434-441.

Senko, M. G. The effects of early, intermediate, and late experiences upon adult macaque sexual behavior. Unpublished M.A. thesis, University of Wisconsin, 1966.

Singh, S. D. Urban monkeys. *Scientific American*, 1969, 221, 108-115.

Southwick, C. H., Beg, M. A., & Siddiqi, M. R. Rhesus monkeys in North India. In I. Devore (Ed.), *Primate behavior*. New York: Holt, Rinehart, & Winston, 1965. Pp. 111-159.

Spitz, R. A. Anaclitic depression. *The Psychoanalytic Study of the Child*, 1946, 2, 313-347.

Suomi, S. J., Domek, C. J., & Harlow, H. F. Effects of repetitive peer separation of young monkeys: Vertical chamber versus individual cage confinement during separation. In preparation, 1971.

Suomi, S. J., & Harlow, H. F. Apparatus conceptualization for psychopathological research in monkeys. *Behavioral Research Methods and Instrumentation*, 1969, 1, 247-250.

Suomi, S. J., Harlow, H. F., & Domek, C. J. Effect of repetitive infant-infant separation of young monkeys. *Journal of Abnormal Psychology*, 1970, 75, in press.

Suomi, S. J., Harlow, H. F., & Kimball, S. D. Behavioral effects of prolonged partial social isolation in the rhesus monkey. In preparation, 1971.

Suomi, S. J., Harlow, H. F., Sprengel, R. D., & Gunderson, W. Depressive effects of vertical chamber confinement early in life in the rhesus monkey. In preparation, 1971.

Suomi, S. J., Sackett, G. P., & Harlow, H. F. Development of sex preference in rhesus monkeys. *Developmental Psychology*, 1970, 2, in press.